# Land of Our Fathers

# History of Clark County, Kentucky

By: A. Goff Bedford

Southern Historical Press, Inc.
Greenville, South Carolina

This volume was reproduced from
An 1958 edition located in the
Publisher's private Library

All rights reserved. No part of this publication may be reproduced,
stored in a retrieval system, transmitted in any form, posted
on to the web in any form or by any means without
the prior written permission of the publisher.

Please direct all correspondence and orders to:

**www.southernhistoricalpress.com**
or
**SOUTHERN HISTORICAL PRESS, Inc.**
**PO Box 1267**
**375 West Broad Street**
**Greenville, SC   29601**
southernhistoricalpress@gmail.com

Originally published: Newport, KY, 1958
Copyright 1958 by A. Geoff Bedford
ISBN #0-89308-893-5
All rights Reserved.
*Printed in the United States of America*

This book on Clark County history is dedicated to Miss Kathryn Owen and Mr. James French, who are the real historians of Clark County. They have helped me immensely.

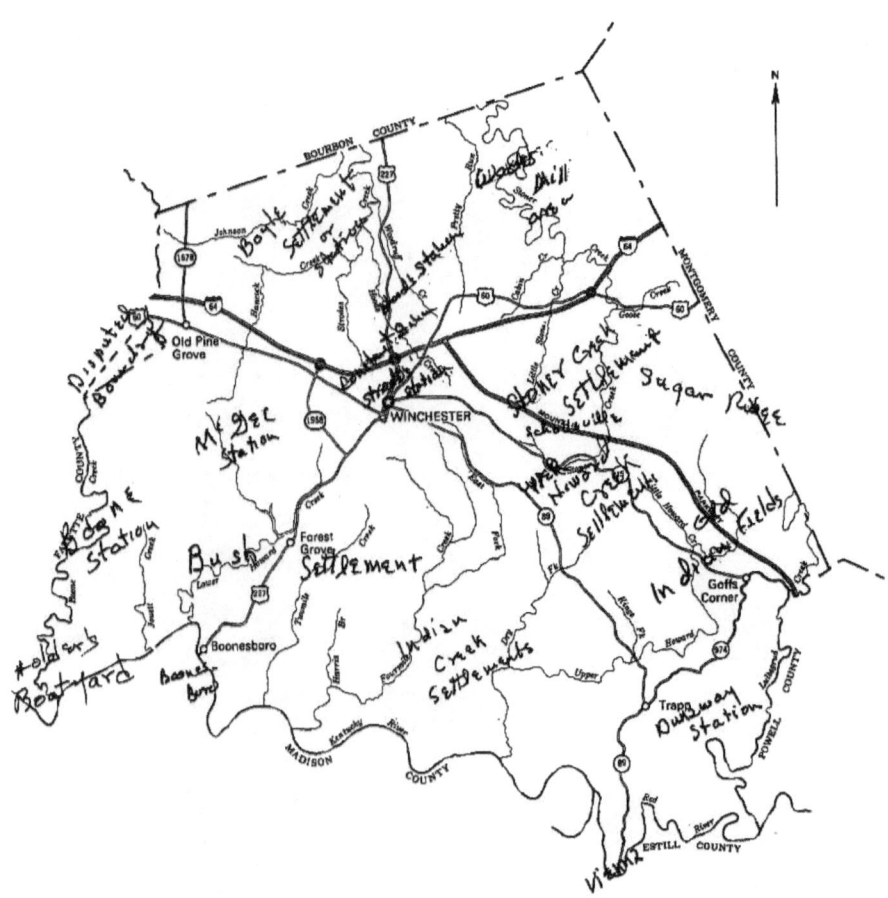

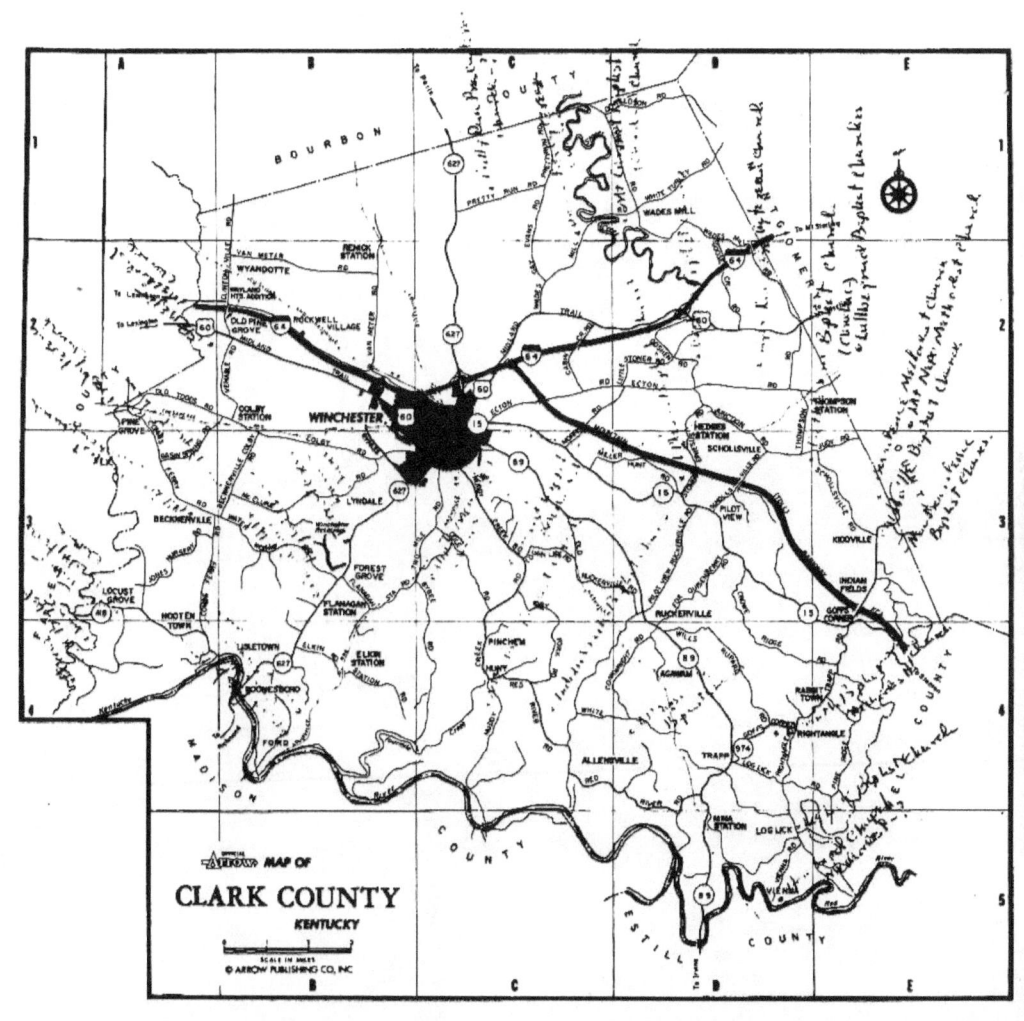

## TABLE OF CONTENTS

| | Page |
|---|---|
| Clark County | 1 |
| Pilot Knob | 1 |
| Prehistoric Kentucky River | 2 |
| Clark County | 2 |
| The Ancient Kentucky | 11 |
| Eskippakithiki | 13 |
| Eskippakithiki and John Findlay | 15 |
| Catahecassa | 17 |
| Lulbegrud | 17 |
| Exploration of Kentucky | 19 |
| John Swift's Silver Mine | 22 |
| The Transylvania Company | 26 |
| The Boone Family | 28 |
| Daniel Boone | 34 |
| Boonesborough | 39 |
| The Kidnapping | 45 |
| Richard Calloway | 47 |
| Michael Stoner | 48 |
| Early Clark County Settlers | 49 |
| Blue Grass | 54 |
| American Revolutionary War Veterans | 56 |
| Clark County Settlements in General | 69 |
| Strode Station | 76 |

|  | Page |
|---|---|
| The Bush Settlement | 80 |
| Providence Baptist Church | 83 |
| McGee's Station | 104 |
| Holder's Boat Yard | 104 |
| Constant's Station | 106 |
| Smaller Stations | 106 |
| Croswaithe's Station | 107 |
| Stockton's Station-Boyle's Station | 108 |
| The Stoner Settlements | 108 |
| Other Communities | 112 |
| Schollsville | 113 |
| Indian Fields | 118 |
| Wades Mill-Pretty Run Communities | 119 |
| Pine Grove | 123 |
| Upper Howard Creek-Ruckerville | 124 |
| Pinchem | 124 |
| Pilot View | 125 |
| Log Lick | 126 |
| Dunaway Station | 126 |
| Ford | 127 |
| Rennick | 127 |
| Sewell Shop | 127 |
| Indian Warfare | 129 |
| Politics on the Frontier | 145 |
| Clark County | 155 |
| Establishment of Clark County | 159 |

|  | Page |
|---|---|
| The County Seat | 166 |
| Further Development of the New County | 168 |
| Montgomery County | 177 |
| Constitutional Changes, 1799 | 182 |
| The Clark County Line | 184 |
| Winchester | 187 |
| Winchester in the 1800's | 193 |
| Life Between 1790 and 1800 | 196 |
| Alien and Sedition Laws | 217 |
| George Rogers Clark | 219 |
| Hubbard Taylor | 220 |
| The McMillans | 222 |
| Richard Hickman | 225 |
| William Sudduth | 225 |
| Achilles Eubank | 226 |
| Joel Hart | 227 |
| Education in the 1790's to 1800 | 228 |
| The Militia | 236 |
| Religion on the Frontier | 247 |
| The Cane Ridge Revival | 254 |
| The Baptists | 256 |
| The North District | 261 |
| The Licking Association of Particular Baptist | 283 |
| Indian Creek Baptist Church | 292 |
| Mt. Olive Baptist Church | 295 |
| Boone Creek Baptist Association | 303 |

|  | Page |
|---|---|
| The French Family of Baptist | 327 |
| The Unity Baptist Church | 328 |
| Friendship Baptist Church | 332 |
| Goshen Baptist Church | 339 |
| Upper Howard Creek Baptist Church | 355 |
| Log Lick Baptist | 360 |
| New Providence and Kiddville Baptist Churches | 364 |
| Ephesus Baptist Church | 367 |
| First Baptist Church, Winchester, Ky. | 376 |
| Mt. Carmel Baptist Church | 377 |
| The Presbyterians | 382 |
| Salem Presbyterian Church | 390 |
| Sugar Ridge Presbyterian Church | 403 |
| First Presbyterian Church | 409 |
| Union Presbyterian Church | 415 |
| The Methodist Church | 419 |
| Kentucky Circuit | 427 |
| Lexington Circuit | 427 |
| Hinkston Circuit | 429 |
| Mt. Sterling Circuit | 441 |
| Winchester Circuit | 444 |
| Mt. Zion Methodist Church | 453 |
| Ebeneazor Methodist Church | 460 |
| Winchester Methodist Church | 466 |
| Dunaway Methodist Church | 469 |
| The Stamper Meeting House | 475 |

|   | Page |
|---|---|
| Buckeye Methodist Church | 477 |
| Providence Methodist Church | 479 |
| Howard's Chapel | 481 |
| Northern Methodist | 482 |
| The Texas-Richmond Circuit | 488 |
| Owen Meeting House, Wool's Chapel, Owen's Chapel | 493 |
| Rev. Lawrence W. Owen | 501 |
| Thomas Hinde | 504 |
| William Kavanaugh | 506 |
| Hubbard Hinde Kavanaugh | 507 |
| Conclusion | 508 |
| Epilog | 509 |
| Index | 510 |

Introduction

This history of Clark County started, as all histories of a county begin, as a one-volume book. However, there is simply so much of interest that it has grown like "Topsy." For awhile, we considered two volumes, and then three, and as we put together the first volume we wonder if it ought not have been in four. The economic factor appears. . . will people be interested in a four-volume history of Clark County? Even at this, there are considerable areas of historical research not yet covered.

We have made little or no effort to read the criminal court cases. Unquestioningly, there would be much of interest. We have done nothing more than barely skim the deed books, and then mostly where they are connected with a church, turnpike, or some other area of interest. Almost nothing has been done with deeds just to see what interesting information they might contain. The governor's papers have hardly been touched. They have been scanned. There is much more. We have not made a complete study of the leigslative journals. We have but scratched the surface of neighboring newspapers. There is a time factor involved. It takes about an hour to read a month of newspapers. A Covington paper will have three news items on Clark County, say for the year 1858. Two of these will not be of real significance. There is hardly time to systematically work through them. Yet, there are papers paralleling Clark County history in Lexington, Louisville, Cincinnati, Frankfort, Covington, Paris, etc., that do have items occasionally of interest. However, there must be a limit somewhere; so we have not adequately examined these sources.

We know there are attics filled with letters, diaries, old church bulletins and reports, and newspapers that would bear a considerable interest on Clark County history. We advertised for such three times and each time got a little. However, there is a great deal more that has never been found. We tremble with fear that when this book comes to the public there will be a great torrent of such material suddenly made available. For example, one of the Jones had an auction a few years ago. They hauled box and trunk full of old magazines and papers after trunk and box full, to be sold. Most of the stuff was interesting, but not really important. There were scattered items that were important, but no one had time to really sit down and see what was there. When I was growing up, I used to rummage in the attic of my cousin, May Goff. There were scads of stuff there. It's all gone now. The house has been sold three times and the attic remodelled. I was too young to recognize what was good or bad. In my own house, I came from a family that seldom threw anything away, I found a stack of letters from my grandfather, who died before my father was born. He was in Jackson, Kentucky, selling bark for the tanning business. It was interesting to see how those letters began optimistic and ended in discouragement as the tanning business collapsed. These are not of historical importance, but if I would ever write Breathitt County history. . .and that would be fascinating. . .they illustrate economic conditions.

Writing county history is like a jigsaw puzzle. A piece will come here and another there. For example, there is a book on the history of stagecoaches in Kentucky. One story is about a stagecoach accident that happened on the Winchester-Mt. Sterling Pike (no date given), between the New Zion Church and the Montgomery line. The stagecoach hit a telegraph pole in its course. We know that the Mt. Zion Methodist Church was called New Zion Church for several years after the building of a new church in the late 1840's. The name of the stagecoach driver was one that drove between Lexington and Owingsville about 1855. Therefore, we have a good date and place. What we did not know, and have as yet not found, is a date for the running of a telegraph line through Winchester. There were state regulations of telegraph companies before 1850. This was within a few years of the invention of the telegraph. The stagecoach book had no interest in telegraph. The bit of information was merely accidental to the story. However, it does give a date when telegraph was available to Clark County.

I often try to explain some historical event by guessing from facts in hand, to an explanation of the fact. For example, there have been certain ministers in the county that have literally married hundreds of couples. One minister married, in Clark County alone, over a thousand couples; another minister five hundred. A dozen or more have married more than a hundred. Among these marrying parsons, there is but one Methodist minister in charge of a circuit. Why? The answer lies in the mobility of the Methodist ministers. In the early days they spent only a year or two in a circuit. They did not have time to establish the kind of communal relations which brought to them large numbers of young couples to marry. Some of the local ministers of the Methodist Church did make the grade. On the other hand, the Christian and Baptist ministers spent their life time in and around the county. One died in his nineties after seventy years of preaching and marrying.

We raise the religious question as to why the Church of Christ, the anti-musical-instrument movement in the Christian Church, had only one church in Clark County, whereas, in Montgomery County they have several. I suggest that the reason for this was in establishing a strong Church of Christ in Winchester, the movement drew supporters out of the other Christian churches. In Montgomery County there was no strong Church of Christ organized in Mt. Sterling until recently; and, therefore, Church of Christ people carried their local churches with them. I have no proof of this, but it seems reasonable.

Roughly, this volume covers Clark County history from earliest times to 1800. There are other items which will be brought up to date or to some other quitting point in history rather than divide the history. Hotels, for example, we bring up to the building of the Brown Proctor Hotel; the Post Office to the point where Civil Service takes over from politics, the appointment of postmasters; churches of a rural nature established before the Civil War, including some that began as one denomination and changed before the Civil War, we bring up to 1922 or to their deaths. I tried to carry the city churches up to the Civil War.

We try to show the relationship of history to the present day. We feel that one reason one studies history is to understand the present and to predict the future. History goes, not in circles as some say, but in spirals, with the same situation duplicating itself with more or less differences over and over again. One can understand, for example, the problems of the draft by a freeminded study of the draft throughout history. One can see the drift of religion, corruption in politics, morals of a nation, etc., in history.

What Clark County offers are graphic illustrations of how the facts of history work out. We read of 90-day enlistments being a problem in the early wars. We see what happens to real live men whose enlistments run out in the middle of a war. We read how the Alliance, and the Populists, shook the nation in the 1890's. In Clark County we can see what actually happened. We can read of the growth of public education, and in Clark County we can see that growth. In this way, it is hoped that these historical volumes will be of interest to more than just local people. In our fondest visions we think of them as a sort of historic "Middletown." "Middletown" was a sociological study of a city in the Middle West during the period following the first World War. Every social studies student in the thirties was required to study the social structure of Middletown. Henry Clay fought for "internal improvements." Our Clark County history will point at some of those internal improvements.

And now an apology. We have in this book thousands of names. It is inevitable that some will be misspelled. Some, because our sources are either misspelled (you should see what the Order books do to Scobee), unreadable or themselves in error. Some have come in the numerous typings and printings. Some are just plain mistakes. If we can, in the second edition, if there is a second edition, we will correct them. In the meantime, we apologize.

## CLARK COUNTY

At the beginning of this history, we must note that Clark County was spelled with an "e," "Clarke" until into the Civil War. The "House Journal" of 1863 still referred to Clark County as Clarke County. The change had been gradual, beginning about 1850. There is no reason given. In passing, we note that George Rogers Clarke also spelled his name with an "e" through most of his life. The local Clark family, Robert and James, a very influential family in county politics, generally did not. The Order books, though putting the "e" to Clark County, did not do so for Robert and James. The use of "e" at the end of many words, shoppe for example, was being dropped at about the same time.

Any history of Clark County must take into consideration the dominating influence of Fayette County and Lexington over the county affairs. Clark County never quite became a suburb of Lexington, but Fayette County influence is constantly being felt, sometimes adversely to Clark County's best interests. There have been many influential Clark Countians whose ties socially and economically have belonged more to Fayette County than to Clark County. This influence is not true, for example, of Bourbon County, where Paris was able to maintain its own personality independent of its overpowering neighbor. Bourbon County did not influence Clark County other than the Wades Mill area. Montgomery County's ties and history flow eastward to Maysville and eastern Kentucky as much as it does to Clark and Fayette Counties to the west. It is surprising how little Montgomery and Clark Counties affect each other.

Powell County has always been closely tied to Clark, as Clark has been to Fayette. There has been rebellion in Powell County against Clark County's influence.

## PILOT KNOB

Pilot Knob is a mountain that sets in the opening of the Red River Valley and Clark County. It is 1441 feet high, not the tallest in the area by any means, but from its top one can see some thirty miles into central Kentucky. The Indians used it as a watch and signal mountain. Christopher Gist visited it in 1751. Boone and Findlay climbed it in 1741.

There has been virtually no effort to develop a park or a tourist attraction out of something that could very easily be both.

## PREHISTORIC KENTUCKY RIVER

J.W. Rouse's "The Geology of Clark County" includes a paragraph of interest. It reports that in prehistoric days the Kentucky River cut directly across Clark County from near the mouth of the present lower Howard's Creek, northward at about a N20° angle coming just west of Winchester and going north to the general vicinity of Georgetown.

## CLARK COUNTY

The Soil Survey of Clark County which was published by the Conservation department contains the foundation to a history of Clark County. Clark County is in the central and western edge of northeastern Kentucky. . .almost a central county and almost a bluegrass county. It is bounded on the north by Bourbon County, which gave a little of its territory to form the original Clark County. Montgomery and Powell Counties, both of which were part of the original Clark County, form the eastern boundary. Fayette, out of which Clark County was originally formed, lies to the west. The southern boundary of contemporary Clark County is the Red and Kentucky Rivers. There was a time when Clark County straddled the Kentucky River to include most of what is now Estill, Powell, and southeastern counties to the Cumberland Gap.

Clark County has 259 square miles or 165,760 acres. At low water mark, the Kentucky River is 525 feet above sea level. The ridge between Stoner Creek and Kiddville is 1,100 feet above sea level, and the ridge along the Clark County-Montgomery County line is 1,051 feet above sea level. Sewell Shop is 1,102 feet above sea level.

The county has four physiological sections with a topography that ranges from gently undulating to steep. It is not included by Berea College among the mountain counties as Madison, Powell and Montgomery are. The western part of the county is the inner bluegrass region, undulating, gently rolling, with many shade tree pastures. It is well watered by creeks and brooks, but these often dry up during dry weather giving a serious water problem. The underground water is usually shallow, also subject to fluctuation, and never in sufficient quantities for irrigation. A few of the better springs were walled up with uncemented stone walls early in the county history. Ponds have been extensively dug, particularly in the last thirty years, to give additional water. Water, therefore, is always a prime need. Most of the homes have cisterns that are dependent on rainfall. The author's aunt and grandmother would never permit water in a tub to be more than a few inches deep. Water hauling in the last twenty years (1976), has become a rather profitable sideline for many farmers and truckers with water tanks.

The second section is called the hills of the bluegrass, and is more rolling than the inner bluegrass. The terrain is hilly, with winding ridges and valleys. The ground is still fertile, though it has considerable erosion problems. Springs are more numerous, but are still mostly surface water or shallow holes.

The third section increases both in the roll of the hills and the depth of the valleys between the ridges. The soil, though still fertile, is apt to be rocky and thin. Water is less of a problem, for the springs are more numerous and the creeks and streams, though smaller than those of the inner bluegrass region, are less apt to dry up. The high ground from Stoner to Kiddville and along the Montgomery County line forms a watershed in which most of the streams of Clark County's eastern section originate. The southeastern section of the county, the Knob Hill section, is rolling except for conical, flat-topped hills. The soil is filled with pieces of slate and is thin.

In the southeast corner of the county is Indian Fields, an interesting geological formation consisting of perhaps five thousand acres of relatively flat, marshy, fertile land surrounded with knob hills and outer bluegrass country. Evidently, it was a lake in the long distant past. Indian Fields is also bordered by numerous mineral springs and seeps oil in places. The area also has extensive slate reserves. None of these natural resources have proven economic advantages, but they keep the door of hope open for the future.

Very important in the early history of Clark County is the system of creeks that flow out of the county. The Order book would refer to So and So on Four Mile Creek, or Bill Smith on Strode's Creek. Roads were too uncertain, always being re-routed in different areas, abandoned and relocated to become map marks. When post offices were located in the country, names other than creeks were used. Political precincts, which came about the same time as post offices, gave other names. However, for the first 50 years a man was located by the creek he lived on.

The Fayette County line is marked by Boone's Creek. Flowing into the Kentucky River, there, are Upper and Lower Howard's Creek that drain much of the area from Winchester to Indian Fields. Two other creeks coming into the Kentucky River are Four Mile and Two Mile. Running the other direction and eventually emptying into the Licking River are Stoner Creek and Little Stoner that drain much of the eastern section of the county. In the western part of the county, Hancock and Strode's Creeks contribute their waters. Along these creeks, most of the early settlements were made.

Clark County has a wide range of temperatures, rainfall, wind and humidity, but it is all well within the range of varied animal and plant life. Southern magnolias and northern pines do seem to be able to live within the county.

The problem in recording history of weather in Clark County lies in its unofficial status. The nearest official weather station is Blue Grass Field. A newspaper of any given date, commenting on the unusual weather of that date, may drift into discussing similar weather conditions of the past. The one thing that is a certainty in Clark County is the uncertainty of the weather. There is scarcely a year that the old timers do not sit back and proclaim that they have lived in Clark County for thirty years and they have never seen weather doing whatever it is doing at the moment. The weather forecasts on the whole are completely undependable. Thirty percent chance of rain in the wintertime is an almost certainty of getting rain. Thirty percent in the summer time is virtually a promise of a clear day. Over and over again, the full effect of a predicted change in weather will be 12 to 24 hours late, or at least, so it seems.

On the whole, the newspapers did not note hot weather other than in reporting drouths. Hot weather does not cause the suffering of cold weather and, therefore, is more apt to be ignored. One can assume when drouth is reported it is also hot. Cathenwood reported that from July 17 to August 11, 1878, it was never below 80 degrees and at noon on July 7, it was 100 degrees. The Winchester News reported July 5, 1911, it was 102 degrees. Winchester's professional ball team nevertheless played baseball.

The temperature will rise to 90 degrees or more on the average of about 29 days a year. A temperature of 100 degrees will occur at least once each year on an average.

When the Winchester DEMOCRAT reported the cold winter of 1899, it also reported the warmest winter up to 1899 was the winter of 1825-26. There was no snow and the coldest was 20 degrees. Another warm winter was in 1889-90 when peach trees bloomed in February, and there was green grass all year long. Unfortunately, there was a 10-day cold spell in March that produced 2 inches of ice on the ponds and death to the peach crops.

Freezing temperatures in Clark County occur about 97 nights in an average winter. However, the temperature will rise above 32 degrees on all but 20 days a year. A daily freeze-thaw cycle is normal for winter. Normally, there will be zero or below weather five to ten times a year.

The length of the growing season, from the last light freeze to the first light freeze averages 190 days. Five out of ten years the growing season is 179 to 202 days. Eight out of ten years the season will be 169 to 211 days. A freeze after April 20 will occur five out of ten years; a freeze after April 29, twice in ten years; a freeze after May 5, once in ten years; a frost before October 7, once in ten years; and a frost before October 12, twice in ten years.

Snowfalls of more than one inch will occur about five times a year. The yearly average snow is 19 inches. The ground is seldom covered more than a few days.

The winter of 1779-80 was called the "hard winter." Snow lay on the ground from the middle of November to late in February. Freezing and subfreezing weather was the rule. The Kentucky River was frozen several times that winter. Zero weather lasted for days several times during the winter. Daniel Boone is reported to have used his last flour in December and did not have any more until late spring when the first pack trains began coming over the mountains. At the Falls of the Ohio, later Louisville, corn was reported selling for $60.00 a bushel. Game was scarce. Suffering among the first settlers was considerable. It must be remembered, concerning the dates, that up into the 1790's, the European world used the Julian Calendar which made no provision for the additional six and a half hours more than 365 days. The result was a slow advance in the calendar so that in 1779 the first day of winter was coming close to the middle of November instead of the middle of December. The calendar was readjusted in the 1790's and Leap Year took care of the six hours. The only saving factor in the "hard winter" was the fact that the Indians were also suffering and kept to their villages in the country north of the Ohio River.

In 1894, there were 5 inches of snow early in May. The DEMOCRAT, reporting a frost May 22, 1894, said snow covered ripened strawberries in that early year. On April 18, 1881, the DEMOCRAT remembered there had been a frost in 1813 every month out of the year and that there had actually been ice in July and August. On March 5, 1890, the DEMOCRAT also remembered that there had been frosts in both June and July in 1816.

The newspapers of Clark County did not mention another hard winter until 1829. The LEXINGTON REPORTER, March 18, 1829, gave a contemporary complaint that the winter had been cold with a great deal of snow. Spring was late. It does not mean that there had been a 12-year period of warm years. The winters weren't so cold that they started legends to be repeated 50 years later. There does seem to be a warming cycle after a period of hard winters from 1786 to 1816.

The DEMOCRAT, shivering in the cold winter of 1892, quoted James Rutledge telling how there were 15 inches of snow November 5, 1818. According to him, it stayed on the ground until the middle of February.

January 19, 1852, was another heavy winter. The Ohio River froze over for the second time in memory. James Rutledge resumed his discussion of weather by reporting that it was so cold in 1863 that chicks froze on their roosts. It was a miserable winter.

On October 3, 1878, Cathenwood reported to the Clark County DEMOCRAT that in 1878 on January 7, it was 16 degrees; on February 8, 19 degrees; March 28, 19 degrees.

Also 1881 was quite a year. The DEMOCRAT, January 19, reported that Four Mile Creek Road was completely blocked, even for men on horseback. Ice and snow 6 inches and 8 inches covered the rivers and ponds. Ice was piled 5 feet high on the banks. The DEMOCRAT reported that the week of the 18th of January the temperature was 40 degrees, but on the 19th a bitter cold wind began to blow. By the 25th it was 8 degrees and there 3 inches of snow. The 31st was a mild lovely day. On April 20, the Log Lick correspondent complained that the weather was so bad that there were no gardens and no grass. August 14 reported that there had been frosts May 10 and June 14.

It snowed so hard in 1884 that the C & O train was stalled at Ewington for two days.

On April 13, 1887, the DEMOCRAT reported in January it had snowed October 1st and 3rd of 1886. In November there was ice. It snowed on December 1 and the snow was on the ground until the 22nd. On December 4, it was -4 degrees. In January it snowed the 1st, 14th, 17th and 21st; on January 18, it was -6 degrees. There was thunder and lightening in February on the 3rd, 4th, and 16th. It was 10 degrees on the 20th. The paper reported that in October, November, December, January, and until the 20th of February there had been only four clear days.

There was a heavy frost on October 2, 1888, that did severe damage to tobacco. It was cold again in 1892. In 1894, it was a -14 degrees at Ford the last of January. May 20, 1894, rain changed to snow; the weight breaking down many fully leafed trees.

October 4, 1895, there was a frost that destroyed nearly a third of the county's tobacco. The worst year was 1899. It was a miserable year in 1916, which started the DEMOCRAT reminiscing; December 6, 1899, it rained all day turning to periods of sleet. The next day, the 7th, the sleet continued, and finally turned into snow covering the county with a layer of ice topped with three or four inches of snow. On the 8th, a cold, fierce wind set in. On the 9th, it was a -12 degrees. On the 10th, it reached a -21 degrees and rose to a -13 degrees in the heat of the day, to drop back to a -15 degrees. On the 11th it got up to zero and dropped to a -9 degrees. On the 12th it was zero but the 13th it dropped back at a -15 degrees and on the 14th it was a -14 degrees.

J. D. Simpson reported a -5 degrees temperature. It was so cold that the river was frozen and the mill at Ford had to close down because the logs were iced in. (In the history of Ford, this was the second time the mill had frozen.) Schools were closed; coal was in shortage; and eight to ten people froze to death.

These are all newspaper reports and most of them went back a decade or more. There has been no effort to find official reports to to verify these news stories. This is the story the old timers would tell. Apparently, there was a period up to 1818 when the winters were severe. They did not appear to be particularly severe again until after 1880 with a few exceptions. For a decade after 1900 winters did not appear to be bad. Perhaps that winter of 1899 was enough.

The next few years the winters were relatively mild. In 1906 there was considerable snow, and in 1909, January 30, the DEMOCRAT reported a blizzard with 50-mile winds. When the blizzard was over, February 1 temperature dropped to a -4 degrees.

The next big snow and the last of this section of the history of Clark County was the winter of 1916-17. There was a heavy snowfall December 19, 1916, but on January 16, 1917, a 20-inch snow fell, one of the heaviest in years. It closed the roads and even delayed the rail connections. The telephone and telegraph lines were out. For a 24-hour period, Winchester was isolated from the outside except for the interrupted rail lines.

The fourth volume of this work will continue the story of cold, wind, and rain from 1916 to present.

The average rainfall in Clark County is 43 inches. On of average, the heaviest one-hour rain will produce one and a half inches. There is a 35 percent of a one-inch rain in July and a 30 percent chance in August. There is less than a one percent chance of a one-inch rain from November to January. Once in ten years, a 4.25-inch rain will fall in a 24-hour period. Thunder storms occur on the average of 47 days per year. Measurable amounts of precipitation will occur on the average of 131 days a year.

Prevailing winds come from the south and southwest on an average of about 11 miles an hour. Calm periods last less than twenty-four hours on an average. The Conservation study does not give any figures on hurricanes or tornadoes.

When a stranger visits Kentucky and sees the rolling green hills and meandering creeks, he finds it difficult to believe that water is a major problem. There is seldom a year when there is not a dry period lasting two to six weeks. Fortunately, it is usually the middle or last of August into the fall, when the crops are made and dry weather is an advantage. Even then, however, it burns the late corn, the gardens, and parches the grass so that fall grazing is hurt. The creeks will dry up and the streams run short.

There are wells reaching down into the subsoil water strata, but in most cases surface water is not of sufficient abundance to do more than partly relieve the situation. In 1881, Kerr was drilling for artesian water and the DEMOCRAT spoke eagerly of unlimited supplies of deep water. This did not materialize. Kerr found some gas, traces of oil, but no water. Most homes, both in the country and the city, were provided water either by springs or by cisterns. Many of the country homes were built with the consideration of the nearness of spring water. Gradually as civilization spread over Kentucky and timber was cut, many of these springs were reduced in size or dried up. Winchester was established on John Baker's land because Baker's spring was large and sufficient for many families. Long before the Civil War it had disappeared and its exact location is uncertain. When the city was first established, Maple Avenue was called Water Street because the city water supply was located in that general area. When the Browning Turkey buildings were erected on the corner of Maple and Broadway, they struck a sizeable vein of water in digging their foundations. In 1881, it was reported that the spring at Clark mansion had been redug after 40 years of disuse. The same year it was reported that the famous Pinchem spring was lower than any time since 1854 but still provided water for 25 families and 200 head of stock.

Therefore, drouth is the weather that haunts the Clark Countians. The two worst drouths in Clark County history occurred in 1854 and 1936. Over and over again the early newspapers refer to the 1854 drouth. June 26, 1901, the SUN SENTINAL described conditions in 1854 as disastrous. It rained the 3rd and 4th of July and did not rain again until the last of October. When one realizes that it takes a rain every five to seven days to keep plants green and growing the conditions of 1854 were obvious. Wheat sold for a dollar a bushel; oats for $5.00 a bundle; timothy at $20.00 a ton; and corn was not available Pinchem spring was the only water in a five-mile radius and hundreds of wagons carried water to Winchester and elsewhere from there. In 1878 it rained 13 days in June; 9 days in July; 11 days in August and 11 days in September.

There was a severe drouth in 1879, and again in 1881, which started the idea of a Winchester water works. In September of 1899, it was stated that the DEMOCRAT wondered whether the Baptists and the Christians would not have to adopt sprinkling and the Presbyterians and Methodists would have to use a damp cloth.

The drouth of 1889 introduced new problem. On dry years before the locks at Boonesboro were built, the Kentucky River would get so low that it could be waded in places. Any shipping that had come upriver when the river was high was forced to remain there until the water rose again. Since the river was the main source of coal, a drouth could stop delivery of early coal which would mean shortages later on.

The SUN SENTINAL reported another dry year in 1902. On November 11, it was reported that the Lexington and Evanston were hauling water for their steam engines. It was dry again in 1904, and there were complaints in 1906.

This new problem was further complicated by the fact that "tides," as high waters on the Kentucky were called, became a necessity of life for Ford. "Tides" on the river brought a rush of logs for Ford's hungry sawmills. Drouth meant that work in the booming community would soon be shut down.

The lack of water was a major threat to Ford's industry. Only twice did the river freeze over, yet there was hardly a year that the supply of logs did not run short because of low water.

Rains and floods have always been important to Kentucky history. It takes a rain every five to seven days to keep crops growing nicely. Even one week's rain, with creeks high and land soaked, will not be enough if it does not rain again in seven to ten days. Those who own river bottoms say that even in 1975 with the lock system complete and some river controls, that the bottom lands will be flooded at least once a year. So the county worries about tides and rains for crops.

A record flood in 1817 destroyed the warehouses and homes along the Kentucky River on both sides of the river around Boonesboro. There had not been any such flood in the thirty or so years. So complete was the destruction that the warehouses were never rebuilt and the exact location of Boonesboro was forgotten. In 1827, for the first three months rain fell nearly every day. In the forty days before January 9, there were only four days of sun. On May 10, 1828, there were hailstones 2 and 3 inches in diameter.

In the year of 1840, a great Boonesboro celebration was planned with politicians, barbecue, military parades, bands, and old timers present. Heavy rains upstream caused the river to rise a foot in one hour, flooding the tables and driving the speakers and participants to higher ground.

John Catherwood was one of the thousands of citizens across the United States that kept weather statistics for the government as a hobby. July 30, 1879, he reported in the DEMOCRAT that it had rained 39 out of the 50 days preceding July 26. The same year, a cyclone, 150 feet wide, swept the eastern part of the county. William Epperson lost his tenant house. Bud Elkins lost a barn and tenant house. Meanwhile, Catherwood reported in 1879 that the warmest day in November had been 78 degrees and the coldest a -3 degrees for a 20-year period.

The Log Lick correspondent reported to the DEMOCRAT, February 25, 1880, the Red River had flooded Vienna in the worst flood since 1817. Vienna was virtually wiped out and was never rebuilt. In 1890 the Red and Kentucky Rivers and Lullibegrud Creek flooded so badly that the Kentucky Central was closed at Ford. May 14, 1895, the DEMOCRAT discussed the 1892 flood reporting that Two-Mile Creek and the river had flooded, drowning seven or eight Negroes and one white woman. The 1892 papers never mentioned such a tragedy.

The SUN SENTINAL reported in 1906 that the February sleet storm was one of the biggest in years. A new factor appeared in sleet and ice storms. In earlier years ice and sleet storms were just another, perhaps more unpleasant, type of winter storm. After 1900, the country was interlaced with a network of telephone and electrical wires. By 1906 the country was already heavily dependent on telephone as a means of communication and the heavy breakdown of wires created considerable havoc.

On May 4, 1909, high winds and rain flooded part of Winchester, including the basement and engine room of the Winchester Roller Mill. Barns were blown down, roofs blown off, chimneys toppled, and homes were wrecked. Many breaks appeared in the telephone lines as falling limbs tore through the wires.

The next year on July 5, the paper reported the heaviest rains ever known. The Winchester Roller Mill was again damaged. Water in

Bucktown was up to the second floors. Street and road damage was immense. The L & N rails were washed out in four places. For awhile, there wasn't a road leading into Winchester that was not at one point or another flooded. Winchester, or at least parts of Broadway and Bucktown, were flooded in 1910.

On February 13, 1910, the river was as high as it had ever been. Then the 19th reported that an ice storm hit Winchester cutting it off from the world. Old Kentucky Telegraph and Telephone managed to keep a few lines working. Only Ford to Richmond of the East Tennessee Telegraph and Telephone was still operating. Western Union and Postal Telegraph to Mt. Sterling were out. Fifty poles were down on the Iron Works Pike and the whole Becknerville line was down. All freight trains were stopped. Central Baptist meeting in the courthouse on Sunday had to use gas lights instead of electricity. It is interesting to note that gas lights were still available.

History of telephone and telegraph will be included in the third volume.

The year of 1911 was a wet one. In April, 1911, the WINCHESTER NEWS reported the biggest tide in 15 years. Boonesboro Road was covered. In September, 1911, the DEMOCRAT reported 5.85 inches of rain in August. It had rained 13 days. In November, 1911, the NEWS reported that October had broken an all-time record for rain in that month. Previously, it had been 1879 with 2.63 inches. In 1911 it was 4.36 inches.

Weather from this point to the present will be reported in Volume Four of this history.

The Ancient Kentucky

When the white man first came to Kentucky, there were only two permanent Indian villages in the entire state, a Shawnee village at Indian Old Fields and another Indian village in the very western part of the state. This was not the historical condition of Kentucky. There is evidence that once Kentucky had a great many villages of an unknown people. We are not going into the entire history of these people, but only those that are related to Clark County. We are referring to the Indian mounds.

The most dramatic of the Indian locations in Kentucky is the Devil's Backbone. The backbone is ridge cut by Stoner Creek, which held Indian graves. It was not a mound as such. Graves were scattered all around it. Even today the mound on Pretty River is a large mound of dirt that is both high and long. It was named the Devil's Backbone, according to tradition, to impress the slaves that they should not run away. There has been some excavation of it, and some Indian graves and bones have been found. There is no indication that the people who buried the Indians in the Devil's Backbone built the mound. There has been little other effort to excavate the Mound because most experts feel it is nothing but a high pile of dirt. Whatever it is, it took a great deal of time and effort to build with the primitive methods that the Indians had at their disposal. The Kentucky Geological Survey of 1928, in an article by W. D. Funkhauser and W. S. Wele entitled "Ancient Life in Kentucky," gives more details. There are other mounds in Kentucky, mostly along the Montgomery-Clark County line. There are also extensive mound developments in Montgomery County, including the mound that originally gave Mt. Sterling its name.

There is also evidence that there was an Indian village at Indian Old Fields that predated the Shawnees. The dance ring located on the bluff overlooking Howard's Creek could not have been made by only a few decades of Indian feet.

We are not quite sure what happened to these Indians in Kentucky. Willard Rouse Jillson and Lucien Beckner, the two leading Kentucky historians of the first half of the 20th century, seldom agreed on the details of anything. One can assume that, if one claimed one thing, the other would take a different position. Both have discussed the disappearance of what we might call the mound-dwelling Indians. Combining their two stories into what seems to be a reasonably historic summation, the story begins with the Dutch settlers in New Amsterdam (New York). They sold guns to the Senecas, one of the original five tribes of the Iroquoian Confederacy. (The term Iroquoian indicates a language group of tribes that started pushing into New York and then southward along the mountain chains. They were aggressive, fiercely savage in battle, and were driving the less warlike, earlier tribes ahead of them. One of the reasons the first American colonists were received by the Indians as well as they were was the hope of these Indians that the white men could stop this Iroquoian expansion. The two main centers of the Iroquois were in New York, where five tribes combined against the French in the Iroquoian Confederacy, and the collection of loosely associated tribes that generally were called Cherokee. There were other tribes, that were not really part of either group. The Tuscororas in North Carolina might be called Cherokee, but after their disastrous war with the white settlers, they moved northward to become the sixth tribe of the Iroquoian Confederacy. The Huron settled mostly in the northern part of the United States and Southern Canada. For some reason, they hated their New York cousins and allied themselves with the Algonquin tribes of the area both in war with the Iroquois and the Kentucky settlers.) This is a hasty generalization and is not completely accurate, but for our purposes is enough.

The Senecas used the guns they had gotten from the Dutch traders to sweep southward, out of western New York, which was their home stamping ground, along the Warrior Trail massacring everything that came before them. They evidently entered Kentucky killing men, women, and children, making no effort to take slaves or prisoners, until the entire area was swept clean of any settled human life. For those that have felt the Indians have been grossly mistreated, and they were, this extermination of an entire people just for the love of killing, might be remembered. The senecas returned to New York making no effort to settle Kentucky, but evidently left a warning to anyone who would.

The Cherokee, moving southward perhaps as part of the same southward drive, though independently, also did not settle in Kentucky but did feel it to be their own hunting ground. They did not object if the Algonquin tribes to the north hunted in it, as long as they did not occupy the territory. In fact there were often joint hunting parties, which showed a certain amount of tolerance. Kentucky had an almost endless supply of game which the Indians could not seriously endanger, and even more important, Kentucky had saltlicks and salt springs that could supply that very needed ingredient to anyone who desired it.

All of this occurred sometime after 1600 and before 1650.

# Eskippakithiki

When the first white men began to enter Kentucky, they found the land largely deserted by Indians other than hunting parties. A hundred years had elapsed since the Senecas had exterminated the Mound Builders, and most of the traces of their communities had disappeared into the wilderness. There were two permanent Indian villages in Kentucky, as it first became known. One was in the most western part, in what was later called the Jackson Purchase. The other was Eskippakithiki. This was a Shawnee village and was located in Indian Fields. Because of the tremendous amount of Indian artifacts, arrow heads and the like, found in the immediate area, it seems likely that there had been other earlier communities in the same area.

One of the better collections of information on the village was written in the <u>Winchester Sun</u>, November 29, 1975, by Mrs. Lucile Goff Clark, whose farm occupied some of the central portions of what had been the village. Thomas Field's <u>Filson Club Historical Quarterly</u> article in Volume 34 gives further information. Willard Jillson has a good deal of the information in his "Early Clark County, 1767-1824."

Mrs. Clark notes that "Kentuck," as a Shawnee Indian word, meant "blue lick" and referred to a salt sulpher springs in the general area. Mrs. Clark also reports that the word "Shawnee" means "southern" in the Algonquin.

With the coming of the white men, there were two language families, indicating related tribes in this general area. The Algonquin were the original, or at least the earlier inhabitants of the entire country from the Great Lakes to the Atlantic Ocean. They were evidently not the Mound Builders, who formed another language group. Into this collection of Algonquins, sometime prior to 1600, came the Iroquoian tribes, five of whom (Mohawks, Senecas, Onondogas, Cayugas, and Oneidas) formed the five-tribe Iroquoian Confederacy. These settled what was to be New York State and waged furious war on all their Algonquin neighbors.

Mrs. Clark says that the Shawnees were part of the Wisconsin Algonquins. Just who the Shawnees were originally, other than being Algonquin, is not clear. There is a suggestion that they were originally Pennsylvania Indians, or perhaps Delawares, that had been driven westward by the white settlers. They were not an indigenous tribe, but were made up of fragments of several tribes. The main body settled on the Miami River shortly before the white men began to appear on the Ohio River.

Sometime after this Miami settlement, a large group of Shawnees moved to Indian Fields and established Eskippakithiki. Mrs. Clark sets the date of the settlement between 1670 and 1754. The 1754 date is much too late. Lucien Beckner maintained that the settlement date was about 1704-1710. Naturally, Dr. Willard Jillson could not agree with his arch rival, so he claimed an earlier date, perhaps as early as 1670 based on the rings of trees and stumps in the area. Christopher Gist listed it on his map in 1751. The French Canadian Census reported by Mrs. Clark, listed the village in 1736 as having eight hundred to a thousand people, some two hundred families.

There is speculation why the Shawnees should go so far from the protection of their kindred to establish a village that had to attract the attention of the Cherokee. There had to be a substantial reason, for Kentucky had become a sort of neutral hunting ground for both Shawnee and other Algonquin tribes, and the Cherokee. They often could be found in the same hunting parties, evidently being peaceful brothers. However, the Cherokee would not permit, for long, a sizable permanent settlement so close to their own territory and towns.

It seems reasonable to presume that the village was originally an outpost of the French religious and economic empire. As Mrs. Clark notes, the entire area was claimed by the French, and the French would naturally want to nail down their claims with some kind of outpost. Indian Fields was a natural, close to the Kentucky River, which would furnish easy communications with the north, and on the Warrior trails that opened up the south. The old fort, or stockade, which formed the central part of the village was built in the white man's style rather than Indian. It was reported that the gates were hung with European hinges. These vanished long before the white man became interested in history.

The fact that the village was listed in the French census of 1736 would confirm the suspicion that this was a French sponsored outpost. However, long before the English began to become aware of the area, the French characteristic had vanished. Left behind was a sprawling scattering of huts and cabins scattered over the entire area instead of being concentrated in one place. These were divided by fields or corn-hacked out of the cane and the underbrush and connected by a haphazard maze of paths. The French had already been defeated and were withdrawing northward when the first English frontiersmen appeared. By this time, a generation of Shawnee had been raised to consider the village home and they did not flee. The Cherokee did not interfere.

The history of Eskippakithiki can never be written. It never occurred to anyone to record it. The village appears now and then in the records as it did in 1736 and in the French Canadian census. Sometime soon thereafter a young French Canadian named Gabriel Arthur was captured by Indians and brought down the Warrior Trail to the village before being released.

Meanwhile, over all the world, the French and English fought a century of warfare. There were periods of peace in Europe; but in the distant parts of the world, where communications could be anything from three to six months behind the fact, protagonists of each other assumed that the old war was not yet over or the new war had already begun.

In 1745, Peter Chartier, a half-breed, came down the Warrior Trail with some four hundred Delaware and Shawnee warriors. The whole English frontier was terrified, not so much with what Chartier was doing, but what he might do. Chartier did not find much harmony, however, at Eskippakithiki. He found opposition among the resident Shawnee to anything that might bring down the rage of the Cherokee. His force broke up and drifted down the southward trails into Mississippi and disappeared from history.

By this time, the country west of the mountains was called Kentucky. Mrs. Clark claims that the name applied first to the Indian Fields area, but in all probability the term applied to the entire area. She notes that, as an Iroquoian name, (which would include the Cherokee who used it extensively), it was derived from the word Kenta, meaning level, and tuckee, which meant meadow land. The word would be Ken-Ta-Ki. The various white explorers were referring to the country as Kentucky, and as the settlements appeared along the Kentucky River or close thereby, they were called the Kentucky Settlements.

Christopher Gist, in his explorations in 1751, evidently came through Clark County and included Eskippakithiki on his map. By this time there was a steady trickle of hunters moving across the mountains westward.

## ESKIPPAKITHIKI AND JOHN FINDLEY

John Findley was a Pennsylvania trader. Lucien Beckner tells his story in the Filson Club Historical Quarterly, Vol. 43, p. 206. In 1751 he floated down the Ohio River in some four large trading canoes looking for Indians in order to swap trade goods for furs. He was not the first trader to do such...in fact, it was evidently a rather common custom. On this particular trip, Findley did not have much luck until he arrived at the mouth of what is now Boone Creek on the Kentucky River. He met a hunting party of Shawnee who invited him to go up the Kentucky River and then inland to the Indian village of Eskippakithiki. He had with him three servants, John Faulkner, William Trent, and one other. It is not clear what their official status was. At any rate, arriving at the Indian village, Findley built a cabin and an animal pound which he surrounded with a low palisaded fence. It was a prosperous year. Beckner claimed that the gate posts were part of an older trading post which has already been mentioned.

This was one of those periodic lulls in the wars between the French and English during the first half of the 18th century. As had been reported there were other white men west of the mountains.

One such group of white men, David Hendricks, James Lowry, Alexander McGinty, Jabez and Jacob Evans, William Powell, and Thomas Hide came up the western branch of the Warrior Trail out of Mississippi and Alabama. They had with them a Cherokee servant. At the time, a band of Ottawas and Choctaw, Canadian and largely Christian Indians, were coming south along the same trail. The Indians were French dominated and hated the Iroquois as traditional enemies. None of the sources explain what such a large group was doing so far south from their usual hunting grounds. Beckner says they planned to raid Choctaw and Cherokee villages.

A full scale battle broke out between the two groups with Findley in the middle. It ended in a complete victory for the northern Indians. Lowry and the Cherokee escaped. The other white men of the party were captured and eventually carried back to Quebec. For some reason, Jacob Evans and Thomas Hide ended up in France. The Indians then turned on Findley. Findley and Faulkner escaped but lost the other two men and the year's profits. James French (1966) claims that this was the first battle of the French and Indian war.

Findley returned to the settlements without anything to show for his year's work, but full of glowing accounts of the western country. By this time, the French and Indian Wars were in full swing. Findley got a job as a wagoner for General Braddock as his army marched grandly in step to the drums and fife into the American wilderness. At nighttime, when in camp, Findley told about the west country. Among his listeners, and soon to be a close friend, was a young Pennsylvanian named Daniel Boone.

When Boone and Findley returned to Kentucky after the French and Indian War, they found the Indian village burned and deserted. There is no historic explanation of what happened. It is not difficult to guess. The Cherokee had permitted the Shawnees to have a village at Indian Old Field because it offered them a good place to trade furs and get the needed white man's inventions. This gave them a certain advantage while they pressed southward and eastward, and finally in their opposition to the white men pushing westward.

However, the French and Indian War ended this relationship. The Cherokees, like all the Iroquois except the Huron, sided with the British. They paid dearly for that mistake, but it seemed like a good idea at the time. No doubt, the fight between the Canadian Indians and the group of white men just described brought to their attention that they had a potential threat in their midst. Sometime thereafter, what must have been a sizeable raiding party swept down on the Shawnees and drove them northward to the protection of the Miami villages. Thus ended what must have been a long and more or less continous settlement of Indians.

It might be worth noting in passing, that the white settlers were not stealing Kentucky from the Indians. The original owners had long since been killed by other Indians, and that the land was up for grabs. Even the Cherokee were invaders and newcomers to the land that they claimed to be their own.

## CATAHECASSA

Mention should be made of Catahecassa, or Black Hoof, a Shawnee Chief. He turns up in history in the War of 1812 when he overheard American prisoners talk. One was Leonard Beall who was from Indian Fields. Catahecassa had been born at Eskippakithiki and saved Beall. Beall was taken to the Indian's cabin, near Detroit, and was adopeted as a "son." Beall, understandably grateful, invited the old Indian to visit him in Clark County. A few years later, in 1816, the old Chief turned up, close to a hundred years old, barefooted, at Beall's home in Clark County. He was gratefully received and spent several weeks there. As Mrs. Clark points out, he showed the early settlers many points of interest about Indian Fields. Unfortunately, no one recorded what he taught. Catahecassa evidently won considerable distinction among the Shawnee. He claimed to have shot at Washington several times during Braddock's Defeat, but ended by feeling Washington had a charmed life.

What has been written above is the tradition...the aged, barefooted Indian. There is another story that Kathryn Owen, who has spent her lifetime working with Clark County history, says was written to her by Colonel Lucien Beckner. Catahecassa visited Winchester some years after the War of 1812 with several members of his family. He lodged at the Clark House, the rival of the National House for the first fifty years of the county's history. They were registered as "Indian King and Lady." Using the Hotel as a base, he went the few miles into the country to visit Leonard Beall. There is very little doubt that Kathryn Owen is correct in her story. However, the picture of an old, tired, savage having ended a long trip to visit his home before he died is much more appealing.

## LULBEGRUD

The final chapter in the history of Eskippakithiki is the story that Boone tells himself.

Daniel Boone, in a deposition concerning a land title, describes the naming of Lulbegrud Creek. Lucien Beckner reports the story in the **Kentucky Historical Quarterly**. About May 1, 1765, Daniel Boone, John Findley, Alexander Neely, John Stuart, a brother-in-law of Daniel who evidently was deeply influenced by his frontiersman in law, Daniel and Joseph Holden, James Mooney, and William Cooley had been exploring and trapping west of the mountains for some weeks.

They finally came out of the mountains and camped on the banks of a small stream which flowed into a small river, which was unnamed(Gist had named it). It was hundreds of miles away from the nearest settlement (though Granny Anderson was reported not to have been too far away). Surrounded by hostile Indians and limited in the space to carry material, these men read sections from a new science fiction novel, **Gulliver's Travels**, written by a man named Jonathan Swift. They decided to name the creek they were camped on Lulbegrud in honor of one of the locations described in the novel.

It was on this expedition that Findley, though sick, and Boone climbed the mountain that Boone labeled Pilot Knob and saw stretching before him the flat lands of Indian Fields and the far distant hills of Kentucky. The party moved and camped at what is now called Hollywood Springs. The Shawnee village was destroyed and deserted. From this camp, Findley started for Fort Pitt and was never heard of again. He was sick at the time and may have died of natural causes.

The rest were attacked by Indians, who stole their horses and furs and scattered the party. Two of the companions of Boone were killed. Boone and Stuart tried to rescue their horses and were captured. They managed to escape. Stuart had had enough and decided to go home. He was killed by Indians on the way. Boone wandered around by himself for nearly a year. Meanwhile, Squire Boone, Daniel's brother, came out hunting Boone and found him at what must have been a predetermined meeting place. Together they hunted until 1770 before they returned to North Carolina.

The Lulbegrud Creek had received its name. Findley had disappeared. Two others had been killed. Stuart was killed going home. Boone, however, lived to explore the mountains east of Clark County even though he wasn't exactly the safest leader to have.

EXPLORATION OF KENTUCKY

In this history we limit ourselves to those early discoveries and explorations in Kentucky affecting Clark County. From the earliest time, there were trails that led north and south. They had been carved out of the land, using the easiest routes, along water and from salt lick to salt lick by generations of wild animals. The bones of mastodons can be found along its routes. The large herds of buffalo that existed in Kentucky before the coming of the white man were also responsible. These trails offered the late-coming humans, avenues of travel from the north to the south. Thomas Connelly makes a report of these trails in the Kentucky Historical Society Review, Vol. 59.

The most important of these, for our history, is the so-called Warrior Trail. It crossed the Ohio somewhere west of Maysville, coming through the Blue Licks, on through Central Kentucky to Indian Fields. Another branch of the trail, less known, crossed the river near Cincinnati, followed the Ohio River southward through what is now called Bone Lick, and then went roughly southward until it joined the other branch at Indian Fields.

At Indian Fields, the trail divided again, one branch swinging eastward through the Cumberland Gap and the other southwestward into eastern Tennessee, Alabama, and Mississippi.

White settlers moving westward had a choice. They either came through the Cumberland Gap, which was the easiest and most accessible opening in the mountains, or down the Ohio, moving inland along what was a prehistoric river bed of the Kentucky River. Clark County's settlers came almost exclusively over the Gap. A glance at Montgomery history would note that the settlers from Cumberland Gap trail would meet those coming from the Ohio. Eastern Kentucky, Fleming County, Mason, etc., drew most of their settlers, so it appears at first glance, from the Ohio route.

From the beginning of the white westward movement from the sea coast, there were white men in Kentucky. Many of them were fugitives from the law; other misfits who just wandered away from the settlements to enjoy life alone; others were Indians who had been raised in white mens' schools or communities or, more often, half-breeds who were not really white or red. Seldom do we get glimpses of these shadowy figures because they did not want to make any mark upon history. At any rate, the general description of Kentucky, the Cumberland Gap, the major rivers, all were reasonably well known before the first so-called explorers, Gist, Walker, etc., made their historic journeys. The men that history records are known because they could write, and did, and because they had sponsors who wanted maps and records.

One such shadowy person was Granny Anderson, who in the 1750's had a cabin, a trading post, or something, close to the present location of Campton. Who she was, or where she came from, or what became of her is unknown. However, Boone and Findley stopped with her for a night on their swing west. Paul Hanson tells of her in his "Lost Silver Mine" and "Buried Treasure of Kentucky" (1972).

In 1653, two scouts of De Sota's, Louvada Moscoca de Alvarado and another, left the main body of that Spanish exploration party and moved northward, up the Tennessee, through the Cumberland Gap, and down the Warrior's Trail until they came upon some Indian villages. De Sota had heard rumors that there were golden streeted cities northward and he was looking for them. They carried the general name of Chisca and must have appeared to the cruder southern Indians as being highly civilized. The expedition was gone some 28 days but returned to report to De Sota that all they found were crude mud villages. (Filson Club Historical Quarterly, Vol. , P.   ) (Kentucky Society Historical Review, Vol. 5, P. 57, Z.F. Smith).

It is impossible, of course, to say exactly where the villages were. One can assume that the Spaniards did go far enough to find something. Spanish greed would make them do this, but the length of time they were gone would preclude any extensive exploration. It seems reasonable to assume that they had reached the Indian Fields section of Clark County since this seems to be the closest of any size Indian encampment during that period. Certainly, if one can judge by the tremendous number of arrow heads and chips of flint that is discovered all over Clark County even to the present day, this area had to be more than an occasional hunting ground.

The Review also goes on to say that the authorities at St. Augustine reported raids from Chiscas in 1676 and that they had sent 30 soldiers and 176 Indians on a village burning expedition. However, it doesn't seem likely that they got as far north as Kentucky or that the Chiscas were the same Indians De Sota was reporting.

A last curious note was reported in the WINCHESTER DEMOCRAT, February 18, 1891, stating that the remains of De Sota had been discovered by a man named Lefforsa, who was reportedly from Winchester.

As early as 1671, according to an old Campton's Picture Encyclopedia (1956), Thomas Botts and Robert Fallon crossed the Allegheny Mountains from Virginia looking for a passage to the South Seas. They were reported going as far as the Ohio Valley. The lay of the lands and the trails that they likely would follow would bring them to Clark County.

The next report of a white man, other than the Spanish and possibly a mythical French trader, in Clark County was in 1730.

The Cherokees captured John Stalling(Sallay) from Williamsburg, Virginia, on the Ohio River, and carried him down the Warrior Trail to Cherokee country before releasing him. This had to bring him close to Clark County territory. The Cherokees may not have actually braved their old enemies, the Shawnees, at Indian Fields, but they had to come close. Gabriel Arthur had much the same experience about the same date.

Soon after this, we find John Findley, who is discussed more extensively in the next section, setting up a trading post at Indian Fields. His story also illustrates how many frontiersmen had crossed into Kentucky and have been lost in the pages of history.

In 1750, Dr. Thomas Walker explored most of Eastern Kentucky (which was originally all part of Clark County) and followed down the Warrior Trail into what is now Powell County. He reported low-grade iron ore in the area. He was back in the area again in 1760.

Christopher Gist came down the Ohio River in 1751, circles up the Kentucky and came through Clark County in 1751. He also noted the presence of iron ore. He called the Kentucky River the Cuttaway River and the Red River, Little Cuttaway.

James McBride was exploring the Kentucky River in 1754. It was already relatively well known, but he made it official, touching bank in Clark County. The same year, a Mrs. Mary Inglis was taken to Indian Fields by Shawnees. She would be the first white woman in Clark County unless we include Granny Anderson.

John Findley returned in 1757 on a sight seeing tour with Daniel Boone and perhaps touched upon Clark County. In 1759, he and Daniel climbed Pilot Knob.

In 1771, Simon Kenton crossed and recrossed the present Clark County. He had extensive grants in Clark County around what became Schollsville and along the Little Stoner Creek which he very early sold to others. James Floyd and James Douglas passed through what is now Clark County in 1774. The next year John Harrod, Benjamin Logan, and Daniel Boone were all busy setting up their settlements. Kentucky and Clark County passed from the country to be explored to the country to be settled.

## JOHN SWIFT'S SILVER MINE

No Clark County history can be written without mention of the John Swift Silver Mine. This section also illustrates the dangers of writing county history. Having collected all that could be found about the Silver Mine and a section written, it seemed safe to assume that the section was closed and it was safe to go on to the next topic. Then the <u>Winchester Sun</u>, February 18, 1976, printed an article on the Silver Mine, which added more information, and, in some cases, opposing evidence to the whole story. The presses had to be stopped and a new section written.

The article quotes a book written by Michael Paul Henson entitled <u>John Swift's Lost Silver Mine</u>. Henson, who is a native of Jackson, claims to have the text of Swift's Journal. Henson claimed that SWift was born in Philadelphia in 1712 and that he went to sea early. Eventually, he reached the post of Ship Captain. The older version is that Swift was an English sailor of somewhat doubtful history. Swift, for some reason, according to Henson and the <u>Sun</u> article, became a trader in the Cherokee and Tennessee country of North Carolina. The <u>Sun</u> reports that Swift fought with Braddock in 1755. Both versions agree that Swift met George Munday, a young Frenchman, at...the <u>Sun</u> said, Alexandria...the traditional story at Jamestown.

The traditional story says that Munday also fought at Braddock's Defeat for the French and had been captured. Eventually, he arrived in Jamestown where he was released. Hungry, discouraged, and hopeless, Munday told Swift of a silver lode in Kentucky. Henson's version is that Munday, his father, and two brothers had found the vein and had worked it in 1750. The Shawnees had attacked them and had killed his brothers and father and had taken him captive. (The Shawnees and French were generally on the best of terms). Munday had escaped and reached Alexandria. At this point, Swift feeds and takes care of Munday and is told about the silver.

Henson says that Swift enlisted a group of veterans from the Braddock campaign, James Ireland, Abrom Flint, Samuel Blackburn, and Isaac Campbell, led by Munday, and went over the mountains to the headwaters of the Big Sandy and pushed westward for "a considerable distance." Swift is said to have reported that three silver mines were discovered and that several other locations were discovered. A Furnace fired by charcoal was built. He returned to the settlements and raised a party of some 17 men. He had worked the mines until 1769 despite raiding Indians and the extortion of a "Sctoch Company."

The older version agrees that Swift returned from this first expedition (without Munday, or anyone else, who had unfortunately been killed by Indians, according to Swift) bringing with him sizable amounts of silver bullion. There were those, according to the older tradition, that speculated that Swift was a pirate operating out of North Carolina (which was a pirate base) and that the silver he produced, much of it in coin, was actually booty off of captured ships. Most of the people accepted his story, however, as genuine. Henson reports that Swift had minted silver coins at the site of the mine. Swift, in both stories, said he had hidden considerable amounts of money in various places. He concealed the mines so that only marks on stones known by him would reveal them. In both versions, Swift sailed to England to raise money for a really extensive development of the mines. He was a strong supporter for the colonists and with the coming of the Revolution was imprisoned for some fifteen years. There is a third story that he was imprisoned for piracy, but usually the British hung pirates. He went blind, or nearly so.

The older version reports that Swift returned after the Revolution and organized several expeditions into the interior, looking for the mines. At this point, there were several nasty stories circulated. One story is that a party discovered the mines; and while the happy expedition slept, the nearly blind Swift quietly cut their throats. Then, on his way back, be became lost again.

Swift was now an old man. He was taken into the home of William McMillan, who looked after the old man until he died. This was not necessarily an act of charity, since this was the normal way for the early county officials to care for the old and destitute. McMillan was a county magistrate and high-ranking militia officer, as will be described later.

McMillan obviously believed the stories told by the old man. In 1810, he organized a stock company that included John Blackburn, John Bush, John Brunner, John Ward, Elijah Crossthwaith, Sam McClure, Thomas Wells, Peter Hall, Isaac Frailey, Zacharia Fields, and Will Lathan. It was agreed that if any should die and the treasure was found, the widow of the deceased would share in the treasure. These men knew Swift personally, and it seems hard to believe they could be duped...yet, by 1817, the treasure was not found and so many of the original company had died that James and John McMillan and John McClure were added to the stockholders. Nothing was ever discovered.

Naturally there was a map. Poor Swift was so blind that he could not find his way, but he could draw maps. The legend was that the map was in code, using the signs of the moon and of the Zodiac as the key. Naturally, the map vanished. Was there really one? The McMillans were hardly the kind of men to be duped for so long a time. One story is that William McMillan's daughter-in-law was a great quilt maker. She needed pieces of paper to go into her quilt making and raided every source available.

Since this period, much has been written about the mine. Paul Hanson's <u>Lost Silver Mine and Buried Treasure of Kentucky</u>, printed in 1972, is one of the best sources.

The <u>Kentucky Historical Society Register</u>, vol. 41, p. 87 reports that, in 1791 Eli Cleveland and John Morton entered 1483 acres of land on a branch of the Red River, in what is now Powell County, in the Fayette County, Virginia entry books. Swift's mine was, reportedly included. If so, nothing was ever done about it.

The mine was reported discovered dozens of times. The <u>Democrat</u> reported, November 20, 1880, that a silver mine was discovered on the farm of Jonathan Newnan, northeast of Winston, in Estill County. It assayed at $5,000 a ton.

The <u>Democrat</u> reported December 3, 1890, that a 113-year-old Cherokee had turned up, with a map, hunting for the silver mine. There was no follow-up story. Again the <u>Democrat</u> reported the Swift Silver Mine was in Morgan County. A philadelphia assayer reported the ore to be as rich as any found in the Black Hills in the Dakotas. Again, in January of 1902, the <u>Democrat</u> reported a Lena Williams of Campton had found a silver mine. The ore was analyzed and was found of good quality. It, apparently, was in a cave. Some old tools were found, and a can containing $1500 was found.

Collins' history notes that a Judge John Haywood reported two old furnaces on Clear Creek, which discharges into the Cumberland River...Henson claimed to have seen the sites. Shafts and charcoal pits have also been discovered in Bell County; but the only silver ore was found in the 1930's by a W. E. Partin, who sold it for four dollars and fifty cents and, evidently, could find no more. There is a report in 1873, that in Carter County a bar of pure silver was found that was believed to be part of this hidden treasure. There was some ore reported.

During the 1930's a group of men went into the mountains of Powell County and emerged with several donkeys loaded down with sacks full of what looked like rocks. It was reported that they had found silver. There was a picture in one of the newspapers of them, but nothing more was heard of it.

There is a story of a farmer in Salyorsville who plowed up a bar of dull, white metal, which he gave to a local blacksmith. He did not recognize it. The blacksmith used it to brace church bells. It was supposed to be pure silver.

The <u>Sun</u> quotes Hambleton Tapp of the State Historical Society as believing that Swift was a real person. Dr. Thomas Clark, a Kentucky historian, is also convinced that Swift was real. Clark claimed he had seen a fragment of what might have been the journal in the possession of a Frenchburg woman, who spent her time looking for the silver. Clark doesn't think that Swift found silver in Kentucky. Geologists say there is none. Still, these stories keep coming up.

As late as 1975, there were still people in Kentucky looking for the lost silver mines. Two parties made the effort, according to the

Lexington Herald, April 14, 1964, in a story written by George Billing, Jr., a Powell County correspondent to the Herald. Ralph W. Griffith, of the Mountaineer Mining and Exploring Company, Clarksburg, W. Virginia, claimed to have found the mine. He was on John Adam's farm near Mill Creek in Wolfe County, one mile south of Pine Ridge. The party hunted in the area for six years, using a reproduction of Swift's Journal. The party leased 300 acres from Adams. They found a tunnel that went 30 feet into the mountain before it was blocked by stone. Billing reported that they planned to dynamite. A later story said they blew the whole side of the mountain unexpertly and gave up. Kelly Dunn Slade was their guide.

The same article reported that an Ed McGaven of the Swift Mines, Inc., Norfolk, Virginia, was hunting two miles north of Griffith. They had hunted for 9 years and had leased 6,000 acres for mineral rights. They thought they had found Swift's furnace. Robert Hill was their guide.

Meanwhile, Dr. Thomas Clark of the University, said he didn't believe there was ever any silver in Kentucky.

## THE TRANSYLVANIA COMPANY

It is not the purpose of this book to go into details of Kentucky history. Yet, to understand Clark County history, a word needs to be said about the Transylvania Company. The Transylvania Company was a stock company in the same manner that we have stock companies today. A group of investors put up the money on a money-making project. The project was to sell or lease land in the Kentucky area over which it had jurisdiction. It was a private corporation with governmental powers. It was in the tradition of various other corporations that had been instrumental in settling various American colonies and in the Dutch and British East India Companies that were in existence at the same time the Transylvania Company was in existence. The Company claimed all south of the Kentucky River.

The authority of the company came from the British Crown. This immediately brought their legal claims in conflict with those of Virginia, which also claimed the entire area. However, Virginia was absorbed in the development of her western counties on the other side of the Shenandoah Valley and was not too interested in the Kentucky settlement. If the American Revolution had not come, the Transylvania Company no doubt would have succeeded in establishing most of her claims. Her idea was not so much to sell the land to the settlers, as to lease the land. Clark County, though bordering Transylvania territory, was not legally in the prescribed area. On the other hand, James Harrod's fort, Ben Logan's stockade, and other settlements in the area, technically, might be Transylvania territory if the grant given to the Company was interpreted literally. This is part of the reason for the extreme rivalry and even hatred between the two settlements.

Richard Henderson and Nathanial Hart were two of the owners of the Transylvania Company that moved westward with their investment. Despite the fact that their grant came from the British Crown, they insured their policy by making the Treaty of Watauga with the Cherokee Indians. In March of 1775, the Company paid the Cherokee 10,000 British pounds for the right to settle in Kentucky.

Of course, the Cherokee did not own Kentucky any more than the Shawnee. They could not, therefore, sell the land. Secondly, the Indians had no idea of private property. Land belonged to a tribe, not to the individuals or the chiefs, who made up the tribe. In paying money to certain chiefs, the white man could feel that they had met all the requirements of being fair and just. To the average Indian, the white man was doing things he did not understand or feel were valid.

Armed with this authority, backed by the prestige of the British Crown, the Transylvania Company was ready to settle in Kentucky in 1775

The American Revolution ended their authority and destroyed their titles. It is important to note that Henderson, a man of means and importance in North Carolina, and whose financial interests were tied with the Tory and British sentiments, nevertheless, supported the cause of the American Revolutionists. By the end of 1776, the dreams of the Transylvania Company were destroyed forever.

We must also note that anywhere in Kentucky, or for that matter anywhere in the west, the land was not free. The legal rights of the Indians were questionable. However, the land did belong to the state...first to the British Crown, and, after the Revolution, at least in Kentucky, to the State of Virginia.

It is true that hundreds of frontiersmen moved westward without authority and squatted on a piece of land without permission or payment. Later, some of these were able to establish legal claim to this land. Many others, after living and developing the land, perhaps for decades, found themselves evicted by legal owners. The Bryans, for example, lost Bryan Station after the Indian fighting.

Even when claims were filed, boundaries were poorly marked. The SUN SENTINAL in 1903 reported a deed, "Beginning at the double Elm and Louis's corner, to Curtis Pendleton, north 35 1/2 east, 107 poles; to a hickory, ash, and sugar Maple trees, thence north 33 west, 12 poles to a hickory...., etc."

Such boundaries were easily identified during the lifetime of the makers. Trees undoubtedly seemed to be eternal. However, trees were cut down, were blown over, or would die. A hundred years later, every land mark on a deed could disappear.

Since much of the western area was never surveyed, grants that covered thousands of acres would overlap. Daniel Boone liked some land around what is now Schollsville. To prove his claim, he chopped the top out of a small locust tree. It was never really identified. Thirty years later the title was challenged.

As payment to veterans of the Revolution, land grants were given in lieu of cash. These grants were often only vaguely marked. They often overlapped. Many times they conflicted with claims of older settlers. Speculators bought all types of titles, good and bad, and then tried to secure them. The result of all this was chaos.

For 50 years, there was a continual struggle over title to land. The surveyor became one of the most important men in a community. Law suits were common. Men who had fought for the land against the Indians found themselves deposed. Anger against the eastern people who promoted some of these land grabs was deep seated.

## THE BOONE FAMILY

One cannot write the history of Clark County without reading the part played in that history by the Boone family. This history does not pretend to be genealogy. To the author, history is made up, however, of the actions of individuals. Social movements do not happen independent of individuals. They cannot be understood apart from individuals. Therefore, it is necessary to at least recognize individuals and try to keep some order among them.

When one mentions the Boone name, the name Daniel immediately comes to mind. Daniel Boone is one of the nation's best known historical personalities. His name would be recognized by more average Americans than any other name unless it was George Washington or Abraham Lincoln. Daniel was the most famous, but he was not the only Boone on the frontier. In fact, dealing with Boonesborough, Bryan Station, and Clark County history there were Boones and Boone in-laws by the dozens. Many Kentucky historians have missed this point. The Boone families were large and healthy. They often married cousins. These large families married into neighboring families, older sisters first, younger sisters later, so that, at least where the Bryans and Scholls were concerned, no less than three Boone women had become wives.

It is not until one takes time to try to unravel the Boone clan in the light of Clark County history, that the interrelationship of these early pioneers is discovered. Mrs. Hazell Utterbery Spraken, whose family genealogy, The Boone Family, is one of the best genealogies this author has discovered, has made this clear. She has a tremendous amount of research, tracing each family down for many generations.

As far as this history is concerned, the Boone family begins with the third generation Boone, George. We might note that the Boone family must have at least 30 George Boones since the name appears in almost every Boone family. Kentucky families are strong for family names.

With the appearance of this George Boone, the family has reached Pennsylvania and are already prosperous farmers, and strong Quakers. He had married a Mary Maugridges and had a family of eight; George (of course), Sarah, Squire (another family name to appear and reappear in each generation), Mary, Joseph, Benjamine, James, and Samuel. Such good Quakers were these people, that they were often in trouble with the "Meeting" over the marriages of daughters and sons with non-Quakers.

Mary married a John Webb, and for this history plays no part. James also has a large family most of whom stayed in Pennsylvania. He did have a daughter named Rachel (another family name) that married a William Wilcoxon, or Wilcox. One of his granddaughters married a William Bryant. Both Bryants and Wilcoxon (and Wilcox) became active in the Boonesborough-Bryan Station areas.

Another of George's sons, James, had a daughter, Ann, who married an Abraham Lincoln. Since the Lincolns were Congregationalists, this was one of the points of difficulty with the Quakers.

Abraham and Ann had ten children among whom was one named Mordecai. In due course of time, Mordecai had a son, among others, he named John. John had a son who was named Abraham. Abraham had a son named Thomas. Thomas married a girl named Hanks who had relations living in Clark County, giving grounds to a theory that Thomas and Nancy Lincoln's son, Abraham, was actually born in Clark County. This Abraham eventually became president of the United States.

Another of George's sons, Judah, married Hannah Lee, whose brother married Judah's sister. This has nothing to do with Clark County history but illustrates what was common custom in these times. Joshua and James, two other sons, married Hannah and Sarah Griffith, sisters. Evidently, the Griffith girls were Catholics since both were married by a priest much to the fury of the Quaker Meeting. Marriage of several brothers to sisters was not uncommon in Clark County.

George's son, George, had a daughter named Sarah, who married a John Wilcox. Her aunt had married a Wilcoxson. Evidently, some of the family were dropping the "son." Sarah, with her family, moved into Bryan's Station, where her son, named Daniel, naturally, barely escaped being killed by Indians. Another daughter, named Elizabeth, married a Ben Cuthburt, who was one of Daniel Boone's favorite hunting partners. Unlike many of Daniel's hunting parners, he was not killed. Another son of George, William, married Sarah Lincoln and was a sheriff...in Pennsylvania and not Kentucky.

Returning to the third generation of George's children we find a son named Samuel. This Samuel had a son named Samuel, who became a gunsmith. Evidently, he was an excellent rifle maker. At one time, his nephew, Squire (Daniel's brother), was apprenticed to him and learned the gunsmith trade which he practiced the rest of his life. Unfortunately, gunsmith Samuel made rifles for the Continental Army during the American Revolution and, according to Spraken and family tradition, was paid in Continental dollars...which were worthless. Ruined, he abandoned Maryland and came to Kentucky where he settled in Shelby County at Squire Boone's station. Among his many children was Elizabeth, who married a Hayden, who may have settled in Clark County. Becknerville was called for 100 years Hayden Corners. One also notes Samuel's politics in that one of his sons was named George Washington Boone.

The son of third-generation George, who was the father of Daniel, was named Squire. His children in order were Sarah, Israel, Samuel,

Jonathan, Elizabeth, Daniel, Mary, George, Edward, Squire, and Hannah. Squire, like his father and brothers, was a good Quaker and constantly in trouble with the "Meeting" for letting his children marry out of the Quaker Church. He moved his family to North Carolina and left the Quaker influence. There is no record of Squire ever moving westward. His wife was a Sarah Morgan and her people followed Daniel into Kentucky.

Squire's third son, Samuel did not move to North Carolina but remained in Pennsylvania. He married a Quaker girl of considerable education named Sarah Day. She taught her young brother-in-law, Daniel, how to read and write. In doing so, she gave to Daniel a precious weapon that few frontiersmen had and that made it possible for him to advertise the merits of Kentucky. This Samuel, eventually, moved to Boone Station and died in Fayette County. Some of his children lived in Clark. One of his sons, Thomas, was killed at Blue Licks. Another son, Levi, also lived in Fayette County for his heirs were sued in 1822.

Squire's daughter, Elizabeth, married a handsome Scotsman named William Grant. Grant, like so many Scots on the frontier, had in Great Britain fought on the wrong side of Cullondon and found England and Scotland definitely unhealthy. They also ended up at Bryan Station and their descendants continued in the area. Mrs. Spracken reports that Elizabeth was very slow in giving up her Quaker faith, but eventually became, like most of the other early Boones, Baptists.

Mary, the daughter next after Daniel, married William Bryan and went with him to help establish Bryan Station. Her husband and son, William, were killed by Indians. Her daughter was raised by Daniel.

The son, George, married a Nancy Linville. In 1777, he was part of the compnay John Holder organized to help Boonesborough in its Indian attack. He did not actually reach Boonesborough, however, until 1779. Evidently, George had a sore on his leg that increasingly crippled him and eventually forced amputation. When he did come to Kentucky, he established a station in Madison County near Richmond and later took part in the establishment of Hoy's Station. One of his daughters married a Wilcox, making the third Boone woman in that family. Several of his children continued to live in the area, though George moved to Missouri for awhile.

Edward married Martha Bryan, who was the sister of Daniel's wife, and sister of the Bryans at Bryan Station. He came to Kentucky in the latter part of 1778. He was hunting with Daniel near Hinkston Creek; they dismounted and were sitting in the shade; Edward was cracking nuts. Daniel got up to do something to the horses when a dozen shots came from the woods. Daniel leapt on his horse and escaped; Edward was killed.

Edward's wife died in Clark County. One of his sons, George, lived on Stoner Creek in Clark County until he died. A second son, Joseph, was wounded in St. Clair's defeat. Other of his children may have settled in the county.

Squire also named one of his son's Squire. This Squire Boone became the second best known Boone on the frontier. He caught from Daniel more of Daniel's wanderlust than any other Boone that managed to survive. In 1765, he went with Daniel to look over the Florida country with the mind of settling, but both agreed Florida was not for them. In 1767, with Daniel, he hunted in the mountains as far west as Floyd County. In 1769, when Daniel Boone had disappeared into the wilderness, Squire went out to find Daniel and succeeded. He took with him a friend named Alexander Neeley, who started home alone and disappeared. It was on this trip that Stewart also disappeared. In 1770, Squire went back to North Carolina for supplies. In 1773, he was building the Wilderness Road with Daniel. He settled in Boonesborough and built a cabin on Silver Creek in what is now Powell County in 1775. He sold it to Joseph Benny and George Smith.

He stayed in Boonesborough fighting through the Indian wars and did not leave till 1779, when he went to Harrodsburg. He was wounded there by Indians and not particularly appreciated by the Boone-hating Harrodsburg people. He moved into Shelby County where he established a station. He was again wounded fighting Indians.

In 1787 he moved to New Orleans after attempting a settlement in Mississippi but came back to Shelby County. He was imprisoned briefly for bad debts. After this, he and most of his family moved to Indiana. Little of his time, or his family's, was spent in Clark County.

Squire's daughter, Daniel's sister, Hannah, was the one who married the John Stewart who was killed, presumably by Indians, while hunting with Boone. She married a second time to Richard Pennington and came to Kentucky.

Squire's oldest daughter, Sarah, married a Wilcoxon (the fourth Boone in that family). Her daughter, Rachel, married a William Bryant, who had spent some of the Revolution in a British prison ship. Together, they helped establish Bryan Station. Biographers of the Bryants, mostly in Missouri where the Bryants eventually settled, referred to Bryan Station as Bryant's Station.

In this confusion of names, Squire's son, Samuel, who has been discussed, had a son named Squire. He fought with Clark in the Piqua Indian campaign and was wounded at Blue Licks. He centered most of his operations out of Bryan Station.

This Squire became a minister and was ordained by the Providence Church in Clark County and served as the minister, according to Spracken, between 1785-87, though other records show him some 10 years later. He married his first couple, Isaac Wilcoxson and Rebecca White, May 25, 1797. He married five other Clark County couples.

The Elizabeth Grant already mentioned had a son named John Grant who established Grant's Station in what is now Bourbon County. This Station was destroyed in 1780 by Virginia Tory Colonel Byrd in a renewal of Indian fighting.

Her son, Israel, married Susan Bryan, who was raised by Daniel after her father had been killed. He was a silversmith as well as a doctor. He moved back and forth between Kentucky and Missouri. Another daughter, Sarah, died in Bourbon County. This Sarah had a daughter named, Elizabeth, who was killed by Indians in 1787 and a son named James who was killed at the Battle of the River Raisin in the war of 1812. Her children helped settle Bourbon and Clark Counties. Elizabeth had a son named John, who married a Mary Neeley. Elizabeth's son, William, married Sally Neeley, her sister. William Grant was wounded in 1780 at Bryan Station by Indians. He later raided with Clark and Ben Logan in Ohio. He eventually settled in Fayette County, when Clark was still part of it, and may have resided in the area that became Clark. Elizabeth's son, Squire Grant, was wounded at Blue Licks. Her son, Samuel Boone Grant, was later killed by Indians in Indiana.

Turning to Daniel's children, Susannah married William Hay. They came to Kentucky with Daniel and a month after arriving in Boonesborough she had a child, the first born of a white woman in Kentucky. Hay became an officer in the militia under John Holder (following the death of Richard Callaway) and was responsible for much of the defense of Bryan Station. For quite some time they lived on the Marble Creek Farm, which is located in Clark County. He eventually moved to Missouri where he was killed in an argument with a son-in-law.

Boone's daughter, Jemina, was the one kidnapped. She married Flanders Callaway and eventually moved to Missouri. Livinia married Joseph Scholl and lived and died in Clark County near Schollsville. Her son, Septimus, left a number of historical statements about early Clark County. Daniel's Rebecca married a Philip Goe, who helped settle Estill and Nicholas Counties. She came back to her sister, Li Livinia, years later to die and was buried in Clark County.

Two of Daniel's sons were killed. James was 12 years old when his family first tried to come to Kentucky in 1773. Daniel was not with them on this dangerous trip. Cherokees attacked and killed the boy. The family retreated to the Clinch River to wait for a safer time and perhaps Daniel's protection. Later, Israel covered Daniel's escape from the defeat of Blue Licks and was killed in so doing. Spracken reports that he could have escaped.

Daniel's sister, Mary, married a Bryan, making a total of three Boone women of the same family married to Bryans and living at Bryan Station.

Daniel's brother, George, who we have reported in part had a daughter named Elizabeth (How many of the Boon women were named Elizabeth, or Rachel, or Rebecca?) who married Jesse Copher. Copher had been one of the very few frontiersmen not intimately associated with Daniel Boone, but instead with Simon Kenton. He had been captured with John Bullock and Simon Kenton and taken to Detroit by the Indians. He had escaped by persuading the wife of the storekeeper at Detroit to give him supplies. He then settled in Clark County having come into the Boone family. His farm was on Stoner Creek. During the War of 1812, he commanded a company of Clark County soldiers under Colonel Davenport.

Another of George's sons, William Linville, married a Nancy Grubbs and settled on Muddy Creek in Clark County. Though he later moved to Missouri, he left children in Clark County.

Edward also had a daughter named Mary who married Peter Scholl ...the third Boone woman in that family. Peter will be discussed more extensively later on in this book.

George's daughter, Mary, (Daniel's brother George) had married Peter Trimble. One of her daughters married George Washington Stoner who settled in Montgomery County and became part of that County's history.

Daniel's brother Samuel's son, Squire, had a son named Thomas who married Sally Muir. Thomas settled at Boone Station and became one of the more prominent early ministers of Clark County. One of his daughters, Harriett, married Nelson Scholl to repeat the cousin-marrying-cousin pattern. Cousin marriages were another family custom in Clark County.

We have not covered the Boone family completely. Information about individual Boones in Mrs. Spracken's books becomes understandably less available as older generations die off and the multitude of children branch in every direction. This brings the family up to 1812 or so and lays the foundation to a dozen Clark County families.

In conclusion, and it has little to do with Clark County, one of Squire's sons (Squire, the brother of Daniel) was named Isaiah and he had a son named Squire Heath Manly Marquis de Lafayette Green Jennings Tipton Boone.

## DANIEL BOONE

Since there is so much written about Daniel Boone, it is not the purpose of this paper to do more than just make a survey of Boone's life and the events that occurred during the years preceding the establishment of Clark County.

Daniel Boone was Squire Boone's son, and among the younger of his children. He was educated by his sister-in-law so that he could both read and write. He used these talents through-out much of his life to help promote Kentucky.

As a youth, he became one of General Braddock's wagoners. The pacifistic Quakers permitted this. It is evident that Daniel did not remain a Quaker long. While hauling supplies for Braddock, he met John Findley, who was also hauling supplies. Around the camp fires at night, Findley told fascinating stories to a fascinated Daniel about Kentucky, its rivers, plains, mountains, and forests. Daniel never forgot. Soon after the end of the French and Indian Wars, old Squire Boone took his family out to the frontier settlements along the Yadkin River in North Carolina.

There, Boone became interested in the Bryan family in which his aunt had married. The Bryans included four strong-minded brothers and several girls, including a fifteen-year-old named Rebecca... However, love and marriage could not keep Daniel at home.

In 1753, he and Squire were wandering around Florida looking for a place to settle. There was no game and plenty of swamp. It did not appeal to Daniel. A few years later, he and Squire were hunting as far west as what is now Floyd County, Kentucky. Then, old, sick, John Findley turned up in the Yadkin Valley on a tired sick mule. He wanted to go to Kentucky, and Daniel was anxious to go with him. This began a 2-year trip to Kentucky that ended with almost everybody getting killed but Daniel and Squire. No record has ever turned up in this book's research to tell who cared for Daniel's young wife and growing family during this period. After being gone for one year, Squire came out to find him and then continued hunting with him. This was the Lulbegrud incident already reported.

Finally, Daniel went back and was almost immediately sent out by the Virginia Governor on a surveying expedition that carried Daniel down to the Falls of the Ohio. In 1773, he was made commander of three small forts in western Virginia that were designed to protect the frontier. It was at this time that Boone tried to start his family to Kentucky, but after Indians killed his son, James, he brought them back to the Clinch River Settlements. Evidently, he spent most of his time hunting and was out of touch with his forts. Richard Henderson had developed the idea of the Transylvania Company and was seeking help in coming to an agreement with the Cherokee. He approached Daniel Boone as the most informed frontiersman with the best relations with the Cherokee. It might be noted that Daniel admitted to killing only two Indians during his entire lifetime.

In 1774, Boone commanded the party of men sent out by the Transylvania Company to widen the road so that pack trains could pass easily. This was one of the most efficient operations of his career and ended with the establishment of a fort on the mouth of Otter Creek in Madison County. The next year he brought his family to help establish Boonesborough.

Once Boonesborough was settled, Boone began his long, aimless hunting as he always had, being gone months at a time. He was in Boonesborough in July of 1776 when his daughter and two Calloway girls were kidnapped. He helped in the rescue operation. Meanwhile, Richard Henderson had arrived in Boonesborough and established a land office for the Transylvania Company to sell 560,000 acres of land. At this point, the American Revolution broke out in serious fighting.

Was Daniel Boone a Tory at heart? The military history of Kentucky notes that John Holder was a Tory. Holder was the second in command under Richard Calloway and succeeded in command when Calloway was killed. Spracken admits that the Bryans were Tories. William Clinkenbeard, some six years later, complains that the whole frontier swarmed with Tories, particularly around Daniel Boone's Station on Boone Creek. He was disgusted because he had to protect them. It was part of the British strategy in the later years of the Revolution to show military strength in the deep southern states. The result was the occupation of Charleston, South Carolina, and the lower part of South Carolina. There was not the expected Tory turnout. The British, feeling their strategy was correct, then marched into the frontier country where the Tory strength was suspected to be strongest. This resulted in the Battles of Cow Pens, Kings Mountain, and Guilford's Chapel...and lead eventually to the surrender of the British at Yorktown. The result saw thousands of Tories fleeing the victors.

What the British had not forseen, though duplication of the situation could be seen in Burgoyne's march through New York towards Saratoga, was the failure of the Indians to inquire the politics of the settler he was scapling. If you lived on the frontier, you fought for your life whether you were a Tory or a Patroit. There were many strong supporters of King George whose descendants would qualify as proud members of the Daughters of the American Revolution.

Daniel Boone continued his hunting despite the worsening of the Indian situation. However, the frontier was on fire. During 1775 and 1776, hundreds of settlers had swarmed over the mountains. Now they were being driven back by large and small parties of Indians, often accompanied by Tories, Canadians, or British officers. One of these Tories was Simon Girty and another was a Virginian named Colonel Byrd. Few, if any, of these Tories were Kentucky settlers.

Colonel John Todd tried to bring powder from Limestone, the present Maysville, which early became a river port for all of central Kentucky. He got as far as Blue Licks and was defeated by the Indians.

George Rogers Clark managed to get the powder to Harrodsburg. As 1776 runs out, Georgetown was attacked. Though successfully defended, the fort was abandoned. On March 7, 1777, Harrodsburg was attacked; April 15, the first attack on Boonesborough was staged; and on the 20th, Logan Station was attacked. During most of this time, Boone was hunting. On July 4, Boonesborough was attacked by 200 Indians.

Boone returned in late 1777 and is given a command of some 28 men to get salt at Blue Lick. In January of 1778, while his party was working at the salt springs, Boone went hunting and was captured by the Indians. On the grounds that the Indians would kill them all, Boone surrendered his party. The loss of 28 men was a serious blow to the white settlements.

Collins reports that in December of 1777 (though the statement would have to come after the Boone debacle) that the Indian attacks had reduced the settlements in Kentucky to Boonesborough with 32 men, Harrodsburg with 65, and St. Asalph, or Logan's Fort, with 15. The Indians had not taken any of the other settlements, but in the face of the hostile pressure they had been abandoned. Many of the settlers' families, including Boone's, had retreated to the protection of the Tennessee settlements.

Meanwhile, Boone was taken near Detroit. The British tried several times to get him from the Indians, but neither Boone nor the Indians were willing. He was received into the tribe of his captors and adopted by his captor chief as a son. He was given considerable freedom and could have escaped almost at will. After several months, Boone noted a build-up of Indians, which he interpreted as a major attack on Kentucky. He easily escaped, covered 150 miles in four days with but one meal, and warned the garrison at Boonesborough of an attack. It did not come.

Wondering what happened to the Indian attack, Boone took a group northward into Indian country that sounded like a frontier list of fighting men. Besides Boone, it included Simon Kenton, John Holder, John Kennedy, John Logan, John Calloway, Pemberton Rolling, Edmund Fear, Alexander Montgomery, John Stapleton, Jesse Hedges, Alexander Barnett, Stephen Hancock, and seven others. They surprised an Indian village of some thirty Indians, killed one, wounded two, and gained some Indian horses. However, they learned that they had missed the main body of Indians, some 400 under Black Fish, Tecumseh's father, and a Canadian named Duquesne with a brass cannon. The white settler party was able to make it back. The Indians stopped about where the water works are today (1976) and prepared for battle. Somehow, the cannon was pushed into a swamp and was lost. Or at least, so the story goes. After a night of dancing, the Indians attacked.

The seige lasted for three days. The garrison lost two men, and had four wounded. Nevertheless, Boone urged surrender in face of such odds. Boone's family had given him up for dead and missed the seige by returning to North Carolina. After the Indians withdrew, Boone went after them and brought them back in time to go through the hard winter of 1779-80.

Meanwhile, George Rogers Clark organized an expedition that pushed into Indian country, capturing the British frontier posts of Vincinnes and Kaskaskia. This has no direct relation to Clark history, though it did break the control of the British on the frontier, pushing their command post back to Detroit. This relieved some pressure on the frontier. Many future settlers of Clark County were members of that expedition.

The same year, 1778, John Bowman lead a sizable force in an attack on old Chillicothe. Though the expedition was basically a Harrodsburg move, John Holder took a Boonesborough contingent and met Bowman in the vicinity of what was to become Lexington. The name was already established, but Lexington was not settled for a another 2 years. After the expedition, Holder furnished a list of his command to Bowman and asked that the plunder taken on the raid, and carried by John Martin, be sold so that he could pay his men. Collins' history carries the list of his command...Uriel Ark, Thomas Bailey, Bland Ballard, John Baughman, G. Michael Bedinger, James Berry, James Bryan, James Bunton, John Butler, John Calloway, Elijah Collins, Jesiah Collins, William Collins, John Constant, David Cook, William Combs, William Cradlebaugh, John Damperd, James Estill, Edmund Fear, David Gass, Stephen Hancock, William Hancock, John Hawiston, William Hays, Jesse Hodges, Jeremiah Horn, Robert Kirkham, Samuel Kirkham, John Lee, Charles Lockhark, John McCullock, William McGee, Ralph Morgan, William Morris, James Perry, John Pleck, Samuel Proctor, Nicholas Proctor, Reuben Proctor, Pemberton Rollins, Hugh Ross, Bartlet Searcey, Rueben Searcey, John South, Jr., John South, Sr., John South, younger, Thomas South, Jacob Stearns, Eenomi Vallandingham, John Weber, Daniel Wilcoxson, Moses Weber...56 men.

It must be remembered that title to land issued by the Transylvania Company was never recognized by Virginia, but was based on a charter issued by the British Government. Naturally, after the Declaration of Independence, these titles had no authority. In 1779, Daniel Boone set out for Virginia with some $29,000 in paper money to establish his land claims. On the way he was robbed and he was never able to validate his possessions.

On returning to Boonesborough, he is charged with treason by Richard Calloway and tried. There is an excellent novel by Allen Eckert about this trial. He was accused of deliberately surrendering his men without a fight, cohorting with the Indians, and friendliness with the British. Boone admitted all these charges but pointed out his reasons, for so doing. The fact that Boonesborough survived proved his case. He was acquitted.

Nevertheless, Boone was through with Boonesborough and established his own station on Boone Creek with property that extended into Clark County. The Boone Creek settlement is still, basically, in Fayette County and we do not concern ourselves with it here. Boone was active in Fayette County. He became sheriff...an appointive position. However, he found himself both in debt and loosing his titles. At the end of the decade, he moves to Maysville to run a store. He spent most of his time hunting, leaving the care of his store to his wife and son-in-law, Philip Goe.

Nothing worked well for Boone, however. He gave up and left Kentucky forever. He moved to Missouri along the Missouri River. He lived with his daughter and son-in-law, Flanders Calloway, and died an old man.

Clark County was his hunting ground. He claimed land in Schollsville and along Boone Creek. When he left Kentucky, Clark County was safely settled.

Daniel Boone was a man of great vision and poor business sense. He was a great hunter, a fine explorer, and a frontiersman.

## BOONESBOROUGH

We are not writing the history of Boonesborough, which has already been done. We have outlined what was important in the section on Daniel Boone. For Clark County, Boonesborough was the mother and the father of the County. In 1774 and 1775, those who dreamed of their own land in freedom of the Transylvania Company used Clark County as a base. It was a stopping place for settlers coming over the mountains for the next 20 years.

If the Transylvania claims were taken seriously, all the area south of the Kentucky River would belong to it, including the settlements that John Harrod had made two or three weeks before the establishment of Boonesborough. The Transylvania Company did not push their charge, but the charge that Harrod was trespassing hung continuously in the air and would sooner or later have to be met by all. The rivalry between Boonesborough and Harrodsburg was bitter, and the relationship between Daniel and men like Harrod and Logan, who had settlements in the area of what is now Harrodsburg and Stanton, was also bitter. It is rather ironic that in the late 1960s, it would be Harrodsburg that would produce "The Legend of Daniel Boone." Neither James Harrod nor Daniel Boone rests comfortably when curtain time comes.

It is at Boonesborough that the proprietors of the Transylvania Company, present in the figure of Richard Henderson, called the first Kentucky Legislature. The legal power of their claims can be seen in that the men of the other settlements did come and recognize the Company's authority. At the same time, the Harrodsburg people sent a petition with some 84 names attached...a rather comprehensive list of settlers from their area for the time...to Virginia asking that they take over the title of the land. In response, Virginia established Kentucky as a county, with Harrodsburg as the county seat, in the latter part of 1776. Boonesborough, as the center of Kentucky government, was forever defeated. From that point on, the Station began to decline.

Boonesborough remained a base of operations and the last line of defense for Clark County. It was also the center of supplies moving up and down the Kentucky River in canoes and flatboats.

During the early Indian fighting, Clark County served as a sort of rest and recreation area for the Indians.

George Ranck's history of Boonesborough reports the first trustees of the town in 1779 when the town was officially incorporated by the Virginia Legislature. They were Richard Calloway, Charles Thurston, Levin Powell, Edward Taylor, James Estre (Estes), Edmond Bradley, John Kennedy, David Gass (Gist), Pemberton Rollins, and Daniel

Boone. The trustees were authorized to lay out streets and sell half-acre lots. None of these men would play a direct role in Clark County history, though most played minor roles during these years.

Boonesborough now spread out from the stockade. Cabins were built outside the palisade. Warehouses were put up along the river bank. The fortress itself became a temporary hotel for transients going elsewhere. The gates stood permanently open. The palisade wall began to sag, and such business as the blacksmith moved outside the fort.

Through the first seventy years of our country, the Kentucky River remained the most dependable avenue of transportation into central Kentucky, particularly for heavy products. As such, Boonesborough remained an important river port, as did the mouths of the various creeks such as Boone, Four Mile, and others where boat landings were built and warehouses began to appear. One of the residents of Boonesborough, who quickly took up land in the Stoner area of Clark County, was John Halley. As early as 1779, he may have had a tobacco crop in Kentucky, and he was apparently the first of the settlers to grow tobacco on a large scale. In 1783, he built a tobacco barn for firing the leaves of his tobacco (same as flue cured tobacco) out of logs. It burned once and he rebuilt it. In 1784, he was deputy surveyor of the new Lincoln County, and in 1788, he was given the right to "retail all kinds of goods, wares, and merchandise in the town of Boonesborough."

In 1797, William Wilkerson built a warehouse for tobacco in Boonesborough. There was a large stone warehouse as late as 1817 being built, and a third warehouse was reported as being large enough to hold 130 hogsheads of tobacco.

In 1792, the new state of Kentucky was seeking a location for state capitol. So began the never ending struggle between Lexington and Louisville for that capitol. Since the two forces pretty well balanced each other out, it became obvious that some other location would eventually qualify.

In 1792, Ranck points out that Boonesborough was still one of the largest communities in Kentucky.

In 1792, the supporters of Boonesborough made a determined effort to get the state capitol. John Holder, William Calk, Robert Clark, William O'Rear, John Moore, James French, John Wilkerson, Richard McMillan, James McMillan, Robert Elkins, Achilles Eubank, Daniel Rainey, Peter Evans, Edmund Hockaday, William Bush, Philip Bush, Frances McKinney, David Bulloch, Robert Clark, Sr., Green Clay, and William Irwin signed petitions pledging 1,727 British pounds and offering 5,758 acres of land (with the possibility of 4,250 more) if the state capitol would be located in Boonesborough, (Kentucky Historical Society Quarterly, Vol. 31, p. 174).

This author discovered no record stating what happened to this petition. The men who signed it were the most important men in the Madison-Clark County (including Montgomery County) area. Other than Green Clay, however, none of them had any state-wide influence. They were opposed by James Wilkerson, who had determined to make Frankfort the state capitol, and had the political power to do so. In all fairness, there was also not sufficient level land bordering the river between the cliffs at Boonesborough for a sizable city. The Kentucky River occasionally became too shallow for larger boats, though at this time this was not an issue.

On the Clark County side of the Kentucky River, a series of warehouses began to appear in competition with those of Boonesborough. When the County was incorporated, the Order Book of the Clark County Court noted that there were warehouses at Cleveland, Holder's and Bush's Landings...on Boone and Four Mile Creeks.

The governor would appoint inspectors, but the task was generally delegated to the Court. These inspectors would investigate the condition of tobacco, hemp, and flour. Nothing was said about corn whiskey. No record of the reports have been found. With one exception, little of the results appear in the Order Books. Nicholas George was inspector of flour; Philip Bush, of hemp; Benjamin D. Wheeler and R. Corbin were tobacco inspectors.

Often, the inspectors would be the owners, or someone who met the approval of the owner. As the county was better organized, roads were built to these landings and the warehouses on them. Presumably, flatboats were floated down river from them. In 1799, the County Court appointed Daniel Harrison, George Sharp, Thomas Scott, and Robert Richards tobacco inspectors of Bush's warehouse.

By 1805, there were three warehouses established in Clark County. John Holder's on Boone Creek was the oldest. It had been originally owned by John Holder, but with his death, it had passed to his heirs. Ambrose Christy was the inspector in 1805. Achilles Eubank owned a warehouse on Four Mile Creek. He was his own inspector. Holder's warehouse was later inspected by William Tinsley. Apparently, there was also a Howard and Bush warehouse at the mouth of Lower Howard's Creek in 1806.

In 1809, Henry Heironymous owned a warehouse on the Kentucky River. On the Red River, at the mouth of Lulbegrud Creek, Joseph McMahan had a warehouse.

The best information, and the only item in the Order Books, giving much detail about the Clark County warehouses appeared in October, 1810. The Bush warehouse was reported to have received 689 hogsheads of tobacco and delivered 731. The report did not say to whom the tobacco was delivered. They had 20 hogsheads left. The report said that the warehouse could hold 500 hogsheads. There were no locks on the doors; the roof leaked, and the scales and weights needed improving.

The Holder warehouse had received 593 hogsheads of tobacco and had delivered 547. It had 94 on hand. It was large enough to hold 500 hogsheads, and it also needed locks and improvements on its scales.

The Heironymous warehouse could hold between 80 and 90 hogsheads. The report was that he had received 95 hogsheads and had delivered 98. He had one hogshead left at the time of the inspection.

Ranck notes that by 1810, Boonesborough had been reduced to a little hamlet. Cabins were left abandoned and were disintegrated. The fort itself had been largely dismantled so that its timbers could become easily available material for newer construction. About the only thing that was left of Boonesborough was the ferry, a scattering of warehouses along the river, and a couple of stores. The huge flood that swept down the Kentucky River in 1817 did some $300,000 worth of damage. More than the damage, it washed away the warehouses and the last few cabins that marked Boonesborough.

The February Court of 1811 reported that Jesse Hampton wished to establish a warehouse on the Kentucky River near that of Eubank's.

In 1812, the Bush warehouse was reported as having two hogsheads for two years. They were to be sold at auction. The warehouse was reported in need of repair.

The Court continued this kind of surveillance warehouses though they became obviously less important. The implication of the inspections is that these warehouses were not in good shape. Be that as it may, these warehouses played much the same role in those early years that the tobacco warehouses played in post World War II days. They provided a market for farm produce that produced hard cash. Most of the farmer's products at the time were either used at home, or in barter with neighbors and townspeople for needed objects. Most of the corn was ground. As will be noted later, nearly every community had a mill for the grinding of corn into flour or meal. The miller usually was paid by keeping some of the product he produced. Some of this meal and flour found its way to the warehouses and eventually down river to New Orleans. Corn, however, was used mostly in the home market. The same was true of hemp. Winchester had hemp factories, or more correctly, hemp walks. Ropes were made by a man walking down a long board walk, weaving the rope as he went. Tobacco represented a cash crop, a means of getting hard money. It was fire cured; grown basically in small lots or acreages. The life blood of the settler went through the warehouse.

By 1815, the warehouses on the Clark County side had cut deeply into Boonesborough's business. The climax came, however, in the winter of 1817-1818 when floods struck the Kentucky River in a way that they had not in the 50 year history of the white man's acquaintance with the River. Boonesborough was completely washed away. So complete was the destruction, that the exact location of the fort was lost. It had been abandoned for several decades by 1818. The village that had grown up outside its walls no longer existed. There seems to have been no serious effort to restore or rebuild it. Boonesborough passed into history.

There was no real effort to rebuild Boonesborough. The raising of tobacco was on the decline. It was no longer used for money. The times were hard, as the first panic in history came in 1818 and 1819. Ranck notes that Boonesborough passed into the ranks of the lost towns of Kentucky.

This does not mean that the river ceased its function as a major transportation method. Steamboats were about to appear, helped by a series of dams and locks. Flatboats as a method of freighting to New Orleans became less and less important. They were still used to float lumber and produce, particularly coal, from up river communities. Little is heard of any river landings until the appearance of Ford in the 1880s. These landings did continue to exist. During the 1870s and 1880s, various newspapers would mention the landing of coal rafts at creek mouths where landings had to be maintained. The various steamboats that worked the river had to have places to tie up. It is safe to say that landings at Boone Creek, Four Mile, and at other points along the Clark County shore, continued until well after the coming of the railroad.

The news and historical sources for the period following 1818 are limited. Boonesborough was no more. It was not until 1840 that Boonesborough again appears briefly in history.

James Flanigan, in the SUN SENTINAL, July 1, 1905, described the celebration held at Boonesborough in 1840. Militia came from all parts of the state, commanded by Clark Countian, G. W. Bush. By this time, the militia had become social units in gay uniforms and the cavalry units were mounted on fine horses. Thousands of Kentuckians came from all around. Mrs. Keziah French, who had been the Calloway girl left behind when her sisters escaped the boredom of a Boonesborough Sunday afternoon to be captured, was the honored guest. With her was an old Negro woman who had been her maid for many years, and who had also been in Boonesborough in those violent years. Coming down the steep hills from Clark County to the River, Mrs. French found the old Negro woman crying. When asked why, the woman answered, "Why Mistress, all them soljers and folk looks zachly like the British and Indians coming to tak de fort...."

About noon, the speeches were going full blast, the dinner tables had been set up, and the barbeque almost ready. Black clouds that had built up over the upper reaches of the river opened up and a deluge caused the river to rise rapidly. Within an hour, there was a foot of water surrounding the tables. The crowd broke up in an undignified rush for higher ground. Among others, Abner Rucker calmly drove his oxen and ox cart across the rapidly rising water from the Madison to the Clark County side, swimming the few feet necessary.

After this great day, Boonesborough relapsed into obscurity. The Boonesborough area eventually became a place where people occasionally went for swimming and picnicking. At the point, the river was shallow and slow moving, though each year someone always drowned. There was no real development of commercial possibilities as there was at Oil Springs.

In 1905, the lock was finished just above the area. Boonesborough did develop into a somewhat sleazy, often disreputable, recreational and boating area.

At the Jamestown Exposition in 1907, a good deal of interest in Boonesborough, the kidnapping of the Calloway girls, and Daniel Boone was renewed. As part of the preparation for Winchester's participation in the Jamestown Exposition, which will be reported in detail in a later volume, on October 10, 1907, 4,000 people gathered at Boonesborough for speeches and a picnic. James B. Headley, Ezekial Reed, and J. W. Harding attended both the 1907 and the 1840 rallies.

The development of Boonesborough into a state park will be discussed in a still later volume of Clark County history covering this period.

The Daughters of the American Revolution dedicated a monument to Boonesborough in 1912, according to the Winchester News, September 20, 1912. Little other official attention was given the area.

A word on Keziah French. She was the daughter of Richard Calloway. She was only fourteen when she married James French, but she was a determined young lady who spun and wove the materials of her marriage clothes, quilts, and sheets. She later designed the Lulbegrud Church in such a way that it had 12 corners, one for each saint. She was evidently a most remarkable woman.

## THE KIDNAPPING

On a Sunday early in July 1776, two of the Calloway girls, Elizabeth and Francis, and Jemima Boone, all thirteen or fourteen, came out of Boonesborough's Sunday worship and wandered down towards the river. Jemima liked water and was nicknamed "Duck." They were bored and restless and wanted to get away from Keziah Calloway, an 8-year old, who wanted to tag along. Jemima had also stabbed her foot on a stob several days before and her "go to meeting shoes" hurt her foot. They got a canoe and despite their Sunday clothes, lazilly paddled across the sluggish Kentucky River. What happened next was told by many with a variety of small differences. Septimus Scholl, a grandson of Daniel Boone, described the incident in a deposition, that the girls actually landed on the Clark County side of the river and picked flowers and berries. The more orthodox story, which the contemporary James French, a descendant of Keziah claims true, that they merely drifted close to the Clark County bank. Jemima sat in the brow of the canoe with her foot dragging in the water.

As the canoe floated under the foilage of the bank, an Indian dropped out of the trees and dragged the canoe onto shore. Several other Indians appeared...evidently five all together, four Shawnees and a Cherokee...and carried the girls into the woods.

Keziah and other children playing along the bank saw the whole action and immediately gave the alarm. Daniel Boone had come home from church (where his brother, Squire, was preaching) and had taken off his shoes but not his good suit. Samuel Henderson who wanted to marry one of the girls had shaved half his face...the other half was not shaved for three days. However, the men of Boonesborough hesitated before they crossed the river. They had no assurance that a large body of Indians might not be lying in ambush for just such action. It was also getting late into the afternoon with night coming on quickly. Much of the information that Winchester's people used in their pageant in 1907 came from a letter written by John Floyd, July 21, 1776, or some two weeks after the kidnapping.

The three Boonesborough men, William Bush, John Martin, and James McMillan, who had staked out claims in what is now Clark County were on the north side of the river. John Martin appeared shortly after the girls had been kidnapped and reported that the north side of the river was clear and that there was no ambush.

It was decided to wait until the next day before following. Two parties were to set out, one under Daniel Boone to swing northward in an effort to head off the Indians if they took a direct route back to Ohio, and the other to follow the trail left by the Indian party.

The Indians rushed rapidly through the woods the first day, along Two Mile Creek and then into what is now Montgomery County, covering some five miles the first day and about fifteen the second. According to Indian philosophy they had pulled their raid off (one that had been a spur of the moment action by a group of young warriors who were really just hunting) and had gotten away with it. According to Indian rules, they were safe. Along the banks of Slate Creek they halted, made camp, built a fire and prepared for some rest. One version says Boone called for the girls to fall flat, but others report that he was not present. The Indians did leave a sentry to watch their back trail but he became hungry and came in to eat.

Meanwhile the rescuing parties followed as rapidly as the new morning would permit. One version reports that Betsy Calloway marked the trail they were taking with bits of cloth from her clothes until her actions were discovered by her captors. The group that was following closely behind the party included John Holder, Sam Henderson Flanders Calloway, William Bailey Smith, John Floyd, Nathanial Hart, John Gess and others. They came upon the unguarded camp of the Indians. The settlers stormed into the camp and rushed the Indians. The best version told how Betsy, wrapped in an Indian blanket, black-haired and dark-skinned, was almost brained by an enthusiastic settler before discovering her identity. He thought she was an Indian woman.

So ended one of the most publicized Indian raids in history. We might note that though this raid ended happily, thousands of women and children, including another child of Richard Calloway, John Calloway, were kidnapped by Indians with less happy results. He and his first cousin, James Hoy, were not returned for two years.

James Fenimore Cooper became so entranced with the story that he patterned the "Last of the Mohicans" and other "Leatherstocking Tales" upon this incident and other adventures of Boone and frontiersmen. This in turn became the base for the unhistoric televis series on Daniel Boone. A French painter, Jean Millet, whose renowned works include the "Reapers" and the "Gleaners" painted a picture of the capture.

All things ended well, however. John Holder married Francis Calloway, Jemima Boone married Flanders Calloway. Elizabeth Calloway married Sam Henderson in August, 1776, to be the first to be married in Kentucky. Keziah married James French.

## RICHARD CALLOWAY

When one thinks of Boonesborough one immediately thinks of Daniel Boone, but it was Richard Calloway who commanded the militia as senior officer and gave to the settlers at Boonesborough the kind of leadership necessary to save them from Indian attack. It was Calloway who insisted on resistance to the British and Indians on the third attack.

According to Mrs. Spracken's "Boone Family," the Calloway family is listed as one of the allied families of the Boones. They came from the Yadkin Valley in North Carolina and had lived near the Boone family. Spracken reports two brothers, James and Richard. James evidently did not come to Kentucky. However, there were several sons of James on the frontier. One son, James, was with the party that Daniel Boone surrendered. Another son, Flanders, was better known. He married one of Daniel's daughters and eventually provided the home in which Daniel lived in his old age. According to the "Filson Club Historical Quarterly," January, 1935, there were four more brothers. The family had originally lived in Virginia, but followed the river of settlers to the Yadkin.

Richard had served in the French and Indian Wars, where he gained his military experience and won his rank. The Quarterly does not say how. His first wife died in 1768, leaving him with nine children. He then married Elizabeth Day. He was with Richard Henderson at Sycamore Shoals, as the ranking military officer of the area and participated in the signing of the treaty. Even though he outranked Boone who held a Captaincy in the Virginia militia, he served under him during the building of the Wilderness Trail. Once in Kentucky, he and Boone, were the only pioneers which received a grant of 640 acres from the company. Calloway was no poverty-ridden frontier tramp. He was a man of considerable wealth in Virginia and had a good education. He owned what some claimed to be the finest horse in Kentucky and had a Negro servant. He held the rank of Colonel in the Virginia militia. As such, he was the senior officer in the Boonesborough area. He was reenforced by militia and a small command of Continentals in the later days of Boonesborough. He successfully defended the area.

He was a close friend of the Boones and Bryants, but he did not hesitate to bring court martial charges against Daniel.

The Indian wars began to fade away in 1778 and 1779, and the worst appeared to be over. It was apparent that a ferry was needed over the Kentucky River. Calloway received the authorization from the Virginia Legislature, to which he had been a delegate, to build such. In 1779, he, Pemberton Rawlings, and some Negro slaves were working on the proposed site. On March 8, Calloway was on the north side of the river when he was attacked and killed by Indians.

He, more than any other man, kept Boonesborough alive in its time of crisis. Yet, as Collins' history notes, he was killed too early in his life to really claim fame.

Later, other Calloways, mostly children of James, came to Kentucky. One of these, Edmund, settled in Clark County.

## MICHAEL STONER

One of Daniel's closest friends and hunting partners was a German by the name of George Michael Holstein. He changed his name to Michael Stoner (Stein in German meant Stone) and as such he goes down into history. He met Boone early and hunted with him up to and through the Cumberland Gap. He was with Boone on the survey of the Ohio River and in 1773, helped build the Wilderness Road. He returned to Carolina during much of the troubles around Boonesborough but did fight at Kings Mountain and was wounded. He was back in Kentucky in 1780 and served in the militia under William Bush. He was wounded at Blue Licks.

Stoner married Frances Trimble and settled in Clark County on the creek that bears his name. In 1797, he moved to Wayne County, but his son remained and his family helped develop the Montgomery County.

## EARLY CLARK COUNTY SETTLERS

The Transylvania Company had title to the land south of the Kentucky River. There was even some question as to whose jurisdiction Harrodsburg and Logan's Station would fall, though the settlers in these places fiercely refused to recognize the Transylvania claims.

There was no question of the territory north of the Kentucky River. That was specifically not in the Transylvania Charter and came under Virginia law. It became very attractive then to those who did not want to have any strings to their legal deeds. From almost the beginning, its lands were being surveyed and the territory which is now Clark County was at a premium. Using Boonesborough as a base, settlers fanned out into the territory north of the river seeking lands.

It is not entirely clear just what one had to do to establish a clear title to a piece of Kentucky land. This comes about because the laws concerning settling new land were numerous, conflicting, contradicting, and continually being changed. It was really impossible to have a single way of gaining title that could not be challenged. Roughly, however, it called for the settler to stake out an identifiable piece of property, build a cabin, and raise a crop of corn. Just exactly how much he could stake out would change, and could be technically evaded...for example he could stake out claims in the name of his children as well as himself. He would have to pay out a certain amount of money, for example, ten shillings for each hundred acres covered by his claim up to four hundred acres. Once established, the claim could be developed with preemptive rights to a thousand acres mores. The added complication came after the Revolutionary War when veterans and certain other privileged people were given large patents of land for services rendered to the State. These would usually be sold off in smaller tracts for the benefit of the owner of the patent.

The next problem was finding any given piece of property on the ground ten years after it was registered. There was a good deal of surveying done. Most any person who could add and use a surveyor's instrument announced himself as a surveyor. The most famous of the surveyors was George Washington. The County Surveyor post was a very important and much desired position.

In 1774, John Floyd and William Preston surveyed the land in what is now Clark County for Patrick Henry, Governor of Virginia. Preston returned the same year to Clark County with Hancock Taylor and James Douglas to continue the survey. Many of the creeks were named after early surveyors and settlers.

The first man to file a claim in Clark County was John Hite as early as 1774. Abraham Hite had been with Floyd on part of this surveying. John might well have been his brother. No other mention of this name appears in Clark County history.

The real rush for Clark County land did not begin until 1775. The first three cabins built in Clark County were built by John Martin, James McMillan, and James Bush. As reported, one of the problems of county history is the separation of like names. There were two John Martins very closely associated with the establishment of Clark County. This John Martin was to be killed by Indians near Cumberland Gap as he brought settlers into Kentucky. The Indians attacked and were driven off, but Martin was badly wounded. He told his party to go back and he would stay and hold off the Indians since he would probably die anyway. His party was saved. His bones were found in a hollow tree where evidently he had climbed.

There is a story that two brothers named Jennings built and lived in a cabin, perhaps the first in Clark County, in the Indian Fields area. One was probably Isreal Jennings and the other brother's name is lost. Both were killed by Indians at the very beginning of the trouble.

The surveying party named the creeks after various men who helped survey the area, or by explorers who were active in the area. Michael Stoner helped survey Bourbon County with Thomas Kennedy in 1774. Just who named Strode's Creek is not clear. There was a Samuel Strode in Mason County in 1774, but it does not seem likely that he or John Strode, who did come to Kentucky soon afterward, gave the creek its name.

The Kentucky Historical Society's "HISTORICAL QUARTERLY," Vol. 14 of 1949, tells of the Marquis de Calmes. The COURIER JOURNAL, October 14, 1934, adds to his story. He was a French nobleman, probably Huguenot, who found the situation in France no more healthy for Protestants than it was in England and Scotland for supporters of the Stewart Kings. Six foot, two inches (in a day when the average height was about five foot five), 200 pounds (a veritable giant), he came down the Ohio River on a flatboat to Limestone and then across country to Clark County. He, with Benjamin and Cuthbert Combs, Benjamin Berry, Marquis Calmes, Jr., nephew of Marquis de Calmes, and Major and William Beasley established claims in the Indian Field area. Calmes did not stay long in Clark County, but moved on to Woodford County where he made considerable history. He did lay claim to Oil Springs, which, in 1795, went to his daughter Miriam and her husband, Thomas Eastin.

By 1777, a good deal of Clark County was already staked out. David McGee was raising corn in Clark County in 1776. This does not mean that all the county was taken up. In the later 1790's, in reading the County Court Order Books, as roads were being surveyed there would often be large tracts of land reported unclaimed or whose ownership was unknown.

Willard Jillson, in his EARLY CLARK COUNTY OF KENTUCKY lists those that preempted land in Kentucky prior to 1780. KENTUCKY STATE HISTORICAL SOCIETY REGISTARY, Vol. 21, 1923, has a list from which this was developed.

| Name | Year | Acres | Location |
|---|---|---|---|
| Joseph Hite | 1774 | 1400 acres | Howard's Creek |
| Ennis Harden | 1775 | 1000 | Stoner's Fork |
| James Wilson | 1775 | 1000 | Two Mile Creek |
| Ebenezzar Frost | 1775 | 1000 | Boone's Creek |
| Elias Harris | 1775 | 1000 | Stoner's Fork |
| Marquis Calmes | 1775 | 1000 | Lulbegrud Creek |
| Samuel Nowell | 1775 | 1000 | Upper Howard's Creek |
| William Nowell | 1775 | 1000 | Howard's Creek |
| James Nowell | 1775 | 1000 | Howard's Creek |
| Jack Starns | 1775 | 1000 | Strode's Fork |
| Valentine Sterns | 1775 | 1000 | Strode's Fork |
| Benjamin Berry | 1775 | 1000 | Lulbegrud Creek |
| Benjamin Combs | 1775 | 1000 | Forks of the Lulbegrud |
| Marques Calmes | 1775 | 1400 | (Indian Old Fields) Indian Town |
| Fredrick Sterns | 1775 | 1000 | Strode's Fork |
| Isreal Boone | 1775 | 1400 | Boone's Creek |
| Daniel Boone | 1775 | 1400 | Head, Licking River |
| Cuthbert Combs | 1775 | 1400 | Indian Town |
| John Howard | 1775 | 1000 | Howard's Creek |
| William Robinson | 1775 | 1000 | Boone Creek |

Altogether 20 had filed claims the first year of Boonesborough, Ennis Harden, Marquis Calmes, Benjamin Combs, Cuthbert Combs, and, of course, the two Boones were to be active in the following years. Benjamin Berry was to pioneer what became Powell County. The others do not appear again in the record.

| | | | |
|---|---|---|---|
| David Robinson | 1776 | 1400 | Boone Creek |
| Robert McMullen | 1776 | 1400 | Howard Creek, South Fork |
| James McMullen | 1776 | 1400 | Forks of the Howard |
| (Obviously the McMillans of later importance) | | | |
| William Bush | 1776 | 1400 | Lower Howard's Creek |
| Ralph Morgan | 1776 | 400 | Strode's Fork |
| William Bird | 1776 | 1000 | Howard's Creek |
| Joshua Barton | 1776 | 1400 | Four Mile Creek |
| John Strode | 1776 | 1000 | Strode's Fork |
| James Strode | 1776 | 1000 | Howard's Creek |
| Benedick Couchman | 1776 | 1000 | Howard and Two Mile |
| John Kennedy | 1776 | 1400 | Stoner's Fork |
| John Kennedy, Jr. | 1776 | 1000 | Stoner's Fork |
| Michjah Wood | 1776 | 1400 | Boone's Creek |
| James Gallaway | 1776 | 1000 | Stoner Fork |

By 1776, many of the characters who would make the next 20 years of Clark County history had appeared, the McMillans, William Bush, the Strode's and the Couchmans.

By 1777 the American Revolution was breaking on the frontier. It was no longer safe to be far from the garrison stations such as Boonesborough and Harrod's Station.

| | | | |
|---|---|---|---|
| Bartlett Searcy | 1777 | 1400 | Four Mile Creek |
| John Booker | 1777 | 1400 | Four Mile Creek |

By 1778 the Indians had failed to break the last ditch resistance in Kentucky, but they still had the upper hand.

| | | | |
|---|---|---|---|
| John Calloway | 1778 | 400 | Stoner's Fork |
| Charles Tate | 1778 | 400 | Kentucky River, North Side |

Settlement and exploration had all but halted. However, by 1779, the Indian raids had let up. The British were obviously being beaten in the east and immigration into Kentucky once again began.

| | | | |
|---|---|---|---|
| Jeremiah Stark | 1779 | 400 | Howard's Upper Creek |
| Morgan Bryant, Jr. (Another Boone in-law) | 1779 | 400 | Boone's Creek |
| James Doster | 1779 | 400 | Head of Stoner's Creek |
| Ralph Morgan (Daniel's mother's people) | 1779 | 400 | Strode's Fork |
| John Donathan | 1779 | 400 | Strode's Fork |
| John Dunaway | 1779 | 400 | Strode's Fork |
| John Constant | 1779 | 400 | Strode's Fork |

By this time the cast of characters for the coming years of Clark history had been added to. Dunaway and Constant had now put in their appearance.

The other names did not appear to be particuarly active. They may have given up their claims or they may have helped settle the county. They possibly sold their title to late-comers. The records available to this study do not give them much attention.

## BLUE GRASS

Blue Grass is the symbol of Kentucky. Nationally, Central Kentucky has become known as the Blue Grass Country and each year thousands of tourists vainly search for "Blue Grass." It comes as a surprise to discover that blue grass was not native to Kentucky, and that it appeared in and around Clark County soon after the white men came. It is not certain where its name comes from. If one has a good imagination, looks in the spring at the right moment, and closes his eyes, there is a faint shade of blue. Another theory is that it was named after a Pennsylvanian named Blue who identified it originally. Another is that it draws its name from the blue limestone needed for the best production.

There are a half a dozen or so stories on its origin. Apparently, it did appear in Indian Fields and at Grassy Lick about the same time. Stories of other origins were definitely questionable. Olympia Springs and the Strode's Creek area are examples.

Lucien Beckner offers this story. John Findley came to Indian Fields to trade with his goods wrapped and cushioned in blue grass that he had gotten near his Pennsylvania home. When he opened his goods he threw away the grass, which seeded the burned-over Indian garden plots. The History of Bath County by John Adair Richards claims that blue grass started in Indian Fields and at Olympia Springs.

Around 1790, blue grass was discovered around Grassy Lick just over the Clark County line in Montgomery County on Big Stoner Creek by Ebeneezer Chorn and Septimus Davis. It is not clear how it got there. One suggestion has been that buffalo, wallowing in mud in Indian Fields, brought it to Grassy Lick where they hunted salt.

The CLARK COUNTY DEMOCRAT in October of 1871 claims that the first blue grass was found by a Goff...it doesn't say which one, in a thimble from England. Appearing as it did in 1790 or earlier, this would have to be Tom Goff. W. M. Beckner, Editor, agreed with the Goff tradition that Elisha Goff, Tom's son, received a thimble of timothy from Virginia which he planted. This being the first of this grass in Kentucky.

The Goffs also claim, and W. H. Lenny's "Report on the Geology of Clark and Montgomery Counties" supports the story that Tom Goff, while driving a herd of cattle to New York in the 1790's, discovered that his cattle did well grazing in Pennsylvania mountains. The Goffs drove cattle north and east for a hundred years. On the way back, he cut several squares of blue grass sod and brought them back with him. These he planted in the land at Indian Fields he had bought for his son, Elisha.

Still another story is that John Constant in 1785 received a quart of seed from John Madison and started planting it on his property on Strode's Creek. At any rate, Isaac Cunningham, who succeeded Matthew Patton in the Strode area, saw the value of blue grass, cutting down trees to give it a better chance.

Fielding Bush planted it on Lower Howard Creek. He reportedly got the seed from Robert Cunningham who claimed to have brought it into Kentucky from the South Fork of the Potomac River about 1800.

Asa Barrow in the Chronicles said Elisha Goff sowed the first timothy and red clover in Clark County (or in Kentucky).

It does not follow that only one of these stories could be true. 1790 seems a little late for blue grass in Kentucky, so the Findley story seems sound. . .and the movement of buffalo before 1775. Its rapid expansion in the area could easily come from other additions of blue grass seed by these various people over the period.

In passing, we note the story that Sam Harmon's father was killed by a bear just about where the present First Christian Church (1976) stands. The SUN SENTINAL, June 8 and 11, 1911, claimed that Billy D. Allen was the source of this story, claiming it happened in 1782. There seemed to be some debate about the story at the time. At any rate, a bear was killed in Indian Fields, in 1800, so the story is not impossible.

Ezra Brown (Braun) had locked his hounds in a shed behind his Stoner Creek settlement. He went into the woods to chop firewood when wolves separated him from his house and forced him up a tree. There he stayed and might have frozen if his desperate calls had not finally caused his dogs to break out of his shed to save him. He did not fasten his dogs again.

## AMERICAN REVOLUTIONARY WAR VETERANS

This is a list of American Revolutionary War Veterans that at one time or another lived in Clark County. We have made no effort to verify the authenticity of these men, or even their existance. We have accepted the word of the primary sources. These are the records of Dr. George Doyle, who sometimes gives his sources, but most generally merely lists the names. These men may not have spent much time in the county to have made Doyle's list. Another contributor is Mrs. Lucile Goff Clark whose lists are probably more accurate, since she was working for the Daughters of American Revolution. Her criteria were who received a pension in Clark County or who had died in Clark County. In addition there have been innumerable magazine, newspaper, and letter references, etc., to this, or that man, saying he was a veteran of the American Revolution. These references may have been made a century later as part of a story concerning other people. To list the source of each name would have added too much to the work in preparing this book. If the name is so listed, someone, somewhere, said that person was a veteran.

Collins' history reported that in 1840 Clark County had eight veterans still alive. They were Smallwood Ecton, (the name Acton seems to be interchangeable; Acton is earlier, but Ecton is the final form), 82; John Arnold, 86; Lincefield Burbridge, 80; James Bush, 83; Vauchel Faudre, 79; Rueben Franklin, 85; Thomas Lowry, 79; and Richard Oliver, 97. Kathryn Owen says there were more than these.

Lucien Beckner in the Clark County REPUBLICAN, November 16, 1914, adds Robert Bush, Drury Scott, Seth Botts, John Dunn, Elisah Estes, Ben Lockett, John Martin, (he does not say which one, there were several), James Wilson, Presley Shepherd, John Fletcher, William Foster Martin Johnson, and Price Key as being alive in 1840. Beckner does not give ages, but it was 64 years since 1776 and 59 years from 1781. Achilles Eubank was also alive in 1840.

It is interesting to note that the great bulk of these veterans are from Virginia; more from North Carolina. They served in the same regiments, fought in the same battles, and came from the same sections of Virginia. They knew each other, were old neighbors, had brothers who had married sisters, and had in-laws among the settlers. The Boone family is just one classic example. The implication is clear; there was a family solidarity to the Kentucky settlements unlike any other westward movement. Clark County, from the beginning, was like a small town, intermarried and intertwined. These men knew each other and what to expect from each other. Settlers that came down the Ohio or from places other than Virginia, North Carolina, or Maryland were strangers and outsiders who were slowly accepted into the community.

Most of these veterans were infantry men. There were a handful of cavalry men and fewer artillery men. Two veterans, one was John Bean, served in the Virginia Navy. Apparently two, Drury Scott and John Morrow, were Negros.

Few of these men fought in the whole war. Kings Mountain, Eutaw Springs, Guilford Chapel, and, particuarly, Yorktown were the battles that had been fought by the majority. Only a few had been at Valley Forge, none had been at Bunker Hill. On the whole they were privates or junior officers. Senior officers had little reason to come west. The majors and colonels in the west largely got their militia ratings while in Kentucky and not before. There would be exceptions such as Charles Scott.

In this list, when possible, we have given the unit the veteran served. Achilles Eubank enlisted some six times. Most enlistments were for 90 days, sometimes six months and near the end of the Revolution, a year. A man could, in the five or six years of the Revolution, enlist, go home for six months, enlist again, go home for a year, enlist a third time, etc. Each time, he could have enlisted in a different unit.

There are a few women, those at Boonesborough, who the Daughters of the American Revolution recognize as soldiers. These were largely wives who fought under attack, like their men.

Militia and regular troops were assigned to the frontier forts by the eastern command. It was not enough to satisfy the settlers and was for years a bitter memory in their minds. It was enough for the seaboard states to consider the settlers ungrateful.

Many of these militia and regulars were also settlers. Every man was automatically a member of the militia. It may be that some of the names listed were omitted on the larger list. They were, when unmarried, constantly shifted from one post to another.

Richard Calloway, commanding officer during the later part of the Indian attacks, killed 1780; Micahjay Calloway, Boonesborough and Blue Licks, where he was captured and spent five years as a prisoner; Sam Boone; Flanders Calloway; James Calloway; Samuel Combs; William Clinkenbeard, who later transferred to Strode's; Achilles Eubank; James and Joseph Kinkaid; Jonathan McMillan; Josiah and George Phelps; James Quisenberry; John Donaldson; Nicholas George; Bartlett Searcy, who married one of the Calloway girls; Enoch Smith, who was to be a founder of Montgomery County; Daniel Wilcoxson.

Estille Station

John Harper and James Berry, who was to move to Clark County.

Strode's Station

Presley Anderson (also served at McGee's); James Bayth, wounded in 1790 at Grassy Lick; John and William Bennett; Cade Chadford; John and Isaac Clinkenbeard; Michael Cassidy, who later established his own station; Capt. John Constant, commanding militia officer at Strode's, who was blamed for the defeat at Blue Licks and was later killed; John Douglas; John Dumpford; John Duncan, who married Strode's daughter; John Hart, who also served at Boone's Station; John Judy; Julian Kirk; Barry Mitchell; Patrick Mooney; Ralph Morgan, who was soon to establish his own station, which was destroyed by Indians on April 3, 1793, in Montgomery County; John McIntyre; George Reynolds; John Rice; Abraham and Joseph Scholl; Matthais and Jacob Sphar, both of whom died by Indian attack; Joshua Stamper; Van Swinger, who was later killed with General Anthony Wayne at Fallen Timbers.

These men might or might not have served in the east as soldiers. They were in the Virginia militia at this time. After 1780, the Revolutionary War veterans were beginning to age. There was a new generation of men. These men were too young to have fought in the eastern Revolution; not by much, but by a few years. Many of these youths served in the militia from 1780 to 1783, and thus justify being called Revolutionary War veterans.

After the first big wave of settlers into Kentucky in 1775 and 1776, the Indian fighting became so fierce that only the three posts, Boonesborough, Harrodsburg, and St. Alph (Logan's Station or more or less where Stanton is) were left. There were no isolated cabins with lonely settlers plowing their fields with rifles strapped to their plow handles. Any effort at such settlements ended. One can note that only two claims were filed for Clark County in 1777.

The situation did not change much in 1778. There were dozens of families, including some of the Boone family and the Bush colony, that had settled along the Clinch and Holston Rivers in the Tennessee settlements. It did not take a military strategist to know that if the Kentucky settlements went down before the Indians, the Tennessee settlements would be next.

By 1779, even before Yorktown, it became clear that the British would not win in the east. They lacked the will in England to push a long war to a successful end. With Yorktown, the presence of a major British force from South Carolina to Maine ended. There would still be fighting in Georgia, along the coast, and elsewhere, but for all practical purposes the War had been won.

In 1778, a trickle began to move westward again. The posts in the west were reenforced with Continentals and militia. Under this protection, waiting families began to move. In 1779, the trickle grew into a stream, and by 1780, it became a torrent that did not end. Even the renewed Indian fighting did not slow it down.

There are a few details that drift down through the various sources about what the Revolutionary War veterans did during the Revolution. Undoubtedly, these stories could be multiplied many times, but there are limits to every book.

According to a story in the NEW YORK TIMES, May 31, 1931, Jack Jouett was sitting in a tavern in North Carolina. It was the first part of the month of June, 1781. The British cavalry leader, Major Tarlton, rode by with 180 dragoons and 70 mounted infantrymen. He intended to capture Monticello and Charlottsville, and to take prisoner the Virginia Legislature and Virginia's Thomas Jefferson. Tarlton was especially hated by the Revolutionists for his cruelty. Jouett took his 6-foot 4-inch, 250 pound frame on horseback and left the Cukoo Tavern where he had overheard some of Tarlton's officers boasting. He rode approximately 150 miles ahead of the British to warn Jefferson. Most of the Virginia Legislature escaped, though Tarlton did capture seven of its members.

Septimus Davis had been a sailor on a British ship. He jumped overboard when the ship was in harbor and joined Washington's army.

James Hamilton was an ensign in 1777. He was captured at Brandywine. He was paroled, which meant that he was released promising not to take up arms again. He reentered the army and was a First Lieutenant at Charleston when he was captured a second time. He might have been hung had the British had any way of checking on parole violators. Because they did not, they were unaware that he had been captured before.

Hercules Conkwright (Kronkhegt) was a Regulator in North Caolina before coming to Kentucky.

Robert McDaniel was in the 3rd Continental Line and was at Valley Forge. His wife served with him, as did many army wives, and many women who were not wives. These women did the cooking, washing, nursing, and many other garrison duties. They also shared the hardships of the campaignes.

Jacob Marx moved from Clark County to Morgan Station in Montgomery County. His sister and children were captured, his mother-in-law killed, one son was killed, and one daughter was never heard of again. A sister and daughter were rescued after Fallen Timbers.

Charles Wood was a youth on the Clinch River when word of Indian attacks on Boonesborough and Harrodsburg came. He joined Boreman and 24 other men to reenforce Boonesborough. His enlistment ran out and he returned east in 1777, but reenlisted to serve under George Davis.

John Howard first came to Kentucky with Boone in 1775. He returned to the east and fought at Guilford's Chapel. He was wounded five times. He lived to return to Clark County and reach 103 years of age.

This is perhaps a good place to tell of John Martin. He was born in Virginia in 1749. He was a Captain in the 2nd Virginia Line and was promoted to Major at Yorktown. He had served with the militia trying to stop Tarlton's raid on Charlottsville and had distinguished himself in that unsuccessful effort. During this same period, he was deputy sheriff of Albemarl County, Virginia. Despite the fact that he was a rather prominent agnostic and scandalized his more religious neighbors by his beliefs, when plaque broke out in Virginia, he without hesitation, would visit the sick and do what he could. He would leave his old clothes in a stump near his home so infection would not be carried home with him. He later became a devoted Methodist. He brought his family to Kentucky in 1782. Martin was reported a cousin to George Rogers Clark and was with him in the campaign of 1788 against the Miami Indians. Later, in 1791, he was with St. Clair but was away on detail when disaster hit St. Clair's army. He became Clark County's first sheriff and settled in the Pine Grove area of Clark County. His son was Dr. Samuel Martin.

The problem of geneology appears here. The first John Martin was appointed to the Quarterly Court when his term of sheriff expired. In one trial he presided over, John Martin was one of the defendants. Presumably, this is the son of the other John Martin who became increasingly active in Clark County. There is no clear indication in the records, other than one assumes that the John Martin who owns a tavern and is a ranking officer in the militia and War of 1812, is the son of the second John Martin.

A second John Martin, perhaps a Clark Countian, the one that was killed, was in the Boonesborough area and settled on Lower Howard Creek Road. He was married to Rachel Pace in 1782. He built the oldest stone house in Kentucky. It was built with gunports, and still stands.

## AMERICAN REVOLUTIONARY WAR VETERANS

### A

William Abney; Smallwood Action or Ecton, wounded at Germantown; John Adams; John or James Adkins (There may be confusions in the records giving John as James or James as John. There seems to be that duplication in places. However, this history does not try to correct such confusions if they exist); Benjamin Alexander, Sr., killed by Indians and eaten by wolves; James Alexander; John Alexander, Sr.; Isaac Allen; Krom Anderson, Virginia Continental Line (The Continental Line regiments were regulars enlisted for longer terms than the militia units and could be classified as genuine soldiers.); James Anderson; Mallory Anderson, Virginia Line; John Arnold; Thomas Ashley.

### B

Edmund Bailey; Isaac Baker; John Baker; John Baldwin; Major Philip Ballard, Yorktown; William Ballard; William Barkley, King's Mountain; Charles and Robert Barnes; David Barrow; William Bartlett; James Baythe, Strode's Station captured 1780, wounded at Blue Licks; Zacheous Beall; John Beesley; John Bean, Virginia State Navy; Richard Bean; William Berkley, King's Mountain; John Berry; Thomas Berry, Virginia Continental Artillery; James Best; William Biggers; Captain John Blackwell; William Booker; Daniel Boone; Samuel Boone; Squire Boone; John Booth; John Boswell; Seth Botts; William Bowman; James and David Brandenburg; James Brasfield; James Bratton; Ezra Brown; Swanson Brown; Solomon Brundage; Thomas Burros, Captain in French and Indian War; Francis Bush, 2nd Virginia Line; James Bush, Virginia Militia; Robert and Philip Bush; John Bush, 7th Virginia Line; William Bush, Clark's Northwest Expedition, Boonesborough; John Bushanon; Captain David Bulloch; James Bulloch; Lincefield Burbridge, Virginia Line; Edmund Butler, Virginia Militia; Neilly Bybee, Wagon Master, Yorktown.

### C

Col. Richard Calloway, Boonesborough; William Calmes, Virginia Militia; Lt. William Campbell; John Carpenter; Peter Cartwright; John Chaney, 13th Virginia Line; Edmond Chapman, Virginia Militia; Ebenezzer Charm; William Chenault, Saratoga, Jersey Campaign, Valley Forge, Charles and Samuel Clark; John Clark; Richard Clark; Capt. Robert and Roger Clark; John Clemmons; Joe Clinkenbeard, Wautauga, Tennessee Militia; William Clinkenbeard; William Clinkenbeard; Gen. McIntosh's Cherokee Campaign of '78, Clark's Miami attack, 1782; Captai

Ben Combs, aide to Washington, Yorktown; Cuthbert Combs, Boonesborough; John and Joseph Combs; Sgt. John Connor; Ensign William Connor, 7th Virginia; Jesse Copher; Charles Cook; John Cornus; William Cornus; Thomas Courtney, Virginia Militia; Isaac Cox; James Crockett; James Crom (broken arm at Blue Licks); Hercules Cronkwright (Kronkhegt) Peter Cronkwright; Jacob Crosthweite; Nicholas Crutchfield; Captain John Cunningham, 7th Virginia; John and William Cunnings.

D

In Mrs. Clark's compiled volume on Clark County Revolutionary War veterans, there is a correction written on a page of notepaper in her hand of an error concerning the two Donaldsons (Donnelsons). Unfortunately, the paper is not securely locked into the book and after three or four students have used the book, the correction will disappear.

Col. John Donaldson was sent out from Washington's headquarters to Boonesborough to take command of the Boonesborough garrison in 1777. He was met by severe objections. He returned to the east, taking with him a number of men whose enlistments had run out. This was done in the face of almost certain Indian attacks. At this point, Donaldson disappears from this history.

Patrick Donaldson was a Revolutionary War veteran. The records available do not show his revolutionary background. He was, however, part of the garrison at Strode's Station. In the first attack on Strode's Station, he looked over the parapet to see what the shooting was about and was shot in the head and killed. His son, John Donaldson, was twelve years old at the time, but was included among those officially listed as hunters who supplied meat to the fort. He apparently was also included as part of the garrison, which technically qualifies him as an American War Veteran. He continued as part of the militia, after long and distinguished service in the state militia, he reached eventually, the rank of General in the War of 1812. His march of Kentucky veterans which eventually ended in the victorious Battle of the Thames River in the War of 1812, is one of the best records of that war.

Beverly Daniels; Major Jesse Daniels; Captain Vivion Daniels; James Daniels; James Davis, Monmouth, Sullivan's Island, wounded at Brandywine; Lt. Septimus Davis, captured at Long Island and later exchanged, Monmouth; Ensign John Day; Abraham Davenport; John Davenport, Strode's Station; Joseph Dark, garrison Strode's Station, murdered by persons'unknown near Mud Lick; Robert and Peter Dewitt (Jouett), Virginia Militia; Jacob Dooley, 1st Virginia Line; James Duncan; John Dunlap; John Dunn, (captured when Daniel Boone surrendered the salt party. He was adopted along with Boone into the same Indian tribe.); John Douglas; Benjamin Drake; Dennis Dudley; Ambrose Dudley; Matthew Duke (Dyches); John Dunlap; John Dyke (Dyche), Virginia Line; First Lt. Jacob Duty.

## E

Thomas Easton; Elisah Easton, Virginia Line; William Edwards; Robert Elkins, Boonesborough; James Elkins, King's Mountain; John Embree, Virginia Militia; John Embs, Illinois Rgt.; John Epperson, Virginia Militia; Abraham and Elisha Estes; Corporal Ethel Monmouth, Stoney Point; Ambrose Eubank; Achilles Eubank, Guilford Courthouse, Yorktown; James Evans; Peter Evans.

## F

Vachel Faudre, Virginia Militia; William Farmer; John Farmer; Thomas and John Ferrall; Jacob Fishback; John Fisher; John Fleet, Virginia Militia; John Fletcher; John Fluty; 1st Lt. John Foster, 5th Maryland Continental Artillery, Monmouth, Eutaw Springs, Yorktown; William Foster, William Fosby, Monmouth and Eutaw Springs; William Foman, Captain, New Hampshire Militia; John Fowler; Benjamin and William Fox; Rueben Franklin, Yorktown; John Fraser; William Fraser, Captain 1st. Maryland Artillery; James French, Virginia Continental Cavalry, Valley Forge.

## G

John Gaul; John Gavo, 5th Virginia; James Gay; Nicholas George; John Gibbs, Scout with 5 years service; Lt. David Gist, Maryland Militia; Nathanial Gist; Thomas Goff, 10th Virginia Line; William Good John Gordon, Yorktown; John Gravitt, Virginia Militia; Jesse and Thomas Green; James, John and Nathanial Greenway, John Griggs; John Grimes, Illinois Rgt.; Robert Groomes; John Gunyon; James Guensey.

## H

James Haggard; John Haggard; John Haggerty, Virginia Militia; John, Benjamin and Richard Haley; Peter Hall, 7th Virginia; William - Hall; Stephen Halliday; Edward Hall; John Haney, Virginia Militia; William Haney, Virginia Militia; Jeremiah and William Hayden, Virginia Militia; John Hathpenny (Halfpenny), Bunker Hill, Long Island, Brandywine, Germantown, wounded at Yorktown; Daniel Hampton; 1st Lt. James Hampton, Germantown, Brandywine, Charleston; Joshua Harms; Charles Harvey, 13th Virginia Line; James Hays, Captain, Virginia Militia; Joseph Hedges; 1st Lt. William Henderson, 7th Virginia Line; John and William Herndon; David Hicks; James, John and Conrad Hieronymous; Joe Higgens; Stephen Holiday, Yorktown; James and John Holiday; George Hope; Tandy Holeman; Wyat Holet; John Hornbeck; Joel Hickman, Yorktown; Edward, William and John Huls.

## J

James and William Jackson; Josiah Jackson; John Jacobs; Isreal Jennings; Martin Johnson, Valley Forge; John, James, Phillip, and William Johnson; Joshua Jones; Nicholas Jones, Camden; J. Joscalm; John Judy; Martin Judy; Jack Jouett.

## K

William Keaton; Thomas Kennedy, captured, Guilford Courthouse; Corporal Price Key, Brandywine, Germantown, Monmouth, Yorktown; Joseph Kincaid, Boonesborough, killed at Blue Licks; Robert Kincaid, Captain, Virginia Militia; John King; William King; James Kincaid; Joseph Kinkaid, Boonesborough; John Kirk; Thomas Knox.

## L

Sgt. Charles Lander, aide to Washington, New York, Jersey Campaign, Valley Forge, Brandywine; Jacob Lander; Jonathan Lander, Yorktown; Thomas Landrum, surgeon, Hospital Department; Dempsey Lasseter; Henry Launch; Henry Lawrence; Thomas Lay, 15th Virginia, Yorktown; James Ledgerwood, 14th Virginia Line, killed at Blue Licks; Charles Lennox, Camden, Cowpens, Eutaw Springs; Stephen and William Lewis; Benjamin Lockett, Guilford Chapel; John Lowe; William Lowe, Sr., 5th Virginia; Thomas Lowry; John Lyle.

## M

Peter Mallious, 5th Virginia; Jacob Manly; James Marion; Hasting Mark, 4th Virginia Line; 1st. Lt. Henry Martin, Guilford Courthouse; Major John Martin; Captain John Martin, Virginia Line; Sgt. John Martin, 2nd Virginia Line; Robert and Matthew Martin; William Martin, Virginia Line, Brandywine, Valley Forge; John McClored, Captain Virginia Militia; Andrew and Alexander McClure; Captain Robert McCreevey; Francis McDonald; Robert McDowell, 3rd Pennsylvania Line, Valley Forge; Thomas McFargo, Lafayette's Command; Captain John McGuire; Samuel McKee, Yorktown; Joseph and Jesse McMahan, Virginia Militia; James McMillan, Boonesborough; Mrs. James McMillan (Margueret White), Boonesborough; James McMillan, Jr., Boonesborough; Robert McMillan, Boonesborough (John McMillan, a scout for the Boonesborough company, killed by Indians in 1775); William McMillan, Boonesborough; William McQueen; Isreal Meadows; Thomas Measley; Thomas Melton (Milton), Virginia Line; Andrew Merrill, New Jersey Line; John Metcalf, 8th Virginia Line; Andrew Merrill, New Jersey Line; John Metcalf, 8th Virginia Line; John Miles; Clayton and George Miller, Virginia Line; Barnay Mitchell; James and John Mitchell; Captain James Montgomery, Virginia Militia; Patrick Moody, Strode's Station;

Charles Morgan, Saratoga, Stillwater; John Morgan, killed at Blue Licks; William Morgan; James Morris; Samuel Morris, 7th Virginia Line; Thomas Morrison; John Morrow, evidently a Negro; Thomas Morrow; John, Richard and Samuel Morton; Benjamin Mosley; James and John Muir; William Myor, Illinois Rgt.

## N

Lt. William Nevios, Virginia Line; John Newland; Isaac Nichol; Joseph Nichol, Point Pleasant, Green Mountain; John and James Noble; James Noel; H. William Norris.

## O

Daniel O'Hara; Patrick O'Hara; John O'Hara; Michael O'Hara; John, Jesse, and Richard Oldham, all of whom were at Guilford Courthouse; John Oldham, was also at Camden and Cowpens; Captain William and Richard Oliver, Virginia Line; John and Daniel O'Rear; George Osbourne; John Owen, Germantown, Maryland Continental Line; Thomas Owen, Virginia First Continental Artillery; William, Sam, and Lawrence Owen (Lawrence carried flag for his brother); John Owsley, Virginia Line.

## P

John Pace; William and John Page, Virginia; Joseph Palmer, Virginia Line, Yorktown; Captain William Parrish, appointed by Washington to be an aide to the newly arrived Lafayette; George Patton, 3rd Virginia Line; Matthew Patton; John Pemberton, Virginia; William Petty; Charles Philips, 9th Virginia Line; John Poole, New Jersey Line, Flatbush, Springfield, Ash Swamp, Brandywine, Yorktown; Robert Prewitt, 5th Virginia Line; William Price, Brandywine, Stoney Point; James Powell.

## Q

James Quisenberry, Virginia Militia, Boonesborough.

## R

James Ragland, 9th Virginia; John Rainey; Alexander Ramsey; John Ramsey, 10th Virginia; William Ramsey; Richard Ray; William Redman; Holman Rice, 1st Bragoons, Virginia Line; Isaac Rice; John Rice, Strode Station; William Richards; John Riley, 12th Pennsylvania Line; William

Riley; Cornelius Ringo; John Ritchie, 7th Virginia; Samuel Ritchie, 7th Virginia; Lt. George Robards, 14th Virginia Line, Brandywine, Germantown, Monmouth, Stoney Point, Camden; Benjamin Robertson, (5th North Carolina Line, Dunsmore War, Monk's Corner, was taken prisoner. He was a musician.); Thomas and John Rollins, Virginia Line; John Roundtree, 1st Virginia; John Rouse, 8th Virginia; George Routt, 5th Virginia Line; George Rucker; Joseph Rutledge.

## S

Thomas Sanders; Joseph Scholl, Blue Licks, lost his horse; Lt. Peter Scholl, Point Pleasant, King's Mountain; General Charles Scott, 2nd Virginia, prisoner at Charleston, exchanged Monmouth. (Later to be ranking general in the Indian Wars); Captain David Scott; Drury Scott, (evidently a Negro though Mrs. Clark does not mention this, only reports "in many battles") Virginia Line; James Scott; Thomas Scott; John Self; Presley Shepherd; Lt. Charles Short, 11th Virginia Line; James Short; Moses Short, 4th Virginia Line; John Sidebottom, Virginia Line; John Smith, Maryland Militia; Thomas Smith; John Sneed; Sgt. Christopher Snail, Maryland Militia; Charles Snowden, had been prisoner; Thomas Snowden; Christopher Sorrell; Jacob Sphar, Strode's Station, killed by Indians; Mattias Sphar, Strode's Station, killed by Indians; James Spillman, Virginia Militia; Jacob Starns, Campaign against Cherokee, 1776; Archibald Steel; Captain David Steel, 13th Virginia Line; Ensign John Stevenson, Maryland Militia; Charles Stewart, 11th Virginia; William Stewart, Valley Forge, Yorktown; Ensign John Stimson; John Strode, Master of a gun factory; James Stuart, Bremmon's Company, Harrodsburg; James Sullivan.

## T

Lt. Isham Talbott, 5th Virginia Line, Jersey Campaign, Paul Talbott, 1st Virginia Line; William Tate; Arthur Taul; Edmond Taylor; Hubbard Taylor, Virginia Militia, Yorktown; Jonathan Taylor, Virginia Convention Guards; Captain Henry Terrell, 5th Virginia Line; James Thomas, North Carolina Militia; Kizziah Hart Thompson, Boonesborough; Captain Lawrence Thompson, North Carolina Militia, Boonesborough; William Thurman, 5th Virginia Line; Charles Tracy, Maryland Line; William Trimble, Boonesborough; Samuel Truman; William Tuggle, Virginia Line.

Mrs. Clark does not mention why she lists a few women as veterans "in their own right." Presumably, they served as fighting defenders of Boonesborough or Strode and must, in the eyes of the Daughters of the American Revolution, be eligible veterans.

## V

George Vanlandingham, Virginia Militia; Col. Garrett Van Meter, New Hampshire Line.

## W

Thomas, Timothy, and Jacob Wade; James Walker; Robert Walker, Virginia Militia; James Wall; Thomas and John Ware; John Warren; William Webster; John Wells; William West; James White; Daniel Wilcoxson, Boonesborough; John Wilcoxson, Virginia Militia; Joseph Wilcoxson; John Wills, 4th Virginia Line; William Wills, Jr, Virginia Line; William Wills, Sr.; Joseph Wilkerson; James Wilson, Maryland Line; John Witcock; John Witt, 9th Virginia Line; Charles Wood, Boonesborough, Illinois Rgt.; Daniel and William Woods, 7th Virginia Line; James Wood, Illinois Rgt.; Thomas Woosley.

Some of these men undoubtedly fought in the French and Indian Wars, though most of the veterans were not old enough. William Hait was wounded at Braddock's Defeat.

## CLARK COUNTY SETTLEMENTS IN GENERAL

The eastern American Revolution, as far as the settlements in Kentucky were concerned, ended with the surrender of Cornwallis' army. There was still fighting in Georgia, but the colonies had been cleared of the presence of the British armies. Thousands of Tories fled from the new country of the "free," in the fear of their lives. They often left behind their properties and businesses. The treatment of the American Tory is a subject that most American historians prefer to overlook. The American Revolutionary Army was disbanded, but the problem of the veteran, as it does after all wars, remained.

The older veterans returned to their homes and resumed their lives, much as they had left it. There was not a lot of property destruction, even in those areas where the fighting was heaviest. The vacuum caused by the flight of the Tories also opened certain areas of economic advancement for those able to take advantage of the situation. The younger men, unmarried, or else married with small children, had less to come home to. Wealth, in those days, was largely measured in land. Opportunity was largely measured in land. Land was becoming scarce and costly east of the mountains. The Colonial Governments, both federal and state, bordered close to bankruptcy. They did not have the means to pay the veterans. On the other hand, there appeared to be endless land west of the mountains. This was the best way to pay off debts--give the veteran the land he wanted--and it would not cost the eastern governments a thing.

In this period of Indian peace, with the feeling that the West was secure, the white man once more began to pour westward. To the alarmed Indians, the new breed of white men were worse than the old. These men were hardened soldiers, disciplined and knowledgeable. They brought with them their wives and children. They came in greater numbers than ever before. They came to stay.

The British took stock of their situation. According to the peace treaty, they were obliged to give up their northern outposts. This they failed to do. Using Detroit as a center for administration, the British maintained a far flung network of trading posts and kept in close contact with the Indian tribes. Also alarmed at the westward flow, down the rivers and over the mountains, of settlers, the British in these trading posts encouraged the Indians to try to stem the tide. Finally, the Congress of the Confederacy discouraged any counterraids into Indian territory. This position, on the part of the eastern politicians, was based partly on misinformation concerning the real situation, and fear that in someway the territories, legally American but actually in the hands of the British, would be lost forever.

By the time the Indians recovered their initiative, however, there was a network of settlements throughout what was to become Clark, Bourbon, Fayette, etc. Counties. Between 1780 and 1783, years that the Revolution was technically in process many of these Indian raids were led by whites such Simon Girty, a Virginia Tory named Byrd, and others, who swept through Bourbon County settlements ...and administered the worst defeat of the frontier forces at Blue Licks, which was officered by Canadian and Tory leaders. This white leadership ended in 1783, when the British accepted the farce of being neutral. With it, the Indian menace lost its danger to the established settlements, but continued the pressure by constant raids on isolated cabins, hunting parties, horse stealing, and similar harassing attacks.

Throughout the 1780's, this was the pattern. It did not appreciably slow down immigration or the settlement of the country, but did cost lives. The effort of the eastern government to prevent raids into Indian territory kept the settlers from retaliating until late in the decade when George Rogers Clark, already in disfavor because of his drinking and political radicalism, lead attacks into the Indian country. By 1790, partly because of these attacks, but mainly because the Kentucky settlements were becoming too strong for Indian raids, the Indian danger was largely over, at least for Clark County. However, Morgan Station in Montgomery County was destroyed in 1793. The record shows militia units being alerted constantly across northern Kentucky for garrison duties.

The settlements in Clark County followed the pattern that was common on the frontier. First, there was the "Station" or "Fort." This was a barricaded village, walled by logs stuck vertically into the ground, with cabins reenforcing the walls. Blockhouses were built on the corners and over the gate. In the center of the fort were locations for blacksmiths, powder storehouses, baking facilities, water, etc. Virtually unconquerable, except by treachery, to any party not armed with cannon, the stations were not pleasant living quarters. A dozen families or more were cramped into a narrow space without privacy, cleanliness, or conveniences. With cattle and horses stationed within the walls at nighttime, animal excretion, human, or otherwise, was a real problem. Odors, flies, and all other difficulties were pressing. These stations protected the citizens in times of danger, but were abandoned as soon as it was safe to do so. Boonesborough, Bryan Station, and Strode's Station were examples of this type of settlement.

A second type of settlement was the building of individual cabins with a neighborhood, and the building of a strong fort, where in times of danger, the settlers could retreat. Here, they could hold out until help came from the stronger settlements. The Bush settlement, based on their church fort, and the Stoner Creek settlement, based about Edmond Ragland's home, are examples. Some of the settlements were small stockades, perhaps consisting of not more than four cabins with some kind of palisade between them. Hood's and Constant's stations were of this type. Gradually, as the Indian threat lessened, cabins were built wherever there was land to claim. Sometimes, they were a mile or so apart. Most of these early isolated cabins were built in such a manner that they could be defended. Wooden shutters could close over windows. Rifle ports were cut in the walls. Given a brief warning, the settler and his wife, perhaps with an older child, could hold off a raiding party of Indians for a few hours. By the middle of the 1780s, most of the Indian raids were small bands, moving fast, looking for booty and not particularly willing to die. If the settler made it back to his cabin, most generally the Indians would fire the outhouses, shoot any animals found loose, and rush off to easier prey.

The next problem was ownership of the land. As reported, just what one had to do to own land was vague and the law contradictory. Each legislature of Virginia and decisions of the Transylvania Company, before 1775, made changes that were often not fully understood. Considering the time lag in distances, it could well be several months before new rules became known. For a frontiersman who could not read, dug in miles from the nearest settlement, threatened by Indians, and fighting for every bit of food, it is not surprising that he often failed to secure his land legally.

The Transylvania Company drew its authority from the British Crown. Naturally, any settler's claim based on a grant from Transylvania was worthless.

Much of the problem lay in the inability to establish hard and fast boundaries. "Surveyors were worth their weight in gold," as one hackneyed expression puts it. Anyone who could figure, from George Washington down to an ordinary school boy, could fill his time with surveying assignments. Many surveyors were incompetent. They made mistakes. For a proper survey, there must be an agreed starting point. These were few and far between. The claims themselves were conflicting. Some Clark County, settlements, in general, were based on land patents that were given before the end of the Revolution and then sold in tracts to many different individuals by their owners. Sometimes the same pieces would be sold to different individuals, or the boundaries of different pieces would overlap. Land scandals were the "Watergate" of the day and included some of the most important men in the east, including George Washington and Thomas Jefferson. Fraudulent land agents were everywhere. They would sell tracts of land many times; they would sell tracts of land that did not exist. Land agents would buy titles, real and imaginary, and then resell them at considerable profit. Hundreds of settlers were cheated, and others found they could not hold onto their lands. The situation was not too different from many mountain real estates even as late as the 1950s.

Many of the early settlers did lose their lands. The Bryans discovered that their fort belonged to someone else...a man named Preston, who had not fought the Indians and suffered the dangers until late in the period. Daniel Boone had 500 acres of Jouett's Creek and sold it for a "song." He had another 1,000 acres at Schollsville, which, after a long and bitter legal struggle with Enos Harden over the title, gave what was left to the Scholls. Twenty years after the establishment of Boonesborough he left Kentucky in disgust for Missouri. Others left for Indiana, Illinois, Mississippi, Missouri, or almost anywhere west. Even Lawrence Owen lost his lands as late as 1811.

The situation in Kentucky was far more complicated than it was to be elsewhere. The confusion of governments, the Revolution, the "innocence" of the first settlers, all made the situation miserable.

The second wave of settlers were more experienced with law and had more time to insure their titles. The county court's order book shows that this was one of the more important items of business ...to give some legality to a claim. Most of this second wave were not frontiersmen or wood runners, but were settlers and farmers. Instead of wanting to move when a neighbor built within three miles, they welcomed the building of the community. They were family men and settlers.

One of these was William Bush. Though a very early settler, Bush was no woods runner. He had accompanied Daniel Boone on the widening of the Wilderness Trail from Wautauga River to the mouth of Otter Creek on the Kentucky River in 1775. He was among the first to stake out his land and to build Boonesborough. He did not, as did Daniel Boone and the Calloways, rush his family into the wilderness. Like the rest of his family, he had belonged to the Church of England before the Revolution. The Church of England, however, had become the haven for Tories and had fallen into disrepute. The Bushs were not Tories, they were landowners, relatively wealthy and stable citizens. He and his family joined the Baptist Church on his westward movement and remained with it. However, with the frontier exploding into violence, Bush did not bring his family into Kentucky until well after the worst was over. He had staked out 1,000 acres in Clark and another in Madison and was wise enough to see that the title, at least of the Clark County land was secure. The Madison County land was too closely related to the rights of the Transylvania Company, which was destroyed by the Revolution. His party waited at Craig Station until 1780, when he felt the time was right.

Another man we ought to mention in passing is John Halley. Here was no frontiersman and hunter, but a businessman. He was in Boonesborough in 1779. He was the first to raise tobacco on a large scale. In 1783, he built a tobacco barn for fire-curing tobacco. Such barns are always easy to set on fire; his burned once, and he promptly rebuilt it. He later owned tobacco warehouses on the Kentucky River in Boonesborough.

In 1784, like any man that could do a little arithmetic, he became deputy surveyor for the new Lincoln County. This was too good an opportunity for any man with any kind of mathematical skill to miss. Surveyors were desperately wanted.

In 1788, Halley obtained the right "to retail all kinds of goods, wares, and merchandise in the town of Boonesborough." The town had by this time broken out of the log fort and now had stre streets, homes, and stores.

However, before actually moving into the story of the Clark County settlements we note that we only cover, for the most part, the area that is now Clark County. Originally, the County extended from the present Fayette County line back to the Virginia border, and included the whole of the present Montgomery, Bath, Powell, Morgan, Breathitt, Owsley, Johnson, Lee, Menifee, and Rowan Counties. In addition, part of the present Floyd, Clay, Estill, Harlan, Perry, Lawrence, Pike, Laurel, Carter, Boyd, Magoffin, Wolfe, Elliott, and Martin Counties were included. The early history shows, however, that the largest development of population in this huge area was in the Clark-Montgomery-Bath area. By the late 1790s, Beaver Pond (Stanton) and some other fortified settlements had appeared in what was to be Powell County, but they (and other early mountain settlements) were negligable in Clark County history.

It is interesting how a county history is largely a self-contained unit. The early Clark records, the Clark County Chronicles, for example, do not include the Montgomery County settlements, even though they were happening at the same time.

From the very beginning, there were differences between the Clark and Montgomery County areas. Clark County was settled almost entirely by settlers crossing the Cumberland Gap, the great body of whom came from Virginia and North Carolina. They came either directly, or stopped temporarily in Virginia and North Carolina during their trek westward. The Montgomery County population benefited heavily from this movement, however, Montgomery County was also populated by those settlers who came down the Ohio River to Limestone (Maysville), and then moved inward. Bath County was to be settled mostly by settlers from the River route.

The settlements in Montgomery County were something of a barrier from Indian attacks for the settlements of Clark in much the same way that Strode's Station was a barrier for Boonesborough. The result was that Indian troubles in Montgomery County were much more violent than in Clark.

The Montgomery settlers came as early as 1775 when William Calk and a few others settled around a spot they called Small Mountain. This settlement had to be abandoned. There was no other real effort to settle Mt. Sterling until about 1790, when the land filled rapidly around Small Mountain, Spencer Creek, Flat Creek, and Aaron's Run. We have made no effort to catalog it. However, the men around Small Mountain felt strong enough to ask that Mt. Sterling be organized as a town...the first in the new Clark County territory, and by 1795 they demanded more recognition and representation on the county court than the more thickly settled western parts of the new county were prepared to give. This story will be discussed in more detail later on.

Looking on the other side of Clark, it is necessary to briefly report on Bryan Station. Bryan Station and Strode's Station were very closely linked in their earlier days.

The Station was established by four Bryan brothers in 1779. The Bryans had married into the Boone family and the Boone men had married Bryan girls. Bryan Station was the exposed front of the settlements sough of the River, and protected the growing number of settler cabins in what is now Clark County. Bryan Station was repeatedly attacked, either directly, or on parties operating out of the Station. Without it, the settling of Clark County might well have been delayed ten years.

Since Lexington dominates the scene for good and bad in Clark County, a paragraph needs to be added. According to Collins' history, as with Clark County, 1775 found many visitors, surveyors, settlers, and explorers within the boundaries of what is now Fayette County. Lexington received its name from a party of hunters who, on hearing the news of the Battle of Lexington, decided to give the name to the site on which they were camped. It, therefore, became a place on the map before any real settlement was made. In April of 1779, Isaac Ruddle reported passing through the spot on the map on his way to establish his own station in Bourbon County. No one lived there. Evidently, there were cabins but they had been deserted. Sometime shortly thereafter, some 14 settlers came up from Harrod's Station to settle around the area called Lexington. These included Robert Patterson and John Morrison. Morrison claimed he was living in Lexington as early as April, 1779. By the end of 1779, however, Lexington was a going community. In the last half of 1787, the KENTUCKY GAZETTE was being printed. Civilization came early with a dancing school in 1788. Transylvania College had its first graduation ceremony in 1790. In short, during much of the next ten years, while Indians haunted the settlements and cabins appeared everywhere, Lexington grew first into a settlement and then into a town. By 1790, it had become the cultural center of the entire area.

Bourbon County did not effect Clark County history in any way. Montgomery County was Clark County's child, and there was always a rivalry between the two. Fayette County, from the very beginning, influenced and effected life in Clark County.

The first census showed Kentucky as having a population of 61,133 whites, 114 free blacks, and 12,430 slaves.

Once settled, and the county lines established, the history of each of the counties went its own way. It is true that state wide historical movements, the struggle between the Campbellites and the Baptists for example, occurred in each county, but the struggles can be studied in each county almost as if they were isolated movements. With the exception of the Montgomery County Lulbegrud Church, and the Grassy Lick Methodist Church, there was little intercounty movement. Politically, each county became involved in its own struggles. Each county formed a part of the larger picture, but once again, they can be studied in isolation. The leadership of one county did not effect the leadership of another. It is true that Clark County followed Henry Clary to the very end, but it was Clark County leadership that followed their idol, not Montgomery or Fayette County leadership. Even families tend to be county centered. One can draw a list of Clark County families, a list of Powell County families, of Montgomery County families, etc., and though there will be some duplication, they are obviously not the same. It even becomes possible to read the Governor's records on militia that did not mention county by regiment, but by recognizing county family names, trace those militia units that effect Clark County. There are exceptions, of course, to these general statements.

Clark County was settled at the same time settlements were being established all through central Kentucky. Beginning in 1779, the settlers fanned out of their fortified bases at Boonesborough, Harrodsburg, Louisville, and Limestone to establish new locations.

## STRODE STATION

The terrible winter of 1779 was over. Kentucky settlers were eager to leave their fortified stockades at Harrodsburg and Boonesborough to claim their lands and build their homes. The Revolution was not over, but it was apparent that the British did not have either the will or the strength to reduce the Colonies into submission. The Tories had been driven from their homes by the thousands and any hope of Tory support swinging the pendulum back to Britian's favor was gone. There had been nearly a year of Indian hesitation. They had not broken the Kentucky settlements. The 1779 winter had left them hungry and suffering. The help they had been getting from the British slackened. Many of the Kentuckians felt that the worst of the Indian wars was over.

There is no evidence of a conscientious plan to settle Clark County or the area that was to become Clark and Fayette Counties. Nevertheless, a pattern did take shape. The Bryans left the river and went to the edge of what was to become the Blue Grass to establish their station giving Boonesborough glank protection and at the same time being close enough for help from Boonesborough. Soon thereafter, John Strode crossed the Kentucky River and planted his station some eighteen miles east of Bryan Station and ten miles north of Boonesboro He was another block in the defense perimeter. Behind the Bryans and Strode, William Bush pushed his people into the hill country north of the Kentucky River, building a fortified church as the center of his defense. The area complemented the Bryan Station-Strode positions by network of cabins and settlers. Daniel Boone would soon move out into the middle ground between Bryan Station and Strode's to establish his station and McGee was to go between Boone and Strode with his. Soon a half a dozen smaller stations appeared, each close enough to its neighbor to give and receive help. Into the protected area behind these strong points came the settlers.

John Strode was from Berkley, Virginia. He had not been among the original group which widened the road from the Cumberland Pass to Kentucky, but had appeared soon afterward. He had helped survey north of the river and had staked out extensive claims along the creek which was given his name. Elizabeth Taylor's "Early History of Clark County says that Strode built a half cabin in 1776. Like the Bryans, he had left the river and the hills for the gently rolling blue grass lands. (Again, note that blue grass was not yet common in Kentucky.) However having staked his claim, in the face of the coming Indian trouble, Strode apparently returned to the east. Clinkenbeard was later to express contempt for this apparent flight in the face of danger.

What Strode did during those few years back in Virginia has not turned up in our records. It was repoted that he made rifles, an occupation of importance and requiring considerable skill. At any rate he was back in Kentucky in 1782 with a firm grant of a 1,000 acres eig miles north of Boonesborough. Taylor says he persuaded a number of men from his home county to come help him.

It provided flank protection for Bryan Station and one of the first acts was to cut a road between the two. (We might note in passing that these roads were for horses and pack animals. Wagons did not appear in Kentucky for another fifteen years.) Much of the information for this section was written by Annie Jones and appeared in the DEMOCRAT on October 15, 1915, and was also repeated in the Clark County CHRONICLES.

Strode had been born in 1736. He married a girl named Mary Boyle and together they would have a dozen children. To entice settlers, Strode offered his land rent free until the end of the Revolution. To each settler living in his station, he offered free a fourth of an acre for a garden and a share in a hundred acres of corn. Clinkenbeard conceded these terms were generous.

His station was a 100' by 300'. Into this small space, along the stockade he squeezed from 18 to 25 cabins. The numbers vary with the descriptions, but it is possible that cabins were added at various times. Block houses guarded the corners. There were gates on the north and east side and a small gate on the west. A dozen men could hold a stockade like this against almost any Indian attack if proper warning was given and the Indians were not lead by white officers.

A station such as Strode's, Bryan's, or Boonesborough could be taken only by surprise as Morgan's Station was, or in case the Indians had artillery, which was the case of Ruddle's Station, or starved out...and Indians never stayed that long. It would have been impossible to store enough food and water for an extensive seige. However, the longest Boonesborough was under attack was three days.

Strode Station now formed the advanced point of settlement and became the jumping off place for settlers wanting to go somewhere else. Bourbon County settlements added to the protection for Clark County.

Clinkenbeard lists the various settlers that lived at Strode Station at one time in its history. They did not stay long, but they do represent a day in Strode's history. Beginning one side was Stephen Boyle who would soon move out and establish his own station. He was Strode's son-in-law which again demonstrates the ever occurring relationship of families on this frontier. Next came Mattais Sphar who was later killed, John Douglas, Jimmy Mathis, Granny West, who was a widow with a grandchild. There is no explanation why she was so far away from any family or how she got to Strode's Station in its earliest days. Next cabin was Joshua Stamper who would also soon help to form Constant's Station and later move out on the Paris-Winchester Road where Hood's Creek crossed the road. The next cabins were Presley Anderson, John Rice,

Robert Taylor, Jacob Sphar, Barney Mitchell, John Constant who was the ranking militia officer at Strode's. Frederick and Benedict Couchman came next, John Dean, Joe Dark who was later to be murdered in what became Bath County, Patrick Mooney, John Hart and Patrick Donaldson who was second in command and would also be killed came next. Finally there was Joshua Bennett and the two Clinkenbeards.

At another time, Clinkenbeard names Pat Donaldson, Thomas and Van Sweinger, John Taylor and son Sam, John McIntyre, Joshua and William Bennett, George Reynolds, who had a finger over the muzzle of his rifle when it went off, John Hart and the two Clinkenbeards, all having come from Berkley County, Virginia.

William Clinkenbeard had arrived at Strode's while the latter was building his first cabin in 1779 and stayed when Strode went back to Virginia. Clinkenbeard, in his Shane interview that eventually became part of the Draper papers (why should the best historical collection concerning Kentucky be found in Wisconsin?), claimed that Roger Clement spent time at Strode's and later at McGee's, so started the false legent that Mark Twain's mother was born in Winchester.

The population of Strode's changed constantly. It would be impossible to list the people who once lived there before moving on. Thomas Parvin taught school there before moving to Constant's Station. John Constant himself was commander of the militia at the station before establishing his own station. David and John Hampton stayed awhile as did William Sudduth. William Haley lived for awhile in its stockade. Jacob and Catherine Sphar occupied a cabin and had Rebecca, the first white child born in Clark County.

The history of Strode was marked with Indian attacks and threats of attack. There is little record of any other events. Strode gave garden space to those who stayed in the fort. There was plenty of grass for stock to graze. But there were other dangers. In 1780 Billy Rayburn was gorged by a buffalo.

In 1785, Tom Goff moved outside the stockade. He was probably the first white man to settle outside the fort. In 1788, John Bean was at Strode's and moved out toward the Paris Road.

With the ever changing population, it can be understood why there was little permanence about the place. There was no formal church until in the 1790s, though it was not difficult to believe that the Joshua Stampers would have some kind of a Methodist meeting going. Dispite this, the first church was to be Baptist. There was evidently a school from almost the first, though the teachers were changing constantly. It can be assumed that there were dances, parties, and with a fort filled with young men, a single girl, regardless of her looks, could have her pick and a new widow need not worry about her future.

By the last of the 1780s and the beginning of 1790s, Strode's Station was no longer needed. The Indian threat had subsided.

Other stations were built. The only permanent resident of Strode's was himself, who used his place as a tavern. The cabins were not used and the palasade fell into disuse. The gates were not closed and were broken up for firewood. The same thing happened to Strode as happened to Boonesborough.

There was a renewal of life about 1792 when the home of Strode was used as a temporary county seat for the new Clark County. It must be noted that Strode's homw was also a tavern. Some of the cabins that could be reclaimed were reconditioned for temporary housing for those who had business with the Court. The smith was reestablished and, if tradition is correct, Strode also operated a dry goods store. The renewed life was short lived. Winchester was established and became the county seat.

Strode Station was deserted. Strode himself died in 1804. After that the exact site of the Station was forgotten. When building the Blue Grass Seed Cleaning building on the Lexington Road, in digging the foundations, enough artifacts of the age were found to locate the Station to at least coincide in part with the building. William Beckner claimed the lines of Strode's Station visible in 1865.

In 1961, the state began to build a by-pass around Winchester from the Lexington Road to the Boonesborough Road. The Lexington Herald of September 18 reported that the bull doziers and earth moving machinery had broken into a cemetery that had hitherto been unknown. The oldest part of the Winchester Cemetery had been thought to be Strode's Station Cemetery. J. O. Tyler, Jr., did the investigation and reported some 67 graves. One of the graves contained an iron casket containing a relatively well preserved body of a young woman and a baby. She was well dressed in clothes of the period; including gloves, scarf, etc. The casket evidently had been filled with water. When unearthened by the bull dozier, it had been broken open. The content rapidly disintegrated.

## THE BUSH SETTLEMENT

Strode was still building his stockade when William Bush began moving his people to Kentucky. The settlement of Kentucky was different from the settlement of the rest of the country. There would be groups that would move from one place to another...for example, there would be some dozen or so members of the Springfield Presbyterian Church from Bathe County who moved to Indiana as a church in the next century. This was a common place in the 18th century. The movement west of Kentucky was largely by individuals who, feeling the rainbow still lead westward, would pull stakes and move. Sometimes a friend or two would accompany them or sometimes they would head for a destination others had gone before. Kentucky was largely, in its early days, a movement of veterans who had fought together, lived together, came from the same communities, were often married into each other's families, and often were members of the same church.

Willaim Bush was a leader of such a group. He received valuable experiences in the French and Indian Wars. Born in 1763, he would have had to be quite young. He came from a substantial family of landowners, who were also members of the Church of England and had good social standing. It is true that they lived in an area that had lost some of its fertility, because it had been abused through ignorance. Actually, though the historians make much of this idea, Virginia land was good when the pioneers left it and has been good throughout the years today.

There was a restlessness afoot in those days that had brought men from Europe to America. It moved them westward in waves, leaving behind some in each wave, to establish a new frontier only to be rolled forward again in the next wave. It was a restlessness that came from ambitions and dreams; a restlessness while taught that just over that hill was a better place to live.

In 1771 Bush left home and wandered west. He met both Christopher Gist and Daniel Boone and became deeply interested in Kentucky. Unlike Gist and Boone, he was not a professional hunter or woodsman. He hunted and he could take care of himself in the woods, but this is not something that drove him into the wilderness for years at a time. He was not, in other words, a woodsrunner. He had an adventure bug, but it did not dominate his entire life. He was looking for an opportunity and once he found that opportunity, he would make it good. Kentucky was different than other areas west, in that the title situation was more confused and uncertain. Land speculators would be found in every step of America westward movement, but Kentucky title was so messed up that they were nearly impossible to validate. Yet, Bush's claim on his property was sound and unchallengable. Where as many of his neighbors would move west because they had lost title to their western land, the Bush party seemed to have their deeds and titles reasonably nailed down. William Bush would loose some land in Madison County but that was because of the instability of the Transylvania Company.

When his father died in 1772, Bush returned to Virginia with every intention of settling down and becoming a respectable citizen. He married Francis Tandy Burrus. However, everywhere there was restlessness in the land. One of the more promising young Baptist ministers of the area, Andrew Tribble, was talking excitedly of the west. In the general area, there were whole Baptist Churches talking about moving as a body to Kentucky. Bush was not happy in Virginia or with his Church of England. He found that his brothers felt the same way. Whether by conviction, or to be part of the excitement, the Bushs turned Baptist and became prominent lay leaders. Perhaps Andrew Tribble had something to do with it.

Whether the Baptist Church was organized in Virginia or later will be discussed in the next section. William Bush moved his party out with the neat efficiency of a military organization. He had been among those that had helped Boone open the Wilderness Trail to pack animals as far as Otter Creek. He had been in Boonesborough long enough to explore the Clark County area and to legalize his claim by building a cabin and planting corn. He saw service against the Indians. In 1779, he thought that the time had come and returned to start his brothers and their neighbors on their westward move.

By the time his group had reached the settlements in eastern Tennessee, the Indian troubles had broken loose again in Kentucky and Bush haulted them along the Holston River near Craig's Station. They stayed there for three years while Bush returned to Boonesborough to be part of the difficulties. He had become the third ranking militia officer in the Boonesborough area behind John Holder and James McMillan. He was with George Rogers Clark on the expedition against the Miami villages.

September 1, 1783, Bush ordered his people forward. He had staked out some 1000 acres between Lower Howard Creek and Two Mile. Next to his property was James McMillan. Besides William's family, there were four other Bush brothers. Philip was perhaps the youngest and very romantic. He loved a girl in Virginia and was heartbroken when she married John Vivion. He swore that some day he would marry her daughter. Some twenty years later, this he did when he married Francis Vivion, her oldest daughter. The fourth brother was Ambrose, who would leave a series of Ambrose Bushs' who would play very important parts in religion and secular history of the county. Like so many other players in Clark County's historical play, it is sometimes hard to know when one Ambrose passes and another begins.

In addition to these brothers, William's sister, Mary, and her husband, Robert Richard, formed another member of the group. All together there were some eight other brother-in-laws in the party...James Quisenberry, Andrew Tribble (both of whom had married Burrus girls), Roger and William Burrus, Joseph Embree and another Embree whose first name seemed to be lost. What we have is a tight family group made up of capable young veterans from the Revolution to which several other families became attached both for safety sake and for the future. The group had their own minister, Robert Elkin, and included Richard Ramsey, Achilles Eubank, and the Gentrys.

John Martin, having been at Boonesborough with William through the fighting, also had his claim in the same general area of the Bush group but was not part of the Bush settlement. Nathanial Haggard, who had married Elizabeth Gentry, moved into the area in 1788. He built a cabin of hewn cherry and ash logs. He had signed Albemarle's Declaration of Independence.

James, Andrew, John, Conrad, and Philip Hieronymous all fought in the Revolution. Andrew died soon after the fighting was over, but some of the others, perhaps all, were in Clark County as early as 1780. Pendleton Hieronymous married Polly Bush, Ambrose Bush's daughter. Their daughter, Julia Ann became Julia Tevis, who helped her husband with the famous Science Hill Academy in Shelbyville.

Henry Lisle, who had married Elizabeth Martin, settled in Clark County in 1795. John Vivion was also closely associated with the Bush settlement and had received a 1500 acre grant from Patrick Henry for services rendered during the Revolution when he had delivered beef to Washington's army. John Tuttle and his wife moved into the Bush settlement about 1801.

The center of the settlement was their church which they built to be a fort as well as a place of worship. We note that Francis Bush's property was southwest of the church, Philip Bush's was west of the church, Ambrose and William were south of the church, and John Martin's land were beside William Bush, and the brother of William, John, was south of his father's land.

Holder's Boat Yard joined the Bush colony.

## PROVIDENCE BAPTIST CHURCH

The history of the Bush settlement and that of the Providence Baptist Church is so closely related that the Church's history will be included at this point. The Providence Church was the mold that united not just the Bush group, but other settlers that arrived more or less independently, but settled in the same area. It was the fort, the defense of the colony. With the screen of stations, Bryan's, Boone's, McGee's and Strode's, protecting it largely in the west and north, the fortified church was enough defense against any Indians that might break into the area. Even after the log church had been replaced by a stone church, the same idea of a fortress was kept.

Romantists like to feel that the Providence Church was one of the genuine traveling churches that marked Kentucky history and are always bitterly hurt when their claims are ignored by Kentucky historians. Julia Tevis in her "Sixty-Six Years in a Class Room" gives excellent information about early Providence and Clark County. She accepts the story that Providence was a traveling church from Virginia and gives a flowery and elaborate description of those origins. A. C. Quisenberry who wrote, among other books, the history of the Quisenberry and Bush families, claims that Providence was Constituted (the Baptist term for organized) in Virginia, but admits that it is a family tradition rather than a historic fact. It would appear that at a time, particularly in Tevis' case, when the original settlers were still living, that the authenticity of this fact would not be questioned. However, as lawyers and historians know, eye witnesses are not always reliable in their memories.

Ambrose G. Bush, grandson of the first Ambrose Bush (founding settler), who was the clerk of the Boone Creek Association for half a century, admits that no one knows for sure. S. J. Conkwright, whose "History of the Boone Creek Baptist Association" is one of the main souces for information for this section, admits that the existence of a church before 1780 is debatable. Bush claims that the church, and the original traveling church, the Upper Spotslanvania Church (which eventually became the Elkhorn Baptist Church in Fayette County) came from the same part of the country as the Providence Church and was made up, partially at least, of the same Virginia members. Conkwright sadly concedes that to be true, but insists that there were only membership similarities.

George W. Rank's "The Traveling Churches of Kentucky" reports that Lewis Craig barely reached his final destination when bodies of Baptists from adjoining counties, particuarly from Orange County, Virginia, had come through the wilderness and were settling nearby. It is quite obvious that he is speaking of Providence. William Paul Livesay, in his B. D. Thesis "Early Baptist and Discipline Relations in Kentucky" reports that the traveling church paused at Craig Station to constitute a group of Baptists living at that place. Later Livesay identified Providence as being the church that Lewis Craig constituted.

There is some question whether Livesay has not over stated Rank at this point, unless Livesay had additional information not footnotted. It is evident from the record of the Elkhorn Church that in coming into Kentucky, Craig discovered a group of Baptists ahead of him, but waiting for word to come into Kentucky. Apparently, he did not know these Baptists or at least, did not know them as he would have known them if they had originally been of his church.

It seems safe to say that the Providence Church was not an organized church until after it had reached the point in Tennessee where it waited three years for permission to go further. There is really no indication that the Bush family were Baptists in Virginia, though the point of their conversion to the Baptist movement is not stated. What does seem certain is that there were a group of Baptists ready to be organized as a church and that no doubt Lewis Craig gave them inspiration.

The actual organization of the church was precipitated by the arrival in the Holston settlement of Robert Elkin and John Vivion who were elders in the Baptist Church. Elkin was an ordained minister. Evidently Andrew Tribble was not a member of the group at this time.

The date was January of 1780. Conkwright claims that Providence was organized before any other church in Kentucky. The original membership included William Bush, Sr.; Franky Bush; William Bush, Jr; Ambrose Bush; Lucy Bush; Philip Bush; Franky Bush (Conkwright repeats this name twice); John Bush; Sarah Bush; Mary Richards; Vinah Jones; Philip Johnson; Anna Johnson; Benjamin Johnson; Mary Johnson; Frank Johnson; Ruth Wall; Thomas Harris; Mary Harris; Sarah Johns; Charles Sinclair (St. Clair); Sarah Sinclair; Suzannah Humphries; Hannah Dungins (Duncan); Hannah Dawson; Leonard Dozier; Rebecca Dozier; Sarah Dozier; Suzannah Dozier; William Fletcher; Daniel Ramey; Elizabeth Baker; John Vivion, Jr; Sebbis Mauw (Maux); Hannah Maux, and Thomas Sutherlin. Elkin was appointed the minister and Philip Bush was appointed church clerk. In April of 1784, Joseph and Milly Embry became members.

The church had a rather shadowy existence in its organization between 1781 and 1783. Conkwright who spent the greatest amount of effort discovering just what did happen in those days, does not interest himself in these missing years.

In passing we repeat that the Bush party included the five married daughters and three sons of Thomas Burrus, one of which was William Bush himself. There were five Bush brothers and nine sisters with their husbands, three of whom were sons of Thomas Burrus. Conkwright notes that there were non-members of the church also that had attached themselves to the party for protection and guidance.

After this long stay in Tennessee, William Bush sent word in 1783 that the situation in Kentucky had opened up sufficiently for the church to move. The church began to move, the majority moving first to Boonesborough, and then across the river onto the property already prepared by William Bush. A minority of the church, according to Quisenberry chose to move to southwestern Kentucky into a section called the "Barrons." One of the better descriptions of the early history of Providence appeared in Lucien Beckner's paper, the CLARK COUNTY REPUBLICAN, June 16, 1916.

The first meeting of the church after arrival was in the home of William Bush, which was already built. During this meeting, John Johnson joined the fellowship.

Katherine Owen lists forty-four names that became part of the Providence Church in Clark County in 1785. Robert Elkin was minister. John Vivion; William Bush; Frank Bush; William Bush, Jr.; Ambrose Bush; John Bush; Philip Bush; Sarah Bush; Mary Richards; Vivion Bush; Philip Johnson; Anna Johnson; Benjamin Johnson; Mary Johnson; Frank Johnson; Ruth Wall; Thomas Harris; John Harris; Mary Harris; Sarah Johns; Charles Sinclair; Sarah Sinclair; Suzannah Turner; Philip Croswaithe; Mary Clark; Mary Cole; Martha Thomas; Suzannah Humphries; Hannah Duncan; Hannah Dawson; Leonard Dozier; Rebecca Dozier; Saray Dozier; Suzannah Dozier; William Fletcher; Daniel Ramey; Elizabeth Baker; John Vivion, Jr; Sebbis Maux; Hannah Maux; Thomas Sutherland, and Ruth Walls.

If any of the group that had organized the church in 1781 went to the Barrons, as Quisenberry suggests, they could hardly be more than two or three. The two lists are virtually the same.

In 1785, James Quisenberry, Thomas and Elizabeth Burrus, and Martin Haggard became members of the church. Later in the year John Ragland joined. In 1786, Andrew Tribble, James and Elizabeth Haggard, Squire Boone (not the brother or the son of Daniel's brother, but the son of another Boone brother, Samuel and Mary Boone), and Samuel and Mary Boone. Francis Bush and Rachel Martin rounded out the list of new members for that year.

In 1787, Providence became a member of the Tates Creek or the South District Association of Separatist Baptist Church.

Conkwright reports the question whether women should be permitted to speak on any subject before the church, petition for the relief of grievances, etc., was answered in affirmative. Providence was a liberal church.

It is not clear when the first building was put-up. Considering the ease that a log cabin could be built, it can be assumed that it went up early, perhaps as early as 1787 or before. It was on land given by Francis and Rachel Bush, and by Mary Richards. The church was not only a religious center, but also the social and military center.

In the Baptist world, the local church was entirely independent from outside control. It had complete disciplinary control of its memberships, its ministry, and its property. Business meetings were held once a month, usually on Saturday afternoon before the preaching services, though they might be held anytime. During these meetings church business meetings orders of business were: trials, charges, questions asked and answered. An additional understanding of these meetings is included in the section on the Goshen Baptist Church.

There were three levels of officials. At the top was the minister. Though actually the minister was only an elder and would be called that for another hundred years (and among the Primitive Baptists until the present), his authority had been growing steadily for the last hundred years. He became the ultimate authority in the church on doctrine. He was the watch dog on morals. His authority on the meaning of the scriptures was considered the final voice. He, and he alone, was empowered with the authority to baptize, to preside over communion and to marry. His authority varied with the groups of Baptist, being strongest among the Regular and weakest among the Separatists, but in each case, growing. However, the minister's authority of his church was subject to the approval of the established majority of his church and could be removed by the establishment at anytime and for any reason without appeal. There were also non-preaching elders in the churches, but these grew steadily fewer in numbers and soon after the turn of the century disappeared entirely. No other Protestant movement would have the complete authority of the Baptist preaching elder. The Presbyterian always had over him the Presbytery and the Synod. The Methodist was strictly an organizational man. The Baptist had just his congregation to satisfy.

Below the elders and in charge of the church were the deacons. These men were elected, usually for life. They held virtually indisputable power within the church. It was such an honor to be elected deacon in a Baptist church that the term deacon, like a military title, might be applied to the man even by his non-Baptist neighbors.

The third officer of the church was the church clerk. To the organization sensitive Baptists, the church clerk became a man, without authority, but with a great deal of prestige. He was the one that kept the records of the church. Because of his position, he was always next to power. He might or might not be a deacon. They felt deeply in their authority over the records. The standing of a Baptist in his church, his letter when leaving that church, the receiving of a letter, was a serious act and belonged to that church clerk.

Baptists almost always felt a deep compulsion to belong to associations. Very early in the development of American history, the Baptists were so inclined to organize. However, this was early in American history, and the development or organizations was still in its early stages. What authority did an Association have over a free church? This also was a growing authority. It was a voluntary authority, admitted, given and accepted by a free church. The association had no weapon to compel obediance other than public opinion or God's will. Baptists felt strongly this opinion (or God's will) did not defy that association lightly. Still, Baptist churches entered and withdrew from associations at will. Indian Creek particularly, and to a lesser degree Unity, moved back and forth between associations. Bethlehem and later in history, Macedonia in Montgomery County, did not always tie itself up with associations. On the whole, a Baptist Church took its association seriously.

A church would send a limited number of men called messengers to the association. The messengers had a limited authority to commit their church to a course of action. Unless actually empowered by the church meeting to act, they could be denied by their local church. They seldom were, although it did happen. The minister was a messenger usually from only one of the churches he served. If he served a church in a different association than his home church, he was automatically barred as a member of that association, though usually he would be seated as a fraternal delegate. The association was the place where questions of orthodoxy would be settled. If a church had a question of its own, or a neighbor's conduct, the question would be asked in the annual church letter that the church prepared for association. These questions and issues would be answered by the association. These answers had the nature of the decisions of the Attorney General of state government but they had no·legal authority. If a church divided, both groups might submit their side to the association in a letter and messengers to carry the letter to the meeting. It would be the task of the association to decide the seating of these messengers and the acceptance of the letters. Sometimes the association would assign a committee the task of solving the division of the church. History records the failures of these committees, in Providence over Unity, in Friendship over the Particular Baptist, in Lullbegrud and Upper Howard Creek over the more liberal fraction, and always, over the Reform of Alexander Campbell. However, these were the exception to the rule. The association was often a stabilizing power that headed off controversy, made the ministers responsible for their orthodoxy, and prevented churches from leaving the straight and narrow way.

The center of the Associational authority would be in its control of the ordained ministry. This also was a growing authority. The local churches had the right to ordain who they liked; deacons, elders, ministers, etc. Increasingly that right was shared with other churches. Increasingly it became a matter of associational business. A minister frowned upon by the association would find the great majority of pulpits closed to him. It was a very serious thing to have charges brought up against a minister. A verdict of guilty would often end a minister's career, at least, in that area. A few, and only a very few, such as Ambrose Dudley and John Racoon Smith, could survive by being part of a new association or organization. They were a minority.

It is a mistake to believe that an entire community belonged to a church. First of all, to become a member of a Baptist church the convert must be able to relate "an experience" in order to be acceptable. As a Calvinist, the concept of predestination was either party or strongly held. In its extreme the Calvinist would take the position that God had already marked those that were to be saved as saved in the beginning of creation. There was nothing really the individual could do, until God chose to reveal to that individual through some kind of experience, that he had been chosen to be among the Saints. There were many people who either did not have those experiences or did not recognize them. There was a suspicion on the part of some of the cynics, that the experiences others had were very convenient. Then the Baptists had their creeds. The most important of these was the Philadelphia Creed that united the Regular Baptists in a monolithic theological rock. The Separatist Baptist did not appreciate these creeds and resisted them. Many in a neighborhood did not believe their provisions. However, more and more the Baptist demanded absolute adherance to the Creed. The more liberal Separatists, unhappy as they were with the creeds, accepted them more and more as the price of unity with the Regular Baptists. Then, in every community, there were those that simply did not accept the discipline and control that a Baptist Church exercised over its members. The member was part of a theological government that insisted on his obedience. This did not appeal to all citizens of the community.

A glance at the total membership will reveal that only a small minority of a community belonged to any one church.

In 1788, the deacons of Providence were Joseph Embree, Nicholas George, James Ragland and Philip Bush. Conkwright reports that James Haggard became an elder and Edward Kindred a deacon in 1791. Haggard would soon move out of the county, but Kindred would soon be ordained and become one of the more effective ministers in the county.

Andrew Tribble appeared to be a member of Providence in 1786. In 1787 he constituted and served as minister of the Tates Creek Baptist Church in Madison County. It is also evident that Tribble would preach on occasion at Providence. Tribble already had, when he came to Kentucky a little late, a reputation as a prominent minister in Baptist circles in Virginia. It is likely that he expected Elkin to give to him the major post of minister in the Providence Church. Apparently there were those in the congregation who would have preferred Tribble over Elkin. Elkin was recognized as an exceeding good man and a devout Christian, but he never won prizes on his preaching.

In 1790, this rivalry came to a head. There did not seem to be any real theological differences between the two because they would appear on various committees, evidently in harmony. Each group charged the other group with disturbance of the peace and threatened to excommunicate them. They wrote letters to the association. A committee was appointed which included William Bledsoe, John Embry, Zachariah Schackleford, and John Bailey to see if they could solve the situation. Conkwright and the record does not make it clear whether this was a local committee or an associational committee. It is not clear who these people were, partisans of one or another, neutrals, or outsiders. They solved the problem by dividing Providence into two churches leaving Elkin and his group in charge of the old Constitution and the property. Elkin's group continued church and from this point on referred to themselves as Providence. The Tribble people moved some two miles on down creek (towards the future site of Winchester), built a cabin church, and called themselves Unity.

As a result of this division, the Providence people began to erect a new stone church. The Indian difficulties were in their last stages but still represented a serious threat to the community. The church was also built as a fortress, with narrow windows more fit for rifle slits than light, and a cellar for the storing of weapons and powder under the pulpit. Philip Bush reports the existence of the stone church in 1793 in relations to the building of a road. Another report, in July of 1793, mentions a log meeting house near Boonesborough. There is no other record of a church in this area. It is a little puzzling since this log meeting house is on the Boonesborough side of Providence rather than the Winchester side. This may be a completely unreported church. The only other recorded church at this time in Clark County was the Presbyterian Church at Salem. In October of 1799, the reports of road maintenance and building, reported a log church near McMillan's. This would probably be the old Unity Church building which may have been still used, though abandoned by Unity itself.

Kentucky Historical Society's Register, Vol. 70, p. 120, gives more details. Providence's early records are on film in various places. At the time of the division, Providence was reporting 187 members to the South District. In 1797, Providence ordained Isaac Crutcher and Matthew Rogers to the ministry. There is no record of either of them serving Clark County churches. There is also no record of Robert Clark, Jr., serving though all the records proclaim him as a Baptist minister. There may well be small meeting houses that existed for a time and disappeared without leaving any record whatsoever that these men might have served. A little more than half of the membership stayed with Providence. Again, like so many divisions, the total membership of the two church and the earliest record does not add up to Providence's old membership. Either this membership was padded, or there were some who just quit organized religion for a time at least. Providence reported to the South District Association in 1796 with 61 members. Unity reported to the Elkhorn Association 58 members.

The South District Association met at Providence in 1797, perhaps in an effort to give Providence stability and strength. If this was the idea, the move succeeded, for Providence began to rebuilt its strength steadily.

Church trials appear frequently in the Providence records. We have not studied the trial record as closely in Providence as we will in Goshen. The analysis of these trials will wait until then. In 1792, a member was expelled for immoral conduct. Another was expelled for vain singing and swearing. Robert Grimes was expelled for kissing his wife in public. John Lisle was expelled for drinking six mule liquor. In 1803, Mary George was excluded (the word used) for scolding her husband.

The SUN SENTINAL, January 18, 1903, carried a report of Providence history which is some different from any other account, though it antidates both Conkwright and Beckner. The report said that Moses Bledsoe and a man named Metcalf served Lullbegrud and Providence about the year 1801. The newspaper does not quote its sources. We have a good deal of information about the Lullbegrud Church, since it is one of those churches outside of the county that is closely associated with county history (Grassy Lick Methodist Church; North Middletown Christian Church; Boone Creek Baptist Church; Walnut Hill Presbyterian Church; and College Hill Methodist Churches are other non-county church that are closely tied with Clark County history), but we have made no effort to work up a complete history. The records of Providence do not show either man as a minister. There is a possibility that Bledsoe was invited to preach on Sundays when Elkin was elsewhere (for example about this time he was preaching at Thatcher's Mill on the edge of Bourbon and Clark Counties in a church whose name is not even recorded). This was often done. A meeting house, particuarly in these days, was generally open to most any minister that wished to use it. Often the deeds of these houses when they were filed would often say whom these meeting houses could be loaned. In the first fity years, only the Methodists drew up their rules in such a way that outsiders could be excluded. Others would limit it to certain denominations, for example, Methodists and Presbyterians. The practice of open meeting houses became increasingly an embarrassment as the great variety of odd-ball preachers increased. They would often introduce turmoil in the religious neighborhoods. The practice just about stopped by 1830 or thereafter.

Moses Bledsoe was no outside or odd-ball preacher. He was a prominent Baptist divine, a regular officer, either clerk or occasionally moderator, of the North District Baptist Association at a time when Providence belonged to that association, and was based in Bourbon County churches. He also had relatives in Clark County and therefore it is very likely that he did preach at Providence and perhaps more or less regularly. If so, considering that he was one of the more important Baptist ministers of his day, Providence can add another great voice sounding from her pulpit.

It is apparent from the beginning that Providence was a Separatist Baptist Church and that both Elkin and Tribble were Separatist preachers. This meant that they were not so strongly Calvinistic or creed-bound as Regular Baptist Churches. This also meant that she was a member of the South District Association. In 1796, she reported 61 members, as reported.

Robert Elkin was deeply involved in the negotiations to bring the Regular Baptist and the Separatist Baptists together into a single organization. It can be presumed that this effort was approved by the Providence Church. Elkin and Tribble both served on the committee designed to unite the two churches. However, Elkin was not sufficiently indignant with the failure to bring together the two movements, that he joined the Tates Creek United Baptist Church. This was later reported as a group lead by Tribble that came out of the Elkhorn Association and were really Separatist Baptist Churches in a Regular Baptist Association. Providence probably did not feel the need to leave the South Association which was in harmony with her views to join a protest movement.

However, the merger between the Separatist and Regular Baptists was accomplished in 1801 through the work of David Barrow, Elkin, and others. The first meeting of the association was held at Providence in which the North District Association was organized and Robert Elkin was elected its first moderator. He would repeatedly be elected, more than any other minister, throughout the rest of his life.

When the North District met in 1802, Providence was still referred to as Lower Howard's Creek Church (there would soon be an Upper Howard's Creek Church). Sometimes it would be just the Howard Creek Church until the second church appeared. In 1802, her messengers were Robert Elkin, James Haggard, Thomas Berry and Daniel Ramey. We can assume that these were leaders in the church, though not necessarily the major leaders. They were the ones who could and would attend the association. It was an honor and a privilege. She was now either the largest or the second largest church in the North District with 197 members.

The issue of slavery was important in Kentucky at this time. It had been an issue at both Kentucky Constitutional Conventions with the ministers of all denominations leading the opposition. In both cases, the pro-slavery position was largely successful. The full weight of the anti-slavery position would not be felt until after 1810, but it was always a minority position in Kentucky.

There does not seem to be much opposition to slavery in Providence. The record reports that Providence voted to permit no slave to preach without the permission of his owner. In the late 1820s when the issue came up whether slaves should be permitted to become members of the church, Robert Elkin opposed and lost. Providence did not support David Barrow, but evidently backed his expulsion from the North District Association over the slavery issue. There was apparently no division in the Providence Church over the issue. (The subject of David Barrow and slavery will be discussed further, as will the history of the North District Association.)

Most histories of Providence, those published in the Minutes of the Boone Creek Church, Spencer's "History of the Baptist in Kentucky," and those in newspapers written either by Ambrose Bush or W. Heiatt claim that in 1812 Providence constituted the Boggs' Fork Church. However, Conkwright notes that the Boggs Fork Church was constituted by Andrew Tribble and Thomas Ammon in 1800. Conkwright therefore speculates that the church constituted by Providence in 1812 was the Durett's (Jouett's) Creek Baptist Church.

However, any Baptist church constituted up to 1810 in the Clark County area would draw members from Providence. She was indeed the mother church of the area.

The question of foreign missions appeared in 1816. The first Baptist missionaries were going to India at the time. Providence refused to support a foreign mission program. She helped force the North District Baptist Association to withdraw pledges of support.

Robert Elkin died in the fall of 1821. He had been a powerful leader of the church and had considerable prestige in the county. His descendents would appear active in many of the churches of the county in the next century. There is some evidence that his last years were stormy, partly over the question of slavery, for his passing was not reported in the Providence records. Enoch Elkin was elected a deacon in 1822.

After the resignation and death of Robert Elkin, Providence was served first by Richard Morton for a few months in 1821, then for a year by William Morton who resigned because of poor health, and then again by Richard Morton until 1827.

In September of 1823, the group of churches interested in the Boone Creek Baptist Association met for the third time and this time completed the organization of the new association. Providence joined them by sending Nathanial Haggard, Morris Miles, Enoch Elkin, P. Bass, and Thomas Vivion as messengers. There is no explanation why Providence changed associations. A few years earlier she had taken a hard position on the new Baptist missionary societies and forced the North District to back down on early cooperative moves. However, that was with Elkin as moderator who, as he grew older, became more conservative and more out of harmony with his church. The Mortons found little in common with the Regular Baptist ministers that dominated the North District Association after the middle 1810s. Providence religious ties were very close with Boone Creek, Mt. Gilead, Bogg's Fork and some of the Fayette County churches. There had been a group within Providence that had wanted to join the Elkhorn Association. Now the Boone Creek Association would being Providence closer to thinking like Baptist and with churches with which she was related to both in families and in proximity.

Very early the Mortons were deeply influenced by the writings of Alexander Campbell which were appearing in print around the

1820s and in the CHRISTIAN BAPTIST which was Campbell's magazine. Providence reported 160 members in 1824. The Mortons had halted a slow slippage of membership. Richard Morton married William Rash, Sr., and Dorcas Lockland for his first county marriage on July 11, 1826. He married some thirty Clark couples. William Morton's first county marriage was Joseph Wood to Rachel Gordon on April 5, 1821. He married a total of 63 couples in the county.

Thomas Vivion followed Gholson as church clerk. He in turn was replaced by Pleasant Bush.

The Baptist movement in Clark County was stirring and feeling the rejuvenating presence of the Reform or Campbellite evangelists who were reaching new converts everywhere. It is always necessary to point out that this same religious revival was being experienced by Methodists and Cumberland Presbyterians, and to a lesser extent, the Presbyterians. In 1826, Providence reported only 144 members representing; again the resumption of a steady loss of members. However, sixty new members were gained in 1827 and many of the older members were reinstated to bring the total membership up to a new high of 280. Providence's messengers to the 1827 association were John Alexander, Enoch Elkin, Thacker Bush, and Pleasant Bush.

George Boone was, in 1827, the minister of Providence and moderator of the Boone Creek Association. His home church was Bogg's Fork though he left her soon after this date. His first county marriage was in February of 1816, Beverly Hicks and Mary Herndon. He had some fourteen Clark County marriages. Boone was another of the thoroughly committed Reform preachers of the association.

The two great clerks of the Providence Church, Ambrose Bush and W. P. Heiatt (WINCHESTER SUN, April 23, 1909) report that Boone served until 1832. S. J. Conkwright in his "History of Boone Creek Association" says that it was only until 1830. The Reform movement reached a climas in 1828. Through the nation, through Kentucky, and throughout Clark County, the Baptists fought desperately to stem the Reform tide. Some Baptist Churches became Christian Churches intact, three in Clark County. Every Baptist Church in Clark County that was in existence in 1830 either divided or lost members with a Christian Church being established as a result. In 1830, Providence reported 208 members.

Sixty-five members of Providence (fifty one white and eleven colored) withdrew to organize the Providence Christian Church. George Boone, the former Baptist minister and new Reform minister, continued to preach to the Christians. They used the same church building on alternating Sundays. There did not appear to be really bitter feelings between the two groups...or at least they do not turn up in this period's records. However, according to the history of the Providence Church printed in 1876, "Boone Creek Association Minutes" Providence did refuse to commune with the Christians. It is a little difficult to place the limits of Boone's ministry to both groups.

In passing, during all the increasing Reform preaching, Providence voted in 1823 that foot washing was not a sacrament, and abolished it. This was essentially the position of the Reformers and can be linked to the shift of Providence from the North District to the Boone Creek as part of the Reform influence. (This Reform influence was not recognized as such at the time.)

As 1831 arrived, Providence was badly hurt, but she was alive. She reported messengers to the association of Esekial Elkin, Ambrose Haggard, M. Miles, and Pleasant Bush. These represented some of the hard-core families that stayed with the Baptists. In 1832, Providence reported only 95 members. All the lost members did not join the Christian Church. Many members were puzzled, upset, and confused by the battling going on by the two extremes. They just didn't want to be involved. Perhaps half of the lost membership represented this group and formed a reservoir of strength that might be won back. For three years, however, Boone Creek Association did not have a minister. The Boone Creek ministry had gone over to the Reform almost to a man. It was unlike the North District where the churches had gone Reform and most of the ministers remained faithful to the Baptist cause. It was out of the North District that Providence got Thomas Boone, T. Ballou, and J. Jarmen to serve occasionally in 1834. Providence's membership had regained to 192, which was stronger than before the Reform preaching had begun. Of those churches that had stayed with the Baptists, only Providence had recovered so completely.

There is no reason for this quick recovery of Providence in the records. Perhaps it was the willingness of the remaining Baptist to stand by their Separatist background rather than revert to a more conservative Calvinist position that so many of the loyal Baptist ministers were holding. This enabled many of those that were attracted to the Reform, but were revolted by the bitter dogmatic attacks on the older ways that marked so many of the Reformers. After all, the Reformers were talking about one's father and grandfather, and about old ministers such as Robert Elkin and James Quisenberry who were now dead. The Reform, like many revolutions, was having difficulty keeping its radical leadership from dominating the movement. They often turned off people who at first leaned toward them. Providence benefited more than other Baptist churches for in her, the gentlier approach drew back these disillusioned. (We have deliberately tried to see this argument in this section from the Baptist point of view. There is another point of view that will be described in the second volume when the Christian Church history is considered.)

Robert Elrod was minister in 1834. Abner D. Jarmen became minister in 1835 and the tendency to look to the North District for minister now had ended. There were to be friendly relations between the Boone Creek Churches and the North District for the next ten years, but Providence led the way in seeking ministers from other sources. Landrum's first marriage in Clark County was Nicholas Johnson to Doshea Pace. He married four other couples in Clark County. Thomas Jarmen, a local county man and better known than Elrod, became minister in 1838. He was a stronger preacher than Jarmen. His first county marriage was Thomas Bush and Harriet Crim. He served Providence until 1842. In 1837, he was able to bring back into Providence some 60 former members. During the years he served, some 116 people joined the church. Pleasant Haggard, Enoch Elkin, Roger Quisenberry, Llewellyn Elkin and Milton Quisenberry were messengers in 1841 to the Boone Creek Association. She reported 286 members. The authoresses of the "Fox Cousins by the Dozen" said some of the members of Friendship, which went to the Reform did not wish to leave the Baptist Church, united with Providence...or at least the rural churches.

E. A. Allen became minister of Providence for the first time in 1842. His home church was the Boone Creek Church with he served throughout this period he served Providence. Allen was to become one of the most influential ministers in the Boone Creek Association and one of the most capable. He brought E. H. Darnaby to Providence as an evangelist and held a series of meetings that reportedly earned 256 new members for Providence. He was to serve Providence three times, for several years each time, that ended just before the Civil War. He would be the moderator of the Boone Creek Association much of the time. Providence was probably stronger than any period in her history including the boom years before the Reform division.

The Baptist had been slow in using the revival as a method of evangelism after the Campbell Reformers had used it against them in the late 1820s. The more Calvinistic ministers never used it again for it did not fit into their theological points of view. However, as pointed out, Providence sought her ministers with background more Separatist than Regular.

It is really not correct to make that statement. The Regular Baptist movement still existed. Even as late as the 1870s, there would be associations such as the Greenville Association centered in Wolfe, Breathitt and surrounding counties that openly claimed to be Regular Baptist. The Philadelphia Confession was not scripture any more, but the statement of Union that had brought the Regular and Separatist Baptist together did become the theological mortar for the Boone Creek Churches. It would be reaffirmed even as late as 1910 in the Boone Creek Association. However, this statement of union was liberal enough to give the Separatists room for maneuver. In the 1840s, the Boone Creek Churches could still find room for change within its context.

During the 1840s, many Baptist Churches including those of the North District Churches turned to the more Conservative, older position of Regular Baptists. They became what was to be known as "Old" Baptists, or "Primitive" Baptists or by several other similar names.

There were tremors in the Boone Creek Churches, but Providence and the others took the turn in the opposite direction. They entered into a developing program that included support of missionaires, cooperative with the state Baptist association and the development of many new ideas of church and its program.

William A. Taliaferro was ordained in 1845. A new Robert Elkin and Pleasant Gentry became deacons in 1843. Ambrose Bush became church clerk in 1846, he was to remain clerk until 1898. He was an immensely popular man who, as a Republican, came very close to being elected to political office against the powerful Democratically controlled machine. His father had been moderator of the Boone Creek Association. Achilles Eubank, (not the original), became deacon in 1846.

B. E. Allen was not in good health and resigned in 1847. Darnaby came to the ministry for the next year. After the withdrawal of the Reform or Campbellite members, foot washing had been reestablished. In 1851, it was once again dropped as an ordinance.

Foot washing was the key issue that represented all types of other issues, such as missions, and issues that had not yet been taken seriously, Sunday schools and instrumental music. In defeating the issue of foot washing, it became clear that Providence had taken its stand.

In 1851, Ambrose Bush, Sr., Steven Quisenberry and Jeremiah Bush were elected deacons. J. M. Elkin became a deacon in 1855 along with Roger Quisenberry. C. W. Boone and Peter Evans became deacons in 1866. If a Baptist deacon changed churches, it did not necessarily mean that he would be a deacon in the new church. Usually he was unless there were some compelling reasons otherwise. C. W. Boone would be among the educators in the public school system that would shift with his teaching post from church to church airing the message of Sunday schools as well as public schools.

B. F. Allen became minister in 1852. Evidently when the church approached him a second time, he told the committee that he was a poor man and had children to educate. He would have to be paid for his effort. Evidently, Providence agreed for Allen came to them. A paid ministry was another step in the direction of a modern church development. He did not remain long. He was old and sick and resigned soon. (There is a very good possibility that Providence did not meet the salary that had been agreed upon. If so, it was the last time that Providence reneged on an agreement.) P. T. Gentry had been ordained in 1852. Following a rather well established custom among the Baptist to call, ordain and invite to preach their own men, Gentry became minister in 1853. He married Joseph Reed and Mary Ann Bush for his first marriage, October 14, 1852. He would marry six Clark County couples. This was the year that Providence came out against dancing and horse racing. Neither position was popular. Horse racing, in the county where fine horses were owned by most everyone, was almost second nature.

B. F. Allen regained his health and was again called as Providence's minister in 1855. He died in 1861. Most of Allen's ministry was in Fayette County and even in the Elkhorn Association. The only church he held in Clark County was Providence, which meant that he had three other churches somewhere. Even at that, he married some 29 Clark County couples. His first marriage was James H. Quisenberry to Margaret Bush on November 11, 1842.

Providence supported missionary societies in 1852 in a program that had been unanimously endorsed by the Boone Creek Association. The association developed a home mission program which sent missionaries to areas where there was little or no Baptist activity...for example into Montgomery and Powell Counties. The Providence people were no longer afraid to let others use their pulpit even though their theology might differ. William Landrum preached at Providence July of 1853 for a service. Landrum was Methodist.

In 1858, Providence helped organize the Baptist Church at Winchester. It is difficult to say how many members Providence lost to this effort to bring the Baptist Church back to Winchester. There still was a weak and struggling Particular Baptist Church at Friendship, but it had lost the support of most Baptists. The history of the Winchester Church will be discussed in the third volume of this series. At this time, Providence was the largest and strongest church in the Boone Creek Association.

She had held her own during the 1850s which were not good years for Clark County. Times were hard. There had been a disastrous drought in the middle 1850s. Literally hundreds of Clark Countians were moving westward. The total population actually fell for the first time since the state was organized. In 1857, Providence reported 271 members. In 1859, it had with the new church and the loss of population, fallen to 189.

In 1860, Providence supported the General Baptist Association's plan to raise money for foreign missions. Her support helped make Boone Creek Baptist Association part of the state work. Conkwright said that this was the first mention of foreign mssions, but Conkwright had reported the one ten years before and the minutes show others. Robert Quisenberry, J. Martin, Enoch Elkin and E. G. M. Elkin were messengers in 1859.

As the Civil War began, however, Providence had regained some of its lost strength reporting in 1862 206 members. Ryland T. Dillard was called to the pastorate. Like most of the ministers in this first half century, Dillard was a mature, able minister with a considerable reputation for his good work and a wide influence among Baptists in the central Kentucky area. He was not, however, a local minister. He would continue preaching throughout the Civil War until 1865. To the 1862 association, Providence sent Robert Quisenberry, J. Bush, E. G. M. Elkin, J. Martin and Enoch Elkin. H. McDonald was to serve Providence in 1865 for a few months and then C. E. W. Dobbs would be the minister until 1867. Providence had survived the Civil War as she had the Reform movement and the effort to keep the Calvinistic traditions. She had been scarred, however, for her membership was now only 168.

W. B. Arvin became minister in 1868 and would remain until 1874. A number of important events occurred during Arvin's administration which in some ways makes it one of the most important periods in Providence's history. First, like Negro members in so many of the white churches, the Negros felt they no longer wanted to integrate but desired their own churches. Nineteen asked for and were given their letters. There were still a good many Negros who stayed on as members.

The Sunday school movement had now reached Clark County. The Boone Creek Association had taken notice and was urging its member churches to organize Sunday schools. To help with this program, Elias Brookshire was made representative for the movement for the association. In 1869, he is listed in the Year Book as the superintendent of Providence Sunday School. The church was also raising money for a library for the Sunday school.

The problem of the two churches, Baptist and Christian in one building, continued to create problems.

This situation was not new, for the two churches had been using the same building since 1830. The two congregations were inter-related and lived in the same community. However, there was bound to be friction. The very presence of the Christians forced the Baptists to draw together their fellowship and sharpen their position. The Christians were not quite as aggressive and critical of Baptist doctrine as they had been, but it was inherent in their position. New ministers particularly were apt to point out the need to reform the old Christianity.

The hostility increased during the 1850s and came to a head in 1858 when John Racoon Smith, now old but still venerated by all, was invited to speak to the Christian Church but on arriving found the church locked. He held services in the yard. The impression from the Forest Grove historians would indicate that the break between the two churches came here, but Julia Tevis reports attending worship at Providence and hearing a Reform preacher as late as 1864. Being married to a Methodist she still considered the Christian Church the Reform movement. She did not report any bitterness or hard feelings but felt that the unnamed minister gave a good sermon. She noted that the Baptist and Reform had alternating Sundays.

A new element came into the scene when the Boonesboro Toll Pike was built along the ridge line missing Providence by a mile or so. Providence was now on a dead-end road. During the Civil War little could be done about the situation, but after the War a drive was started to build a new church on the new road. This was done in 1868. R. G. Bush gave two acres of land. The Christians did not participate in the new church and the old building was turned over the the Negros. It has remained an active Negro church ever since.

Probably for the same reason the Baptists moved out on the new road, the Christians moved closer to town, into Germantown which was now called Forest Grove.

At this time the messengers from Providence included James Haggard, Ambrose Bush, E. J. M. Elkin and L. Quisenberry. She reported 142 members. It was down considerably from its pre war height. In 1872, membership was heading up again with 185.

G. T. Strassberry followed Arvin in 1874 for a few months and then in turn was followed by George Yeiser. The Boone Creek Association met at Providence and as had been their custom they continued their circular letter. However instead of a theological essay, they began a series of the histories of the host churches of the association. Providence was the first. It contained most of the material that appears in later history and in Conkwright. However, it does repeat the claim that in 1812, she helped organize the Bogg's Fork Church. Providence did report that up to this date, she had received 1,946 by experience and baptism and 227 by letter.

In 1878, A. F. Baker was called to the pulpit. Baker was a new type of minister for Clark County, a city man who was connected with the Academy in Winchester, an outsider who had other interests than the church. The introduction of men who preached on the side for the length of their residence in Clark County, but who would leave the county when their basic profession would call them to do so, changed the character of the ministry. Up to this time, most ministers had farms or occasionally stores. Some, like Dillard were professional men, lawyers, doctors, etc., but they were permanent in the community. They changed churches, but lived in the same location. Baker also served Mt. Olive which was most often tied with Providence in using ministers. Services were held, like most Baptist churches, on Saturday night and Sundays, once or twice depending on the church. Providence's day was the first Saturday and Sunday. The church records are not supplemented by a continuous file of county newspapers.

Providence reported 148 members. The association reports showed that she thought her building worth $3500...a goodly sum for those days.

By 1886, the association was printing complete sets of statistics. Providence was paying her minister $250.00 and giving a total amount of $534.40. She gave something to each cause the association espoused. She was paying $340.00 in 1887 but reported only 119 members. Her messengers in 1890 were K. J. Hampton, James Haggard, Sr., and S. J. Conkwright. Providence reported 161 members in 1892.

John Garner told the story on Providence that after a rather successful revival, the church was having Baptism. There had been a large number of converts and the minister in his enthusiasm wanted more. He would reach out and grab one convert after another, pulling them into the pond, baptize and then hurriedly grasp for another.

One man resisted violently, but since the minister was a big man, the baptism was accomplished. On coming out of the water, the convert sputtered, "You've played hell now. I'm a Methodist steward".

I. T. Creek accepted the pastorate until 1894. It would appear in reading the newspapers of the time, that there was a real effort to establish a full time ministry. The effort failed and Providence returned to a twice a month schedule. He then also served Mt. Olive and Allansville.

A second of these new ministers, J. Pike Powers, became minister in 1881. He was the cashier in one of the Winchester banks. He was to be influential in the Clark County churches for a decade, and would help establish the Baptist Church in Mt. Sterling. However, he was not a native son, and when the time came, he left the county to find his home elsewhere. He was, in the meantime, a very effective minister. A. F. Baker, E. J. M. Elkin, A. S. Hampton, James Hampton and Jackson Epperson were messengers to the association. Membership was down to 148.

All rural churches were entering into a period when their fortunes seem to go down. They did not share in the prosperity of the county until nearer the close of the century. Perhaps it was the changing type of ministry, though good men, they lacked the hold on their congregations the earlier type had. J. Dallas Simmons followed in 1887. During his administration the church took a strong stand on alcoholic beverages. Without a dissenting vote, Providence insisted on total abstinance. In the third volume of this series, we will discuss the effect that alcohol had on Clark County politics for over fifty years.

Simmons was also serving Ephesus during this period. J. Pike Powers returned for a second ministry in 1888 to 1889. Providence had the first Saturday and Sunday, Mt. Olive had the third Saturday and Sunday, and Ephesus the second. Unfortuantely, Powers was sick and unable to do the kind of work he had done before. In 1890, he left the county for his health.

Lloyd Quisenberry became a deacon in 1866; A. S. Hampton in 1876; Jackson Epperson, 1876; Bartlett S. Haggard, 1893; Thomas Tucker, 1893; Clayton Strode and S. J. Conkwright in 1902. A. H. Anthony became minister between 1890 and 1891. H. A. Hunt followed in 1894.

J. N. Conkwright was reported as Providence's Sunday School superintendent from 1884 until 1891.

Providence may or may not have had a Sunday School since the time Brookshire organized one until 1872 when Ambrose Haggard was superintendent. The next superintendent was reported to the association in 1880 to be Ambrose Bush. After this date the association makes yearly reports of the Sunday school superintendents and statistics. It seems likely that Providence had a Sunday school between

1872 and 1880. J. N. Conkwright moved into the Providence neighborhood teaching school and promptly became active in the church. Conkwright, Cyrus Boone and others of the county's teachers would inevitably develop the Sunday schools of the nearby Baptist churches. It is a concidence that three of the county's best male teachers who made a career of teaching were dedicated Baptists and Sunday school men. It helped account for the superior development of the Baptist Sunday school system and an association wide Sunday school convention yearly since 1884. Conkwright left the Providence community in 1891 and his place as superintendent was taken by W. T. Heiatt. Heiatt remained superintendent until 1907 when Clayton Strode took over the job.

Providence's messengers in 1901 were W. P. Heiatt, A. S. Hampton, Clayton Strode, Woodie Ecton and R. D. Hunter. Ecton had been active in Ephesus even to being Sunday school superintendent. He moved and spent his last few years of life working for Providence as he had worked for Ephesus. Providence reported 199 members. J. S. Wilson became minister after 1898 and continued to 1903.

He apparently held high respect and reputation through the association. We do not have a record of where he went after he left Providence, but he did reappear as the minister of the Mt. Sterling Baptist Church in 1918. He seemed to have such influence that he brought Mt. Sterling to the Boone Creek Association out of Bracken Association. He did not remain, for after that 1918 session, Mt. Sterling reported a new minister and the next year returned to the Bracken Association. W. P. Heiatt also replaced the elderly, ailing Ambrose Bush as church clerk. Bush had served for fifty years. He passed on soon thereafter. He had been a church member for 61 years. Heiatt was to remain clerk until his death in 1919. He wrote a history of Providence that appeared in the WINCHESTER DEMOCRAT, April 23, 1909. He reported that since the church was established there had been 1,280 baptisms and 307 received by letter for a total addition of 1587.

T. C. Ecton became minister in 1904 and 1905. At this time the building was remodeled and improved. On the committee was A. S. Hampton, R. D. Hunt, W. P. Heiatt, Clayton Strode, Bert Haggard and A. T. Tucker. Oscar Brown was ordained in 1903. That fall, Providence reported 200 members.

A. R. Willett became pastor in 1906 and was followed by B. J. Davis in 1908-1912. Wallace McCormack and W. P. Heiatt became deacons in 1908. The messengers in 1911 were James Dykes, W. P. Heiatt, Clinton Dykes and Walter Hampton. Her membership was down to 170. Walter Hampton replaced Clayton Strode as Sunday school superintendent. Ray Flynn was Sunday school superintendent in 1915. Providence took part in the Kentucky Governor's Sunday School Contest in 1914. The Winchester News, May 8, 1916, reported Providence with 40 in Sunday school. She also was having a Sunday school contest with Kiddville.

B. J. Davis is the first identifiable student minister from Southern Seminary. There may have been others, including Wilson, but Davis' address was in Louisville. He came in over weekends. Hereafter most of the ministers, if not all, are students. They either attended Southern Seminary or Georgetown College. Occasionally a University of Kentucky man will turn up and one or two who might be going to Richmond. However, the Baptist schools dominated the student ministry field. Sometimes a student minister will start in Georgetown and stay with a church through seminary. This will be discussed further in the history of the Boone Creek Association.

We do have another interesting side light on student ministers. Providence reported to the association meeting in 1913 as not having any minister. This is a pattern that occurs more and more. Every two or three years, several of the rural churches will report no minister at association. What has happened is the departure of their former student minister in June after graduation. The Seminary has not begun by the time the association met, so the new student minister hasn't been sent out from the college or seminary. We also find an interesting unofficial "sending" of student ministers. The seminary will send a certain student to a certain church. Other students will be sent to other churches. If the local church refuses to take the student sent, they might find the other desirable students already taken, or find the seminary a little slow in sending a replacement. Usually the country church took what they got. They had some consolation in knowing that the student minister usually had an advisor to help him over the rough spots.

The association meeting of 1913 reported Providence with no minister. W. S. Taylor appeared soon thereafter. R. B. Jones came in 1917. S. A. Taylor in 1921. Joseph W. Thomas was elected a deacon in 1918.

It is difficult to note sociological changes. However, in reading the association minutes and the churches' records, adding to them the newspaper accounts one gets a distinct feeling that the status of the rural minister was changing. First of all the city churches were growing. Up to 1890, Winchester Baptist and Providence were about the same size, though admittedly there was more money in the city church. But by 1910, the rural churches were no longer growing and the city churches were. Providence was, in say 1880, the leading church in the Boone Creek Association. By 1910, she was just another country church.

The ministers who held the city church before 1900 were ministers of possibly a little more education, but little more ability. Men like S. V. Potts, T. I. Wills, Richard French were every bit as prestigious and as capable as their city brethren. However, even by 1900 these old style county preachers were disappearing. The new emphasis on education often discouraged a layman of mature years and successful business experience in becoming a minister. The new program that was developing which included Sunday school, youth work, visitation, etc., took far more time than the old minister who did little but preach, marry and bury. The expense of being a minister also had gone up so that the rural church who was now paying twenty or thirty dollars a preaching service was expecting a good deal more than the old church. Conversely, in an era of increasing competition, a man could not afford to leave his business, store, profession or farm and spend much time preaching. The old time minister was fading from the scenes. The result is a widening of leadership between the city churches and the country churches.

Elmer Barker became Sunday school superintendent in 1917. In 1918, James Hunter became Sunday school superintendent. The school reported 29 students to the association. With the death of Heiatt, Paul Shepherd became the new church clerk.

The women's work had now developed until it was a part of the association reports. Miss Kitty Hampton was reported president in 1920. There were only four churches in the association: First Baptist, Central, Providence and Ephesus that reported a woman's organization.

As this section closes, Providence reported in 1922 141 members. Besides their minister, J. N. Thomas, Andy and Clinton Dykes and Armstead Brookshire were messengers.

Providence in 1922 was paying her ministers $436.00 a year, somewhat less than all the other country churches save Corinth. She was giving to all causes about $300.71.

As this part of Providence's history closes, it becomes evident that Providence had accepted the full program of the Baptist missionary movement. She had not yet reported a Baptist Young People's Training Union which was also now being reported by the association. Nevertheless, her program seemed to be nearly complete.

Church statistics like most statistics are often questionable. On the whole, the Baptists, particularly an active church, keeps fairly dependable statistics. We note that Providence had 280 members before the Reform difficulties in 1828. She was reduced to 95 as a result of that division. She peaked again in 1841 with 286 members. She dropped steadily thereafter, particularly after the Civil War when she reported only 119 members. As Clark County entered into an economic and population boom that reached the rural areas, Providence membership began once again to build until it reached 200 in 1902. From that point on she began to loose steadily so that she was down to 170 in 1911 and as this period closes 141. It must be remembered that every Baptist Church established before 1810 drew some members out of Providence. Winchester Baptist pulled heavily on Providence members. As new Baptist Churches appeared in the same area, the number of members Providence would draw became steadily smaller. However, as we close this history of Providence up to 1822, she is weaker in numbers, richer in money, and better organized than anytime in her history.

## MCGEE'S STATION

David McGee first came to Kentucky in 1775 with John Floyd. He did not stay in Kentucky but went back east. He returned in 1782 claiming some 1400 acres of land west of Howard's Creek that ran from the West Fork of Lower Howard's Creek to the headwaters of Jouett Creek. It was some 2 1/2 miles north of Boonesboro and was somewhat between Strode's and Boonesboro on the edge of what was soon to be the Bush settlement. Elizabeth Taylor's history reports that his station was adjoining the survey of James Hickman and claims that it was the first station built in Clark County, even before the larger and better known Strode's Station...some seven miles away. It is in the general area of what became Hayden's Corners and later Becknerville...an area that is generally covered in this history as part of Pine Grove...perhaps wrongly.

There is no reason for history's failure to pay attention to McGee's Station. Strode's was built just a little later but had been started earlier. It is not quite clear whether Strode's was abandoned when John Strode went back east or whether it remained as a fort before Strode's return.

There were about fifteen or twenty families connected with McGee's. These included: John Fleming, who would go eastward later on, John McGuire, James McGuire, Bea Waller, Alexander Neely... Ben Walker and James Chenault are supposed to have spent time at McGee's. Clinkenbeard reports that Joe and Page Proctor first came to McGee's. Like Strode's, McGee's Station was a way station for settlers going somewhere else. It was abandoned not long after 1785 with its settlers who were to stay taking up grants and buying farms. Clinkenbeard with seven militia had been assigned to guard Boone's Station and had reached McGee's when the Indians attacked Strode's.

## HOLDER'S BOAT YARD

John Holder was one of the more interesting men of the frontier and certainly one of Clark County's greats. According to the official state history of the Kentucky militia, Holder was a Tory in political sentiments, but, faced with the Indian trouble, he fought because he had to. Actually, Holder's loyalty lay not with the United States but with Virginia and the official government of Virginia commanded the militia. He was a militia officer and like many a Virginian ninety years later who did not approve of succession, he obeyed his state. There were other Tories on the frontier. Evidently the Bryans were. Perhaps even Daniel Boone for it was for treason that he was tried and found innocent. Unlike Daniel Boone, however, Holder never compromised his career with any questionable relationship with the British.

When Richard Calloway was killed, Holder became the next rating officer at Boonesboro and in Clark County. He was to remain active in the militia, a magistrate on the county court, and a man of considerable importance until his death. He had some 1000 acre grant at the mouth of Upper Howard's Creek and touching Boone Creek. In addition he bought half of Robert Preston's 1600 acres. The other half of Preston was divided between Preston's three heirs. One of these shares eventually passed to Chilton Allan who was the heir's lawyer. Preston was the real owner of Bryan Station as well.

Holder built a boat yard and maintained warehouses for tobacco, wheat and corn. The boats that he built were mostly rafts on which the area products were floated southward. It was the most important area in Clark County besides the county seat. As the county magistrates developed the county road systems next to Winchester, more roads ran out to Holder's boat yard to various places in Clark and Fayette Counties than any other one location.

Evidently Holder had his property staked out as early as 1781, if Dr. Doyles' notes are correct. Like McGee's Station, it has not received the recognition in history that it might. Unlike McGee's Station, it did not disappear from history.

It was the port for the Bush settlement, and was busy with sending goods to market. It was the first Clark County warehouse to be inspected by the state appointed inspectors. Besides Holder's warehouse, William Bush maintained a warehouse there also. Katherine Owen suggests that there were some 80 people living in and around the boat yard. If so, Holder's would be next only to Winchester in size in Clark County.

Holder's daughter, Theodocia, married Samuel Combs, and as Holder sickened and aged near the end of the century, Combs bought the boat yard. Holder died, but as late as 1812, the county court referred to the area as Holder's or Holder's Boat Yard. The great flood that swept the river in 1818 wiped out Holder's, but Sam Combs restored it. The flat boat business declined as steam developed on the river. Combs, however, did establish a ferry across the river as well as maintained a river port. The ferry became Comb's Ferry. The river port was one that coal and other items from up stream was landed and transported inland and the steam boats, as they pushed up river, would land down river products and passengers.

John Holder had been with Boone on the raids into Ohio in 1777. He was at the seige of Boonesboro and with the scarcity of ammunition, threw rocks at the Indians. He was with Bowman in the attack on Chillicothe and was at Upper Blue Licks (or Holder's defeat).

## CONSTANT'S STATION

John Constant was the ranking militia officer at Strode's Station. He was involved in a minor skirmish that is almost unknown to historians called Boyle's defeat and was blamed for it. Because of this criticism, he left Strode's Station and established his own station a half mile down stream on Strode's Creek.

His station was not as permanent a station as Strode's, though many families did live with him for awhile. The Constant descendants lived and owned land in the area and William Landrum, who taught school in the area in the 1810s referred to the community as the Constant Community rather than the Strode Community.

He took with him four families when he moved out of Strode Station: Andrew Hood's, John Morgan's, Thomas Parvin's and an M. Stueben. Both Hood and Morgan later moved out to establish their own stations. Hood came back once under Indian pressure and then returned to his own station. Morgan's Station was to be destroyed by Indians some ten years after this date. Parvin was to move to Lexington to help print the Kentucky Gazaette. In their place, came a Methodist family named Joshua Stamper.

The station was a quadrangle with cabins in each corner. It was much smaller than either Strode or McGee's. It was not really built to stand attack as was Strode or Boonesboro, but when it was built it was presumed that the worst of the Indian attacks were over. As in other places, we find the intermarriage of the frontier. John Constant and Andrew Hood had married sisters.

In 1785, the station was attacked and two of Constant's children were killed. Kathryn Owen says the children's identity is not clear in Clinkenbeard's description. Constant had a leg broken. The Hoods came back to Constant for a brief stay and then returned to their own station. Whether this was fear of Indians or to help out in the crisis is not clear. After 1787, the station broke up.

## SMALLER STATIONS

There are several other "stations" found in Clark County, most of which were established after 1783. Most of these should not be so called in the sense that Strode, Boone, Bryan and Boonesboro were stations. These were large fortified areas capable of handling dozens of families and served as a starting point for the adventurous and protection for the timorous.

The smaller stations which really included Constant's Station, were more fortified homes with a few out buildings that had some

kind of palisade or fence around it. Usually it was the home of
one or two families and a couple of transient families going or
coming. Most of these lasted but a few years before they broke up
with the members building more comfortable cabins on their farms.

The Hood Station was perhaps the second of these that comes
to mind. The Hoods, father and sons, were extremely colorful people.
Clinkenbeard called them low Dutchmen. Andrew Hood came down the
Ohio to Limestone, later called Maysville, with four other families
by flatboat. As such, he is among the few that chose that mode of
transportation in Clark County. The eastern sections of Kentucky
were populated more and more as one goes east by this route. The
Hoods were Pennsylvania Dutchmen. Andrew had married John Constant's
sister and we can presume that Constant also came from the same
area. He later married Massa Sudduth. Andrew had some military experience, presumedly in the French and Indian Wars and was
called Major. He did not seem to exercise that rank, and considering that he was born in 1743, he would have been relatively young
for the last French and Indian War. Yet there had also been constant
fighting with the Indians along the frontier. Andrew's son, Luke,
was to become quite famous as an Indian fighter during the 1790s.

Andrew spent some time at Strode's and then moved out with
Constant to his station. With the end of the Revolution, Hood
established a station about five miles north of Strode's Station.
It was the advanced post of the settlements along the Kentucky, and
though Bourbon County had filled up, the last British drive before
the end of the War had weakened them considerably.

Hood abandoned his station in 1786 and retreated back to
Constant's. He stayed until 1789 when he returned to his old
station and reopened it.

The Sudduth family and the Hoods were closely affiliated with
Hood's Station and it is the beginning of the Pretty Run and Wades
Mill communities.

## CROSWAITHE'S STATION

Lucian Beckner, Filson Club Quarterly, Vol. 22, 1948, called
Croswaithe Winchester's first resident. It is questionable whether
he had more than a cabin, but sometimes his home was referred to as
a station. At any rate, it was about a half mile below where John
Baker was to build his cabin.

Unfortunately, this first Croswaithe managed to get himself
in trouble, being convicted in 1794 of counterfeiting. His companion, a man named Wilcox, was sentenced to hang while Croswaithe
was to go to prison. Some 8,000 gathered to send Wilcox off, but,
with the rope already around his neck, a rider dashed up to the
gallows with a reprieve. One wonders whether these theatrical
rescues are not staged out of some form of grim humor.

## STOCKTON'S STATION-BOYLE'S STATION

George Stockton established a station two miles from the present Winchester. He was a half brother to John Fleming. Around his station the Williams and Barnes families settled. Little is said of Stockton, his best source being Mrs. W. P. Ardery's "Kentucky in Retrospect".

Boyle's Station was about a mile from Strode's and Constant's, and was a square with cabins in each corner. Lucian Beckner describes it in the Filson Club Quarterly, 1931. James Walker, John Miller, old Mrs. Clifford, Paul Hulse, Stephen Boyle and Benjamin Allen lived there for a time. The settlement was established about 1785 and is sometimes referred to as the Johnson Creek Settlement. Allen evidently taught school for awhile at Boyle's Station before moving to Indian Fields.

## THE STONER SETTLEMENTS

These stations that were being established along a line from Strode's Station north toward the settlements in Bourbon County were largely fortified way stations. The Bush settlement had been one of a large number of interrelated families moving into an area where they permanently settled. On the whole, they knew where they were going to settle when they came, unlike many of the pilgrims who stopped at Boonesboro, Strode and the other stations, and settled when they arrived and largely did not move again.

Contemporary with these settlements was another like the Bush settlement along the two Stoner Creeks in eastern Clark County. These settlers knew what they were going to do and worked together to accomplish it. They were not a single family, in-laws, and friends of relatives as the Bush settlement, though the Taylor history refers to the settlement as the Tracy Settlement.

They did consist of some fifteen families or so from the same section of Virginia, who had served together in the same Revolutionary units, and came west together. They were not related in the same manner as the Bush party, but they were old friends and comrade in arms.

Nor was this group a movement of poverty stricken frontiersmen. They were, if anything, better financially than the Bush people and infinitely more than the wanderers who moved in and out of the various stations. They carried with them their stock, their slaves, their equipment.

Altogether counting men and full grown boys, slaves and free men, they had some thirty able-bodied, experienced men, most with military training. Among this group was Edmond Ragland, Charles Tracy, Richard Hainey, Wyatt Hulett, Ezra Braun (Brown), William Haley, William Jackson, Erastus Tracy (cousin to Charles), a Mr. Todd,

William Ragland (Charles' brother) and some five other families who for unknown reasons are not written up in the Clark County Chronicles where most of the information about this settlement comes.

Their first act was to plant potatoes, beans, pumpkins, etc., for food. Within a month they had cleaned up some 20 to 30 acres of land for gardens and began to build cabins. Charles Tracy was evidently the great fisherman who would bring home 50 to 60 pounds of fish regularly. Evidently in these days Stoner Creek had as much water as Red River.

Most old homes were built near springs which account for the reason why so many are built so far off of roads. There were no cisterns or wells during this early period. This was true of the Stoner settlement. Early roads would follow the creek beds and later, when roads were built they often followed the ridges. It didn't matter in the least where the roads were located, fences were rails or non existent and could easily be hurtled so that the traveler would go directly to where he wanted.

Most of the cabins were one room affairs and if two rooms were built, a breezeway would connect them. However, like the Bush settlement, a need of a strong refuge for danger was needed. There was not the same religious impulse that the Bush settlement had. Eventually the area would have more churches than the Bush's Providence: Lullbegrud, Bethlehem and Grassy Lick on the edges, and Goshen and Sugar Ridge in the middle. (This is not exactly fair since Upper Howard Creek, the Winchester Churches and Unity might be called on the edges of the Bush settlement.) However, there was no church as part of the original plans or dominating the settlement. The fortress was Edmond Ragland's house. Ragland was the oldest and richest of the settlers though he did not play the part that William Bush played in his settlement.

Ragland's house was a big, two story log house located on top of a hill instead of in the valley. The second floor extended over the first with rifle holes in the projecting floor so as to shoot anyone trying to get cover by leaning against the ground floor walls. Ammunition, guns and food were stocked for emergency and Ragland kept a fox horn whose two note blast could be heard for miles as a warning.

Like the Bush Church, the house was never truly tested. Once when the horn sounded and the settlers rushed their women to protection, they turned and caught the Indians in the act of burning Haley's cabin. Three Indians were killed, some livestock destroyed ...there was never another raid of that size and only an occasional Indian reported in the area.

Richard Hainey also built his house on high ground. He was Charles Tracy's brother-in-law. His house was not as large or fortified as the Ragland home. He built one of the first mills if not the first mill in Clark County in 1786. David Petty actually did the work. Sam Petty was his miller. Petty would find himself in continual trouble with the Goshen Church and Baptist court system. Hainey later built a saw mill into his operation. Again, apparently Stoner Creek had a good deal more water than present. Edmond Ragland was to bring a copper still down the Ohio River and overland from Limestone. Liquid corn was much easier to move and brought more money than the solid corn. Ragland was the first to operate a distillery in Clark County. The business once was one of Clark County's more important industries.

On the heels of the first settlers came more. Septimus Davis and Ebenezer Chorn settled in the area in 1790. Alexander Ramsey and William Wills had settled on Sugar Ridge by 1788. David Brandenburg arrived about the same time and built a bigger and better mill than the Haineys. Evidently the first mill was washed out and not replaced. Brandenburg could grind both wheat and corn. James French after several moves, Madison County and Four Mile, bought land that crossed the county line between Clark and Montgomery Counties. At one time he owned 225,000 acres in various places, to be one of the largest land owners in Kentucky. Once settled, the French family was to operate from this cross-country land for the next two hundred years playing important parts in both counties. Some place in this period the Paynes came, for William furnished the house in which Goshen was organized and Jilson was to be just over the county line in Montgomery.

Sugar Ridge was located in the Stoner Creek area. Tanner Store was also later to be in the area and would be an important center of the area. Actually the Stoner Creek Settlement, almost from the beginning, was never the unified cohesive settlement the Bush settlement had been. Providence had stood like a monument of solidarity in the Bush settlement, but Goshen never played that part for the Stoner area. Almost from the beginning the Sugar Ridge Presbyterians and Bethlehem Baptist Church divided the settlement into different congregations. The fact that Montgomery County felt that the Stoner Creek area ought to have been in Montgomery showed the relationship between the Stoner area, Winchester and Mt. Sterling.

John Rupard settled on Stoner near what would later by the L. and E. Junction in 1785. Absolum March, who was a large slave owner, moved into the area soon afterward. David and John Hampton stopped first at Strode's Station and then settled more in the Ruckerville area than Stoner, but on the edges. With William Wills there moved into the Stoner area his family of seven sons and three daughters. The first marriage in the settlement was between Luke Hood and Francis Wills. Both Ebenezer Chorn and Septimus Davis were educated men. Davis brought blue grass from Grassy Lick and planted it on the banks of the Stoner.

The main road from Winchester to Mount Sterling ran through the center of the Stoner Settlement. This road at a very early date became the main road from Lexington to Olympia Springs were the elite vacationed in the hot weather. It also became a secondary but never the less important road to Maysville. There were two taverns that dominated the road between Winchester and the county line...since a stage had to stop every seven to ten miles for new horses. The Blue Ball Tavern was the most famous and would become a voting center before the Civil War and lend its name to the entire precinct until well after the Civil War when new precincts were created. The White Ball Tavern was owned by Jack Wills who had a dream of some day owning all the land from his Tavern to Winchester. He never quite made it.

Buford Allen Tracy apparently wrote most of the material in Clark County Chronicles that contains information about this settlement. He was relating the information that his father told him in the 1890s. He admitted that the Indian was not a threat in reality, but did tell such stories as Braun and the wolves we have related.

Tracy reported that sugar making was a common practice in 1784. Maple sugar and syrup provided the only sweetener available. Little and big Frederick tobacco was raised from the beginning of the settlement. It was mostly for chewing. It was hickory fire cured. Flax was raised for the making of linen cloth and there was some cotton planted. Cotton did not do well in Clark County, but it did provide some material for thread. Very few sheep were raised because of wolves. Most of the wool used was carried over the mountains on pack animals or floated down the Ohio from Pennsylvania and pack muled inland.

The present (1976) crafts, as demonstrated in the Boonesborough Fort at the Boonesborough State Park, gives a very clear picture of what was done to keep body and soul together.

## OTHER COMMUNITIES

By 1787, there was a change in the style of settlement in Clark County. No longer did a group move into an area, building their cabins around a strong point or a stockade as an organized or a semi-organized community. From this point on, they came as families or two or three families at the most...usually related. Often we find a father with two or three married sons or daughters and their families. Often they had to buy the land from others who had been there before them or had claims on large acreages. Incidently, their rights to the land would often prove more sound than the original settlers. These late-comers were generally operating within the frame work of the law, where as the settlers that had gone before had operated before the laws were formulated, or before they were changed two or three times, or in ignorance of them.

Of course there were those who were sold illegal claims, who were swindled, cheated or abused. For those who are proud of their ancestors, we can note that if one had a forefather who came to Clark County in the 1780s, and the family is still here, he can rest assured that those ancestors were able to beat the game. The west was full of speculators and gamblers, but those who survived proved their superiority.

## SCHOLLSVILLE

William Scholl came from Virginia as did most of the early settlers from Clark County. He had been with Boone in some of the early days. It was not until 1779 that he brought his wife and ten children to Kentucky and settled on Marble Creek on land bought from Daniel Boone. In 1791, his three sons established their homes in what is now called Schollsville. Peter married Mary Boone, daughter of Edward, the brother of Daniel who was killed while Daniel escaped. Joseph married Lavina, one of Daniel Boone's daughters. Abraham was the third brother. Early in 1779, Daniel Boone and his son-in-law, Flanders Calloway, had hunted the Schollsville area. Boone liked it so he marked several trees to substantiate his claim. Unfortunately, trees change their shapes as they grow. The location or the existence of those trees became a legal question that went largely against Daniel. The difficulty appeared almost immediately with Boone's land titles. Enos Harden was the first to enter suit with the Scholls and won some of their land. George Fry, Ephram Drake and John Price also had some of the Scholl land before the titles were settled. Not only did Daniel Boone finally give up in disgust and move westward, but so did Abraham Scholl.

Besides the Scholls, the Vivions-James, Jesse, Beverly, and Daniel-spilled over from the Upper Howard Creek area. James was a Captain and Jesse a Major in the Revolution. The Upper Creek Baptist Church's charter list gives an impressive list of these Vivions who settled in both communities. John Baker also moved from Winchester and established a farm, sometimes called a Station but it wasn't in this full scale, on the edge of the Schollsville-Stoner Creek neighborhood.

Peter Scholl was in a sense the leader though not in the same way that William Bush had led his people. He was just the oldest and most experienced. He had fought at Point Pleasant before the Revolution and at Kings Mountain and had spent some 2 years-six months in the Continentals. He was a lieutenant under Boone at the Miami Campaign and fought at Blue Licks. It is not quite clear whether it was he or a son by the same name that was wounded there, though Kathryn Owens says it was the father Peter. He was knicked and blood poured down his face. He cried out, "I'm dead." Since he wasn't, he was never allowed to forget that statement of crisis.

Schollsville remained an identifiable community early in Clark County history. Landrum taught school there in the 1820s but did not mention the name. It was identifable in the 1830s and Sam Martin includes it in his accounts in the 1850s. Asa Barrow wrote a rather lengthy series of accounts of the Schollsville area for the Clark County Chronicles.

Abraham Scholl served three months in the militia during the Revolutionary War while in Virginia. He fought at Blue Licks, was unwounded, and escaped. However, he did see Isreal Boone go down fighting to let his father, Daniel, escape which Daniel did. After coming to Clark County he fell deeply in love with Fannie Hardesty and went as far as having her initials tattooed into his arm. (This is evidence that teenage madness is not just a modern disease.) Unfortunately, Fannie loved another and eventually married Ezekial Flynn. Abraham did not stay love-lost long, he soon married Nellie Humble and later after Nellie passed on, married Tabitha Noe. Altogether he had some eighteen children, two of his sons were Achilles and Morgan. Evidently in these days it was quite the custom for a daring young man who was facing parental opposition to his love, to elope with the girl fleeing ahead of a wild pursuit. Achilles eloped with his girl, but it was Morgan and not her father that lead the pursuit. Eventually Achilles escaped and married the girl. Another daughter Rachel married Hinchia Gilliam Barrow, who was the son of David Barrow. This reinforced the unproved evidence that David Barrow preached at Bethlehem Baptist Church for many years after its organization. Abraham was an abolitionish, and he refused to work his wife's slaves.

William Scholl married but lost his land and moved westward. He had a daughter named Elizabeth who married Arnold Custer. Elizabeth was captured by Indians and carried to Canada where she was held prisoner for years. She was finally released and came home and learned that her husband was looking for her. She started backtracking her husband northward until one day she met some men closing a new grave. They told her that it was a stranger in that community that had just died of fever. She found out his name was Custer. She had found her husband.

Peter Scholl had fourteen children. Eight of these were born on George's Fork of Stoner Creek in Clark County. The rest were born near the Boone Creek Station of Daniel Boone. Joseph Scholl had seven children. Septimus Scholl was one of his sons. Septimus left considerable information concerning Schollsville.

Rachel Scholl married David Denton, and lived briefly at Schollsville. Later they moved to Logan County. One of his sons was named David Barrow Benton. It is obvious that David Barrow made considerable impression on the community. Denton had an Indian adventure that is related in the section on Indian Warfare.

The three Scholl boys had together some 38 children. There wasn't sufficient land for all of them and most of them moved westward.

Asa Barrow lists other families in the Schollsville community to include Zacharia Haggard who wife was named Zilpah. Barrow claimed that this is the only case in county history where the given names of both man and wife began with "Z." Another was John N. Conkwright who

who married Mary Jane Taul. One John Conkwright was a Methodist lay minister. This Conkwright played a lengthy part in the Boone County history. The Tauls were a border family, active in both Clark and Montgomery Counties. In Clark they would be magistrates, sheriffs and even a Congressman. They would be classified as Stoner Creek or Grassy Lick (Montgomery) families.

The Taylor history of the county adds William Hays, Robert Shortridge, Keith Monroe and Sam Boone to the early settlers of the Schollsville area. Nathanial Hart had grants in the Schollsville area. He died in 1782 and his land went to Lawrence Thomson (without the p). This started a long line of active Clark countians. Robert Peoples inherited some of the land and in the KENTUCKY REPORTS 36, page 387, one of the Clark County legal cases made the higher courts.

Asa Barrow describes the recreation in a frontier community which usually in some way combined work with play. Parties turned into wood chopping, log rolling, corn husking, flax pulling, and wood combing activities that combined in getting people together for social entertainment and a job that had to be done finished enjoyably.

Another of Schollsville early inhabitants was Sampson Harmon. He taught music schools...moving into a community for two or three weeks of intensive training in music, both instrumental and voice. Again, as mentioned in connection with Goshen Baptist Church history, the singing was taught by the notes-fay,so,la,etc. The students would learn the music by the notes and once the music was learned, would then supply the words. It was usually a five note scale instead of seven. Its effect is melancholy and sometimes almost weird, but also deeply moving and beautiful. The modern survival can be seen in the Sacred Harp singing in Alabama and North Georgia. Evidently, however, Samson was not above teaching popular songs, and, even worse, playing the "fiddle" for dances and parties. Barrow reported that Samson Harmon's voice was such that if lifted could be heard a half mile away and a whisper could shake a house.

The general store was centered in Schollsville. The first owners were James and John Hinde and would be dated sometime after the War of 1812. The store eventually passed into the hands of a Clark and Fry and just after the Civil War, to Landrum and Ware. Eventually Ware became the sole owner.

The country general store was almost all things to the community. The storekeeper bought the goods, sold them products (often on a barter system), kept their money and loaned them their needs. Ware ended up owning one of the largest estates in Clark County.

The other important profession was blacksmiths. Glenmore Combs and Peter Glover were early blacksmiths in the Schollsville area. They not only shoed the horses, but usually were practicing veterinarians (as were most of the early doctors), and also made wagons, plows, and whatever was needed out of iron.

William Wadkins was the first suicide in Indian Fields. He sent his family away and used a squirrel rifle. Sam Davenport was the first Indian Field's blacksmith. The Indians had a burial ground near the mouth of Combs Creek almost beside the Old Baptist Church site.

John Goff reported that the first race track in Clark County was in Indian Fields. There is a poster owned by Stanley Clay that advertised preaching in the morning and evening at Bethlehem Christian Church while the minister offered to take all challengers with his blooded mare in the afternoon.

John Hedges Goff had the name of Indian Old Fields changed to Indian Fields when the railroad went through and the station built.

Much of the social life of the area centered around Old Barfoot Tavern...one of the more rough drinking establishments in the county. It was a two-story, log building, the owner, whose name is not mentioned in any of the available sources, never wore shoes.

Up on Pine Ridge there was a haunted house, scene of one of the worst crimes in Clark County...which will be discussed in the third volume of this history.

In 1818, the widow, Mrs. William Burgess Kidd settled. The Kidd family plays an important part in the development of Kiddville that will be discussed in the second volume.

After the Indian danger lessened, well after 1785, it began to fill up rapidly. Because of its dangerous exposure, there were quite a few transients who moved in and decided later that other areas were safer. However, Conkwright notes that the Goffs, Combs, Hisles, Landrums, Harrisons, and Calmes were early settlers.

Tom Goff made his main base of operations on Strode's Creek, but he never lost his interest in Indian Fields. He helped his son, Elisha, to obtain sizeable holdings on the edge of the great flat plain which made up the main part of the Fields on the Iron Works Road that lead out of the Red River country. Elisha would have twin sons, John Hedges and Tom, who would develop much of the area. Thomas Eastin married Meriam Calmes, daughter of Marquis Calmes. Kathryn Owns says in "Old Homes and Landmarks of Clark County" that the Calmes tract totaled 3,800 acres. In 1795, Meriam's father left her the Oil Springs area. Before 1800, Eastin was developing the resort potential of the 17 different mineral springs in the area. It had become popular enough that the widowed Judith Gist came here for rest and recreation to meet the crusty old Indian fighter and militia general, Charles Scott, who also was seeking rest and recreation. He was sufficiently rejuvenated to woo and win the beautiful Mrs. Gist. Eastin also claimed that he had the first steam engine in Clark County, with which he ran his grist and saw mill when the waters in Lulbegrud fell.

John Goff adds to Conkwright's list of early settler families; the Hornbecks, Waskins, Watts, Hempsteads and Allans. Benjamin Allan particularly was one of the first settlers...there being two Allans. The father was killed by Indians and the other kidnapped to Ohio. William Foster and Zachery Beall were also early settlers. The Daniel family, whose main property lay in Montgomery County, were nevertheless active in the area.

Indian Fields property lies in Clark County for despite Montomery County's efforts, Lullbegrud Creek became the county line leaving the entire area in the old county. Once again, there were several efforts to create a new county out of Indian Fields, the Red River Valley and related areas of Montgomery and Estill Counties. Finally the Red River was divided out of Clark County leaving Lullbegrud again the line.

Unlike the Stoner, Strode, Wades Mill and Bush settlements, no main road went through Indian Fields. It was considerably off center from the rest of the county. Along the edge, the Iron Works Road provided some travel.

A massive pigeon roost was located near Lullbegrud Creek and Pilot Knob. Passenger pigeons by the thousands would roose for the summer. John Hedges Goff reported that he had killed as many as 21 with one shot. By the middle of the 1800s, however, the birds had all been killed.

## INDIAN FIELDS

Indian Old Fields attracted the attention of the frontiersmen very early in the settlement of Clark County. It was fertile, though somewhat swampy; well watered, different geologically which attracted attention; rich in game; covered with mineral springs and salt licks; and so located that a resident of Old Fields could move quickly to the Kentucky River for transportation, up the Red River into the mountains or reach the Bush and Strode settlements with little difficulty.

On the other hand, because of these very advantages, because of the Old Indian trails from the north and south converged at this point, it was particularly subject to Indian raiding parties. Actually there was little or no real fighting in and around the Old Fields, but the potential was always there which pehaps accounts why so little occurred.

In 1775, we find the six foot-2 inches, powerful French Huegonot noble, the Marquis de Calmes, with Benhamin Beny, a nephew and Cuthbert Combs and two brothers named Beasley were staking out the Old Fields for themselves. The Marquis name would be translated into a given name which would be handed down to his children. He had evidently come down the Ohio and cross-country. Benjamin Combs is generally reported to be the Marquis' son-in-law, though one source called him a grandson-in-law. Evidently, this is false because Kathryn Owens says Ben Comb's wife was Sarah Richardson. Benjamin's son, Sam, would buy Holder's Boat Yard a quarter of a centruy from this date.

Indian Fields was far too exposed, however, for settlement in Indian troubles. Two brothers whose names have been lost though they may have been Jennings...there is a spring named Jennings Springs ..tried it and were killed. The Indians beheaded them which is not normal for most Indians of the east with the possible exception of the Abernacki. Tom Goff was attracted to the area and was hunting there in 1787. He saw a deer and started to shoot when another shot rang out and the deer fell. An Indian, unaware of Tom Goff as Goff had been of him, stepped out of the bushes to claim his kill. Not knowing how many other Indians were around, Goff decided that a careful retreat was in order.

One of Thomas's great-grandsons', John Goff, wrote for the Clark County Chronicles a good deal of the early history of Indian Fields. Since its odd geographical features draw attention, there are many other scattering reports about it. John Hedges Goff, Tom's grandson, also wrote a journal that has never been published which contains a good deal of information about the area.

## WADES MILL-PRETTY RUN COMMUNITIES

This area like most of the others was settled by individuals and not by groups and relatively late in the period. The Indian threat was almost over which accounted both for the lateness of settlement and the fact that it was being settled. Pretty Run is a creek. Stoner Creek also runs through the area. It was never called Wades Mill until recently (at least not before the Civil War). It is probable that those people felt themselves closer to Bourbon County, particularly North Middletown, than to Clark, where as the Pretty Run communities were largely Fayette County oriented. Before the name of Wades Mill, the owner of the mill was a man named Judy. However, it was not referred to as Judy's Mill Community. Perhaps, when names were used, it should be thought of as being in the Blue Ball precinct. It was for convenience that we call it Wades Mill.

It was good land, but it was also exposed to Indian attacks after the destruction of the early settlements in what was to be Bourbon County. John Hinkston and 18 others had established a station in Bourbon County in 1776 on the creek that got his name. Thomas Kennedy and Michael Stoner had thoroughly surveyed the area prior to this. However, Hinkston gave up his settlement and many of his people fled back to the east. Isaac Ruddle moved into the abaondoned cabins in 1779 and set up Ruddle's Station. Others were soon established, Miller's Station at what is now Millersburg, Huston's Station where Paris soon developed, a settlement at Cane Ridge, Lowe's Station...all before 1790. But at the very end of the Revolution, Morgan and Ruddle Stations and some of the others were captured in the last Tory sweep of the War.

When the settlement did develop, it was largely out of Bourbon and Fayette Counties rather than the rest of Clark County. The families were different and had their ties elsewhere. They included the Stuarts, Lewis, Judy, Pendleton, Wades, Dooleys, Scobees, Gaitskill, Evans, Brattons, Gays, Deans and Harmen among others. The old familiar names of Hampton, Vivion, Haggard, Bush, Elkin, etc., that so dominate the other settlements do not appear. Nor do the Ramseys, Tracys, Haleys, Haineys, etc., of the Stoner settlement.

The most famous figure of the area was that of Nathaniel Gist. Nathaniel's father, Christopher, had been one of the major explorers of Kentucky doing far more effective work of mapping and exploring than anyone else. Part of his reward for these services was a 1,000 acre tract of land that would lie in Clark County.

Nathaniel was old enough to travel with his father on some of these explorations. When Gist was appointed agent to the Cherokee nation, he took his now teenage son. While Christopher was negotiating with the Cherokee chiefs, Nathanial had diplomatic relations with the Cherokee girls. Eventually he took upon himself a Cherokee wife, on a temporary basis. Such unions were not frowned upon by the Cherokee and were not looked upon as permanent or binding by either party. Out of this marriage, a child was born as they often are after such affairs. Later the Congregational missionaires would name him George Guess (an earlier spelling for Gist), but the Cherokees called him Sequoya. Sequoya was to become the most famous Cherokee in history...one of the most famous of all Indians. He was well educated in the missionary schools in Connecticut and elsewhere. He became the spokesman for the Indians. He developed a written language for the Cherokee and printed a newspaper. He represented the pinnicle of the Cherokee effort to become "civilized."

Meanwhile Nathaniel returned to "civilization" and in due course married a white woman and inherited his father's Clark County lands. He moved there and built Canewood, one of the more famous houses in Kentucky. Nathaniel died about the turn of the century in 1796.

In 1801, his daughters, Sarah Howard Gist and Judith Bell Gist, married Jesse Bledsoe and Joseph Boswell in a society double wedding that literally swept the dazzled Clark Countians off their feet. Fayette County had seen nothing like it. It was a sign that the frontier was over.

In 1807, the grizzled, yet dashing warrior, Charles Scott, met Judity Gist at the Oil Springs Resort, courter her and married her. In 1813, Scott returned to her holdings in Clark County and became Clark County's first governor. He died soon thereafter.

In 1828, Sequoya on his way to Washington, came through Clark County and stopped at Canewood to meet his cousins. He was well received.

Another of Gist's daughters, Maria, married Benjamin Gratz, a young and growing merchant from Lexington, in another of the stunning social events of Fayette and Clark Counties. No longer was the frontier of lindsey and buckskin alive, but it was silks and satins of the old south aristocracy. The ties of Gists were with Lexington and not Winchester. Maria Gist inherited Canewood and the land that surrounded the house...which had shrunk to 177.5 acres. Canewood was later sold, in 1852, to Matthew Hume who would be involved in the section on Lincoln later in the second volume of this book. David Gist, a cousin, whose efforts continued Richard Calloway's ferry across the Kentucky at Boonesborough, built Oakley on Pretty Run near the Devil's Back Bone.

Thomas Lewis first appeared in Fayette County tax books as early as 1787. He was from the beginning no leather-jacketed frontiersman and Indian fighter, but an able and successful businessman. He owned a store in the newly established Lexington with Edward Payne as a partner. He had a mill about three miles out of Lexington. He was elected to the legislature from Fayette County in 1792 and was a magistrate.

With the Indian danger over, he sought land on which he could build a home, move his family, and invest his money. Fayette County land already had been taken up largely and was getting expensive. He was told of the Gist tract and that Nathanial was anxious to sell some of it. He investigated and bought the southern half (well within the Wades Mill area) for 900 British pounds. It is difficult to say that Thomas ever became part of Clark County. He did build a house but never moved his family there for his ties in Fayette County kept him in Lexington much of the time. Whether Clark County was his official home or not, he passed out of the Fayette political picture and never entered that of Clark. In 1804, he became involved in a quarrel with Rev. Jacob Creath, then minister of the Town Fork Baptist Church, over slavery which eventually split the Baptist Church as will be discussed later in this book.

In 1829, the estate was divided between the Lewis' sons. Asa Lewis inherited 560 acres. He met and married Peggy Ellerzly, a mountain girl of considerable beauty, but of frontier culture. Both the family and society was scandalized, but Peggy learned what had to be learned to be a Lewis wife and the shocked voices stilled. She was eighteen years his junior. Thornton Lewis inherited 580 acres and Stephen 690. Alpheus became the most active of the sons in the Clark County area building "Oakwoods" as his home. He would also build a distillery on Stoner Creek to become one of the more famous makers of whiskey in Clark County.

Along the Bourbon County line a settlement grew up mostly in Bourbon County, but crossing the line that was first known as Thatcher's Mill which was built by a Daniel Thatcher about 1799. This mill would play a part in the Lincoln section later on. The mill was eventually taken over by Homback's, but the area became known as Stoney Point. John Fox, Sr., would establish his famous school near the mill and the store that went with the mill on the Winchester-Paris road. His son, Jr., Jr., would write such books as "Little Shepherd of Kingdom Come" as well as teach in Clark County.

There were others, of course, that moved into the area. Roughly this would be the area where Hood's Station was originally (near Pretty Run) and it would also be the general area for Stamper's Chapel and the Stamper family. Thomas Wright, reported in the Clark County as early as 1780, was also a settler in the area in the '90s. Henry Gaitskill and James Stuart (church records often spelled it Stewart) had settled here in 1800. William Sudduth, Benjamin Ely, Elias Mynrt, Jacob Smith, Henry Lander, David Allen, Levi Ashbrook,

John and Benjamin Foreman, Ephriam Harmon, Thomas Talbott, and Thomas Little all settled in the area by the turn of the century.

## PINE GROVE

Pine Grove has been called Hayden's Corners and Becknerville over the years, though the latter two names were more down the road toward what is now Pine Grove. Pine Grove proper was originally on the old Winchester Lexington turnpike and became known as such because of the heavy stand of trees that marked the road at this point. Before this, the area was often called the Ebeneazor community, since the Methodist Church was one of the early landmarks. When the C.& O. came through, Pine Grove was moved three miles to the railroad and a station built. For awhile, it was called New Pine Grove. Hayden's Corners was a crossroad that lead to the Holder's Boat Yard and later Comb's Ferry and Winchester. In the 1900s, it was renamed Becknerville in honor of William Beckner.

The land originally belonged to Dr. Thomas Hinde who had received a blank land warrant from Patrick Henry in return for the services he had done the State. He filled in the number of acres - some say for as much as 20,000 acres. Hinde hired Hubbard Taylor to make a survey of the land in return for a tract that would belong to Taylor. Taylor did this and built his family home, Spring Hill. Hinde actually sold much of his land before he came to Kentucky thinking he would never see it, for much less than its worth. John Martin bought some of this land and established his home.

William and Ben Hayden built first at Fort Lexington before moving to Clark County and giving the area their name. Others who settled in the area included Jacob Fishback in the early 1790s, James Gay who built Mound Hill after 1785, Robert Prewitt who reportedly built the first brick home on Strode's Road and others.

## UPPER HOWARD CREEK-RUCKERVILLE

Archibald Crawford settled in 1790 in what was Upper Howard Creek sometime before 1790 and later moved up into Wolfe County. John Fox, Jr., who wrote "Little Shepherd of Kingdom Come", and other books about the Kentucky mountains, had a theory that the mountain people were those who somehow did not have the energy to push on to more valuable land, but became side tracked in the mountain valleys and coves. Without trying to make a scientific study of the fact and looking at the migration of people into Clark County, it strikes me almost the opposite. Many of the settlers came first to the flat country and then deliberately turned back into the mountains and valleys of Appalachia. Most of this area was settled well after the first settlers in Clark County had been established, but long before the good land had disappeared, or before the population push would drive out the less successful. Moving into the mountains was a deliberate act of men seeking homesites that would have water, a few acres of fertile bottom land soil, plenty of game, which was becoming scarce in the flat country, and room to expand. They moved up the rivers such as the Red River in the present Powell County. They were no more isolated in the beginning than any other settler and somewhat safer from Indians. Their problem was of being bypassed. Their mountains would not support a heavy population and the geography would prevent easy communication with roads built for wagons and heavier vehicles. Outside of the iron forge areas, Powell County wasn't really settled until well after 1810. Hardwick Station was much earlier. However, Wolfe County was settled even later. When Estill County was created, it was still virtually virgin territory.

The Vivion families, James, Jesse, Beverly, and Daniel moved into this area early. Older generations and other Vivions had settled in the Bush area. This Creek was really an extension of the Bush settlement.

Herculius Kraukhegt whose family name would soon become Conkwright came to this area about 1790. As noted, he had been a "Regulator" in North Carolina in his younger days. He was considerably older than most settlers. Richard Oliver settled in 1802. Bryant McDonald had 400 acres on the Upper Fork of the Creek. The name Ruckerville did not come till very much later. Rueben Rucker was the man for whom the community was named. It would eventually become a prosperous community consisting of a grist mill, two stores, two blacksmiths, a hotel and a church that once had three church organizations meeting in the same building. This, however, would be much later. At this time it was the Upper Howard Creek Baptist Church that gave the community a sense of unity and a name.

## PINCHEM

Two Mile and Four Mile Creeks were so named by Daniel Boone (according to legend) because they were roughly two miles and four miles away from Boonesboro. Four Mile was also called Muddy Creek which is confusing to old records in that there is also a Muddy Creek in Madison County.

After the Civil War, the area was called Pinchem. The name, and many stories seem to all agree, came from some jokester who noted that the boys on the creeks were romantic boys who liked to pinch the girls slyly. Kathryn Owen says the Pinchem name came from a stingy storekeeper who traded his merchandise for the farmers' produce and always managed to get the best out of a deal. Farmers would say they were pinched in trade and called the store Pinchem Store. So for reasons that forbade logic, the area became known as Pinchem.

Simon Kenton had extensive patents along these creek bottoms. James French bought 400 acres of this land and first moved to it. He was later to move to a farm on the Montgomery-Clark County line.

In 1790, Francis Cullum built a log house on Four Mile Creek which he sold to his nephew, Horatio Owen. Owen would add two stone rooms, two rooms on an ell, a store room and a lean-to. This was very typical, each generation adding what they want permitting the house to grow like Topsy.

Achiles Eubank was very early developing properties on the river and along the creeks. James Quisenberry also was to settle early and by 1798 John Rutledge had established himself.

To some degree the later Unity Church and definitely the Indian Creek churches were part of this community and the names of their early members would be early settlers in the area, such as the Hampton family.

One extreme of the Four Mile-Two Mile or Pinchem area as it was later called, was what eventually became known as Allanville. Here again, the name was not common until well after the Civil War when the Allan family was prominent in the area. Indian Creek formed a part of this community. Joseph Combs had a 1000 acres on Howard Creek that reached into this area. There was a little community at the mouth called Charleston before the Civil War that has almost escaped history. It was at the mouth of Indian Creek and consisted of a store, post office, hotel and most important, a coal yard. The Baldwin family evidently settled this area originally.

Oliver established a distillery early in the history, though probably not till after the War of 1812. His mill, however, was there much earlier.

The Clark County Chronicles never described this area despite the fact that some of the earliest and heaviest settlements occurred here. They were largely an outgrowth of the Bush settlement. First mill at Pinchem Creek was built by Rev. Laurence Owen Circa 1791.

## PILOT VIEW

Along the edge of the Stoner settlement, or along Upper Howard Creek area or for that matter, along the edges of Indian Fields, is Pilot View. The name did not come into being until 1868-69 when the Iron Works Pike was built and a pike from Schollsville was extended to join it. A crowd of neighbors had gathered to celebrate the merging roads. John Hedges Goff was instrumental in building the Iron Works Pike...the history of the pikes will be in the third volume. It was obvious that the junction of the roads would be a little community. Several names were suggested such as Scholl-Goff.

This was rejected as too cumbersome. John N. Conkwright suggested Grand View since the point was on a ridge and the view was indeed grand. Someone noted that Pilot Knob was clearly visible from the point and thus, Pilot View was developed.

To initiate the name, the Lexington-Estell stage had arrived and a somewhat inebriated Irish buyer of pig iron stood in the open door. Impressed by the crowd and the occasion, he entered into a lengthy speech and in so doing, frightened the horses. The stage coach lurged, the Irishman fell out, and the stage raced on down the road. When last seen, the Irishman was racing after the stage as fast as his legs could take him.

Apparently a Timothy Carrington built a cabin a mile from Pilot View in 1775, on a 300 acre land bought from Patrick Henry. He returned later after the first Indian troubles. Jeremiah Moore was also a very early settler. Frank Ramsey owned the first store in what became Pilot View.

## LOG LICK

Log Lick first appeared in history as a place where the prehistoric sea had left a long dried-up salt pool which in turn had impregnated the soil with salt. Animals would come to this point and lick the ground. Thomas Goff and Daniel Boone were hunting the area in the late 1780s with Goff's Negro servant and a William and Major Beazley. (Major was a name and not a title.) They had built a corral of logs and were intending to drive game into the corral where they could be killed wholesale. Indians surprised the group and, true to his reputation of being the fastest runner in Kentucky, Daniel with Tom Goff right behind, took off for Boonesboro. The Indians, however, were fascinated in Goff's Negro servant. There were a number of Negros in and around Boonesboro, in the Stoner settlement, and some in the Bush settlement, but this Negro was the first these Indians had ever seen. They gave up the white man and pursued the Negro. The Negro escaped but didn't stop until he had reached Goff's home stamping grounds in Virginia (now part of West Virginia) where he turned himself into Goff's relatives and begged never to be sent back to that awful place. He was not!

## DUNAWAY STATION

Perhaps the least reported of the early settlements is Dunaway Station. Actually, like Pretty Run is combined with Wades Mill for ease, Dunaway Station is combined with Log Lick. There is nothing in the records about Dunaway Station save a single mention in the records of Dr. Doyle on the history of Clark County physicians concerning Nelson Tuttle. Landrum's book mentions a Dunaway Station but it is not clear whether he was referring to the area about the present Dunaway or a station on Hardwick Creek in what is now Powell County.

Doyle reports that Nelson Tuttle, who was born in 1797, moved with his family to Dunaway Station in 1800. The father was evidently John Tuttle who came from Culpepper, Virginia. He was evidently a Williams College student. Nelson married Nancy Conkwright. James Elkin was an early settler.

Obviously John Dunaway had to be an early settler. However, there is virtually nothing concerning him in the records discovered up to date. He was an American War Veteran and the church took his name....and another in what became Powell County.

The community of Trap is also part of this Log Lick-Dunaway neighborhood. The story is that the name came at a time when a rural post office was being established. The area is heavy with Fox families and there has been a Fox store in Trap for many years. The neighbors gathered to decide on a name for their post office. Several names were suggested but some place there was always another post office with that name. Finally, imagination running out, one of the neighbors waved at a bunch of traps hanging on the store wall and said, "Call the d___ place Trap." So came the name... or at least so that legend tells.

## FORD

Ford proper does not develop until after 1880 and will be discussed fully in the third volume. Evidently, John and Jesse Dyche settled near Ford. They were carpenters and did a good deal of barn work and some house carpentering in the area. Another John Dyche or Dykes as the name becomes, was one of the county's early law men, a long time constable and deputy sheriff.

## RENNICK

The name really is a railroad station and therefore, does not appear until after the railroads....so this will not be discussed until the third volume. Matthew Patton, Isaac Cunningham, Thomas Goff were all residents of the area and the Van Meters were to follow as in-laws of Isaac Cunningham. Thomas Goff was to sell shorthorns to Matthew Patton to begin the shorthorn development in Clark County which is a second volume subject.

## SWELL SHOP

Really part of the Stoner settlement. Joseph Sewell who was

a Methodist local minister had a blacksmith shop which was to be run by the Sewells for nearly a hundred years.

Most of the other communities were developments of the railraod that went through. Stations would be placed about every seven miles along each railroad and around each settlement would often develop. These will be considered later.

By this time, there is also a Beaver Pond on the Red River, which contained a church and probably a store. This was the beginning of Stanton. We have reached well into the 1800s and there was no longer a frontier. Kentucky had been settled.

## INDIAN WARFARE

At this point we need to say a few words about Indians and their methods of warfare. The experts divide the Indians into language groups. The Iroquian which includes the Cherokees has already been mentioned. They were a late tribe into the United States, arriving contemporaneously with the white settlers along the eastern coasts. They became enemies of the French and usually were allied with the English. With the exception of the Senaca massacre of the Mount Builders already mentioned, only the Cherokee and the Huron branch of the Iroquois effected Clark County history. Actually, the Cherokee threat was more a threat to the supply lines going over the mountains than to the central Kentucky colonies.

The main enemy of Clark County settlers were Alquonquin Indians from a dozen or so tribes. The Shawnees, Ottawas, Wyandots, Miamis were some of these. Mingos was another name for the Iroquois Huron. There were Indians coming up out of the south that endangered other areas of the state such as the Choctaws and Creeks. They did not effect Clark County.

The Indians raiding Kentucky were pretty much alike in customs and thinking. On the whole, they were matriarchal by that the final authority would rest in the women and not the men. Most American fiction writers from John Smith of Jamestown down to the present overlook this fact. The woman to marry in an Indian village was the chief's sister, not his daughter, for if there were any inherited lines of authority it would go to the sister and her husband, or the chief's niece. The immediate authority rested with men, however, who held two leadership positions. The hereditary authority was largely administrative, though it is hard to claim that the woods Indians had hereditary chiefs. They kept order in the tribe, moved the villages when they became so unsanitary that living in them was impossible, divided the food, and in general, did what any administrator had to do. He was often an older man and respected for his wisdom.

The war chief was a different man. Any warrior could be a war chief. Let a young warrior make a name for himself on a raid, and the next time he might be able to recruit two or three of his friends for his own raid. If this raid was successful, he might find himself leading a band of fifteen or twenty. Thus, a war chief would build a reputation by success. There would be several such chiefs with different reputations in any given tribe.

Discipline always depended on the force of character of the chief. If he was a strong leader, he would hold his warriors tightly. At any time, however, some of the younger and up and coming chiefs might challenge his authority and break from his control. This explains why the white officers could not assert their authority absolutely over their Indian troups.

The Indians loved war, but to them it was a game. The object of the game was to win glory and trophies. It was a method by which a poor Indian brave could become a wealthy and respected member of the tribe virtually overnight. The Indians were perfectly willing to take risks to win this booty and glory. However, this did not go as far as getting killed. The Indians felt that being killed had certain drawbacks. There was no way an Indian war chief could lose his authority and popularity faster than to lose a few of his followers on a raid. This does not mean that the Indians were not willing to fight to the death if need be, it just wasn't popular with them.

Glory and booty was the main object of Indian warfare. He was not interested in territory as such. Sometimes when a village grew too large, a portion of it would break off and follow a new chief, perhaps an old war chief that was crossing over into the administrative field to establish a new village. They might move into disputed territory as the Iroquoians were doing. Normally, Indians did not seek territory or control of an enemy. They took prisoners, particularly women and children. These prisoners were usually worked into the tribe. The women would generally marry. Life for such women was hard, but not much harder than what they had known on a frontier farm. Once they had children, they often found their ties with the Indians very strong. Add this to the uncertain welcome they would expect on returning to their white families, many a captured woman preferred to stay with their Indian husbands and had to be literally forced to return.

The need for children was always pressing among the Indians. There was no real problem in integrating children of other tribes into a tribe. If captured young enough, they grew up without stigma or prejudice. It did not occur to the Indians that they could not work white (or in the deeper south, Negro) children into the tribe in the same way. Many of the Indians of the south, the Siminoles and Creeks for example, were heavily shot through with Negro blood. The Cherokee had Negro slaves, but a Negro slave could always hope to be elevated to tribal membership. If an Indian took a Negro mistress, she usually became his wife in a full Indian sense of the word and their children would be part of the tribe.

It is also true that many of the white children did prefer their Indian adopted parents. Hundreds of children, and this is a literal fact, disappeared into the tribal ranks and became full blooded Indians. Others would shift back and forth from white settlement to Indian. The most famous perhaps of these during this period was Simon Girty.

Glory was also killing an enemy. It didn't really matter whether the enemy was man, woman or child. A child was a potential

warrior and killing it was the same as killing the man. The woman
was the mother of a warrior and in killing her, a potential source
of enemy was cut off. True, it was a greater glory to kill a
warrior, but this entailed considerable risk. It was no disgrace
to obtain glory the easier way. There are some novels written
about Indians seeking to kill a particularly great enemy. Most of
these are novels.

The Indian did not shrink from hand to hand combat if necessary,
but only when necessary. If an enemy could be killed from conceal-
ment or by surprise, there was just as much glory and considerably
more safety. If any attack appeared to be too costly, the Indian
quickly lost his interest in it. Hence, the frontier settler who
could make it to his cabin, hold the Indians off an hour or two,
had a good chance of coming through alive. The woods Indians would
not persist in such an attack. In an hour or two they would wander
off looking for easier and more profitable prey. This is not to
infer that the Indians were cowards. They would fight furiously
and fanatically if necessary. They would willingly die if necessary.
It's just that they did not do these things unless they were
necessary.

Where they had white leadership, or more correctly white spon-
sorship for in most cases the white officers that accompanied an
Indian raiding party did not command directly, but through the
chiefs, Indians would stand and fight for long periods of time.
They attacked Boonesboro for three days before they gave up the
effort. Seldom, without white leadership, did large numbers of
woods Indians come together for battle. The average Indian raiding party would consist of anywhere from ten to twenty warriors.
Sometimes a half dozen or so raiding parties would work together,
but not as a unit. Where the white influence could be felt, these
raiding parties would often number several hundred warriors, but
even here, small groups were always breaking off for some indi-
vidualistic raiding, or returning home.

After the American Revolution when white leadership stopped,
the Indians were never really a threat again. They would strike,
kill, hurt, carry off, and loot, but they never again threatened
the frontier. In the 1790s, the Indians fought and often won,
knock down and drag out battles with the whites. Actually, the
record of the frontier of Kentucky largely favored the Indians
except on the final battle, the one that counted. These battles,
however, were being fought in the Indian country, around the
Indian villages. The Indians were fighting for their lives. They
fought well. They did not follow their victories and therefore,
could not reap the potential rewards. They seldom kept a reserve
that could be used to turn the tide of a losing battle. They
did not fight in depth so that losing one battle they could fall
back to fight another. These were military tactics that came
after long development in western warfare and were not always
practiced even by the west.

The years between 1779 and 1789 brought an increasing wave of settlers into Kentucky. Many of these were military men and had experience in the Revolution. There had been a lull in the Indian struggle following the failure to drive the settlers out of the Boonsboro, Harrodsburg and St. Alph. The Indians were disheartened. The hard winter of 1779 and 1780 had also crippled them. Their white leadership was confused and uncertain. There were not the expected victories in the west. With entrance of the French, and few people realize it, the Spanish also, on the side of the Revolutionists, it became reasonably clear that Britian would not be able to hold the eastern coast. The question now developed just how much was the British going to be able to hold?

The control of the British on the then called Northwest, the country that included Ohio, Indiana and Illinois had been badly shaken by George Rogers Clark campaign that took Vincinnes, Kaskaiskia and other villages and forts in the center of the country. John Bowman's raid in 1779 on the Indian villages at Chillicothe was not really successful, but it proved again to the Indians that their own villages could be and would be subject to attack.

The British in Detroit before the end of the Revolution in 1782, came out with a gracious plan, continental in scope in which they planned to seize control of the entire country north of the Ohio and the Mississippi Rivers from St. Louis to New Orleans. It was a magnificant plan that never got off the planning table. However, as part of the plan, a Virginian Tory, gallant and gentlemanly, named Harry Byrd, with six field cannon and some six hundred Indians and Canadians swept into Kentucky. Most historians have not noticed the potential of this attack. There was not a military force in Kentucky that could have resisted. The militia was scattered in garrisons and disunited in command. There were probably not as many cannon (though small) in the whole state. Against cannon and a determined enemy, there was not a station that could have resisted a day. Byrd's problems were logistics and not Kentuckians. It was virtually impossible to supply such an army over an extended period of time. Even by living off the country, the raiding force could not expect to feed itself for a long period of time and its supply of ammunition was limited. Nevertheless, the damage that Byrd might have done in Kentucky could have been of a deadly nature. However, as he swept the stations in Bourbon County capturing Ruddle's Stations and Morgan's Stations, he found it increasingly difficult to control his Indians. After a bitter dispute with the Indian leadership, Byrd returned to Canada. The threat was over. The proposed attacks on St. Louis and New Orleans never developed.

This did not effect Clark County directly, but it did open the new forts at Strode's, Bryan's and Boone's to direct attack.

In retaliation, George Rogers Clark in July of 1780 drove into the northwest destroying Indian villages at Chillicothe, Pique and Laramie. This was the first aggressive attack into the northwest since Clark had taken the British forts at Vincinnes and Kaskaskia.

Meanwhile, Colonel Todd, ranking officer in the Blue Grass, tried to set up protection for the area. Daniel Boone was promoted to Lieutenant Colonel which was the first time after his court martial that any real confidence was placed in him by the militia officers. The various stations were staffed with militia and a flying horse squadron was set up to work between them. At this time, most of the settlers had some military experience in the Revolution in the east.

In 1781, according to Clinkenbeard, he, John Douglas, John McIntyre, John Hart, Frederick Couchman and Sam Taylor were moved out of Strode's to guard Boone's Station. After milking time in the evening John Judy and a youth named Bruner were driving the cows in from pasture. Jacob Sphar was outside the fort chopping wood. Sphar saw the Indians coming and broke for the stockade. He didn't make it. The children heard the shooting and broke for the stockade at the first shots. Bruner made it unhurt, but Judy was hurt. Patrick Donaldson was the ranking militia officer in the fort at the time; he rushed to the palasade and looked over it. He was shot and killed. The Indians burned out some buildings, shot some cows, and then moved on. Throughout 1781, Indians prowled around Strode's but there were no major attacks. One man, a Van Swearinger, was killed as a result. He was a militia officer.

Another skirmish, really part of the same raid, became known as Boyle's defeat. John Flemming was wounded. According to Clinkenbeard, Constant was blamed and in bitterness he moved out of Strode's Station.

Early in March of 1782, a band of some twenty-five Wyandots came down the Warrior Trail and took a few shots at Strode's Stations, burned some cabins that had been built outside the fort, and killed some cattle. They wandered off into what is now Madison and Estill Counties. James Estill, a minor militia officer, gathered about twenty-five men and started off in pursuit. The Indians did not want to fight a party about their own size and they fled across Clark County into Montgomery County.

Estill caught the Indians near Little Mountain or Mt. Sterling and one of the bloodiest battles of the Indian frontier followed. It was a hand to hand, toe to toe melee. Estill and his second in command were killed. Joe Proctor, a Methodist lay minister, tried to shoot the Indian before he killed Estill, but Estill was in the way. He killed the Indian immediately afterwards. Five others of the settler party were killed and most of the others were wounded. Among the killed was Jonathan McMillan, the younger son of James McMillan. The Indians lost seventeen (wounded that were not carried off were naturally killed by the settlers) including the chief. The surviving settlers were the ones that backed off, but the Indians were too badly hurt to follow. They turned and returned to their own country. This became known as Estill's defeat.

Encouraged by the success of such hit and run attacks, other bands of Indians came out of the north and raided Strode' Station, took some shots at Holder's and then crossed into Madison County and attacked Hoy's Station. They kidnapped another son of Richard Calloway and a step-son. John Holder gathered together a small group of militia mostly from McGee's and Strode's Stations and pursued one group to the Upper Blue Licks. He had some seventeen or eighteen men. He was ambushed on the Blue Licks, lost four men, killed or wounded, but was able to get the rest out without further loss. The Indians, not liking the resistance they had met even though more or less successful, withdrew. This was called either the Battle of Upper Blue Licks or Holder's Defeat. Roger Clement was one of this party. Page Proctor was part of the rear guard.

It was obvious that the Revolution had been lost by the British. The British had made no real effort to launch an offensive since the fall of Yorktown and the surrender of Cornwallis. It was known that peace negotiations were going on in Paris. In Canada, the British leaders decided on one more effort to establish their hold on the northwest so completey that anything done in Paris would have no effect. The plan was somewhat like that of Harry Byrd's expedition though without the coordinating plans for St. Louis and New Orleans. The plan was simple, to send a large body of Canadians and Indians into Kentucky with the objective of destroying the nest of stations, Bryan Station, Strode Station and Boonesboro that defended the east flank of the Kentucky settlements. With them gone, the supply lines to western Kentucky settlements would be wide open and might force a withdrawal of western settlements.

The instigator of the plan was a Captain William Caldwell with another Canadian, Captain Alexander McKee. They had some 26 Canadian Rangers. They went to the Upper Sandusky base of Simon Girty. The force was disappointingly small. Harry Byrd had three times that number and cannon. Crawford had no cannon. The British in charge of Canada did not really encourage the operation or give to it the kind of muscle it needed.

Simon Girty is one of the most interesting characters on the frontier. He was one of the most hated of the British Tories, but had the British defeated the Americans, he might well have been the Daniel Boone of the revised history.

The Indians swept down the Warrior Trail and hit Bryan Station. The Station had had warning that they were coming and was not surprised. However, the size of the Indian and Canadian attack was more than had been expected. Messengers from the Station did escape to spread the message, and the militia began coming from all over the area. The first fifteen or so reinforcements managed to fight their way into the Station, but the next party found the opposition too strong, so they had to remain outside the battle area until still more reinforcements came up.

Meanwhile the Indians had taken a considerable mauling and the white leaders were very much aware of the gathering army of militia to their rear. There was a real danger that they might be surrounded themselves. Crawford therefore, decided to give up the attack that had already failed in its original purpose, and retreated back across Clark and Bourbon Counties, along the Trail toward Ohio.

Some 160 militia gathered at Bryan Station under the leadership of Colonel John Todd of the Fayette County (which included Clark County) militia. The rest of the men were drawn largely from the same area, plus Madison County. For this reason, the Battle of Blue Licks takes on a special importance. Nearly half the family names of the survivors will appear at some time or another in Clark County history. Todd knew that Ben Logan was coming up from the St. Alph-Harrodsburg settlements with some 600 more militia.

Todd could not decide whether to wait for the reinforcements or go after the Indians. However, he really did not have an opportunity to decide. The average frontiersman felt that any Kentuckian was worth five Indians and that delay would let this large body of the enemy get away. The overwhelming opinion was to pursue the Indians and let Logan catch up when he could. The Kentuckians moved out. Todd was the colonel. His brother, Levi, was a major. Levi Todd would become one of the most popular lawyers serving the Clark County bar and for a time would be Clark County Attorney, though a resident of Lexington. A third brother, not at the battle, was Robert Todd who would become the father-in-law of Abraham Lincoln. In addition to Major Todd, there were two lieutenant colonels, Stephen Trigg and Daniel Boone. Edward Bolger, Hugh McGary, Silas Harlan were majors. John Allison, John Bolger, Samuel Johnson, Gabriel Madison, Clugh Overton, John Beasley, John Gordon, Joseph Kincaid, William McBride, Robert Patterson, were captains. William Given, John Kennedy, Thomas Hinson, James McGuire and Barnett Rogers were lieutenants. John McMurty was an ensign and Joseph Lindsay was commissary officer. This was a rather high proportion of officers for a command of this size, but it also reflects the experience of the group.

Two days later, the Indians had been chased across the Licking River without any real problems. As the Kentuckians crossed the country between Strode's and Licking River, their confidence grew. They arrived on a point of the Licking River where the east bank was very rugged, but the west bank, though steep, had been largely cleared of underbrush by the buffalo that had come to the wallow. It had been a relatively dry year and the river itself was easily fordable in most parts, though waist deep on the west bank side. There was also a wide stoney strip of barred river bottom on the east side.

The militia leadership was acutely aware of the danger. Indian fires could be seen in the darkness on the top of the cliffs across the river. It was decided that they should all wait until daylight. Logan was still far behind, not yet to Bryan Station.

Several Kentuckians argued that they ought to wait on the river bank for Logan to come up. Daniel Boone was one of these, but it must be remembered and was, that Boone had advocated surrender of Boonesboro and had, at these very Licks, lost a group of settlers that he had surrendered without a fight to the British. Boone had been found innocent in his treason trial, and had been promoted, but there was deep suspicion of him among the settlers. As the argument waxed back and forth, Hugh McGary leapt to his feet, shouted, "all those that are not cowards, follow me," and plunged into the river. Immediately the whole contingent of Kentuckians poured after him. As the Kentuckians hit the water, struggling to keep their powder dry, and coming out on the flat stretch of dried bottom, the Indians opened fire. The whole east bank exploded with fire.

The Kentuckians went down by the dozens, many of them not even able to get their guns into action. The water was full of struggling men, downed and terrified horses and shouting Indians who rushed out to meet the Kentuckians. Peter Scholl caught a splinter in his face as already described. Interestingly enough, it was not reported as wounded as many of the minor wounds were not.

The right wing of the Kentuckians, under Daniel Boone received the full force of the ambush.

The Kentuckians broke, trying to get back to safety. The Indians followed. Israel Boone went down covering the retreat of his father, Daniel, who escaped unharmed, evidently by swimming under water to a safe place.

Of the 182 settlers that had ridden into the attack, seventy-two were killed including all the high brass except for Boone. The number killed was unusually high because in the flight, the more seriously wounded were left behind to be tomahawked. Twelve more were wounded who got away and some seven were captured. The defeated fled back across the territory between Blue Licks and Bryan Station. By this time, Logan and his men had come up. He had some six hundred men with him, but he felt that it was best to wait a day before advancing toward the Licking. He wanted to see how strong the Indians were. Strode's, McGee's and the settlements along the Stoner and around Providence Church (the stone church had not yet been built) area.....all of which were hardly established.

When Logan reached the Licking, he found the Indians gone. They had not made any effort to follow up the worst defeat that whites had taken at the hands of the Indians up to that point and the first in a series of defeats of rather large numbers of troops. The fact that the Indians were not or could not follow up their victory reveals their major problem. They had won the last major battle of the Revolution, but were unable to stop the rush of settlers into the west.

Among the officers killed were John Todd, Stephen Trigg, Silas Harner, Edward Bulger, who died later of wounds, John Bulger, Clugh Overton, John Gordon, Joseph Kincaid, William McBride, William Givens, John Kennedy, Thomas Hinson, James McGuire, Barnett Rogers, John McMurty and Joseph Lundsay. Robert Patterson would have been killed had it not been for another soldier who gave him a horse to escape. John Beasley was captured. Of the twenty-four officers, fifteen were killed. Among the enlisted men (if they were called that in those days) were Charles Black, Israel Boone, Samuel Brown, James Brown, Esua Corn, Hugh Cunningham, John Douglas, William Eads, Homas Farrier, Charles Ferguson, John Folley, John Gry, Ezekial Fields, Daniel Foster, Jervis Green, Little James Graham, Daniel Gregg, Francis Harper, William Harris, Matthew Harper, John Jolly, James Ledgerwood, who was killed after being captured, Francis McBride, Isaac McCracken, Henry Miller, Andrew McConnell, Gilbert Marshall, John Nelson, John Nutt, Joseph Oldfield, John O'Neal, Drury Polly, John Prise, Matthias Rose, William Robertson, James Smith, John Stableton, Valentine Sterns, William Steward, William Smith, William Stephens, John Stevenson, William Shannon, Richard Tomlinson, John Wilson, John Willson, Israel Wilson, Matthew Wylie and Archibald Wood. This is a total of 49 killed. Besides the few living officers, Thomas Acres, William Aldridge, Elijah Allen, James Allen, Abraham Bowman, Robert Bowman, Thomas Brooks, William Barbee, Squire Boone, Jr., who was wounded, Samuel Boone, James Coleman, who was wounded, Jacob Coffman, Edward Corn, William Corn, William Custer, George Corn, Whitfield Craig, Benjamin Cooper, Jerry Craig, Richard Davis, Theodore Davis, Peter Durby, Thomas Finklen, Henry French, William Field, Henry Grider, James Graham, Edward Graham, Squire Grant, Peter Harget, Benjamin Hayden, John Hamblin, John Hart, James Harrod, Henry Higgins, Jacob Hunter, James January, Ephriam January, Wainwright Lea, John Morgan, Andrew Morgan, James McCollough, James McBride, William May, James Morgan, who was captured but later escaped, James McConnell, Mordecai Morgan, Henry Nixon, James Norton, Benjamin Netherland, John Pittman, Matthew Patterson, John Peake, Alexander Perkin, Robert Poague, Elisha Pruit (Prewitt), Andrew Rule, James Ray, James Rose, Aaron Reynolds, Lewis Rose, who was captured, Joseph Scholl, Samuel Scott, Andrew Steele, Thomas Stevenson, James Steward, James Stuart, Abraham Scholl, Jon Smith, Peter Scholl, Jacob Stevens, Jacob Stucker, Robert Scott, Samuel Shortridge, Edmund Singleton, George Smith, Bartlett Searcy, John Searcy, William Shott, Anthony Showdusky, John Sumner, James Twyman, James E. Wood, who was captured, Josiah Wilson, Henry Wilson, Samuel Wood and Jesse Yokum, who were captured. This is a total of 90 men.

This totals some 162. There is one side of the monument at the Blue Licks State Park that is dedicated to unknown heros. There are some ten who are unaccounted for either among the dead in most cases, or among those that escaped.

Since this is the last battle of the Revolution, all could be listed as Revolutionary veterans for those who seek to relate with such. Since there is no definite proof that all these men ever lived in Clark County, they are not listed among Clark County's veterans unless listed elsewhere as veterans of this battle. Perhaps they should be.

One wonders where certain others who certainly were Indian fighters and whose courage could not be questioned, were at this time. The McMillans, Hoods, and Bushes are all missing. So also is Constant, Holder, Clinkenbeard and others of Clark County. Part of the answer is that much of this strength came out of what became Fayette County that was not threatened while the Clark Countians were dug in waiting for Indian attacks on their own settlements. However, as stated, many of these names became family names in Clark County.

In passing, we note that Major Hugh McGary who led the unwise attack was not killed.

George Rogers Clark, following his belief that attack called for counterattack, hastily organized an army of 1,050 men from all the settlements and struck north into the Ohio country and laid it waste. The Indians were not prepared for the counterattack and it drove them back off the Ohio River. The Indians had villages along the smaller rivers leading off the Ohio. The Shawnee were the closest to Kentucky and the Huron were largely a Canadian tribe.

They were not nomads. They built semi-permanent villages in which they lived for years. They would move only a few miles to a cleaner camp site. They lived by hunting but they also had extensive agricultural practices, growing corn, beans and other crops.

It never seemed to occur to Indians that retaliation was the next thing to happen. According to the rules of the game, if the raiders could swoop down, take a scalp or two, a horse and a captive, and get away a day or so, they were safe. The kidnapping of the Calloway girls was an example. As far as the Indians were concerned they were home free. They had raided and gotten away. Now they should have the right to enjoy their leisure.

Now a new factor struck the Indians. For seven years the British had given them a free hand in raiding. They had provided guns and ammunition. They had lent leadership. For a period in 1777, they had come close to sweeping the settlers out of Kentucky. Had the British cared to give them more support, they might easily have cleared Kentucky and opened the back door of the sea board colonies and changed the history of the Revolutionary War. Somebody in Britian did not see the opportunity.

As stated, despite the disaster on the Licking, the settlers continued to pour into Kentucky and into Ohio. They jammed the Ohio River with rafts and swept beyond Kentucky into Indiana, Illinois, Missouri, Iowa and down the Spanish Mississippi River into Mississippi, Arkansas and Louisiana.

The Kentuckians had also shown their ability to strike hard at the Indian villages and that the Indians without their white leaders were even more vulnerable in their own lands than the whites in Kentucky.

Had George Rogers Clark been in charge, it is possible that the whole frontier history might have been different. He was able, aggressive and capable as his first two attacks against Vincinnes and against the Miami villages proved. He was also drinking harder and harder, he had a disappointing love affair and he was growing more radical each year... or perhaps more correctly, the country was growing more conservative each year. With the end of the American Revolution, George Rogers Clark had become a man that no longer inspired enthusiasm among the leadership of the east and less and less among Kentuckians.

Clark made another effort to attack the north which never really got off the ground because of wrangling among Kentucky leaders. John Bowman took many of the men and attacked the Indian villages.

With the end of the Revolution, the style of Indian attack changed. No longer were there massive raids, including hundreds of Indians ram rodded by British, Tory or Canadian leadership. Now they were small groups, dozen, twenty or so hit and run types.

Not only did the British stop leading the Indians, they began to insist on the return of white women and children captured in raids going back over the years. As reported, the white woman with two or three dusky children faced an uncertain welcome back in the white settlements.

Did the British continue to supply the Indians and encourage them? The Kentuckians thought so. They felt that the British senior official in Detroit offered the Indians guns and other equipment. This seemed to be true, but whether it was a calculated policy or merely the result of normal trade is not clear. Innocent trade or not, the British knew what was going on and did not try to stop it. Nor did they obey the treaty obligations to abandon their posts and give up Detroit. On the other hand, other than protesting mildly, the Americans were in no position to do much about the British violations.

In 1784, the horn in the Stoner Creek blew again in the Stoner settlements and the settlers gathered at Ragland's house. Once their women were secured, the Stoner settlers tried to find the Indians. They were gathered around William Halley's house which they had set on fire after looting. Three Indians were killed. The remainder fled toward what became Winchester. The Stoner settlers followed and surprised a second camp of Indians near the present sight of Winchester. They killed another Indian and drove off the rest.

Matthias Sphar, Josua Bennett and Michael Cassidy were hunting near Grassy Lick on Plum Creek when they were attacked by Indians. Bennett and Sphar were killed and Cassidy was badly wounded but escaped.

Polly Donaldson and Rebecca Sphar were two of the girls kidnapped from near Strode's Station and carried into Canada. They were recovered some ten years later after the Battle of Fallen Timber.

James Baythe was captured by Indians at about the same time and was given up for dead. His wife was about to remarry when he returned just in time. (We might note that on the frontier it was almost necessary for a wife to remarry if her husband died, but she did have a rather wide choice since men out numbered women many times and all wanted to get married.)

In 1784, there were almost constant raids and skirmishes. Seventeen eighty five started about as badly when Constant's Station was attacked. Two of Constant's children were trapped outside of the compound and were killed. Constant had a leg broken with a rifle but the Indian did not get a chance to kill him. Thirty militia hastily assembled and went after the Indians. They escaped. Another band of Indians raided a group of slaves picking blackberries and carried off two of them. Captain Stucker led a militia party in pursuit and claimed he killed two, but the Indians escaped with their prisoners.

In 1785, Hood had returned to his station. In March, the Indians shot up Hood's Station and stole four horses. Hood, breathing fire and brimstone wanted to pursue, but found only three men willing to go. The Indians hit him again in April and stole more horses. This time, Hood got his posse, but the Indians escaped. Indian raids into Kentucky were getting dangerous.

George Rogers Clark organized an expedition based on the Falls (which would become Louisville) to raid again into Indian country in retaliation. Again the expedition did not get off the ground because of bickering, politics and Clark's now very heavy drinking. Ben Logan lead a smaller detachment on an Ohio raid soon thereafter, but it was not a glowing success. Kentucky now lacked a leader that was capable of really carrying the fight into Indian country.

In 1787, Daniel Denton saw an Indian stealing a horse in Schollsville. Denton fired and raced to a tree to get cover to reload his rifle. He discovered a second Indian hiding on the other side of the tree. Both fired, missed and ran in opposite directions. The Indians earlier had stolen a Negro girl on her way to a spring. In revenge, the Scholls organized a raid into Ohio and stole an Indian girl which they sold, despite their anti-slavery views. The same year, 1787, Indians raided Strode's Station stealing horses. A company of militia poured out of Strode's Station and caught up with the Indians. The Indians, surprised when they shouldn't have been, lost several, most escaped, but the Shawnee chief, Blue Jacket, was captured. Blue Jacket was one of the better known war chiefs of the Shawnees and his capture was quite a triumph. It was this group that had killed Ezekial Sudduth.

Blue Jacket was bound and James Baythe, who was now back home, and old Stephen Boyle were posted guards over him. With disgust, Clinkenbeard reported that the guards went to sleep and Blue Jacket promptly worked out of his bounds and escaped.

In May of 1788, Strode's Station was again raided, and the militia was in pursuit. They caught up with the Indians near Mud Springs and killed one. The Kentucky militia system was working. It must be remembered, however, that the Congress in the Articles of Confederation refused to permit raids into Indian country. This was to be a political debate which is discussed in the next chapter.

In 1790, Benjamin Allen, Sr., was killed and Benjamin Allen, Jr. was carried off to Ohio as a captive. He was staked out on a sand bar in the river to attract flat boats close enough for the Indians to capture them. He was able to free himself and escape.

In June 1790, a raid near Hood's Station killed a man named Dickerson and wounded Isaac Baker. Major Hood again organized a posse using the militia that was stationed to protect the furnace along Slate Creek in Bath County. John Wade and J. Muir scouted for the posse and ran into the Indians trying to set up an ambush. In getting out, Wade with another member of the posse, Rueben Coffee, were wounded but got to Baker's Station on Stoner Creek. By the next day, more than a hundred militia were in pursuit of the Indians.

One tradition is that John Constant was the last man killed by Indians in the county. Constant family history states he died October 10, 1788, in Bourbon County; he died of "Wildfire".

The picture of Indian warfare now shifts. In October of 1791, William Sudduth who is rising as a militia officer in Clark County, led a company after Indians who had been horse stealing in Mason County. He joined with other militia units under a Colonel John Edwards and raided close to Sandusky, Ohio.

Meanwhile, the ban on raids into the north country was lifted. Washington was President and he sent westward a Revolutionary War veteran named Brigadier General Josiah Harmar in April of 1790 with 100 Regulars and 250 Kentucky volunteers under Charles Scott to mouse-trap a band of Indians at Maysville. It failed. Harmer was then reinforced by another 200 Regulars and moved down the Ohio to Cincinnati. Harmer then attacked the Miami villages with both Regulars and militia and walked into a double ambush, suffered heavy casualties, and caused him to retreat in disaster. Great bitterness arose between Harmer and the militia which he accused of cowardice. He was charged with trying to have his cannon fire on the militia. At the court martial that followed, Colonel James McMillan who had served with the militia along with other Clark Countains testified.

The Kentuckians carried their protest to Washington who, though not accepting their version that all to blame was Harmer, did permit General Charles Scott to make a raid against the Miami villages with state militia. He was moderately successful, but Kentuckians felt that in Scott they had the first general since Clark that might carry an attack into Indian country successfully. He had not been truly successful. Nothing decisive was decided.

Washington then authorized a second regular army officer, General St. Clair, a gout ridden, pompous old Revolutionary officer to command some 1400 regulars and order to punish the Indians. He proved undiplomatic and became very unpopular with the Kentuckians. To raise Kentucky's share of the militia, Isaac Shelby, the new Governor of Kentucky, had to institute a draft. St. Clair with a 1000 Kentucky militia advanced against the Wabash Indians. The non-volunteer Kentuckians deserted by the dozens....in one case a whole regiment going home. St. Clair was again surprised, surrounded, and had to fight furiously out of a trap back to Fort Jeffers some 29 miles away. He lost 890 men and 16 officers out of 1400 men and 86 officers he went into combat with. Wilkerson then lead a cavalry attack on the battlefield where the Indians were looting and celebrating in an effort to save what wounded he could. He in turn surprised the Indians and drove them off recapturing supplies and saving some lives.

The last raid into Clark County came in 1793 when a band of Indians stole horses from around Strode's Station. They were followed by James McMillan to the Red River where they camped. McMillan did not have enough men to challenge them so he returned to Strode to get more help. By the time he got back, the Indians had gone. Still, by this time, the fears of Indian attack in Clark County had largely abated.

Morgan Station was a typical palasaded fortress type settlement west and somewhat north of the site of Mt. Sterling which had been incorporated the year before. The settlers were careless and Indians in 1793 surprised them with their gates open. The Cherokee carried nineteen women and children off. A Mrs. Begraft was beaten, scalped and left for dead, but lived. A Clauda Ellington, twelve at the time, was carried off by a Tuscarora (the record said a chief naturally) and by him had three children, John, Sallie and William. The legislature in 1797 authorized a sum of money be spent by one of her relatives who sought to find her among the Cherokee. She was returned to Kentucky about 1810 and married a Jacob Ellington and had a second set of children. Enoch Smith led the pursuit without much luck.

At the same time Sam Trimble's wife heard a commotion in her yard. She and her slave, Rosa, armed with fire tongs, discovered a wolf in the chicken pen. They killed it. Looking up, on the edge of the clearing, they saw several Indians watching with considerable interest. The show over, the Indians quietly withdrew into the woods without offering any harm. These were apparently of the same band that had attacked Morgan's Station.

Meanwhile, Washington sent a third general, an Anthony Wayne, who had made quite a reputation in the Revolution, the most important campaign being the successful capture of Crown Point from the British, to take command of the campaign against the Indians. Wayne's first task was to win the confidence of the Kentuckians who by this time had an almost complete low regard to the regular army. Finally, under Charles Scott, a sizeable Kentucky detachment arrived. Wayne made a favorable impression on the volunteers and as some had served with him in the Revolution, finally was able to get some 1600 militia. Wayne was not able to get his attack off the ground in 1793, and there was some loss as enlistments ran out. However, in 1794, Wayne with regular and militia moved out. He fought the battle of Fallen Timbers (August 20, 1794) which he won decisively. He went on to destroy the Indian villages and crops. A British trading post offered no help to the Indians. The result was the almost complete destruction of Indian power in Ohio and along the river. They were driven out of Kentucky. The river was made safe.

The Indians were not completely defeated, but were driven back into Illinois and Indiana. There they would be rallied and reorganized by Tecumseh for one final effort to hold back the white flood. This would be ended in 1811 by William Harrison at Tippacanoe. However, for the future of the Kentuckians, particularly those in and around Clark County, the danger was ended.

A good many Clark Countians were at each of these battles. Only a few of the names have come down to us. Both Luke Hood and Jonas Goff fought with Wayne.

Richard Calloway was one of the negotiators with Richard Henderson that signed the treaty at Watauga River with the Cherokee giving the Transylvania Company an opportunity to claim legal rights from the Cherokee for Kentucky.

Micajah Calloway was captured by the Indians at Blue Licks in 1778 and was held prisoner for five years. He later became an interpretor and a spy for Anthony Wayne in his expedition against the Indians.

James Calloway was captured with Daniel Boone and spent five years of captivity in Quebec.

Sam Boone was one of those early men with his uncle Daniel, who fought in the Revoluntionary Battle of '96, helped build Strode's Station and Boone's Station. He and Andrew Huls scouted the territory between Licking River and Blue Licks for some thirty days and tried to give warning of the impending disaster at Blue Licks.

John Martin, who had been with Boone among the original 30, one of the three original cabin buildings in Clark County was leading a party through the Cumberland Gap about 1780. They were ambushed by Indians and Martin was wounded. He knew that he was critical and that his party had to move rapidly or all would be destroyed. He requested that he be left with ammunition and food to act as rear guard knowing that he would be killed. He was killed and some years later, his rusted gun and bones were found and buried.

Black Hoof, one of the Indians from Indian Fields, was born about 1711 and died in 1831. He fought at Oriskany, was at Braddock's defeat and fought Anthony Wayne.

Lucas Hood was born in 1770 and came to Kentucky in 1784. He had been scalped and left for dead, but lived to be at Harmar's defeat, was a spy for Anthony Wayne's expedition and fought at Fallen Timbers. He died on September 30, 1843.

Joseph Nichol was with the Virginia expedition that fought Cornstalk and the Shawnee in western Virginia in 1774. This victory opened the Ohio country and Kentucky for immigration. It also drove the Shawnee out of West Virginia and western Pennsylvania.

Griffin Kelly, in 1790, belonged to Moses Hale's militia company and fought in the three battles in the Miami country of Ohio. He was wounded at Harmar's defeat. Later he worked as a spy or as a scout for Harmar and St. Clair. In 1792, with Jacob Rucker and James Tucker he was at Big Bone Lick. Two years later, he fought under John Hall and Simon Kenton with Anthony Wayne at Fallen Timbers.

Thomas Kennedy had been kidnapped at the age of six or seven by slavers from Ireland. He was brought to this country as had thousands of young children and sold as an endentured servant. He moved naturally toward the frontier. He had helped Stoner survey much of Clark and Bourbon Counties. He had helped Strode build his fort and had helped Stoner clear his land.

## POLITICS ON THE FRONTIER

Kentucky had 12,000 people in 1783. Seven years later her population had grown to 70,000. By 1800 her population had reached 200,000. It slowed then, and much of the torrent either continued westward or replaced those in Kentucky who for one reason or another, had lost the dream and moved westward looking for it.

Clark County was still unheard of. It belonged to Fayette County, and as such was merely the outskirts of the rapidly growing and developing Lexington and its agricultural suburbs. As we have said, the frontier was made up largely of young men. They were veterans of the American Revolution. Originally they had come as closely related and interlocked bands who fought and settled together as a unit. After 1790, really after 1785, this characterization disappeared and immigrants were coming over individually or at least in little more than family groups to settle in areas where already there were older settlers.

It is a mistake to think of these settlers from 1779 on, and increasing so, as ignorant misfits of the nation. There was some of that in the beginning and there would always be the woods-runner wandering ahead of the main body of immigration. On the whole, however, the Kentucky settlers of the 1780s were educated....for their times...men, and often men of considerable wealth and resources. Despite this, they were also usually what we might call liberal men.

For the purpose of this work, a liberal is one who is ready to trade the past for the future, who dreams of a utopia ahead that would never come, and stands ready to change the old for the new. The conservative is one who sees value in the old and a glorious day of the past which he is always seeking to restore.... though such a glorious moment in the past probaby never existed. He is slow to make changes, suspicious of the new, and those who advocated the new, and always struggling to promote or restore what he believes to be the true ideals of his forefather.

However, there were conservative elements on the frontier also. Clinkenbeard commenting why he and seven others had not been at Strode's Station when the Indians attacked, stated that he had been sent to Boone's Station to protect the Tories that swarmed (his word) about the place. We note that Daniel Boone had an interesting record. He admitted that in all the fighting that he had participated in, he knew of killing only two Indians. He had advocated the surrender of Boonesboro and had been tried for being too friendly with the British and the Indians. He did not deny the charge, but won acquittal by arguing that what he did was necessary to save lives and the best interests of the settlements. Holder, as reported, was originally a Tory as had been the Bryans. These viewpoints were washed away by the necessities of survival, but one can assume there were on the frontiers many who were not really anxious to break with Great Britian and once done, were conservative in their views on government. A third factor, besides the liberal frontiersmen and the Tories, was an increasing number of men of considerable wealth and education who came west in the third wave of settlers, moving into relatively safe neighborhoods with their slaves, building not log cabins, but fine homes that would include glass windows and imported furniture. These reinforced a concern for more conservative politics. They were businessmen who established stores, sold goods eastward and handled the sales of their neighbors, did what took the place of banking at this early day, and started an economic middle class.

George Washington was the hero of all Americans. As late as 1790, we find Richard Hainey and Charles Tracy walking back to Virginia where they could choose between John Hancock and George Washington, to vote for Washington. Washington was a powerful conservative influence, and despite his failure to produce a general who could defeat the Indians for many years, his position was respected and accepted by many of the more prominent leadership.

At the same time, we find that the Kentucky delegation in the Virginia House of Burgesses, voting against the Constitution 11 to 3. This was not so much because these 11 were liberals, but because they respected and were influenced by Patrick Henry. Actually, if they had voted their opinions, the vote would have been more closely split. There was a strong conservative element as well as a strong liberal element on the frontier. Like so many conservative movements, however, the conservative element is more concerned with its own affairs and less apt to be militant. It is the liberal leader and issues that draw the attention of the historian far beyond his actual deserts.

There was an interesting similarity between the complaints of the Kentuckians and the complaints of the Colonies. The difference being that the Colonies were complaining against England and the Kentuckians against the Colonies. There was a deep seated resentment against those left behind, a feeling that the eastern states were not interested in the western well-being; that all the east wanted was to fatten their purses, as the saying went, at the expense of the west. Kentucky felt that the east did not give them enough political rights and taxed them without representation.

The major issues were, obviously, those that concerned the west directly. The first was the Indian problem. During the 1780s, the Congress of the Articles of Confederation forbade any retaliation of Indian raids into Indian country. This made the Kentuckians bitter and made men like George Rogers Clark, who was always ready to carry the war to the Indian villages, furious. Congress felt that raids into Indian country would only make the situation worse, forcing the Indians to band together, and in turn, forcing the British to support the Indians. The Congressional leadership was afraid that such a reaction would end forever the hopes of winning the northwest back from the British.

The Kentuckians, however, felt that first of all the Congress did not understand that it was Kentucky women and children being killed and carried off. The east was trading Kentucky blood for political and economic gains. They also felt that the help the Continental armies had given them during the Revolution was insignificant and that there was no help to speak of at all now that the Revolution was over. Even powder and shot were hard to come by and often had to be paid for by individuals.

We find the militia leaders meeting repeatedly to see what could be done to promote a better Indian defense system. The militia was technically Virginian, but they found themselves working virtually without authority or direction. Repeatedly, delegations and individuals went eastward to protest this policy of no retaliation. It is not until the change to the Constitution and the election of Washington that this obstacle to the country raids into Ohio and Indiana was lifted.

The second issue that was felt throughout the state was the need for a way of selling their goods to gain capital. The trip eastward from Kentucky was both long and difficult. As we have noted, the roads coming over the mountains were good only for horses and pack animals. There were no covered wagons moving whole families as there would be in later days. The first wagons other than homemade two wheel ox carts would be freight wagons coming in from Limestone and the ports around Cincinnati, but these were still two or three decades off. Pack animals can only carry a limited amount of goods and the costs of packing products eastward was exhorbitive. Animal drives did begin almost at once. We find William McMillan driving cattle northward to Cincinnati in 1790 to help provide food for the armed forces gathering there. However, in face of Indian trouble, these drives were dangerous until after 1790. There was also little surplus livestock to be sold till the same date. The settlers were raising corn, tobacco and to a limited extent, wheat, flax and rye, for the market. These could not be sent eastward by pack train economically. The only way the Kentuckians could sell was down the Mississippi. There was little or no way to go upstream. Against the river, only rowed craft which by their nature had to be small, was the only way. Obviously then, for commercial use, there was no way to travel up the Ohio from the falls in the river to eastern centers.

We have reported that not only the French but the Spanish were allies of the United States during the American Revolution. Good relations existed in the early days of Kentucky with Spain. River travel was dangerous with Indians and savage white men haunting the river ways. Still, it could be done though in the early 1780s there was not much down river traffic. Still, that was what Holder's boatyard made, rafts for the down river trade.

As the population of Kentucky increased and the Indian trouble slacked off, more and more rafts went down river. Without much warning, the Spanish suddenly closed the river. The motives of the act are not clear. The situation in Europe was getting rough, with France breaking off into a bloody rebellion that sent shock waves throughout Europe. The Spanish, not knowing exactly how the United States was going to move, might well be jittery. The rush of settlers into Kentucky, Tennessee and Georgia was also spilling over into Spanish territories in Florida, Missouri, Iowa and into what would become the state of Mississippi. This was frightening the Spanish a little as they were a Catholic-Spanish people seeing the on-coming wave of Protestant-English. The new crop of Spanish officials also saw an excellent chance to increase their own income through bribes. This was a customary and acceptable way to enrich oneself and knowing that the Kentuckians had to trade, laws against trading opened all sorts of possibilities for additional revenue for Spanish officials in the various river ports up and down the Mississippi. Finally, with the disturbed condition of the relationship between the west and the east, made the idea of stirring the pot and adding to the American's trouble, enticing.

Before carrying this Mississippi-Spanish problem a step further, we return to the political relationship between the west and the east. Kentucky felt that Virginia did not care. The same situation was true in Tennessee which was a part of North Carolina. In each case, there was a good deal of truth in the charge. Both states had frontier counties east of the mountains that were undeveloped and needed attention. Kentucky and Tennessee were far away and far from the minds of the Virginia and North Carolina legislatures. This resentment took form in Tennessee with the organization of the state of Franklin under the leadership of John Sevier. North Carolina shouted treason and threatened to send the militia into the western counties to punish Franklin. She didn't quite do it, but Franklin stood ready to resist attack. This feeling of rebellion was finding reflection in Kentucky.

This was a period of national disturbance also. Shays Rebellion had occurred in Massachusetts. Rhode Island had created cheap money that was by law legal, thereby undermining the creditor class. The government of the Articles of Confederation was too weak to do much of anything. Vermont was virtually in a state of rebellion from New York. Maryland and Pennsylvania were making threatenting noises over their boundaries and finally called in two surveyors, one named Mason and another Dixon, to work it out. The New England states and New York were bitterly quarrelling with Virginia about their territories in the northwest which was already controlled by the British. There were military plots by ex-service men to take over the government at Philadelphia and talked dictatorship or establishing a King with various candidates including George Washington (who didn't have a son to inherit the line which made him more attractive). It looked like a strong possibility that the Confederacy of the thirteen states would break up either into individual states or regional confederacies. The British were hopefully expecting the Colonies to return humbly to the Crown, as the English sick of Cromwell, had returned to their kings.

There were several possibilities for Kentucky. She could remain part of Virginia, hoping that Virginia would improve conditions when she could. There were those who felt that this would be best and that Virginia would in time improve Kentucky. In fact, Virginia reached in this direction by creating new counties and offering more and more county government and more recognition in the Burgesses which was the Virginia legislature. Kentucky could withdraw from Virginia as had Franklin. If Virginia would not recognize the new state, then she could do what she could to stop them. Most Kentuckians felt that neither North Carolina had the power to crush Franklin, nor a Virginian free state in Kentucky.

However, going a step further, there were those that felt if need be Kentucky could declare its independence. Perhaps taking in some of Tennessee and even Ohio country, a western state of real potentiality could be produced. The drawback with both these plans lay in communication. Virginia might not be able to conquer a rebelious Kentucky, but she could cut off supplies and new immigrants. She could control the up waters of the Ohio and the passes in the mountains. Such an independent state would be at the mercy of the British, Indians and Spanish.

The next logical question then was whether it would be wise to give up independence and become part, either of Britian or of Spain. The Kentuckians at this time hated the British too much to seriously consider that possibility, and there was some uncertainty whether the British did not prefer the Indians anyway. Spain, however, offered another possibility. Spain controlled the Mississippi. If Kentucky became a part of the Spanish empire,then the Mississippi would be opened to them. Whether this was really part of the thinking of any sizable number of Kentuckians is unclear. However, what is called the Spanish Conspiracy is a very real part of Kentucky history. There was a move on foot, certainly once between 1783 and 1800, and really twice, to bring Kentucky into the Spanish empire. It is not really likely that there was any real danger to the idea, but it was discussed in the taverns across the state.

Into this picture appears James Wilkerson who is undoubtedly one of the most interesting men in American history. It is very easy to call him a rogue and a scoundrel. He had shown himself to be a better than average officer during the Revolution. He came to Kentucky and settled in Lexington. He owed money to Hart and Rochester, merchants of Winchester, not too much and evidently paid. He also owed money and owned a warehouse at Boonesboro. As such, he becomes a borderline character in Clark County history.

How far into these questions Wilkerson is found is hard to say. He gathered around him what became known as the Court Party because it was made up largely of lawyers. It perhaps is not fair to say, "gathered around him," for most of those who would become prominent in Kentucky's politics in the next twenty years were also members of the same group. They threatened the Virginia authority and represented the left in economics and politics. They were ready for something new.

Just before the first Spanish conspiracy broke, Wilkerson went down the Mississippi and did some strange and unreported maneuverings and managed to open up the river. Perhaps Spain had become disturbed by one more move in Kentucky, and that was to organize an army and take the Mississippi away from Spain. Even with the opposition of the Confederacy in Philadelphia, the Spanish had no desire to find a hungry, deadly shooting army of frontiersmen swarming into their lands. With the Mississippi open, the fight talk died down, the drive for independence also went with it. The question remained, did Wilkerson accept bribes from the Spanish, was he actually on the Spanish payroll? The answer is very likely. However, again, this is not then as dastardly as it is today. Several English Kings took financial support from the French at the very times their armies were fighting. Morals and ethics were different. Whatever happened, Wilkerson remained one of the more powerful political figures in Kentucky.

Now the struggle came for statehood. Against statehood which was favored by the Court Party was what was called the Country Party. They were led by men such as Thomas Martin, George Newton and Joseph Crockett....able men but whose names were lost among the defeated. There were a series of clubs being organized in Kentucky, particularly in and around Danville which had every possibility of becoming the state capitol. One might read Janice Holt Cile's "Land Beyond the Mountain" for a fictionalized account of this time.)

There was a series of conventions held in Danville, virtually one a year that accomplished little. One was swept away by George Rogers Clark's attack into Indian country in 1786. This attack had only half-hearted permission from the east. It accomplished little.

At this point a vote was taken on statehood in Kentucky. It carried 8,804 to 3,049, decisively yes, but no way unanimous. With the coming of the Constitution and the organization of the United States, three new states were admitted in rapid succession, Vermont, Tennessee and Kentucky; Kentucky becoming a state in 1792. There is no record how the Clark County area voted, nor have we found one for Fayette County. We now have the Court Party leaders coming to the fore to take the spoils of victory, John Brown, Henry Innes, Callab Wallace, Isaac Shelby, Christopher Greenup, Benjamin Sebastian, Richard Anderson and Alexander Bullitt. None of these came from Clark County though some from Fayette and Bourbon. There is every reason to believe they represented the majority opinion in Clark County.

Another sudden change occurred that reversed Kentucky politics. The French Revolution had gone through its extremes. Many Americans were shocked at the bitterness shown, the blood, the purges, and then the final elevating a Corsican artillery officer named Napoleon Bonaparte to First Council.

In the various maneuvers on the European front (reported much more thoroughly than the news from the Clark County area of Fayette County or even the local news of Lexington, by the Kentucky Gazette), the Mississippi River passed into the hands of the French.

Before this was to happen, however, there is another incident in Kentucky history that should be briefly recorded. In 1793, the French Ambassador to the United States sent four agents to Kentucky to enlist help for an attack on Spanish New Orleans which was still in the hands of Spain. They enlisted the help of George Rogers Clark. Clark was at this time far gone in his alcoholism. Still, he was not without influence. Had Clark been the hard hitting, effective leader of his earlier days, Genet's plans might have worked. Both Isaac Shelby as head of the state and Washington acting as president took steps to prevent Clark from taking an army down river. He had been appointed major general in the French army. An early Clark might have been able to swing the invasion of Spanish territory against this type of opposition, but he wasn't the earlier Clark. Also, the French government changed again, and Genet was ordered home. Genet was much too smart to return to France, he married the daughter of the Governor of New York and settled down in New York City. Clark was nearly court martialled and only his immense prestige and gratitude of his country saved him from this final insult. He died soon afterwards.

However, the idea of taking New Orleans by force did not die with him. The idea was very much alive, and no doubt the possibility of a Kentucky army either alone or coupled with the power of the British, no doubt had much to do with the offer that France made President Jefferson....to sell the whole of Louisiana to the United States.

Indians, the Mississippi River, the Spanish question, political relations of the state question, were the major issues of the time. There were others of course. The problem of money was a serious one. British money was still the most trusted....... pennies, shillings and pounds were the most common, though Spanish money also was available. However, none of it was available enough to meet the demand. The result is a barter system with tobacco as the main item for value. To some degree whiskey made out of corn was a second. A third problem was to find some way out of the land title mess. How was a man to nail down what he owned and prevent the loss of his hard won property? Several commissions worked their way through the state hearing cases and making decisions. One of these proved that the Bryans did not own the land on which their stations stood.

None of these and all of these effected the territory that was to become Clark County. We do not find any of the earlier inhabitants active in the state conventions until the constitutional conventions come up. Then they are not leaders but followers. Still, we can assume that the common issues were also common in Clark County and that Clark County broke up much like the state, every fourth man being against statehood and seeking a more conservative tie with the past and the other three willing to gamble with something new in the future.

One of the first political organizations in the county and giving a list of some of the younger men was formed October 22, 1793 by William McMillan. It called itself the "Democratic Society". It included William Sudduth, James Lane, John Baker, John Crawford, Mark Chadford, Robert Higgins, William Jennings, Nelson Hackett, Azariah Martin, William Barnes, Andrew Kinkaid, Robert Trimble, Andrew Hood, John Strode and Levi Lockhart. There is no report on what their political position was, but we can assume it was in line with other societies, such as the Danville Society, formed elsewhere. It belonged to the Court or Liberal Party.

Beginning in 1784 there were a series of state conventions to deal with the problems of Kentucky. The Convention of 1785 met at Danville, Clark County was still part of Fayette and her delegates represented the whole huge county. However, among those delegates were John Martin, Robert Clark and Richard Taylor that more or less represented what was to become Clark County. None of these men represented the leadership of the state. They did, however, reflect the general feeling of anger and unhappiness with the political situation.

The Constitutional Convention of 1792 found Fayette County represented by Hubbard Taylor, Thomas Lewis, George S. Smith, Robert Fraser and James Crawford. Hubbard Taylor had newly arrived in Kentucky, but had inherited the Taylor prestige and immediately became a leader of the Clark County area. Lewis would eventually buy into the Clark County territory, but it is questionable whether he ever felt himself a Clark Countain. James Crawford was a pioneer Presbyterian minister who was also involved with the Salem Church in the future Clark County. At least the borderline strip of what was to be the county was well represented. However, one critic discussing the Fayette delegation said of them that they were honest and worthy but....not one of them were any more than mediocre.

With the establishing of the new state, John Brown was elected to the Senate unanimously. The Senator had to be elected by the State Legislature. The second Senator was elected in 1794. John Edwards, John Breckinridge, John Fowler and Humphrey Marshall sought the post. On the first ballot, Edwards got 7, Breckinridge 16, Fowler 8 and Humphrey Marshall 18. Edwards and Fowler dropped out and Marshall beat Breckinridge 22 to 28. Marshall was to be one of the few federalists that eventually came out of the Country

Party that was to hold office. Even he was under constant attack, and came close to being impeached for his support of the Adams Administration.

Isaac Shelby was the first Governor. No study of county politics can be reported without a little appreciation of the Governor. He was a man of tremendous power in the state as long as he was in office. Being limited to one term at a time, did limit his individual power, but it did not limit the group around the Governor who had brought him to power and in turn, would follow him in power. Fortunately, perhaps for democracy, politics were not so organized as to use that power to its fullest. An Andrew Jackson later would draw pictures how such power could be used, and the Democratic courthouse organizations after 1900 would demonstrate how it could be used. The potential was there.

Shelby had been born on December 11, 1750, in Frederick's, Maryland according to Glen Cliff in his "Governors of Kentucky". He had fought at Point Pleasant, surveyed for the Transylvania Company and supplied munitions to various frontier militia posts. He had brought George Rogers Clark the munitions he needed for his Indiana campaign. He advocated the separation of Kentucky from Virginia.

His election is typical of the information source. Cliff has spent much of his life working over old records. The only announcement of Shelby's first election appeared in the Kentucky GAZETTE, May 19, 1792. "On Tuesday the 15th", the report read, "the electors from the different counties in the state of Kentucky convened in Lexington agreeable with the Constitution and proceeded with the election of a Governor and a Senator. Isaac Shelby, esq., was elected Governor." There was nothing more.

Of course, Shelby had much more. He dominated the frontier for twenty years. He had served in the Virginia legislature. He had fought at Fort Anderson, Musgrove's Mill, Kings Mountain and Fairlawn. He came to Kentucky in 1783 already an important man. He was one of Transylvania's first trustees. He was chairman of the militia officers considering an attack on the Indians and separation from Congress. He was everything George Rogers Clark might have been if Clark had not drank so much.

He never lost his influence and was elected the first Governor of Kentucky to be elected a second time in 1812. He handled Kentucky's part in the War of 1812 with efficiency and decisiveness, and personally lead the Kentucky contingent to support Jackson at New Orleans. He was offered the Secretary of War post in 1812 but refused. He and Jackson worked out the Chicasaw Treaty in 1818. He had married Susannah Hart, daughter of Nathanial Hart of the Transylvania Company, once again revealing the interrelation between the frontier leadership. He died in 1826.

We note that the first Constitution did not call for direct election of governors. This would be the case after 1800. Instead the people voted for electors. There apparently is no way of finding out who were the electors in Clark County or Fayette County for that matter.

In the first state legislature, Fayette's Senator was Robert Todd. The representatives included Thomas Lewis, Hubbard Taylor, John Martin, James McMillan, William Russell, John Hawkins, James Trotter, Joseph Crockett, John McDowell, Robert Patterson, William Campbell, Edward Page, Abraham Bowren, Robert Todd, John Morrison. Taylor, Martin and James McMillan came from what would be Clark County. Lewis had property in Clark County. Thomas Lewis did not live in Clark County.

We might note that all of these men came from areas that bordered Fayette County. Taylor and McMillan represented the Bush Settlement. Politically in Clark County, these two areas, the Bush Settlement and the western part of the county in that order was to dominate Clark County politics for sixty years. Martin came from Pine Grove.

We note that in the constitutional Convention of 1792, slavery was an issue just as abolition of slavery was a religious issue among the churches. Hubbard Taylor, though a slave owner himself, supported those that sought to limit slavery in the state. He and his side lost.

The ministerial faction largely opposed the slavery issues that might in any way encourage slavery. William McKinney and Ambrose Dudley particularly were active. It is with this group that Hubbard Taylor was siding. It is not clear which of the churches Hubbard Taylor gave his support, but the Taylors would in the next twenty-five years become Salem Presbyterians and Ebeneazor Methodists. We can assume that the religious elements of the county were also on this side. However, it is also evident that they are not fanatically antislavery.

It is evident that Clark County supported Shelby for Governor as did most of the state. When Clark County was organized, Shelby turned to James McMillan who had been close to him, as had been the senior James McMillan, in the militia, for guidance as to whom to appoint to the first Clark County offices. There is no way of telling just who the McMillans recommended and how far Shelby followed that advice. James was very active in the first legislation, but more or less drops out of politics when Montgomery County is organized into which he had moved. However, his brother, William, becomes a power in Clark County politics for the next thirty years.

## CLARK COUNTY

Prior to the Revolution, Kentucky had been divided between the authority of Virginia based on explorations and the authority of the Transylvania Company based on the authority of the British Crown and subsequent treaties with the Cherokee. With the Revolution, the Transylvania Company passed from existence and any claims based on Transylvania authority became very uncertain. Had there been no Revolution, it would have been interesting to see what would have happened between the two contending forces. However, Virginia was left in charge.

Even before the Transylvania Company, Virginia claimed Kentucky because it was out there somewhat west of what was known Virginia. Virginia claimed everything west. It was all part of Orange County. No one really knew what the western boundary was. It was not at that time an issue. As Virginian population moved westward, but still east of the mountains, in 1773, Orange County was divided and Augusta County inherited the west and this in turn, became Fincastle. It was with Fincastle County that Boone's early efforts involved. Partly because of the Transylvania interference in 1776, Fincastle was broken into two counties and the west of the mountain area became the Kentucky district. Kentucky became, not fully a county, but with some of the rights of a county, particularly in relationship to justice and militia. Richard Calloway and James Todd represented the Kentucky District in 1777 and again in 1779.

To meet the needs of a booming population, Virginia broke the Kentucky district into three counties; Jefferson, northwest of the Salt River; Fayette, east of the Salt and north of the Kentucky; Lincoln taking in the rest of the state. Fayette County included all of the territory beginning with the mouth of the Kentucky River extending all the way up the river, up the Middle Fork to its headwaters and all the land east. Clark County was very much part of the Fayette County, not just geographically, but spiritually as well. The area including the Bush Settlement, McGee's, Strode's, Hood's....what is now roughtly west of the Boonesboro and the Paris highways from the Kentucky River to the Bourbon County line, was really part of Fayette County proper. Going east there was the Stoner Settlement that phased into the Montgomery County settlements around Grassy Lick, Little Mountain, and about the Old Fort in which became Camargo, on along Flat Creek into Bath County. Still, most of Fayette County was remote and wilderness. Its settlers were not particularly influenced by the going on of Lexington and Fayette County.

In 1784, Jefferson County was divided into Jefferson and Nelson Counties. In 1785, Bourbon County was created out of Fayette County. Most of what was to be Clark County remained in Fayette County. Before 1785 was over, Lincoln was divided to form Mercer and Madison Counties. In 1788, Bourbon County gives birth to Mason County (a violation of the 20 miles between county seat rule). Maysville was already an important town and river port.

The territories of these new counties were almost as bloated as the old counties and no way did they resemble the present boundaries. However, there was little apparent objection from the older county to the creation of the newer counties. The rule of the ideal thumb was that every man should be within a days ride of the county seat so that he could reach the seat in a day, do his business and be back home the second day. Fifteen to twenty miles was about the limit that a man could easily do this. Hence, the old counties, knowing that new counties were inevitable, were concerned mostly in just where the boundaries would be. Ambitious men planned their settlements to be the county seat. Some, like Mt. Sterling and Winchester, were designed as county seats before anyone actually lived in them. Others were establishing cross road communities that were promoted into becoming county seats. Ambitious men about every twenty miles or so from, say Lexington, began looking about them for a proposed county seat and began campaigning for a new county. In turn, as these county seats were established, they realized that they could not hold the vast territories that had been awarded them by the old county. Hence, moving out from Lexington, some place around what became Winchester was a logical choice for a county seat, not forty miles away even though forty miles might have been close to the geographical center of the new county. Once Clark County was established however, it became obvious that Mt. Sterling or some county seat in that general direction would become the seat of a new county. In turn, it became fairly obvious that a town somewhere around Owingsville or Sharpsburg would become a county seat of still a third county. The same process was going on working out of Maysville. It was certain that a county would be organized somewhere around what became Flemingsburg and someplace beyond Flemingsburg and Owingsville would soon grow still another county based around a settlement somewhere in or about Morehead.

It came then as no surprise to the older counties that new counties would be organized. Later, when efforts to organize counties within that ten to twenty mile riding range, the old counties would fight back. Hence, Winchester would resist the effort of Kiddville to carve out a county, as would Mt. Sterling, from Montgomery and Clark County. On the other hand, Clark County did not seriously resist the creating of Powell County with its county seat at Beaver Pond (Stanton). The issue was always just where the boundary would be drawn.

In 1792, Nelson County was divided to form Washington, and again with part of Lincoln County, to form Green County. The same year, Fayette divided to form Woodford County and before Woodford could hardly be established it divided to form Scott County. Shelby County was formed out of Jefferson. Lincoln was again divided to form Logan.

At last, as 1792 was nearly over, Clark County was formed out of Fayette and Bourbon Counties. Clark County was the ninth county to be formed in Kentucky. In the year 1792, it was hard for a settler to know just what county he actually did live in. Clark County was surveyed, and there were several errors in the survey which will be discussed somewhat later in this book. Thomas Scott was appointed to run the Fayette County line, and Enoch Smith was to run between Bourbon County and Clark County.

The county as created was enormous. We have already outlined the number of future counties and parts of counties that would emerge from it.

At the time Clark County was established, there was no community that could be dignified by the term town. There were stations, the largest of which was Strode's that were scattered over the entire area. Though perhaps as many as a hundred fifty to two hundred people lived at Strode at any one time, it could hardly be called town. It had no self feeling as a town. The people who lived in it knew they would be moving out just as soon as it became safe enough and they found a place to build.

The same year that Clark County was established, Mt. Sterling was incorporated. There was no town in Little Mountain as it had been called until the state legislature dignified it by changing the name to Mt. Sterling. Its promoters were obviously hoping that by incorporating it, and laying out streets, selling lots, it would become the natural choice for a county seat. It was closer to the center of the whole county than any other possible place. In other words, the settlers of the Montgomery area, had planned a taking-over of the administrative end of the county. In all fairness, they had chosen well. Mt. Sterling would grow rapidly, catch Winchester after the War of 1812, and become a larger and more important center until after the Civil War. Winchester always hurt because of its closeness to Lexington. The difference after the Civil War between Winchester and Lexington would lie in railroads, the story of which will be considered in the third volume of this history.

There were other locations in the enlarged Clark County that demanded attention. The area along Flat Creek had several sites that promoters were suggesting could be developed into a county seat. The discovery of iron ore and the development of an iron forge in this area helped with these claims. The early foundations of Sharpsburg and Owingsville had appeared and though not incorporated were clamouring for attention. Even this early,

Olympia Springs was developing into the recreational center for the entire area and by 1800 would become more important than any other site as far as the state was concerned. However, Olympia Springs was too interested in developing her recreational facilities to be interested in becoming the county seat.

What all these areas had overlooked was the principal already mentioned of a county seat being not more than ten miles ride from the seat to its furthest citizen and about twenty miles from the nearest county seat. This eliminated the Montgomery County sites for a county seat and guaranteed that the seat would be somewhere in the present Clark County. It also gauranteed that there would be other counties out of Clark County at a very early point in history.

However, before this could be done, Clark County was organized as a functioning county unit. It would then pick a county seat and let the chips fall where they may.

## THE ESTABLISHMENT OF CLARK COUNTY

It is not easy to establish a new government. New officials must be either elected or appointed. A whole new political establishment was to be made. The boundaries of the new county must be established with the agreement of all concerned. A new taxing system must be set up and some decision what to do about delinquent taxes. A similar problem will exist in criminal and civil jurisdiction. Which courts will try crimes or civil suits that occurred before the new county, but within the boundaries of the old counties? How do the militia units which existed across the boundaries of the new and old county be maintained or divided?

Unfortunately, records simply do not exist. We have mentioned the newspaper report of the election of the first governor. Election results if ever recorded have been lost. G. Glenn Cliff has searched the records and come up with only a few for the first decade of the county's existence on state level. There is almost nothing on the local level. The records of the county court are most inadequate when legible. In the whole county, there are virtually no other records other than church records. These are also usually very inadequate. Providence Church alone has records that still exist. Goshen records for this early period were taken into Winchester by its' city division in 1904 and apparently have been lost. There are Baptist and Presbyterian records for this early period, but they concern associational and Presbyterial history and not local.

Local history is more than anywhere else odd bits of information put together. Clark County did not have a local paper until 1812, and only a copy or two are reported in the record. Elections were held, however. Often unofficial elections would be held for local officials even though the results would not be binding. The governor would usually appoint the winner.

All county officials were appointed. This meant a tremendous power vested in the Governor and his group. Once in power, it was difficult to remove.

The Fayette County magistrate court in 1792 included James McMillan, Hubbard Taylor, Thomas Lewis, Robert Todd (Mary Todd Lincoln's father), John McDaniels, Edward Payne, James Trotter, Joseph Crocker, Abraham Bowren, William Campbell, Broward Butler and Walter Carr. The state senators from Fayette were Peyton Shrout and Robert Todd. (There seems to be no objection in holding magistrate and legislative positions at the same time save in 1794.) Representatives in the lower house of the legislature were Thomas Lewis, Hubbard Taylor, James McMillan,

William Russell, John Hawkins, James Trotter, Joseph Crockett, John McDowell and Robert Patterson.

It is quite obvious in this situation that Clark County's area was represented in the county court and state legislature, but only that strip of Clark County that bordered Fayette County and felt itself to be part of Fayette County. Taylor and McMillan being the two leading figures in Fayette County's delegation from Clark County, we assume that they were part of the establishment and underlay the political strength of the time.

It is not surprising then to find James McMillan representing the new county in the state legislature. What was surprising was to find that Hubbard Taylor was defeated by a younger and rising young man named Richard Hickman. Hickman came from the Pine Grove area close to the Taylors so that the area of Clark County represented had not changed. There is no record of this first and direct election from Clark County. Taylor had only been in the county some four years. He had stepped into influence partly because of his influential kinfolk. He was, however, a man of ability and was appointed Quarterly Court Magistrate. There was no state senator chosen until 1794 to keep the proper rotation. It was generally understood that Taylor would be that senator.

A check on the House Journal for 1793 in an effort to get some feel of the politics of the age compared 19 votes. McMillan was on the winning side thirteen times against Hickman's 10. McMillan was on the loosing side five times against Hickman's six times. The other times were not voted. The two voted against each other only six times. It would be safe to say that the two, though not completely obedient to the wishes of the majority, pretty largely supported the majority. They also worked together on most issues. Many of these issues were unimportant, routine or amendments to a major motion voted on later. Unfortunately, the record does not give enough information to know the issues involved in each vote or the debate about them.

Hickman opposes and McMillan supported the inspection of tobacco law. McMillan was with the majority. Both favored a circuit court system. Both supported widening the civil rights of individuals. McMillan did not want the state to pay for damaged tobacco in warehouses. They supported the establishment of Winchester. Both Hickman and McMillan wanted to give the Revolutionary War veterans more time to get their surveys of grants done. Both supported a new county on the Green River.

Basically, Hickman was a trivial more liberal in his voting than McMillan, though McMillan apparently worked better with the establishment.

Hickman was to be re-elected each year until 1798. He was to be the most popular man in Clark County and the most influential Clark countain in the state. Hubbard Taylor would re-enter politics later to be State Senator and would share with Hickman these honors.

As reported, November 13, 1793, the Shelby papers reported that the Governor asked James McMillan to submit a list of men who would be acceptable for appointment for magistrate from Clark County. The report did not say anyone else was asked, though this does not mean that they were not. However, it does mean that Shelby considered McMillan part of the Court Party and therefore, part of the establishment.

The magistrates were divided into two categories. The first was the Quarterly Court which handled minor criminal cases and more important civil cases. The Quarterly Court would also supervise grand juries, both for the supervision and investigation of problems of the county and to indict those who needed to be for higher court which would be held in Lexington. The lower or county court handled the administration of the county affairs. The magistrates were also justices of the peace. Later, they would have definite court days and locations. This probably was done at this time also. If they did at this time, it never appeared in the record. There is one case where a magistrate did send a man up from his court to the county court for contempt. This magistrate never sat with the county court and lived in what became Estill County. No other mention of him or his court was made again in the county records. There is not enough information to state firmly what he did. In likelihood, he was assigned the task of taking care of some of the court's work in the sparsely settled section of what would become Estill County.

There were eleven magistrates appointed. The first three were the judges of the Quarterly Court and they were Hubbard Taylor, John McGuire, and Robert Clark, Sr. The remaining magistrates were James McMillan, John Hood, John Holder, Enoch Smith, James Baker, Jilson Payne, William Sudduth and Abijah Brooks. Smith and McGuire came from the Montgomery area as did Brooks though the latter also could be classified as a Clark County citizen. McMillan was from the Bush Settlement but he would move later to Montgomery County. He was eventually a major in the militia and served under Gen. Arthur St. Clair in his disasterous campaign against the Indians. Baker would help establish Winchester but then move to the Stoner area. Sudduth and Hood came from the Pretty Run part of Wades Mill section. On the whole they were representative of the more prestigious citizens of the county, though there were some notable omissions. None of the Bushes or Scholls were included. No Boone was included though at least two Boone families lived in Clark County. The Haggards were perhaps too new to the area, but the Vivions were not included. There were no Ramseys, Tracys, Haineys or any other of the original Stoner Creek Settlement. Daniel Boone had been sheriff of Fayette County before the creation of Clark County, but for some reason the Boone clan did not belong to the Court

Party. The Stoner Creek people, and the other settlements in Montgomery were simply not part of the Clark County-Fayette County establishment and therefore not included. There was no one from Powell, Estill or that vast bit of Clark County that reached back to the Cumberland Gap. There were a few settlers scattered in this region, but they made little impression on the Governor's supporters.

John Martin was appointed the first sheriff. He was not one of those that had first staked out his claim in Clark County, nor was he the John Martin that had been on the Clark County side when the Boone and Calloway girls were kidnapped. This Martin came to Kentucky in 1784. He had rated high in the militia, but like so many of the Clark County militia, did not become involved in Blue Licks. At one time, as Quarterly Judge, John Martin had to try John Martin. It was a minor case, but the records do not say just who the defendent John Martin was....possibly his son. Martin was a loud, and agressive deist who later became a converted Methodist. Now at this point we have an unresolved problem. There was a John Martin who was a member of the original Providence Baptist Church group. This Martin was the one on the other side of the river at the kidnapping. He married Rachel Pace and had 13 children. He was a lieutenant in the Virginia militia and was one of the orignal settlers of Clark County on lower Howard Creek in an old stone house built in 1782 which according to Katherine Owen still stands. After his term as Sheriff, the first John Martin would become a Quarterly Judge. One of his sons, Dr. Samuel Martin would leave behind one of the better descriptions of the early period of Clark County after the War of 1812. It is difficult to separate similarly named Clark Countians.

**The last** county official was the coroner which had traditionally been created by the British Kings as a check on the sheriffs.... technically he was the only official in the British structure that had the authority to arrest a high sheriff. In the American system he was the least important in the county system. The first Clark County coroner was John Strode.

The county court met first at Strode's Station in the house of John Strode. This was now "an ordinary", a drinking and eating establishment that had been enlarged by the combining of several cabins into one establishment. He was paid for the use of his establishment. It is nothing unusual for a tavern to be used by public officials. In the first place, it usually provided a room, small in our comparisons, but large enough for a dozen men to sit comfortably. Often it would provide a table on which writing material could be placed. The ordinary also provided food and drink. Many of the court would have been in the saddle at an early hour and would be hungry on arrival. There was no opposition to drinking in these days. It was considered very much part of the necessities of eating. The ordinary would often provide rooming, or better, sleeping accommodations.

The problem of getting a place to sleep on a trip was not an easy one. There were plenty of taverns. However, usually the sleeping accommodations would be a loft, a second floor room in which three or four travellers might be compelled to sleep. It was often far more convenient and sanitary to sleep in clean hay in the stable. One could often find accommodations in private homes. However, in a one or two room cabin which housed a family of two adults, three or four half-grown children, and another half-dozen little children, privacy was difficult to come by.

There is in the Methodist history an itinerant minister named Watson who was tried by the Conference for immorality. They had him on two charges, one with having boasted that he had slept between two sisters. He explained this charge by saying he was offered a bed in a small house. The two older girls, teenagers, dressed, climbed in bed with him on either side and the older brother slept in the same room by the fire on the floor. This is the beginning of a century of farmer's daughter jokes.

Returning to the organization of the court. The WINCHESTER SUN, April 28, 1933, claimed that Daniel Harrison was the first sheriff. It is not clear where the Sun came up with that story for it was not repeated. Harrison had been a deputy sheriff in the old Fayette County as a young man just before the creation of Clark County.

The court met and appointed David Bullock county clerk. The appointment would be validated by the Governor. Between David and his son, the Bullock family would hold the court clerk's position for fifty years, until it became elective. Micah Taul described him as one of the laziest men Taul ever knew. However, his court records appeared to be effective. He held his office about two miles out of Winchester proper. He would have a staff of up to a half-dozen young men, including Micah Taul at the end of this decade. Taul was 12 when he went to work for Bullock. Their job was the copying of the records, providing the needed documents for the lawyers. On the whole, their writing is legible after one adjusts to it. There are differences however, in their written English and present day.

In 1793, Clark County did not have an official seal to close documents. A seal was a wood or metal device, sometimes on a ring, more often on a stamp. A letter or a document would be folded into a convenient package and the open ends sealed with a blob of hot wax. Into this wax the seal would be pressed giving the letter or document an official status represented by whatever the seal represented. Until Clark County's seal could be deviced, Bullock was given permission to use his family's seal.

Perhaps the most important item of business in the establishment of the county was to pick a courthouse. The residents of Montgomery area had incorporated Mt. Sterling, a little before the county was legally established. Their intent was quite clear.

Mt. Sterling would be an established and legal town and would be the obvious and logical place to establish the county seat. Enoch Smith, Hugh Forbes, John Judy and Samuel Spurgeon had been back of the 240 acres of land set aside around and including the Indian Mound that was called Little Mountain.

We have noted, however, that county seats appeared about twenty miles away from the older seat and Mt. Sterling was twice that distance from Lexington. Enoch Smith was perhaps the best known of Mt. Sterling's backers, but it was quite obvious that it was not in the center of the county's heaviest population. Even in this area, it was not the unanimous choice. Some of the settlers around what is now Sharpsburg offered that spot for the county seat. Flat Creek was suggested. Some of the Daniels and Vivions had suggested Indian Fields as in the center of the population, close to the river, and offering flat land for a growth of a town. Further up the Red River, the Hardwicks suggested Beaver Pond. The Hood's felt that their station was ideally located and Strode's Station was already acting as county seat.

Strode's Station was the center of early activity in the county. Settlers came to Strode's first before going elsewhere. The early court had begun the county road system with Strode's as the center. It was the logical county seat.

Into this picture came John Baker. Baker was from Winchester, Virginia. He had purchased some 319 acres from the Edward Wilson patent that was on the road that led from Lexington through Strode's Station to the already important Olympia Springs. According to Ben Allen's interview with Dr. Shane, Baker's first wife was a Miss Welch, second wife Aga Williams, and his third wife was a Polly Combs. Together they built a cabin with a large room and a loft. In one end of the room he set up a board table braced on a couple of barrels of whiskey and opened an ordinary.

Baker's land was a wilderness. He owned a farm of cane covered hills. He did have one advantage, a spring that was large enough to provide water for many people. He went to the magistrates and offered his site as the county seat. He would break it up into lots, lay out streets, and provide free land to the county for a courthouse, a school, a jail, and a stray animal pen. He would sell at reasonable prices, 66 acres for a building program. He claimed the spring would provide water for five to six hundred people. He would lay out two broad streets (not the narrow raods most new communities grudgingly gave the public, which he would call Main Street and Main Cross Street).

To top this proposal, on the day when the magistrates would decide on the county seat, Baker provided a full fledged meal. James McMillan and William Sudduth were for Baker's site. Enoch Smith and John Holder opposed Smith because he wanted Mt. Sterling and Holder because he favored Strode's. Baker, of course voted for himself and with the promise of public land, he brought Robert

Clark and Hubbard Taylor in favor. Payne, Brooks and McGuire voted against both Strode's and Baker for a five to five tie. Hood was not present but would have opposed both Winchester and Strode's, but was also against Mt. Sterling. As it stood, there was a five to five tie.

John Garner, prominent Clark County politician about the last quarter of the 19th century and three times mayor of Winchester, was a humorist and a historian of sorts. He reported that John Strode broke the tie by voting against his own station on the grounds that he did not want to raise his children in a city with all its corrupt elements. There is no way of telling where Garner got his story. However, Strode was not a magistrate and therefore, had no vote. However, the story might not be entirely wrong. Undoubtedly since the court meeting was at Strode's Station, Strode was present. He certainly knew the men involved and was a close friend to all. He could well have expressed his opinion. As a result, both Holder and Hood who had arrived at that time, voted for Winchester. Baker's site was therefore the winner. The legend about Strode's vote does not die easily but is repeated over and over again by eager but not always thorough historians.

There is another interesting legend. The contemporary, James French, said that each of the proposed sites sent a wrestling champion to Strode's to battle out who would win. French said that Hood did not change his vote until his champion was beaten by Baker's and that Holder did not change until Strode's man was beaten. French does not tell his sources.

The KENTUCKY GAZETTE reported the establishment of Winchester, named after Baker's former home, December 21, 1793. Mt. Sterling's supporters, angry, immediately demanded that the county be divided.

There had been opposition to the establishment of Winchester. There is no indication who was at the bottom of this opposition but presumedly it was the Mt. Sterling advocates. The House Journal of 1793 unfortunately, like most of the early records, does not explain what really was going on. However, both James McMillan and Richard Hickman threw their weight behind the new town.

## THE COUNTY SEAT

We will consider early Winchester in detail in a following section. However, the establishing of a county seat was of primary importance to the new county and a short word of it must be included now.

The first cabin in what is now the area of downtown Winchester was built by a man named Patrick, but he was a squatter and did not own the land. Baker's cabin was second. The Croswaithe Station a mile away from the spring came before either. It was originally a half faced cabin of red oak logs located a mile east of where Maple and Broadway meet.

The first task after the incorporation of Winchester in December of 1793 was to lay out the town into lots. This task was given to John Elliott, Benjamin Combs and Hubbard Taylor. Sixty-six acres was divided into 72 lots of 99' by 208' and 24 lots of 106' by 200'. Baker laid out Main Street and Main Cross Street which was to bisect Main Street and connect with the road that reached out to Strode's Station and Lexington. North of Main Cross Street was Washington Street which was named, obviously for George Washington. South of Main Cross Street which did not become Broadway until after the Civil War, was Fairfax Street, once again showing Baker's love of Virginia. After 1900, the name of Fairfax was changed to Lexington Avenue. It had been called unofficially, the Lexington Road ever since the Lexington Pike came through along it rather than along Main Cross Street. West of Main Street was Water Street indicating the nearness of the spring. It would become Maple Street sometime after the Civil War. The spring had long before disappeared. East of Main Street was High Street. This constituted the original Winchester. The whole center portion, from Main Street to Water Street and from Main Cross Street to Wall Street was reserved for county buildings.

Thomas Hart of the Transylvania Company had obtained land in Clark County up and above his interest in the company. He left some 800 acres of this land to his son, Josiah Hart. Much of this property ran along Washington Street. Josiah Hart sold to the town another ten and a half acres to be divided into lots. This gave Winchester a total of 76 1/2 acres. Winchester would not grow any larger until 1831 when 640 more acres would be added to the city limits. Lots were sold readily, but there was not a rush to build. Nearly every important Clark Countain tried not only to have a farm, but also a lot in town on which he pannned some day to build. Most of these land owners were more interested in building up their farm family home. By 1797, Winchester consisted of just eleven homes, connected by a series of paths leading through the cane, and streets that were laid out, but not really cleared. There would be stumps in the middle of Main Street until well into 1800. Thomas Scott actually did the work of laying out and surveying the streets.

Evidently, John Frame was one of the earliest settlers. Among the other early residents were the Towbridges and the Lamptons. One of the early histories of Winchester appeared in the WINCHESTER SUN March 13, 1924.

The lots were auctioned off, March 24, Court Day, 1794 and were so advertised in the KENTUCKY GAZETTE. John Strode bought Lot 1; John O'bryan, 2; William Barnes, 3; Josiah Bullock, 4; Rueben Crosthwait, 5; William Mim, 6; John Baker bought 23, 27, 17, 18 and 24; for some reason, the purchase of Lot 25 to David Hughs, 35 and 36 by Rice Pendleton, and Lots 33, 24 and 34 by Samuel Warner were crossed out.

By March 1795, Lot 60 had been sold to Isaiah Nichols, Thomas Scott bought 30, Judah Heming, 29; Jeremiah Power, 41; William Denwill, 65; Robert Higgins, 42; Berryman Kirtley, 64; Charles Beeman, 87; in April, Jeremiah Strode bought 48; John Strode, 89; James Kidd, 28; John Ritchie, 63; Samuel Ritchie, 46; John Sphar, 37 and 39; Stephen Boyle 38 and a little later, 30; William McMillan, 40; Edward Nelson, 80; John Ireland, 81 and 82; Samuel Thompson, 92; Thomas Johnson, 22; Jeremiah Nichol, 21; Josiah Hart, 91; John Frame, 20; William Frame, 19; Robert Hogge, 66; Pleasant Hardwick, 67; John Hood,12; Andrew Hood, 70; John Sphar, 69; John Hannor, 27; and John Warner, 32. This totals some 50 lots.

Winchester was not a glowing success. Baker died in 1803; only then did the estate convey title to the six acres for public buildings until 1803 for the courthouse and 1810 for the school. Richard Hickman was elected the first chairman of the Board of Trustees....in a vague sort of way, he might be called the first mayor of Winchester. Both the Board of Trustees for Winchester and the county court now met at Baker's Tavern instead of Strode's. Other of Winchester's first trustees were David Bullock, Josiah Hart, John Elliott, Benjamin Combs, William Bush and Hubbard Taylor. Naturally, these were all appointed by the Governor and would be until well after the Civil War. There would be elections, however, at various times for trustees, the results of which would be unofficial and verified only at the will of the Governor. The first trustee's meeting was February 6, 1794.

## FURTHER DEVELOPMENT OF THE NEW COUNTY

Once the county seat was established and developed, the next problem was to bring into being buildings to meet the governmental requirements of the new county. In 1794, the KENTUCKY GAZETTE called for the lowest bids to build a cabin courthouse, jails, stocks, and a stray pen. Hubbard Taylor, the two Robert Clarks, Junior and Senior, and Edmond Hockaday were on the committee. For reasons not explained, Hockaday was replaced by Thomas Scott. The May court records of 1794 contained the plans for the courthouse.

By 1795, a two room courthouse was built. Hubbard Taylor, Original Young, Robert McKinney and Dillard Collins were appointed to supervise the construction. It would be a two room building, one room 20' by 20' and the other 20' by 10'. The total building would be 42' by 30' with 2' walls set 18' from the ground. A chimney was to be built in either end of the courthouse with fireplaces for heat. There would be six, 8' by 10' windows with 24 lites (glass was still a novelty and a luxury in Clark County) in each.

The rest of the county buildings came harder. The stray pen produced no trouble. In the days when there were either no fences, or rail fences, zig-zagging across the country, stray animals were a major problem. Every newspaper that has been preserved carrys ads for lost animals. There would not be a half way satisfactory jail until 1811. The school would not be built until at least 1803, though there was a school in Winchester before that.

The county rounded out its organization by appointing Austin Webb and William Harris the first constables. Charles Cade, William Bush, William Higgins and Samuel Plummer were appointed superintendents of the poor in districts outlined by the court.

Five new magistrates were added to the county court in 1794. The Quarterly Judges remained the same and also served with the county court. Richard Hickman was naturally added to the court. He was a rising young legislator already attracting state wide attention for his ability. He was also a rising officer in the militia which was almost a requirement for a politician at this time. James McMillan had overlooked William Bush, the last of the regular frontiersmen, when he advised the county court. It was an error not deliberately done, and it was now rectified. Bush was to remain judge for quite some time and then serve as sheriff before his death. These two were added to Hood, Holder, Sudduth and Baker, plus the Quarterly Court Judges giving that area including the Bush Settlement along the Boonesboro Road and the Paris Road nine men.

The third new magistrate was William Crawford who had as many ties in Fayette County as in Clark, but would have to be counted with the majority giving them ten. Arthur Kinkaid was generally felt to come from the new county area not yet named Montgomery, and of course, James Poague was one of the stronger new county men, influential even in Frankfort and a ranking officer in the militia. The new county people had these two plus Enoch Smith and Jilson Payne to give four. James McMillan and Abijah Brooks were the swing vote which often supported the new county people. McMillan did so particularly in the legislature. Even with these, the new county people had only six to the Winchester court nine.

This division was not violent. It could be seen, however, in the way roads were laid out, giving Winchester most, Mt. Sterling some and the rest of the county very little.

Kinkaid dropped out withn a year. John Hood was the owner of an ordinary in Winchester. He stayed magistrate only two years. He was, however, active as a trustee to Winchester during most of these early years. He did various jobs for the county such as the janitor (name not used) of the courthouse after it was built, and for a period used his house as a jail...he had a storeoom that had been built out of logs and could be closed with a reinforced door. In normal times he would use it to store barrels of whiskey, pelts of wild animals he had bought from the trappers in the area, or whatever needed a relatively safe room.

Holder would be a mgistrate until his death in 1798. Enoch Smith was magistrate until 1794 when he, and Abijah Brooks left the county courthouse in protest to the Clark County contingent. Smith was the leader in the establishment of the new county. Jilson Payne was also for the county but he remained as magistrate until 1797. Payne lived near Lullbegrud Church and was deeply involved in its affairs. His home was close to the present Clark County line.

William Sudduth emerged as perhaps the most influential Clark Countian that did not go upward in politics. He was magistrate until elected sheriff and was elected or chosen magistrate after that time...one of the few sheriffs who had been magistrate that returned to the magistrate job in time. He rated next to Hickman and McMillan in the militia. He was county surveyor from 1796 until after the War of 1812. As such he had considerable influence.

The job of tax commissioner revolved. Edmond Hockaday succeeded Jilson Payne and John Young replaced John Elliott as tax commissioner. It was felt during these times it was the duty of a citizen to hold office regardless of the injury it might do to a personal business. It is true that it was apt to do less damage than in later years. However, this attitude was pretty largely the popular attitude until 1900 and later. Once, however, having served a term in some public office, the duty was fulfilled and the citizen no longer expected to make sacrifices.

The United States Senators were elected by the state legislature in joint session. Unfortunately, the Legislative Journals do not break down the vote to the various counties. John Brown became Kentucky's first Senator and was elected unanimously. He was to remain in office until 1805. To provide the proper rotation of Senators which only a third are elected every two years, the second Kentucky Senator was not elected until 1794. By that time, the division in the state politics had become evident. The so-called Court and Country Parties had disappeared, mainly because the Court Party so dominated all, that merely belonging to the Country Party was a kiss of death. Therefore, regardless of what one felt, they belonged to the same party... and in this case, only very dimly related to the Jeffersonian-Burr Republicans. They were more or less held together by being anti-Federalist. This party situation has been repeated over and over in Kentucky, first with this situation, later with the triumph of the Whig party to the exclusion of the Democrats, and finally with the triumph of the Democratic Party with the exclusion of the Republicans.

The exclusion was not complete, however. Representatives of the minority party would surface from time to time temporarily. Also, since many of the majority party actually felt and voted like the minority party when able, occasionally, a majority victor would actually reflect minority principles. So it happened in the 1794 election for the United States Senate. The candidates were John Edwards, John Brickinridge, John Fowler and Humphrey Marshall. Marshall represented the old Country Party that had now taken on Federalist coloration. The definition of conservativism offered hold. The Country Party had tried to maintain the good of the old system. They were beaten. The Federalist power became centered in Washington. It still offered allegiance to the old, tried formula and though many of the Federalist ideas were actually the opposite to Patrick Henry's position that had attracted the Country Party, Federalist still provided the emotional tie with the past. This shifting of political ground, often a reversal of positions held by conservatives and liberals become confusing if this principle is not recognized. On the first ballott, Edwards received 7 votes, Breckinridge 17, Fowler 8 and Marshall, 18. The problem with a majority vote is that personalities often splinter it permitting the minority to gain a victory. Breckinridge clearly represented a majority position as he would demonstrate in later elections. However, the majority fell to pieces as Marshall was elected over Breckinridge 22 to 28. Marshall would serve out his term despite constant attacks and as reported, near impeachment. He supported the Federalist administration politics including the alien and sedition acts. In 1801 when his term was over, Marshall was retired from Kentucky politics.

Congressmen were elected by popular vote. This office and the state lower house were the only two the people were called on to vote that they had the right to elect. In the Presidential elections even unto this day, no one votes for President but only for presidential electors which theoretically are pledged to support a certain candidate but are not legally bound to. There seems to be no election results by county. In 1792, Christopher Greenup became Kentucky's first and only Congressman. He was to be elected until 1797. In 1794, the state had grown sufficiently that two congressmen were elected from a northern and southern district. Greenup remained the congressman for the northern district which included Clark County. James Fowler became the second congressman.

There simply are no political records. We assume that they must be somewhere, and kept by someone. They have probably been lost. The county court would assign magistrates to run the election polls. They must have recorded the results and reported them to the court...they were probably noted but never recorded. There were no newspapers interested. Occasionally, some election result would appear in the KENTUCKY GAZETTE but since the GAZETTE could hardly care less about Clark County, these are not her figures. This report would also have to be given to the sheriff who in turn would report them to the Governor. Sometimes election figures would appear in the Governor's papers. More often they did not.. at least those available. Merely the results, that so and so was chosen. Often the opponent is not even mentioned. These, in turn, were taken to one of the committees of the House and Senate who examined the results and certified that some person was eligible to sit in the seat of some specific county. This committee was interested only in eligibility and not how that eligibility was obtained.

For some reason James McMillan is not returned to the political front in 1794. He generally disappears from politics. We do not have a death date for him, but we believe that it does not occur for a good many more years. Trying to guess what happened was a political defeat that retired him to his lands in Clark County to live out his days as a citizen. Katherine Owen suggests that after the killing of Peter Harper, McMillan began heavy drinking.

Robert Dougherty was elected as Clark County's second representative. Presumedly this was the growing feeling of the eastern part of Clark County that there should either be a new county seat in or around Mt. Sterling, or that a new county should be formed. The areas of what is now Montgomery and Bath Counties were being filled with settlers who felt themselves a long way from Winchester. The fact that enough of them were willing to make the long ride into Winchester to vote shows their determination; Dougherty was their man.

Apparently there are no results of local elections that have been preserved. State Senators, National Senators and Governors were all originally elected, under the first Constitution, by an electoral college. All local officials were appointed by the

Governor. After the Constitution of 1799 became effective, the Governor was added to the list of popularly elected officers.

However, the task of providing a list of officers to be nominated by the Governor for everything in a county from magistrate to coroner, from sheriff to militia officers, was staggering. There would often be an election, unofficial and without legal authority to choose this or that official. The result of these elections would then be handed on to the Governor by the county as their recommendations. This was particularly true in the militia where the men of a company would quite often elect their captains, lieutenants and ensigns, even though the Governor would have to make those appointments with the consent of the Senate to make them legal.

Actually, the electorate in Kentucky was quite a broad one. Article III of the first Constitution gave the ballot to any free, white, male who had lived within the state two years and the county where he voted. There were no property or educational limitations. A poll tax would be demanded at a later date, but the poll tax was never so large that a man could not pay it if he really cared to vote. The poll taxes would later be used as a method of meeting the election costs.

It was the responsibility of the county court to see that elections were held and that the reports were forwarded to Frankfort. The Shelby papers made it clear that the official responsible for the holding of the elections, the assigning of the time and place would belong to the sheriff. An election, the paper notes would be from 9 o'clock to sunset for three consecutive days. The court would furnish the officials for that election.

The April Court of 1795 appointed William Bush and John Baker to supervise the election of representations, sheriff and coroners for that year. The December Court of 1796 paid Dillard Collins 12 shillings for three days work holding elections.

Unfortunately, though appointed and performing their function, they did not report the results to the county court. The sheriff did report the final result to the Governor, but seldom the actual statistics. They would certify that so and so was elected. There would be no mention of who the opponents were, what the issues were, or what the problems had been.

The location of the voting booth for nearly thirty years would be at the courthouse. The purpose of the three days would allow even the most distant voter to get a chance at voting.

There was no such thing as a secret ballot. Micah Taul gives a very vivid description of an election place. The election officers sat at a table, if the weather permitted, outside under the trees. The voter would ride in, hitch his horse somewhere and

and approach the table. The election officials would check his name against lists and then ask him how he wished to vote. The voter would then declare his candidates for all to hear. He would be greeted as he approached the polling place and as he voted by the cheers of those who knew that he was on their side and boos by who were opposed to him. Along the way, he would often be threatened with physical violence and his name insulted. Sometimes he would become angry even before he got to the polling place and have to fight. Usually however, the election faction would keep handy a few rough bully boys who would keep the weaker members of its side from getting too badly hurt. Sometimes the bully boys on each side would end up in a riot. The sheriff and his deputies after permitting a good deal to go on, would step in to break up the disturbances. Peace restored, the sheriff would step out and the process would start all over again. Having voted, the citizen would quite often join the side of his candidate to join in the fun.

There would always be taverns nearby which kept a plentiful supply of spirits going and which would house the leaders of each group who would continue the argument inside with words and blows, that outside was carried with jeers and blows. As time increased, the candidates themselves would furnish free drinks. Descriptions of Clark County elections, particularly the 1840 election which reached its peak, whiskey barrels were placed on posts around the court yard. At the end of the third day, Garner, who was describing the scene, said that the court yard looked like the day after a battle, with bodies covering almost every square foot of ground.

It took courage to vote, particularly if you knew you were voting against the majority. The chance of fraud in the voting were slim; the chances of intimidation and violence good.

The elections that produced the 1795 House must have increased Clark County's fear of the future. Hickman was, of course, safe in his legislative seat. However, the threat of the eastern part of the county continued. Simon Adams was elected to join Hickman.

A number of things happened in the 1795 legislature that is worth noting in passing. John Gano was elected chaplain. Gano was a popular minister of a liberal bend of mind, suspected of universalism, and would eventually become part of the Campbell Reform. Already controversy was stirring about him. He symbolized the religious unrest of the day that would be further described in Volume II.

The previous two accrediting committees, 1792 and 1793, had seated the elected representatives without a challenge. This time, 1795, the committee refused noting that many of the newly elected legislators also held other positions in government, for example, judges of the Quarterly Court. There was no challenge to Clark Countains. James French,**then** elected from Madison County, was refused a seat because he was Quarterly Judge in Madison County.

The legislature was paralyzed for the first several weeks of the session because of a lack of majority. It must have been decided in favor of those who held other seats, though Quarterly Judges may have been eliminated, for the conflict of offices continued without further question.

The debate over a new county out of Clark continues, but will be discussed later.

The road from Virginia to Kentucky through the Cumberland Gap was to be improved and widened for wagons. Seventeen ninety-five was 20 years from the time the first large settler body crossed the mountains and came down the road. Wagons had tried, but the going was rough and unsatisfactory, pack trains were more common. In Clark County, a new insistance that the roads being built should be wide enough for wagons was present.

Humphrey Marshall was the United States Senator and represented the right wing of Kentucky politics. He supported the Jay Treaty, favored the alien and sedition acts and could in general be classified as a Federalist. Charges were placed against him in the 1795 legislature for gross fraud and public and willful perjury. Wilkerson was evidently behind the effort to unseat Marshall. The legislature, without condemning Marshall, called for an investigation which Marshall felt would be rigged against him. Hickman avoided voting growing himself more conservative as the years went on. We have part of the reason why Hickman's rising career went only so high. Kentucky was not yet ready for conservatives. Simon Adams, however, voted for the investigation. The Montgomery area would always be more apt to be liberal than Clark County. Both Adams and Hickman were voting with the majority two-thirds of the time. They voted together about half the time, though we note that Hickman didn't vote on about four called votes.

Hubbard Taylor becomes Clark County's first State Senator in 1796. McMillan is re-elected to the legislature in 1796. He served with Hickman, Doughtery and Poague. This would give Clark County a four man delegation. However, it must be remembered that Clark County reached to the Cumberland Gap. The number of delegates to the lower house of the legislature varied election to election; no reason has as yet been discovered. It was based on population.

Adams', Doughtery's and Poague's call came from the area that would be Montgomery in a few years. Robert Clark, Jr., and Dillard Collins would replace Doughtery and Poague giving the Clark County area all three votes. The four men, Senator Hubbard Taylor, and Legislators Hickman, Clark and Collins represent considerable political power in the county. Taylor and Clark both had considerable standing statewide. Add to this group James McMillan who was now ranking officer of the state militia, and the power establishment of the Clark County area was completed.

George G. Taylor and Achilles Eubank step into the legislative seats.

Jacob Fishback replaces Collins in 1798 serving with Hickman and Clark. Fishback is another strong political figure of the time, though his influence is largely limited to what is now the Becknerville area. He had considerable influence in Fayette County also. Two Clark County businessmen (all men owned farms and Eubank was one of the largest) and store owners, George Taylor and Achilles Eubank join Clark in 1799. Richard Hickman goes to the state senate in 1800.

As the decade closes, several names have appeared on the political scene over the others. Hubbard Taylor and Richard Hickman are definitely leaders. James McMillan, though not so much politically, has important militia post. These three men were perhaps the best known Clark Countains. On a more local level, the names of Robert Clark, Jr., Dillard Collins, Jacob Fishback, George G. Taylor and Achilles Eubank were men of considerable influence.

Isaac Shelby's first term expired in 1796. The election of the new Governor was done by electing electors. The two main contenders were James Garrard and Ben Logan with Thomas Todd a poor third. Logan had wide respect as an Indian fighter and long a hero of the frontiersmen. He was not, however, a member of the Court Party that had placed Shelby and Brown in office. When vote was made, as reported by the Shelby Papers in 1796, Logan received 21 votes, James Garrard 17, Thomas Todd 14 and John Brown 1. Logan claimed that he had won, but the electors insisted on a run-off vote. Todd and Brown were dropped and this time, with the Todd vote swinging largely to Garrard, Garrard won.

Logan's people shouted foul, and for awhile the whole state became tense waiting for an explosion. There would not be another situation like this until the bitter Democrat-Republican struggle with the killing of Senator Goebel. Clark County was largely behind Garrard. Logan appealed to the State Senate, but the Senate let the vote stand. Garrard became the second Governor and the state settled down.

Garrard like most of the Kentuckians at this time, had been born in Virginia in 1749. Like Shelby, he came to Kentucky already a prominent man among Virginians hence carried his popularity to Kentucky. He had served in the Virginia House of Deputies in 1779. He represented Fayette early in the Virginia Legislature in 1785. He had been a colonel in the Virginia militia. He had opposed the Constitution but had changed his position when Kentucky was promised statehood.

Garrard was also a Baptist minister of the Separatist group. He organized or helped organize a Separatist Baptist church at Cooper's Run in what is now Bourbon County. He preached for them for several years. Looking ahead in this work we might note that the Elkhorn Association which Cooper's Run joined, was basically a regular Baptist body and did not always look with sympathy on Cooper's Run liberalism. Garrard also became interested in what was then called, the Hell Redemptionist movement....the idea that even those in hell would eventually be redeemed and saved by God's grace...the present day, Universalism. His Secretary of State and close friend, Harry Toulmin, also a Baptist minister, was an ardent supporter of Universalism. There is no real evidence that either Garrard or Cooper's Run were won to the Hell redemption position, but they were influenced. The Elkhorn Association would later try to discipline the church with some success.

This made Garrard a center of turbulence in the religious world then carried over into the political field. Clark County lost their love for Garrard over this issue despite the fact that Garrard owned land near Indian Fields which he sold to his son who, for a time, lived in Clark County. Clark County's Baptist movement was much too conservative to support a Hell Redemptionist.

Despite Clark County, as we will note, Garrard was re-elected to a second term of Governor, this time as the first popularly elected Governor of Kentucky. However, after this, he was never able to get back into successful politics. He would make a couple of efforts but all of them futile. He became deeply interested in the ideas of Barton Stone and those of Alexander Campbell and his church, Cooper's Run, was strongly Reform. It did not actually join the reform movement. Garrard could not quite make up his mind in the greatest struggle of the 1820s which did not help him politically. He died in 1832.

He married Elizabeth Mountjoy. One of his daughters married John Edwards, the second Senator from Kentucky, and another married Isham Talbot, who also became a United States Senator. Even out of office, Garrard was not without political strength.

## MONTGOMERY COUNTY

As 1796 turned up, the division between Montgomery (still not officially named), and Clark County was a certainty. Clark County was too large to administer successfully from any section and certainly from Winchester. It was state policy to encourage the organization of new counties as immigration filled in the uninhabited spots. Nearly every legislature was busy establishing one or two new counties from some older organization. The issue, between Clark and Montgomery was just where the new county lines would be run.

James McMillan had handled most of the county debate for the new county. Perhaps this was partly why he was dropped from the legislature by the county. He was back again for one year in 1796.

A petition had been offered to the state legislature by a large number of Montgomery people requesting the new county and seeking to include most of what is now Clark County up to the Boonesboro-Paris Roads. This was too much since the suggestion on the part of the new county people that additional territory of Fayette and Madison be added to Clark County to round it out. McMillan then submitted a counter petition with more than a 1000 names pointing out that what would be left of Clark County would be too small and that the new county proposal would be better to take in parts of Maidson, what is now Estill, Powell as well as some of what is now Montgomery County. That petition was, in 1976, in the Doyle collection in the Winchester Library.

Meanwhile, Clark County had made some effort in bringing representation to the Montgomery County area with magistrates and to encourage the building of roads with Mt. Sterling as the central hub for that area.

In 1796, John Martin's term as sheriff expired and he became a Quarterly Court Magistrate. In his place was Bob Higgins who had done most of the sheriff's work during Martin's administration. Higgins came from the Grassy Lick section which was generally thought of as in the new county. He had bought a lot in Winchester, however. Enoch Smith was also made the county surveyor which was a very important job.

There is really very little information concerning the actual struggle. One reads between the lines, looks at possibilities, weighs results for causes and comes up with a sort of fictionalized account of what must have happened. The advocates of the new county wanted the Stoner Creek area and the Indian Fields area, plus Powell and hunks of Estill (what would become Powell and Estill). They were trying to strip Clark County of all but the more heavily established centers around the Bush Settlement, Upper Howard's Creek around what is now Ruckerville and northward to Pretty Run area which was close to the Bourbon County line.

This proposal was unreasonable even on the surface of it, and the legislature did not support it. However, the loss in the county struggle was merely a round.

A second petition introduced that went another direction was kept among the Shelby Papers asking that the magistrates be assigned or be drawn from specific neighborhoods. This petition was dated 1795 and included the signatures of John Pleickerslaver, John Mornell (writing illegible), Peter Cuthwright, ? Swearenger, Dick Taylor, David Ellington, Jonathan Allington, Joseph Moore, James Brown, Abraham Becraft (writing illegible), Rueben Copher, John Scott, Lawson Wade, Thomas Pinter (writing illegible), William Payne, John Burroughs, Peter Detweilt (writing illegible), Edmond Burroughs, Martin Demerett (writing illegible), Edward Roberts, James Payne, Moses Frazee, Felix Baker, John Baker, Elias Sanchez, Peter Toler, M ? Harrison and Jonathan Lanter. There were some 32 more names on another page, but these were even more illegible.

Perhaps as response to this request, McMillan offered a petition requesting more magistrates to administer the huge area. Specifically, James McEltheny was asked for Flat Creek and Grassy Lick, William Roseberry for the mouth of said creek, John Mockaby for the Iron Works, and David Hughs for Flat Creek.

Some of these names, both of proposed magistrates and petitioners, were residents or at least owned property in Clark County proper...particularly in the Stoner area and from the Wades Mill area.

Josiah Bullock was recommended for the Stoner Creek area, Jessie Woodray for the Grassy Lick, William Copher for Slate Creek, Simon Adams was from Grassy Lick. The sessionists were strong enough to elect him to the legislature.

Behind much of these petitions apparently was Enoch Smith. At least it would be his name that was attached to the correspondence going to Isaac Shelby's office.

As counter to the 1795 petition, James Clark, John Martin, David Hamilton, Achilles Eubank (the official record spelled his name Killes), Dillard Collins, Robert McKinney, Original Young, George Taylor, Joseph Smith, Robert Daugherty, James Ward, James McElhassy, Jesse Woodruff and William Roseberry opposed.

Again in 1796, a bill to divide Clark County was up before the House and would divide Clark County at Indian Creek and include all of Powell County in the new county. It failed.

The legislature also saw the need for a new Constitution and the three year process for a new constitution was begun. The legislature was not interested in a tax supported wagon road to run from Frankfort to Cincinnati.

The legislature came back to the question of new counties. Nelson County was formed out of Jefferson. There was no doubt that it was a question of time before Montgomery County would be formed. The question that then developed in the 1796 legislature was just how much of Clark County should be cut off to form the county. There is no record of the struggle behind the scenes, of the conferences between Montgomery and Clark County people and the influential men of the state. Unfortunately for Montgomery County, men like William McMillan, Richard Hickman and Hubbard Taylor had more weight than any of their leading men. Enoch Smith, Jilson Payne and the others had not sufficient contacts. As a result Montgomery County lost the Red River Valley, the Log Lick area, Indian Fields and the Stoner Creek communities. This would be added to Clark County's undisputed areas of the Bush community, Winchester, Wades Mill and what would leave all the future Powell, Wolf and Estill Counties in Clark County. On the other hand, Montgomery had her county which included all of what is now Bath County and considerable other territories.

Among those from the Montgomery County territory, at least James McElhassy was not a strong new county supporter. He had turned up on petitions that were basically in favor of the old county. The control of the county court still remained firmly in the hands of the Clark Countains. James Ward might be considered a Montgomery County man also, but he had strong ties in Winchester business that made him an old county supporter. Dillard Collins was one of the up and coming younger men in the county. He was willing for the new county to be established but did want to keep Stoner Creek in the old county. Later, when Collins would be up for sheriff, some of the Stoner Creek people would challenge him on these grounds. Robert Clark, Jr., was filling the place of his father who was rapidly dropping out of politics because of sickness. Young Robert was one of the brightest and most promising of the younger generation of Clark Countians. He was also deeply interested in pushing the iron industry along Red River into which he had heavily bought. He also was not against the new county, but was not anxious to lose the Red River Valley to it. Like others, he was active in the militia and was entering state politics when he abruptly died.

There was one final effort to defeat. The new county people made one last effort to move the county seat from Winchester to Mt. Sterling. This was defeated, but narrowly. The purpose was to frighten Winchester. The hand writing was on the wall. The eastern parts of Clark County was filling rapidly. If a new county was not formed, it would be only a question of time before the political center would shift and Mt. Sterling would become the county seat. Montgomery County became a fact, Mt. Sterling became its county seat. Winchester settled down with relief. Later in 1808, when Estill County sought her existence as a new county, there was virtually no opposition and no controversy. Much later, the independence for Powell County would come as a punishment to Clark County for its long adherence to Clay politics in the state. That story will be covered in the second volume of this series.

December 17, 1796, Governor Garrard appointed Jilson Payne, James McElhany and James Poague to the new Montgomery Quarterly Court.

To replace the Montgomery County magistrates, new Clark County magistrates would have to be appointed. Jacob Fishback, James McMillan who still lived within the county, and Macajah Clark were appointed magistrates. Garrard's paper reports that Clark County legislative seats would be limited to three. After the bills were paid, the treasurer of the county was to be divided equally.

The Clark County Quarterly Court remained the same, John Martin, Original Young and Robert Clark, Sr., William Sudduth replaced Enoch Smith as county surveyor. He was immediately given the task of surveying the new county line.

In so doing, Sudduth discovered that the original county line between Bourbon County and Clark County had been wrongly surveyed. He was authorized by the county court to correct the line and the result was a sliver of Bourbon County that included what is now Donaldson Road, the Gist-Scott home, and about half of Wades Mill was added to Clark County. There is no indication as to the reaction of the people in the area, or of Bourbon County. The error was evidently not unknown and it was just a question of time before the boundary would be rectified. However, the inhabitants of the sliver of land, still looked to the thriving crossroads town of North Middletown for economic and social ties. There was even, briefly, talk of a new county with North Middletown as a county seat cut out of Bourbon and Clark, but this talk was firmly opposed by both older counties. Bourbon County particularly had too much influence to be so divided.

Dillard Collins was appointed Clark County's third sheriff. There was evidently some kind of election to decide just whom the county court should recommend and the Governor appoint. There is no indication as to Collins' opponent. George Halley appeared before the July Court in 1797, challenging Collins' right to serve as sheriff. The court does not say why other than to report charges of irregularity. The court delayed seating Collins until Halley had a chance to make his charges heard. He did not appear. James McMillan was appointed to investigate the charges. Nearly a year later, in 1798, Collins appeared before the court with his commission, and demanded to be installed. The court then appointed a commission, Daniel Ramey, Edmond Hockaday, John Susner, William Smith and William McMillan....all younger men and fairly well distributed over Clark County, to look into the charges. Evidently, their report was favorable to Collins for he was installed as sheriff.

Collins later was to sue Halley for damages, though the outcome of the suit had not been reported. In 1799, Collins appointed James Sympson as his deputy. For the next fifteen years, Sympson was to be tied closely with the law enforcement of Clark County, active in the militia and eventually magistrate of the county. He was the "Wyatt Earp" of Clark County.

The Collins affair was the last flair of the Montgomery question. The county was divided. It was still nearly three times the size of the final Clark County, but Montgomery County would soon be divided to form other counties. Actually, politics in Clark County settled down largely to individual popularities until religion divides the county in the 1820s and 1830s. After 1830 the Jackson people fight furiously with the Clay people in a two pronged political struggle.

George Taylor and David Hampton were added to the county court. Taylor was one of the up and coming and more successful businessman-farmer (all business men in Clark County were also farmers). He owned a store in Winchester, a grist mill on Lower Howard's Creek, and warehouses on the Ohio River. Hampton was one of the long line of David Hamptons. Among the magistrates of Montgomery County was David Hampton. Apparently these David Hamptons were the same men. Whether Hampton lived in Montgomery County and moved back to Clark or whether his appointment to Montgomery court was a mistake, is not clear. At any rate there would be a long line of David Hamptons which would hold political positions in Clark County over the next hundred and fifty years.

## CONSTITUTIONAL CHANGES, 1799

A new Constitution was almost a certainty from the beginning of the state. The old constitution had been much too conservative for the people of Kentucky. It looked backward to the forms favored both by the United States Constitution and some of the state's viewpoints as well. In the decade since the Constitution of 1792, the older generation was passing.

In Clark County more new names were appearing in power. In 1798, Henry Chiles, Daniel Harrison and Thomas Scott were added to the court. Chiles was a Winchester businessman and tavern owner whose name would eventually locate the western side of Winchester's Negro districts. Harrison was, according to Lucien Beckner, closely related to the rather aristocratic William H. Harrison. Beckner suggests that it was in Clark County that William Harrison associated with the crude log cabin that became his political symbol... and eventually the political symbol for the Republican Party in Kentucky. Like some claims for glory, it would be hard to support such a claim. Harrison was the Governor of Indiana territory at a time when the land north of the Ohio was more primitive than Kentucky.

Thomas Scott was a popular figure around Clark County and was a trustee of Winchester's early board. He was a surveyor along with Smith and Sudduth, but he made some errors in his surveys....as Sudduth discovered on the Bourbon line and as we will discuss about the Fayette line in the next session. No one seemed to hold this against him, however. He was a favorite to appoint on a variety of commissions to do a variety of jobs for the county and the town. He was a big, good natured, heavy drinking man who eventually lost everything he owned and died in poverty.

Meanwhile, the discussion whether the Constitution should be changed or not was going on. The major change as far as Clark County was concerned was the popular election of governors. There was also changes in the Judicial system that would affect Clark County.

There was a campaign meeting in favor of the new Constitution held at Bryan's Station. Issues were not reported or speakers. We do note that there was also considerable agitation concerning the alien and sedition laws in which Henry Clay had first made his appearance in public. This may have produced a reaction calling for change.

The vote, whether or not a Constitutional Convention was to be held in Clark County, and the Garrard Papers reported the results... 481 for a new Constitution and 12 against. However, the paper reported that some 610 had voted, but the difference had voted to remain silent on the issue. There is a faint hint of intimidation at this point. It takes a courageous man to stand up against a heavy majority in a public vote.

There was a county election for delegates to the Constitutional Convention but no report of either who the loosers were or what the issues were. The winners were Richard Hickman, Robert Clark, Jr., and William Sudduth. These were without question among the four most infuential men in the county at this time...Hubbard Taylor would perhaps be the fourth.

The new Constitution was passed. It did set up direct election for Governors and provided for changes in the judicial system. It did protect slavery which had grown to a tune of 224.5%. Opposition to slavery was also growing but would not reach its peak for another ten years.

The state voted in favor of the new Constitution 5,446 to 440. In Clark County the vote was 775 to 38. There is little question that the new Constitution was popular.

The county continued peacefully. The Grand Jury for 1798 included Charles Teeter, Foreman, Charles Stewart, John Quisenberry, John Skinner, Truman Marshall, Charles Gentry, Henry Landers, Henry Welsch, William Martin, Ambrose Christy, Leonard Hall, James Steward, A. Bronough, Robert Wallace and Isaac Reese...Benjamin Wheeler was appointed coroner in 1798.

In 1799, two more magistrates were added to the court, George Sharp and Josiah Combs. Sharp, for reasons never stated, dropped off the court after a year. As the decade closed, Nicholas George and Benjamin Taul were added to the court. Taul's baby brother, Micah, perhaps with his brother's influence, became a clerk in the county clerk's office. Micah was to live in Clark County, eventually become a lawyer, serve in the militia and in the War of 1812 and become Clark County's first Congressman.

As the century closed, 1800, John Baker, William Sudduth, Richard Hickman, William Bush, Achilles Eubank, Robert Clark, Jr., James Ward, George Taylor, Micajah Clark, David Hampton, Henry Chiles, Daniel Harrison, Thomas Scott, Joshua Combs, Nicholas George and Benjamin Taul were the magistrates. This is a total of sixteen. Martin, Original Young and Robert Clark, Sr., were Quarterly Court Justices. Young would often hold court in the magisterial court as well as Quarterly Court.

Many of these men were legal trustees of Winchester and other appointive courts. It did not seem to matter. One did resign from the court to be sheriff and that seemed to be the only conflict of office at this time.

## THE CLARK COUNTY LINE

There was next a task of establishing a permanent county line. This had been a first priority of the county and had been placed in the hands of Thomas Scott. We have noted that there had been an error concerning the Bourbon County line. There was also some minor adjustments in the Montgomery County line during the late 1830s that shifted some property back to Clark County. The real problem came over the Clark County-Fayette County line.

Fayette County was a proud county and there were those along the proposed boundary who were not really enthusaists for the new county. We will note continually in this history that many of these Clark County citizens retained contacts with Fayette County, economically, socially and particularly medically even to the present. One group of these citizens decided to do something about it.

Thomas Scott was a genial and popular man, but he was also a man who was known to be interested in good whiskey and fellowship. These Fayette citizens turned the surveying party from a business expedition to a drinking party. By the time the surveyors had gotten to the head waters of the Boone Creek, no one was feeling any pain. The Fayette County people therefore, found it relatively easy to bend the survey lines to meet their desires.

The cut that was left in Fayette County was not a large amount of territory. The WINCHESTER SUN, August 14, 1914, reported that it consisted of 6,000 acres and contained some 9 square miles. Once established, it became impossible to move. Periodically, Clark County tried to get the line straightened out. In 1849-50, Henry Clay Hart surveyed the line and Clark County sought to make the change. Fayette County had much too much influence for Clark County to succeed.

Clark County, however, persisted. After the Civil War, another survey was made, but the surveying party representing both counties could not agree and again the idea was dropped.

After the Civil War, it also became evident that the state capitol was too small for a growing and ambitious state like Kentucky and that a new capitol building would have to be built. Naturally, the question where this building should be built became an issue. No one liked Frankfort. Louisville and Lexington both dug in and announced that the state capitol should be moved to one of their cities and naturally they did not agree as to which one. Editorials were written, speeches were made, offers of money and land were proposed. Each year the problem got worse.

It had been the plan of Richard Henderson to make Boonesboro the capitol of the Transylvania Company in Kentucky and thusly, the capitol of Kentucky. The first legislature of a sort, was called and held at Boonesboro. However, Boonesboro and the company were much too unpopular for any consideration to be given after the collapse of the company.

The idea of Boonesboro did not die altogether. During the 1790s, Robert Clark, Junior and Senior, John Holder, William Calk (Montgomery County's pioneer), Robert McMillan, James French, Robert Elkin and Philip Bush along with a group of Madison County men headed by Green Clay pushed for Boonesboro with an offer of land and money. The effort failed. There is no record of how it was received or what happened to it. Green Clay was one of the powers in the state legislature, but unfortunately for him, he was on the wrong side of the political battles.

For quite sometime, Danville seemed to be the logical place for a capitol, but then Lexington and Louisville both were growing and demanding the capitol for them. Frankfort was a project of James Wilkerson among others. It was along the river at a point where it was navigable all times through the year. There was adequate space between the cliffs for a sizable town and though there was constant flood danger, it was not as bad as Boonesboro. However, no matter how one added up the advantages of Frankfort as a town or as a capitol, they could not surpass Louisville or Lexington. It's one advantage lay in the rivalry between Louisville and Lexington and the dislike of the rest of the state for both cities. Frankfort was an unhappy compromise on which all parties could agree.

The need for a new capitol building opened the controversy again. The climax for the political struggle came in 1894.

Meanwhile, quite apart from this struggle for a state capitol, Clark County was trying to get its boundary straightened. In the fall of 1891, D. J. Pendleton, who was county surveyor for many of the years after the Civil War, was secured to resurvey the line. This he did with the same results as all the other surveyors. The Clark people took it before a hearing in Frankfort. Pendleton had surveyed the line from south to north, from the mouth of Boones Creek to the Bourbon County line. The Fayette representative demanded that Pendleton describe the line from north to south which he could not do. Fayette County attacked the survey as erronious.

In a speech, the Fayette County legislature roared with amusement and solemnly offered to support Clark County's claim if they would agree to move their county line a little further to the left so that it would take in the home and farm of a potential rival for the State Senate. The legislature filled with laughter at the joke and Clark County's claim was ignored.

Furious but impotent, Clark County was left in the cold. Meanwhile the debate over the proposed new capitol reached new heights. So engrossed in the combat that the two cities did not notice that William Beckner, then representative of Clark County, introduced a bill making Winchester the new state capitol and forced a vote in the lower house. To everyone's amazement, Winchester beat Lexington by 31 votes, Louisville by 29 and Frankfort by 11. The legislature also appropriated $500,000 to start the capitol.

Lexington and Louisville were shaken to the bottom of their ballot boxes. The State Senate was suddenly adjourned for the day before a vote could be taken. By the time the Senate met, the Louisville and Lexington people had reorganized. Beckner withdrew his bill and Winchester threw its support to Lexington. This time the southeastern part of the state, the Republican faction which was growing steadily in power during these years, tried to make Lebanon the state capitol. This failed, but it did bring both sides to the realization that Frankfort was still the only place in the state, that all could agree to be the state capitol. Winchester and her hopes of being the state capitol died. The idea wasn't too bad. Winchester was a railroad center. It was high and dry and out of flood danger. It had all the arguments that Lexington had. It did not have the political power. She lost the state capitol and her county line was not straightened out.

In 1914, Stephen Davis, then county attorney took up the issue but got nowhere. The people who inhabited the little cut into Clark County territory had no desire to be Clark Countians. Fayette County was not about to lose them.

Since that time, R. W. Craft and Rodney Thompson when they were city and county attorneys since World War II, made some effort to straighten the boundary. In each case the issue never was able to get off the ground.

The situation remains the same. The error in the original survey is admitted by all, but after 150 years and in the face of Fayette County opposition there is no change. However, we submit, had it not been for those 9 square miles, Lexington would have been the state capitol of Kentucky.

## WINCHESTER

Winchester was chosen as the county seat of Clark County. It is impossible to ferret out all the reasons. There is no doubt that John Baker's salesmanship had much to do with it. No other station had thought out so carefully their proposition. Mt. Sterling had been incorporated and had made some steps toward becoming a city, but had not reached the point of planning that Baker had. A glance at other central Kentucky cities very quickly shows the genius of Baker's planning. Main Street was unusually wide and it was crossed by an unusually wide cross street. Despite the hills, the original blocks were largely square, the streets were straight and the plan neat. The public building space given was centrally located and generous. The only other city in the central part of Kentucky that showed the same forethought in building was Lexington itself.

Partly, because Winchester was not a living community, gave the spot added advantage. It could be developed from scratch. It was also some three miles deeper into Clark County than Strode's Station and more centrally located in the heavist populated area. Three miles might not sound like a great deal in an era of automobiles, but three miles was an hour's walk or three quarters of an hour ride. What Winchester did not have, was central location in the expanded county. Once Montgomery and Estill Counties were cut out of Clark County, Winchester became reasonably located in the center of Clark County.

Winchester, as county seat, immediately took on life. As the county seat, it played host to perhaps half the county's population at least once a year. These people would come to court, to business deals, to sell animals, to meet friends, to train for the militia. They had to be housed if they stayed overnight, fed, and refreshed. Because Winchester overnight became a center of population, there were opportunities for stores, blacksmiths, leather merchants, wood and coal yards, tanneries, haberdasheries. The community would need lawyers, doctors, teachers and the like. It was a town that had to grow. Many of the landowners who would visit Winchester often would find it expedient to own a town house as well as a family house. Some of them would find it simpler to live in town and visit the farm than live on the farm and visit town. Widows would find the town house a better place than the rural isolation. Winchester was bound to grow.

Therefore, when one says that in 1797, Winchester consisted of a dozen log houses, the importance of these could not be ignored. Several would be taverns which refreshed, fed and housed. Their owners were respectable and influential businessmen as such owners are not today. New people were moving in regularly. In 1797, Peter and James Flannigan moved to Winchester. Three years later, James Flannigan was to build a horse powered grist mill for Josiah Hart. Prior to this time, it had been necessary to go to Brandenburg's mill on Stoner or any of the half dozen mills on Lower Howard Creek. A horse power mill could not do a large business but it made it possible for the residents to take care of their individual needs. Peter Plannigan would build in 1804 another log cabin tavern that would start a history of hostelry that would not end until 1976.

It would not be until 1808 that James Sympson would build the first brick house in Winchester. There were many already built in the county. John Ward would be the second, using it for a home and tavern combined.

The center of everything would be the courthouse. The square on which the courthouse stood originally would include the block where the courthouse is, the McEldowney and Post Office, and the buildings behind the present courthouse to Maple Street. The courthouse would be the center of town until the railroads came to the edges of town to build their stations. Then the center would shift and the court buildings would lose some of their importance. But that was still seventy years away.

Mical Taul's memories are found in the Kentucky Historical Society's Quarterly, Vol. 27, 1929. It describes the pre-1800 Winchester. If the town, Winchester, had but seventeen or so cabins, it was a roaring little village. Its taverns were open most of the night. Fights were common. Horses were raced on the downtown streets. Dogs, pigs and mud were everywhere. To the rustic, living far out of town, now that the Indian danger was over, Winchester must have appeared an utterly new world, and for the grim faced Calvinistic preachers, it must have been very close to what John Strode feared it would become...a den of iniquity.

The first trustees of Winchester were, naturally, appointed by the Governor. In later times there would be elections for the trustees but the elections would have no official standing. These met at Baker's tavern, February 6, 1794. They included Richard Hickman, who was chairman. The chairman of the trustees could hardly be called mayor. The others were David Bullock who was county clerk, Josiah Hart, Benjamin Combs and Hubbard Taylor. There may have been others, William Bush probably. If these names are familiar, it is not surprising. The small group of men that dominated Clark County seemed to appear in other offices as soon as they were established.

New laws had to be established for the city. There was to be no washing or rinsing of clothes within thirty feet of the public spring. The fine would be three shillings. No one could water his horse, mare or gelding within thirty feet of the spring. No one could use a dirty bucket, pail or tub...this referred to the outside of the bucket which was to be dipped into the spring. If a child was guilty of any of these crimes, his parents would be held liable for the fines. The problem of safe-guarding the water supply was the first major problem for the trustees. Unfortunately, all the old records save those that accidently turn up in deeds and wills have been lost.

Winchester was not an organized community, Bullock resigned as town clerk and is replaced first with Richard Jones and then later with Samuel Taylor. The next list of trustees for Winchester were in 1796, Robert McKinney, Robert Hogge, John Hood, Thomas Scott, John Lander, John Ireland, Josiah Hart and James Campbell. William Smith replaced Thomas Scott who had probably moved out of town or perhaps up to the county court for there are now no county magistrates on the city trustee board. McKinney was the second chairman....or possibly we might give him the credit of the second mayor.

There is no list of trustees for 1797, though the deeds showed John Buner, John Baker and John Frame as trustees among others.

The list of 1797 included John Hood, Robert Higgins, William Smith, Josiah Hart, John Crawford, Robert Jones, John Ireland and Dillard Collins. There was no report of who was chairman though usually the first name was so considered.

Josiah Hart was chairman of the trustees in 1798....though now they referred to him as President. John Lander, John Ireland, William Smith, of the old board, and James Simpson. Robert Higgins, Dillard Collins and Joseph Arthur were added. The next year, Hart was still President and the board included McKinney, Higgins, John Hood, John Stevens, John Loveland, and Jonathan Baden. Whether there is any significance in the substantial change in trustees is not reported. There is a faint chance that the election of Garrard Governor is finally reaching into local politics.

We have no list for 1799, but in 1800, the trustees were Thomas Scott, James Ward, James Spillman, James Sympson, John Hood, Peter Flannigan, John Bruner and George Webb. Ward, Hood, Flannigan and Webb either were or had an interest in tavern owners. In 1797, Higgins was just coming into his own after being deputy under Martin. Sympson was his deputy. Dillard Collins was to become sheriff and was now a magistrate.

Beside the settlement around the courthouse, there was also considerable industrial development some three to five miles south of Winchester on Lower Howard's Creek. The approximate location would be the 1976 community of Forest Grove which was earlier called Germantown. Some have called it the largest concentration of industry west of the mountains. Cottrell reports factories that made iron and wood items, tanneries (Bruner owned one), several grist and saw mills, carding factories and hempwalks. It was a rough area with cabins and shanties squatting along the creek and hill sides.

Fights were common. Into this area crowded the later immigrant who did not wish to farm or had not the fortitude to carve out his own land. Many of them were Germans which at this time began to pour into Kentucky from the Netherlands and the German states. Several had been Hessians in the British Army, left behind after the war.

Mical Taul adds to the picture of Winchester before 1800 in his memories. A common pasttime which the clerks in the stores, the loafers around the courthouse, and the customers at the taverns, would partake was pitching bullets on a line. This is identical to the pitching of pennies found today in areas where there is, momentarily, little to do. Wrestling was a number one sport. There was no skill, no holds, no methods, just brute force against brute force which quite often ended just this side of mayhem. Many a man had an ear bitten off, an eye gouged out, or hair yanked out by the roots. Most wrestling was on a friendly basis and no hard feelings. Fist fights were common and formed an appreciated part of the town's recreation. Usually fights of this nature were not as friendly as the wrestling and the worst kind would combine the best and worst features both of fist fights and wrestling. Very little was done to stop these fights as long as they were reasonably balanced and it was not gentleman against rough neck...unless the gentleman was willing which often they were.

Cock fighting was a favorite spectator sport. It was also the major source of gambling. Most every man who had any property at all, kept a few fighting cocks, and the most prized slave in many a man's possession was the one who grew and trained his fighting cocks. There was a small amphitheatre built in a lower corner of the courtyard behind the courthouse cabin which could provide comfortable seating for between twenty to a hundred spectators.

Horse racing was the most popular participant sport. Nearly everyone had horses. Good horses turned up in Kentucky from the east almost as soon as men did. Racing on Main Street was a common and daily, almost hourly, occurrence. These races were not formal. They started when two or more men started arguing, usually over the ever present corn whiskey, as to the merits of their animals. To solve these arguments, the men would boil out of the taverns, line up along the street, and the race was on. There is a tradition that Winchester streets, as Main and Broadway in Lexington, were deliberately made unusually wide so that horse racing and the usual traffic could go on simultaneously. Sometimes the ladies would complain that racing made the streets dangerous for pedestrians. No one paid much attention to them. There were no fine carriages or even well built wagons in Clark County until well into the 1800s. Some farmers built home-made ox carts, usually of the two wheel varieties, but even these were few and far between. The streets then were virtually left to the horseman.

Marksmanship was very important. Most men carried rifles wherever they went well into the 1800s. This wasn't just for protection from Indians, but to shoot a little game on the way to and from town. Most of these rifles were made by various craftsmen... Squire Boone and John Strode were both gunsmiths....and varied greatly in their effectiveness. Shooting matches were common. Pistols were yet something that only a cavalry man could carry... too large and cumbersome when a man could carry a much more effective rifle....and were usually single shot. Dueling pistols were another affair. These were usually finely made and most every "gentleman" had a pair. Dueling became illegal under the Constitution and even today, a public official from the lowest to the Governor must swear that he never fought a duel. The oath like many which the government forced on people, was not really obeyed. However, though there were Clark Countians in duels, there has been no record yet found of a duel fought in Winchester. There may well have been some, but several were fought in the county.

There were, however, constant shootings, knifings, the knife was still more or less a heavy version of a butcher knife, homemade by some blacksmith. The famous Bowie knife was still twenty years away. There are several shootings and fights that will be recorded in later volumes. Violence is very much a part of the American tradition. Perhaps it is wrong, but part of the vitality and the power of these early men can be traced to violence. Only the strong and the able survived. This was a period when the Harpe brothers were terrorizing the Natchez Trail and western Kentucky. Violence even on a violent frontier could get out of hand. However, within limits, it eliminated the unfit and put a premium on intelligence and physical ability. It also meant that courage was common for a man that was afraid, stayed home in England or at least on the east coast.

One story that comes from this period, however, which appeared in the Comb's family records kept by Dr. Doyle is about Ben Combs. This was quite a man...one of the first to settle Indian Fields, Indian fighter, rough and tumble brawler, successful in business and planter. He obviously stood well with the establishment for he is included in the Winchester trustees. The story for what it is worth is that as an old man, in his late eighties or nineties... some versions even make him a hundred...got into a fight with four Bush brothers...who were never named. In the course of the fight, Comb's throat was cut. The tradition is that he grasped his spouting juglar vein with his fingers...some say he dictated his will... but all agreed that he told those standing around...."now, you will see how a man should die...." released his vein and bled to death. Another version reported by Kathryn Owen was that Samuel Richardson Combs, sone of Ben, who was murdered by the Bushs'. S. R. Combs was John Holder's son-in-law having married Theodoria Holder. Whether he made the traditional famous statement is not reported.

The bleeding hearts can cry all they want, but violence breeds a certain amount of vitality that the gentler people lose.

Behind all of this is the tavern which is so important in this period that we have dedicated a whole section to it. The tavern is the heart and center of these communities. The tavern was the political party, the social club, the psychologist's couch, the newspaper and the public opinion maker...its importance overshadowed all.

# WINCHESTER IN THE 1800s

Winchester was a vital, exciting little town in 1800, despite its smallness in size, certainly not more than 400 people. In 1812, the figure was put at 412. There probably was very little real growth during this twelve year period, though if one added the industrial section that lay unincorporated outside the city limits, Winchester might well have touched a thousand. Even four hundred and twelve people made Winchester the seventh largest town in Kentucky, behind Louisville, Lexington, Harrodsburg, Danville, Paris and Washington, though not in that order. Still in those days, it must have seemed a metropolis.

In 1801, the trustees were John Landers, Thomas Scott, Clem Wood, Jonathan Baker, John Hood, James Sympson, James Spillman, John Brunner, Peter Flanigan and George Webb. Landers was probably the President.

In 1804, the trustees were Robert Clark (does not say senior or junior, but presumedly the son), John Landers, John Martin, Peter Flanigan, James Clark, James Spillman, John Hood, Jonathan Baker and George Webb. Landers was still President despite the order of names in the list.

He remained President the next year when Robert Clark, James Sympson, John Ward, Peter Flanigan, John Martin, James Clark, James Spillman, Thomas Scott, Samuel Tipton, Josiah Hart and Anthony Pool served with him.

Landers evidently was the President for about five years during this period. The honor does not necessarily mean that Landers had great importance. Being President of the trustees of Winchester was scarcely that important. Still it does show that he enjoyed a certain respect during this period. We see certain names appearing repeatedly in this list.

First of these repeaters were the tavern keepers or owners. John Hood and John Ward appear often. Martin and Webb also operated taverns, though more in the background. Peter Flanigan operated a tavern until the end of the War of 1812 when he went into banking. Merchants such as Hart and Robert Clark appeared regularly. Other merchants in Winchester had their homes out in the country and were not usually found among the trustees. There are new comers appearing among the trustees and then disappearing. It was a restless age, and men were looking for opportunity. They would move into a community, stay a few years, and then move on somewhere else seeking better opportunity. The confusion of land titles helped this movement. It would be another fifteen years before a man could buy a piece of property with assurance that it would not be challenged. Titles in Indiana, Illinois, and west of the Mississippi in Iowa and Missouri were far more secure, having been protected by the bitter lessons learned in Kentucky and Tennessee. So Clem Wood in 1801, Anthony Pool and Samuel Tipton in 1805, appeared for a few years and then moved elsewhere.

The Acts of 1813 legalized the accepted system of local election whereby the citizens could nominate and elect their own trustees. These elections were spasmodic and often omitted. The Governor either before or after the Act of 1813 was not bound to the winner. According to this law, however, any person who was male and over 20, and who had lived in Winchester for three months could vote. The trustees had to be residents of Winchester. The first Monday in June was chosen as election day. At this time, the trustees were limited to five. In addition, the town would elect a clerk and a tax accessor. Election was, in most cases, tantamont to being in office.

The same act gave Winchester control over the Market House and the ownership and control of the land within thirty feet of the spring which was the main source of water for the community. Cisterns and wells were not yet being dug.

The trustees did not have a great deal of power. They had virtually no taxing power of their own, but depended largely on the county for many services. They had the right to license and to collect fines. This gave them a very limited amount of money to spend. They were responsible for law and order within the city limits. This was done largely through a constable appointed by the county court to take care of Winchester. There is no indication of exactly when the constable ceased being a county officer and became strictly a town officer. This happened some time after the War of 1812.

We find the city struggling with the problem of her streets. This also was, at this time, a county problem, but it was always and mainly a city problem from the beginning. Even without wagons and other vehicles to rut a road, the city streets were quickly to become a bog. Board walks were built across them by 1812 to permit pedestrians a chance to cross without mudding their feet. These walks were always being broken up. Ox carts became more numerous after 1800 and an occasional wagon was making its appearance. Wilkerson came back from the east with a carriage and soon others appeared. Both wagons and carriages soon would be produced locally. One of the Smith's along Howard's Creek had combined with a saw mill and was beginning to make wagons. These would break up the boards, drive them deeper into the mud, and to make matters worse, in winter time they would occasionally be stolen for fire wood.

Winchester did not grow much between 1800 and 1812. Lots were still being sold from the original plot as late as 1811. However, Winchester had grown beyond its suburbs. High Street had been developed on both sides of the street as had Water (Maple) Street. Houses were reaching down the Boonesboro Road connecting the industrial district. James Clark built his house beyond the edge of town, and yet the town was beginning to reach out towards him.

The town trustees in 1806 included Josiah Hart, John Ward, James Sympson, Thomas Scott, Peter Flanigan, Anthony Pool, James Spillman, John Martin, John Bruner, Robert Clark, James Clark, John Lander and Samuel Taylor....12 trustees. There were fifteen in 1808, William Miller, James Duncan and Jonathan Baker being added. Robert Clark had died. One report said that there were eighteen trustees in 1809. Evidently the custom was to add any new man in town that appeared worthy without dropping anyone of the old court. However, the state law changed that and we find that in 1810 only five trustees....Thomas Scott, John Bruner, James Sympson, John Ward and Thomas Pickett. Pickett was dropped in 1812 and Anthony Pool was added.

Several of the prominent Winchester businessmen, such as Nicholas George, George Taylor, John Ward, etc..were county magistrates. At last there seems to be objections to men holding too many appointive posts. However, there still was no law against it since Scott was also a magistrate. Bruner had been a businessman in the town for twenty years, running a tannery. He had apparently no upward ambitions and was a steady, dependable man. Ward represented the tavern influence which still was recognized as one of the most important community institutions. We might note, however, that already there were three types of taverns or ordinaries. Just what the distinction is between an ordinary and a tavern is not clear. The term seemed to be used alternatively and yet with some differences. Ordinaries were earlier, taverns later. It had something to do with providing food as well as drink. Most taverns also kept rooms for overnight guests. There were growing distinctions between the taverns and ordinaries in the industrial area which were rough and even dangerous to visit if one was a stranger, and the tavern in the town itself that catered to the courthouse group. Ward was one of the best of these. Sympson was still the lawman of Winchester. Sheriffs came and went, but Sympson remained deputy doing much of the work.

## LIFE BETWEEN 1790 AND 1800

It is the purpose of this section, and similar sections in other decades to make an effort to draw a picture of the life of the county in that period of time designated. Many of the incidents reported will probably not be of historic interest, but they will be part of the life of the people of the time. It is not easy to get information of this sort for the period before the War of 1812 and after the Indian troubles. There were letters and memories of the pioneer fathers in their travail with Indians and wild animals, but this particular period does not attract too much interest. Later, there would be a few old men who would remember back to 1812 and afterward whose memories would be printed in newspapers before their death. There would even be an occasional newspaper to keep reports fresh and contemporary.

At this time, however, there was only one newspaper and that was Lexington's KENTUCKY GAZETTE. Micro film files can be found for it at the University and in the Lexington Library. Unfortunately, the Gazette is more interested in the maneuvering of Napoleon's armies and the political situation in London than the situation in Clark County. It would report an Indian attack briefly on the Ohio River, but it would dedicate pages to speeches given by Congress or the State Legislature. It would also occasionally give reports of incidents that were happening in Boston or New York or Charleston, but it has no interest in Winchester and very little in Lexington. The best information it had to offer was largely in ads. One could catch a glimpse of what was happening by an ad now and then from Clark County. The reason for this lack of news no doubt would be that everyone knew what was happening in Lexington and Winchester and what was happening wasn't really important anyways.

The best source of information about Clark County during this period comes from the county court records. Unfortunately, these give only an official report and it requires a little imagination to fill in the details. Normally the plan for these sections on life in other volumes is chronological, but for this section we will follow more or less a typical arrangement. The county court reports many interesting items, most of them routine. We generally pick some examples of the routine and report them.

A second source of information are the governor's papers on micro film in the historical society. During this particular period the papers of Isaac Shelby and James Garrard are available. Unfortunately, they are not systematically organized from the point of view of this book. It is interesting, however, that certain family names belong to certain counties. Once one is familiar with these names, a few appearing, for example, in a list of militia officers, will identify the home county of that list. Once again, there is not a lot of detail, which we filled in after some high level speculation.

Undoubtedly, the other records, the deed books for example, would hold information, but they hold so little that is new or different, that time and space does not present opportunities to use them to the fullest.

By the time that Kentucky is settled, marriage had become a legal ceremony that required state attention. Marriage licenses were not to be required until another forty years, but both ministers and marriages had to be registered with the county government. Robert Elkin was the first minister to register. There were four Baptist ministers, including Robert Clark, registered before the first non-Baptist, Lawrence Owen, a Methodist, was registered. Donald How, a Presbyterian, was registered early. Later, we have such men as David Lyle and John Kavannaugh registered, Presbyterian and Episcopalian. It is obvious, however, that some of those ministers who registered to marry in Clark County never held churches within the county. It is also obvious that only a small handful of ministers ever bothered to register and evidently the county never seriously enforced this requirement. Even as late as 1865, ministers were marrying in Clark County without listing themselves on county records and nothing was ever said.

This brings up the interesting question as to how many early Kentuckians actually did get married, and how many just quietly moved into a family situation. Certainly the churches represented a relatively small part of the population. Ministers were few and far between. Interestingly enough, there is very little evidence that the magistrates married often. A scattering of names, William Bush married about four couples, James Sympson later as magistrate was to marry a few. However, the numbers were very few. There were not a lot of ministers available in this decade. Later, about the War of 1812, there would be ministers behind every hillock and in every dale. Religion also at this period was not influential. The great revivals that would shake the frontier were yet to come. It was not unusual for a circuit minister to appear in a community and marry two or three couples with children in their arms.

Likewise, one wonders how many marriages were never reported. It is obvious from the records that some ministers, James Quisenberry, for example, often would not report his marriages until months after they occurred and then put them in the record by a list. Sometimes these delinquent reports would not have dates showing that the minister was forgetting. How many simply were not reported, much to the annoyance of some geneologically oriented descendants trying to trace down a line.

The first mrriage in the county on the record books was performed by Robert Elkin to Nathanial Vice and Elizabeth White.

Elkin also married the second couple, George Routt and Margaret Holder. Jilson Payne, who was a magistrate, though he came from a preaching family, performed the next two, William Taes to Suzanna Higgins and Michael Pault to Betty Hughs.

A few marriages at random were James Hazelrigg to Lucy Fleming, October 30, 1793, by William Payne. Payne was a Baptist minister who helped organize and may have served Goshen Baptist Church and possibly Lullbegrud Baptist Church, but spent most of his ministry in the Brachen Association. May 8, 1794, Robert Elkin married Andrew Goff and Anne Cocker. The next year, December 20, 1795, David Brandinburg was married to Agnes Morton by Elkin. James Rash married Mary Terrell, August 11, 1796, by W. E. Waller. Waller's name does not appear in any of the available church records nor is he a county magistrate. James Quisenberry married William Dunaway to Margaret Bradshaw, August 4, 1796. Quisenberry was a Baptist and Dunaway was to become one of the early local ministers of the Methodist movement. There were Methodist ministers available at this time, Owen, Kavanaugh among others. Perhaps Dunaway had not yet been won. A Donald Holmes married Andrew Downing and Emma Cochran, February 2, 1797. Holmes is another of the names that is never listed in the available sources, yet he married some four or five couples. John Conkwright married Nettie Lewis, June 4, 1799 by James Quisenberry. Assuming our names are correct, John Conkwright was to be one of the most successful of the local Methodist ministers in the next forty years. There is a possibility that the minister Conkwright could be a son. The problem of the same name always haunts the county historian who is not writing genology.

William Payne married John Hulse and Mary Anne Davenport, June 23, 1800.

A side interest is names. Suzanna, Anne, Deborah, Rachell were very common women's names for the period. William, John, James, etc.., were even more common than today among the men. Biblical names, Isaac, Mordecai, Abraham, etc.., would appear occasionally, but not in large numbers.

Any government had to have lawyers. The government is so set up that lawyers are necessary in order that a simple man can get justice. Since the business of a lawyer is the law and therefore, governemnt, he has the time and it is in his interest to take the time, to be interested in politics. In order to serve before a court, the lawyer had to receive some type of legal recognition. Many of these lawyers would appear before the county court to receive permission to practice in Clark County. There are those that do not appear in the records, but this was probably an oversight on a clerk's part for so important a requirement would not have been just ignored. For example, there is no place in the record studied that Henry Clay was ever formally admitted to the Clark County courts.

The first to register was Keith Marshall who was Clark County's first assistant United Stated Attorney, the equivalent to a county prosecutor. The second to qualify was Patterson Bullock. We note that in the January Court of 1796, that James Brown, who was the first Kentucky Senator, Levi Todd and Isaac Barnett were also registered. Bullock and Todd were to be the most influential lawyers at this time in Clark County. Levi Todd would follow Marshall as the United States Attorney. Todd was paid 12 shillings for his services. None of these early lawyers lived in Clark County. Bullock kept residence of sorts with his relatives. Bullock became Assistant United States Attorney in 1799. It would not be for another decade that lawyers would actually live in Clark County.

The first Clark County bar is quite late in this period. It included James Clark, George Webb, Chilton Allan, James Simpson, Richard French, Ryland Dillard, Robert Wickliffe, John C. Childs, and P. B. Hockaday. This could not have been much earlier than the end of the War of 1812. Even many of these names are not Clark Countians. Webb, Allan, Simpson and Clark were. French lived on the county line and chose Clark County for the early part of his legal practice before moving to Montgomery. Hockaday had much the same situation in the Fayette-Clark County area, but probably lived in Fayette County.

Prior to this, most of the lawyers lived in Fayette County and commuted, certainly this was true before 1800. George Webb and James Simpson would be the first local lawyers to appear in the 1800s.

We noted that Robert Trimble was admitted before 1800 to practice before the bar in Clark County. Trimble was from an established Clark and Montgomery County family, but he practiced mostly in Bourbon County. He would eventually become a Supreme Court Justice.

There are two kinds of juries, then and now. The Grand Jury's task was to study the evidence to see if arrested criminals ought to be brought to trial. They were not concerned with guilt or innocence as much as whether on the fact of the evidence there was a case against the arrested man. Their job was also to investigate any question of illegal actions on part of the county officials, to see that the county was being handled in an efficient and capable manner, and to make recommendations on anything that the jury felt needed to be reported on. Usually the Grand Jury indicted those who needed indicting and did not pay much attention to the county situation. After all, the jury was usually part of the establishment and was not about to begin to look under every rock for some wrongdoing. Also, on the whole, the membership of the Grand Jury was that of nonlegal rank and file. Unless there was some official, a prosecuting attorney for example, or a rare fellow juror with some legal knowledge, most Grand Juries would not know how to investigate wrong doing. Occasionally, however, a Grand Jury would stir the situation as they did in 1796 about the condition of the roads.

The Petit Jury was chosen for each case to be tried and concerned itself only with the case, either civil or criminal before it. During these days there were all kinds of juries, coroner juries to investigate the causes of death, juries to decide on the legality of an application for a mill pond, and most anything else. There is no report on how the juries were selected, but there is evidence that most of them were made up of men who just happened to qualify and be avialable. Then, like now, there would be men who would hang around the courthouse just seeing what happened. We find, for example, Absolum Hanks (a relation of Abraham's mother) on six juries in a row over a three year period. In any of the taverns, there were usually those who would be eligible and willing to sit on a trial. After all, the court system was the greatest show available to the bored and isolated frontiersmen. Imagine, no T.V., no radios, no newspapers, no movies. Each jury had a foreman who was, technically, in charge of the jury.

The first Grand Jury met in 1793. Daniel Ramey was foreman. Richard Hickman, John Frame, James Hazelrigg, Nicholas George, Thomas Burrus, Achilles Eubank, Philip Bush, John Vivion, James Eubank, Jacob Keitley, James McQuin, William Trimble, David Highs, David Martin and William Gray were the other members. Such a list is to blue ribbon a list of Clark Countians to be accidential. They must have been very aware that they were Clark County's first Grand Jury. They found nothing to present, however, and were discharged. The first petit or trial jury included William Braun as foreman, Jim Yates, William Ellis, Denis Burkham, John Huddleston, John Jones, John Young, John Frame, Benjamin Eli, Jerome Wilson, James Hulse and Francis Price.

The first trial was held in John Strode's house or tavern in 1793. Jacob Croswaithe, who seemed to have a knack of staying in trouble, was charged with stealing Rachel Hedrick's horse. Later John Petty would be called before a Grand Jury charged with stealing Daniel O'Hara's horse. John Wood made the mistake of stealing the sheriff's horse. Both were sent to higher courts. Horse stealing seems to be very common in these days.

A trial of John Middletown versus Waller Cunningham forced Middletown to pay sixteen pounds, three shillings and ten pounds of tobacco. In another case, Jonathan Holland versus David Harrow, Harrow had to pay thirty pounds, nine shillings and 110 pounds of tobacco. We will return to these monetary units in a few paragraphs.

Witnesses were also paid. In 1794, William Wilson had to pay his witness, Hezekiah Harrison, six pounds, five shillings for one days attendance plus riding to and from the court, in a case of William Wilson versus Levi Lockhart. He paid John Morgan, Theodore Arnett, Lucus Hood, Robert Butler, James Morrow, Andrew Hood, Daniel Shosberry and John Burham as witnesses in the same trial.

There is no doubt that Clark County was a rough county. In 1793, Stephen Kelly and Linchfield Sharp were indicted for breach of peace. Also were Joseph Whiteside and William Browser. In 1795, Pleasant Hendrick broke the peace. There were tax suits entered against John and Thomas Strode and against James Williams, Archibald Crawford and John Jones were charged with breaking into the house of Elias Tobin and stealing iron utensils. This would be an interesting case to know more of, since both Crawford and Jones were men of considerable prestige in the community and related to strong families. They were found innocent.

Grand Jury foreman included James Quisenberry in 1793, Robert McMillan in 1794, William Trimble in 1795. The rest of the 1795 jury included William Reid, Elias Tolen, Anthony Griffin, Macajah Clark, William Moffatt, James Young, Allen Bibley and Jesse Bledsoe. In 1796, Robert Doughterty and Garland Bullock headed grand juries. William Trimble was again foreman of a grand jury in 1797. Jesse Bledsoe would be Secretary of State in the Charles Scott administration.

Grand Jury in 1798 had Charles Teeter as foreman and included Charles Stewart, John Quisenberry, John Skinner, Truman Marshall, Charles Gentry, Henry Landers, Henry Welch, William Martin, Ambrose Christy, Leonard Hall, James Stewart, A. Bronough, Robert Wallace and Isaac Reese.

The worst crime in Clark County which at this time extended all the way back to Cumberland Gap occurred in July of 1793. As one went back up the Red River beyond what is now Stanton, the country was virtually untouched. B. C. Caudell tells the story in "Remembering Lee County".

July of 1793, Michael Stoner, James Harrard and a man named Bridges were in this wilderness near what would later be called Three Forks hunting for Swift's Lost Silver Mine...Swift was still alive and no one seemed to question his story. For some reason, Stoner remained in camp on the morning in question while Bridges and Harrard went out hunting. Sometime during the morning, Stoner reported that he heard distant shots and later Bridges came rushing into camp saying that Indians had killed Harrard and that they were in danger. This was country that was open to Cherokee raids, and Stoner left with Bridges never doubting his word. Sometime later, Bridges tried to sell some gold buttons. These buttons were identified by Mrs. Harrard as being on the hunting jacket that her husband had worn. Harrard's body was not found, and Caudill's tale fails to tell whether Bridges was ever tried for the crime. It was assumed that Bridges murdered Harrard for some reason and tried to blame the Indians.

All of this court system required a jail and there came a hitch in the organization of the county. John Baker had agreed to provide land for a jail in his proposed building of the county seat. The November court authorized a call for bids for the buiding of the jail in the KENTUCKY GAZETTE. At this point, something goes wrong, for either there were no bids or they wanted more than the county wanted to pay. At any rate, the March Court of 1794, paid Nathanial Saunders 156 pennies for being in charge of Thomas Harris in his own home while Harris was in custody. Obviously a jail was needed and the May Court appointed William Sudduth, John Bush and John Baker to draw up plans for a jail or gaol as it was then called. Plans were drawn but there were no bids upon them, so a second less expensive plan was drawn. There appeared in the minutes of the May, 1794 court plans for stocks. These would be two sills, 10' long, 14" square. Two posts were to be emplaced 10' high, to be braced 5' from the platform to form an A. The prisoners hands would be fastened to the cross bars of the A. There was no way that a prisoner could sit down or take care of his special needs. This was relatively simple, and we find the July Court, 1794, paying Rice Pendleton for building the stocks. The jail, however, remained unbuilt.

In 1795, Hubbard Taylor, Dillard Clark and (a name unrecognizable in the records) Bullock were authorized to draw up still another set of plans. It is possible that something was built because some sources say the jail was built in 1796.

The court did not hear about it, however, or what was built was unsatisfactory. In 1797, the home of John Hood was made the jail. Higgins, the new sheriff, appeared before the court and protested the inadequacy of the jail. This was to become a routine function of each new sheriff. Presumedly, by making this protest before there was an escape, they freed themselves from responsibility. In passing, we note that the sheriff was also responsible to see that the courthouse was cleaned. This responsibility was passed, by Higgins, to John Hood. Hood also ran a tavern in Winchester. Politics being what they are, after Dillard Collins became sheriff in 1799, Hood was replaced both as jailer and keeper of the courthouse by another tavern keeper, Edmond Callaway. Even as he did so, Collins protested that Calloway's house was not adequate. Why tavern keepers? As for cleaning of the courthouse, both Hood and Calloway had several slaves or indentured servants that were used in the stables and taverns for the purpose of cleaning as well as several employees in more responsible jobs. This gave to a tavern keeper of a large labor supply that could easily take on the extra work. In addition, the tavern keeper would have one or two reinforced rooms in which whiskey and other valuable merchandise could be placed and locked. It would be a simple matter to clean one of these rooms out for temporary placing of a prisoner. If he was chained with leg irons, even these could be fastened to the wall. Later Winchester would become a relatively important slave market. Even at this date there would be places again controlled by the tavern keepers because their facilities would be demanded to house and feed chains of slaves and their owners and guards. This movement of slaves either for sale in the Kentucky areas or to be transported southward to the larger markets in the deep south were just beginning to appear at this time. We note that in 1796, the county paid John Hood for making hand cuffs and fettors.

The county did not often have prisoners that could not be kept in the stocks. In 1799, the court reported that a Robert Toulgier had both ears bitten off in a fight. They did not seem to have the man that did it, and were not much upset by the incidents. Fights often included biting, butting and stumping. In October the court decided, frustrated, that it did need a jail and would build one on the old site, presumedly the 1796 site. There was no report what happened to that jail, but it may have burned immediately after it was built. Josiah Hart was contracted to build a new jail so the century ended with no real jail.

In passing we have noted that John Strode was the first county coroner. In Clark County he was a relatively minor official whose major task was to decide how a person who died unexpectedly, died. Strode either resigned or was not reappointed coroner in 1795, his place being taken by William Craig. There are a few faint hints that John Strode was on the wrong side of the political battles of the day. The May Court, 1798, reported that Benjamin Wheeler was coroner.

Besides the sheriff, Clark County had for each magistrate a constable. The first constables in 1792 were Augustus Webb, William Harris and Peter Terrill. Actually, there were never as many constables as magistrates and there was not a recognizable relationship until after the 1849 Constitution. The constable was a law enforcing officer that might come close to being a policeman in a community like Winchester, but he was more of a process server than a law officer. On the whole, they were so minor that his history has not seriously tried to keep tract of them other than as they appeared in some record. However, in 1793, Augustus Webb, William Harris, Peter Dewitt, Richard Wills, Samuel Plumer, William Owlsey, Peter Dewitt, Jr. and Matthew Lander were constables. In 1794, Martin Elliott and John Cooner were listed as constables though presumedly most of the former were still on duty and these two were replacements. In 1795, the constables were William Johnson, John Evans, John Dykes, Isam Wright, William Jennings, Philip Dethridge, Julius Watts, John Harris and William Willard. John Dykes becomes a figure in the law enforcing groups in Clark County for the next fifteen years. Dykes will turn up as a constable or a deputy second only to James Sympson.

In 1797, the constables had among them Robert Campbell and John Young.

Dillard Collins divided the county up into four districts and assigned a constable to each district. William Witt was assigned the third district, but withdrew and was replaced by Henry Dooley. John Young was constable of the third district. John Dykes was assigned to the first which was mostly Winchester. The district system never worked out and if new constables had districts they were not mentioned in the records. The county was being crossed and criss-crossed with districts for constables, patrols, tax purposes, welfare, etc... The boundaries of the districts were usually in terms of property owned, from so and so far, down the road to this and that, and...

Another law enforcing body in Clark County appeared in the December Court of 1796 when James Duncan, John Fains, John Williams and Thomas Burrus were listed as patrol members. They were expected to give twelve hours a month to patrolling the roads in Clark County. There is nothing in the records that we have studied concerning its duties. Obviously, it was a police function, and also obviously against the movement of slaves without express approval of their owners. They were to be nicknamed the "Patty Rollers" by the Negros.

We should note that Clark County never had any serious problem with runaway slaves. Of course, in the earlier days, this period, there was no where for the escaping slave to go...other than to join some Indian tribe. The Cherokee kept the Negro as slaves themselves, a custom that eventually would place the Cherokee on the side of the Confederacy in the Civil War. However, the Indian type of slavery was entirely different from the white. Indian children by a slave woman would have full standing in the tribe. An Indian could marry a slave and have her fully accepted by his people. It was also possible for a slave to gain recognition as a free man through bravery or some service and become fully part of the tribe. In the deeper south, among the Creeks and even more so among the Seminoles, there were many runaway slaves living as full members of the tribes.

However, as the north became increasingly free soil, the nearness of freedom must have been tempting. Again, it was not until close to the Civil War that escape into the northern states meant freedom. Usually they would be picked up by the authorities and sent back again. However, an increasing number of slaves did escape north and become free. Yet, actually, there was very little loss among the slaves. The number of runaway slaves in Clark County was very small. Perhaps some of them did not know where to go, or were afraid to leave the protected areas.

In any slave society, there was also the fear of slave rebellion. Just about this period in history, the slaves of Haiti rose and drove out their Spanish owners in a bloody, violent massacre and then withstood a French effort to subdue them. However, despite the fact that in 1800 most of the slaves in Kentucky were but third generation away from Africa, there were very little signs of rebellion. New slaves that came into the country came largely from the West Indies where slave ships from Africa had first stopped or where older slave populations were sold off. A much more detailed history of the Negro in Clark County is carried in the third volume of this series.

However, the major reason for the patrol was merely to prevent movement between areas at night time, largely to keep down petty pilferage. There is no indication that the patrol was looked upon either as a distasteful or prestigious job. Unlike the militia, being on the patrol did not lend any prestige to its members. The patrol was, at this time, appointed at random over the county, though there would be efforts to appoint patrols for specific districts. Basically it was a pleasant way that a handful of youths could earn a little extra money without doing too much work and taking too much risk.

The patrol was in continued existence, though sometimes changes were not made of record. Somebody would drop out, and the patrol would pick up a substitute. We note that in 1800 Peter Flanigan would replace John Brunner, who was getting a little too old to ride around all night, as captain of the patrol that operated around Winchester. Flanigan would be the chief figure of the patrol for the next decade.

There probably is buried in the Deed and Will books a good deal of information if one wishes to take the time to plod through pages of unprofitable material for an item or two. The first deed was April 22, 1784, conveying from Garnett and Elizabeth Hanson to William Morgan of Scott County, a tract of land on the Licking River. The second deed was from John and Rachel Quisenberry to Benjamin Drake for the sale of some land on Two Mile Crrek. The first will recorded in Clark was that of Isaac Baker, brother of John Baker; will probated March 26, 1793. The second will was filed for Martha Boone, widow of Edward Boone, dividing her property between her children, George, Gantry Ellendry, Jane Morgan, who inherited the Negro house servant, Lilly, Mary Scholl and Sarah Hunter. Martha Boone's will was probated July 23, 1793.

The October Court, 1798 summoned Frederick and Elizabeth Couchman and Violet Ritchie to explain why the will of Jane Ritchie had not been filed. The August Court of 1800 concerned itself with the process of setting a mulatto girl, Lucy Taylor, free. Her former owner, Price Key, had set her free in his will, but the process was somewhat complicated. It was the task of the court to carry out the terms of the will.

We note that December 26, 1797, that David and Susannah Bullock sold to Henry Hickell 1000 acres for twenty shillings a piece. There were twenty shillings to a pound or a shilling was worth about 12 pennies. There was no American money. Therefore, it is impossible to say how much the land was worth. When dollars did come onto the scene, the British pound would be worth close to six dollars. Roughly, then, a shilling would be worth about $.25 cents American money of about 1900. (We note that in 1976, the British pound was worth $1.57). A 1000 acres of Clark County land in 1797 was selling for about $5.00 an acre. It was not until January 19, 1797, that a Bertron Ewell of Mason County sold to a Robert Camp, a Philadelphia merchant, property along Slate Creek which eventually would be in Montgomery and Bath Counties in which dollars were used. This is the first time in the records that dollars appear as a medium of exchange.

One task of the court was to make a statement as to the legality of the boundaries of a particular piece of property. The court met perhaps ten months out of the year, and always there would be three or four of these validation cases before it. Slowly, as the 1800s began, these cases would dwindle until they vanished by 1805 from the court all together. There is no indication how much weight the court's approval of a land title would have, but it did give the owners a little more secure feeling.

The court personally supervised land transfers for much the same reason. The legality of shakey titles needed every kind of legal support. However, there were transactions that appeared in the deed book that were not recorded by the court. The author has not discovered why some were and others were not.

There were problems with the deeds....in July 25, 1797, John and Rebecca Hasty sold to James Flanigan...in consideration of forty pounds current... In February 18, 1797, David and Nancy Snowden sold to James Jenkins...one hundred pounds current money of Kentucky.... In August 1797, Henry and Nancy Gardner sold Abijah Brooks....fifty pounds, good and lawful money of the state aforesaid...

Here, as appears elsewhere in this section, the problem is what is the lawful money of the state...and how does one get a hold of it...the settlers were not poor...they had land, they had furs, they had crops and livestock. They were making iron products, wooden equipment, walking hemp into ropes, manufacturing rifles, building flat boats...but how does one get a hold of hard cash for these products and what kind of cash?

The court records reveal one little corner of history not otherwise mentioned. A Thomas Clark had built near Upper Blue Licks, in 1775, before the fear of Indians, a station consisting of five cabins. In the face of Indians, Clark abandoned these cabins and fled. Somehow, the cabins were not destroyed by Indians and after 1781, they were reoccupied by others than Clark's original party. Now, in 1795, came the issue of ownership. Before the issue could be decided, Montgomery County was established and the case passed out of Clark County courts.

One of the many cases coming up of this nature was reported in the January Court of 1796, at the request of Cuthbert Combs to establish the boundaries of a hundred acres on the lower side of the spring where Beasleys had their cabin to an old Indian tower on the north side of the Kentucky River and between Lullbegrud and Howard Creek....The court ordered Jilson Payne, John Duncan, James McMillan and Elisah Collins to look into the subject and report back. Enoch Smith was the county surveyor until Montgomery County withdrew when William Sudduth took over the job.

A similar task was given to Beverly Daniel, William Edwards and John Duncan to perpetuate the title of Joseph Combs, 1775, on Upper Hancock Creek. There are too many more of these to report them all, but this was a major function of the court of the day.

Taxation and land were closely related since the only tax that really amounted to much was the land tax. The first tax commissioner was Jilson Payne. In 1795, he was replaced by Robert Elliott who in turn gave way to John Young in 1796. The January Court of 1799 divided the county into three districts. Edmond Hockaday was appointed the tax commissioner of the first district, which we can assume would be the western part of the county; Joseph Combs the second, which would be the southern part; and Benjamin Taul the third district which would be the western part of the county. The district method would remain the method of tax collection until well after the War of 1812.

One of the first acts of the court was to require the sheriff to see that the Fayette County sheriff stopped collecting taxes from Clark County citizens. There evidently was some hard feelings as the Fayette County men continued to tax Clark County people. This was particularly true until the county line was successfully drawn.

While the 1793 court was establishing its authority by fining William Brown five shillings for contempt, and the November Court fined Nicholas Hadden for several false oaths, the May Court of 1794 subpoenas Robert McDaniel, Jesse Kenton, William Flower, Thomas Pemperton, Benajmin Rankin and Jesse Young to explain why they did not list their taxable property. In 1796, Stephen Boyle was fined for not listing property. The Clark County Court was not going to take much off anyone. In March of 1798, they fined the sheriff 20 shillings for neglect of duty.

James G. Hunter, who evidently owned a store in Winchester, appeared before the Court July 1799 to protest his taxes. Evidently, the clerk had gotten them mixed up with Barnett Fields. The same year, James Clark complained that he was being taxed for a stud horse that was not his. The November Court, 1799, hauled David Gist into court for failure to pay taxes on 200 acres of land that had belonged to Nathanial Gist since 1792. The March 1794 court reported that the sheriff's share of the tavern tax was 6,222 pennies. The December Court, of 1796, found itself so overworked that it adjourned one session of the court to John Hood's tavern.

The December Court, 1800, listed for tax purposes landowners in Clark County. Some of the larger ones were Elisha Collins, 700 acres; Ebenezar Chaims, 500; Abejah Constant, 804; Lewis Grigsby, 1000; Nathanial Haggard, 550; John Kindred, 5,000; Peter Scholl, 1200; James Stivers, 1,150; Jesse Coyle, 1,150; Richard Halley, 1,150; Thomas Brundage, 1,146; Samuel McKee, 650; Robert Clark, Jr., 550; John Frame, 477 1/2; William Bush, 7,280; John Bush, 2,500; Philip Bush, 812; John Hood, 670; Cuthbert Combs, 5,398; Robert Rankin, 705; William Sudduth, 1,238.

In reading this history, particularly concerning the political and economic leadership, one becomes sharply aware of an establishment that depends largely on itself. The same men appear as office holders, commissioners, militia leaders, politicians and the like. Fifty names would just about sum up the men who apparently dominate the county. Yet, looking over the land owner list, one is impressed at the number of men that had to be influential, that were obviously rich, and no doubt exerted great influence on the county government and affairs, that do not appear in the apparent establishment. This is the invisible government and some writers describe. Men who themselves never appear in public, but who behind the scenes pull the strings.

The Bible says that "the poor ye will have with you always." The court found much of its attention taken up with the poor, the orphan, the sick, the old and the injured. Most of what was done would be called foster home care today. The old peoples or orphans home did not come about until after the Civil War.

The November Court of 1793, ordered the overseer of the poor to bind Thomas Clement, infant of Sally Clement, to William Harris. Harris was reported willing to accept the responsibility. The court did not say whether Sally Clement was dead, sick or just poor. One way or the other, she could not care for her son. Legally, an infant could be a teenager. Harris would be paid room and board and some clothing for the child. In this case, it was probably a small child. In 1797, John Ramsey was appointed guardian over Peggy, Sally, Polly, Henry, Betsy and Nancy Smith, orphans of Joseph Smith. 1793, the court appointed John Donaldson and William Sudduth guardians over William, John and Thomas Flavey, orphans of John Flavey.

The poor were under the supervision of overseers of the poor. The first district was assigned to Charles Cade; William Higgins the second and Samuel Plummer the third. The poor districts were more or less the same as the tax districts.

The August Court, 1794, appointed Ambrose Bush to take care of James Burgess, an infirmed man, for one year. The November Court, 1794, reported paying William Higgins for cost of providing food and raiment to John Mounts since August 15. No reason given for Mounts' problems. One assumes that he was just old or he might have been a prisoner. The same court paid William Wilson to take care of Thomas Smith, a wounded man. He died as a result of his wounds. The court doesn't say how he was wounded. The June Court of 1795 was to give John Rear, age five, son of Winnie Rear, to John Wells to raise. The December Court of 1796 appointed Thomas Scott to look after the infant orphans, John and Polly Cheaton, children of John Cheaton, deceased. Sometimes for no reason visible, the court would be specific. The October Court of 1799, ordered Robert McKinney to take into his care Mary Ann Crouch and furnish her with sufficient diet and clothes until next court when he would be paid. Presumably, Mary Ann was an older girl. The May Court of 1799 permitted Joel Ellis, presumedly an older youth, though not old enough to apprentice, to pick Timothy Parrish as his guardian.

There were problems concerning the assigning of children, particularly of girls. The November Court considered the case of Betsy Jacobs who complained of the treatment her guardian, John People, gave her. People was warned by the court to desist doing what he was doing with the threat of punishment. Specifically, the court warned him not to beat or misuse her in any way. The January Court of 1795, took up the charges that Mary Wells made who evidently was either apprenticed or warded out to Daniel Sphar. The problem must have been worked out to the satisfaction of everyone for no other mention of the case was made. April of the same year, John Wells, no relationship to Mary, was accused by Nancy Adkins of bastardy at the instance of Thomas Atkins, father... Trial does not mean conviction. June Court, 1796, tried Alexander McGinty for vagrancy and found him innocent.

There were scandals that shook the whole county. Nearly as serious as James Quisenberry's second marriage was the romance between elderly, wealthy, "Killes" Eubank in the 1830's with his court assigned ward, 15 years old. This is discussed more in a later section.

August Court, 1800, made George Bruner overseer of the poor for the Winchester district.

The November Court, 1799, granted Berry his grist mill on Lullbegrud near the stone quarry.

It is difficult to decide whether the following cases are welfare or education. They probably should be listed as education though usually the youths involved came from poor families and this was one way of getting rid of an extra mouth without actually becoming welfare cases.

In March of 1798, John McCort, son of Henry McCort, apprenticed himself to John Brunner, a tanner, to learn his art or history, for four years...to serve faithfully...shall not absent himself at night... his Master shall provide for him sufficient meat, drink, apparel, lodging, washing and all other necessities...he shall have the offals of the tan yard...horns...horse, dog and sheep skins...to tan for himself, at the end of his apprenticeship he shall be provided with tools of his trade and a freedom suit.

The apprenticeship of William Holeman, son of Tandy Holeman, included for some reason some additional requirements not found with McCort...shall not commit fornification or contract marriage...shall not play at cards, dice or any other unlawful games...and at the end of his apprenticeship shall receive 11 pounds in trade goods and 3 pounds 10 shillings case after 12 years and 7 months.

A tanner is one who took the green hides of animals and put them through a chemical process which turned them into leather that would not rot. It was a dirty and stinking trade but most respectable in a rough sort of way. Brunner was to have a good reputation and appear in other capacities in Winchester for the next ten or more years.

In May 22, 1798, Flavel Vivion, son of John Vivion, on his own accord and with the consent of his mother, entered into an apprenticeship with Robert Morrow of Montgomery County to become a wheelwright for a term of four years two months among other things, the contract said that Flavel would not embezzle, waste or loose the employer's property...or shall not indulge in games...shall not play in taverns and ale houses...not marry...and he would get his tools. A wheelwright made wheels, wagons, carriages, which was at this time becoming an important item of trade, and would also often do cabinet work, furniture making, etc.

We note that Mrs. William Kavanaugh and Clifton Allan's mother all apprenticed their children as they reached the teens. It was the usual way of getting their children economic opportunities otherwise beyond their financial reach. It was no disgrace or degradation to be an apprentice. Many young men would not fill out their terms and would run away, however. Legally they could be picked up by the law and returned to their masters. Usually this was not done even when the so-called master would know where his fugitive apprentice was. After the apprentice reached proper age, he was free from any danger of arrest.

On the whole, it was good cheap labor that was made available to men with a trade. This might be a good place to insert a list of cabinet makers who lived in this community during these years as written by Mrs. Wade Hampton Whitley in "A Check List of Kentucky Cabinet Makers, 1795 to 1895."

1780: William Clinkenbeard made a chair while living at Strode Station. He may have made more. 1781: Enos Terry was making buckeye trenchers and a turner. 1790: Daniel Weible was advertising in the KENTUCKY GAZETTE, January 23, 1790 homemade furniture while living at Strode Station. Jerry West made a cherry slant desk in 1797 and perhaps other pieces. William Horton was a master cabinet maker living in Winchester in 1800. Robert Morris was 13 when apprenticed to Horton and began to make furniture. In 1803, Wiley Brassfield was making coffins and became Clark County's first "undertaker."

One of the most interesting descriptions of Clark County life is reported by the Kentucky Historical Society's Register, Vol. 27, 1929. In 1798, Micah Taul went to work in the county clerk's office as a copiest at 13 years of age. A frontier society had no time to permit the young to waste their teenage. They were expected to do a man's work from the very beginning. Taul reports that David Collins, Joshua Baker and Edmond Shropshire were other and older clerks. He considered David Bullock the laziest man he had ever known.

The March Court of 1794 excused Julius Webb from paying county levies which means the requirement to work on the roads because he was infirmed. We note that every male, free or slave, was obligated to put so much time maintaining roads. He could do this himself, hire someone to do his work, or contribute money to the road fund so that it could hire someone. This will be covered in more detail on the section on roads.

Water was and is a major problem in Clark County. Normally there is adequate water for all purposes. However, rivers and creeks were all subject to drying up. Dry spells created real problems particularly for those in what would be called the blue grass. Isaac Dickerson is given credit for digging the first well, September 20, 1792. After that most of the better homes as they were built, were served by huge cisterns dug by slave labor and bricked to be water tight.

The grist mill was one of the most important businesses in any community. To it the farmer would bring his corn, wheat or other grains to be gound. Usually the miller would take a portion of that which he was grinding as payment. This was an essential function in any community. Corn meal was a vital part of the diet. Millers were needed everywhere, every three to six miles apart.

Grist mills and an occasional saw mill could be powered by mule or ox harnessed and walking around a circle. Where water was insufficient, this was a method. However, a mill pond which would build up a sufficient body of water to operate a water wheel could turn mill stones of various sizes. The problem with every mill pond was a shortage of water.

The process of getting a mill, for a mill with a pond included many things. First it called for making an application to the county court. The court would then assign in the earlier days the case to the sheriff who in turn would send his deputy Robert Higgins and in later days organize a jury, who would inspect the sight and see what was involved. If the mill pond would run on other's property, what it would hurt, who might oppose, would be reported. Then the court would decide on whether or not to grant or deny the application. The court did seem to have the power to condemn land for a mill if needed.

In 1793, we had in the July Court a request from John Ray for a mill on Howard's Creek. William and Joel Higgins wanted to build a mill at Grassy Lick. In the August Court, William Said requested a grist mill on Stoner Creek. Johnathian Bryan and Richard Oliver wanted to build mills on Howard's Creek.

The August Court, 1793, brought in the report on the first requests. John Ray's dam would be fifteen feet high. The passage of fish and navigation would not be affected. No mansion, house, garden, orchard or cultivated land would be underwater. The health of no peron would be injured. Deputy Sheriff Higgins recommended that the mill be permitted. The Higgins dam would be 10 feet high. Twelve good and lawful men had examined the Oliver dam and had their approval. It would be 9'5" high. Williams' dam would be 10 feet high. There is no way of knowing whether these dams were built but in all likelihood they were.

The March Court of 1794 noticed that Edward Traube wanted a grist mill on Hinkston Creek near Payton Lick. Bennett Clark wanted a grist mill on Somerset Creek. Bennett Clark also wanted a mill on Hancock Creek. Once again the process was started.

The May Court was asked by Cornelius Ringo to build a grist mill on Peter Ringo's land below the mouth of Enoch Springs Branch. Henry Gardner wanted to build a grist mill on Slate Creek above the mouth of Stepstone Creek. All but one of these last requests were in the Montgomery area of the county.

The July Court of 1794 reported that Bennett Clark's grist mill on Somerset would be 10' high, but it would damage four acres of land owned by Rhodes Ragland. Nothing was ever said about the result of this problem, but evidently Clark and Ragland got together and settled their problem. So also did Cornelius Ringo over the land that his dam would damage belonging to Peter Ringo and Hugh Forbes. Since the dam was already on Peter Ringo's land, it is evident that this was a method of determining how much Cornelius would have to pay Peter.

More grist mills were needed. Arthur Conally and George Berry wanted to build a mill on Berry's land. There seems to be no similar problem here that the Ringo's had. Evidently Berry owned the land and Conally was to run the mill. Thomas Goff wanted a grist mill on Hancock Creek. So did John Peebles. Harold Ralls wanted a grist mill on Lullbegrud. Harold Ralls' dam on Lane's Branch of Hinkston was to be 10 feet and saw no problems. Arnett's mill would damage a half acre of John Prewitt. Evidently this could not be worked out for the project was dropped. Arnett requested that he be permitted to have a grist mill and powder mill on Stoner Creek. This met with no opposition. The other requests were approved.

The applications for more mills poured in. It must be remembered that what we are recording is merely the formal application of men who wanted to build mills. There is no evidence from the court records that they were all built. No doubt some were not for financial and other reasons. Also, the earth moving job was difficult. Dams were usually flimsily built and the first big rain would wash away the dam depriving the mill of its power. Sometimes these dams would be reestablished but more often than not they would be abandoned. Other mills would be operated for a few years and then shut down because of the health of the operator or poor financial situation. Often again, these mills would be owned by one man, for example, Tom Goff, but would be operated by a second on a share basis or a straight wage. Good millers were hard to come by and when such an employee would leave, sometimes the owner would just close down. Other mills would operate right into the 20th century when commercial flours pushed the smaller miller out of business. Many of the older citizens in 1976 could remember in their youths, mills operating full capacity, but by World War I, most of the neighborhood mills were disappearing.

John Yocum wanted a mill on Slate Creek in October of 1796. Sam Smith applied for permission for the west fork of Howard Creek. O. Martin was operating a saw mill and wanted to add a grist mill to his operation. Since he already had the water, there was no problem. The separation of Montgomery County slowed considerably the number of applications. Many of the mills in Clark County dated to the 1780's before Clark County was established, but the new Montgomery territory was filling up fast and the need was pressing.

The Quarterly Court was active. In February 1797 the county had a case against William Said whose mill pond was flooding the Winchester Mt. Sterling Road. Another case was William Nelson versus Peter Small and wife. A jury of bystanders was drawn. The list is interesting in that it reveals who came to court out of curiosity. Samuel Crosthwaite, Andrew Hughs, James Ward, John Bailey, James Turley, John Whiteside, James Ries, Jacob Crosthwaite, Hugh Forbes, William Goodlawn, Samuel Spurgeon and Job Glover. The defendant was found not guilty.

1797 Thomas Goff whose mill was operating on Hancock Creek asked to raise his dam two feet. Once again we note the problem of water. The dry weather during the summer would virtually stop water flowing in the creeks. A larger pond would provide more water to use during these dry spells. The March Court, 1798 granted Jacob Fishback the right to build a mill on Upper Howard's Creek. In July of 1798, Richard Hickman, George Taylor, Henry Chiles, James Beatty joined together to build a mill on Bean's Creek near the mouth of Bogg's Creek. To do so, they had an acre condemned on the opposite bank for their dam. James Beatty wanted to build his own mill, but the August Court refused to condemn an acre on the west bank of Boone's Creek because it lay in Fayette County. The October Court, 1798, was requested for permission from William Myers to build a mill on Four Mile Creek. James Fishback finished this mill. John Gordon requested the May Court of 1799 to build a mill on Stoner Creek. He also applied for permission to build a mill on Four Mile. The July, 1799, Court permitted James Gowan to condemn an acre for a grist mill on a fork of Boone Creek.

Thomas Berry had applied for permission to build a mill as reported earlier, but evidently had lost interest and had not completed his mill. In November of 1799, he asked permission to finish it. David Gist applied for permission to build a mill on Stoner Creek.

George Sharp asked the court to build a grist mill on his and Adam Sharp's land on Hardwick Creek, July of 1800. This is one of the earlier mentioned events in what would become Powell County. The North District Baptist records would report churches in what is now Spout Springs, Beaver Pond (Stanton) and perhaps one or two other places; there was a Methodist operating on Harwick Creek sometime in this period and a Presbyterian Church near Beaver Pond. There were people then, along the Red River by 1800. They were seldom mentioned by the court. The August jury for Sharp included Samuel Woodard, Nicholas Burgy, Alexander Harrison, Augustus Crowe, Peter Worley, James McNichor, Sam Powell, Jesse Robertson, Richard Wharton,

James McMahon, James Stewart and Samuel Eaton. Already we note that there were not the usual names one generally finds in Clark County. Some are not unknown families in Clark County, but they do not represent the big block of families such as the Bushes, Hamptons, Haggards, Goffs, Ramseys, Haileys, Owens, etc.

August of 1799, William Robinson wanted to build a mill on Boone Creek near the forks of middle and east fork. January, 1800 William Downey and David Brandenburg both were faced with water problems. Already the amount of water in Stoner Creek was falling. They wanted to raise the level of their dams and condemn two acres to do so.

This is by no means a complete list of dams. Because they have been so important in the history of the county, we have tried to report them more extensively than other forms of county activity. The mill, like the tavern became a gathering ground of people, a country club for the farmer. Usually around a mill one or two other establishments would appear, a blacksmith, a crossroads store. Mrs. Pearl Delaney who was raised in the Schollsville section about 1900 to 1910 described what it was like in her day. It was not much different a hundred or so years earlier. The farmer would bring his corn to the mill and the miller would grind it while he waited. It was one of the trips that often he would take the middle children and was something eagerly looked forward to. Sometimes the wife would come if the farmer would bring the wagon. While the corn was being ground, the children and wife would go to the store. There was always some kind of hard candy available which was a rarity and a treat for the children. Often there would be another farmer's wife or two coming to the store for the same reasons. For people who were isolated for days without seeing anyone save the nearest neighbor or two except on Sunday, this was a rare social treat. After getting a little candy, the children would meet with some other children for an opportunity to play with someone other than older or younger brothers and sisters. Around the mill, there would be another two or three farmers with grain to be ground. If there was a horse or mule that needed shoeing or some broken machine that needed fixing, this would be done during grinding. The miller, the smith and the farmers would talk politics, religion, weather, farming and gossip a bit. There would be no real hurry in getting the grain ground and when it was finally finished and the farmer would load up his family; it had been a pleasant afternoon for all.

One other curious incident about millers and mills really belongs to a later period of time than this section, but since we have spent so much time on mills here, we will add this story instead of later where it belongs.

The Taylors began their mill during this period and conducted a mill for more than a hundred years. One of the Taylors, probably George, had a son who was blind or nearly so. This boy became the miller of the Taylor mill. Like most blind, he had a knowledge of where everything was in the mill and as long as he was free to move about without obstacles put in his way he had no troubles. He discovered that it was easier to grind at night time when all other people had left. He needed no light. Of course, in grinding there was a great deal of flour dust in the air that also dusted every object, moving and still.

Hence a traveler, riding up the road from Boonesborough late at night, would suddenly come upon the Taylor mill, running full blast, without a light. Moving weirdly in the dark was a white ghostly figure. It was enough to jolt many a sinner into religion and it was one section where the slaves did not travel at night.

Even by 1800, Clark County was still a wild territory with game available to the hunter. Deer would be seen in Clark County into the 1970's. Wolves were a major problem so a price was paid by the state government for wolf scalps including the ears. In 1800 Samuel Plumner was paid three shillings for killing a young wolf. Wiley Brassfield was paid for a wolf scalp. Julius Watts was paid seven pounds, which was a lot of money in these days, for killing wolves. William Oldham collected on a wolf scalp.

This drive on wolves evidently began in 1799 for Henry Chiles was paid for eight wolf heads. In 1801 Joshua Hoy was paid for one. After 1801, there is no more mention of paying for wolf heads in the court books. Perhaps the menace was finished.

In a land where fences were nothing but rails, snaking back and forth across pasture land, the problems of stray animals were serious. The few newspapers were filled with advertisements for lost horses, cattle, etc. A stray pen was operated long after the War of 1812. Any lost animals could be herded into Winchester's stray pen and there held for four days before being sold. The county also began to register brands so that the hundreds of head of half wild cattle that wondered the woods could be identified.

The July Court of 1793 registered the brand of John Strode as 1S and that of John Baker as 1B. David Hughs' brand was a little more imaginative. Ear notches were also registered. However, by the end of the decade these were no longer registered. Few men were large enough operators to go to the bother of registering brands. Also as the country filled up, the yearly round-ups of stray animals halted. However, ear notches and occasionally branding is still done by many animal raisers, but they are no longer registered. The law still is on the books, however.

Another very important aspect of Clark County economic life was the development of warehouses along the Kentucky River. These ranged from a crude lean-to beside a crude landing at a creek mouth, to a reasonably sizable dock and a full fledged warehouse. During this period, travel on the river was mostly down stream. A canoe with a strong arm pilot was about the only method of going up stream. It was simpler to go over land. The traffic down stream, however, was vital. Already in the 1790's, some coal was being floated down from up stream docks on rafts of walnut and poplar loaded also with corn and livestock from the crude mountain settlements along the Kentucky. In the next fifty years, the down stream coal trade would boom into a torrent for there was never enough coal to last a cold winter unless it was imported early in the summer and to the very cold spell itself.

The big task of the warehouses, however, was to house the tobacco, corn, wheat, flax, or the ground flour of each grain, to keep barrels of whiskey that poured out of the crude stills and to provide some kind of barracoon for slaves who would man the rafts and be sold in turn.

The major creek beds would be deep enough to pole rafts out of the river and usually the current would not be so strong that they could not be moved into the sheltering mouth of the creek. Hence these warehouses appeared on the banks of the creeks...Boone's, the Two Howard Creeks, Four Mile and Two Mile, and, across the River at Boonesborough and along the Madison County shore.

Very early, the new State of Kentucky assigned inspectors to examine the stocks of agricultural products for their worth, to keep an eye on the scales, and to some extent the warehouses. As state men, they were responsible to the Governor, but generally came under the over sight of the county court who recommended their personnel and received the reports. The warehouse owners and the magistrates of the court were often the same men. The inspectors would often be the warehousemen themselves or a friend or relative.

The inspectors for Stafford's Landing in 1792 were Walter Carr, John Martin and Abram Venerable and was located on the Fayette side of the Kentucky...and evidently was the only landing and warehouse on the north bank in this general area. For Boonesborough, the inspectors were Idom South, David Lee Cruse and Francis Holiday.

By 1794 and 1795, however, there were several warehouses in Clark County. John Holder and William Bush had warehouses at Holder's Landing...or Boat Yard. Philip Bush was their inspector. The March Court approved the appointment of William Means, Frederick Moss and James Hawkins to inspect the warehouses of James Wilkerson at the mouth of Four Mile Creek. The number of warehouses would multiply in the next decade. Later, when steam boats began to work the river, the shallow draft river boats would put into land almost anywhere there might be a shipment.

James Wilkerson is not a Clark County figure and does not play any large part in the county's history. Yet he was always there like a dark cloud, involved with politics, economic deals, and in the social life of Fayette County. He was the ranking army officer for years in the area. He had stores and warehouses. He was involved in land deals sometimes of questionable nature. He was charged with being in the pay of the Spanish even while he was an officer in the army. He performed reasonably well in the Indian campaigns as he had the Revolutionary War. He was closely associated with Aaron Burr but escaped being tarred with the same brush of charges. According to the WINCHESTER NEWS, December 13, 1910, he owed the firm of Rochester and Hart, in December of 1792, 41 pounds, 8 shillings and four pennies for castings. He had an older bill also but evidently paid.

Meanwhile, there was a stirring among those who were making money to build finer homes. A third wave of settlers were coming in, wealthy land owners who sent their slaves first to build a brick house, with fireplaces and glass windows instead of greased paper, and planked floors instead of stamped clay. They would send their furniture and silver, lace and linens. When all was ready, they brought their wives and children. The marriage of the Gist girls accelerated the movement. Society was touching Clark County. In 1797, Richard Hickman was building Caveland.

Among the businesses that were in Clark County, besides Brunner's tannery, Rochester and Hart's Mercantile business, the court records revealed that James Hunter, John Warren and Barnett Fields were partners in a mercantile business. At least three taverns were in Winchester at this time, plus a number of smiths, carpenters and brick and stone masons.

According to the census in 1800, Clark County had 7,656 white males, 6,075 white females, 1,568 slaves and 17 free Negros. It was obviously a woman's opportunity for marriage if those were her desires.

## ALIEN AND SEDITION LAWS

Clark County had, by the end of the 18th century, become a safe, relatively prosperous, well settled country. There were still deer, wild turkey and an occasional bear to be found. Wolves were a problem. The Indian danger was now a recent memory. The economics of the county was already in the process of turning her politically into a conservative bastion of the Whig Party...but not yet.

The Kentucky Senator Humphrey Marshall had supported the Federalist administration of George Washington including the Alien and Sedition acts. Clark County and Kentucky might well revere the name of George Washington but many did not accept his politics. Marshall was in serious trouble over his stand. Had there been "recall" in Kentucky he would have been recalled. As it was he narrowly missed impeachment. The dislike of the Alien and Sedition laws reached well into Clark County as well as the rest of the state.

Vice President Jefferson had led the attack accusing John Adams of planning to make himself King. Adams had threatened those that supported Jefferson with punishment under the Alien and Sedition acts. Jefferson turned to North Carolina, which was a politically radical state for support. Before such was forthcoming, Kentucky acted and Clark County lead the attack.

Jacob Fishback called a meeting in Winchester to protest the acts. The meeting met with Robert Higgins as secretary August 1, 1798. It met and drew up articles of protest that would form the basis of the Kentucky protest. Clark County claimed the honor of being first to take this position in the state. Copies were sent to the President, Congress, Governor and any other official that might be interested.

## GEORGE ROGERS CLARK

George Rogers Clark was never a Clark Countian, but he was certainly most influential in Clark history. When the county was established, his name was eagerly sought as a memorial for the great things Clark had done.

He had been born in Albermarle, Virginia 1752. He became a youthful surveyor, a profession on the frontier that was in great demand. He commanded a company in Dunmore's War against the Cherokee and was offered a commission in the British Army. He refused. He was in Kentucky during the spring and summer of 1775, but was commanding Virginia regular militia on the Virginia frontier for a time. In 1776, he returned to Kentucky. In the bitter struggle between the Transylvania Company's Henderson and Virginia, Clark was furiously on the side of the radical opposition. He took the position that Kentucky ought not be part of either North Carolina or Virginia, much less of the Transylvania proporietory, but should act as a free agent negotiating with the eastern states for all things. He was never the less elected to the Virginia legislature in 1776.

He negotiated successfully with Patrick Henry, the Virginia Governor, and less successfully with the executive council for large amounts of powder and other military aid for Kentucky. The Virginians were not happy with his and with others' attitudes toward Virginia authority.

Clark returned to Kentucky determined to make it independent of Virginia. As such he represented the left wing of Kentucky thinking. Virginia did back down from their position and did furnish the powder, only to have most of it captured by the Indians on the way down the Ohio River. Other powder did reach the settlements however providing what Collins' History considered an adequate supply.

George Rogers Clark's determination to capture the British outposts of Kaskaskia and Vincennes and perhaps eventually Detroit was not only to cut at the root the source of supplies of the Indians, but to add to the settlements vast new territories that would augment the size of a western nation. He sold Virginia on the idea and received money and supplies for his expedition from Virginia.

There followed a series of attacks into Ohio and Indiana designed both to cut off Indian attacks into Kentucky and prevent the British from retaking Kaskaskia and Vincennes. In the process of this, the falls of the Ohio, was used as a base of operations. It was also the natural stopping place of down river traffic since all rafts had to be unloaded and taken around the falls. Louisville was born.

In 1780 Clark was back in Virginia trying to set up an expedition against Detroit, but found himself facing an invasion of vengeance by British troops under Benedict Arnold. He was placed under the command of Baron Von Steuben. This taken care of, Clark got his permission for the Detroit attack and was raised to the command of a Brigadier General.

He failed to get the troops necessary for the operation. Political enemies undermined him. He was drinking steadily and this fact was used to discredit him. After the disaster at Blue Licks, however, he roused the country side and swept northward again destroying the Indians. He tried again in 1786, but now, without the stimulus of a Blue Lick, he could not rouse the needed support. His command was divided and his efforts made ineffective.

He was now openly arguing the necessity of a breaking away from the control of Virginia, perhaps even of the whole eastern nation. Most of the arguments used by the American Rebels were being used by Clark, Wilkerson and the Danville group of like minded thinkers. It was this same type of thinking that caused the Kentucky delegates to oppose the adopting of the Constitution by a three to one ratio.

Citizen Genet, Representative of Revolutionary France, whose visits to Kentucky caused great excitement and enthusiasm, commissioned Clark a Major General in the armies of Revolutionary France giving him the objective conquering Spanish Louisiana...and its queen city, New Orleans. Clark proceeded to raise the necessary army and evidently had considerable success. Before Clark was actually able to carry out his mission, faced by extremely strong opposition from Virginia and the Washington administration just going into office, weakened politically by the creation of Kentucky as a State of the Union, Genet was disgraced and recalled. The Spanish turned the administration of Louisiana over to the French and before anyone could figure out what was next, Jefferson quite illegally bought the whole works.

Clark now found himself out of favor politically. There was no place in a peaceful Kentucky for a fire eater soldier. He was sick physically and mentally, bitter and angry. Though his ideas no longer fitted Kentucky politics, Clark Countians named their county after him because there were few others who contributed more to the creation of a new land. He was Clark County's first hero.

## HUBBARD TAYLOR

During this decade a number of other names have appeared and some deserve a little more attention than we have given them. Robert Clark certainly would have had, if he had lived. He followed closely in the steps of his father who also had carved a strong place among the settlers of Clark County and, as Judge of the Quarterly Court, had gained their respect. But the Senior Robert Clark grew old and soon dropped out of the picture. The young Robert Clark grew steadily, politically into the state picture as representative, economically with his interest in the iron forges along the Red River, and as one of the more impressive social figures. Just how far he would have gone or what he might have done is one of those unfortunate questions that can never be answered for he died suddenly. There were other Clarks to take up the family reputation, but the most important is James Clark who makes his appearance in the next decade, but does not reach his importance until the part we cover in the second volume.

William Bush continues as one of the old timers to play considerable part in Clark County history, until he passes from the scene as one of the most active and important Clark County men. However, we have discussed him before.

The Taylor family very early emerged as one of the most influential families in the county. Hubbard Taylor came from Orange County, Virginia in 1789. He had been in Kentucky, however, off and on, since 1781 when he was employed as a deputy surveyor for Lincoln County. He was related to other Taylors who were active in various parts of the state and in the state legislature. He came from the same area of Virginia that Dr. Hinde who will be discussed later in the section on Methodism, to survey his extensive grants of land in Clark County. Taylor had married Dr. Hinde's niece. Evidently, Hinde never expected to come to Clark County and was generous with his property, offering Taylor a large tract of land in return for the surveying. Taylor accepted and cut out of Hinde's land a piece of excellent farm land in what became the Pine Grove-Becknerville area, close to the Fayette County line. In 1789 he built a house, at the time one of the first and best homes in the county, which he called Spring Hill that still remains and is used.

Taylor is a good example of the third wave of settlers, educated, financially well off, who sent his slaves to build his home and to establish himself comfortably before bringing his family west.

Hubbard was immediately recognized as an important man. So many people were coming out of Virginia that prestige was carried with one and a newcomer who was actually important in Virginia, found it rather easy to assume a life of leadership in Kentucky as if he were still in Virginia.

Taylor became a magistrate in Fayette County, served on some of the early delegations to conventions and was elected to the state legislature where he supported James McMillan in the creation of the new county.

Somewhat to everyone's surprise, Richard Hickman replaced Taylor in the state legislature, but Hubbard was repaid by being appointed as one of the county's first quarterly judges. In 1794, he became Clark County's first State Senator. He will hold this position until 1800 when he is again replaced by Richard Hickman. He does not enter active politics again until 1815 when he returns to the State Senate for another four year term. As according to the Constitution, no one votes for a national president but for electors. In the early days, the electors were far more important politically than they are today, though being pledged to a candidate, they were legally permitted to vote as they pleased. Taylor was elected elector in 1805 and thereafter in every presidential race until 1825. He voted for Presidents Jefferson and James Madison and James Monroe twice each. In the 1825 election Taylor was not a Clay supporter until public pressure forced him into it. Taylor would have much preferred John Q. Adams which is perhaps indicative of his political viewpoint. This might also account for his occasional political defeat since these views were considerably right of the standard political viewpoint of the state or county until well after the Warof 1812 when Clay represented the right and Jackson the left of the American political spectrum... though there were those both further right and left than these who held the middle.

Hubbard Taylor became sort of a senior citizen, or respected patriarch of the county. Famous men moved in and out of his house at Spring Hill with regularity. Beverly Besuden in an article in the WINCHESTER SUN, June 4, 1965, notes that Henry Clay, James Madison and Aaron Burr were all guests at Spring Hill. Beverly Besuden notes that reflecting her uncle's Methodism, Mrs. Taylor did not approve of alcoholic drinks, so Hubbard and Henry Clay would have to retreat to the spring house in the rear to enjoy their mint juleps.

Collins' history notes that Taylor was one of the five cattle judges at the first cattle show in Kentucky, July 1816. He passes in 1842. His children were: Mildred T., Lucy, Hubbard Jr., Elizabeth, Alice, John Pendleton, Nancy, Thomas M., and J.K. (died before 1840). Hubbard Taylor, Jr. would play a very important part in later county history.

## THE MCMILLANS

The McMillan clan was one of the most influential families in the early history of Clark County. James McMillan, like William Bush, was one of those that helped Daniel Boone open the Wilderness Road before the settlement of Boonesborough. Like Bush, he was not a professional frontiersman always seeking the will of the wisp in the next mountain valley. He was, on the other hand, a genuine frontiersman and Indian fighter that was seeking an opportunity to carve for himself and his family an opportunity for the better life. He belonged to a Scottish clan that had clung stubbornly to the lost hopes of the Stuart Kings and found red-skinned Indians less dangerous than red-coated English soldiers. Like many of the early settlers he was an educated man having studied logic and metaphysics at the University of Edinburg in 1734.

Arriving in Virginia, he did what many of the young men did with some education, he taught school while he looked around. Part of his looking was to find Margeret White whom he married. He was among the first settlers to stake out land in Clark County (out of claims of the Transylvania Company), but he did not bring his family over the mountains until the worst of the dangers had passed.

James, Senior, was active in the militia, second only to John Holder in the early days. There is one grim story that reveals much about the grim old man. There was at Strode's a young man named Peter Harper. Harper was known and a companion of Clinkenbeard who tells the story. Peter's mother had been captured by Indians in the 1750's and had lived with the Indians for several years. The result was the birth of Peter who grew up dark-skinned, black, long lank hair...obviously more Indian than white. Peter's mother had married a man named Harper and together they had moved to Strode's Station. Harper had adopted Peter and there was a contented family situation. Peter was fully accepted around Strode's Station; had hunted with most of the young men and had belonged to the militia like most of the young men. Near the end of 1780, he was found shot dead near Lullbegrud Creek. No one knew who did it. The next day, James McMillan returned to Boonesborough where he was living reporting that he had killed an Indian while hunting on Lullbegrud Creek. There was no proof that the Indian was Peter, but Clinkenbeard reported that McMillan felt it was and was deeply grieved.

As is so often, there are other versions. Kathryn Owen says that Col. Lucian Beckner, "on July 4, 1753, Peter Harper and Eve Deal, a young German couple, were married in Philadelphia. They moved to the frontier and there Eve and her children were captured by Shawnees and taken into Ohio. She was forced to marry a Shawnee Indian. The union resulted in the birth of a son, Peter Harper. After Boquet's victory at Brushy Run, the white captives were surrendered and in the fall of 1779, Peter Harper came to Kentucky and enlisted in the garrison at Strode's. In many respects, the half breed white man became on the most useful and picturesque characters of his time and place."

Miss Owen also quotes Ben Allan, another of the frontier men who was interviewed by John Shane. Allan claimed that Harper had ridden to the forks of Salt and Mud Lick in search of his two dogs. He met Benjamin Allan and told him he planned to ride over to Beaver Pond, some two miles away, where he hoped to find his dogs. On the next Monday, Harper's horse came riderless into Morgan's Station on Slate Creek. Harper was never seen again.

James McMillan had been hunting in the woods the day that Harper disappeared. He reported that he had shot an Indian off a horse, and though, afterward he could never admit his mistake, his conscience was profoundly troubled. According to Allan, the incident occurred near Mud Luck which became Olympia Springs.

The two stories, one by Clinkenbeard and one by Allan, reveal the difficulty at coming up with the actual facts of an incident in history. Both were contemporaries of Peter Harper and James McMillan. However, Allan actually saw Harper that day. Kathryn Owen thinks the story is more correct. She also wonders if it wasn't James McMillan, the son, rather than the father involved.

James McMillan, Sr. died in 1799 closing the chapter on one of the leaders of the county and the father of two of the power houses of Clark county politics and life.

Somewhere in the 1780's, James McMillan drops out of history and his son, James, appeared. Like his father, James was active in the militia and was one of the rating officers in the new Clark County. He had been elected to the legislature and served from 1793 to 1796...he had been largely responsible to the legislature creating Clark County and had done much of the legislative work for Montgomery County.

Even while James was at the height of his power after Montgomery County was created, James dropped out of the political picture, William was gaining favor in the eyes of the public.

William also was active in the militia and had been in the Indian campaigns as had James. (This was probably the Senior for he was a Colonel. He testified at the court marshall of General Harmar.) About 1790, William McMillan had driven cattle northward to the posts as far north as Detroit. He met Simon Girty and reported him a charming individual. He also met the Indian who very likely had killed a young brother, Jonathan, at Estill's Defeat.

William rose in the militia and was for a time commander of the 8th Regiment and the brigade with a rank of Brigadier General. The army gave him a full title of Major at the outbreak of the War of 1812 and made him in charge of recruitment. He did a good job and was given a rank of Colonel in the United States 17th Regiment. He was elected to the legislature in 1801, a seat which he held until the War of 1812. He went to the Senate in 1827 and followed James Clark in 1831 as Senator after Clark was elected Governor. During most of this period he was also a magistrate. His son, William later became mayor of Houston.

There was a fourth McMillan active in the 1790's named Robert McMillan. In 1792, he was an officer in the 8th Kentucky Militia Regiment under Levi Todd when the Regiment was Fayette County. After the creation of Clark County, he became the Major of the second battalion of the new 17th Regiment under Col. John Holder. He also held a legislative seat.

A will filed in the October 1799 Will Book records the death of James McMillan, Senior and helps straighten some of the confusion the records have left of his children. He left his eldest son, Robert, 100 acres of 300 acres he owned on Lullbegrud and a 100 acres on Howard Creek. James also received 100 acres on both creeks. Both James and Robert moved to the Lullbegrud area where they became Montgomery citizens. Robert returned to Clark County briefly. A daughter, Elizabeth, also received 100 acres. William McMillan inherited 300 acres in Howard Creek. The rest of the property and monies were divided between the two girls, Elizabeth and Mary.

## RICHARD HICKMAN

Perhaps the most prominent of the Clark Countians, at least politically was Richard Hickman. He was the son of James Hickman and like most of his generation, served briefly in the American Revolution. He came to Kentucky in 1784 and settled near the Fayette County line in the Bush-Taylor area building a home he called Caveland which still stands. It is particularly marked by a large cave in its front yard that leads down to the River. The Hickmans were never so numerous as the Bushes, Martins, Taylors, etc. who were their neighbors, but there is no question as to their importance in this period.

Hickman entered politics and replaced Hubbard Taylor in the legislature. He was a magistrate and served on most of the early committees. He was one of the first trustees of Winchester. In 1799, he was one of the delegates to the new state constitutional convention. In 1800, he became State Senator once again replacing Hubbard Taylor and remained so until 1812. He became the most influential senator in the state. In 1812, he ran for and won easily the Lieutenant Governor's chair serving under Isaac Shelby who had won a second term as Governor.

Hickman had always been active in the militia, Hickman, McMillan and Sudduth being the three highest officers in the county. As such, he wanted to partake actively in the War of 1812, but Isaac Shelby out ranked him and left him as acting Governor while Shelby went to New Orleans to help Jackson.

For some reason, Hickman lost the political popularity poll for he was unable to win state office in 1816. He was still popular in the county and was promptly elected State Senator in 1819 until 1823.

He married a widowed Calloway girl, Mrs. Lydia Calloway Irving.

## WILLIAM SUDDUTH

William Sudduth became one of the second generation leaders of Clark County and was during his hey-day perhaps the most influential man in the county that did not hold a state elective position. He was born in 1765 which made him a little too young for leadership in the new settlements at first. He arrived early in Kentucky, in the middle 1780's and ended at Strode's. Beckner gives an account of him in the Historical Society's Quarterly of June 1928. The histories of the time, however, do not give him the credit that reading the county court records and the militia rolls would indicate.

He had a better than average education for he was among the first school teachers at Strode's. However, he was too well educated to waste time with teaching school and became one of the more able and sought after surveyors of the area. He joined the militia though evidently he was too late to make the Revolution even on the frontier. However, he was a competent soldier and a good Indian fighter and rose rapidly in the ranks, popular with his men. He was, by 1790, third rating officer, after Holder and James McMillan. In another ten years he was to be the rating officer in the Clark County militia.

With the lessening of the Indian threat he moved into the Pretty Run area, for awhile associated with Hood's Station. He continued surveying and after the establishment of Montgomery took Enoch Smith out of Clark County became the county surveyor...a post he held for most of the rest of his life. He served with Wayne in 1793 with distinction. He was a magistrate for more than twenty years and served as one of the Clark County representatives at the Constitutional Convention of 1799. He was the last surviving member of that Convention.

His health took a bad turn in the 1810's which kept him out of most of the War of 1812. However, he lived until 1845 when he died at the age of 79.

## ACHILLES EUBANK

Achilles Eubank was old enough to serve in the Revolution. He was in the militia at Boonesborough in 1777, but his enlistment expired and he was among those that returned to Virginia that year. He continued to serve in various military outfits and fought at Guilford Courthouse and Yorktown. All together he enlisted some six times. He continued in the militia and rose in rank until he stood behind Sudduth in the military hierarchy and eventually became colonel of the Clark County militia. He served in the War of 1812 and was captured at the River Raisin. He ran the gauntlet and came through alive.

He first married Polly Bush which related him to most of the Bush Settlement. He bought 282 acres of land on Four Mile Creek from Nathanial Massie. He was a shrewd businessman and a good farmer. At one time he was the largest slave holder in Clark County and was second in the census of 1810. He owned warehouses on the mouth of Four Mile and operated a grist and saw mill. In 1812, he built a large brick home with out buildings that were eventually attached to the house itself. The house stands in good repair in 1976 though in somewhat reduced size. He was a very active magistrate through most of his life.

However, near the end of 1820's, his wife passed away. As was customary, the Eubanks had taken into their home to raise an orphan girl. When the girl was fifteen the old man, now in his seventies, announced that he intended to marry her. Achilles'...called "Killes". children protested angrily and in such a manner that Achilles felt that all they wanted was his property. He divided the land between them, giving everything he owned, married and left the state for Missouri. There he struggled to reestablish himself, an old man who had once been one of the wealthiest in Clark County. He now had a new and growing family and in desperation applied in 1837 for a Revolutionary War pension. He was then able to get back on his feet and finally died in his nineties. The Kentucky children had lost track of him completely and it was not until after his death and the reaching of maturity of his Missouri children, that contact was made between them.

## JOEL HART

Joel Hart was the son of Josiah and Judith Tanner Hart. It was unfortunate in that his father had lost most of his money before the boy had reached adulthood. Joel had about three months of formal education. As a youth he lived in Owingsville working with stone, on chimneys and building stone fencing. He moved to Lexington in 1830. He met Stobell Clevenger of Cincinnati who carved tombstones. Hart began carving. His first bust was that of Cassius Clay. In 1848, he moved to Florence, Italy where he continued to sculpt. He did Andrew Jackson, John J. Crittenden and in three years' work he did Henry Clay. Later he did Zach Taylor and Robert Wickcliff.

## EDUCATION IN THE 1790's TO 1800

One of the basic requirements of any culture at any time is to provide an adequate number of emotionally balanced trained children. Without this requirement, any given culture will, and has, died. However, how much education is needed on the frontier? In 1790, there were probably less than a half dozen stores in Clark County and by 1800 probably not more than twenty which would require some math, some bookkeeping and the ability to read on the part of at least one of those engaged. Add to these, another half dozen taverns where the same requirement would be needed. By 1800, there are about ten churches of a variety of types which would require some reading, at least on the part of the minister. A half dozen lawyers, several medical doctors (though until Dr. Hinde appears in the county, there is no record discovered of any before 1812 when there were several), and a dozen surveyors would make up the professional classes. From a technical sense, an education played a part in perhaps fifty lives in the county. The rest could live reasonably comfortably illiterate. The more important knowledge was to know the right time to plant wheat, to recognize a deer track in the soil, to care and keep a rifle, to be able to make soap from ashes and grease, to wield an axe, etc. Extensive education to help a person adjust to living was not needed. A man could learn enough to read his Bible, to write his name, to add and subtract, and learn a little about his country, in two or three years of education. Since girls often had nothing better to do, like hunting and fishing, they quite often got a little better education than the boys.

The frontier, however, was not without culture. A surprising number of men were well educated who carried a long rifle and in moccasined feet walked the forests' paths. Men such as James McMillan or the Marquis Calmes were university men. Many had attended European and particularly Scottish Universities. Others had gone to eastern schools such as Liberty Hall which eventually became Washington and Lee, William and Mary, and even an occasional Harvard or Yale man. Even in the west, before the war whoops of the Indians had halted, the Presbyterians were trying to establish a college called Pisgah. Before 1790 Transylvania was a going institution of learning, basically Presbyterian at this time, though the Presbyterians had a hard time holding on to it. As a center of learning it became the best west of the mountains for another fifty years. There were also schools in every settlement of any size from the very beginning. From modern standards they were very crude, but they met the needs of the time.

A teacher would meet with a dozen or so children, with virtually no books, often using charcoal and bits of wood for school boards and writing material, they taught reading, writing, the Bible, a surprising amount of history, politics, theology; and classical literature

Already the age when anything that sounded like Greek and Roman was venerated. Towns were being named Paris, Versailes, etc.; buildings were being built with what was presumed to be Greek oriented styles, etc. These teachers would vary. Ministers made up most of the more permanent instructors and founded more schools. Where ever the Presbyterians went, schools were started. David Lyle is a good example. When a Presbyterian moved, he often moved not only to a church, but to the school that the former minister had established...Walnut Hill in Fayette County was a good example. In Clark County the Presbyterians in Winchester either dominated the Academy with their men, or conducted rival schools as late as 1890. The other movements did not have the educated men as did the Presbyterians, but where there was education, particularly among the Baptists, schools would also appear. The Methodists were generally too much on the move to establish church related schools particularly at this time. Later, Methodist sponsored schools would appear in Mt. Sterling, in Millersburg, in Shelbyville and elsewhere. Usually these were organized and taught not by circuit riding ministers but settled men who made no effort to hold an official pastorate. Women often were teachers though the record does not in the early days speak often of them. They were there but taken for granted. These were mothers who would take in a few children including their own to teach. We have mentioned Daniel Boone's sister-in-law who taught him how to read. Most of the teachers that made the record were young men who had education and while they were looking for a place to settle and a final occupation to enter into, became teachers. James McMillan, William Sudduth, Hubbard Taylor and many others fell into this group. Outside of the ministers, however, one does not find full time, professional teachers in Clark County until after the Civil War. These men were teaching to mark time. Once they found their spot to settle, made a little money or started a profession, they left teaching to another young man just beginning.

Most of the professional training was individual to individual. A lawyer would have in his office two or three young men who would do his clerking, write his briefs, do some of his research and read his law books. With his training they would become lawyers who in turn would train other lawyers. Medical doctors were also trained in this way. It is not until after the Civil War that medical and law schools become common, though they did exist in these early days. Transylvania had a law shool in the 1790's though it was not separate from the other curriculum and was taught often by ministers and non law instructors.

We have already reported the apprentice system where a man taught a youth a trade. It was also not unusual for the apprentice to also be taught to read, write and something of literate knowledge. This happened to David Lyle's students and apprentists.

To the non-literate mind of many readers the interest of the people in these communities are sometimes a shock. This was after the Civil War, but we find a literary society in Rabbit Town which is located roughly in the Crow Ridge area. The Bean School which was one of the oldest would have debates on highly technical subjects. Winchester had poetry clubs as well as literary societies and debate societies. It is hard to say how early these went back.

Winchester had a library society as early as 1810. The history of the library effort in Clark County is found in the fourth volume.

Any layman knew his theology well and was ready at "a drop of the hat" to debate some other equally versed layman the questions of predestination and free will, immersion or infant baptism, universal damnation or universal salvation.

Asa Barrow reported a Mr. Doniphan who taught pupils at Boonesborough in 1779.

Jo Delta Albund in her thesis, History of the Education of Women in Kentucky, 1934, reports that the first school was that of Mrs. William Coons. C. P. Johnson's "History of Kentucky" said that schools were started as soon as a settlement was firmly established.

We see Daniel Boone as a very young man learning to read and write from his gentle Quaker aunt-in-law. A mother with some education would find time to teach her children the essentials. Since the community in Clark County at least was filled with relations, she would not mind adding to her children those of an uncle or an aunt, or a cousin, or the friend in the next cabin. She might have a half dozen or more crowded around her. Her methods might be simple. Her teachings crude, but then, what was needed was not elaborate.

The settlement felt its duty to provide some kind of school. The mother teacher might be adequate. On the other hand, it might be that the education of the young was more than the mother-teacher could handle. Something more was needed. The solution was simple. Find one of these young men, or more rarely, young women, who had a somewhat better education and hire him to teach one's children. Naturally, the neighbor's children could come. Ruth Wood Wilson's thesis, 1959, the History of Education in Clark County quotes a Mrs. William R. Wooten describing how her mother hired a woman to come in to teach. Her home was virtually turned into a boarding school since some of the neighbor's children had to be kept all night or all week when it was difficult to get them home.

Wilson suggests that Strode Station had a school as early as 1779. There is no record of a regular school however, though the settlers undoubtedly did something in the line of education. Jilson in the Historical Society's Quarterly, Vol. 34, reports that a Nick Thomas was teaching at Strode's in 1789. William Sudduth, John Rice and Thomas Parvin were teaching also at Strode's during this general period...Parvin was probably first since he was at Constant's Station during the Indian attacks. He became the printer of John

Bradley's KENTUCKY GAZETTE in Lexington. About 1790, Benjamin Allen was teaching school at Boyles' Station. It is safe to assume that any of the stations where more than three or four families were based had some type of school.

Lucien Beckner considered William Kavanaugh in the Quarterly, Vol. 11, was Clark County's third teacher, but there were others before him for this honor. However, Kavanaugh was teaching shortly after 1790. Settler children living in and around Strode's Station were never without a teacher.

He also described a method of teaching the alphabet with wooden paddles. A letter would be written on each paddle. The teacher would hold one up and the student or students would read it aloud.

It is not clear whether the Independent School House is related to the Bush School or not. At any rate, the Deed Book for June 26, 1-807, reported that David McGee had given the school an acre and a half including the use of a spring. The house was already built. The school was bordered by the property of William Moore and William Robinson. This was the first reported property used exclusively for a school house, legally deeded, in Clark County.

On the whole, the supply of teachers met the needs. When there were not enough teachers seeking the jobs, the school trustees would look around in the community for someone that had had a little education for the job. So it was that William Landrum reports that when he had worked his way through the accepted math book and had had all the available schooling offered, his neighbors considered him educated enough to teach. He was eighteen.

Micah Taul describes his school before 1800. By present standards it was meager. Two or three books were all that were available to the whole school...however, in the KENTUCKY GAZETTE there were always advertisements of book companies. This was true right down until 1900. The school houses were a log cabin, usually even cheaper made than usual. If it had windows, and windows in a log cabin were always difficult to make, they would be covered with greased paper that let in a little light but little else. A fireplace would be placed in one end and the door in the other. Often the fireplace did not draw well so there would be smoke in the one room. Often the only furniture would be a chair for the teacher and slab benches without backs. As the school became older in use, and by 1900 most of the more important rural schools were already established, there would be a slow accumulation of equipment. A map, a few extra books, a globe, perhaps a few desks for the older students made out of slabs and hastily put together, ink wells, and the like. Often it was easier to build new cabins that to repair the old, so as the old building fell to pieces a better one would be constructed.

The books would be the Kentucky Speller, Duball's Arithmetic, the Bible, Dillsworth's Spelling Book, and other books that might be available. Considering the story of Daniel Boone's party on Lullbegrud Creek in the middle of Indian territory far away from the nearest settlement with Gulliver's Travels would indicate that there were more books available than might be expected.

Apparently there were two types of early schools.....the loud school where the students would repeat their lessons out loud and in unison... a method used by Arabic and south European schools for a thousand years. This verbalization of lessons would help those who did not have a book. John E. Garner remembered such schools as late as 1840. Mrs. Julia Tevis remembers attending school in the Bush Settlemen in 1803 with a man whose unlikely name was Mr. Petticord.

The method of teaching was simultaneous, auditory reading with the older children helping the younger children. The birch switch was ever present and discipline was harsh and hard. It was often a necessity for the teacher to be able to whip any student who might be a nearly full grown son of a farmer, or any combination of students. Teaching on the frontier was no place for a feminine teacher.

There apparently was a log school house in the yard of Providence Church after the building of the stone church in 1798. It was probably there much earlier and could have been the old log church building itself. William Beckner said the school building was still standing in 1888. The August Court of 1798 reports, incidently, the existence of a school house on the Kentucky River at the mouth of Two Mile in connection with the surveying of a public road. This school could not have been the school of Providence Church.

We have noted the existence of a school in Strode's Station. Thomas Parvin moved out of Strode's early into Constant's Station before he went to Lexington. We can presume he was teaching there until 1788. Fred Eagle's thesis, the History of Education in Clark County, 1928, claims that the oldest school house in Clark County was on Four Mile Creek on what was later known as the Muddy Creek Pike. This was reported in the records as early as 1793. There was evidently a school associated with the Owen Meeting House by 1794. These two could be the same.

The same road reports, incidently list a school in 1802 between Jackson's Ferry and Fred Buchanon. (We have made no effort to locate Buchanon's) but it would be at the lower part of Four Mile. A school is repeatedly reported to be about Barnett's on Four Mile in connection with the report to the county court. Again, the exact location of such a school could perhaps be discovered from the road records if it was worth it, but presumedly it would be about where the present Barnett's store is located (1976). This school is reported in the road reports in 1802, 1806, 1808 and 1816. It may be the same school earlier reported at Owen's Meeting House.

In 1798, a school was reported on Two Mile near Tom Burney The same year a school house was reported on the land of William Bybee. David Barrow opened the Lullbegrud school just over the county line in Montgomery Count in 1800. This school was operating well into the Civil War in that James French tells how his father relates an incident of bullets whipping in and around the school house during a Civil War skirmish. All the students laid flat on the floor.

The first school in Indian Fields was near the old fort on Nelson Bush's land. It may have not been operating until late in the 1820s.

William Landrum gives perhaps the most extensive record of early schools in Clark County that has come across in this research. He moved into an area that must have been close to the Pilot View area in that on one side of him was a school that included children of such families as the Noes, Gibbs, Boones, Christies, Muiers, Bunches, Combs, Edwards, Moriss, Hornbacks and Eldridges and taught by such teachers as Isham Landrum, Alexander Jones, Thomas Boone and Thomas Philips, a Methodist minister. On the other side of Landrum's home there was another school that included the Fues, Scholls, Huls, Donahoes, Fowlers, Ricks, Clarks, Tyners, Walkers and Davises and had been taught by John Wills, James Bibb, a Mr. McGee, a Mr.Hunt, Thomas Maffett and Martin Haggard...Schollsville-Bethlehem area and the Ruckerville country.

Landrum's first teaching job was in one of these schools. In 1822, he was teaching at the Bethlehem School which also probably started with David Barrow and continued a hundred years as one of the best rural schools. Here Landrum taught a year and received $7.00 per student. Evidently, no child was refused, however, if the parent was too poor to pay. There may have been a social distinction when a teacher listed his patrons and then added "and others", but this was to be expected. Those whose children attended Landrum's Bethlehem School included George Fry, and the school was on his land, James Clark, William Clark, Matthew Davis, Joseph Scholl, Anderson Johns, Robbin Kincaid, James Edmonson, William Rupard, Erasmus Rupard, Joseph Rupard, William Haley, Bird Clewson, Isaac Wills, Thorton Wills, Austin Trimble, Henry Fritts, Jack Bonney, Berryman Adams, Septimus Davis and John Rupard.

In 1827, he was teaching in the school in the Gardner neighborhood which must have been near Hood's Station for this school included such families as the Gardners, the backbone of the Methodist Church, Constants, Sphars, Skinners, Beans, Caspers, Redman, Wilson and Bryants.

In 1827, Landrum was teaching at Sugar Ridge which he considered one of the best neighborhoods in the county. His patrons included

William Ramsey, John Ramsey, Alexander Ramsey, Andrew Ramsey, James Ramsey, Henry Judy, Fielding Watts, Dr. Andrew Hood, John Flynn, Michael Fields, Merine Bowfield, William Stevenson, Bird Clewson, Isaac Wills, Thornton Wills, James Stevenson and David Brandenburg.

This school no doubt dates back to John Lyle in 1800. It was closely related to the Presbyterian Church. Some families had sent their children to him at Bethlehem.

Part of John Baker's agreement to win the county seat for Winchester was to give land for a school. The land was not actually deeded by his son, John Baker, until after the father's death and a school built until 1810. The location was the corner of Hickman and Highland. The school, however, was operating many years before this date and would continue to operate on that sight until 1974.

On December 18, 1798, the legislature established the Winchester Academy along with several other schools in neighboring towns. The county court implemented its establishment. Originally there were thirteen trustees: Robert Clark, Junior and Senior, Hubbard Taylor, John Lyle, Richard Hickman, William Kavanaugh, Jacob Fishback, David Bullock, William Sudduth, Dillard Collins, John Irving, Patterson Bullock, and Robert Elkin according to the history written by Elizabeth Taylor. This was quickly reduced to seven, Robert Clark, Jr., William Sudduth, David Bullock, Dillard Collins, John Irving, Patterson Bullock and Robert Elkin. The earlier list is interesting in that it includes the name of David Lyle who had just arrived in Clark County. It is possible that there was some plan that he might teach at the Academy. Kavanaugh also might have been interested. However, Lyle did not and went ahead with organizing a school in the Salem area .... which also accounts for the dropping of Fishback from the trusteeship. The Acts of 1813 said that new trustees would have to be appointed when only seven were left. It may be that this number seven was a minimun amount permitted by law. The school lay just out of the city limits.

To finance this school, the state endowed the school with 6,000 acres of state land that could be sold to obtain money for the school. In 1809 land was sold in Christian County and 1811 in Caldwell County for the benefit of the Academy and so listed in the deed books. In 1808 the state had extended the time the school had to organize properly. Even though the trustess had been given the power to levy a tax to pay Thomas Scott for the surveying he had done in Winchester, there is no indication that any such support came to finance the school In 1803, several trustees of the school had been ousted for failure to attend meetings. The legislature did, in addition to the grant of land give Winchester Academy the right to have a lottery. We have not discovered whether it was ever held.

No doubt there was a school of sorts in Winchester as Micah Taul described it before 1810. It is also obvious in the record that very little was done to organize the school. However, with Winchester growth it became necessary to build a school. Hence, the sudden activity which forced Baker to fulfill his father's promises and deed the land..the second in Clark County to be deeded for strictly educational purposes. There was also a building constructed at this time. It must have been brick and remained largely the same building that appears in very early photos after the Civil War. The Presbyterians and later the Methodists used it to hold meetings. It is very likely it was in this building that the Quakers held their meeting for their short lived church. At any rate, the school building became the center of not only educational life, but also the religious and social life as well.

Amsi Lewis was still listed as a teacher in the KENTUCKY ADVERTISER in 1816. Thomas Dudley names an Amzi Martin in his recollections of this period, but he probably has the name confused. Willis Collins taught sometime after Lewis, perhaps as the second teacher. In 1814, the KENTUCKY ADVERTISER reported that Ameziah Lewis (who was also an active Presbyterian), from New York state, was the head master. He offered to teach spelling and reading for $6.00; writing, math and English grammar for $8.00 and Latin and Greek for $12.00.

The trustees of the Academy of 1811 were Thomas Pickett who was president, Thomas Irwin, Chilton Allan, Samuel Hanson, Peter Evans, Jr., Thruston M. Taylor, John Ward, David Dodge and Samuel Taylor. They were at that time selling land in Caldwell County.

The old school which may have met in John Strode's house (which also was used as a jail and a tavern) was moved back to the Hickman site.

As stated, the stronger rural communities had their schools well established by this time. However, schools would appear and disappear with the needs of the communities' children, the personalities of the parents and the availability of teachers.

There was a settler school established close to 1800 in what is now called the Becknerville area by a Mrs. Gray and Mrs. Throckmorton. This was apparently a girl's school (though John Lyle is given the credit for the first girl boarding school in Paris in 1804) and taught among other things the harp, harpsicord, needlecarft, knitting and tufting. Thomas Dudley reported that Silas Robbins was teaching in the general area of Wades Mill during his early adult life.

During the War of 1812, the KENTUCKY ADVERTISER reported a military school being organized in Clark County. Easton also mentions a Magrudder School taught by two sisters. This may have been the school that connected Kavanaugh's school in 1800 with the 1808 effort.

## THE MILITIA

The frontier needed a military organization. The militia was the military that served the frontier from its outset until it finally dissolved in Kentucky in 1850. Many of the military titles that Kentuckians bore throughout their lives came from service, even though brief, in the militia. The best source of the first twenty years of the militia's history is of the Cornstalk Militia by G. Glen Clift in the Frankfort's library of the Kentucky Historical Association.

Clift's name, Cornstalk, is somewhat derisive. The militia in the eyes of many was a joke. During the American Revolution, the history of militia units were spotty. They won very decisive victories at Bunker Hill and elsewhere. They broke and ran at Brandywine and Germantown. On the whole however, they were an adequate military force for what they were organized for...to protect the frontier from Indian attack. They were not, on the whole, organized for a first class war. Militia units as such were not used in the War of 1812 or the Indian wars. Entirely new units, often based on militia, would be organized.

During the American Revolution, Virginia militia was assigned to the frontier to defend the various fortified stations, Boonesboro, Harrodsburg, St. Asaph and later Strode's, Boones's, Bryan's, etc. These military services were just as much American Revolutionary war services as those fighting in the east. Most of the men that were important during the Revolution, Simon Kenton, Daniel Boone, Richard Calloway, John Holder, etc... held military titles in the militia that ranged from colonel downward. In the Battle of Blue Licks, most of Kentucky's brass was present and much of it was killed.

For the Clark County area, Richard Calloway was the ranking officer at Boonesboro from about 1777 onward. After his death, the ranking officer was John Holder. No Clark Countian had high rank as far as the rest of the state was concerned. The first uniformed militia was in 1788.

One of the first acts that Isaac Shelby did when he was elected governor was to establish the militia. Previously, it had been Virginia militia.

All white male citizens, 18 to 50, were subject to the draft by the Governor. They could hire a substitute but otherwise there was no appeal. This was considered part of the duties a citizen owed his state.

According to the Military History of Kentucky which was part of the American Guard Series, 1939, every company would have a captain, a lieutenant and an ensign. The ensign would be the equivalent of the present second lieutenant. The company would have three sergeants, three corporals, a drummer and a fife and not less than forty or more than sixty enlisted men.

There was a long list of those not eligible for the draft: judges of the Superior Court, members of Congress, Attorney Generals, registrars and clerks of the land offices, inspectors of tobacco, professors and tutors of any public seminary, all ministers of the gospel (those licensed to preach according to their sect), keepers of the public goals (jails), millers, iron workers.

There were draft dodgers. They were legally dead and any property would be passed on to their next heir. It made no difference as to politics. If you were able bodied, Tory or not, you served your time. It is this history that notes John Holder who was to become a ranking officer in the militia was a Tory.

In 1782, horse units were formed. Every sixteenth man was to have a horse at least 14 hands high with a saddle and bridle. He was to furnish the horse and equipment. The state would furnish the sword, pistol and a pair of saddle holsters. (The guns of those days were too big and heavy to wear on the hip.)

Legally, the militia was to have two musters a year as regiments. Every company was to drill every other month except for December. (The calendar which had been based on the Julian calendar had no provision for leap year. The result was a steady gaining of winter on the calendar so that December was now actually January. This was changed in Washington's administration). For all practical purposes, there was no muster days in winter.

A better unit would drill monthly and occasionally even weekly, at a given point, usually the county seat. On the whole, uniforms and equipment, even ammunition were furnished by the soldier. Gradually the equipment was furnished by the state to non-commission and private soldiers. The officers were required to furnish most of their own equipment right down to the Civil War. There was some effort to standardize uniforms, but save in some of the social militia units in the larger town like Lexington, little was done along these lines. The social units would often design their own uniforms with the usual fancy designs of the military day. Privates who could not supply their own needs were to report the fact. Presumedly something was done to help them.

Militia day, or often called muster day in the earlier period, was as much social as military. The militia was basically a young organization. The young men of the county would ride or walk in on muster day leaving behind the worrisome work and chores of a mostly agricultural existence. They would go through a period of drilling, a period that varied with the influence and ability of the officers.

Most of the officers in the earlier days had some military training in the Revolution and others had fought in the various Indian campaigns. Most of the militia outfits had a core of old veterans to give experience to the youngsters. Discpline was slight. Attendance though mandatory was not enforced. The drill varied in its effectiveness. There was little training for field work. Actually the drill not only drew the young men, but a reasonable number of girls whould show up to watch the fun along with a collecton of parents, interested citizens and loiters. All together, muster day was an important day to a cross-road community.

There is one story of Chilton Allan that should be added here. No date is given but it would have to be about 1810... perhaps even later. It was muster day and there was an effort to form a new company in the pasture where the recruits had gathered. Allan had not signed up, but being a young man who had just begun to climb the ladder of life, had wandered out to see what was happening. It was obvious that one of the town's leading men expected to be elected as captain, but instead of electing him, the recruits elected Allan. Allan protested that he had not even signed up and was not part of the militia. The recruits insisted. Allan argued that he had no military experience. This made no difference and he agreed to accept the captaincy. With that, the militia adjourned and went to the nearest tavern to attest their bravery and hard work.

In the month before the next muster day, Allan found a copy of Baron Von Stuepen's drill manual. Allan then cut out a series of small wooden blocks which he arranged as the company and learned to drill. When the muster came again, he was prepared.

The militia was an opportunity for the bored country boy to come to town, to parade before the girls, to pretend to be soldier, and to drink a little before going home. Again the system worked. When the Indian wars came and the War of 1812 called many of these young men up to prove their ability, on the whole, they performed well. The problem was in the officer class. Given good officers, the militia generally did creditably. Where the militia performed poorly, it could generally be traced to leadership.

When the Kentucky militia was organized, most of the rank that had been recognized as Virginian, became Kentuckian. Officially, officers were appointed by the Governor with the approval of the State Senate. Much of his official papers were concerned with the organization and upkeep of the militia. Actually, during the Indian dangers, it was perhaps the most important function of the state and the one function that effected nearly every citizen. Actually, officers of company level were elected by the men under whom they served, and could be removed by popular vote. The results of these elections were passed upward for Governor's signature. The system often broke down. Strong disciplinarians often were found without a command. However, on the whole, the system worked well. If a man was going to fight an enemy, he would prefer a good leader. If the system occasionally ditched a man of ability, it also eliminated many incompetents.

Officers above company level were usually nominated by their fellow officers. Actually there was more and more a tendency to elect all officers by fellow officers rather than full company vote. This was particularly true after the establishment was created in which a single group dominated the militia and after a campaign was well underway. Company vote usually came with the initial organization. Occasionally, the Governor would exercise his right and promote an officer. Usually the staff, if regiment or division, would be chosen by the commanding officer. An officer could drop out after a period of service, but he would always be known thereafter by his rank. Only a handful really stayed in the militia for a career (there were no full time militia even at the top), and was promoted up to general. In 1790, the officers were paid by the month. The lieutenants received $22.00; Ensigns $18.00; sergeants $5.00; corporals $4.00 and privates $3.00, but only were they paid when drilling. Actually it did provide a source of cash money, something scarce in the county during this period and so was attractive.

The muster day celebration would continue until midnight or later, when one by one the soldier boys would stagger to their horses or find their way home unaided.

Most of the fighting, Estill's Defeat, Blue Licks, etc..,were militia ooperations. The stations at Boonesboro, Harrodsburg and St. Asaph, and later at Strode's, McGee's, Bryan Station, etc.., were garrisoned by militia and the defense was militia responsibility. Every frontiersman was automatically a militia member in times of trouble.

When Daniel Boone took some men to Blue Licks to get salt, he was doing so as a captain in the militia. He surrendered them to the enemy for which Calloway, his commanding officer, court martialled him. Boone was acquitted and promoted to major.

In 1790, Charles Scott took a command of Kentucky militia to help in the Harmar campaign...230 Kentucky cavalry mostly from Fayette and Bourbon Counties. Officers were not elected until after the command had crossed the Ohio. Evidently, the Bourbon County men were in minority and there was fear they would go home if all the officers went to Fayette County. A number of Clark County men (not yet established) was with this group.

Shelby divided the state into two divisions, four brigades and fifteen regiments. From the very beginning it proved inadequate. The militia laws were in constant change so that it is difficult to say what was lawful or what was not over a period of time. In 1792 Fayette County (which included what became Clark County) had 1,954 enlisted men and 179 officers.

Regiments, brigades, divisions, etc., had definite geographical territories which the Governor had considerable right to change.

In 1792, with the establishment of the militia, Clark County area was served by the second division, the 3rd brigade and the 8th, 9th, and 10th regiments. Most of Clark County's men were in the 8th.

With the establishment of Clark County, the 17th became her regiment though some Clark County residents remained in the 8th. After the creation of Montgomery County, the 17th remained Clark County and the 31st became Montgomery County. Again, there were a few Clark Countians in the 31st.

There were radical changes in 1799. Clark County became part of the 5th division, the 5th brigade. The 5th brigade included Fayette's 8th (the rest of Fayette's regiments were in the 3rd brigade), the Clark County's 17th and 36th, Montgomery's 31st and 34th and Bourbon County regiments were the 14th and 47th. Again, some Clark men could be found in the 14th.

It must be remembered that the number of men in a unit was, in comparison with today, quite small and very flexible. Usually replacements were not sent to a regiment that had heavy casualties but new regiments would be formed. A company would seldom have more than a hundred men and companies of fifty were not uncommon. The platoon and squad did not usually have a definite form but were formed out of the company depending on the duty and the number of officers or non-commissioned officers. A regiment would have about five hundred men or less...usually three or four companies with some supporting forces, staff, quartermasters, etc..

The Governor had the power to call to duty small units of the militia with the appropriate officers. One might therefore, find a captain or even a major, in command of fifteen or twenty men. The Governor had the power to draft men to service. Usually the time of service was small.

In 1792, Thomas Kennedy was appointed general for the second division, but for some reason was declared ineligible. Charles Scott was thereby appointed. Third brigade senior officers were Peter Moore, Alexander Parker and Robert Todd, none from Clark.

Levi Todd was the commanding officer of the 8th regiment. As already reported, Todd was one of the chief lawyers to serve before the county courts. He was well known to Clark Countians. The ranking major in command of a batallion was James McMillan. John Martin was the second major and John South the third major. The captains were Philip Bush, William Campbell, William Dudley, James Hickman, Richard Hickman, Garrard Hume, Robert McMillan, James Stevens. Lieutenants were Elijah Chinn, Bennett Clark, William McMillan (William McMillan in 1792 was part of the Kentucky attack based at Fort Washington on Wabash Indians) David Hampton, Jacob Landers, Bird Price, John Price, Joseph Scholl and William Whiteside. The ensigns were Thomas Baxter, William Boswell,

Nathanial Bullock, Martin Johnson, Thomas Jones, Richard Mitchell and John Waller. Nathanial Wilson was cornett, Levi Todd was promoted to brigade and John Tetter became commanding officer. Waller Overton was paymaster and quartermaster.

The WINCHESTER SUN, April 3, 1924, carries the names of McMillan's 1793 company. Sergeants were Milton Vivion, William Wilson and Mark Chadford; corporals were James Beall. In addition there were James Moore, Thomas Randall Moore, John Crabtree, David McGee, Jesse Milton, Samuel Vissor, William Trusdell, Jonathan Hunt, Mitchell Hardwick, William Nelson, William Downing, James Dunlap, Joseph Blackburn, James Williams, Matthew Wills, Thomas Owen, James Jackson, Jacob Casinger and Robert Craig.

With the creation of Clark County, the 17th regiment was organized. John Holder was lieutenant colonel in command. Richard Hickman was the first major and Robert McMillan second major. Later, William Sudduth became major. The captains were Simon Adams, Joseph Blackburn, Sam Downing, David Hughs, William McMillan, James McGill, James Maupin, Thomas Miner, John Martin, William Rodgers, Ambrose Christy, Isaac Crabtree, John Dooley, Robert Higgins (of the Light Horse Company) and James Young. The lieutenants were Anderson Bryan, Uriah Humble, Martin Johnson, Henry Kelso, Miltheny McClung, Robert McGary, John Ray, Alexander Ritcher, William Tinsley, James Wade, Benjamin Yates, Hugh Doublas, Lewis Grigsby, Joseph Martin, John Moore, Henry Moore (Light Horse cavalry) and Stephen Strode. The ensigns were Abihew Anderson, James Browning, David Hathaway, John Judy, William Oakley, George Richter, Isaac Spurgeon, Jeremiah Strode, Daniel Wilson, John Yarborough, Peter Goosey, John Knight, and unknown Kelly.

Evidently, this list covers a period of several years for all of these men did not serve at the same time. The court book shows some differences in rank and names that are not recorded in the Cornstalk militia. In the December Court Book of 1793, James McMillan was proposed as lieutenant colonel and John Martin and John Baker were proposed as majors. This could well have been a court proposal, James McMillan being the senior McMillan in this case who would have sufficient rank to be a lieutenant colonel. The Governor may well have seen fit to appoint others. This might well be the end of James McMillan's military career for he dies soon afterward. Martin becomes a quarterly judge and being sheriff he would not be eligible in either case. The court does not continue making such appointment recommendations. It becomes a matter of through channels.

March 4, 1796, the Shelby papers reported that Edmund Baxter and George Redmond were captains, Lynch Brooks was lieutenant and Peter Hackett as ensign.

The same year the court makes its recommendation, lieutenant William McMillan with 26 men were sent to guard the iron works on Slate Creek near Morgan's Station. It is this command that first reaches Morgan's Station when attacked and tried a futile pursuit of the Indians. Evidently, McMillan was not with them at the time.

December 10, 1793, Lieutenant James McMillan was ordered to service with fifteen men and sent to Madison County for thirty days. The same orders had Richard Hickman, William Bush, Andrew Kinkaid, James Poague and William Caldwell stand alert for possible orders to Indian duties.

In March of 1794, John Holder, then the ranking officer of the 7th in the county, was ordered to send two squads to protect the extended parts of Clark County (back towards Cumberland Gap and most around the iron works along Slate Creek). These iron works were vital to the interest of Kentucky and had to be protected at all costs from Indian destruction.

Changes were made in 1796 with Henry Lee becoming the commander of the 5th brigade and William Ward his inspector. The Shelby papers, March 4, 1796, reported that Edmond Baxter and George Raymond were made captains with Lynch Brooks lieutenant and Peter Hackett ensign. This must have been a new company being organized in the Montgomery area.

With 1799 there were changes within the militia. Fifth division general was Levi Todd. He has been mentioned as the most popular lawyer practicing before the Clark County quarterly court. Montgomery's John South moved up into the brigadier general's command of the 5th brigade. Hezekiah Harrison was the brigade inspector.

Clark County now is populous enough that she has two regiments. The 17th which was already organized and operational. The 36th was new and never did reach full strength. It included some of the Montgomery people and generally pulled its recruits from the eastern and northern parts of the county leaving the 17th with the western and southern. William Sudduth was promoted to the colonelcy of the 17th and Richard Hickman moved into Sudduth's old command. The majors were Achilles Eubank, Robert Clark and John Donaldson. Sudduth resigned from the battalion soon afterward to become brigade general and Hickman was promoted. John Holder was now old and sick and dies in 1798.

The captains of the 17th were Jonas Browning, Philip Bush, who had been somewhat upset with having to leave the 8th with the formation of Clark County and had dropped out of the militia for five years, Ambrose Christy, Dillard Collins, Isaac Crabtree, John Dooley and William Frame. William Chiles was a captain in 17th, but he was promoted to major and transferred to the 36th. The lieutenants were Amzi Anderson, James Box, who had been promoted from ensign, John Christy, Joseph Clark, John Corum, Halley Crump, John Deal, Thomas Embree, Caleb Embree, Ambrose Eubank and Churchill Garner. Ensigns were John Christy, Archibald Daniel, James Daniel, Peter Daniel was quartermaster. Dillard Collins was adjutant but he resigns in 1800 and James Holliday became adjutant.

The 36th started with Robert Clark, John Donaldson and William Chiles as majors. All three were originally 17th officers. Clark became the commanding officer. The captains were John Bean who had been promoted from ensign to lieutenant in the 17th, Wiley Brassfield and Robert Cunningham. The lieutenants were promoted from ensigns and were Archibald Bristow, Jonathan Bryan and John Douglas. Hubbard Taylor, Jr., became quartermaster. Cornelius Skinner became captain in 1800.

The May County Court, 1800, confirmed for officers, captain, Christopher Martin, lieutenants, Christopher Calvert and Smith Turner, in Robert Clark's battalion of the 36th. In 1801, George Taylor became paymaster for the 36th.

The period between 1799 and 1805 was a period of declining interest in the militia. The Indians had been driven well out of the Kentucky area. There was no real need from a military point of view for an active militia. It was becoming more and more a drinking and social gathering rather than one with definite military objectives.

James Stephens replaces Robert McMillan as major of the 17th. Smallwood Ecton becomes a captain in the 17th. The entire brass of the 36th changes in 1804. John Bean is promoted to fill William Chiles' position as major and William McMillan replaces the sick Robert Clark as the other major. Only Donaldson holds his command. The 17th also changes in 1808. James Browning, Philip Bush, Jr., Abner Wiseman and Matthew Frame become majors in the 2nd, 3rd and 1st battalion. Bush moves up to staff.

Philip Bush resigns as major and is replaced by James Browning. James Stephens resigns and is replaced by Matthew Frame. Abner Wiseman was the third major. They commanded the 2nd, 3rd and 1st battalion in that order.

The 17th in 1802 showed a roster: Moses Scott, Ambrose Eubank and Joseph Christy, lieutenants; Reason Halsey, ensign; Henry Moore, James Fox, John Christy, lieutenants and Jonathan Morton, Wilburn Aldham and William Bush, ensigns.

This history has largely confined itself to the Clark County regiments, the 17th and the 36th. We note, however, that there were Clark Countians in all the surrounding militia units. For example, the 8th which was in the 5th brigade along with the Clark County regiments, had as major in 1804 William Porter. He resigned. John Edmonson was senior captain; Benjamin Graves, second captain. Lt. John Wills was promoted to replace captain John Jones who had resigned. Ensign William Sphar was promoted to Winn's place. Hezekiah Ellis promoted to Lt. Robert Prewitt's post; Elijah Montgomery went to Ellis's. Ensign John Hart was promoted to Lt. Charles Carn's William Dudley was the lieutenant colonel of the 8th. Lieutenants Charles Carn and William Dudley were promoted.

Of these men, Edmonson, Winn, Jones, Sparr and Prewitt were all Clark County people, largely from what is now known as the Beckernville area. Once again we see the strong influence that Fayette County had over this area. Their ties were as much with Lexington as with Winchester.

After 1805, the militia receives a new spurt. Henry Clay and other Kentuckians wanted war with Great Britian. They wanted the British out of Detroit and out of Florida. They wanted Canada as part of the United States. Slowly they were able to swing the thinking of the Republican Party away from sympathy with France...which no longer represented democracy and individual rights....to a neutrality. They were increasingly successful in forcing the government to take stronger and stronger positions against the British.

With this in the minds of Kentucky leaders, a strong militia that could be used as a striking force in such a war became a necessity.

It is difficult to get the right order of promotions. The Governor's papers are not always in order and sometimes not even dated. Other sources do not always reflect the dating.

A major change was made in the electing of officers in 1806 when by act of the legislature officers were given the right to nominate other officers. This was making official what had been going on for quite some time. On the other hand, it did not end the custom of the ranks electing their company officers. It was at least an effort to head off a serious problem.

According to the Greenup Papers the musical chairs of rank again started taking place in 1805. Sudduth resigned from the 5th brigade and Richard Hickman was again advanced from regiment to brigade and the rank of brigadier general. In November John Donaldson was advanced from battalion major to lieutenant colonel in command of the 36th. Achilles Eubank resigned from the militia, possibly a little irritated that Donaldson was promoted over him. Philip Bush stepped up into the major of the 1st battalion.

Another 1805 promotion was James Gibson as ensign in the 17th. The 36th must have been virtually inactive. Most appointments were for the 17th in this period.

For brass, William Russel, a brigadier general, takes command of the 5th division in 1806. Philip Bush becomes major of the 1st battalion of the 17th. Francis Cullum goes rapidly up the ladder being appointed ensign in 1806 early and seven months later being made a captain of the 17th. James Jackson became a captain also. Gholson Bush was promoted to lieutenant as was John V. Bush, Joseph McMahon and Daniel Railsback. The one exception to the 17th in 1806 was the appointment of John Bean as major of the 2nd battalion of the 36th.

Incidently, there is a Philip Bush who is an officer in the 22nd regiment who does not belong to Clark County. Since the militia does not note what counties men live in, the two names are occasionally conflicting. Katheryn Owen thinks this Philip Bush may be the son of Josiah Bush, one of the brothers who did not come to Kentucky but his widow and children did.

Joseph Clark was a captain in 1807 and James Clark was an ensign, both in the 17th.

At any rate, we have in 1807, October 13, the report that the 17th met at the house of Captain John Martin. The majors were Philip Bush and William Farrior. The captains were Dillard Collins, John Martin, A. Eubank (Ambrose), William Tuttle and Francis Allen. The regiment nominated for captain William White; for lieutenant Isham Baber and for ensign John Owen. Further changes in the 17th were reported in February of 1808 in the Greenup Papers when James Browning became major of the 1st battalion and William Frame the 2nd battalion replacing James Stevenson who resigned. Then there is the very odd note in the Greenup Papers that Philip Bush was a captain in the 22nd. Did Bush again shift back to a Lexington regiment or was this Bush an entirely different Bush?

February, 1808, the Greenup Papers again summed up the 17th. In battalion was William Frame with captains, Comb, Clark and Cullum. The second battalion was James Browning with captains Collins, Eubank, Mallord and William White. Hickman told Greenup that Major Browning was a good officer.

May 5, 1808, the 1st battalion met with William Frame directing and captains D. Collins, John Martin, Ambrose Eubank, John Hatton (spelling in many of these reports are doubtful or the writing is illegible), James Clark and Henry Moore. It is not clear whether the officers are nominating replacements at these meetings or whether the officers are the only ones listed and the lower ranks just assumed. Three captains are made, James Davis to replace Lt. Brown who was promoted; H. Davis replacing Isham Baber who was removed for failure to attend; and Stephen Trigg in Abner Wiseman's place who has been promoted.

Other 17th officers in the 1808s were Benjamin Culver, captain, Henry Moore, captain; James Daniel, lieutenant; Isham Giddons, lieutenant; and William McMahon and Thomas F. Marrow who were ensigns

A similar meeting in March of 1809 was held with Frame presiding New officers were elected by their fellow officers. The idea of the rank and file electing officers is not entirely dead for it appears again in the War of 1812, but the move toward some kind of discipline which requires officers whose rank depends on something besides popularity was taking hold. James Browning, the second battalion major and Captains John Martin, Ambrose Eubank, John Combs, Josiah Clark and William White were present. They nominate for captains Henry

Moore to replace James Browning; John W. Bush lieutenant, replacing Henry Mason who also was promoted and Thomas Morrow ensign, replacing James Gibson who resigned. Joel Hickman was paymaster for the 17th in 1809.

Richard Hickman was still rising in the promotion ladder. He replaced Benjamin South as brigadier of the 4th division. William Frame made lieutenant colonel of the 17th replacing Hickman. John Martin became major of the 1st battalion of the 17th. In 1811, he was replaced by John Morton. John Posey was quartermaster of the 17th.

The second administration of Isaac Shelby's Papers noted a change in the boundaries of the regimental lines in Clark County between the 17th and the 36th. Beginning at Boonesboro Road opposite Peter Evan's gate, a line was drawn through the center of Samuel Taylor's house to the EG mark at the corner of John Gorden's lot, turning to the southwest corner of John Irwin's lot to Fairfax street, to the southeastern corner of Rueben Elkin, northwest to John Martin's lot on Main Street, up the alley to Edmund Calloway's to the Mt. Sterling Road to John Hampton's house. The border line between the 17th and the new 78th regiment was the new Estill County line. Roughly speaking, the western third of the county belonged to the 17th and the rest went to the 36th.

Micah Taul was a lieutenant colonel in the 90th which was not a Clark County regiment but came from Wayne County. Wiley Brassfield in 1812 was major of 1st battalion of the 36th. Isaac Cunningham was the new paymaster for the 36th and Christopher Morrow for the 17th.

## RELIGION ON THE FRONTIER

We have reported the establishing of the Providence Baptist Church as an integral part of the Bush Settlement. No other Clark County settlement was related to a church in the same way. However, it was not long after a settlement was established that religion followed. A Church of England or an Episcopal minister preached May 28, 1775, at Boonesboro. We have found no record of what happened to him after that. Squire Boone, Daniel's brother, held services regularly at Boonesboro during his residency there. He was a Separatist Baptist. There is no evidence of a church being organized.

However, there were church men among the settlers. One report stated that there was one Baptist church for every 23 Kentuckians, but this does not fit the facts in Clark County. During the 1880s there was evidence that Baptist, Methodist and Presbyterian ministers had held services in the county but only two churches were organized during this period. There were no church buildings until the middle of 1880s and then only in Providence and Salem churches. Most services were held in homes, under trees, in barns, wherever a few people could gather together. When a group grew large enough to organize a church, there was no problem in throwing up a log cabin in the corner of some member's farm. It is hard to assess the strength of the churches and of religion. A glance at the records show very little evidence of any real influence until 1800. On the other hand, in the 1792 Constitutional Convention there were seven ministers including George Smith and James Garrard from Bourbon County, David Rice from Mercer County and Charles Kavanaugh from Madison.

What churches there were usually were very small. However, it ought not be forgotten that the official membership as reported to associations or presbytries, did not include the community support by non members who attended, gave financial support and were influenced.

Strode's Station's church never reported over 11 to 12 members. Many churches were not much more than a single family with a few in-laws. Providence was the strongest church in the Boone Creek Association for years with about 250 members.

Churches were served by three types of ministers. Most generally and particularly among the Baptist, the ministers were residents in the area of the church. Generally they owned farms and supported themselves outside of their ministry. These would preach on Sunday, marry and bury, but this ended their ministry. They were known throughout the communities as ministers, however, but otherwise were not set apart from the rest of the people. It was customary, again particularly among the Baptists, if an adequate supply of ministers failed, the neighboring churches would search among their own people to find some young man and bring him into the ministry. In a movement that expected a "call", that is, some divine message to tell the young man he was to preach, the cynic might note that such a call almost always came soon after the deacons of the various chruches interested made the request. The believer would note that the young man, so challenged, would seek God's advice in prayer and God would answer the prayer. The local ministers of the Methodist church would also be in this category. Their names are not often recorded in the Methodist records, yet they did much to hold the various circuit churches together during the constant parade of circuit riders.

The circuit rider is the second type of minister. Of course, even to some degree the resident minister rode circuit. He would have four, perhaps even more churches, scattered over a radius of fifty or even a hundred miles from his home. He would often be called upon to preach special services where churches were not available, or help organize churches. Revivals, particularly after 1800 might also take his time, though not so much among the Baptist. A minister might well be in the saddle several days a week and travel long distances. The real circuit rider was operating on a full time basis, his support being drawn from the churches he served. The Methodist and Cumberland Presbyterians favored this type of ministry. Since the Methodists were continually moving their men, often to different conferences which could cover several states, it was not practical to own a farm or business. The Circuit rider in this case often would be on the road literally for weeks, preaching at dozens of stops which would range from a family gathered in a single cabin to a fully organized church. He was continually exposed to Indians until that danger ended, and thieves thereafter. It was a dangerous, hard life which did not contribute greatly to family life. For this reason, ministers were often leaving the itinerary in favor of being local ministers.

The Presbyterians had a form of ministry that somewhat combined the two types. The Presbyterian was not as apt to ride circuit as the Methodists, though it was done among the Cumberland Presbyterians, and even occasionally among the other types of Presbyterians. Often the Presbytery would serve a dozen or so churches too small to have a resident minister very much like the Methodist circuits. On the whole, however, the Presbyterian ministers were more apt to be residential in a certain area. They were apt to buy farms knowing that if they would move, they would move in a more localized area than the Methodists. Other Prebyterians would have businesses such as book binding, wheel rights, smithing, etc., which they would establish besides their churches and operate as long as they were in the area. Above all, the Presbyterians would teach school. This was the most common side income of the Presbyterian minister and would be the first thing he would do in a new parish. As noted earlier, often when a Presbyterian church issued a call to a minister, they also had a school as part of the bargain.

It should also be noted that worship services could be held at any time during the week when the minister arrived in the community. One writer boasted how his church had regular Thursday morning services at least once a month. The service would be held whenever the circuit rider would appear. The time schedule was usually known in advance, but if it wasn't, it would not take long before the news would be sent out and the faithful and the curious would gather.

During this period, there were few forms of recreation. Preaching became an important event whether one belonged to a church or not. It was almost always a whole day affair. A person who lived three to five miles away from the church would load the family into a wagon or on horse back, with blankets, food and other necessities. Later on, in the 1870s, in the Clark County Democrat, First Christian Church would announce that tables would be provided and other facilities would be available for those who came from long away. Goshen Baptist Church arranged crude sleeping quarters in the back of their church for those who had to spend the night.

Since preaching was once a month, the ministers would often come in on Saturdays in many churches. Business meetings would be held on Saturday afternoon, and preaching services at night, again Sunday morning and often on Sunday evenings. Usually the evening services would come early so that it might be possible to get home before dark.

Services were long. Ministers often preached an hour or an hour and a half. They were usually informal and there might well be two or three sermons by different visiting ministers. Singing would intersperse the sermons. There were no hymn books. These would begin coming out after 1800 and met with vigorous opposition. Without hymn books, some one would "line" out the song until the congregation would know it, and then all would sing. Songs were also taught by the fa so la te do system...the notes were sung first, but this was after hymn books became more common. Many churches refused to sing any hymns but psalms. There was great opposition against using "ditties like those the Wesleys were writing". There were almost always no instruments in the church. All of these items would become bitterly controversial in the next half century.

Theology was not limited to the ministers and the theologians. Every church layman had an exact knowledge of his church's doctrine. Even non church people had strong ideas upon the subject. The layman would listen intently to their ministers, nodding their agreement in places, and sharply taking issue on something that was not, in their minds, theologically correct. The minister might say something in a sermon that would bring angry division in the church, dividing congregations and providing everyone in the community with a fascinating topic of conversation.

Such guardianship of the orthodox was important. Denominations, and factions in denominations...there were at least four types of Presbyterians in Fayette County in the late 1790s and early 1800s, two types of Baptists, and a definite division among the Methodists relating to the position James O'Kelley had taken in regards to itineracy of the ministry. In addition there were many strange ideas that might appear in a minister's sermon, such as Hell redemption...or the possibility of saving people even though they were in hell. Later there would be Shakers, Mormons, and other sects seeking converts. The Cumberland Presbyterians would plague the orthodox Presbyterians and finally the ideas of Alexander Campbell and Barton Stone would be presented, supported and opposed.

There was plenty within orthodox denominations to debate about. There was Predestination...was the fate of a man preordained in the beginning of creation so that he had no chance but to wait for God to let him know whether he was among the saints....or did a man possess a free will and could through his own efforts find God's Grace? Jonathan Edwards in the east had preached a sermon describing hell paved with the skulls of unbaptized babies. Was original sin so deadly that a baby who died without baptism was a lost soul, or was there a period of time up to an age of unaccountability when a child was not responsible for sin...in short, the question of infant and adult baptism.

Evangelism was just beginning to influence the churches. George Whitfield had swept the east coast with emotional appeals for faith in God that had divided Congregational, Baptist and Presbyterian denominations into "Old Light", and "New Light" factions, and set up the Cane Ridge Revival just across the county line from Clark in Bourbon County. The Methodists were from the beginning evangelistic since their theology was Arminianism rather than Calvinistic emphasizing free will. There is very little evidence of the use of revival until after 1800. Then it came upon the frontier like a hurricane, furiously opposed, but sweeping much of the opposition before it. Camp meetings became a regular feature of the religious scene. William Landrum's journal, concerning the Methodist churches centered around Clark County, reported yearly camp meetings at Owen Meeting House, at Grassy Lick and Ebenezzar, and, among the Presbyterians at Sugar Ridge. A camp meeting would come soon as the crops were in the ground and the farmers had a little leisure time. They would last for days, perhaps even weeks, with wagon loads of faithful coming and going. Gradually as the Civil War approached, the camp meeting began to become less used. Roads had improved, communications were better, there were more churches. Camp meetings would remain an evangelistic instrument even to the present among more conservative groups. They would often be sponsored by evangelists as a money making side line to revivals.

If camp meeting declined, revivals did not. They became part of the church's program, often being held yearly at the same time. Mt. Olive's May Meeting, or Ephesus's June Meeting among the

Baptists, became calendar events that were able to draw people from many miles away.

The main purpose of church services, camp meetings and revivals was to spread religion. They did more than that. In an age when there was little communication beyond a few miles from a man's home and almost no recreation, any break would dispell the boredom and isolation that surrounded the settler. Court days and church services furnished an outing for the whole family that was eagerly anticipated. It was a time when courting girls and boys had a little more freedom than the old home place afforded. More, the selection was greatly enhanced. Under normal conditions the girl might know a half dozen boys. Even if she went to school as she usually did, the number of older boys in her school slimmed down each year as the boys grew older. In church, however, she might meet boys from three, four, even five miles away from other neighborhoods.

Such gatherings were filled with non sacred activities. One handbill advertising a church service at Bethlehem Christian Church before the Civil War proclaimed preaching in the morning and in the later afternoon a challenge by the preacher that his horse could beat any other horse in the community. Opposition to liquor was not widespread until after the Civil War. The charge that some camp meetings were drunken brawls were not entirely without foundation. Violence was also part of the church scene. Theological quarrels could often be decided by use of fists. It was not unusual for the local toughs to roust a church service, even shooting into the open doors and windows. Just as it was permissable to break up rival political meetings with hecklars, it was not unknown to break up rival church services as well. The popular hymn of the late 1960s, "The Reverent Mr. Black" is not over done.

As preaching points built church buildings, these would become the center of the community. Many of them openly stated that any accepted minister of any faith could preach. The result was that services would usually be held nearly every Sunday even though the church's offical meetings would be once a month. This caused no end of difficulties. As long as the church was a "meeting house", it belonged to the community. Gradually the deeds began to limit who could and could not preach. The Methodist deeds particularly by 1830 had developed a formula that limited their churches to Methodists. Others stated that only Baptist, Presbyterians and Methodists could use them...an effort to close out the Hell Redemptionist Universalists, for example. (It might be noted that Gov. James Garrard's administration was continually under attack because his Secretary of State, Henry Toulmin, was so charged, that Transylvania University was nearly destroyed by charges of Universalism, and that Barton Stone was heavily attacked because he was vague as to the nature of the Trinity.) Some churches began to put in their deeds, statements of faith admonishing that only those who agree with that statement, whether in majority or minority, would have control of the church. For example, the control of the Fairfax Church's property belongs to that group who will not use instrumental music.

In a world of limited social and emotional outlets, speaking became a favorite pasttime. Men would discuss the merits of this preacher or that lawyer, or some politician by speaking ability much as modern people might discuss the batting averages of professional ball players. When certain lawyers were to speak at court, people would come from miles to hear him. The same was particularly true of ministers. Part of the attraction on Sunday was to listen to the preacher preach, not necessarily hear what he had to say but how he said it. When he began to thunder, even the loafers on the fences outside the church would stop their gossiping and listen.

There was also, in most cases, a strong sense of sin. Those who had Calvinistic feelings often looked for, prayed for and desired a sign which would place them into the elect group. The excesses that were part of every revival, shouting, jumping up and down, tongues, trances, etc., were all part of the effort to help a person overcome the hold of the devil. There were those who openly declared their athiesm, sneered at the Bible and at the churches. But even these people often had deep down within themselves a sense of sin. This made the revival and camp meeting such an effective religious tool. People attended them not only for religious reasons, but for social and political. They were always possible candidates.... those who "came to sneer left to serve" type of thing.

Even during the frontier period, the total number of church members was small, and even if one would add those who attended churches with some regularity whether they were members or not, we would still have a very small minority of the population. It might be noted that attendance in churches in those days was nearly compulsory. Basically, it was who belonged to the church that made the difference. The great majority of influential citizens either belonged or more or less supported a church during this period. It gave to the church an influence far beyond the numbers who adhered to it.

The early churches were not interested in social issues. The exception was slavery, though as the Civil War approached this was extended to alcohol. Slavery was a part of Clark County history from the very beginning, as it was in the entire state. There was also very strong opposition to slavery from the beginning of the settlements. On the whole, the opposition rose out of the ministers and centered in the churches. The Quakers were quite strongly opposed to slavery, but they were never able to establish themselves in any numbers in the state. Most of their members, as we have seen in the Boone family, became members of other churches. However, the opposition of Baptist and Methodist seem to be quite strong.

The Methodists came close to being officially opposed to slavery from the very first. It was not until well after the War of 1812, that the issue died and actually the Methodists changed sides. The Baptists were strongly divided. David Barrow led the Baptist forces in this area and divided association and churches on the issue. At least one church would be established in Clark County as an abolitionist church.

In the long run, however, slavery was not an issue in Clark County. When the northern and southern Baptist movements divided nationally, the Clark County churches continued without even seemingly noticing the change of membership of their old associations and continued using what ties they had with the state and national work with the Southern Baptists. If the Clark County Methodists were divided slavery, it can't be demonstrated. There would be northern Methodists, but not until after the Civil War. Neither the Christians nor the Presbyterians seemed to be particularly interested in the slavery question before the Civil War.

At first, denominationalism was both extremely strong and equally weak. We have noted that deeds of some churches called for toleration of any who sought to use the church. It is also quite apparent that ministers of various groups, for example William Landrum, would preach in other denominational services. Landrum would quite often attend the Baptist Associational Meetings and apparently found a second home among the Sugar Ridge Cumberland Presbyterians. There was a Flatswood Meeting House near Bradshaw's Mill in what became Montgomery County that never appeared by that name, at least, in any of the denominational records. Robert Elkin was preaching at a church near Thatcher's Mill on the Clark and Montgomery line that never was reported as Baptist. Most of these were weak and died.

Many churches were strictly family churches. The Stampers, Landrums, among the Methodists, for example, had churches that were evidently basically made up of family. Landrum tells how when an uncle moved, the family church on the uncle's property was closed.

## THE CANE RIDGE REVIVAL

The Cane Ridge Revival was not in Clark County but it was over the county line from Clark County in Bourbon County. Because of this, we will not go into the story of Barton Stone and his separation from the Presbyterians until the second volume of this history which takes up the story of the county after 1820. However, one could not describe the religious life in any county in Kentucky after 1801 without giving some attention to the Cane Ridge Revival. Up to 1801, religion was largely a formal affair of conflicting theologies. The revival movement was already well developed in the eastern colonies as the results of George Whitfield. However, it did not change the fact that most churches were small...perhaps not more than a dozen members....and tightly knit theologically. After the Cane Ridge Revival, though the theological differences would remain, the great evangelistic drive to convert the sinner was by direct and aggressive action.

Briefly, Barton Stone was a Presbyterian who had been born in Maryland in 1777. He started out to be a lawyer, but after attending Guildford Academy and Hampton Sidney College, he turned to religion. He sought to preach in the Presbyterian Church in 1793. He had, like most ministers of the Presbyterian movement, taught school along with his religious duties. This teaching brought him into contact with a Republican Methodist school that had been organized but a few years before by James O'Kelley and was essentially a protest of a movement against Methodist itineracy and organization.

He arrived in Kentucky and became minister of two Presbyterian churches, Cane Ridge and Concord, one in Bourbon and the other in Montgomery County. Nothing is said just how the revival got started. However, John T. Brown in his "History of the Churches of Christ" describes the Thursday and Friday before August, 1801. The roads were literally crowded with wagons, carriages, horsemen and footmen moving into the solemn camp...it was judged by military men on the ground...twenty to thirty thousand...four or five preachers were frequently preaching at the same time in various parts of the woods and fields surrounding the Cane Ridge Church....they included Methodists and Baptists...

Besides these movements, there were men of most every color of religious feeling from Shakers to Hell Redemptionists. The revival continued for several days and finally ran out as food began to become short and the sanitary conditions of the area worsened. However, the revival broke out in all directions. Redford's History of Methodistism in Kentucky claimed it came to Clark County at Owen's Meeting House. It burst loose, of all places, in Salem Presbyterian

Church, dumbfounding John Lisle, Salem's minister. The revival was finished by Methodist circuit riders. Revivals appeared all over Kentucky in great profusion. There was a tremendous religious revival. New churches were organized. Older churches grew in size. New denominations appeared and old denominations divided. The effect was profound.

By the end of the 1810s, the first fever was to have petered out, though revivalism was now firmly established. It was to reappear in the 1820s both in the new camp meeting idea and in the reform revivalism of the Campbells. This also would pass after ten years or so, but would break out again though never in history with such force as these two times.

## THE BAPTISTS

It is a mistake to think of the Baptists as a single movement. About the only thing that Baptists agreed upon was baptism. They were all immersionists by definition. There are more than 30 Baptist groups that remain today in some part of the country as distinct denominations. However, for Clark County, we are concerned mainly with two groups of Baptists that were in existence at the end of the Revolution. They were the Regular Baptists and the Separatist Baptists.

The Regular Baptists were the older of the two movements. In 1770, there was a general association meeting in which the Regular Baptists drew up a statement of faith or a confession which became known as the Philadelphia Confession. This was a strongly Calvinistic document and was immediately accepted by Regular Baptists as just short of scripture. In fact, the Regular Baptists would argue that the Confession merely codified and clarified the scriptures and therefore, was to be obeyed absolutely.

The Confession did give some respectability to the Baptist movement that had been looked upon by its contemporaries at least as a nuisance and at the worst as heretics and trouble makers. It did reduce some of the emotional excesses of the earlier Baptists and gave a measuring stick for the layman to judge its ministers. On the other hand, its very nature kept the Baptist appeal to a minimum. Regular Baptist churches spread slowly over the colonies before the Revolutionary War without making a great impression on them.

In the middle of the 18th century (1740-174]), there occurred in New England what could be classified as the "Great Awakening", a religious stirring and a breaking out of the Calvanistic shell that held both Baptist and Congregationalist. Its main spokesman was George Whitefield.

This produced a new breed of Baptist who were told to separate out of the old churches and hence, their name Separatist Baptists. They were generally Calvinistic, though they were not much interested in its extremes. Calvinistic though their thinking might be, they did not place much emphasis in creeds or statements of faith. They held for open communion (open to all Christians regardless of denomination) and their approach to religion was simpler and evangelical. They felt that salvation was offered to all, though they did feel that God must send an experience before conversion was official.

Their version of Baptists thinking spread rapidly down the colonies from New England. Master's history of the Baptist movement points out that during the Revolution they had nearly stolen the back country from the Church of England.

The Regular Baptists were always suspicious of the Separatist looseness in theology. They felt that this opened the doors to heresy. To prove their point they pointed to the Hell Redemptionist movement that had found some favor among Separatists. The Regular Baptists were not happy with the revival and suspicious of those who were converted in the revival. If God had chosen those to be saved in the beginning, what use was there of a revival. A man had but to wait until chosen and once called, then join the Saints.

However, there was more to hold them together than divide them. They could belong to each other's churches, a little uncomfortably, but faithfully. Soon after the American Revolution, the Separatists and Regular Baptists united in Virginia under the name United Baptists. It was not long before there was a union movement in Kentucky.

Though these were the two movements that appeared in Clark County, they did not exhaust the possibilities of the Baptist for division. Alexander Campbell in the first volume of the Milliniger Harbinger (p. 214), reported that these were: Particular Baptist from England and Wales; Mennonites from Holland; Scotch or Weekly Communion Baptist; Associated or Calvinistic Baptist started at Providence in 1639; Seven Day Baptist which appeared in Rhode Island in 1671; Six Principal Baptist which Campbell admitted had only twenty churches, the American Mennonites; the Free Will Baptist.

Clark County was dominated by the Baptist movement in the early days of its life. Every church was constantly aware of the necessity of keeping itself pure from heresy. Repeatedly, even before the Campbell Reform, and perhaps leading to the success of the Reform, churches had divided and subdivided. It is not until after the middle of the 19th centry, that the Baptist reached some semblance of stability.

In 1801, there was a merger between the two churches which became known as the United Baptist. It was largely from this merger that the Particular Baptist withdrew. However, the United Baptist Church becomes the main stream of the Baptist movement in Clark County. We might note in passing that the disturbing element that ripped the Baptist movement after the merger was the election of James Garrard, a Baptist minister-soldier, to the Governor's chair in 1796. He appointed Harry Toulmin Secretary of State who was leaning in the direction of Unitarianism.

The position that the United Baptist held such points as: The Old and New Testament are the infallible Work of God and is the only rule for obedience. The Trinity was reaffirmed, One God, but in the Godhead there are three Divine personalities, Father, Son and Holy Ghost. Men are totally depraved and fallen and there can be no hope for them. Salvation, regeneration, sanctification and justification can be had only by the life, death, resurrection and ascension of Jesus Christ. The Saints are preserved through the Grace of Glory. Believer's Baptism is the absolute requirement for the participation in the Communion. The Baptist believed in the salvation of the righteous and punishment for the wicked, both eternally.

There was also an accompanied list that controlled the life of its members. Reading any of the minutes of these early Baptist churches, the present day man is amused and sometimes puzzled by the series of church trials that dominate the early minutes.

What the contemporary man of today sometimes overlooks is that a Baptist church was the entire life of its members. It claimed the right to police every action and to supervise every phase of life. Church was not a voluntary function. If you did not live up to the rules and regulations, if you were not guided by church discipline, then you were excluded from the church. Attendance was required. In reading history, one must note that John Calvin actually did impose a theocracy on Geneva with the full powers of state. A Baptist church felt itself no less authoritative. In reading Goshen history, this will be brought out in more detail.

Besides theology, the Baptist church was divided almost from the beginning over slavery. This was reflected in the establishment of the Bethlehem Baptist Church in 1810 and by David Barrow, one of the leading exponents of the anti-slave position in Clark County. The anti-slave men and churches referred to themselves as the "Friends of Humanity". They organized the Baptist Licking-Locust Association, but it soon died, killed largely by the Campbell Reform which was uninterested in slavery but attracted the more liberal anti-slavery ministers.

The Campbell Reform movement will be gone into in more detail, both in this volume, but also the next for this effort shattered the churches in Clark County, created a powerful new movement, but left the more liberal United Baptist intact and more unified than ever before. Hardly had this been settled when a new struggle between the missionary and the anti missionary-minded, really the more conservative and the less conservative wings of the movement. At first, the division in Clark County was relatively equal... Providence, Ephesus, Mt. Olive going with the missionary-minded groups, soon to expand their numbers to include First Baptist in Winchester, Kiddville, Allansville and Corinth after the Civil War. The more conservative Baptist included Goshen, Ruckerville or Upper Howards Creek, Mt. Carmel, Log Lick, New Providence and Friendship.

Weakened as the Civil War period came on, by 1910 all had died save Goshen and the one new "Old Baptist" church in Winchester that had been established. Today (1976) of this entire group, only Goshen remains. It must be noted that these churches also were not united. Mt. Carmel was Particular Baptist as was Friendship until they divided in 1848. Log Lick tended to hold Separatist doctrines. In the face of declining strength, there was some effort to bring them together, at least for fellowship. William Rupard, Goshen's minister, would visit the various association meetings as would to a lesser extent other members. They were generally known as Old Baptist, though this applied more to the Regular Baptist groups such as Goshen. The word Primitive Baptist becomes a later application that does not appear in the newspapers until after World War I.

Perhaps the man who most represents the effort of the Baptist to bring together their divided forces and, at the same time, the dividing issues among them is David Barrow. His descendant, Asa Barrow wrote for the April 1933 Filson Club Historical Quarterly a good deal of information concerning Barrow. Essentially, he is a Montgomery County figure though he probably did preach at Bethlehem about 1806 or '07. His influence, however, marked Clark County as well as the Baptist movement. He was born in Brunswick County, Virginia in 1753. He was ordained a Baptist minister in 1772 and served in the Revolutionary War. He came to Kentucky in 1798 as the minister of the Mt. Sterling Baptist Church serving Goshen and Lullbegrud...and as noted, probably Bethlehem at a later date. He married his first couple in Clark County, April 1, 1806, James Sphar to Roxana Tracy. His last couple in Clark County married October 10, 1816, Simpson McMerry and Jane Clark. In between he performed some 39 Clark County weddings.

He was particularly active in bringing together the Regular and the Separatist Baptist creating the union of United Baptist, but he then turned around and divided the Baptist by insisting that slaveholders should not be given fellowship. For this the North District Baptist expelled him from their ranks in 1808. According to Collins, he and other prominent Kentucky Baptist divines organized the Friends of Humanity and the emancipationist Baptist Licking-Locust Association of Friends of Humanity. The association died with Barrow.

However, his influence is even felt in other quarters. He was obviously not a theological absolutist though he did oppose the Unitarian movement of the day. He sympathized and counciled with the young, questioning, tragedy ridden John Raccoon Smith who was serving Montgomery County churches, often the same churches he had served. In a very real way, Barrow opened the door to Campbellism in Clark and Montgomery Counties though Barrow himself was dead before Alexander Campbell seriously began to put his ideas into words.

One of the ministers that appear in and out of the Baptist churches that effected greatly the life and character of the Baptist churches during this period of church history is Ryland T. Dillard. Again, like so many early Kentuckians, he was born in Virginia in 1797 and came to Kentucky in 1818 settling in Winchester. He studied law under Hubbard Taylor and in 1821 was partner of Richard French working out of Mt. Sterling. He became a Baptist minister in 1825. He became a minister of the East Hickman Baptist Church in Lexington for 47 years. He was minister of the David Fork Baptist Church, one of the great country Baptist churches of Fayette County for thirty years. More than 4000 people came into the church through his life's activities and he married some 873 couples. His first Clark County marriage was Barnett Watts and Delia Sympson, August 23, 1825, and his last marriage in Clark County was in 1864. He had seen service in the War of 1812. He also owned a farm and was an early raiser of shorthorn cattle. It was customary for the state to appoint ministers as Superintendents of Education. In 1842, Dillard became Superintendent for a six year term (he was proceeded by an Episcopalian bishop) and did a good deal to promote the still fledging public education. Politically, like most Kentuckians, Dillard was a Whig. Reluctantly, as the Whig Party disintegrated, he became a Republican.

## THE NORTH DISTRICT

There are, of course, two types of church policies. One where the authority within the church rests within the local congregation and the other where the authority rests in a higher body than the local congregation. The need for the individual to draw together like thinking individuals to form churches is reflected in the need for like thinking churches to draw together to form larger fellowships. All the churches in this first volume belonged to one or another organization above their local churches that were called by various names, parishes, conventions, conferences, associations, presbyteries, etc. Among the Methodist, official records are kept by circuits and it is difficult to know which churches belong to these circuits. Therefore, the history of Clark County Methodistism is directly related to the circuit. The history of the Methodist district or the conference is not particularly important for local history. The Presbyterians were also organized into Presbyteries, but these never played a serious part in Clark County history. It wasn't that they were not important. The local Presbyterians were sufficiently independent in their local bodies and few in number within the county. The larger Presbyterian units play little part in Clark County history, the same will be true in the third volume when the Catholics and Episcopalians appear. Both had strong authority in their upper structure, but their single county church can be studied with very little reference to that structure. To the Christian churches, their district and state organizations play little part in local church history until after 1920.

The Baptist are congregational in church policy. By this, we mean that each church is independent from outside control, owning its own property, calling and dismissing its own ministers, deciding its own creed and theology, and setting its own policies. Hence, it is possible for a Baptist church to go its own way, for any reason, without regard for the rest of the movement. This is done even today (1976). The country is spotted with independent Baptist churches, or with small associations claiming some particular doctrine and fellowshipping with one one else.

However, the Baptist have an almost compulsive desire to associate. From the very beginning they have come together into groups of like thinking churches, giving voluntarily considerable powers to those associations, and adjusting their programs around those associations. The associations often provide the discipline, particularly of ministers, to protect the unwarry church. They decide doctrinal points and warn member churches of the danger of heresy. The local church, though free not to do so, often bound itself to the association decision. In fact, the control of the Baptist association, at least to one who is neither Presbyterian, Methodist or Baptist appears nearly as strong as the Methodist control and stronger than Presbyterian. The fact that it is voluntary makes this all the more amazing.

There are several Baptist associations that effect Clark County. The oldest and original is the North District Association. It was the parent body of most of the other associations, or at least the parent body of the Clark County churches of those other associations. The Boone Creek Baptist Association is the one that intimately relates to the local Baptist churches by 1930; all the Baptist churches in Clark County save one belonging to the North Association had died. Believing that history has meaning, it is interesting to contrast the North District Association and the Boone Creek Association to see why one association lived and one died.

Roughly, the North District Association served more the western part of Clark County and what is now Montgomery, Bath and Menifee Counties. This became particularly true after the formation of the Boone Creek Association. The minutes were printed almost from the beginning. Southern Baptist Seminary has in its possession about half of these printed minutes. William Rupard has a few more. In all, however, one can get a reasonably adequate picture of the North District Association. Many of its churches, particularly in the Montgomery County area, went to the Disciples. After 1845, it had definitely become anti-missionary and lost others.

Collins reports that in 1785, less than ten years from the date when the settler was fighting an almost loosing battle in three small enclaves against overwhelming Indian might, that there were three Baptist associations in Kentucky.

Five Regular Baptist churches came together to form the Elkhorn Association; none from Clark County though Andrew Tribble's Tates Creek Baptist Church in Maidson County was one. The next year it added a sixth, from Limestone (Maysville). Three more united in 1786 including Bryan Station's and Boone Creek's Baptist Churches. In 1789, the association met at Bryan Station and added three more churches.

Meanwhile, in 1789, the Regular Baptist and the Separatist Baptist of Virginia had united to form the United Baptist Church. There were immediate calls for such a merger in Kentucky and immediate opposition.

In 1793, a Grassy Lick Baptist Church from Montgomery County joined the association. This church eventually became Somerset Christian Church. In the 1793 meeting there had been a long and bitter argument between the Regular and Separatist leaders over union. The Regular Baptist insisted on the Philadelphia Confession virtually in tact and the Separatists were unwilling to make any serious compromise. Angry over the defeat, four churches withdrew and joined the Tates Creek Baptist Association in 1793. This movement was lead by Andrew Tribble and was based on his Tates Creek Baptist Church. They announced that their movement would be the United Baptist Church. The majority of the churches were Separatist, though there was at least one, later two Regular Baptist Churches in the association. Unity Baptist Church joined this association the next year. Considering Unity's relationship with Tribble, this is not surprising. Ambrose Dudley had been moderator in 1794 and was one of the most influential ministers in or out of office.

In 1797, the discussion between the Separatist Baptist and the Elkhorn Baptist Association started again. In 1800, Elkhorn Association had 27 churches. David Barrow was moderator in 1801 and James Price was clerk in 1798 and continued in that post.

While the Regular Baptist were organizing in Fayette County, the Salem Association was organized with four Regular Baptist Churches in the area west of Frankfort, mostly around Louisville, Harden and Nelson Counties. This association also grew, but its history had nothing to do with Clark County.

The Separatist organized the South Baptist Association in 1787 and included Providence Baptist Church. There was also a Boone Creek Baptist Church. Whether this church had belonged to the Elkhorn Association and changed its membership or whether it was one of Boone Creek's many divisions is not clear. Houston Creek Baptist Church in Bourbon County was a member. This was the home church of Moses Bledsoe who was to be active in association history and with Clark County.

In 1790, the South District had grown to 19 churches including Tribble's Tates Creek and Unity. It reported 1311 members. In 1791, the more liberal Separatist Baptist were having trouble with the Hell Redemptionists. Andrew Tribble and Robert Elkin were appointed on the committee to investigate the question and eventually ordered the expulsion of John Bailey who had defended the position at the association meeting. The fact that a Separatist Baptist would actually defend the position at the association no doubt frightened the Regular Baptist and caused the failure of the 1793 merger efforts.

The organization of the Tates Creek Association, drawing as it did from the South Association, showed an irritation at the Separatist's refusal to take a compromising step towards the Regular Baptist's creed as much as irritation at the Regular's insistence on their position.

In 1794, the South Association met at Howard's Creek Baptist Church, as the association referred to Providence until well after 1800. It was the first of many associations, conventions, conferences and Presbyteries that would meet in Clark County over the next years. At this meeting, negotiations with the Elkhorn Association were once again begun. Ambrose Dudley, Robert Elkin, Moses Bledsoe and John Price were among those negotiating.

The result of this series of negotiating meetings with David Barrow acting as moderator of the Elkhorn Association and given the credit for a final success of the talks, the Regular Baptist Elkhorn and the Separatist Baptist South District again met at Providence with Robert Elkin as host pastor and David Barrow as moderator voted to organize the North District Association of United Baptist. Robert Elkin was elected moderator. All the churches north of the Kentucky River, east of the Elkhorn Association area, regardless of whether they were Separatist or Regular would be members. Similar mergers were accomplished in other parts of the state.

In 1802, the North District Church met at Unity. At this time she included Spencer Creek (71), Lullbegrud (49), Bofman's Fork (43), Salt Lick (116), Howard's Creek (Providence) (197), Unity (188), Bald Eagle (61), Mount Pleasant (184), Blue Ash (104), Log Meeting House Tates Creek (168), Locust Creek (39), Salem (138), John's Fork (12), Red River (25), Sycamore (131), Jessamine (62), Greer's Creek (18), Upper Howard Creek (38), Station Camp (12), Brush Creek (28), Long Branch (45), Morton's Meeting House (22), Hopewell (135), Slate Union (45). This is a total of 24 churches with 1,928 members. Elkin was moderator and Bledsoe clerk. Ordained ministers included David Scott, Robert Elkin and James Haggard from Providence, James Quisenberry from Unity, Leonard Turley, Isaac Crutcher and Joseph Craig, Moses Bledsoe, Mahaleal Shackle, Charles Finnel, Daniel Williams, John Davis, Edward Kindred from Upper Howard's Creek, Henry Blackgrave and Isaac Crutcher.

Noting also, David Barrow and Jilson Payne were messengers from the Elkhorn District. Payne was a magistrate of Clark County before Montgomery divided and later active in Montgomery County. Tates Creek Association sent a Boon (Boone did not use an "e" in his name), but does not say which Boone.

Like all church mergers, all were not happy. There remained the extremes of each group who felt that too much had been given up. On one side were the Baptist of strong Calvinistic trends who were becoming interested in the Particular Baptist position of Old England. The Hell Redemptionists were still bothersome, and particularly in Garrard's Church of Cooper's Run in Bourbon County. The Cane Ridge Revival had sent a dozen variety of preachers wandering the woods and by-ways ready to expond their views if someone would listen. Among these were the Shakers and Mormans. Barton Stone himself had now broken with the Presbyterian Church and was advocating what he called a Christian Church which denied all creeds and man made theologies and urged union....an idea that many Separatist Baptist found appealing.

David Barrow became minister of the Mt. Sterling Baptist Church, **the Lullbegrud Baptist Church and probably** one or two more North District Churches. He transferred his standing from the Elkhorn to the North District. Anti-slavery feelings were running strong at this time, and there were many Baptist and Methodist with a few Presbyterians, that were insisting on forbidding fellowship with slaveholders. Barrow was very sympathetic with this position though there is no indication at this time he was ready to go that far. In 1803, he attended the Bracken Baptist Association as a fraternal messenger from the North District Association. One of the Bracken churches, Licking Locust, was divided over the issue of slavery. Though a guest, Barrow took sides in the debate that had been more or less compromised by the ruling heads of the Bracken Association and ripped the issue wide open and destroyed the compromise.

The next year, Bracken County prepared charges against Barrow and had him expelled from the North District Association. Actually, it was not so much his slavery position as his interference in Bracken policies, but the basic issue was slavery. The North District was not really happy with Barrow. The Elkhorn though it had been a Regular Baptist Association, had been a lot more tolerant to a variety of ideas than the North District. Most of the churches of the North District had come from Regular Baptist sources and were conservative. Even churches like Providence and Boone Creek, who had been Separatist Baptist were now being swept along in the conservative tide. Robert Elkin as he grew older was growing more conservative and he was setting the tone.

Barrow was ousted not only from the association, but also from his churches except for Mt. Sterling. Barrow organized the Licking Locust Association for the Friends of Humanity with nine churches and 190 members. It was not a strong movement. Licking Locust went for a time with Barrow, but in two or three years, the anti-slavery people were expelled and had to organize their own church. Most of the others were splinters of Baptist churches that would not go along with the anti-slavery position.

One of the results of this association, however, was the organization of the Bethlehem Baptist Church sometime after 1806 at Schollsville. Its membership was anti-slavery factions from Goshen, Lulbegrud, Ruckerville and New Providence in Kiddville (which wasn't organized until after 1806). Barrow became its minister until his death in 1819. Thus started the history of the Maverick Baptist Church of Clark County whose history will be carried in the second volume of this work.

In 1803, the association met at Bethel in what became Bath County. The minutes were printed by Daniel Bradford of the KENTUCKY GAZETTE in Lexington. The 1802 minutes are missing. The 1803 moderator was Elkin and he can be presumed to have been the moderator in 1802. He also preached the introductory sermon which was an honor in the North District Association. Moses Bledsoe was clerk.

In 1804, the year of the expulsion of Barrow, Moses Bledsoe was moderator and James French was clerk. Isaac Crutcher was the introductory speaker.

A list of the churches and their messengers might have some value. Spencer Creek, Joseph Rice, James Rice, Benjamin Cave and Dawson Wade (70). Rice was listed as an ordained minister and presumedly, though not necessarily, minister of the church. Lullbegrud, James French, Jilson Payne and William O'Rear (51). Both of these churches were in the present Montgomery. As Baptist churches in 1976, both were dead. Spencer Creek continued as a Church of Christ. Providence, Robert Elkin, James Haggard and Thomas Berry (172). Unity, James Quisenberry, John Haggard, David Routt, Jonathan Fugate and Moses Sharp. Of course, Elkin and Quisenberry were ministers. Red River had Nelson Burger and Cornelius Newkirk. Red River is the Salem Baptist Church in the present Estill County on the Powell County line. Upper Howard Creek, Edward Kindred, James Elkins, and William Haggard. East Fork of Four Mile, David Brandenburg. The other churches are out of the Clark County or Montgomery County area.

Slate Union which was a church from the Bath County area asked how many messengers should a church have; the answer was four.

The 1804 district meeting reported 12 churches. Log Lick is added to the list. So is the church at Strode Station which would soon be called Friendship. This is large for a Baptist Association which generally runs between ten to fifteen churches. In a day when transportation was either horseback or wagon, distances were important.

The 1805 association was held at Bethel again. Jilson Payne gave the introductory sermon and James French was the clerk. The 1805 association forgave Barrow and tried to get him to return. He wouldn't.

Providence and Boone Creek Baptist Churches inquired what to do about a minister who promoted false doctrine. The Hell Redemptionist position was still being advocated strongly and James Garrard's Cooper Run Church in Bourbon County was still suspected of heresay. There were several other ministers advocating this position. Then the abolitionist ministers were quite numerous. These did not upset the Clark County churches as much as it did the Bracken or other North District churches. What is more, the abolitionist position was growing in Kentucky and would until around 1820. However, the present problems were not those on the more liberal side, but those on the more conservative, the Particular Baptist. The answer was to withdraw authority from those heretics.

The 1809 minutes, which are the next minutes to survive, reported that Moses Bledsoe had died. The meeting was at Bald Eagle which was then still part of Montgomery County. The total churches had risen to 28, but the membership was down to 1,445. New churches were Bethel (Bath County), Red Lick, Long Branch, Cane Springs (David Chenault's home church in Madison County), Goshen, Grassy Lick (Montgomery County), Friendship, Log Lick, East Fork of Flat Creek (Bath County), Ohio River, Tygart's Creek and Poplar Run. Missing were Blue Ash, Log Meeting House, Tates Creek, (this may be Cane Springs), Station Camp, Brush Creek, Long Branch, Morton's Meeting House. It may be that some of these churches are reported in the 1809 minutes under different names. Robert Elkin was again chosen moderator and James French was to begin a long term as clerk. Jessamine was dismissed to join a closer association. Unity did not report either by letter or messengers. The minutes made no other comment.

Eighteen hundred nine and ten was the beginning of the Particular Baptist troubles in Fayette County. It did not effect the North District until sometime later, but it would then divide a number of North District churches.

Evangelistic fever swept Kentucky in 1810 and 1811 with revivals and camp meetings held by many denominations and churches. During this period the North District reported 1,078 converts bring the total membership up to 2,383 members in 28 churches. The Campbell ideas were not yet within the area. This evangelism largely stemmed from old Separatist backgrounds. It did revive the Separatist feelings and thoughts that had been sinking under the Regular Baptist Calvinism. It opened the area unto Campbell and the evangelistic methods of Walter Scott.

The 1810 meeting was back at Bethel, a favorite meeting place for the association for some reason. Thomas Smith who succeeded David Bradford was the printer. The association now reported 1461 members. Edward Kindred preached the introductory sermon. The next association met at Hopewell which was in Woodford County. David Chenault preached the introductory sermon. These are about the earliest appearances of Kindred and Chenault into the religious field. T. L. Patterson replaced James French as clerk. East Fork had disappeared from the roles. One can assume it continued living another year or two half life.

The pressure by the Particular Baptist was strong. The Licking Association was being organized. The Association warned that churches ought to be careful how they invited traveling preachers to preach. The problem lay in many of the deeds to the meeting houses allowing anyone who wished to preach.

Providence was host to the north District in 1812. Again, Elkin and French were moderator and clerk. French probably had not been able to attend the 1811 association being so far from his established area. Indian Creek marked its first appearance.

The introductory preacher in 1812 was Isaac Crutcher. The North District now had 2,383 members. The struggle for control of churches with the Particular Baptist continued. Bald Eagle is captured by them and withdraws from the association to become part of the Licking Association. Jilson Payne and James French were the moderator and clerk for 1813.

The 1814 and 1815 minutes have not been accounted for. In 1816, Thomas Moseley was the moderator, Nathan Lipscomb the clerk and David Chenault gave the introductory sermon. Indian Creek has withdrawn. The relationship with Unity was so poor that they did not want to be in the same association. N. Patton printed the minutes. He was a Winchester printer and editor of the KENTUCKY ADVERTISER.

In 1817, a faction of the Bald Eagle Church returned to the North District. The other faction remained with the Licking Association. David Chenault was elected moderator. James Mason was clerk.

Evidently in the 1816 association meeting, the North District Association agreed to enter into correspondence with the Baptist Board of Foreign Missions. Since those minutes are not available, and since the minutes are themselves minimal, just how close that vote was and who supported or did not support it, is unknown.

However, in the 1817 association, Providence, Friendship, Upper Howard Creek, Unity, Log Lick, Mt. Tabor, and Goshen demanded that any correspondence between the North District and the Missionary Society be halted. It is assumed that the other members of the association were either neutral or favoring the societies. However, in the face of such a block of powerful Clark County churches (only Mt. Tabor was not Clark County), the North District withdrew their support.

In 1818 minutes are missing. David Chenault was again the moderator of the North District in 1819. French was clerk and Thomas White was the introductory preacher. The minutes were printed by the KENTUCKY ADVERTISER in Winchester. Besides the ultra conservative Chenault, James Fishback, George Boone and Richard Morton were scheduled to speak. These were men who would be instrumental in the organization of the Boone Creek Association and would then become won over to the Reform of Alexander Campbell. Reading between the lines and using hindsight, one can see a stirring of unhappiness among the North District churches.

On the other side of the theological aisle, Friendship requested that the North District take up correspondence with the Licking Particular Baptist Association. By this time several of the North District churches had been split and at least one stolen by the Particular Baptist. This was no time to ask the North District to take to its bosom the source of discord. The district refused! Friendship was to return to Winchester where some of its members were to brood about the lack of true Christianity in the North District and among its own members and then explode into division... as did New Providence in the flat acres of Indian Fields.

John Racoon Smith was the introductory speaker of the 1820 association. He was as yet no reformer. He was unhappy with the Regular Baptist and not really content with the more liberal Separatist. His tragic life had smoothed out in Kentucky and with the gentle hands of his second wife, Nancy Hurt, was beginning to become normal. He had been called to preach at Lullbegrud, Grassy

Lick, Spencer Creek and Bethel. He had almost immediately come under the influence of David Barrow. He had met and liked Barton Stone. He had begun to read some of the writings of Alexander Campbell. He would soon be ousted from Lullbegrud but then he was immediately called by the Mt. Sterling Baptist Church to fill the pulpit left by the death of David Barrow. Smith was becoming a power in the North District despite the opposition of the old Calvinists of Lullbegrud.

Samuel Kelly was the introductory speaker in 1821, somewhat balancing the previous year's Smith with Calvinism. The control structure of the North District, however, remained firmly in the hands of David Chenault and James French.

In passing, we note that not only has David Barrow died leaving a gap in history that few could fill, but also Robert Elkin who had been moderator of the North District more than any other man. He died in 1822, not too happy over the divisions that were threatenting in both the Providence Church and the North District Association. He was 77 years old and had been preaching for 51 years. His death opened the way for Providence to leave the North District and join the new association named Boone Creek that was being formed by some of the Fayette churches.

David Chenault remained moderator of the North District in 1822 with James French his clerk. Their control was sufficient that Edward Kindred was the introductory minister. Kindred was a good man, neither offensive to the Calvinists or those with less strict theologies. Still, he was not a man who would introduce the new ideas that were being promoted by the Campbells in their newspaper, the Christian Baptist. Nearly a hundred copies of the Christian Baptist would make its appearance in Clark County with each issue.

With Kindred the introductory preacher, it was logical to expect that his church, Bethlehem, should be admitted to the North District. She applied. What was overlooked was the bitterness that remained for anything that had been David Barrow. Next to Mt. Sterling, Bethlehem had been his strongest supporter. It had been organized for anti-slavery purposes. It had drawn members from Goshen and Lullbegrud. James French might forgive Kindred of being pastor of Bethlehem, but French wanted no more strengthening of the liberal elements in the North District. Bethlehem was refused. It is the only case that this research has turned up that a church has been refused admission to either the North District or the Boone Creek Associations.

The North District also tried to find a solution for the division that was tearing apart the Friendship Church. The issue was first of all the Particular Baptist versus the Separatist learnings of James Quisenberry for he was not really that liberal. He had served Friendship for ten years without trouble. The problem in back of Quisenberry was a solid group of laymen that were becoming increasingly influenced by the ideas of Barton Stone.

The North District under Chenault could not really support the faction that was supporting Quisenberry. On the other hand, they could not give approval to the Particular Baptist group that had taken over the majority of the church. So often when one tried to find a compromise, neither side was happy. The Particular Baptist group joined the Licking Association. The Quisenberry faction dropping Quisenberry themselves, turning to the Mortons for leadership, joined the Boone Creek District Association.

The more conservative establishment began loosing control in the North District. John Smith was again the introductory preacher in 1824. He was without doubt, the strongest and most influential minister in the North District, or for that matter, the Boone Creek Association. The full force of the Campbell doctrines were beginning to strike both associations.

The 1825 minutes are among the missing. But David Chenault and James French were once again moderator and clerk in 1826. One of John Smith's churches, Bethel, dissolved as a Baptist Church. It did not go out of existence but continued as an independent church. It was adhering closely to the ideas of the Restoration.

The whole situation was bound to come to a head and in the 1827 North District Association, the explosion came. Chenault was again the moderator with James French as clerk. Thomas Boone had the introductory sermon. The association was held at Cane Springs Baptist Church which was out of the usual area for the North District, south of the Kentucky River. At the time of the organization of the North District, it had felt closer to the Clark County churches than the other churches in the South District. James French of the Lullbegrud Church lead the attack. He accused Smith of using Campbell's translation of the Bible, changing of the words used in the ordinance of baptism, changing the method of serving the bread in communion and intimidating that the Philadelphia Confession was called a man's opinion. To this, Smith confessed guilty and a good deal more. He defended his position as being scriptural and called for the restoration of the "ancient order of things". The association moderator realized he could not control the vote and postponed the show down until next year when the association would meet in Lullbegrud.

The 1878 association met at Lullbegrud. Once again, the establishment was returned to authority. Chenault was made moderator and French was the clerk. This is interesting for it is reasonably clear that at any time the Reformers could have ousted Chenault and French from their offices. The inbred habit of the Baptist to return to office good men without opposition seemed to be so deeply ingrained that it overruled politics. It is also possible that in the face of the opposition among the ministers, Smith felt that he had the votes among the laymen and it would not hurt to let the ministers control the offices.

Once again, the messengers from Lullbegrud, Goshen and Upper Howard Creek pressed to the attack. They accused Smith of a new mode of breaking the bread for communion. The bread should be broken by the minister as the scriptures called for, thundered Rupard, and not by each individual for himself as the Reformers did. By a parliamentary decision, Smith was kept from speaking in his own defense. However, it was apparent that if a vote was taken, Smith would win and, it was even possible that the Calvinists could be censured as being the party of disorder. Even Cane Springs, Chenault's own church, was showing signs of weakening. Chenault adjourned the meeting, putting off all disciplinary matters until the next year.

Meanwhile, one of Smith's own churches divided, Grassy Lick. The Reformers and the majority willingly left the old church building and organized a new church. James Mason had opposed the move, pleading for unity. Smith offered to resign but was told that the majority of the church would merely call another Reformer. The result was the organization of the Somerset Baptist Church of Christ. A few months later, the church dropped the word Baptist.

The 1829 meeting was held at Unity. Once again Chenault and French were moderator and clerk.

The churches in the district were Spencer Creek (313), Lullbegrud (200), Salem (42), Upper Howard's Creek (150), Mount Tabor (21), Sycamore (54), Cane Spring (102), Goshen (123), Log Lick (86), Cane Creek (20), Unity (149), Beaver Pond (74), Licking Providence (33), Slate Union (54), Salt Lick (53), New Providence (108), Mt. Sterling (155), Owingsville (95), South Fork, Red River (40), Sharpsburg (81), Slate Liberty (105), Upper White Oak (35) and Friendship Sweet Spring (56), for a total of 2,268 members.

This list is more familiar than the 1802 list. Upper Howard's Creek, Goshen, Log Lick, Unity, New Providence, were Clark County churches. Providence, Indian Creek, Friendship, Mt. Zion now belonged to the Boone Creek Association. Spencer Creek, Lullbegrud, GrassyLick, Slate Union, Salt Lick, Mt. Sterling, Owingsville, Sharpsburg, Slate Liberty, Upper White Oak were either in Montgomery or Bath Counties. Beaver Pond and South Fork Red River were in Powell County. The others are at this writing unidentified.

From reading the minutes, one can get little indication of trouble. Chenault and French were firmly in the saddle as the controlling officers. Thomas White, whose home church was Beaver Pond which name would eventually become Stanton in Powell County, was not a Reformer and the next meeting would hear Thomas Boone.

During the year of 1829, all over the state of Kentucky, there had been trouble. Showdowns were coming in the Boone Creek Association for this year and there was little doubt that the Boone Creek Association would dissolve. On the other hand, the Frankfort Association had expelled many of the Reformer churches and had sent

to the North District Association a Silas Noel who rose in the
meeting and demanded that the North District withdraw correspondence
with any Reform church or Reform members. David Chenault took up
the attack charging that the Reformers rejected creeds, covenants
and constitutions, that they did not require experience before
Baptism or church membership; that Baptism and the Lord's Supper
could be administered by laymen; that they rejected a special call
for ministers and refused special rights for the ordained clergy.
He called for a withdrawal from the Reformers. However, with
French calling for a vote, Jeremiah Vardeman stood up and started
the Benediction and the meeting was adjourned.

The 1829 minutes reflect none of these violent events. Louis
Cochran has written a fictionalized biography of Racoon John Smith
in which he gives a very vivid account of these events. The only
thing that the 1829 minutes noted was that the circular letter prepared by James French was rejected.

It was now quite apparent that the Reformers controlled the
North District Association and that the association would meet in
1830 at Spencer Creek, one of John Smith's supporting churches,
and would abolish the constitution.

The Calvinists of the Frankfort Association had withdrawn from
their association knowing they would be defeated by a vote. Noel
was encouraging the Calvinists of the North District to do the same.
During the winter James French contacted those churches that he felt
were safe. The Goshen minutes report such a message in her minutes
and went through a series of agonizing meetings deciding what to do.

April of 1830, two months before the Spencer Creek meeting,
Lullbegrud, Salem, Upper Howard's Creek, Goshen, Unity, Mt. Tabor
and New Providence met at Lullbegrud. Their minutes read "Proceedings of the Messengers of Seven Baptist Churches of the North
District Association". Thomas Boone was elected moderator and James
Edmonson clerk.

This meeting, after a study of the North District and South
District records, reached the conclusion that the function of
the association was to preserve the ways and the traditions of
the Baptists. The meeting protested that these ways were being
changed and the protests of their churches to preserve the true
spirit of the Baptist movement was ignored. They repeated the
past struggles, how Lullbegrud had protested the change in
communion in 1828, how Goshen and Cane Springs had protested
in 1829 only to be ignored. They did not say that it had been
their men as moderator and clerk that had kept order in the
meeting, handled the business and had deliberately dismissed
the meeting rather than face defeat by a vote.....or at least
this is the way Louis Cochran describes it in his novel. It
was also agreed that James French was to hold the records
of the North District Baptist Association until duly relieved
by a Baptist Association.

The second volume of Campbell's Mellinial Harbinger, July 23, 1831, reported that the North District Association met at Somerset with 382 members and had dissolved its constitution. This meeting had met at Somerset July of 1830.

Unity, New Providence, Lullbegrud, Salem, Upper Howard's Creek, Mt. Tabor, Goshen or Grassy Lick did not attend. Spencer Creek sent T. Mosely, D. Bruton, J. Coons and Joseph Bondurant as messengers and reported 309 members. Sycamore sent Joseph Famming, John Gradshaw, R. Trimble and Shelby Daniel with 54 members. Cane Springs messengers were Isaac Thornsburg, Josiah Harris, Thomas Reed and Nathan Lipscomb with 71 members. Log Lick sent Absolom Stivers and H. Farney and reported 30 members. Beaver Pond sent Thomas White, Thomas Dickey, John Foreman and Alexander Collins and reported 64 members. Providence on the Licking reported 38 members and sent William Reed, Barnabas Kinder, David Hopkins and William Hedges. Slate Union had 53 members and sent Rueben Randolph, Jacob Ragan, George Randolph and Andrew McNabb. Salt Lick reported 60 members and Timothy Carrington, William and James Lane and William Crouch. Mt. Sterling reported 148 members and was represented by John Smith, William O'Rear, Adam Dickey and Buckner Payne. Owingsville had 98 members and sent Sinnet Young, Edwin Young, James Johnson and James Sudduth. South Fork of Red River had 40 members and sent Joseph Hon, Hugh Johnson, William and John Hon. Sharpsburg had 96 members and sent Moses Ryan, Asa Maxey, James Rafferty and John Payne. Slate Liberty sent J. Parker, D. M. Cartmill and J. Shultz. They had 105 members. Upper White Oak sent Lewis Templeman, James Duval, William and Thomas Swetman and reported 42 members. Friendship (not Clark County's) sent A. Stewart, L. Jones and J. M. Harris and reported 40 members. Two new churches were received into the association, Somerset which had grown out of Grassy Lick sent H. Darnal, M. Badger, James Allan and Jonathan Masterson. They reported 127 members. Triplet Union sent Isaac Evans, Senator William Logan and I. Evans, Jr., they reported 23.

Thomas White was elected moderator. White was basically a conservative and would like to have gone along with Chenault and Rupard but he was caught up in a rush that was too much for him. His churches were all Reformers. Buckner Payne was elected clerk.

There was no question of the vote. The constitution was abolished. The name Baptist was cast out of the association's name. Chenault, who was there, saw his own church messengers voting for the Reform. He would see to it that they were expelled, but it did hurt his feelings at the time.

Feeling confident, the association set Somerset for their next meeting.

The Unreformed Baptist's meeting, according to the minutes, called for the next meeting June 4th at Goshen for all churches or parts of churches that are content with the old usages. Ten churches attended this second meeting, Lullbegrud, Cane Springs, Goshen,

Grassy Lick, Salem, Upper Howard's Creek, Mount Tabor, Log Lick, Unity and New Providence sent messengers. David Chenault was elected moderator and James French clerk. The meeting began to endorse the actions of the other unofficial meeting. Rueben McDonald (Grassy Lick), Jesse Noland (Mt. Tabor), and John Treadway (Lullbegrud) were appointed on a committee with the moderator and clerk to report the business of the next day. It is interresting to note that of the ten churches in attendance, five were Clark County churches. Only one of the committee were from Clark County.

The meeting admitted that they were acting as a minority and that they were acting without the majority which were more or less committed to the Reform. It was agreed that such was necessary if the Baptist movement was to survive. They called the 1831 meeting at Upper Howard's Creek Baptist Church. Any church attending this meeting would have to state their loyalties to the old Baptist forms.

In the course of time, the regularly called meeting of the North District Baptist Association met at Spencer Creek in July of 1830.

As 1830 closed, it was clear that the Baptist movement in Montgomery and Bath Counties had been smashed. The great majority of churches had gone to the Reformers and though here and there a rump group would struggle; most of these would not survive the middle of the century. However, the North District in Clark County remained strong and loyal Baptist.

The difference can also be seen in the Boone Creek Association. In Clark County, only Mt. Zion and Friendship had gone to the Reformers. Bethlehem had also gone to the Reformers, but it had never belonged either to Boone Creek or the North District. It may have been a member of the Locust Licking Association, the anti-slavery organization of David Barrow. When this association broke up, even though their minister was orthodox Edward Kindred, they may have joined the Elkhorn Association. In Clark County, therefore, there was still a network of Baptist churches. From the numbers and statistics, the North District was the stronger of the two and the most likely to succeed.

Seeking reasons for the survival of the Clark County Baptist, one can merely point out personalities. In Bath and Montgomery, Racoon John Smith was an unswerving supporter of the Reform, a powerful preacher and a good organizer. In Clark County, though Smith's influence included Bethlehem and he was known throughout the rest of the county, he did not have the same influence. On the other hand, in Clark County, holding both Goshen and Lullbegrud was the combination of minister and layman, Thomas Boone and James French. As back-up team to this powerful pair was David Chenault. The Clark County reformers, the Mortons and George Boone, though individually good men and fine ministers, did not have the power that these men had. There were no such Baptist ministers and laymen in Montgomery and Bath Counties.

It is not until 1832 that the North District came up with statistics. It had grown to 12 churches. Lullbegrud now had 171 members and was the strongest Baptist church of the two associations. It had lost only about 30 members. However, since Lullbegrud was the only functioning Baptist church left in Montgomery, refugees from Mt. Sterling Baptist and even Grassy Lick had placed their membership there. This fact was in the end to be the final blow to Lullbegrud. As for the moment it gave her considerable strength. Actually, she lost closer to sixty members than thirty. Goshen reported 102 members. This represented some loss, but not much more than one might have expected over a three year period. What losses she had went to Bethlehem as did those of the Lullbegrud Church. Grassy Lick, which had been the strongest church in 1829, dropped from 313 to 30. Most of these went to Somerset Christian Church. Even the rump group were not to be able to last out the decade. Upper Howard's Creek dropped to 99, some 50 members. Most of these would remain in the community and there would be an occasional report of a Christian Church meeting in the same building with the Baptist. This would eventually consolidate into Pharis Hill and Ruckerville Christian Churches. Log Lick lost thirty members to 48. Here also we would have the pattern of the Christians meeting in the same building with the Baptist evidently harmoniously. Unity lost forty members to 105. Most of these went to Antioch Christian Church. New Providence lost thirty members to 77. Most of these, the Elisha Goff family, for example, joined Bethlehem.

The loss of Baptist membership is not balanced with Christian gain. At least half of the Baptist loss dropped out of both churches.

There were other factors in these disputes besides religious. James French had married a daughter of James Prewitt. French's wife died in child birth soon thereafter and French, after a reasonable time, remarried. Nevertheless, there was bad blood between French and Prewitt which just naturally put the two families on opposite sides in any quarrel. The Prewitts in mass joined Bethlehem.

The North District had grown to 15 churches in 1836. Most of the intact churches were showing gains in strength. Chenault was moderator in 1833 and in 1836. We can presume that he was moderator each of the intervening years. In 1834, Lewis Ford was clerk, but in 1836, Jeremiah Clark was clerk. The North District reported 15 churches in 1836,

There are holes in the available minutes for this period. In 1840, Thomas Boone was moderator and J.L. Carson was clerk. The North District Association was recovering slowly from the losses to the Reformers. The recovery was not as rapid as that of the Boone Creek Association which by 1844 was almost as strong as it had been in 1824 before the Reform boom. There is no similar gain to the recovery of Providence. Actually, Goshen had lost membership. Some place in this period the Particular Baptist Church had dissolved in Indian Fields and a few of its surviving members drifted back into

New Providence. The Boone Creek Association had been successful in winning back many of those that had either stayed home or gone to the Christian churches. The North District was not so successful.

The seeking of the answer for the difference with limited records is not easy. The very strength that carried the North District through the Reform crisis lead to its destruction. In the Boone Creek Association it was the leadership that had gone to the Reform and the membership that stayed with traditional Baptist position. The membership did not want a narrow ministry and they were not narrow Calvinists. They just preferred the religion of the Baptist movement as they esperienced it. On the other hand, the leadership of the North District Association had remained faithful. They were able, at least in Clark County, to control their own churches. They did this by ruthlessly eliminating any layman that felt inclined to any deviation to the Baptist tradition. As the years continued, they prevented any minister who felt inclined to anything less than their rigid standards from serving in their pulpits. They fought furious battles in Upper Howard Creek and Lullbegrud to maintain that purity. In each case, they purified their congregations and weakened their church to a degree that it would never really recover. Their rigid Calvinism prevented the addition of large numbers of converts.

After the struggle with the Reformers, Goshen began to purge her own ranks of heretics until 1840 when she reported 98 members. Now determined to hold herself true, she refused new members as well as old who might not be truly Calvinistic. Her membership shrunk to 76 in 1844. Incidently, a young man named William Rupard, the third with that name, was a messenger. This was his first appearance in North District history. By 1856, she was down to 59. Upper Howard Creek had also divided again by 1844 with a faction still using the building, reporting to Boone Creek Association. She just had 50 members. New Providence reported 42 and Log Lick only 27.

The Reformers of the 1820s were a clear cut body with a definite program of changes. The issues in the 1840s were less distinct and less organized. They were not so much differences, but degrees of emphasis. Foot washing was an issue. In many ways, it became the issue around which the other issues revolved though not so important in itself. Foot washing had bothered the Boone Creek Churches also, but it was not a fighting issue there. The method of receiving new members was the issue that divided Lullbegrud. The Calvinists demanded an experience feeling that God would call and a man could be nothing but His passive agent, waiting to be notified of his salvation. The less Calvinistic found the revival a method of hurrying this notification. There were stirrings of missions, both at home and abroad. The Congregationalists had started the movement, but the Baptist had followed quickly. In fact, the Baptist had converted the first group of Congregational missionaries heading for India. There was even some talk of Sabbath Schools, though this was to be an issue a little later. Instrumental music had a part, though most Baptist churches were too poor and too remote to have organs, melodians or even a violin. Pianos were not yet in the picture. By the time instrumental music became common, the division had already been accomplished and the explosion in this issue would go to the Christians. By 1850, there were obviously two schools of Baptist thinking, the old school which held to the old (Regular), Calvinistic position and the new school that reflected many of the attitudes of the Separatist and in a sense a reaction to accommodate those Reformers who did not want to leave the Baptist church and to adjust to new ideas and developments.

Purity may well be a good thing, but it was not blessed by the flavor of success. In 1859, the North District reported only 9 churches and 417 members. What the Reformers could not do, their own position had. The North District was broken.

By 1853, where the next available minutes appeared, the North District had changed its name to the North District Association of Old Baptists. The Association had expanded its boundaries so that it no longer represented the churches north of the Kentucky River. The 1853 association was held at Swift's Camp in Morgan County.

Thomas Boone was no longer physically able to be moderator. James Edmonson was moderator and William Rupard (the third by this name) was the clerk. Montgomery County was represented by Lullbegrud and Spencer Creek. Clark County had Goshen, Howard's Creek, Log Lick and New Providence. Unity had combined with Indian Creek to form Mt. Olive that had chosen the Boone Creek Association. Lullbegrud reported 72, Goshen 64, Howard Creek 60, Log Lick 21. None of the Clark or Montgomery churches were strong.

In 1856, the pillar of the North District, Thomas Boone, died. In his foot steps however, followed William Rupard, a young man that had been born in 1825, converted at Goshen and ordained in 1852. He was preaching at Log Lick and Liberty in Estill County in 1855. When Boone died, he also took over Goshen and the old Lullbegrud Church. Edmonson was still moderator.

Rupard was elected moderator of the North District in 1859 and remained moderator until 1904. One year he was sick and S. E. Reed was elected moderator pro temp. Log Lick changed pastors in 1855 and Rupard took Cane Springs in Madison County.

In 1859, the North District churches adopted the name of "Old Baptist" and sometimes the North District would be referred to as the Old Baptist Association. In 1880, there were only 9 churches in the association, four of these were served by William Rupard, with a total membership of 414 members, most of these being Rupard's members. His churches grew slowly as country churches generally grew, but the others didn't. By 1890, the North District consisted only of the four churches Rupard served and Lullbegrud.

North District Association minutes between 1856 and the 1890s are virtually non existent. There is a single page of minutes for 1870 that had been used by someone to make notes for the Goshen minutes in the Goshen record book. The meeting was at Log Lick. William Rupard was the moderator and C. H. Thompson was the clerk. The association reported 12 churches. Lullbegrud reported 70 members; Goshen 117; Howard Creek 34; Salem 11; Liberty had no report; Cane Springs 82; Stone Pound 11; Mt. Gilead 55; Poplar Grove 52; White Oak 18; Licking Locust not reported. Most of these churches were not in Clark County and we have not sought to track them down to their location. There are some unanswered questions, however. Is Mt. Gilead the Mt. Gilead that had stood firm in the Boone Creek Association? Is the Licking Locust church the same church that gave David Barrow's abolitionist association its name? It is obvious that the only churches that were reasonably healthy were those served by William Rupard.

One little side note... A. C. Noland, fraternal messenger from the Tates Creek Association of Particular Baptist, was left to preach to the people (presumedly out of doors) while the official messengers of the association retired to a school house to conduct association business. Unfortunately, the rest of the minutes are missing so that business is not recorded.

The Southern Baptist Seminary does not have many association minutes after the Civil War. A few are found in William Rupard, IV's possession and in the newspapers.

The 1890 meeting was at Goshen. A. H. Rupard became clerk in the 1893 meeting. In 1897 the association included Goshen, Lullbegrud, Cane Springs, Liberty in Estill and Rock Springs in Wesley. She received messengers from the Tates Creek Old Baptist Association.

A new and unexplained spurt of life appeared in the association in the 1900 meeting. For many years a Madison County minister named J. N. Culton had been serving the Baptist church at Log Lick. Evidenty both he and the church belonged either to the Red River Association which had met at Log Lick in 1890 or perhaps to the Tates Creek Association of Old Baptist. The Red River Association was an association of Baptist churches in Lee, Powell and Wolfe Counties. It is not to be confused with the contemporary Red River Association. The Southern Seminary has a few of their association meeting records but not enough to learn much of their nature or of the period about this time. It could be that Log Lick had found their ministerial supply in Red River. On the other hand, Culton apparently belonged to the Tates Creek Association.

The SUN SENTINEL, August 17, 1901, reported the North District meeting at Goshen. It noted that there were only four churches that were members, Goshen, Liberty (Estill), Lullbegrud and Cane Springs (Madison). William Rupard was elected moderator. The paper noted that he had served these churches for 55 years without pay. This, of course, was not entirely accurate. Old Baptist churches did not pay salaries at this time. Individuals would often give the minister gifts, quite often in the hand shake on departure on the theory that the right hand should not know what the left hand was doing. What was meant was that the churches did not pay an agreed salary. Here again, this was not always quite accurate since often a group of members would get together and guarantee the minister a certain sum in return for his services.

The change that came in 1904 was dramatic with the death of William Rupard. Evidently it brought into the association several other churches including Log Lick. It moved Culton into a position of leadership. It is again mostly conjecture at this point whether the actual death of Rupard removed obstacles to this sudden flare of life or whether it would happen anyway. Apparently Rupard had controlled his churches with an iron hand. No other minister had any real say in the business of the association. It is interesting to note that William Kash, who became minister of Goshen and some of these other churches, never accepted the role as moderator. Whether this was deliberate or accidental can only be guessed at.

The other result of the death of William Rupard was the immediate division of Goshen. A group left the country church, as had the neighboring Sugar Ridge Church (Cumberland Presbyterian), with every effort to move the organization into Winchester. Unlike Sugar Ridge, a minority held to the country church and kept it open. The fact that there were hard feelings is not only clear in the Goshen side of the controversy, but also clear in the attitude of T. M. Osbourne, the last minister of the city church, when he refused to let this author see the minutes of the city church. The city group never affiliated with any association, a fact that is unusual in itself for a Baptist church.

Culton served briefly Goshen after Rupard's death as well as Log Lick. He also became moderator. There isn't a clear report as to how long he was moderator of the association. During this time he held together the tattered remains of the country church and if he did not rebuild it, he at least kept alive the one church that also kept the North District alive. The WINCHESTER SUN, August 24, 1917, reported Culton still moderator. The meeting was held at Goshen.

A. H. Rupard, who had been the church clerk through these years, a member of the Cane Springs Church and a brother to William, became moderator. Apparently there was dissatisfaction with Culton. Presumedly he was not completely orthodox in the viewpoint of the Goshen people. He would remain on the edges of the association, serving briefly at Irving in Estill County, for a few more years, and then he disappears from the boundaries of the North Association. A. H. Rupard was not a minister but a layman. E. B. Bartlet became the clerk of the association. For the rest of North District's history, mostly laymen were moderators.

In some ways the association was stronger during this period than at any time in the last twenty-five years. There are several other churches, mostly in Estill, Powell and Wolfe Counties that came and went. In 1924, she reported ten churches including Lullbegrud, Log Lick and Goshen. A new church was organized in Irving.

There are no records available through the teens. In 1919, we find that J. H. Oliphant was the moderator and he may have been moderator earlier. J. S. Stephens is the clerk. In 1924, A. H. Rupard is again the moderator. The next year William Kash became minister of Goshen and several of the other churches of the association. He was to remain minister for 33 years but never asserted himself as the official leader of the association. In 1929, William Rupard, IV, became moderator. He was a layman. In 1937, Rupard was still moderator. The association had 8 churches.

The churches not served by Kash suffered. Lullbegrud finally gives up its stormy life. What few members are left shifted to Goshen with no apparent change in Goshen's strength. There is another "Old" Baptist Church on the Levee Road in Montgomery County that has not played any part of this history. A few of its members may have gone there. Log Lick also dies during this period. In the Licking Association, Mt. Carmel had passed on. A church dies slowly and takes a long time, but there was something about the rural depression that preceeded the so-called great depression of the thirties that left the bones of dozens of churches scattered throughout the country. By 1932, there were only five churches, two in Estill, one in Madison, Powell Valley a new (old) church for the association in Powell County and Goshen. Another church united with the association from along the railroad to Jackson in 1935, but in 1939, the association was back down to 4. Henry C. Jones became association clerk in 1942.

For all practical purposes, the North District Association had become the yearly meeting of the parish served by William Kash. In 1952 there were only three churches left as Cane Springs dropped out. It does not mean that these churches had all died. It does mean that the association had become so closely tied to the set of churches administered by one man that there seemed to be no place for any other. The city Old Baptist Church was operating fairly vigorously in the 1930s and 1940s, and did not really begin to die until in the 1950s. There is no evidence that it was ever approached. We have mentioned an "Old" church on the Levee Road in Montgomery County. We have made no effort to study its history, but it existed close to but never a part of the North District. There were a number of churches in Powell and related counties that dated back to the trouble with the Christians in 1830. These were roughly the Red River Association. The Boone Creek Baptist have approached them several times and have been rejected. The Boone Creek missionary efforts in this area were largely with new groups. Occasionally one or two of these churches would appear in the North District for a few years and then drop out. Powell Valley after a short time as a member of the North District went back to the Boone Creek.

There are records available for this period 1848-1954, but none show anything significant to report. In 1960, there was a disturbance in Irving. Kash had left the association in 1958. As always when a long term, strong minister leaves, he is hard to replace. William Rupard reported that it was obvious that the association would have to take sides in the case. It was felt it was better just not to meet. There was no meeting in 1961 or any year thereafter. Technically the North District Association still lived since it had never officially been disbanded.

The Kentucky Baptist Historical Society has an article entitled, "The Boone Family and Kentucky Baptist Ministers" by a Leo Crisman, 1949. It contains the history of Squire, Daniel's brother, the second Squire in Kentucky's history, Samuel's son and Daniel's nephew, and Thomas and George. Thomas was Squire's son. George, Crisman noted, was not listed in Stricker's Boone family geneology, but he also was probably Squire's son. Kathryn Owen says he is likely George Green Boon of Virginia.

For the North District, Thomas Boone was one of the three most important ministers of the North District. He was born in Fayette County about 1790. He joined the Boggs Creek Church and married Sallie Muir. He was ordained and began to serve the Log Lick Church. He was close to their first minister. The records are missing. His name did appear on the North District records from there in 1817. He began to serve Goshen in 1816 and continued until his death in 1855. He also served Lullbegrud from 1823 to 1843. He evidently served Indian Creek and Providence in 1830. He was always active in the North District Association being moderator in 1830, 1840 and 1844. He became Log Lick's and New Providence's minister in 1855 just before his death.

A second of the outstanding men of the North District and of the county was William Rupard. Strictly speaking, Thomas Boone lived his life in Fayette County, the Rupards were 100% Clark. The best description of the Rupard family was given by a contemporary mother, whose son was dating one of the contemporary Rupard girls. She was pleased, "The Rupard name means solidarity in Clark County", was her explanation.

John Rupard came from Rowan County, North Carolina to Kentucky in 1784. He went first to what is now Jessamine County, but soon moved to Clark County settling in the Stoner Creek area. He married a Hannah Roberts and together they had seven sons and two girls. One of these sons was named William. He married Patsy Haggard and together they had ten children. Only two survived, however. One that did was William Rupard who was born in 1825. He was converted in the Goshen Church in 1841. He started teaching school at 18. He was ordained in 1852. In the middle 50s he went west, but returned at the death of Thomas Boone. In 1855, he started serving Log Lick and Liberty (Estill County). In 1856, he added Goshen and Lullbegrud.

The Clark County Republican, October 20, 1916, in commenting on the Rupard family noted that seven of the sons served the Union forces during the Civil War. Fifteen voted for local option in 1916. Tradition also says that it was William Rupard who voted the lone Lincoln vote in 1860 that was recorded in Clark County.

The third name that is important in the North District Baptist Association is that of David Chenault. Chenault came out of Madison County where he had been deeply influenced by Andrew Tribble. He had married Andrew's daughter, Nancy. He was converted in the revivals that burst out over the frontier in 1801 and began to preach almost immediately. He was a dogmatic but dynamic minister, who became steadily more conservative as he grew older. Both A. C. Quisenberry and Conkwright describe him as a hyper-Calvinist. Like most ministers of the day, he spent most of his life in a few churches, Cane Springs, Lullbegrud, Log Lick, Oak Pond and Stoner's Branch (Unity).

With his base of operation on Madison County, he influenced the churches in Clark and Montgomery Counties. Before the break with the Reformers, he had repeatedly led his churches in an attack on the new ideas. He bitterly protested that he was ignored. In 1830, backed by Thomas Boone and James French, he fought to hold what he could of the North District together for the Baptist. He was the North District moderator through the thin years of the 1830s. He was instrumental in laying the theological background that turned the surviving North District Churches into the "Old" Baptist road.

In addition to being a strong minister, he was also an excellent businessman.

## THE LICKING ASSOCIATION OF PARTICULAR BAPTIST

The Licking Association of Particular Baptist came into being in 1809. According to Collins, the whole affair began over a dispute between Jacob Creath and Clark County landowner, Thomas Lewis, over a purchase of a slave. Collins does not go any further into the matter and so far no other source has produced more information. This is obviously an over-simplification. There were deeper theological troubles that would underlie any superficial dispute such as this.

The Particular Baptist movement had its roots in Great Britian where there were associations of Particular Baptist. They were extreme Calvinists. Specifically, the Particular Baptist denied that God's grace was freely given to all people, but instead grace was given to those particular individuals that God had preordained in the beginning of creation to be saved. This group did not accept the Philadelphia Confession. As a matter of fact, the Licking Association minutes did not list a confession of faith or articles of faith.

The Union of Regular and Separatist Baptist was a compromise. The Separatist had given up a good deal more than had the Regular as the liberals quite often will to perfect a desired merger. However, such accommodation seldom makes happy the more extreme of either group. The stronger Calvinists were not happy with the Union and became more restless as those who leaned toward the Separatist position increased more rapidly in the United Churches than the Regular.

Whatever the origin, Particular Baptist movement spread quickly among the more conservative ministers and churches. Ambrose Dudley was the leading minister and the logical exponent of the new association. He was the first moderator and was re-elected regularly.

The first minutes preserved by the Louisville Southern Baptist Seminary is 1812. One of the first churches to go to the Particular Baptist was the Mt. Carmel Church of Clark County. The meeting was at Bryan Station. Eighteen churches belonged to the association with total membership of 895. Very little happened in these early minutes....1817, the meeting was at Town Fork; 1818 at Mt. Carmel; 1819, at Mt. Carmel, the first of many association meetings in Clark County. This was the first year that the word Particular was used to describe the association.

Eighteen twenty was perhaps the last year when the Baptist were not affected by the stirring Reform that was to sweep them.

However, the Reform did not seriously affect the Particular Baptist. The association now had 16 churches with 802 members. In eighteen twenty-one, the meeting was held at Dry Run in Scott County; eighteen twenty-two, at Elizabeth in Boyle County. Friendship had now joined the association, being one of the largest churches with 72 members. Mt. Carmel still had 25 members. In fairness to these conservative Baptist, there were a great many more people who attended regularly and financed these churches than appeared on the rolls. Several Licking Association Churches joined the Boone Creek Association. These were apt to be divisions of older churches.

In 1823, the meeting was held at Versailles and the next two years at Mt. Carmel. In 1827, the number in the churches had increased to 22 and the associaton reported 1352 members. There had been 159 baptisms. Mt. Carmel had grown to 91 members. Even the Particular Baptist were gaining in membership in these years.

Ambrose Dudley died and in 1830 Lewis Corbin was moderator. There were now 31 churches in the association making it one of the largest Baptist associations in the area and they were reporting 1400 members.

There seems to be little Reform activity among the Particular Baptist in 1831, they reported 29 churches and 1322 members. Thomas Dudley was now the moderator. Also with Dudley the minutes take up new interest. They were deliberately and joyously controversial.

Evidently Dudley sent Alexander Campbell a copy of the 1831 minutes. The Millenial Harbinger reported a letter from the association. It had met at Friendship. Campbell noted that they had 14 ministers who had been ordained. They had 50 baptisms, 125 dismissals, 26 deaths and had excluded 5 for a total of 1460 members. Campbell noted that this was about three baptisms per minister. He was "astonished at the unprecidented oneness of the language spoken". In 1834, the association refused to fellowship with the Kentucky Baptist State Association.

Dudley was moderator in 1839 and would continue to be till his death. James Peck was the clerk. Bald Eagle had left the North District and joined the Licking Association. Later a splinter group of the Bald Eagle Church was to return to the North District. It is interesting that even as conservative as the North District was, there were still those that thought it ought to bo further.

Evidently 1841 was a good year for the Licking for they added more churches for a total of 1331 members. This was the highest membership record since 1828. Meetings were scattered, 1839 at Bryan's, 1841 at Elizabeth, 1842 at Elk Lick in Scott and 1843 at Long Ridge in Owen County. The Licking Association included most of northern and central Kentucky.

In 1843, the Licking Association got in a running skirmish with the Elkhorn Association over missions. They charged the Elkhorn with sending missionaries to the Indians in 1792 and as late as 1814 would not give up its missionary program. Apparently, this was one of the issues that had caused the Licking Association to withdraw from the South Elkhorn.

The 1849 meeting was interesting for several reasons. The original association meeting was to have been held at Rockbridge, but because of the cholera epidemic, it had moved to Mt. Carmel. Cholera was a plague that could not be ignored. Campbell's Millinial Harbinger and the Old Christian Messenger took time out to have articles on cholera. The association took a variety of positions against chaplains for Congress, the Army and the Navy, military schools or for Indian agencies.

The associational minutes over the years have been interesting reading. They corresponded with a variety of other associations. The Tates Creek and Salem Presbyterian associations were brother associations. The association also corresponded with the Mt. Pleasant Association of Regular Baptist. Minutes were sent to the Warwick Baptist Association in New York. There had been a long standing running debate on theological points with this association. Minutes went also to the Ketocton Baptist Association in Virginian, the Red River Association in Tennessee and the First Northwestern Regular Baptist Association in Wisconsin. Over the years, the Circulatory Letter which was part of every Baptist association minutes, had become the personal vehicle for the ideas of Thomas Dudley who authored them. In 1849, he authored one concerning Particular Godliness. Having read the Circulatory address and the Circulatory Letter, both would appear to be merely a strongly Calvinistic dissertation emphasizing the sovereignty of God, the predetermined salvation of the saints, and the resulting good works that arise out of the condition of salvation that the saint finds himself in. It does not seem to a person unversed in Particular Baptist theology to be anyway obnoxious, but it evidently did thoroughly upset some of the churches, among which was Friendship in Clark County.

Friendship had remained one of the stronger churches in the Licking Association, but it was not pastored by Thomas Dudley as was Mt. Carmel. In its power structure was the Rash family, some of which had gone to the Reform, but the others had been fairly entrenched in the Particular approach. In 1849, a new young Rash had been sent to the association as a delegate, A. D. Rash. The minister was William Rash.

If there is not a too obvious point of departure to Calvinistic theology, it might be speculated that some of the difficulty arose out of the iron hand domination that Thomas Dudley had over the Licking Association. Apparently, the Baptist of any of these early associations saw nothing wrong in electing the same man as moderator for his life time. This by necessity squeezes out any other ambitious minister that might feel he was entitled to recognition.

Whatever the reason, the next available minutes, 1854 shows the Licking Association down to 18 churches and Friendship gone.

In referring to the incident, Dudley was later to comment that only two churches had actually left the association, one of which was dead and the other almost dead. He hinted that ambition had indeed been the real cause for the revolt. There is no way of knowing where these two churches went, but presumedly they would affiliate with the Tates Creek Particular Baptist Association. There is also a Tates Creek Baptist Association. The records of the former are not at the Southern Baptist Seminary as are so many records. William Rash would die in the next few years and as was so often done, Friendship chose out of its own group, William's successor, A. D. Rash. There is no questioning A. D. Rash's ability. He would, in 1959, join the effort to establish a missionary (though that term had not yet been fully accepted) Baptist Church in Winchester that would be part of the Boone Creek Association. He would be accepted by the Boone Creek Association, made minister of the Winchester Church and go on to become one of the most influential men in the Boone Creek Association. It is true that the Boone Creek Association was far looser in its discipline than the North District or the Particular Baptist Association, but they would hardly take so completely into their association a man who represented a decisive theology position unless they were certain of his conversion. Rash was certainly the most important secondary result of the establishing of the Baptist Church in Winchester.

It is not really clear what happened to the Friendship Particular Baptist Church. It obviously died very soon thereafter. Some of its members, perhaps all, united with Winchester.

Meanwhile, the Licking Association meetings note a slow disintegration of the association. In 1865, there were only 15 churches left. The association had in 1859 changed its name to the "Old School" Baptist Association, but had returned to the Particular Baptist name in 1870. A J. R. Royster was the associational clerk in 1865. The association continued to decline. Two more churches had died by 1872, but the old fire was there. The minutes published again a history of the Elkhorn-Licking relationship. New churches were added occasionally, others died, but in 1882, there were still only 15 churches and but a few hundred members.

After a long life, Dudley is no longer able to function. In 1883, J. M. Theobald became moderator. Curiously, the printing of the minutes is now being done by a New York printing house that evidently was clearing and publishing house for Particular Baptist and their allies throughout the nation. There seems to be far more national consciousness in this group than in either of the other two associations.

In 1884, Mt. Carmel sent a colored messenger. There is no record of how he was received. He was not on Mt. Carmel's list for the next year. There has in most of the Kentucky churches, been Negro members but never had one been sent to the association meetings as a messenger.

Dudley is dead by the 1886 association. H. Cox is moderator. J. T. Moore was moderator in 1887. Now the meetings when they are held in Mt. Carmel are reported by the Winchester newspapers. They are not given the attention that is given the Boone Creek Association understandably, but some information is gleamed from these reports. In 1890 the association met at Mt. Carmel. There were only ten churches reporting. William Rupard was a welcome guest as he had been for the last twenty years. The differences between these old school Baptist associations were fading as hard times crept upon them. The newspapers reported the association as peaceful and cooperative. The association was at Mt. Carmel in 1891 and in 1894. In 1894, the DEMOCRAT listed Bald Eagle, Bethel (Shelby County), Elk Lick, Goshen (not Clark County's Goshen), Little Rock, Mt. Carmel, Mayslick, Sardis and Salt River as members. Even the Bryan Church, home church of the Dudleys, is no longer reported.

The meeting in 1909 was also at Mt. Carmel. Mt. Carmel's minister, J. G. Eubank, was moderator. The meeting perhaps was one desperate effort to save the church at Mt. Carmel now completely in the hands of the Christians. The meeting failed. Mt. Carmel now had only one member and she ceased to function as a church.

The association again met at Mt. Carmel for the 99th annual meeting in 1911. At this time, it called itself the Licking Association of Old Baptist.

Despite the fact that the newspapers which reported the Licking Association meetings when held at Mt. Carmel, also reported William Rupard in attendance and evidently well received. He was occasionally asked to preach. There is no mention of such relationship in the minutes of the North District.

There are now no Clark County churches in the Licking Association and we make no effort to follow its modern history.

What happened to the churches of the North District and the Licking Associations? In Clark County they were all dead by 1930 save Goshen. Most of them had ceased being an effective religious organization by 1900.

They were all small churches. Their hyper-Calvinism made the use of revival and Sunday School impossible. To become a member, one had to have an experience which would let the individual know that he was among the elect. God just didn't send enough experiences to keep these churches alive.

Since World War II, there was a development among the Southern Primitive Baptist Church which brought the use of Sunday schools, youth groups and other instruments that have been used successfully by other churches to survive. They call themselves the Progressive Primitive Baptist Church. William Dudley, a farmer in Bourbon County and a descendent of Ambrose Dudley and a member of one of the last Primitive Churches in that area, tells the author that he approves of this movement and had a history of it. However, there is no sign that any of this movement reached the remains of the "Old" Baptist in Clark County or elsewhere in the state.

For Clark County and for the association, the leading Particular Baptist was Ambrose Dudley. He was born in 1750 in the Spotsylvania area of Virginia. He came to Kentucky in 1793 from Virginia where he already had a reputation for a minister. He settled in Fayette County and became minister of the Bryan Station Church in 1786. Later he served the David Fork Church also. Probably he was magistrate in Fayette County in 1795. He never held any Clark County churches, but he did play considerable part in the county. His first county marriage was Jonathan West to Rachel Alexander. He married a total of sixteen couples within the county. He married Nancy Parker. He died at the age of 73, in 1828 leaving fourteen children, eleven sons and three daughters. Most of these became themselves prominent citizens of the state. He had over 100 grandchildren.

For the history of Clark County, however, it was Ambrose's son, Thomas, that ranked important. A good account of him is found in Masters History of the Baptist of Kentucky. He was born in 1792. He fought in the War of 1812, fighting at the Battle of River Raisen. He was captured and later released. He was later quartermaster for Andrew Jackson at New Orleans. Returning to Kentucky in 1816, he spent the next eight years as cashier to the State Bank which had offices in Washington, Winchester, Paris and Richmond. He helped close out these offices, carrying literally hundreds of thousands of dollars in a wagon back to the home offices. He joined his father's church in 1820 and was licensed to preach in 1822. He was ordinaed in 1823. He followed his father as minister of Bryan Station in 1825 and remained its minister for 55 years. He was the minister of the Elizabeth Baptist Church in Bourbon County for 53 years. He served Mt. Carmel in Clark County for 46 years and the Georgetown Church for a mere 44 years. The WINCHESTER DEMOCRAT reported that at 87 he rode forty miles each Sunday in his buggy and preached two sermons each Sabbath. He died in 1885 at the age of 94. He wrote several rambling memories of Clark County and Winchester in the 1830s which are the best source for this period.

Dudley's first Clark County marriage was William Chandler and Isabell Richardson in 1824. He had a total of 45 marriages in the county.

There is virtually no reason to believe that Red River Baptist Association had anything more than a passing relationship with Clark County. In 1890, Log Lick was host to its associational meeting. In 1807, a New Providence Church with William Payne as messenger was reported in one of the half dozen minutes of the Red River Association available. In 1877, the association included churches of Clear Branch, Slade in Powell County, Hopewell, Means on the Montgomery County-Menifee County line, Pine Hill near Zacharia in Lee County and Mt. Chapel which location is uncertain. It was probably in Wolfe County from the little information that has crossed our path.

Without any more information than this, we assume that when the Plan of Union was formed, these churches or at least churches in this area formed their own association rather than joining the North District Association partly because they were strongly Regular Baptist and partly because they had little in common with the people who made up the churches of the North District. Already, without anyone really being aware of it, the mountain coves and valleys were slowly filling up, but at the same time becoming more and more isolated from the rest of Kentucky.

Another thing that is interesting that has nothing to do with Clark County history is that the 1917 Red River Association report included a member church named Samaria... in Winconsin. After the Civil War, a Greenville Regular Baptist Association was organized that included some Red River churches. Sometime after the 1917 meeting the Red River Association disappears. The Greenville Association becomes an unenthusiastic missionary Baptist Association and continues as such until after World War II.

A number of churches were organized before and after World War II partly by Boone Creek Association along the Red River. Some of these joined the Greenville Association. There was a struggle between these churches and the older churches. The result was, in the 1950s, the organization of the Red River Baptist Association of Churches in Powell, Wolfe and Breathitt Counties, contemporary leadership of the Red River Association has no information as to what happened to the older Red River Association.

It is difficult for a church to replace a strong minister. Unity had been served by James Quisenberry since 1793. Even if they could not agree with all his ideas and theology, even if he had become puzzled and uncertain in his old age, he was still the great minister. Unity had already lost nearly half of her membership. It is not clear where they had done because there was not a Christian church in the area...at least not for another fifteen years.

John N. Johnson became their minister in 1834. Johnson came out of the more conservative churches. His first county marriage was between Lewis Niblic and Elizabeth Vivion. He would either be a product of Upper Howard Creek or Goshen, probably the former. He had some nine marriages in the county which would indicate that he was not a minister for many years. Soon after William Chenault became Unity's minister and remained so until his death in 1842. In 1836, Isham Baber, Lewis Allen and William Johnson were messengers. In 1840, William Johnson, Eli Bruce and James Carson were messengers. In 1842, Unity reported only 70 members. James Carson, Eli Bruce and John Haggard, Jr., were the messengers.

Once again Unity shifted to Boone Creek. Evidently in 1842, Edward Darnaby became minister. Darnaby signed the county court record as a United Baptist which indicated that he adhered to the Plan of Union of 1801. His first Clark County marriage was Ambrose Hall and Elizabeth Chism. He would marry six Clark County couples. The difference between Darnaby and the Calvinistic preachers that dominated the North District was among other things, a positive approach to evangelism. He favored revivals.

Evidently Darnaby also became minister of Indian Creek close to the 1842 date that brought him to Unity. He became instantly aware that here were two churches, niether too strong, nor too far apart, made up of relatives of the same families. It was obvious that if the two churches could be united there might well be one strong church. Darnaby brought in W. F. Broadhus, a well educated Baptist evangelist. To the two churches, Broadhus was something new. Quisenberry had been a fine man, humble, gentle, who had become part of every family of his church. He had not been a preacher. He had presented his sermons well enough, but in an age where oratory was considered with the same interest as an American baseball players batting average, it was not good enough. Broadhus was more like the Reform evangelists, fervant, articulate and sensible, but with the Baptist flavor.

In themselves, neither revival was a startling success, but they did bring Unity and Indian Creek to the opinion that my merging their two churches a single strong church could result. Unity appointe John Haggard, Jr., Joel Quisenberry, Pleasant Haggard and Donald Haggard to meet with a committee from Indian Creek. The discussions were successfully carried out.

Indian Creek and Unity had been referred to as old line Baptist churches. Their location placed themselves in the North District area which was strongly Calvinistic. There was not yet really that much difference in theology between the North District and the Boone Creek ministers, though already it was becoming noticeable. The place where it was most noticeable was in evangelism and this was sufficient to turn the trick. Both churches became one of the strongest churches in the Boone Creek Association.

In closing this section, we might note that Lullbegrud whose history lies outside this discussion, during this same period also brought in an evangelist who held a revival for the church. The result was a division that fought through the law courts and ended with two churches, one in the Boone Creek and one in the North District.

## INDIAN CREEK BAPTIST CHURCH

Less is known about Indian Creek than about Unity. Like Unity, it moved restless from association to association. It lacked the leadership that Unity had and never had the size and strength. Still, it was in an area that was largely unserved by any other church. On its edges was the Methodist Dunaway Chapel. Between Dunaway and Unity was a wide area of Red River territory that had little attention from religious institutions. The Red River was a county line which made little difference to everyday lives of people in the area. There was an area of Estill County close to Indian Creek that also did not have a great deal of religious organization. There was need for a church in that general area.

Though Indian Creek was made up and controlled by the same families that made up and controlled Unity, there were other families in Indian Creek that did not have these ties. These people were not necessarily more or less Calvinistic than the controlling faction.

Unfortunately, there is not enough information to speculate on the intra church feeling about merging with Unity. At least Unity had a clear cut record left in the various associational records. Indian Creek does not. There were periods of her history where she either did not belong to any association, or they were associations outside the Clark area. To complicate the matter further, there is an Indian Creek chruch that appears in the various associations, particularly the Elkhorn Association that was established in 1803, or at least was first reported about that time, that is not Clark County's Indian Creek. After a period of confusion in my research, this study eliminated its statistics. The problem may well be that the two Indian Creeks were sometimes mixed even in the records.

Indian Creek Baptist Church was organized in 1812 as a result of James Quisenberry's second and somewhat hasty marriage. Tradition says that it was Quisenberry's son-in-law who had just been married, led the revolt, but the Unity history shows that John Haggard, Jr., was always a loyal member unto the merger.

Nathanial Haggard had moved to Kentucky with three grown sons in 1788. The father and two sons, Bartlet and James, had settled in the Bush country and became members of Providence. The fourth member of the family, John, moved further north into the Four Mile-Upper Howard Creek area about six miles out of Winchester in what was later known as the Haggard-Hampton community. Conkwright points out that it was this John Haggard and not the son-in-law that led the revolt.

This makes one wonder just how extensive the resentment to the second marriage was, and whether there were other factors involved. Experience shows that such a reason did not point out the depth of the quarrel. If there were other factors, they simply can't be guessed at from the data available.

The church was organized on Indian Creek which is roughly in the general area of the Allensville Baptist Church today (1976). There are no records from its founding in 1812 to 1823 when deed book 20, reports that John and Mary Haggard conveyed to the trustees of the Indian Creek Church an acre of land and the church house which was already built. Conkwright thought that Indian Creek's affiliation might be with the Tates Creek Baptist Association in Madison County these years.

Apparently, Edward Kindred was minister during much of this period. Kindred was an able country minister. William Landrum reports that he was nicknamed Nolly Kindred. He married first in Clark County, Thomas Reynolds to Maud Wills, June 11, 1821, and performed 314 marriages in Clark County during his lifetime making him the second only to Quisenberry as a marrying minister in early years and among the top five for the total history of Clark County. Why he should start his marrying career so late is puzzling for he must have been preaching at Indian Creek at least five or six years before that date, serving Bethlehem at least since 1818 and Upper Howard's Creek for at least ten years or more before that. He was evidently well received and spoke often at both the Boone Creek and North District Associations. Like Quisenberry, he was deeply swayed by the message of the Reform preachers. However, he was less influenced than Quisenberry, though he seemed to play different roles in different churches. At Upper Howard Creek he supported the Calvinistic members that opposed sternly the Reform. At Bethlehem he apparently went along the Reform tide that built up and swept that church. He, like Quisenberry, was old by the time the Reform question broke out in the associations and died before he had to make a final choice.

In 1826, Indian Creek appeared for the first time in a Clark County association at Boone Creek. Kindred, D. Reid, J. T. Watts and John Hampton were the messengers. This was the same period that Unity came from the North District for a couple of years before going back. Perhaps the more liberal leadership in the Boone Creek attracted Kindred as it had Quisenberry. She reported 105 members which was the strongest she would ever be. Unlike Unity, Indian Creek stayed in the Boone Creek Association. In the session of the Boone Creek Association in 1830, she, Mt. Gilead, Bogg's Ford, Boone Creek, Hickman and Providence held true to the Baptist banner. There is no indication that Kindred was still minister. She reported 95 members. This would indicate little real trouble within the church. Nothing that a change of minister might not account for. In 1832, she was down to 88 members.

In 1830, Thomas Boone, stretching himself as far as he could to help those loyal churches, served for a year. The next year William Pigg served as minister according to the Boone Creek Association. In 1832, the Goshen minutes report a request from Indian Creek for the ordination of James Edmunson to preach. We can assume that he served thereafter. In 1833, the membership hit a low of 76 and rose in 1835 to 85.

W. T. Watts may have been minister in 1840. The churches had a custom of choosing one of their own number when ministers were scarce and making him preach. The skimpy evidence of the association minutes are not clear enough as to Mr. Watt's function. At any rate, in 1841, Dennis Doyle, Elisha Ryan, David Reed, Thomas Rigg (or perhaps Pigg) and T. L. Haggard were the messengers. It is interesting to note that Indian Creek was not strictly a family church of Haggards and Hamptons as Unity had become. Indian Creek was actually on the edge or perhaps a little beyond the edge of the Haggard-Hampton-Quisenberry-Bush country.

S. V. Potts makes his first appearance in Clark County history evidently as minister to Indian Creek in this year. S. V. Potts was never to become a famous minister, but few men have contributed more to the life and well-being of the county than Potts whose efforts to bring Christianity to Clark County would last another fifty years.

Apparently Darnaby became minister the next year and was instrumental in calling W. F. Broadhus as evangelist. The result was to convince both Indian Creek and Unity of the value of merger. To the meeting to merge the churches, Indian Creek sent David Haggard, Jesse Hampton and David Reed, sons or sons-in-law of John Hampton, Sr. The merger came about.

This does not end the story of Indian Creek. Evidently, the merger satisfied the Haggard-Hampton elements of Indian Creek for they returned to form a family church. The desire for something for the Indian Creek community itself did not die. The newspapers of the 1870s and 1880s reported continued services being held in the Indian Creek School. One of the strongest Sunday schools not sponsored by a church was reported in the school building for years in the 1880s and 1890s. Ministers such as William Rupard or William Harding often preached. They did not seem to be particularly denominationally minded hence, no church actually emerged from these meetings.

However, the Baptist did meet the need in 1887 by the organization of the Allensville Church. The immediate success of the Allensville Church can be attributed to this latent desire for a church in the community. The fact that it did not entirely satisfy the need can be seen in a continuation for a few more years of the school house church. Since no other group took advantage of this activity, it gradually died out and left the field to Allensville Baptist Church.

## MT. OLIVE BAPTIST CHURCH

Because of the fires, there are not many records of Mt. Olive's early days. The outlines of the merger between Unity and Indian Creek were clear. The two churches agreed to build a new building about half way between the two old churches to serve the two communities better.

The building committee included Joel Quisenberry, Jesse Hampton, David Reed, David T. Hampton and John Haggard, Jr., all sons-in-law or sons of John Haggard, Sr. The new church was built on Jackson Ferry Road where it not only could draw on the Unity and Indian Creek area, but by Jackson's Ferry from the Estill County area across the Red River.

In keeping with its membership in Boone Creek Association, the new church had a revival that brought some 55 additions, some of those that had dropped out during the last fifteen years of warfare and some new. The land had been given by George Robinson. David Haggard was elected church clerk. Eli Bruce would become one of its charter members.

What exactly the roll of S. V. Potts was during these years is not clear from the association records. In 1845, he was the minister of the Mt. Olive Church. He may have been there all the time acting as sort of an assistant to Darnaby.

S. V. Potts, E. Ryan and L. Hampton were messengers to the 1848 Boone Creek Association and reported 159 members. A few members were discharged from Mt.Olive that year to help build the Ephesus Baptist Church. They could not have been many, but they did include S. V. Potts who went to help organize the new church. Since the membership of Mt. Olive was reported in 1849 as 213, the loss did not do any real damage.

Conkwright, working largely from his own recollections, reported that Darnaby resigned in 1850. The association records do not show him as minister during this period, but it is possible he returned when Potts left. Conkwright does not mention Potts in connection with Mt. Olive, but the association records do. At any rate, T. I. Wills is called. Wills is discussed more in connection with Ephesus which he and Potts were serving jointly at this time, than with Mt. Olive. Enough to add here that he was one of the new generation of ministers, as was Potts, who would direct the county Baptist movement for some time. Mt. Olive's messengers in 1850 were D. V. Haggard, Eli Bruce, A. H. Hampton and E. T. Woodward. She reported 202 members.

It would be interesting to know just what Conkwright meant when he referred to Indian Creek and Unity as "old school" Baptist. Presumedly, this would refer to what the North District had become to which they referred as "Old" Baptist. The Particular Baptist sometimes thought of themselves as the "Old School" Baptist, but neither Unity or Indian Creek ever belonged to this group.

Whatever they were before their merger, Mt. Olive from the very beginning became one of the more progressive and capable churches of the Boone Creek Baptist Association. Most often, it would affiliate itself with Providence in the support of a minister. This was a natural parrish including many of the same families in both churches and roughly, the same part of the county.

T. I. Wills was still pastor in 1853 and David Hampton was the clerk. Wills was followed the next year by N. D. Creed. He married that year G. W. Broadhus to Nellie Hunt...March 17, 1853. He had only two marriages within the county. Creed was to become a union sympathizer and a Methodist before the next decade was over. Conkwright does not report his ministry. Mt. Olive reported 179 members. The messengers in 1859 were N. R. Creed, A. H. Hampton and F. S. Allen. Her membership was down to 154. This again, as noted in the histories of other churches in Clark County, reflects the heavy westward movement of Clark Countians during the 1850s. It must have appeared that half the county were going west...Texas, California, Illinois, Missouri, Kansas and Nebraska,etc...

Eighteen hundred fifty-eight was also the year that Mt. Olive voted to have a three day meeting each May beginning with the Friday of the third Sunday. This became the famous May meeting of Mt. Olive and reflects the Camp Meeting methods of the Methodist and Cumberland Presbyterians. The Baptist never did enter fully in the camp meeting concept. It is interesting that Mt. Olive would in light of Conkwright's statement that but twenty years earlier they were leaning towards the "Old" Baptist.

T. I. Wills was again the minister of Mt. Olive replacing Creed in 1859. He was also serving Ephesus. F. S. Allen also became church clerk. Conkwright reports that Broadhus was called in 1861 and served a few months. It is more likely that Broadhus conducted the revivals that Mt. Olive had in 1861 that left her with 176 members going into the Civil War. Wills served in '62 and '63 being called on a yearly basis. Wills, however, does not seem happy at Mt. Olive for he resigns because of the "difficult times". There was considerable "union" sentiment in Mt. Olive and this may have conflicted with Wills' own views. A. D. Rash became minister from 1863 to 1868. In passing, we note that Pleasant J. Conkwright became a deacon in 1860.

The war over, T. I. Mills returns to Mt. Olive in 1868. At this time, her messengers were Wills, A. L. Haggard, P. J. Conkwright, A. S. Haggard and F. S. Allen. She reported 176 members. She had survived the war without damage. The next few years were not as good.

By 1875, her membership had dropped to 137. D. G. Heironymous, A. H. Hampton, A. S. Heironymous, P. J. Conkwright and F. S. Allen were the messengers.

Mt. Olive began showing interest in the social problems of the time. In 1861, she came out firmly against drinking and dancing. The association voted in 1868 to set up a home mission program within the limits of the association. Mt. Olive sent a committee to help with the plans and later was made the permanent headquarters of the executive committee that would supervise the missions. This began a series of efforts to expand the Baptist movement into Montgomery, Powell, Wolfe, Breathitt and Estill Counties where the Baptist movement was extremely weak. In 1869, Elias Brookshire was ordained by Mt. Olive, his home church. She helped with the establishing of the Corinth Church in 1871. In 1872, Henry A. Hampton became clerk.

T. I. Wills died in 1872. He had served in three pastorates fifteen years as Mt. Olive's minister. He had left Mt. Olive a strong rural church.

From the last months of 1872 to 1874, W. B. Arvin was pastor. During this period, according to the associational records, Mt. Olive gave $50.00 to missions, her first recorded gift. In 1873, F. S. Allen was elected clerk but did not serve. His son, James L. Allen, became clerk. F. S. Allen was moderator of the Boone Creek Association in 1879 and 1880. He was also the county judge. Fifty cents a member was assessed for missions in 1874. There is no record as how successful the collection was.

J. L. Smith supplied the pulpit in 1875. Then A. F. Baker became minister. Baker represented a change in ministerial types. He was a banker in Winchester, a stranger in the county who stayed and served while he taught and then moved elsewhere never to return to the pages of Clark County history. Mt. Olive met at this time the third Saturday and Sunday of each month. Baker also served Providence at this time. If he had any other churches they were outside of Clark County and we have no record of them. We note in passing that A. Fleet held services October 9, 1878. Fleet was a teacher in Winchester and did a good deal of preaching for local Baptist churches.

Allen Lipscomb was reported Sunday school superintendant in 1879, by the Winchester newspapers. There was no report when the Sunday school was opened, nor is there a report how long there had been a Sunday school at Mt. Olive.

Conkwright reported that the Sunday school was authorized by the church in 1882 but that it had existed as an independent body perhaps as early as 1876. The association was pushing the organization of Sunday schools as part of the churches' program and had organized association wide Sunday school convention meetings on a yearly basis. The Sunday school movement will be more fully discussed in the third volume of this work.

J. L. Smith was again minister in 1880. The newspaper, DEMOCRAT, reported that J. Pike Powers was serving Mt. Olive as he was serving Providence, Ephesus and Kiddville, but this must have been in error. Smith stayed only a year. J. Dallas Simmons was called 1881 to 1887. George Doyle became church clerk. A history of Mt. Olive appeared in the Boone Creek minutes in 1881.

The Sunday school superintendent was James Woodard. The messengers for 1881 were J. D. Simmons, A. S. Haggard, James Haggard and W. T. Eubank. S. P. Hodgkin became clerk in 1882.

James Woodard was made Sunday school superintendent in 1882. The Sunday school was given permission to purchase an organ in 1884 on the condition that it would be removed any time a member would request it. This is the second mention among the Baptist of an organ. Providence already had one installed. It must be remembered that the "Old" Baptist were anti-instrumental and that the anti-instrumental movement among the Christians was gaining headway and would explode in Clark County in 1888. The move shows a number of things that will be discussed later in the Sunday school section of this history. Enough to note them now. It reveals that even with the Baptist official support of the Sunday school both on association and local levels, it is still looked upon as something different from the church. It also reveals how explosive the instrumental issue was, not just among the Christians, but among the Baptist. Finally, it reveals that even though the Boone Creek churches had turned to the missionary approach, a strong conservative sentiment still ran through the churches. S. F. Hodgkins was reported as Sunday school superintendent in 1883. Hodgkins was, as we have noted, clerk. It is interesting to note that in the association, quite often the church ckerk was the Sunday school superintendent. Of course, the clerks were usually men that were active in the church, quite often deacons in their own right, so it is not surprising that many would be Sunday school superintendents. Yet, one might wonder whether the associational pressure for Sunday schools had become so great that a clerk would write his own name into the blank to make his church appear better in the records. Statistics, and no doubt the prestige of a good report, was rapidly becoming a very important item in the association.

The Baptist had always taken a firm stand opposed by dancing. A glance at their records will show that many times members were excluded for taking part in such parties. This attitude was generally true of all the movements, though the Baptist with their better records, appear to be the strongest opposition. However, the county newspapers and diaries reported many dances and parties in progress. Evidently, the problem hit Mt.Olive hard. In 1886, the church offered a blanket amnesty for all those who had danced and promised not to do it again.

In 1886, Mt. Olive was paying, according to the associational minutes, her minister $250.00 a year and with the exception of state missions contributed something to each cause listed in the Baptist program. Her total giving was $436.00. Eli Bruce became Sunday school superintendent. (We have a name problem at this point in that there are at least two Eli Bruces, we think in county history and we do not know one from the other.) Mt. Olive's messengers for that year were Allie and Nannie Lipscomb. This is the first woman to be listed as a messenger in either Mt. Olive or any other associational church. Both Providence and Winchester would send women as messengers in 1887. T. S. Allen became church clerk.

In 1887, fifteen members of Mt. Olive were dismissed to help organize the Allensville Church. The loss did not materially hurt Mt. Olive though some of the transfers were excellent members.

J. Pike Powers became minister in 1888 to 1890. Eli Bruce was still Sunday school superintendent. She reported 176 members and was giving a total of $413.00 for all causes. Things evidently were not going well in 1887 with the loss of the Allensville members and the general situation. The association printed abstracts of the church letters reporting to the association. Mt. Olive reported "no cheery news". The next year they reported still slipping but that she had made some repairs on the church building. Dallas Simmons, another of the new working outsiders, who was serving churches during this period, was minister of Mt. Olive, Ephesus and Providence. The services were the third Saturday and Sunday. Mt. Olive did not send messengers in the 1891 association.

There is no indication of what the trouble was in the records. Perhaps the organization of Allensville indicated more local trouble than had been apparent. J. Pike Powers had been an excellent minister and had organized Mt. Sterling Baptist Church, but during this round of preaching he had been physically sick and far below his previous levels of activities. All the churches that Powers served this last time seemed to be having trouble. Powers left the county after resigning.

A successful revival was held in 1889 which brought thirty people into the church. A. H. Anthony became minister in 1890 and the next year Richard French took control of the church. His history is also reported in connection with Ephesus. As reported elsewhere, French came from an old and influential Clerk and Montgomery family and represented the older school of ministers. Like the other ministers of his day, Baker, Powers, Simmons, etc., he had business interests in Winchester and was not primarily a farmer though he did own land. He was a man of considerable ability and leadership. Membership was reported in 1897 as 183. This was the most members reported since 1850.

Robert Cole was reported Sunday school superintendent in 1893. However, the next year there was no Sunday school reported so one can assume that there was no Sunday school. No Sunday school is reported at Mt. Olive until 1899 when Minor Hisle was listed as Sunday school superintendent. Apparently, whatever his virtues, Richard French was not particularly interested in Sunday school work despite the fact he had been Sunday school superintendent of Winchester's Baptist Church before he became a minister. J. I. Creek became minister in 1895. Mt. Olive tried for two Sundays a month, but found it financially impossible. J. S. Wilson became minister in 1896. Wilson was the beginning of a still newer type of preacher, the student. Older than most students, capable, he was to serve in 1899 Providence and Boone Creek. According to the authoresses of a book, "Fox Cousins", etc., Nellie Adams and Bertha Walton, Wilson became a missionary to Indians in Oklahoma. In 1899 Mt. Olive's messengers were R. B. Quisenberry, A. H. Hampton, S. A. Lipscomb and D. B. Hampton.

P. J. Conkwright became minister in 1902. T. S. Hubert was minister next briefly and was followed by the three year ministry of Otis Hughson. James Eubank, R. E. Quisenberry and Minor Hisle were elected deacons in 1902. Allen Ecton became deacon in 1906.

Messengers in 1901 were H. G. Hisle, B. B. Hampton and Earnest Cole. It is interesting to note the family turnover in the names of the messengers over these years. She was paying her minister $212.00 a year and her total giving was $268.40. She had no Sunday school.

Hughson was another student minister, inspired by his seminary, was seeking to bring their enlightened ways to his church. He did have a Sunday school going in 1903 with S. A. Lipscomb as superintendent. He then introduced the envelope system of church giving in 1903. The church approved, but the system never functioned. Hughson left the church for wider fields as student ministers of country churches do when they graduate, no doubt puzzled and perhaps a little wiser. He was replaced by another student, O. P. Bush who wondered how come new and modern ideas had not been introduced into Mt. Olive. Minor Hisle was Sunday school superintendent but with the change of ministers there was no Sunday school in 1904. The new minister reorganized the Sunday school and A. Haggard became Sunday school superintendent.

Two deaths occurred during these years that need noting. Ninety-three year old Sallie Gordon passed on after a long illness. T. S. Allen died in 1905. He had been clerk for eight years, but more, he had been the community doctor. His passing marks also the passing of the medical men who lived in a rural community and gave personal attention to their neighbors. Gordon Haggard became clerk.

Once again, it was time to change ministers. The last year of a student minister becomes difficult. He has struggled for two years and has not made a great deal of progress. He was in his final year of seminary. His thinking was towards his graduation, his future work and his own plans. Mt. Olive's Sunday school went unreported in 1907. Robert Cole was Sunday school superintendent in 1907. In 1908 J. E. Brandenburg was superintendent. He closed the school for the winter and it did not reopen. The new minister, T. C. Duke, was called in 1909. The 1908 association reported no minister, no Sunday school. Duke promptly organized a Sunday school with J. R. Cole as superintendent. Duke was a Southern Seminary student. Duke did a better than average job for a student. He left in 1911, Mt. Olive was negotiating and called George Shepherd, a local minister who wanted to come back to Clark County. He accepted instead the call of the New Winchester Central Church. The church had abandoned any effort to use envelopes, but the Sunday school was going under Audley Haggard. She reported 183 members. She paid her minister $300.00 a year. Her giving to the association causes were well rounded other than to state missions. She had a building valued at $2,000. Her messengers for 1912 were Gordon Haggard, E. A. Ecton, H. Hisle, D. B. Hampton and Sherman Jewell.

The association lists Don C. Smith as minister in 1911, but he must not have lasted long. Conkwright does not report him. Duke left earlier that year and the 1912 association reports neither minister or Sunday school. Conkwright says that C. E. Wanford became minister in 1912 but he is not reported at association time and therefore, presumed gone.

A. J. Gravett was chosen deacon in 1910. Student ministers have now become the rule. Wanford was followed by E. D. Poe. Poe was from North Carolina and after several months went home for a vacation. The newspapers reported that he had been killed, March 16. He appeared in Kentucky very much alive April 5 with the not too original report that his death had been somewhat exaggerated.

In 1914, the governor had encouraged a state-wide Sunday school contest and many of the Clark County churches, including Mt. Olive, participated. She reported her Sunday school with fifty members.

The students continued to come and go. In 1915, A. Y. Ammerson became minister and the next year, A. N. Nicholson was minister and continued at Mt. Olive until 1920. Revivals were now a yearly feature, but under Nicholson, the 1917 revival won seventeen new members to the church. It is perhaps, the expression of the change of effectiveness of a revival when seventeen converts is a matter of rejoicing. Everett Gravitt was elected deacon in 1920.

Nicholason was followed by a home boy, W. S. Shearer. Shearer left, however, after one year. Audley Haggard was elected a deacon in 1920. A minister named ARbuckle served so briefly that Conkwright could not even record his initials.

As with Providence, as the 1920s came, Mt. Olive was perhaps weaker than any time since 1890. The heavy change over of minister made a three year ministry seem extremely stable. From a non-Baptist observed, the saving power that held Mt. Olive together was the leadership and the inspiration that the association was able to give. It was the associational program that provided the continuation from one student minister to another.

# BOONE CREEK BAPTIST ASSOCIATION

The most influential Baptist Association in Clark County history is the Boone Creek Baptist Association. Its history and the history of the member churches have been written by S. J. Conkwright. His history is the main stay of this section. Spencer's "History of the Baptist Church in Kentucky" adds a bit more. The newspapers, particularly after the Civil War, will add their bit. The minutes of the association are on microfilm down to the date of 1957. This volume will carry the history of the association, and the rural churches in Clark County that belonged to the association, to 1922. This date is a good place to stop for somewhere in the early twenties, there is a turning point in all Clark County church history and needs to be studied separately in a long historical account.

Conkwright gave the reasons for the establishing of the Boone Creek Association in 1820 of churches that would come from the North District, the Licking, the Elkhorn, the Tates Creek Baptist Associations as the unwieldiness and size of the parent bodies. However, it is obvious that studying the member churches of the old association and those who helped form the new, or became a member of the new association, that distance and unwieldiness is only a partial answer. The distances traveled by many of the churches that remained in the old association was much larger than those of the new. However, the new association did form a geographically reasonable pattern.

It is quite obvious that this is an association of Separatist Baptist who were pulling out of associations largely dominated by Regular or Particular Baptist Calvinists. The Union was now twenty years old. Neither side, liberal or conservative, showed themselves to be really happy with the merger. The Licking Baptist that had grown out of the Elkhorn under Ambrose Dudley represented the conservative wing. It is true that the North District Association held men and churches that were not regular or Calvinistic Baptist. Their leader, however, John Racoon Smith, had begun a Regular Baptist and had not showed signs of changing until his contract with David Barrow, and then with Alexander Campbell and other Baptist liberals in Kentucky. The establishment of the North District Baptist Association and the Licking Association was dominated by men of strong Calvinistic convictions. The establishment of the Boone Creek Baptist Association was to, at least in part, shake free of that domination.

The Boone Creek Association was strictly a non-Clark County effort. Mt. Gilead, a Fayette County church, canvassed her neighbors about the possibilities of a new association. In 1822, Mt. Gilead, Bogg's Fork, Boone Creek, Mt. Union and First Baptist of Lexington met at Cross Plains (Athens or even more precise the Boone Creek Church). This did not appear to be a rush of churches to take up the new possibility. A Constitution was adopted to which the Lexington First Church objected and voted against. Being defeated, First Church did not return to the next meeting. Jacob Fishback had been elected moderator and William Boone clerk. Fishback was part of a strong Presbyterian family that resided in Clark County. He had been converted to the Baptist church from the Presbyterians because of his interest in Barton Stone and Alexander Campbell.

In 1923, Mt. Gilead, Boone Creek, Bogg's Fork, Mt. Union, Hinds Creek, Hickman, Lower Bethel, a Mt. Moriah and Providence in Clark County joined, making nine churches. Hickman was in Jessamine County which was quite a distance from the center of the association. James Quisenberry and Thomas Boone of the North District attended as fraternal delegates. George Boone was elected moderator. Unlike Thomas Boone, he was not a Calvinist and was to show increasing interest in the Reform movement of Campbell.

To these early meetings men like J. Vardeman, Jacob Creach, John Smith, John Collins, William Thurman attended. Many of these men were already in revolt against Calvinistic extremes and were interested in the Stone-Campbell ideas.

The nine churches in 1824 reported 760 members. Hickman was in Jessamine (65 members), Hind Fork was in Madison (26). Providence was in Clark. The rest were all Fayette County churches. Mt. Gilead 126, Bogg's Ford 144, Mt. Union 61, Lower Bethel 55, Mt. Moriah 37. Providence was the largest with 160 members. Richard Morton was elected moderator for 1823 and 1824. B. W. Riley was the clerk. Morton was to become one of the leaders in the Campbell Reform movement. Morton was Friendship's minister.

The Friendship Church, which had split originally from the Strode's Station Church, and had split again with one section going to the Licking Association and the other moving into Winchester, was, by 1825, calling itself a Christian Church and showing considerable influence of Barton Stone. Though never actually a member of the Stone movement, even while applying for membership in the Boone Creek Baptist Association, it was for all practical purposes, a Stone's church in Clark County. Barton Stone had a dozen more in Bourbon and Fayette Counties. Friendship joined the association in 1825. She was the largest church in the association reporting 230 members. The Boone Creek Association reported 918 members.

George Boone became moderator between 1825 and 1828. Eighteen twenty-eight was the peak year for the association. The Campbell Reform was in full swing and the Walter Scott evangelistic five points program, Faith, Repentence, Confession, Baptist and the Gift of the Holy Spirit being used extensively. Eight hundred and nine baptisms were reported by thirteen churches with a total membership up to 1,835. Never would the Boone Creek report such an influx of new members. Some churches doubled their membership in three years. Strangely after Mt. Zion Baptist Church, no new churches were organized. It would not be until 1900 when the Boone Creek Baptist Association was much larger would this number of baptisms be matched. In passing however, we ought to note that there was everywhere a religious excitement. The Methodists were growing so fast during this period that they assigned two extra ministers to handle the work. The Sugar Ridge Presbyterians had one of their most successful camp meetings during this period and the Winchester Presbyterians finally were able to build their church building (as did the Methodists) and become a self supporting church.

William Landrum attended one of the association meetings under George Boone and was very complimentary seeing nothing wrong. But then Landrum never did report seeing anything wrong about any church or religious meeting.

During the first seven years of the association's life she met at Mt. Gilead, Bogg's Fork, Boone Creek, Hickman, Providence, Mt. Gilead and in the 1828 meeting at Friendship. Richard Morton had preached the introductory sermon, which was a high honor, in 1823; Benjamin W. Riley in 1824. George Boone preached the sermon in 1825 and 1826; John Sacre in 1827. William Morton preached the introductory sermon in 1828, but John Racoon Smith preached on Sunday morning. A motion was entered into the association calling for the abolition of the Constitution. The motion was deferred until the next year. This was the Reform effort to bring the Baptist movement into line with their conceptions. Their ideas and issues will be dealt with in the second volume in the section concerning the Christian Church. Certainly it is obvious that the leadership were Reformers. The great bulk of church membership that joined in 1828, joined under the Reform leadership. There was every indication that the association would abolish the Boone Creek Association's Constitution.

William Boone was clerk in 1825 and 1826. Thomas Faulconer was the clerk in 1826, 27 and 28.

The Reformers kept the pressure on the Baptist. Like most campaigns, it was fairly clear which churches would oppose a reformation of the association. The Christian Messenger reported in February how one of Stone's ministers, John Roberts, preached in Clark County at the end of the Four Mile Creek at Jackson's Ferry. On Sunday he preached at Jackson's home. That evening he visited and preached at a meeting at John Hawkins and reported that seven were converted. Monday he preached at Thomas Burgess and Wednesday at Sam Tribbles' .... claiming to have won a conversion at each. These services remind one of the Methodist circuit riders in the early days of their movement.

On Thursday, Roberts was joined by a Baptist whom he called J... S... (undoubtedly John Smith). Together they went to Indian Creek Baptist Church to hold services, but the church was locked. Finally the deacons of the church agreed to open the church to John Smith but not to Roberts. Saturday, Roberts and Smith returned to Jackson's and lodged with a D____ S____ in site of his church. (This would have to be Unity.) D____ S____ would not have to be the minister but could be a layman. S____ would not go with Smith to church and once again the church was found locked, windows nailed shut. A large and respectable congregation gathered and a fire was built in the yard because it was so cold. Finally one of the members demanded the keys to the church and opened the church to Smith.

This picture of Smith and other Reformers going from church to church in an almost comic struggle with the Baptist strongholds for keys and opportunity to preach was duplicated all over the area, not just in Clark County, but Montgomery, Madison and others.

It is interesting to note that Roberts always refers to Smith as a Baptist. To the Stone Christians, the Methodists and to the majority of Baptist, the Reformers were Baptist and would remain Baptist Reformers for another quarter century.

The Christian Messenger, June of 1828 (the publication of the Barton Stone churches), reported a call or resolution submitted at the request of the churches, after mature debate stated that it does not feel the Word of God does authorize or prescribe any form of Constitution but authorized the Assembly of Saints to come together only for worship by the Boone Creek Baptist Association and that they voted to abolish their present Constitution. The Reformers objected to an association that could be turned into a formal court of inquiry and resolutions.

The church roll in 1828 reported Mt. Gilead, 125 members; Bogg's Fork, 124; Boone Creek, 151; Hickman, 109; Mt. Union, 55; Providence, 280; Hind's Creek, 31; Lower Bethel, 152. Each of these churches showed very substantial increase in membership. Some were actual double of their 1824 reports. New churches were added to the Boone Creek, Nicholasville, 180; Friendship, 265; Mt. Zion, 160 (both the last two were Clark County churches); Liberty, 97; and Clark County's Indian Creek, 108. The total association membership was 1,835.

Elisha Bibb was elected moderator in 1829 and John M. Johnson of Providence was elected clerk. They were not able to stop the association from voting to abolish the association Constitution. William Morton and George Boone were principal speakers. The majority of the 1829 association favored abolishing the Constitution.

Nicholasville, Friendship, Lower Bethel, Mt. Zion, Liberty and Mt. Union voted with the majority. It might be noted that only one of the churches who belonged to this association before 1824 voted with the majority. The others were churches that had joined the association after 1824.

What Bibb and Johnson were able to do was to save the records. The Boone Creek Baptist Association met in 1830. There is no indication of other meetings such as happened in the North District Association. The churches that had voted not to keep the Constitution did not attend. Unlike the North District Reform churches, there is no indication or record that they ever met as a unit. Later, they joined the Montgomery Reform churches in a weak district organization. The churches that reported to the Boone Creek in 1830 were Mt. Gilead, Bogg's Fork, Boone Creek, Hickman, Providence and Indian Creek. We have noted that Unity was one of the seven that supported the Baptist in the North District. Of all the Baptist churches in both associations in Clark County, only Friendship and Mt. Zion went intact to the Reform. Bethlehem belonged to neither association.

Ambrose Bush became moderator and would be until 1849. He was not a minister but he was a strong and determined layman. His son would carry both the name and tradition. The introductory sermons during this period were preached by Edward Kindred, Thomas Boone, Robert Elrod, A. D. Landrum, Thomas Boone, Landrum twice again, Josiah Leake, William Hickey, James Edmonson, B. E. Allen, W. F. Broadhus, Mason Owen, Allen again, A. R. Macy, S. V. Potts.... names that become increasingly related to Clark County history as the years progress. A few, Boone, Edmonson, for example, would go with the "old" Baptist group, but the majority were identified with the missionary group as that group emerged. This apparently was a right compromise for the Boone Creek churches who rejected the extreme of the Reformers and the ultra Calvinism of the "old" Baptist.

Membership was to continue downward until in 1836 it sank to 412 for seven churches. Only 11 baptisms were reported that year. The member churches at this time were Bogg's Fork, Boone Creek, Hickman, Providence, Indian Creek, Mt. Gilead and Mt. Freedom. Unity had belonged to the Boone Creek briefly in 1832 but had gone back to the North District. J. C. Christopher became clerk in 1831 to 1835. B. E. Allen was to serve for the next two years. This is Allen's first introduction to Clark County history. He was a rising young man, preaching at Boone Creek as his home church. In 1837, the bottom was hit with 409 members and no baptisms reported.

There were serious doubts that the association could survive. The North District, under stronger leadership, was recovering faster. There was not in the Boone Creek men like Chenault, Boone or a layman like James French. The nearest to it was Ambrose Bush who lacked the dogmatism or the inflexibility of French.

The churches began to strengthen. Providence went back over 200 members. Boone Creek under Allen began to strengthen. Unity returned to the Boone Creek. The "old" Baptist Church at Ruckerville (Upper Howard Creek) divided and the more moderate element came to Boone Creek...making three groups at Ruckerville, two Baptist and a Christian, using the one building...some new ministers like S.V. Potts were joining Allen. Broadhus was conducting the first really successful revivals (without using the Reformer technique) that the association had seen since the division. The association in 1840 voted for missions to the heathen without delay.

In 1842, the association reported 223 baptisms, the most since 1829 and would be the most until 1902. New life ran through the association churches and new excitement spread. It is standard operational procedure that any church that grows rapidly will have a disruption between the old members and the new. Associations are no different than churches and just as it happened in 1828, so it developed in the 1840s. There was a difference in disputes. The Reformers were an organized and capable group of men who felt that they were going to Reform Christianity. The approach was simple, evangelistic and aggressive. It was obviously a planned revolt from the Baptist tradition. The struggle in 1840 was basically over what was Calvinism and how it should be interpreted though it is doubtful whether many of the lay participants had ever heard of Calvin. Calvinism may be logically and intellectually satisfying but it is seldom inspiring. The Boone Creek churches were feeling the urge toward something that might be called progress. The Calvinism of the "old" Baptist ministers would halt this progress. The bitter struggle and law suit involving the Lullbegrud Church in Montgomery was a classic example of the kind of struggle that went on in Upper Howard Creek at Ruckerville and to a lesser degree in other Clark County churches. There was no reorganization, no cohesive movement as among the Reformers driving to change the Baptist way, nor was there a conscious organized movement on the part of Baptist laymen to preserve a certain way. It was a battle that was fought out intra church by intra church and sometimes almost by individual by individual. The younger ministers, though intelligent men, often lacked the education to appreciate the fine points of theological Calvinism. They were feeling the pressure of the Methodist and Reform....more and more called the Christian Churches in Clark County... to move ahead to some kind of church program.

The Christian or Reform movement had stripped the North District Baptist Association of any moderate ministers. In the Boone Creek Baptist Association, the remaining Baptist ministers themselves were more apt to be moderate or separatist in viewpoint. The break with the Campbellites had been less bitter and the fears of being contaminated anew by new ideas were not so prevalent. Upper Howard Creek divided and the more liberal group organized and joined Boone Creek Association. Unity which had been under John Quisenberry for much of its history came back to the Boone Creek. The Boone Creek stopped using North Dsitrict ministers, not perhaps deliberately, but because they did not like their approach.

This does not mean that the Boone Creek Association was having any doubts about its position. In an effort to assert its position, the association in 1846 once again ratified the Plan of Union of 1801 as its guide and the theological standard. The two associations, therefore, parted company in a division that became increasingly apparent as the years went by. Providence, Unity, Indian Creek, in Clark County, went along with the Boone Creek Association towards a more progressive position on such questions as missions, Sunday schools, paid ministers, cooperation with the State Baptist Association and the National Mission Boards. Goshen, Upper Howard's Creek, New Providence, turned to the "old" Baptist ways with the North District. Mt. Carmel remained loyal to the Licking and virtually in another world of church activity. Floundering more or less by itself, deserting the Licking Association but not joining the Boone Creek, gutted by the issues over Particular Baptist, Friendship continued to weaken alone and soon died.

There is absolutely no mention of the slavery issue that divided the country at this time. None of the churches in either association was affected and there was no anti slavery effort. All of Clark County's churches continued without even so much as mentioning the issue in any of the minutes that have been available.

During the forties, membership in the Boone Creek hardly faltered. Seven hundred sixty-six after the splendered record of baptisms in 1842; 832 the next year; dropping to 766 in 1845, but back again to a high since the Reform of 959 in 1830.

The Boone Creek gained confidence as the decade went on. Unity and Indian Creek were combined in 1844 to form Mt. Olive and Ephesus was organized in 1848. Of course, the Boone Creek's Upper Howard Creek church disappeared after Ephesus. The Unity and Indian Creek merger meant a net loss of a church, but on the whole the association was stronger because of the two actions.

B. E. Allen was to become moderator in 1850 to remain until 1855; then one year more of Treadway's clerkship; then four years of John Hunton. Smith V. Potts would be moderator in 1856 and then Allen until 1860.

The 1850s were not good years for the county. Economically, save for the shorthorn industry, the county stagnated. Population decreased as hundreds of Clark Countians moved westward. The growing threat of the Civil War kept the atmosphere stirred. The collapse of the Whig Party brought a desperate feeling to Clark County politics as the abandoned Whigs hunted for an alternate. One cannot separate the total picture from the specific.

However, the Boone Creek Association prospered....mildly. Her total membership into the nine hundreds and generally stayed there. In 1858, it was 968. One hundred thirty-three were baptised in 1848; 120 in 1852; 117 in 1856. There were bad years, only 5 in 1854.

Besides Ephesus and Mt. Olive, new churches came into the association, Salem (a division in the "old" Baptist Church) and Cow Creek from Estill County. Later on, Union in Madison County was added. Most important Winchester Baptist Church was organized in 1858. After the Reform movement, there had been no churches in Winchester of the Baptist movement. Presbyterians, Christians and Methodists all had reasonably strong churches in the county seat, but Winchester Baptist belonged to country churches, mostly Providence. As the decade closed, the demand for a church in Winchester grew. Once established, Winchester Baptist Church was not an over night success, but it did add to the overall strength of the association.

Other churches now appeared, South Fork of the Kentucky, in Owsley, Mt. Freedom which had been a member was revived with 8 members. This was the beginning of the associational missionary work. As early as 1843, the association appointed a committee to employ a missionary to work in the association boundaries. Samuel Cleam was treasurer. S. V. Potts was closely connected with it from the beginning. In 1859, the association was reporting ten churches, Providence, Mt. Olive, Ephesus and Winchester in Clark County, Lullbegrud's missionary faction in Montgomery, Salem and Cow Creek in Estill, Union and Madison and South Fork in Owsley. Mt. Freedom had collapsed again.

James French was clerk for three years beginning in 1855. James French was the brother of Richard French and the son of James French who had saved the North District. The contemporary James French (1976) said that Richard was not particularly religious in that he went into politics and was a Congressman. James, however, resumed the traditions of his father, but in a more non Calvinistic way. He had been county judge in Montgomery County, but later moved to Winchester where he became active in the Winchester Baptist Church. In 1848, Nathan Edmunson became clerk until 1864. The introductory sermons were almost entirely by men deeply involved in Clark County history.... T. I. Wills in 1848, S. V. Potts again in 1849, then N.D. Creed, T. I. Wills, John Hunton, Smith V. Potts for a third time in 1853; B. E. Allen, P. T. Gentry, T. I. Wills for a second time; B. E. Allen for the fourth time and in 1858 once again S. V. Potts. N. D. Creed spoke again the next year and in 1860 the very interesting A. D. Rash.

Rash had been the minister of the Friendship Particular Baptist Church outside of Winchester. He had been disturbed by the friction that had developed in the Licking Association and had left that association with his church. However, he gave material aid to the establishing of the Winchester Baptist Church and was rewarded by becoming its first minister. Rash was always a strange cross between strong Calvinism and a willingness to follow the missionary program. He became sort of the fireman of the Boone Creek Association, going where needed to prevent trouble. He became moderator in 1861 and was to continue until 1867.

The association met at Providence, 1834; Indian Creek, 1836; Providence, 1839; Indian Creek, 1842; Unity, 1844; Howard's Upper Creek, 1845; Lullbegrud, 1846; Ephesus, 1849; Providence, 1850; Mt. Olive, 1853; Lullbegrud, 1854; Mt. Olive, 1855; Ephesus, 1857; Providence, 1859; Winchester First, 1861, Lullbegrud, 1864; Ephesus, 1866; Providence, 1868; Winchester First, 1870; Kiddville, 1871; Mt. Olive, 1873; Corinth, 1879; Allenville, 1884; Providence, 1885; Winchester First, 1888; Corinth, 1889; Allensville, 1890; Mt. Olive, 1892; Ephesus, 1893; Kiddville, 1894; Providence, 1895; Winchester First, 1897 and 1898; Corinth, 1899; Allensville, 1900; Mt. Olive, 1902; Ephesus, 1903; Kiddville, 1904; Corinth, 1908; Winchester First, 1909, Allensville, 1910; Mt. Olive, 1913; Winchester Central, 1914; Ephesus, 1915; Kiddville, 1916; Providence, 1917; Corinth, 1920 and Winchester First in 1921.

The Civil War was disruptive, but it actually did very little damage to Clark County. No real battles were fought in the county. Morgan's men moved repeatedly through the county several times but always moving. There was only a touch of the guerrilla warfare that was to tear Powell County so badly. No homes were burned. A few horses and vehicles were confiscated by one army or the other, but nothing really harmful. Even the loss of slaves was delayed in that the Emancipation Act applied only to seceded states and not to Kentucky. The slave owners had time to make some adjustments.

The Boone Creek Association did not make progress during this period but neither did it lose. T. I. Wills, in 1861, Nathan Edmunson, A. D. Rash for the second time, E. D. Isbell, A. D. Rash for the third time, Thomas Stevenson, A. D. Rash for the fourth time, T. I. Wills for the second time and Nathan Edmunson for the fourth time preached the introductory sermons. Except for Isbell, all were closely connected to the association.

As never before, the association is led by home-grown ministers. Those of the pre-1850s were not county residents. Thomas Boone was from Fayette, Chenault from Madison...hardly a local minister. Now the core of the Boone Creek ministers were resident men, mostly from county families. A. D. Rash, S. V. Potts, T. I. Wills, Nathan Edmunson, and a little later on, Richard French, T. C. Ecton, etc. They will be joined later by a group of ministers, largely locally based, but not native to Clark County. Among these will be J. Pike Powers, Dallas Simmons, A. Baker, etc. These were mature able men. If they lacked advanced theological education, they were excellent Bible students, and dedicated Christians. The latter group were business men of considerable ability.

There was basically no difference between the ministers who served in the country and those who served in the city churches until late in the 19th century. Usually they would be the same men. Winchester was more apt to import ministers than the country church. The quality did not change on the whole, until the country ministry began to deteriorate after 1900.

The association was very much aware of the Civil War. In 1861, the circular letter reported the horrors of Civil War.... of citizens divided and of animosities and distrust... and the necessities of trusting God. The association shows little signs of being badly hurt by the Civil War. Membership from 1860 to 1865 averaged out about 850 with low reports 1863 (778) and 1865 (649), but also high reports of 932 in 1862 and 953 in 1864. Baptist, which may be a better sign of church activity than membership, showed disruption of normal activities, however. In 1863, when there was intense action in Kentucky, reported only 2 baptisms. Again, in 1865, when the turmoil and disruption in the county was at its height reported only 6.

The association interests both during the Civil War and afterward was expanding. Besides the objective of establishing more churches in the association, the association took a very active interest in Sunday school. The larger picture of the Sunday school movement will be reported in the third volume. However, the Baptist never seriously cooperated with the larger movement so there will be little overlapping by a summary of Baptist Sunday school work.

Even as early as 1854, Ephesus was raising money to buy Sunday school books (for a library), but her Sunday school did not really take shape. She sold the books somewhat later. The association was giving some time to Sunday school work in the middle 1860s, urging churches to organize. The association at this time did not report Sunday school statistics so it is hard to know how many churches followed suit...though evidently not many. Winchester Baptist had a Sunday school since the end of the Civil War and perhaps earlier. The association appointed Elias Brookshire to the task of organizing Sunday schools in the association in the 1867 meeting. The next year Brookshire turned up at Providence as Sunday school superintendent. He must have done a good job because Providence had a Sunday school thereafter. The association heard a report in 1876 showing the association had 380 students with 55 teachers in five Sunday schools. There were 15 churches in the association owning 13 meeting houses. The association also reported that it had over 200 books in its Sunday school libraries. In 1878, only Winchester and Ephesus had Sunday schools under A. Fleet of the Winchester Seminary and another Sunday school at Kiddville which was one of the more permanent schools. We now get the pattern of professional educators, organizing and developing Sunday schools near their homes. Mt. Olive and Boone Creek had Sunday schools but they did not report that year. The next year only Winchester and Kiddville had Sunday schools. Cyrus Boone was responsible for Kiddville.

Sunday schools depended largely on the interest of the minister and on the weather. Most schools stopped each winter and were reorganized in the springtime. At this time, the majority of schools were held in the afternoon away from church services and as a semi-independent organization. For example, we note that one church permitted the Sunday school to buy an organ, even though the organ was not used in the church services.

Sunday schools were coming into their own in 1886. Providence, Mt. Olive, Ephesus, Winchester, Kiddville, Corinth, Macedonia, Jeffersonwille and Powell Valley had Sunday schools. There were now yearly Baptist Sunday school conventions.

The WINCHESTER DEMOCRAT reported that the Boone Creek Sunday School Convention held June, 1887, at Ephesus had 1200 people attending the first day and 1500 the second. It is possible that the convention was held in conjunction with Ephesus's June meeting.. a point that the newspaper may have overlooked.

The next year the DEMOCRAT reported the program of the conventions: L. N. Conkwright, opened with "The Relation of the Sunday School and Church". Thereafter, Richard French, "What Authority Do We Have for Sunday Schools?" R. R. Perry, "The Cost and Value of Sunday Schools". A. D. Rash, "What are the Qualifications of a Sunday School Superintendent?" W. H. French, "What Should the Objectives of the Sunday School Be?" Stonewall Conkwright, "What are the Duties of a Sunday School Treasury?" T. W. Hampton, "Should the Older Members be Interested in Sunday School?"

The 1887 meeting showed Providence with 119 students, Mt. Olive with 176, Ephesus with 146, Winchester with 176, Kiddville with 65 and Corinth with 64.

Cyrus W. Boone who was one of the county's veteran male teachers had taken over the Kiddville Sunday School. L. N. Conkwright was also a Sunday school superintendent wherever he taught...Sunday schools also served as a starting point for some of the ministers. Richard French and P. J. Conkwright were both Sunday school superintendents (Winchester and Allensville) before they entered into the ministry.

Already, by 1900, however, one can see the Baptist Sunday school growing into the effective tool that it was to become. More and more, the Baptist found their Sunday school an instrument around which to build a church. Ministers could come and go, but the Sunday school went on. By 1922, reinforced by the county convention which passed out of use in World War I, but replaced by other effective means of Sunday school training and control, the Sunday school was a powerful tool for churchmanship.

Interest in associational missions continued. In 1853, the association asked either for money or for time given to missions. P. T. Gentry pledged ten hours, B. E. Allen 5, S. V. Potts 5, T.I. Wills 5, etc. It was with these funds and time that the association began to reach beyond the limits of its association into Estill County and into Powell. For example, it was S. V. Potts that worked with Salem and Cow Creek in Estill that brought them into the association. In 1860, the Home Mission Board of the association confessed they had stopped working because they were "destitute of funds".

There were problems with this mission work. Almost at once, in 1866, Cow Creek and the revived New Freedom Church wanted out of the Boone Creek Association to join a closer association. The work was renewed again after the Civil War and as a result, we find a half dozen new churches coming into the association. In Clark County, Kiddville and Corinth, and then later Allensville were established. In each case, there appeared to be good solid Baptist support, strengthened by the family ties that ran through the county, and reinforced by the nearness of other Baptist churches. In 1874, there are a raft of non county mission points, Snow Creek, Mt. Zion, New Salem, Macedonia, Friendship, Spruce, North Fork of the Red River, Zion, etc., all of whom were listed in the 1875 minutes. Later churches were added including Beattyville, Jeffersonville, Filson, Irving First, Boonesville, and Heidleburg. Many of these churches were on the right-of-way of the Kentucky Union Railroad, or later called the L and E Railroad which ran from Winchester or actually outside Winchester at the L and E Junction, to the coal fields east. The Reform or the Christian Church had swept Powell County and very largely Estill in the 1830s. What was left was a series of "old" Baptist churches, mostly in remote areas. Since that time, both Estill and Powell Counties had grown some, but were still very rural. The railroad reaching up through Jackson, Wolfe and Breathitt opened up the whole region. The history of the railroads is in the third volume of this history.

The Boone Creek Association was making a tremendous effort to expand the Baptist movement and spending, what for those times was a considerable amount of money. However, the total results were not encouraging. The new chruches in Clark County all blossomed almost immediately into good rural churches. It was another story outside of the county. Many of these new churches would be organized with maybe ten or fifteen members. This was all many a strong Baptist church had started with, but times and locations were different. Many of the new churches were located in sites that obviously had no future. Others collapsed as soon as the evangelist left the territory. Some would operate rather well for a few years and then die. They would be reported in the associational minutes for a few years and then be dropped. It is difficult to assess such a program. There were successes. J. Pike Powers reorganized the Baptist Church in Mt. Sterling. The original church had gone in a body to the Campbellites and had become First Christian. In the 1870s Powers reorganized and brought together many local Baptists and the church was started and grew steadily if not spectacularly. Powers, despite his help from the Boone Creek, took his church into the Brachen Association which generally claimed Montgomery for its own. The organizing of Mt. Sterling also killed the feeble branch of the Lullbegrud Church that belonged to the Boone Creek Association. Other churches, Powell Valley, Beattyville, Irving would finally make the grade, but only after a long struggle that usually ended in another association.

There were grumbles in the Boone Creek about the mission work but the Baptist did not discourage easily. The association reported in 1891 to the newspapers that C. H. Anthony was being sent into Powell County as an evangelist. The total cost of running the association that year was $4,000.

Committees from the association continually went out to see what could be done to bolster the sagging new churches. In the early 1900s, L. N. Conkwright, though not formally a minister, went to Beattyville to see if that church could be brought back to life. It had a rather spotty beginning. Beattyville was a river port and a supply point for the back country. Lumber and coal were being floated down the river, but it was not until the L and N Railroad finally reached the community that it grew substantially. In 1911, the Boone Creek Baptist Association held their annual meeting at Irving. The boat, "C. W. Burks" was chartered to carry delegates from Ford to Irving. It was sort of a vacation and excursion built into an association meeting.

Still, despite the high rate of loss, the Baptist were once again in Powell, Estill, Montgomery and into the mountains. If the Boone Creek did not profit greatly from the effort, the Baptist movement as a whole did.

The Boone Creek did seek to analyze the situation. J. N. Conkwright did admit in one of the later minutes that mistakes were made. There has to be other reasons than just the mistake of very small groups trying to establish a church. Many Baptist churches began with small groups. Ten or twelve people are hardly enough to organize a church, yet many churches have begun with that limited number. After discussing the situation with a number of lay and ordained Baptist personalities, Conkwright offered these reasons for the failure of the Home Mission Program.

First of all, Boone Creek was moving into areas where the Baptist movement either was non-existing, or was already dominated by small, but tightly organized "old" Baptist churches. The Reform movement had nearly wiped out the base of Baptist in Montgomery and in Powell. Having gathered together a handful of faithful, there simply were no more people to convert. The few would battle valiently, but there simply were not enough people interested. In most of the areas where these churches were being established, there were already old and established churches of other denominations or "old" Baptists.

Secondly, there had been a time when ministers were largely self-financed. They owned farms or businesses and did not heed expenses. This was no longer true. Even with a railroad, it cost money to send a minister to a church group. Churches like Goshen among the "old" Baptist could operate for decades with less than fifty members because their ministers were still largely self-supporting. There was never adequate funds in the associational treasure to finance sufficiently, and long enough, a program in any of these preaching points. The association also tried to establish too many churches at the same time.

Third, the investment was too much. In the old days, a church could be built over night by a handful of members out of logs. By 1900, to build a church took money and skills usually not possessed by a local congregation. Even the well established country churches in Clark County were facing difficulties. The "old" Baptist churches were dying. Rural churches of the Christians, Methodists and Presbyterians were in trouble. The rural areas were being bled of its youth going to the cities in numbers that were even worse than the westward movement before the Civil War. The best rural minds and leaders were deserting the country for wider economic opportunities in the county seats. Many who remained in the country joined the city churches.

Finally there was a change in attitude among the people. The revival was always a fickle instrument, immensely successful at times and indifferent at other times. It no longer was simple to hold a successful revival. It did require an evangelist which could catch the imagination of the neighborhood, and it took long hard work on the part of the membership to get the neighborhood to attend. Revivals were becoming common. A church had one every year. There was a lessening of the interest in theology on the part of the layman. Churches, to be successful, had to offer a great deal more than just a preaching service on a Saturday and Sunday once a month.

There is little change in the minutes of the North District Association from early days to the days before it died. The association would meet, perhaps on a Saturday. A chosen minister would give the introductory sermon. There would be two or three other sermons throughout the meeting. The meeting would elect officers, quite often merely returning those that were already in office. Letters from corresponding associations would be read and their messengers seated. Usually messengers would be appointed to attend the associational meetings of corresponding associations. Business would be conducted though little of it would appear in the minutes. Most debatable issues would be settled behind the scenes. Letters from the local churches would be read or at least reported in some manner or other. Boone Creek would sometimes print exerts from them, other times give a digest. Eventually they were not reported at all. It would be at this time that a church would ask questions of the association such as in 1809, the Cane Creek Church of the North District asked whether it was permissable to commune with other societies not of "our faith and order". The association said it was not. Through these questions one can sometimes get a feeling of what was going on. On the whole, this type of question disappears from the Boone Creek Association as early as the Civil War. It will reappear as resolutions or motions for the business meeting. A good deal of time would be given to the preparation of a circular letter. Originally this was a theological exhortation, from a historian's point of view, of little value. After the Civil War, the Boone Creek Association used the circular letter to outline the history of the host churches or the Boone Creek Association itself. After a brief return to an inspirational circulatory letter, it became a "it was a good meeting, wish you were here" type and then dropped. Some place in the minutes a list of messengers from member churches would be given and some statistics, mostly baptisms, dismissals and membership would be reported. Generally, these minutes would be printed. The North District printed their meetings from 1802 to its death. The microfilm records of the Boone Creek show handwritten records largely until after the Civil War. It appears however, that there were also printed reports.

This description pretty largely reflected the Boone Creek minutes until after the Civil War. The Home Mission effort was the first report to creep into the minutes that broke this pattern. Next the Sunday school reports began to fill the minutes.

However, the transformation of the minutes from such minutes as described to one filled with reports from a half dozen different agencies came rather suddenly. By 1875, the minutes were giving the report of the executive committee, the report of the orphan's home, a report on state missions (which for some reason would be the agency most neglected by the churches' giving), education, meaning colleges and seminaries, Sabbath Schools, home missions (Salem, Macedonia, Jeffersonville, Bethel, Laurel Springs and Zion receiving help but sending no messengers), foreign missions and a report on destitution in the associational area. Instead of having many visiting messengers from other associations as of old, the guest list would include secretaries and chairmen or other executive leadership of one or more of these agencies. At the same time, the statistics began to blossom. The old report on baptism, dismissals, deaths, etc., and membership was continued often with the names and addresses of the minister, church clerk and Sunday school superintendent. Usually Sunday school statistics would also appear. Now, however, an associational breakdown of giving to the various agencies also became important.

There was still inspirational preaching. The association was now a three day affair. The introductory sermon was extremely important as recognition of outstanding ministers (or as a new minister), but often they became more pep talks, than thoughtful haurangues on theology. The Sunday sermon would also be important usually by the host minister. Here again, it often gave the host minister a chance to express his own ideas on how things were going. Often in the evenings there would be other inspiration worship services. On the whole however, the association was becoming the agency through which the state and national agencies worked. A similar development would appear among the Christian churches and had always been present among the Methodist.

The association in 1849 sent a letter and messengers to the General Association of Kentucky meeting that year in Lexington.

In 1871, the association voted to help defray the expenses of her messengers attending the Southern Baptist Convention. From this point on, Boone Creek was represented at every level of the Baptist movement.

In 1871, the minutes gave the effort to bring the Greenville Theological Institute from Greenville, South Carolina to Louisville. The resolution was repeated in "73 in giving support to the Southern Baptist Seminary, and again in 1878, the association supported the one year old Louisville seminary. The association also gave support to Georgetown College and to occasional other Baptist educational institutions. The effect of the Seminary was not really felt until after 1900 when the student minister became the basic source for ministerial supply for the country church.

T. I. Wills became moderator of the association in 1868 and would remain til 1871. James French became clerk for two years in 1865 and then A. L. Haggard for two years. French was again clerk in 1869 for three years. J. N. Conkwright was clerk for three years. In 1875 the clerk was F. S. Allen. Conkwright again became clerk until 1885. James French became moderator of the association from 1872 to 1878. F.S. Allen was moderator then for two years. A. D. Rash returned to be moderator in 1881. James French was again moderator for four years. J. N. Conkwright became moderator in 1886 (after thirteen total years as clerk) and remained moderator until 1917. W. D. Strode became clerk in 1886 and remained clerk until 1905. The introductory speakers in 1881 with T. I. Wills and the next years Nathan Edmunson, A. D. Rash, A. D. Isbell, who was not closely related to the Clark County churches, A. D. Rash again, Thomas Stevenson and A. D. Rash, T. I. Wills in 1868 was moderator and introductory speaker. He was followed by Nathan Edmunson, no one listed for 1870, D. B. Ray, J. L. Wray, William Tyree (who was from the mission points) in 1873. In 1874, the preacher was Smith V. Potts, and thereafter J. Pike Powers, J. L. Smith, A. F. Baker, B. Manly, A. D. Rash, T. C. Stackhouse and A. D. Rash in 1879. T. C. Stackhouse, again, W. M. Pratt, J. D. Warder, Simmons, William Stewart and for the last time, A. D. Rash. He had spoken to the association seven times. The use of Winchester's ministers immediately after being called can be seen in the use of Stackhouse and Stewart. Richard French gave the sermon in 1891, J. I. Wills and I. T. Creek, in 1893 and 1894. For some reason, the newspapers were excited over Creek. Providence tried a full time program with him and when it did not work out reluctantly shared him with other churches. Creek obviously was not satisfied with the arrangement and left the area. Another of Winchester's new preachers, B. B. Bailey preached in 1894 followed by Richard French, Bailey, J. S. Wilson, Bailey, J. S. Wilson...no reason for the alternating of these names up to 1900. Then came T. C. Ecton, W. L. Shearer, B. B. Bailey, W. E. Thayer, Bailey's successor, and once again Richard French in 1906.

J. J. Porter gave the introductory sermon in 1908. He was Winchester's new minister who dies soon thereafter. The next year an agency preacher, J. W. Porter, used the introductory sermon to push the Baptist program. This is the first time this was done. Porter died and Winchester called his brother, T. J. Porter, who gave the next two years introductory sermons. Richard French preached his last introductory sermon (five) in 1912.

In passing, we note that William Rupard was asked to preach (not the introductory sermon) to the 1883 association.

Membership in the association topped 1,037 in 1872. It did not materially change until 1889 when it reached 1,407. It continued in a steady growth until 1892 when it topped at 1,776. The growth was largely in the Winchester church. Winchester was in a boom period with railroads being built through it and population rapidly expanding. The boom slacked off in the 1890s and can be reflected in a relatively stable period of membership until it again started going upward in 1900 with 1,909 members. It crossed the 2,000 mark in 1902 with 2,102 and continued steadily upward until 1919 when it peaked at 3,010, was stable for a few years and reached a record high in 1922 of 3,163.

Baptisms also showed an irregular but steady upward movement. Four times, 1871, 1872, 1884 and 1887 baptisms topped a hundred: beginning with 1890, with 178 baptisms, the average stayed over a 100. In 1902 the association reported 204 baptisms that broke the century old record of 1828. In 1921 baptisms topped 287. Again, much of this growth can be seen in the development of First Baptist and Central Baptist churches in Winchester which grew rapidly during this period.

The Baptist were definitely against alcohol. During the 1880s, several of the minutes reported resolutions condemning the manufacturing and sale, and of course, the use of alcoholic beverages. This reappeared again in the middle 1890s. This does not mean that the Baptist drank in the years they did not officially condemn alcohol. The position was strongly held. In 1894 and 1895, there was again a flurry of resolutions against alcohol.

The first women messengers appeared in Providence in 1887.

One must deviate here from the religious to county politics. During the 1890s the Democratic Party split wide open. On one side was the Bryan free silver forces backed by the Farmer's Alliance and on the other, the old Democrats who supported gold standard. The struggle was bitter. Each side preferred to have the Republicans win the offices than the other side to control the Democratic Party. As a result in 1894, the Republicans elected the governor. They elected him again in 1898 but the Democrats led by William Goebel, by using the heavily Democratic majority in the Legislature, threw out the elected. Then Goebel was assassinated. Bryan ran twice for president. In each case, the Democrats fought each other furiously, the Courthouse Democrats who supported Bryan organizing down to the last voter to keep the anti-Bryan men out. In the background, behind all of this struggle, was also the liquor issue. There was a more or less open alliance between the liquor interests and the official county machine so that a fight against them and the corruption that a lot of money brought into politics was also a fight against free silver. One after another of the powerful Democratic figures of the past broke with the party and tried to break the courthouse control. Together they might have succeeded, but each stood by while the others fought and then, when it was his turn, each fought alone. The last to break with the Courthouse Democratic machine was L. N. Conkwright who was the long time moderator of the Boone Creek Association. His major concern was the liquor question rather than the question of free silver that had caused the opposition of Rodney Haggard, or corruption that had fired William Beckner, or party control which had motivated John Garner.

The Baptist were sympathetic to Conkwright's position. There had been a time when the prohibitionist party, who had been headed by ministers had boasted they would replace the Republicans as a second party. Those times were gone, however, to support Conkwright, a resolution was entered into the Boone Creek Baptist Association's annual meeting calling for support of Conkwright at the polls. Almost immediately the situation nearly exploded. The WINCHESTER DEMOCRAT mentioned there was trouble but never gave any details. Some years later, the SUN SENTINEL printed the story. The editor of the SUN SENTINEL was R. R. Perry who was also superintendent at that time of the Winchester Baptist Church's Sunday school and very active in Baptist affairs.

After the motion was made there was an explosion of feelings. Angry shouts came from various corners, arguments, a near fist fight...for a while it appeared that the associational meeting would break up in turmoil. Conkwright, who was moderator, stepped in and got order. He persuaded the sponsors of the motion to withdraw it. It was withdrawn and the meeting continued on an uneasy, but normal basis. Resolutions against alcohol was permissable in association meetings, but it was too much to ask Clark County Democrats who were also Baptists to break with the county Democratic Party over the issue. In 1905, the association expressed its approval of the Anti Saloon League, but this did not call for members to support it against their political party. Nothing more is said of significance against alcohol until 1912 when once again the drys were pushing their resolutions through the association. Liquor had become the number one issue in the state that was dividing both parties in bitter primaries. The struggle in the county continued to a climax in the 1914 elections. The results were somewhat clouded in that the candidates were not nearly as against liquor as the voters and the final victory once again eluded the prohibitionists. In 1915, resolutions passed the association calling on all voters, Baptist in this case, to support those who opposed liquor regardless of their party label. This was essentially the same motion that had nearly torn up the association thirteen years earlier. The resolution did not name which candidates were against liquor.

In 1890, a question as to the conduct of the church appeared in the minutes, the first in almost forty years. The question asked whether communion should be shared with those who were not baptized by a Baptist minister. The answer was "no".

In 1891, the Boone Creek Baptist Association reaffirmed the merger Constitution of the Separatist and Regular Baptist of 1801. These two actions represent a certain amount of unrest in the rank and file of the Baptist movement that had not really been vocal since the 1840s. There were changes being made. During the last part of the 19th century, there was wide cooperation between churches, such as combining services on Sunday evenings during the summer, joint revival services, loaning out of the buildings to other groups....for example, the Presbyterians met in the Baptist church while building their new building in 1890. (The Baptist had used the Presbyterian building in organizing in 1858). A county wide Sunday school convention generally included the Baptist churches and many Baptist were active in its program. The Baptist had their own associational Baptist Sunday school conventions at the same time. Student ministers were appearing increasingly in the ranks of the ministry. The older men were tried and true from old church families and whose ideas and beliefs well known. They were often farmers, or men from the community. However, times were changing. A minister in the early days preached, married and buried. He was responsible for sermons, perhaps three or four of them once a month....Saturday night, Sunday morning and Sunday early evening or late afternoon at least. Now with the new century, the minister found that he was also responsible for a Sunday school, men's clubs, women's auxiliaries, etc., he was expected to work with youth groups, he was not expected to be a community leader. Once it was the usual for the minister to have another job, perhaps even a farm. There were several churches that actually furnished their minister a farm. Lullbegrud was one.

Gradually the city churches, in this case Winchester grew larger. The community itself doubled and tripled in size. From a crossroads of a few hundred in the first quarter of the 19th century, Winchester had reached about a 1,000 by the Civil War. It was five thousand by 1900. The city churches went full time. First the Presbyterians, then the Christians, finally about 1890, the Methodist and Baptist.

While the city churches improved and developed, the rural churches stagnated and declined. It was noted that in 1820, there were 16 Bush widows attending Providence. By 1900 there was a tendency for the widows to move to town. On a farm there was room for only one or two children to make a life's work.

The others moved off, to the west, to the cities, anywhere that work was available. As roads bettered, the landowner and better educated began to move their membership to the city church. This became very obvious after World War I. They would remember fondly the church of their fathers. They would return on Homecoming Day, give a hundred or so dollars to a special fund, but beyond this they did little or nothing for the church. This is clear in the records of Providence.

For the first half of the 19th century, the country minister was an important community figure. He exercised authority and influence. This was largely true until 1900. Gradually, the city church minister became more dominant. He was better educated, better trained, and had more time. He was closer to the power centers of the establishment. At the same time, the country preacher remained largely ministers with another job, students, or a struggling person living on an inadequate income until he was able to get something better. Whereas in the early part of the county histories, the rural churches were as important or even more so at the city church, the city churches soon out distances them. Now a rising young minister took a rural church only as a stepping stone to something better.

The new element in the preaching picture of the association as 1900 came and a new century began were the student ministers. These young men came to the Boone Creek Association mostly from the Southern Seminary in Louisville, from Georgetown College and occasionally from the University of Kentucky or the Richmond Colleges. Eventually, they would live on the property of the church they served, but at this time they would come in on Saturday, spend the night at a layman's house, preach, and rush back to school as soon as the last service was over.

They were often bright, able, eager young men filled with enthusiasm and dedication to the Lord and to the church. Usually no one had ever heard of them until they had gotten off the train with a letter from the school as introduction. These student ministers were largely strangers to all and they represented a new idea, seminary trained men. The rank and file Baptist were not at all sure they liked the idea. The organizational work was now firmly established and it held the association in firm grips. Most of the associational meeting was given to reports of various boards. The Christian churches were in a battle over missionary organizations as well as the use of instrumental music. It was inevitable that the unrest on one denomination would over flow into others. There was obviously a fear on the part of some that the Baptist purity would once again be contaminated. It is interesting to note, however, that there was no desertion to the "old" Baptist churches which were beginning to show signs of collapse.

While this under current was going on, the Baptist quietly dropped the name "United" from both individual church names and the associational name in 1897. There does not seem to be anything in the associational minutes that called for such an action. No doubt it was discussed for the dropping of the "United" was done the same year throughout the association.

The question of alien baptism rose in 1908. The Baptist stood firm against any policy that might admit candidates to membership of the church by any other baptism other than that administered by Baptist ministers. In 1910, the association issued a warning against any Sunday school using literature other than that from a Baptist publishing company. During this period, a city wide revival was conducted with the support of all but the Baptist churches. A Tabernacle was built back of the courthouse and a great deal of publicity was given to it. It was a highly successful revival which perhaps marked the high point of inter-church and community wide cooperation in such a program. The Baptist were severely criticized for not cooperating. The Baptist answered, particularly C. C. Carroll of First Baptist, in point by point defense of Baptist actions.

The need returns to the advent of Seminary students as ministers about 1900. This fact was to change the whole picture of the country church, and not necessarily for the better.

Laymen who had served their churches and the Lord for half a century discovered that their pastor was young enough to be their son, even their grandson. These young men were learning the "right way" of running a church and they were very anxious to impart this new found knowledge upon the strangers there were now their parishioners. It was often a rude awakening and the cause of great agony for both the church and the minister when these new ideas were not always found suitable. For example, Mt. Olive adopted an envelope system to finance the church early in the new century. Two years later it was abolished. There was also a growing gap between the layman and the minister. In the old days, the minister and the layman had about the same education, very much of the same background, quite often came out of the same community. The minister would add to his religious knowledge as the years would go on, but it would be very much of the same, just more of it. The young seminary minister had all kinds of new ideas. He spoke, sometimes Greek, Hebrew and Latin. He quoted from books written by famous and unheard-of men. His theology would be worded in long and strange terms and phrases. Occasionally, there were even theological differences between the layman and the young man which disturbed the laymen and caused the young minister to complain of the hard nuts he had to crack. If the young man had just come from the neighborhood...or had be been a member of one of the county families... but these students might come from anywhere in the United States or even elsewhere. They had never been in the county before their call, and in many cases, they would never return after their student pastorate was over.

This perhaps explains why the Winchester ministers so dominated the introductory sermons of the association. The city men were better educated; better trained; stronger speakers. They offered associational leadership. Their churches were rapidly growing until they raised more money and had more members than all the country churches put together...or so it seemed. However, by 1913, when C.C. Carroll, in many ways one of the strongest Baptist ministers ever to hold a Winchester pulpit, was the introductory speaker, the danger in too much Winchester spotlight became evident. The rural churches and ministers were restless and were feeling a little dominated and patronized. J. T. Turpin was the introductory speaker in 1914. He was a survivor of the old type of minister. R. L. Motley, E. C. Nall, Motley for a second time in 1916 showing again the Winchester dominance, A. M. Nicholson, C. M. Thompson, J. W. Mahan and in the last year of this study, 1922, W. M. Nevins.

In 1900, the ladies of the Allenville Church, invited the women attending the association at their church to be present at a woman's meeting. This was the first women's meeting held in conjunction with the association.

In passing, we note that the association took a strong stand on prize fighting in 1902.

In 1908, the Winchester Baptist Church split with the Central Baptist Church being organized as a result. The Central Baptist Church grew fairly rapidly giving the association two strong city churches in Winchester. Under R. L. Motley, Central's influence in the association grew. From a statistical point of view, the association was greatly strenthened by the two large churches, but the relationship between the two churches would be such that it would, in the next decade, nearly destroy the Boone Creek Association. This history is covered in the third and fourth volume of this series.

There was no mention of break-up of Winchester Baptist in the successive associations that followed during the division. In 1912, Central joined the association along with Winchester Baptist who now became known as First Baptist. This was a little confusing in that the Negros also had a First Baptist Church. Central's minister, George W. Shepherd, died suddenly that year. The 1912 association reported First Baptist with 395 members and Central with 100. The association had a total membership of 2,444. The association took a strong stand against divorce in 1912.

The development of a modern church with a full state and national program is clearly seen in the associations of these years. Only Corinth and Ephesus did not report a regular Sunday school.

In 1915, the associational meetings were reduced from three to two days.

By the 1917 association the local mission program is in full swing. J. T. Turpin was the associational evangelist. He reported holding meetings at White Oak, Macedonia, Powell Valley, two at Beach Grove, at Pine Hill, at Garrett's school house, at Cobb Mountain, two at Black Mountain, one at Lone Oak School House and another at Nada for a total of fourteen. Turpin reported that he had visited 30 communities, traveled 900 miles by rail, a hundred miles by buggy and 300 miles on foot. He had visited 534 families, 10 churches, 20 Sunday schools, 15 prayer meetings, preached 168 sermons, gave 9 Sunday school addresses, baptized 56, restored 30 to membership, received 18 by letter, organized 7 Sunday schools, gave away 15,000 tracts, sold 2 Bibles and received 3 subscriptions to the Western Recorder. He also raised $92.75.

In 1918, the Mt. Sterling Baptist Church sought membership in the Boone Creek Association. They were to stay in the association for only three years before going back to the Bracken Association.

The women's work was now being fully reported by the association. Ephesus, Kiddville, Mount Olive, Providence, Central and First all reported women's organizations. First Baptist had a Young Women's Auxiliary and Central a Girls' Auxiliary.

Temperance reports were specially emphasized in the association in 1918. Victory was apparently at hand.

Finally, J. N. Conkwright died. He had joined the church at 12 at Providence. He had been baptized by S. V. Potts. He had been the clerk of the association for thirteen years and had been moderator from 1896 to 1917. He had been Sunday School Superintendent of Providence for years and then on moving to Winchester, he had been First Baptist Sunday School Superintendent for seventeen years. He had been a deacon most of his adult life.

Sick and ailing, W. P. Heiatt was elevated to the moderator's chair. It was an effort to honor another of the old Baptist knights who had fought her battles for so long. S. J. Conkwright became the clerk.

The sad report in the 1919 association was that Heiatt had died. The association then continued its policy of electing laymen to the moderatorship by elevating R. F. Scudder to the moderatorship. Scudder represented the newer churches that had come to fill much of the association ranks. He belonged to Union City in Madison County. This was the first time since 1860 a Clark County man had not been moderator.

The Southern Baptist Convention had launched a five year campaign to raise $75,000,000. Kentucky was to raise $6,500,000. Boone Creek was asked to raise $200,000. The request was accpeted without a dissenting vote. Conkwright proudly notes that the Boone Creek Association was the seventh association in missions and benevolances.

The association also authorized S. V. Conkwright to write a history of the Baptist churches and of the Boone Creek Association. This was completed in 1922.

As this section closes in 1922, the association was strong and rapidly expanding. Conkwright reports that some fourteen churches had in the last few years been added to the association. Five or six had died, but there was a net gain. The association had pushed into Powell and Estill Counties and had frontier churches in Wolfe, Lee and Breathitt Counties...mostly up the railroad from Winchester to Jackson and to Irving.

Altogether in 1922, the Boone Creek Association had 21 churches, seven were in Clark County, three in Madison, two in Lee, one in Powell, one in Owsley, five in Estill and one in Fayette County.

Calvery Baptist Church in Irving was a missionary church whose pastor is supported by the association. There is now a fledging laymen's movement. The head of the association woman's missionary society for 1921 is Miss Mary Emma Bright. Central, First and Ephesus have Baptist Young People's Union. First, Central, Providence and Ephesus had women's societies. The association was sponsoring a tithing drive.

There is proposed a Baptist school for Beattyville. The 1922 association thought that the possibilities were good. The association raised for missionary purposes some $22,249.28, more than enough to meet the associational quota.

One gets the feeling that the association is a strong organization with a solid hard core of progressive, healthy, well organized churches, mostly in Clark County, and with a satellite ring of mission churches some not doing well, but on the whole making progress. Beneath the surface, many of the rural churches were having increasing problem, but it did not reflect in the association.

The only faint note of discord, not so much discord, as solidarity came when C. G. Bush suggested that the by-laws be revised. The opposition was solid and based on "the old time religion was good enough." The motion was defeated. Despite all the modern organizational trappings, the heart and core of the Boone Creek Association was solidly old Baptist.

## THE FRENCH FAMILY OF BAPTIST

James French came from one of the leading families of Montgomery and Clark Counties. The first James French came into Madison County. His property covered originally 225,000 acres. He married Keziah Calloway when she was only fifteen. After residing for awhile in Madison County, he moved to the edge of Montgomery and Clark Counties and became a power in the Lullbegrud Church. As clerk of Lullbegrud and of the North District, he was instrumental in bringing some semblance of Baptist order out of the holecost of the Reform Movement that nearly brought it down.

His sons were James, Richard and Charles French. The contemporary James French (1976), whose father was Richard, says of his uncle that he was not as religiously motivated as his father and grandfather. He, therefore entered politics and became a judge, a congressman, and ran an unsuccessful race for governor. The next James was born in 1828. After a stay in Montgomery County, where he became county judge,he moved to Winchester. There he was instrumental in establishing the Winchester Baptist Church and was deacon and powerful in that church for years. He was for eight years the clerk of the association, and moderator for eleven years. He died in 1900.

A second son of James was Charles S. French. He was also a member of the Winchester Church, serving as clerk for a good many years. He was county judge in Winchester and found more often in the political pages than the religious. He was nevertheless, one of the standbys of the baptist in Winchester. His daughters were active in the educational world of Winchester.

The third son was Richard French. He was born in 1842. He had been active in the Winchester Baptist Church being Sunday School superintendent. He was a successful merchant in Winchester. As was customary when ministers were in short supply, the association looked among its own. Ephesus asked for the licensing and ordination of Richard French in 1890, a man who had already reached his late thirties.

Richard French preached for most of the Clark County rural churches at one time or another. He also established with association money the Howell Mill Baptist Church in Montgomery County. He was long associated with the Ephesus Church. He died in April of 1914. French was the highest type of old fashioned country Baptist minister. In a very real way, his death ended this type of minister. An era had closed.

## THE UNITY BAPTIST CHURCH

The second Baptist church to be established in Clark County was the Unity Baptist Church. There was a Presbyterian church, Salem, in Clark County at the time, so in 1790, Unity was the third church within the present county boundary. It was on the edge of the Bush-Quisenberry-Haggard settlement, but still very much part of the southern part of the county history. The only records of the church appear to be in the associational minutes and L. N. Conkwright's book on Boone Creek history. There were several fires that destroyed any actual records of the church.

Unity came about as a division with the Providence Church. The quarrel apparently began with a personal quarrel between Robert Elkin and Andrew Tribble over who should be the minister of Providence, then reported as the Lower Howard Creek Baptist Church. Tribble was a minister of some reputation before he came to Kentucky having served in the Spotsylvania area of Virginia. He had organized, or had been instrumental in organizing the Tates Creek Baptist Church in what is now Madison County in the middle 1780s. He had been very active in the various associational beginnings. He no doubt felt that Elkin should give to him priority, a gift Elkin did not intend to give. There does not seem to be any theological differences between the two men since they both appear on the same side in subsequent disputes. Evidently the Elkin people met and excluded the Tribble people. The latter group then met and returned the threat.

As reported in the Providence history, Joseph and William Bledsoe, John Embry, Zachariah Shackleford and John Bailey were on the committee to solve the problem and did so by dividing the church. In passing we note that John Bailey was later excluded from the association by a committee that included both Tribble and Elkin for supporting hell redemption.

Unity was established in 1790. It is not surprising to discover it joining the Tates Creek Baptist Association in 1794 which had pulled out of the Elkhorn and South District Association to form the first United Baptist group west of the mountains under the influence of Tribble.

Unity more than any other church in the association moved back and forth between associations....sometimes in North District, her usual home, but shifting now and then to the Boone Creek Association where she finally ended.

The history of Unity is not one of Tribble, however, but James Quisenberry. The first location of the Unity Church was some two miles downstream from Providence. A log church was built, according to Conkwright about where the pumping station (1923) for the Winchester water works was located. Zacheriah Fields built a road from the log church and his property on which the church was built to Winchester.

In 1792, it moved again, further away from Providence and built a second church. There is a possibility that the first log church was continued in use for a time but it then quickly passed from history. A. C. Quisenberry's geneology of the Quisenberry family indicates that James Quisenberry did not become a minister until after the new church was built.

Certainly, as we examine the men already important in Clark County history, the Boones, William Bush, the McMillans, Hubbard Taylor, Robert Elkin, John Strode, John Martin, etc., Quisenberry deserves a high rank. He was one of the most popular ministers of his day. One of the best measurements of popularity lies in the number of marriages performed in a lifetime in Clark County. He married a total of 462 Clark County couples to make him one of the top five marrying ministers of all time in the county. Robert Elkin married 89, Lawrence Owen 49 and William Morris 48 among contemporary ministers. He served Unity until his death in 1830. He was also minister of Friendship for a decade between 1810 and 1820. He served Red River which is in what is now Estill County.

He was born in Virginia. He saw service in Boonesboro during the Indian troubles as a member of the Virginia militia. He was a big man, six foot five, according to his descendent, A. C. Quisenberry, in a day when the average height was about 5'7". By family tradition he was a gentle loving man. The Baptist historian, Spencer, unkindly described his preaching ability as meager.

Whatever his nature and preaching ability, he seemed to get himself into a number of sharp disputes. The first split the Unity Church. The second was when he was ousted by Friendship as minister. Not only did he lose the conservative group of Friendship, but the more liberal group did not call upon him to serve them. There is some indication, by his associations as much as anything, with ministers leaning toward the Reform movement among Baptist that he was leaning in that direction. Yet his church, Unity, was one of the few in the North District that stayed with the Baptist movement.

It was controversy in his own church of Unity that makes the most interesting reading. Like William Bush and Andrew Tribble he had married one of the Burrus girls, the sister named Jane. This accounts for his support for Tribble in the Providence division. He moved out on Four Mile Creek where he offered a stone mason one hundred fifty acres to build chimneys on either end of his cabin. Apparently it was a happy marriage that produced seven sons and six daughters. Unfortunately Jane became ill and after a lingering illness died. During these last days, a neighboring girl, Chloe Shipp, spent a good deal of time at the Quisenberry house looking after Jane and the children and in general keeping things together.

There is no doubt about Quisenberry's grief at the death of his wife. After a short but respectable period of mourning, Quisenberry's daughter married John Haggard, Jr. Evidently, the wave of loneliness for a man who had always had the loving attention of a woman and the problems of a growing family of motherless children was too much for him to bear. Two days after his daughter's wedding, he married Chloe. The neighborhood was scandalized. Gossip was rife.

Tradition says that it was the younger Haggard that angerly rebelled against this action of his new father-in-law, but as Conkwright points out, the son-in-law never left the Unity Church. It was John Haggard, Sr., that led the scandalized group of Unity Church members out from the new church and organized what became known as Indian Creek Baptist Church.

The majority of members, however, closed ranks behind Quisenberry and his new wife, and Unity continued with a few tolerant smiles, worshipping together. The new marriage was also a success and in due course of time produced eleven more Quisenberrys. Number 14 and 15 of Chloe's were twins. Quisenberry died in August, 1830 at the age of 71. His youngest child was one year old.

In 1802, Unity was one of the members of the North District Association. After her formation in 1790, she had become a member of the Elkhorn Association. When Tribble organized the Tates Creek Association of United Baptist, in protest to the failure to create such a union that year, Unity became a member in 1794. We can presume she remained a member of that association until 1802. John Haggard, David Shinall and Samuel Douglas were messengers to that meeting. She reported 188 members making her second to Providence as the largest church in the new association. James Quisenberry, John Haggard, Daniel Routt, Jonathan Fugate and Moses Sharp were messengers in 1803. Quisenberry was still the minister.

Unity does not appear in the next few North District minutes. Eighteen hundred and four minutes are not available. Quisenberry was a supporter of David Barrow in the abolitionist problem. Quisenberry himself had not been active in the slave issue and did own slaves. However, he felt that Barrow was within his rights. Whether Unity joined the Licking Locust Association is not known.

In 1807, Unity was back in the North District Association. Quisenberry, David Routt and John Haggard were messengers. She reported 122 members.

In 1811, Ambrose Bush, Daniel Routt and James Barnett were the messengers. The church reported 180 members. Quisenberry was minister in 1812 so we can assume that he was the minister through all these years. This would be after the Indian Creek division which is reported for the first time in the North District. George Allen is among the messengers for this year.

Quisenberry is still the minister in the 1816 report. He and Joseph Ship were the messengers. The church reported 149 members. The loss probably could be traced to the Indian Creek division. Indian Creek was no longer in the North District. Isham Baber and Anderson Piggs were the messengers. The membership was 141. Unity seemed to hand around the position of messenger more than many churches. On the other hand, if her membership was as large as she reported, she would have the members to share in the responsibilities.

The 1819 North District shows Quisenberry as still the minister.

The association met at Unity in 1820. John Raccoon Smith was the introductory speaker. It was a happy association meeting where the theology was loosely interpreted which pleased Unity. Only John Haggard is mentioned as messenger in 1821. Quisenberry is now involved in his struggle with Friendship. He is not mentioned as having attended the association and there is no hint as to whether he was still minister of Unity. One presumes he was, however.

Quisenberry is again mentioned as minister of Unity in 1823. Routt, James Baber and James Haggard made up the rest of the messengers. Unity now shifts over to the Boone Creek Association during the next few years. The leadership of the Boone Creek Association was definitely Reform by this time. The Calvinists still control the administration of the North District. Quisenberry is not a Reform minister, but he is leaning in that direction.

Unity moved to the South District in 1826. T. Berryman and D. Jones were the messengers and reported 74. In 1827, D. Jones and C. Combs were messengers. They had 73 members.

Unity is back in the North District in 1828. It had been a spectacular year for her. She had baptized 81 people for a total membership of 171, the largest that she had ever been. Quisenberry was not again mentioned in connection with Unity. It may well be that he was no longer minister. He was getting old. No doubt his health was breaking. It may well be that he was no longer able to lead Unity and the rank and file of the church wanted to go back to the more conservative leadership of the North District.

Unity was to be among the seven churches that responded to James French's call for churches at Lullbegrud to take a stand against the Reformers. There is also a Unity at the next meeting at Goshen in which the North District's minority organized a district free of radical changes. Her messengers were Daniel Routt, Eli Bruce, Lewis Allen and the two James Elkins, father and son.

For some reason Unity again shifted to the Boone Creek Association. In 1832, she showed that she had paid dearly for her loyalty in the Baptist cause. She had but 88 members left. Again not happy, she was once again in the North District in the same year. This is the only case where a church has been listed in the minutes of both associations at the same year.

## FRIENDSHIP BAPTIST CHURCH

The Strode's Creek, or Stroud's Creek Church, was reported in the minutes of the Marble Creek (East Hickman) Baptist Church when John Price and Flanders Callaway were sent as messengers to an association meeting in 1791. The church evidently had just been constituted, to use the Baptist term, though it is likely that there had been religious services at Strode's Station more or less regularly for a decade. During the Indian troubles, the crowded conditions in a stockade were not conducive to an exclusive band of believers regardless of what their religious views were. Associations, fellowship meetings, conventions were luxuries that most communities could not afford in the face of Indian troubles. Ministers were usually as foot loose as the layman, wandering from place to place, seeking to settle and make a living in secular ways, preaching on the side. By 1790, there was an increasing need for specific churches. Baptist wanted Baptist churches and their own kind of Baptist particularly. The Presbyterian wanted their own kind of church and so it went. The acceptance of anything that might come through was gone.

Strode Station's Baptist Church had different problems than Providence, Unity or Indian Creek. The latter churches served a permanent, land owning class of people. Strode's Station had become a stopping point for settlers going somewhere else.

Conkwright says that most of the churches around Clark County were largely Separatist Baptist, whereas, the Elkhorn Association churches were largely Regular Baptist. Strode Station did join the Elkhorn Association which indicates the more conservative, Calvinistic theology of its members. In 1791, she only reported 9 members, in 1793 she dropped to seven and never got more than 11. From 1796 to 1804, she made no report which would indicate that she had died or at least became more or less inactive. In 1804, she united with the North District Association as would be natural under the merger of the two Baptist groups and called herself Friendship Baptist Church of Christ.

In 1797, Deed Book 3, page 73, Clark County reports that Thomas and Abegail Constant sold to John Strode, one acre of land including the old meeting house to be occupied as a place of worship. Conkwright claims that this is the oldest deed in Kentucky for land to be used for religious purposes. The church was located on Constant Creek on the road between Winchester and Strode's Station.

Conkwright does not speculate as to what might have happened. In the best historical fiction manner, we suggest that there might have been no less than three churches involved. First was the one church at Strode' Station that reported to the Elkhorn Association which broke up as member families moved elsewhere...with nine to twelve members only one or two families could do this. Secondly was a church of unknown denomination, perhaps even Methodist, that served the Constant Station group...Methodist because the Stampers were residents of Constant Station about this time. This also broke up, perhaps as the Stampers moved out to settle near Hood's Station. This brought the effort of John Strode, perhaps some other Baptist who might or might not have been Separatist Baptist, to reorganize a church in that area. Strode therefore, bought the old Constant Church with the understanding that any minister of the Baptist, Methodist or Presbyterian Church could use the building when not used by the regular church, and reorganized his church.

The hesitancy of this church to unite with the new North District Baptist Association shows a strong Regular Baptist influence in its ministry. However, the North District was the logical association for Friendship and she united. Its minister by this time is William Morris. He and William Rash (the first Rash to be reported in this history) were messengers. They reported 30 members which would not indicate a very strong church in an area that was already well settled. This reemphasizes the fact that religion on the frontier was not a strong influence, or at least in its church form. This would also indicate that this new church was more Regular Baptist than Separatist. William Morris also seems to have served only Friendship in Clark County. His popularity was strong. His first marriage was March 20, 1802, which is a good date to say that he was preaching at Friendship, united James Green and Polly Indadus. Altogether, he married 96 couples in a little less than a decade. In 1804, Friendship reported 23 members with the same messengers. Perhaps there were those who did not approve of entering the North District. Benajmin Blackwell and Maximillan Bauren were the 1805 messengers and the membership had worked up to 37. It was still called Strode's Station in the association minutes. By 1809 when the next minutes were available, membership went up to 50 and her messengers were Abraham Weldon and Joseph Kelly. The turnover of messengers might indicate that the Strode Station area was still a stopping place for transients rather than a permanent home for settlers. These two men however, were stable residents of the area. The church was now known as Friendship. The messenger list was increased to include Weldon and Kelly in 1810 and Pervin Mosely and Rueben McDonald.

The church had doubled in size by 1812 reporting 109 members. Joseph Kelly, Ransdale Petty, William Rash and Pervin Mason were messengers. It seems unlikely that two men in the same church would be named Pervin. Someone has made a mistake in the minutes.

It is difficult to say who was minister during this period. Morris might have served in 1810. However, there is a possibility that James Haggard served a year in there, perhaps in 1809.

James Quisenberry became minister in 1810. He converted William Vaughn who was a leading athiest and anti-church man of his age. Vaughn was to become one of the leading ministers and theologians of Kentucky. The same year Friendship granted Vaughn ordination, they also licensed James Haggard, Anson Mills and Ninninan Ridgeway to preach. It is presumed that each of these men preached somewhere because a church would not usually grant a license unless requested by another church who was seeking a minister. There are no records of their service in Clark County though this may well be lack of evidence rather than absence of service.

Deed Book 9, page 187, 1811, reported that John and Sally Skinner deeded Joseph Kelly and William Rash of Friendship a lot on Constant Creek of Strode's Creek on the main road from Winchester to Strode...with the intention of erecting a new brick building. Conkwright thinks this is a different location, closer to Winchester than the old location. There is no report of what happened to the old church. The deed did say that "No person should be denied the privilege of preaching if morally suited and not repugnant to scriptures."

Friendship reported, in 1814, 113 members. Under Quisenberry the church had grown and prospered. The DEMOCRAT reported August 27, 1879, that Thomas Dudley was minister in 1816...this is no doubt an error. Dudley was the son of a very prominant minister and had just returned from a successful military service. He was beginning an important business career, but he had not yet been converted, nor had he started to preach. It is possible, however, that as a layman he preached in Friendship.

The high point of Friendship's early life was in 1817 when it reached a total of 167 members. The messengers were the same. Winchester had grown during this period from a few hundred to almost a thousand. Joseph Kelly, Ransdale Pretty, William Rash and Pervin Mosely were messengers.

It is inevitable that any church that makes a sudden growth will find discord among its new and old members. The older members feel that the new members are not sound theologically as they ought, and the newer members feel that the old members are too set in their ways.

Quisenberry also was finding an increasing gulf between his more Calvinistic members and his separatist background. He had not yet become interested in Alexander Campbell and though he had met, discussed and shown an interest in Barton Stone, Stone was still a Presbyterian. However, there was enough difference between the Separatist and Regular Baptist positions to permit friction. The Particular Baptist movement was causing trouble all over the North District. It was particularly at home in Friendship.

Friendship was one of the seven churches that forced the North District Association to halt correspondence with the Baptist Foreign Missionary Society. In 1819, she requested that the North District Association take up correspondence with the Licking Association, a request that was denied.

The effect of this fighting was seen in Friendship's 1819 membership which was down to 135. Josiah Ashley, Pervin Mosely, Joseph Kelly and William Rash were messengers. Ashley represented the newer and more liberal elements. The other three were strong Calvinists. The next year Robert Brooking would replace Pervin Mosely for a still loosening of the Calvinist learnings.

By this time, Quisenberry was reflecting the early thinking of Alexander Campbell, particularly the views he had shown on the "Law". More than this, now in Clark County there were a half dozen ministers that were unhappy with the tight theology of Calvinists....the Mortons, John Smith from Montgomery, the Creaths, Jacob Fishback who was deeply impressed with Barton Stone, a George Boone who was as liberal as Thomas Boone was conservative. It was everywhere a period of church growth and the disturbances in Friendship were not strong enough to discourage it.

In 1821, she reported 125 members. Quisenberry was ousted as minister. The minutes of Friendship, which are on microfilm, reported that the church, March 16, 1822, with James Kelly moderating, give much of the details. She had 128 members.

Two factions presented themselves to the North District Association each representing Friendship. One group calling itself the Friendship Baptist Christian Church and the other the Friendship Particular Baptist Church. The first group almost from the beginning dropped the word Baptist except in Baptist meetings and were called Christian Church, a Barton Stone name. This was considerably before the teachings of Alexander Campbell had reached full epidemic proportion, but Barton Stone's group who called themselves just Christians had great influence in this part of the state. The North District in this quarrel dodged the question of who was right but gave moral support to the first group.

The second group, lead by William Rash, among others, now became members of the Licking Particular Baptist Association. There had been, before this point, a petition asking for restoration of Quisenberry as minister. Sam McClain moved in Friendship's meeting, that Friendship leave the North District and seek fellowship in the Licking Association. At the same meeting, Laura McClain, apologized for having signed the petition favoring Quisenberry. James Kelly and William Rash were elected deacons. In the 1826 Deed Book, Thomas and Lewis Berry, the old trustees, were replaced by Joseph Kelly, William Rash and Robert Ricketts. Rash was moderator of the meeting, and signed the transfer.

Isaiah Cornelius became minister in 1822. His first marriage was Smallwood Acton to Nancy Coons, December 13, 1823. He was to have seven county marriages.

The North District did appoint a committee to look into the situation. Conkwright reports "That party which wrote a long letter to the association last year, in which letter they informed the association that they had excluded that whole party which wrote the other letter to the association, which excluded the party the was and is, the majority of members, and the party which was the excluded party had restored some..."

The North District then accepted the faction which sought to continue membership in the district. Abraham Weldon, Josiah Ashley, Griffen Kelly and Zacheria Ridgeway were the messengers. They reported 72 members in 1822. In 1825, they reported 227 members and had joined the Boone Creek Association. Deed Book 21, page 171, 1825, lists John Ashley, John D. Thomas and Zacheria Ridgeway as trustees.

The Particular Baptist now went their way. They struggled over who would control the church building. There has been a rather disgraceful episode over who should own the key. There was no joint meetings as in other churches. In 1825, Robert Ricketts and Sam McClain were added to the deconate. H. N. Brooking was the clerk. In 1825, Lewis Barry and N. Jones were deacons.

The North District showed its bitterness. The Unity Church refused to give Steven Brook a letter of transfer. Providence would not give a letter to the slaves of William Counchman who had moved his letter to Friendship.

Isaiah Cornelius was not a particularly successful minister. In a year he had left the church. Like so many Baptist churches, particularly among the more conservative, when a minister is needed, the church would look to itself. In 1823, the church called William Rash, Jr. to preach. His father had been one of the leading men in the division and had stood for the particular position. William, Jr. had been active in the church being a messenger to the North District. Rash was ordained by Ambrose Dudley, Henry Fore and John Shackleford. Before going on we should note that Ambrose Dudley did not serve at any time, a church in Clark County other than the first few months of Goshen while she was being organized. He performed his first marriage in Clark County in 1798 to Jonathan West and Rachel Anderson. Throughout the years he married only 22 couples in Clark County. John Shackleford never held a church in Clark County but was one of the Baptist divines that had associated himself with the Particular Baptist cause. He must have preached at Friendship for he had married S. A. Dudley to Sally Woodford, December 4, 1820. There is no other record of any Clark County marriages. There is no record of Fore having any contact with Clark County than this.

William Rash performed his first marriage in Clark County September 18, 1823, between Roger Robinson and Lucy McCargo. Altogether he was to have 109 marriages making him one of the more popular Baptist ministers in the county.

Rash was to continue as the minister of Friendship until in the 1850s when at his death he was succeeded by his son, Ambrose. It is also presumed that the other Rashs that appear in the church history are also related,but this history has not sought out geneological links.

We will not follow the history of the Friendship Church that joined the Boone Creek Baptist Association until we begin the section on the Baptist-Christian struggles of the 1828-30, and the history of the county's Christian churches. The only record we have of the Particular Baptist Church lies in the Licking Association reports. The church minutes that are microfilmed at the University of Kentucky Library ends with 1828.

The Particular Baptist group reports 72 members in 1823. From the very beginning the Friendship Particular Baptist Church was not successful. In 1834, its membership dropped to 60. A. R. Batterson was the messenger. During the period when most churches of every denomination were booming, and the other branch of the Friendship division went to 227 members and more, the Particular Baptist Church at Friendship reported in 1827 -67, 1828 - 78, 1830 - 75, and in 1830 - 90. It is evident that some of the disgruntled Baptist left the Winchester Christian Church and went to Friendship instead of Providence where others went. The numbers leaving the Christian church when it left the Baptist were so few and the number of new members so many that it made little difference to them.

Unfortunately, for Friendship, they could not hold their new members. The next Licking minutes available, 1839, reported Friendship with 65 members. William Rash, S. Jefferies, L. Berry and L. Bell were messengers. An E. Stuart and an A. Cast replaced L. Berry and L. Bell as messengers in 1841. The membership reported as 68. The next year it was up to 78. Jefferies was licensed by the association to preach in 1842. Her messengers in 1843 were Rash and Jefferies, G. E. Monroe, J. Estes and Cast. She reported 77. She was back down in 1849. As reported in the Licking history, the Friendship Church took acception to something in Dudley's 1849 Circulatory Letter and withdrew from fellowship. Dudley later commenting, said that one of the two churches which withdrew was dead and one nearly so. The latter must have been Friendship. We have no other statistics.

With the establishing of the Winchester Baptist Church, the association historian reported that A. D. Rash, pastor of the Friendship Particular Baptist Church, was giving support. Eventually, Rash is called as Winchester's first minister and served them from 1861 to 1866. He then became one of the more important ministers of the Boone Creek Association, belonging to the small group of very active local Baptist ministers which kept the Boone Creek Association moving forward.

It is not clear what happend to Friendship. There is no way of knowing how many of its members joined the Winchester Baptist church with their minister. At any rate, Friendship was dead in 1863. The WINCHESTER SUN, December 13, 1923 said the Friendship Church died in 1861 and was sold. The money was given to Goshen Baptist Church. Interestingly enough, William Rash, Sr., though an old man, was alive during this period for he did not die until 1862. There is no information whether the defection from the Particular Baptist Church met his approval or not. Since the leaving from the Licking Association was the senior Rash's doing, we can presume that by 1858, he was not in objection to his son's switching churches. Samuel Beall was evidently minister in Friendship through these last years. He arranged the sell of Friendship and the donation of the proceeds to Goshen. He later joined Goshen.

Once again we note the barreness of appeal of the old Calvinist position in the county during this period of history. Rash was unable to build the Friendship Church though it was located on the edge of a community of a 1000 people which did not have a local Baptist Church. Later on as a Baptist minister of the Boone's Creek Association, the same Rash showed himself to be a very competent and able minister. In this case it was definitely not the minister's fault, but the theology and the church.

The problem of the William Rashs is the problem of so much of this county history. It is hard to tell where the father left off and the son began. The original William Rash was born in 1783. He came to Clark County and settled in Winchester where he became a maker of hats. He married Elizabeth Berry. In 1801, he was converted at David Fork's Church. Sometime after that he moved his membership to Friendship where it stayed for the next 47 years. He was immediately given recognition in the church and appeared as messenger and was no doubt a deacon. He was an advocate of the Particular Baptist and helped oust James Quisenberry.

The second William Rash fought in the War of 1812 and was at the disasterous Battle of the River Raison. Returning to Winchester he followed his father in his interest in the Friendship Church and was at one time messenger. When his church needed a minister, he accepted the call and was ordained in 1823. He served Friendship, and at various times, Nepo in Madison County, Boone's Creek, Town Fork and Stoney Point...presumedly the Particular Baptist faction in each area. Eventually, he returned to the North District when his son became minister of First Baptist in Winchester. He said of the Licking Association that it was infected with Americanism (presumedly the Know Nothing political party) as well as modern missionarism. He died in 1877.

## GOSHEN BAPTIST CHURCH

There were now three Baptist churches in Clark County, Providence, Unity and Friendship. There may have been more, but they left no traces in county history other than log meeting houses mentioned incidently in some road report. The Presbyterians were active in Salem and in Mt. Sterling which was still part of Clark County. There were also Methodist stirrings on Four Mile Creek and around Strode's Station.

The Stoner Creek area was a rolling country of good fertility that had been settled now for nearly ten years. They had been a close knit band of comrade in arms that had served in the same units in the Revolution in Virginia. By the middle of the 1790s, new people had filled the Stoner community and in and around Grassy Lick until the area had become more an agricultural settlement than a frontier settlement.

William Payne lived in the Stoner Creek area. He was the first minister and the first Baptist minister to register with the county to marry. His first marriage was William Yeates and Suzannah Higgins, July 11, 1793. Soon thereafter he married Isaac Newton to Margaret Wade and Daniel Darry to Agnes McFadden. Altogether he married some 31 couples in Clark County which in those days included Montgomery County. It seems likely that he preached in the general area in the ten years preceding the establishment of Goshen. However, there does not seem to be any record thereof.

It finally became time to organize a church, Ambrose Dudley and Donald How organized Goshen in Payne's home. Ambrose Dudley was to be the minister. The charter membership listed included William Payne, Moses Frazee, Dreselda Frazee, John Baker, Aconey Barker, Daniel Maurice, Peter Scholl, Levi Ashbrook, James Thomson, Mark Chadford, Abner Ashbrook, Glory Chadford, Elizabeth Lloyd, Moses Baker, James Ingersoll, Mary Golden, Rachel Deaton, Massa Baker, Susan Dowden, Sister Williams, Robert Scott, Abraham Miller, William Said, Susan Said, Elizabeth Green, William Haley and wife, David Thompson, Charles Tracy, Sarah Tracy, Mary Baker, George Weddel, Felix Baker, Tabitha Rowland, Robert Rowland, Kannoah Morris, Robinson Hunt, James Payne, Lea Scholl, Jacob Marsh, Lucy Richardson, Elizabeth Barnett, Philade Hampton, Elizabeth Huls, William Wells, James Hampton, Elizabeth Thomson, Elizabeth Swango, Frank Young, Daniel Winn, Sarah Morris, Robert Franks, Patsy Thomson and Elizabeth Fugar.

There is no other record on William Payne in Goshen history. Evidently he served churches during the period he lived in Clark County. In 1807, the Red River Baptist Association reported

William Payne as a messenger from New Providence Baptist Church. Whether this is the same William Payne is not clear, or whether this New Providence in Clark County is also not clear, though both are likely. However, if he served New Providence in 1807, he held other churches at the same time elsewhere for in 1804, he was the moderator of the Brachen Baptist Association. Brachen Baptist Association stretched from Maysville to Mt. Sterling. During this period, Payne was minister of the Washington, Kentucky Baptist Church. He was serving that church in 1807 when evidently he either died or left the area.

Goshen's first deed was in Deed Book 3, 1798, John McKee and John Baker gave to Moses Frazee, Robert Scott, Charles Tracy and Peter Scholl, trustees for the Regular Baptist Church at Goshen. Providence and Unity were Separatist Baptist churches. Goshen and Friendship were Regular Baptist churches.

The ownership of the church of Goshen was to be in the hands of those that believed in the items of faith listed in the deed. There were three equal persons in the Godhead. The church believed in the doctrine of personal election, the doctrine of original sin, in particular redemption, free justification of the righteousness of Christ, the efficacious of Grace in regeneration, the final preservation of the Saints in the Resurrection and in life everlasting.

The church was also Particular Baptist in its theology which perhaps can be accounted for by Ambrose Dudley's interest. Dudley could not have stayed with Goshen for more than a few months, perhaps even but a few weeks until the church was fully operative. Without the early records it is difficult to fill in the gaps. In all probability William Payne carried much of these early years as minister to Goshen.

The first church was a log cabin located in the valley below the present location, near the existing bridge across the Stoner Creek. One old man is supposed to have drowned in high water when he insisted on crossing the rain swollen creek in order to come to church. The official name of the new church was the Baptist Christian Church of Christ at Goshen. Charles Tracy and Thomas Edmonson were its trustees.

According to the record, David Barrow was minister of Goshen in 1799. This would mean that Payne was no longer minister. If Payne had been minister of New Providence and Goshen, which was then briefly part of the North District, he would have more likely been a delegate from the larger and stronger Goshen which was also closer to his home. It is more likely that Payne was already located near Washington and New Providence was his last Clark County church.

It is impossible to say how long David Barrow remained minister. In 1802, Goshen reported to the Elkhorn Association, James Thompson and Levi Ashbrook were messengers and the church reported 84 members.

Again, in 1804, Goshen appears in Elkhorn records, this time with David Thomson (no "p" in the name) and Charles Tracy as messengers and reported a membership of 71. This fits the facts because during these years David Barrow was a member of the Elkhorn Association. In 1804 and 1805, Barrow became the minister of the Mt. Sterling church and came to the North District Association.

Barrow would now be serving Lullbegrud, Mt. Sterling and Goshen. It is at this point that the Brachen Association brings charges against him in the North District to which he had just transferred. Evidently Goshen, like Lullbegrud, disassociated themselves from Barrow. Barrow at this time, or perhaps as late as 1807, helped organize the Bethlehem Baptist Church near Schollsville taking with him several of Goshen's members. Barrow became minister of Bethlehem until his death.

Goshen was a Regular Baptist Church with some Particular Baptist learnings. She was not really happy with the Plan of Union and did not join the North District Association until 1805. At that time, her messengers were Charles Tracy and David Thomson. The church had 63 members.

It is generally believed by contemporary Goshen members that when the members who organized the Winchester church left Goshen in 1904, that they took all the minutes of the Goshen Church. In a reasonable time, the Winchester church returned the minutes from 1825 onward but nothing was done about returning the earlier minutes. This author was told that they were still in the possession of the city church. Talking with the last minister of the Winchester church, he denied having the earlier minutes, just the ones of the Winchester church since 1904.

The June 1893 minutes, which happened ten years before the devision while William Rupard was still minister, a committee was appointed to find the missing records from 1807 to 1825. There is no subsequent report of those records ever being found and no trace of any records earlier than 1807. It would be a very good possibility that the Winchester church was innocent of having or losing those early records, a point that caused considerable bitterness between the two organizations. It is also very likely that the earliest records may have disappeared in the division over slavery, the turmoil over Barrow and the bitterness over members leaving for Bethlehem.

In 1807, Goshen, angry over the turmoil in the North District and hurt badly, returned to the Elkhorn Association. William Morris and Charles Tracy were the messengers. This is the only reference to Morris as a member of Goshen, but he was probably the minister of the time. At the time he was serving Friendship as well. However, his standing was in the Elkhorn Association which would account for the membership of Goshen.

In 1809, Goshen reported only 28 members. It is clear that Morris had not been able to stem or repair the shattering loss to Bethlehem (whose history is reported in the second volume). At this time, Morris left Friendship and presumedly Goshen.

In the 1907 minutes where Goshen puts on record her side of the division with the Winchester church, Edward Kindred is listed as a minister of Goshen. The only time that Goshen could have had Kindred is from 1809 to 1815 when Thomas Boone becomes minister. Nothing is said of Morris, but Morris never again appears in Clark County history. He evidently had been a popular and capable minister. So also was Kindred and he was from a good Clark County family and spent his entire life preaching to Clark County churches. It is obvious why Morris would have been forgotten a century later and Kindred would not. Most likely Kindred preached from 1809 to 1811. Whether Kindred preached the entire time is not clear. Perhaps he shared the years with Nininan Ridgeway.

Goshen membership continued to sink in 1810 to 24. Nininan Ridgeway was licensed to preach by Friendship in 1810. Evidently Goshen was following the Baptist custom of bringing forth one of their own in time of need. We can assume that Ridgeway performed the ministerial duties for several years at this time. His work showed results. In 1811, the membership went up to 29. William Whitsitt was the messenger. James Thomson was messenger in 1812. Goshen is reported with only 13 members in 1816. John Berry and Charles Tracy were messengers. She had not reported in 1813. In 1814 North District minutes are not available.

It is possible that the life at Goshen flickered very low during these years. The anti-slavery movement was strong. Barrow was at Bethlehem. The War of 1812 had drawn some of the young men out of the county. However, about this time, perhaps 1815, Thomas Boone becomes minister. He is not reported from Goshen for his home church apparently was Log Lick.

The tide was turned again. In 1817, with John Christopher and Charles Tracy as messengers, Goshen's membership went back to 22. Thomas Boone is a messenger from Goshen in 1819 along with Nininan Ridgeway and Isaiah Cornelius. Cornelius was soon called to Friendship Particular Baptist Church. The Deed Book 16, 1820, shows renewed strength in the church by naming Charles Tracy, Nininan Ridgeway and Thomas Edmunson as trustees. The 1820 North District minutes reports Goshen with 135 members, tripling its year before record. Even if the record is somewhat padded as often membership records will be with inactive and absent members, Goshen had had a tremendous year.

William Landrum's journal reported that there was a singing school at Goshen sometime during his youth which would be in these years. This is the only other mention of Goshen between these years outside of the minutes of the North Association.

Singing school would be conducted by some song master, usually itinerant and in this case unnamed. Often he would teach on the side instruments such as the violin, but at this age, a singing school would be just that. Those who came would sing without instruments using the old five note fa-so-la type of music. Many of the songs would be in minor key and were often ancient melodies. The students would sing the notes until the tune was learned, and then they would substitute the words. There is a survival of this type of singing in the "Sacred Harp" music of Alabama and Georgia. Landrum reported that such songs as "Salvation", "Ninety-five", "Bold Soldier", "Bunker Hill", "Rockbridge", "Windham" were sung. They did not have to be religious, but the Calvinistic Baptist often frowned on the frivolity of non religious songs. Many of the songs were psalms set to music. There were segments of the Presbyterian Church that sang only psalms. Landrum said later that Joseph Trowbridge and Thomas Maffett were conducting music schools in private homes around the church.

The North District was held at Goshen in 1822.

The Deed Book 21, 1825, page 39, describes Goshen as simply the Goshen Meeting House. It would be interesting to find out whether the change of name was incidental or whether it was trying to get away from the names that the Reformers were advocating. Thomas Edmonson, Richard Haynes, James Edmonson and George Thomson were named as trustees for the church.

The North District Reports do not give as much information as Boone Creek. Therefore, we have paid closer attention to the Goshen minutes than any other Baptist church in the county. Because of this closer study, an interesting viewpoint can be developed. Much of what was true of Goshen in 1820-1860 was true of all the county Baptist.

The Goshen Saturday meeting was generally the business meeting of the church. Discipline was firm. No one was permitted to take communion who had not been baptized by a minister of a Baptist church. If a member missed a meeting he could be called to explain his absence. Two absences could subject him to an inquiry from the deacons and perhaps even dismissal.

The present Goshen records begin January 22, 1825. In 1825, Thomas Boone was minister. Boone had become minister in 1816 in conjunction with Nininan Ridgeway. Boone evidently was the senior minister with Ridgeway operating as supply and relief minister. Boone had taught school for a few years about 1816 or before. His other major church was to be Lullbegrud where he followed John Racoon Smith. He was an old time Regular Calvinistic Baptist. He would be moderator of the North District Baptist Association in 1830, 1840 and 1844. He, David Chenault and his Lullbegrud church clerk, James French, would be credited with saving the North District from destruction.

Most of these business meetings were concerned with trials. On the 22nd, it was J. Henning's man, Jack, who was subject to trial. He was charged with intoxication. Slaves were members of Goshen from the beginning. It is evident that they were expected to have the same standards as white members. James Edmonson was clerk.

The August meeting of 1827 found the church contributed $1.75 toward having the North District Association Minutes printed. We find that Tom Rupard was blind and the church was seeking ways of helping him. Also, Brother Fleming, a man of color (but evidently free), was guilty of drunkenness and profane swearing. He was to be visited by the deacons. At this meeting Sister Nancy Trowbridge was dismissed for having joined the Dunkard Society. This is an interesting comment in that there is no other mention of Dunkards in Clark County.

January of 1827 started off with something of a scandal. Evidently a Mr. Watkins, who does not seem to be a member of Goshen but lived in the community, put on a ball for the Christmas season. Thomas Petty was tried for drunkenness at this party. He acknowledged his guilt and was forgiven. Francis Petty was also charged with wrong doing, acknowledged and was forgiven. However, Sally Clem made no such confession and her case was carried to the February meeting. Sally still would not acknowledge wrong doing and her case was continued. Finally, in June, she was excluded from the church. Somehow, Francis's confession did not last long for he was charged with drinking again in October of 1827 and for having left his wife. He was excluded.

In October 1827, Edmonson was absent and James Walker was the clerk pro temp. Edmonson was back for the February meeting.

In April of 1828, the question of foot washing came up and was approved as a sacrament of the church. It had been disapproved by Providence several years earlier and was generally opposed by the Reform. This demonstrates the fact that Goshen was thoroughly in the hands of the Baptist other than the Reform which did not see foot washing as a sacrament. In May, Edmonson presented the letter he was giving to the association as Goshen's report for the year. It was approved. On June 25, Nancy, woman of color, was received into membership by experience. In July, Johnny Pace was received back into fellowship and promptly granted a letter.

These were not the only things that happened during the meetings, but the purpose of this and the following is to give some feeling as to how and why a Baptist church operated. We note the discipline over the membership, but we also note the difficulties. A member can be excluded. In the eyes of the church, being out of fellowship meant being out with God. Yet, Baptist doctrine would prevent the church from taking away from the person their saved status. The concept of once saved always saved, weakened the position.

Obviously, however, many members were anxious to remain in good standing and recognized that their sins were real. To stand before the church and confess their authority was a strengthening of the soul. The willingness of the church to forgive could be equaled with God's willingness to forgive. There were others who wanted to be in good standing with the church and would seek forgiveness, and then to show their disapproval, would take their letter elsewhere. Finally, there were some that did not care. Slowly, and in the Baptist this change did not really come until after the Civil War, a change was taking place. More and more people would disregard the authority of the church.

Eighteen twenty-nine carried an interesting report that Malinda Hanks had lost her letter of dismisal and she wished to join New Providence. This item notes that there was a relationship between the two churches and just how important to a Baptist these letters of good standing were.

At the January meeting of 1829, a very serious question was raised. For information, a member wanted to know whether Goshen intended to adhere to the Constitutional principles and in her form usage and customs, and in the celebration of the Lord's Supper, and in the administration of the ordinance of Baptism. In short, was Goshen going to support the Reform movement? Questions like this must have been asked in every Baptist Church in Clark County and elsewhere during these years. In Goshen, there was sufficient question that a full answer was delayed until the next meeting.

The February meeting did not give any of the discussion. It merely stated that there would be no alteration of the church's position at this time. A question asked on the church's stand on experience as a requirement for Baptism, the church said that there would be no change.

The March meeting firmly stated that Goshen would not fellowship with any church or person who had accepted any change in the old ways. The church went on to reaffirm its adherence to the Union Constitution of 1801. Considering how unhappy Goshen had been over this constitution, it was a concession to the liberalizing effect of the years.

There is no way of knowing how many members left the church to go, say to Bethlehem which was the nearest church that did leave the old ways. In 1829, the North District meeting at Unity found Goshen reporting 200. Goshen was one of the seven churches to stand firm in the North District for the Association in the April meeting of 1830 at Lullbegrud. Thomas Boone was elected moderator. James Edmonson was clerk, both were Goshen men. Goshen messengers were John C. Rogers, Martin Haggard, and James Edmonson. There were no reports of membership at this meeting. She invited the Regular Baptist Association meeting to come to Goshen for the fall meeting. Statistics are not available until the 1832 association when Goshen reported only 103 members. Through this crisis Thomas Boone held the church firmly to the Baptist way. Landrum reported Boone in his old age as strict in his profession and orderly in the whole department.

The March, 1830, meeting reported the preparation Goshen was giving to these two meetings. The request for the first came from James French. He wanted advice from Goshen as to what to do with the records and papers of the association. French also wanted to know which translation of the Bible is scripture.

James Edmonson, Thomas Boone, John Rogers and George Thomson were messengers to the various meetings with instructions to act on their own discretion.

The turmoil in the church, the loss of a hundred members in two years, show just how deeply even Goshen was hurt in the Reform battle. The mystery, just as with the district, is what happened to the lost membership. The minutes do not reveal any such massive losses. For example, in March of 1830, a woman of color, was eccluded for having a child without a husband. In September George Thomson and James Edmonson were elected trustees of the Goshen Church and so registered in the county clerk's office in replacement for Richard Hainey and Thomas Edmonson. In June 1831, the meeting noticed that James and Susan Walker still had their letters of dismissal given two years ago. They were ordered to return them. The Walkers refused.

That month, Log Lick requested that Goshen give up John C. Rogers that he might be ordained for their benefit. In May of 1830, he and his wife, Deborah, were dismissed. They remained, however, active in the church though it is assumed that they preached at Log Lick also. They were farmers and no doubt their Log Lick call took only one week a month. In May also, James Edmonson responded to the lack of ministers among the Baptist by seeking to refill their pulpits. Indian Creek was to request Edmonson's ordination in February of 1832.

Now the problem is what has happened to the lost members. This is also true of all the Clark County churches which survived. The Christian Church got a part of them, but only a part. For example, Bethlehem received most of the Prewitts, a scattering of New Providence families and some from Goshen. However, Bethlehem statistics do not show anywhere near the growth that should have come from Goshen's losses alone. Like Providence, many of those in the Goshen Church just quit church. A few of them might have gone elsewhere, for example, Sugar Ridge which does show an increase in membership at this time. No matter how one figures, perhaps half of Goshen losses are literally lost to religion.

If there were any problems for Goshen they do not appear in her minutes. Martin Haggard is substituting for Edmonson as church clerk, presumedly so that he would serve New Providence. All seemed routine.

Among other things, the April 1832 meeting considered selling the old church building. Catherine and Margaret Scobee joined by experience. The colored brethern requested the use of the church building for segregated worship. Similar requests were to be made of Ephesus at a much later date. There is no report of the action of the church, but later reports would indicate that the request was turned down. By this time the abolitionist movement in Kentucky was completely dead. The slave holders were not anxious to have groups of slaves from various plantations meeting in unsupervised meetings.

Martin Haggard was sick in 1832, so he was unable to attend the association meeting. W. Smithson was sent in his place. Edmonson resigns the clerk's post and Charles       was elected pro temp. The spiritual problems of the church were revealed partly by an agreement with Cane Springs Baptist Church in Madison County to meet together in October for a meeting which would in part be prayer and fasting. The messengers that attended the 1835 North District were Thomas Boone, James Edmonson, George Thomson and William Smithson. She reported 103 members.

Of course, the supervision of the members' lives continued. Henry Judy confessed to horse racing but refused to say he was sorry. He was excluded. His case was reheard in November. Meanwhile, Goshen is determined never again to have non Baptist take control of the church. George Thomson, David Judy, John Tribble, William Rupard (presumedly the senior), Asa Tracy and Thomas Boone revised the rules of the deacons eliminating article 17.

Asa Tracy is elected the new clerk. His hand writing was beautiful. All records, county or otherwise, were written in hand writing and of all reported by this study, his was the most clear.

Having straightened out the rules, Goshen tried to elect a new deacon in early 1833. No unanimous choice could be reached so the subject was deferred. In March, Johnny Pace was elected deacon. Boone, Edmonson and Thomson were still messengers. John Tribble was added to the messenger group.

Evidently, the earlier report of slave activity did cause the church to set up a series of meetings held on different plantations by white ministers for the slaves. The September meeting, 1833, report the successful results of these meetings by adding numerous slaves to the church role including eight or nine white converts with them. Edmonson and James Clark had done the preaching. There was no reason to believe that this James Clark was the Governor.

In December, Joseph Scholl was elected as a deacon.

May 1834, the records report that Betsy Haggard had joined "a people who call themselves Reformers..." and was excluded. This is the only example of a member going to the Christians reported.

With both the North District and Boone Creek Association in trouble, Goshen asked their messengers to suggest to the North District that the two associations should be united. Nothing came of the report. Already the differences between the two associations were growing. Meanwhile, Lewis, who was owned by Mrs. James Patton, had run away to escape punishment. He was excluded. In July of 834, the church paid William Smithson to make needed repairs. Grassy Lick Baptist Church, which is in Montgomery County, was struggling to survive, asked that Goshen help ordain their new deacons. To the Baptist, particularly in the shattered Montgomery area, Goshen had become a symbol of strength.

Goshen apparently was strong. The term, when there were no charges or struggles used by Baptist churches was "Fellowship at Peace." The same term would appear in Ephesus minutes. Goshen reported 124 members.

Another phase of the Goshen minutes reappeared in November of 1835. Francis Petty had a broken leg. Goshen Church contributed $11.00 to his relief. Considering the value of money, carefully spent, $11.00 could keep a man alive for a month in 1835.

Goshen apparently is a strange church in 1836. Thomas Boone, James Edmonson, G. V. Thompson and John Tribble were messengers. There was no indication, unlike Providence, that Goshen had made any real membership come back. Still she is a healthy Baptist church that survived the holicost. In October of 1836, Otter Creek Baptist Church invited Goshen to help ordain Howell Searcy to the ministry. August of 1837, Margaret Rogers is given $16.00. She is old and informed. Gbed Tracy was chosen janitor for 1837 and was paid $8.00 for his year's service.

The minutes have their usual housekeeping reports. George Thomson is to buy in November of 1837 a water bucket. In December, the church leaves one end of the church for accommodation for those who come to church over long distances. Kentucky weather can be very severe so they were now permitted the privilege of sleeping over in the church.

March of 1838 notes that Jesse, a man of color, was hurt with the church. There is obvious concern in the minutes. Jesse evidently was a slave highly regarded who had the call to preach. The church sent a committee of deacons to visit him to find out the problem. There obviously is a genuine concern on the part of the church. It is worth repeating to make the emphasis.

The problem with Jesse is related to the church's refusal to let him use the church building for his religious meeting. Jesse evidently felt that what he wanted had been granted in the past. (It had been granted at Bethlehem but seldom used). The committee to deal with the subject researched the minutes and reported that there never had been a right to use the building. It is evident that the Negros had used the building on occasion, however, in times past. There is no record of what the church did, if anything, to make Jesse happy. It was evidently not enough. The August meeting of 1838, complained that the section of seats reserved for black members was not being filled.

Meanwhile regular business at Goshen continued. David Brandenburg moved his letter from the East Fork of Four Mile Baptist Church, a church long since dissolved. The East Fork does appear in some of the early North District minutes but it is not reported after 1812. One wonders what Brandenburg had been doing in the years between.

The North District records report Goshen's membership at 98. This is some five members less than what had been reported a decade ago. The messengers to the association had not changed, Thomas Boone, James Edmonson, George Thomson, and Asa Tracy. Martin Haggard had been replaced as messenger by Zach Haggard. Now Tracy replaces Zach.

We learn in March of 1840, that Francis Petty is up and around. However, another member brought up charges against Petty of having legally evaded a just and moral debt. The church decided that Petty ought to pay.

In September of 1840, Upper Howard's Creek asked Goshen to help ordain her elders. Upper Howard's Creek was having difficulties within their congregation and obviously hoped that Goshen's stabilizing influence and their long time powerful minister, Thomas Boone, could help. Goshen reported 98 members.

The routine continued. Joseph Scholl became janitor. Inflation had set in for now, the salary for taking care of the church was $10.00. There are of course, many other things in the minutes. We are trying mostly to give the feel of the church.

July of 1841, the church reported that Savory House had joined the Reformers. There then is a steady drainage. Goshen had not changed much over the years, but in 1844, she reported only 76 members to the district association.

Meanwhile, in September of 1841, Goshen wanted to enlarge its lot by buying about an acre off of William Ramsey. Zach Haggard and James Edmonson were the committee. It would cost $50.00. In December of 1841, Humphrey and Harrison Miller agreed to be the church's janitors. No pay was reported.

Our history of the North District revealed that there was a stirring of division once again during the 1840s. Lullbegrud and Upper Howard Creek would divide. One can understand how the memory of the Reform still fresh in the minds of the Baptist, they were anxious not to permit anything to destroy their movement again.

Whether what happened next in Goshen is related to this back drop, or whether the two incidents about to be reported are even linked, is not clear. There simply is no way of finding out unless someone comes up with an old letter or diary in a trunk long forgotten.

In January 1842, William Read and John Rupard were charged with becoming free Masons. We might note that the anti-Masonic movement was very strong nationally in American politics. Those who were anti slavery were also quite often anti-Masonic. It was part of the effort to clean up the multitude of sins real and imaginary that haunted the 1840 America. Evidently, neither Reed nor Rupart were willing to withdraw from the Masons so they were excluded. The church waited until April in hopes that the men would obey.

At the same time, James Edmonson suddenly became church clerk. Something had happened to Asa Tracy. For a decade, the Goshen records had been kept in the beautiful, neat, readable hand of Tracy. A church clerk is high in the Baptist heirarchy, following after the minister and the deacons. Tracy had been a messenger to the association, a further concession to his importance. There is nothing in the minutes that states why Tracy left the church.

It was not that the leadership of Goshen did not try. For the next two months a variety of delegations consisting of deacons, of the minister, and of others visited him. Whatever was wrong, Tracy would not yield. Finally, nevertheless, in the April meeting, the last committee brought back the church's records and papers and recommended that Tracy be excluded. He was.

In a very real way, this ended a phase of Goshen's life. She had taken a turn which would bind her to a different future from the rest of the Clark County churches which belonged to Boone Creek. Her fate was now linked with Lullbegrud, with New Providence, with Upper Howard's Creek and to a lesser degree with Log Lick and Mt. Carmel. Of the entire group, only she would survive (1976). She was never to really recover her membership. There would be short term gains, but nothing that would last. On the other hand, she would be able to hold her own until the devastating division that came in 1904.

This closes one of the record books of the church. A modern reading the Baptist records, whether it be Goshen's or Providence's or Friendship's that have been aptly preserved on microfilm, or Ephesus's which has been photographed, these church trials and tribulations appear at first both tragic and comic. Usually they are recorded with a dry sense of humor to break the drudgery of history.

It is only after going through these records, meeting after meeting, does it suddenly become clear that what we are dealing with is not a church in the modern sense whose members take it or leave it. Goshen, Providence or Friendship, or any other of the churches involved were establishing a theocratic society. They sought to create a situation in which the church would become the total state for its members. The church would provide justice, would provide moral judgement, would provide welfare, would provide fellowship. No other agency was needed or wanted. In the background one can see John Calvin's church state of Geneva, or Oliver Cromwell's England, or the Puritan colony of Massachusetts. The Baptist did not have the power and control that Calvin, or the Puritans had, but the intent was there. In theory, the Baptist church at Goshen was all that was needed. It the state and county would disappear, the church could continue. It was an organic body with authority over all its members. With this in mind, these monthly church trials were not the work of busy bodies interfering with the rights of others. The monthly church meetings were the working of the theocratic state.

There is another viewpoint that will be reported here but taken up in more detail in a third volume. A Negro was a slave, but in the eyes of Goshen, he was still an important person. He obviously had sufficient freedome to get drunk, to commit crimes, to even run away. He had sufficient freedom of choice, he did not have to come to church if he did not want to, and sufficient freedom of action, that he could come to church if he desired. It is also obvious that despite the fact that he was a slave, he was expected to live in moral circumstances. Illegitimacy is as bad for a Negro as it was for a white girl. Marriage was blessed and a slave was expected to be married to have a family. This gives a little different viewpoint on slavery that some of the modern novels have ignored. There were injustices and brutalities in the system. Yet there was another side to the system that comes as a surprise to those who accept the modern novelists viewpoints as historic.

Goshen membership dropped to 76 in 1844. Besides Thomas Boone and Edmonson, Z. Higgins and two William Rupards were messengers. This is a father and son team. William Rupard, II now appears in Goshen history for the first time. The loss shows the steadfast determination of Goshen to remain true to its strict Calvinistic background. There is no indication where the membership loss went if it went anywhere.

The loss in membership continued. In 1853, when the next North District minutes are available, she had but 67 members. William Rupard, Sr. and James Edmunson were messengers. Rupard was church clerk. Thomas Boone was sick much of this period and James Edmonson was preaching in his stay. William's son was at this time out of the state.

James Edmonson became minister when Boone died in 1855. Boone's passing ended the career of one of the power houses of the Baptist movement. His loyalty to the old Calvinistic traditions never wavered. Had it not been for him, there is some question whether the Baptist movement would have survived at all in the North District.

James French could not have been able to hold the remenant against the Campbellites without him. He was not able or was unwilling to make the transition to a more modern Baptist program as the Boone Creek ministers had done. In 1856, Edmonson, J. Hilley and the two Rupards were again messengers. Young Rupard had returned to Kentucky evidently with the intentions of filling Boone's pastorate. Edmonson did not remain as pastor. Whether this was of his own doing is not clear. His son turned up soon thereafter in the Boone Creek Association, and served as minister.

William Rupard became minister of Goshen in 1857. He held the church, being elected for one year terms each year, until 1904. William Landrum attended Goshen in 1859. He reported Rupard's sermon to be strongly Calvinistic, but that he was an interesting speaker. Landrum liked Rupard's sincerity and honesty.

In 1870, the district meeting was at Log Lick. William Rupard, C. Rupard, N. G. Haggard were the messengers. The church reported 117 members. Rupard had done well in repairing the church and had brought it through the Civil War virtually unscarred. As the Winchester newspapers became available, Rupard and his church appear regularly in the list on the mast head of the newspapers. The Goshen Church met every fourth Saturday and Sunday.

The minutes of Goshen Church had definitely changed by 1883. The phrase, the church is at peace, was repeated regularly. The minutes of the monthly meetings often covered no more than three or four lines. No longer was Goshen trying to be a small theocracy. Trials virtually disappeared.

During this period Columbus Thomson was the church clerk. Other names appear occasionally. For example, James B. Lampton was moderator of the March congregational meeting in absence of William Rupard. Since his name does not reappear, it seems likely he was a visiting minister. The messengers in 1883 were William Rupard, S. Reid, Seth Rupard, Johnson Watts and C. Thomson. The church does not report its membership to itself or read into the minutes the official letter it sends to the association.

The official name of Goshen during this period was the Baptist Church of Christ at Goshen. In 1891, the name became the Old Baptist Church of Jesus Christ at Goshen. After about three years, the Jesus is dropped and the Old retained, the Old Baptist Church of Christ at Goshen.

Not a lot happened during these meetings. Sarah Blackwell, Lizzy Thomson, Elizabeth and Mollie Evans were baptized in October of 1883. The biggest problem that seemed to face the church was caretaker. William Reid took the job in 1883. It paid $15.00

Win some, lose some, in 1884 Lou Raney joined the Presbyterian church and was excluded. In 1887, the messengers to the association were W. E. Pace, R. T. Scobee, H. R. Watts, B. A. Tracy, William

Rupard, William Reid and C. Thompson who stays the clerk. Each year in October, a secret ballot as to whom shall be minister for the next year is held. William Rupard is always elected unanimously.

In 1890, Seth Rupard and S. E. Reid were sent to see Mr. and Mrs. William Tracy concerning their non-attendance. In September of 1890, Henry and Sally Hall were received into membership from the sister church of Liberty.

Each year there appears now to be three major items of business, the election of minister, the appointment of a housekeeper and the preparation for the association meeting. Occasionally, something of the old spirit would appear. Eight new members were reported in June of 1893 who were W. H. and Tinkey Rash, Nancy Scobee, the wife of James Scobee, Nancy Sewell, Malinda Rupard, Belle Allan, Lena Haggard and Nannie Kate Rupard.

Evidently the joining of his wife, her confession of faith and baptism, made a profound effect on the mind and life of James Scobee for in February, 1894, he appeared before the meeting and confessed immoral conduct and begged to be forgiven. This was granted. The Scobees became the pillars of Goshen strength.

The messengers for this period besides William Rupard, were S. E. Reed, B. A. Tracy and Columbus Thomson. B. A. Tracy died in December of 1894. R. T. Scobee and Seth Rupard appeared on the delegation list in 1896.

There were costs. In February of 1898, the church paid $11.00 for two dozen hymn books. Goshen at this time was perhaps stronger than she had been for many years. It was this prosperity that brought problems.

Many of Goshen's members lived in Winchester. They represented a very important part of the congregation, much of the money, a great deal of economic and social prestige. The trip out to Goshen was not easy. Roads were not paved and in some periods of the year would dissolve into mud quagmires. The new railroad, the Kentucky Union, was built along the Ecton Pike and came within two miles of the church, but those two miles could not easily be walked. Goshen's neighbor, Sugar Ridge Cumberland Presbyterian Church which was located further down the ridge in an even less desirable location, decided to move to Winchester in the 1890s and made the change without difficulty, establishing a new church on Washington Street in Winchester. The Sugar Ridge Church was dismantled and its furniture sold. However, William Rupard was against any suggestion of moving which settled the problem.

Messengers to the 1896 association included the two Guys and Z. F. Elkin. In 1897 Goshen reported 97 members, about her largest membership in later history. In 1901 the membership had slipped to 88.

Messengers to the 1901 association according to the SUN SENTINEL, August 17, 1901, were William Rupard, W. D. Stuart, C. C. Thomson, Seth Rupard and Murry Bass.

William Rupard died in 1904. For more than a half a century the power of the man's personality had completely dominated the North District and his churches. He was the "Old" Baptist movement in central Kentucky. Under him, the district had slowly disintegrated. His churches had showed slow, very slow, growth but not sufficient growth to provide a future operation.

Almost immediately after his death, a faction that represented the majority of Goshen members voted to move the church into Winchester. The leading element of this drive came from the Scobee family which were prominent in the social, economic and political life of Winchester. To drive out to the country in horse and buggy was a difficult task. There were other "Old" Baptist in Winchester besides Goshen members and it was hoped that these could be brought into the fold. Elizabeth Hunt wrote the story August 10, 1959, which explained the history of the Old Baptist Church in Winchester. This history will consider its history in the next volume.

The group that met had some thirty voting members of Goshen. The minority bitterly charged that there was no effort to notify all the members of the church of the meeting. Even at that the vote was twenty to ten. The ten called a meeting of the rest of the church which voted to remain at Goshen.

There was bitterness. Much of this came over the minutes. The church clerk had been with the town faction and took the minutes with him on the theory that the Winchester church was the continuing Goshen. However, as it became evident that Goshen would continue and that perhaps had a majority of the members when the dust settled, the minutes from 1825 were returned to Goshen. The question remained over what happened to the missing minutes. It has never been solved.

Evidently with the death of Rupard and the division of the church, J. N. Culton stepped in and served as minister. Culton evidently came from the Red River Association which is different from the modern Red River Association. It had, evidently, broken up about 1900 and Culton may have joined the Tates Creek Predestinarian Baptist Association on which were a group of Old Baptist centered in Madison County. The 1905 minutes of the North District, of which Culton became moderator, showed Goshen with 45 members. Seth Rupard, William Rash and Henry Hon were the messengers. The church called J. W. Anderson to be minister and elected Seth Rupard clerk. Sam Rupard and Henry Hall were elected deacons.

Since this is a turning point for the Goshen Church, we will drop its history at this point and will renew it in the fourth volume of this history. Goshen, reorganized, reduced in strength and without its city support, continued to operate. It was without William Rupard and the transition was painful.

## UPPER HOWARD CREEK BAPTIST CHURCH

The religious scene in Clark County by 1800 now included Providence, Unity and Goshen. The Presbyterians had Salem and Lawrence Owen had established the Owen Meeting House for the Methodist. All of these churches except for Goshen were in the Haggard-Quisenberry-Bush-Hampton area...the southern half of Clark County. Upper Howard Creek Baptist Church was still within that area. It became the seventh church to be established in Clark County. It was established in what was to be known as Ruckerville.

The history of Upper Howard Creek is complicated because it is the history of not one, but three churches, an "Old" Baptist, a missionary Baptist and a Christian church all of which met for a time in the same building. We will make no effort in this book to follow the Christian church. The records of the early Christian church are so few that for all practical purposes we will start with a later Christian church. The two Baptist churches we will try to trace.

At this time outside of the North District records, a scattering of other references are the only records. The "Fox Cousins by the Dozen" contains a short history of Upper Howard Creek that includes some of the earliest records.

According to the Fox cousins, Upper Howard Creek Baptist Church was organized, (the Baptist used the word Constituted), April 3, 1802. The charter membership list included James Elkin, John Vivion, Milton Vivion, Thomas Vivion, Thacker Vivion, Flavel Vivion, Isaiah Vivion, Henry Vivion, Mary Vivion, Shelby Vivion, Elizabeth Vivion, James Muir, Barnett Wills, William McDole, Nancy Vivion, Martha Newton, Mary Jones, May Towbridge, Elizabeth Kelly, Sarah Oliver, Mary Penland, Catherine White, Dolly Conkrite, James Wells plus three Negro members, Vivion's Ellick and Rachel and Duncan's Grace.

James Muir and Smith Vivion were elected elders and Richard Oliver was elected deacon. In 1805, William Haggard became a deacon. Milton Vivion was clerk.

The 1802 association messengers were Edward Kindred, James Elkins and James Muir; the membership was 38. Edward Kindred was the first minister.

The North District Baptist Association reported that Upper Howard Creek Baptist Church was among eight churches that united with the association that year. There was obviously no hesitation in Upper Howard Creek about the new association as there was among Goshen's poeple. Upper Howard Creek was made up basically of the same families that made up Providence, Unity and Indian Creek. James Elkin, James Muir and Edward Kindred were their messengers. It is interesting that there was not a Vivion in the first delegation. Kindred was to be their minister for the next thirty years.

Elkin, Quisenberry, Morris and Kindred made the four ministers that dominated this particular period. To this group would have to be added Lawrence Owen, but Owen has a strange position in the Methodist movement that is not entirely clear. There were no Prebyterians that had anywhere near the influence of these four men. Kindred had begun at Providence Church first as a deacon and then as an elder. On September 2, 1802, he married Harvey Vivion to Mildren Ryan. He would marry 187 couples before his death. Upper Howard Creek was to be his base.

James Elkin and William Haggard were the messengers in 1803 along with Kindred. In 1805, Vachel Faudre was added to this list of messengers and the membership had increased to 93. The situation was largely the same in 1809 with Kindred, Smith Vivion and James Elkin messengers, and the membership down some to 73.

The work did well in the next few years for in 1811, the membership had grown to 147. Jesse Wilcox was added to the messenger list. James Muir returned to the messenger list in 1812 and the membership continued upward to 152. The next year it had dropped to 142. This was the time that the Particular Baptist controversy was ripping the North Association but there is no reason to feel that this loss was significant. However, by 1816, Kindred and Harvey Vivion as messengers the membership was down to 134. This is more reflective to the War of 1812, the westward movement of many of the people of the area. Hundreds of Kentuckians were now moving into Indiana, Illinois and Missouri. Much of the west was being opened by the victories at Detroit over the Indians.

The minutes are full of the usual church trials. As with Goshen, a Bpatist church thought of itself as a minute government with controls over its membership that resembled a government. Sarah Oliver was charged with letting a falsity. She confessed and was forgiven. James Wells was charged with trading on the Sabbath. The church is referred to in the October Court 1816 as Dry Fork Meeting House.

In 1811, a building committee has been appointed consisting of John Gibbs and Jesse Wilcoxon, trustees, three acres on Dry Fork, a branch of Upper Howard Creek.

Even ministers could be charged with wrong doing. Kindred confessed in 1811 that he had whipped an apprentice boy too hard. He was forgiven by the church. Nothing was said how the apprentice boy felt.

Howard Creek was one of the seven churches that forced the North District to withdraw from correspondence with the Baptist

Foreign Missionary Society. In this, they were not completely out of line with Clark County viewpoint in that of the seven, six were Clark County churches including Providence.

In 1819 the messengers were the same except for Henry Bunch. The membership had grown to 236. The membership of North District churches were all strong this year. In 1821, a James Wood was included in the messengers. The membership dropped to 231.

Something happened that we have not commented on in the North District churches at the organization of the Boone Creek Association. We have indicated that there were shifts in theology, the Boone Creek Association controlled by those of more Separatist and now Reform views and the North District by those who were more Calvinistic despite John Racoon Smith's influence.

The 1823 association reported Upper Howard's Creek as having 177 members. Her messengers were James Wood, John T. Watts and Jesse Hampton. There is a similar drop in other church memberships, Providence from 183 to 169; Lullbegrud and Unity all showing drops. This was the year that Friendship split. Perhaps even more relevant to the situation was the organization of New Providence Church in Indian Fields that would include some of the Vivions, so presumedly Howard Creek members. If so, the memories of New Providence was not to Howard Creek, but to old Providence from whence came the name. It would appear that Upper Howard Creek was not a happy church.

In 1829 as the Baptist associations were rushing into division, Upper Howard Creek reported 150 members. Lewis Bledsoe, Archibald, Tucker, Smith and Milton Vivion were the messengers. She was the fourth largest church in the North District association, behind Spencer Creek, Lullbegrud and Mt. Sterling. There is no indication who her minister was. It is very possible that Kindred is no longer minister. If so, this might account for the slump in membership when most churches were booming.

Upper Howard's Creek was one of the seven that responded to James French's call for loyal Baptist North Association churches. Her messengers were Smith Vivion, Zach Ridgeway, Lewis Bledsoe and David Hampton. Smith Vivion was one of the committee that was asked "to examine the records....and report". At the second associational meeting the same delegation attended. It is interesting to note that previously Zach Ridgeway had been a Friendship member though the Ridgeways had lived in the Goshen area. The 1831 North District Association was called to meet at the Upper Howard Creek Church. There was no questioning its orthodoxy. Next to Goshen and Lullbegrud, it was solid.

Like all Baptist churches she was hurt. In 1832 she reported 99 members. There is no indication what happened to the lost members. A Christian church would be organized at Howard Creek and would use the building along with the other factions. It is impossible to say how early for the first mention we have at this point of research for the Christian Church at Ruckerville is 1848. She was a more or less operating church. Therefore, some of this loss would be accounted as going to the Christian Church.

She began a slow recovery. In 1834 she reported 114. Her messengers in 1836 were James Muir, David Haggard, James Wood and Nelson Bush. She showed signs of increasing controversy for in 1840 she reported 70 members. Her messengers were William S. Hickey, James Muir and Tarlton Embs, a shift in membership of the delegation would show reflections of a shift in the make up of the congregation. She also requested Goshen, according to Goshen's September 1840 minutes, to help ordain her decaons. This could be an act of fellowship, or it could be an effort to bolster the more Calvinistic faction of the church.

Whatever the difficulties, they were not abated. Conkwright reports that Howard Creek had 105 members in 1842. Deed Book 40, 1842, did not mention the name Baptist in relationship with Howard Creek and listed the trustess as Nelson Bush, Robert Lawrence, Nathanial Ragland and David Berryman. A few days after the North Association meeting in 1842, a group of Upper Howard Creek Church requested admission to the Boone Creek Association.

In 1844, N. Ragland, T. Embree (we note that this is probably the same man whose name was spelled Embs in 1840), J. T. Watts and James Elkins. The church reported 82 members. There is no record as to who were the deacons or church clerk for this period but usually the messengers represented the active leadership of a church. In 1846, N. Ragland, T. Embree, J. T. Watts, and D. R. Twynmen were the messengers and the church reported 50 members.

The Ephesus Church was organized in 1848 with the Upper Howard Creek Baptist Church giving many of the members, or at least theoretically. None of the messengers appear on Ephesus's list. What was done was the other Baptist church disappeared from the area.

The next North District Association list that is available is for 1853. Ragland, Watts and Nelson Bush were messengers. The church reported 60 members. There is no indication of who the minister might have been.

No other North District Association minutes have been discovered between this date and 1870, when someone had written Goshen minutes on the back of one. At this time Howard Creek reported 34 members. Its messengers were T. B. White, Nelson Bush, J. Christy and W. T. White. Evidently T. B. White was the minister.

The Clark County Democrat as early as October 9, 1878, does not list the Upper Howard Creek Church on its mast head as it did most of the county churches. Nor did it appear in 1887. This does not mean that the church was dead. Other churches were not so listed.

February 15, 1899, the WINCHESTER SUN reported that William Rupard preached a sermon at Upper Howard Creek on the same day he preached a sermon on Mt. Carmel. On the 25th, the paper reported that John Adams became minister. Much earlier, in August 6, 1879, the WINCHESTER SUN reported that Adams had taken up residence and farming in Ruckerville and that he was a minister. Whether this information concerned the Baptist Church or the Christian Church at Ruckerville is not clear, but we believe that it was the last gasp of the Baptist Church. When North District minutes reappear, in the 1890s, Upper Howard Creek Church is no longer reported. It is presumed to have died though it may have clung half alive until 1900.

The other Upper Howard Creek Baptist Church applied for admission to the Boone Creek Baptist Association in 1842. She reported 28 members. Nathan Haggard, J. Acton (Ecton), Smallwood Acton and Horatio Acton were the messengers. She reported 28 members which would be about the loss of membership reported by the North District Church. Conkwright reported that the new group would call themselves Missionary Baptist. It seems that this is a little too early to use that name in connection with any other of the Boone Creek churches. They would, in the next twenty years proudly call themselves missionary Baptist. Certainly there were theological difficulties in Upper Howard Creek. It seems more likely that this was a struggle between the churches old establishment and a group of members not previously recognized. None of these Boone Creek factions had represented Howard Creek before. Obviously we are dealing with the Ectons, two or three families of them which would be a sizable portion of the 28 members. As much as anything, this was a struggle over personalities.

In 1845, her messengers were N. Haggard, H. Ecton, J. Rucker, H. G. Porter and J. Ecton. Outside of the appearance of the name that would eventually be assigned to the location, Ruckerville, this group appears normal. A few new, a few old members..... In 1846, she reported 49 members. The Ephesus Church was organized in 1848. Conkwright reports that members from Upper Howard Creek made up the majority of that group. Ephesus' charter membership was 26 white and six negro members. This certainly does not account for the entire Upper Howard Creek group. One can assume that after the charter members were closed...and there is not a list available for Ephesus... that other Upper Howard Creek members joined. The Ecton family appear almost immediately in Ephesus history. Even the messengers to the Boone Creek Association of 1842 are not among the charter members or half the messengers of 1845. It seems reasonable to raise a doubt that the majority of Upper Creek members did make the change. Enough did, no doubt, that it killed the missionary church at Howard Creek. The "Old" Baptist membership shows the loss and never gains it back. It is the Christian church that becomes more active after 1848 though here the records are scarce.

## LOG LICK BAPTIST CHURCH

The records of Log Lick Baptist Church apparently have disappeared. They may be residing in someone's attic, or in an old trunk in the backroom. Like so many such treasures, sooner or later some unknowing daughter-in-law will be cleaning out the mess and burn them. Log Lick survived longer than any other of the "Old Baptist" except for Goshen and its Winchester off-spring.

Unfortunately, Log Lick moved the association membership that have left no records. There are a few newspaper reports, but the problem with these is the difficulty distinguishing what is Baptist and what is Christian in them since both churches used the same building for many years.

Log Lick reported to the North District Association in 1804. Her messengers were David Snowden and William McMahon. She had 16 members. Considering the size of membership, this would very likely be the first year of her existence. There is no mention of a Log Lick Church, or a church that might be Log Lick under a different name in the records of South or North District, or the Elkhorn Associations before this date. The 1805 North District records show that Log Lick had increased her membership to 25. Along with Snowden as messenger Samuel K. Whitley served.

The next available North District minutes are in 1809. The church had grown spectacularly to 86. She had had 36 baptisms that year and 12 members received by letter. James Elkins and James Fox were messengers. The next year membership had dropped back to 57. Snowden and Joseph McMahan were messengers. In 1812, the membership had once again increased to 82. Richard Stevens, Samuel Williams, Jesse MaMahon and Charles Snowden were the messengers.

According to the court record in 1816, a road was mentioned in October that extended from the Log Lick Church (no denomination mentioned) to Tuttle's Mill. Solomon Bunsford, Nicholas Merrill, Abraham Miller and Thomas Stone were responsible for the road. It is most likely that this Log Lick Church was the Baptist church though it is also possible that none of these men belonged. However, in Deed Book 21, Nicholas Merrill deeded the Log Lick Church one acre. Evidently the church already occupied the acre. Another court record told of a road, evidently a continuation of the earlier one, that would run from the Log Lick Church to Lullbegrud Creek. The church was located on the Red River near a ford crossing into Estill County. There is no hint as to who was the minister during these years.

There is a break in the available minutes until 1816. The membership is back to 40. Thomas Boone is the minister and Dan Lassity is the other messenger. This is the first time a minister has been identified with Log Lick. There is no way of telling how long he was there. The fact that Boone was a messenger from Log Lick would indicate that this might be his home church. If a minister represents several churches, he is a messenger from only one. For example, Boone was messenger in 1319 from Goshen. Log Lick's people were Abraham Miller and Rueben Franklin. The membership had sunk to 30. There is no indication of what Log Lick's problems were. During this ten years, a half dozen of the North District churches divided over the Particular Baptist question including New Providence and Friendship in Clark County. There is no reason other than this loss of membership to believe this might have happened to Log Lick.

There are no minutes available between 1813 and 1816. However, at sometime between these dates, the North District Baptist Association was approached by the Baptist Board of Foreign Missions. In 1817, Log Lick, along with Providence, Friendship, Upper Howard Creek, Unity, Mt. Tabor and Goshen, went on record as opposing any further correspondence with the Board. The North District listened to their requests. The missionary issue was dead in Clark County for another twenty years and in Log Lick it was never resurrected. Membership was back up to 70 in 1821. A Thomas Palt was listed among the messengers that had not before been mentioned.

The messengers of 1824 were John House, James Fox and Thomas Palt. As 1829 came with the threat of the Reformers hanging over the North District, Log Lick reported 86.

Log Lick did not attend the first meeting of the North District at Lullbegrud, but she did attend the second meeting at Goshen in 1830. It was one of the ten churches of the North District that carried on. Wilson Stobers and the two James Elkins, father and son, were reported as messengers. There is no membership report.

The April minutes of the Goshen Baptist Church carried a request from Log Lick that John C. Rogers be set aside for their benefit to act as minister. This was done, and we can presume that Rogers did preach at Log Lick for a time. He was occasionally active at Goshen in whose neighborhood presumedly he lived. There is no indication how long he may have served Log Lick. The messengers were Don Routt, Eli Bruce, L. Allen and Winn Johnson. Some of these names would later appear on Mt. Olive's rolls. The territory that Log Lick drew its members in 1830 must have dovetailed into Unity and Indian Creek.

There is no record of what happened to them in the struggle with the Campbell refromers. Up to this writing, we have not turned up any records of the Christian Church prior to 1881 though the church was considerably older than that. Whether it goes back to this division in 1830 between the Campbellites and Baptist is not yet affirmed. However, in 1832, Log Lick's messengers to the North District included James Elkins, Cuthbert Combs and James Elkins, Jr. The membership had dropped to 45 which would indicate that there had been a Reformer division.

In 1836, the messengers were James Elkins and James Fox. Membership had grown slightly to 52. The Foxes lived roughly in the area of Corinth Baptist Church where they later were to be strong members. Corinth would not be established until after the Civil War and in the twilight of Log Lick's existence. In 1840, James Elkins and William White were messengers. Both the James Elkins and White evidently shifted their membership to that church since in 1846, Elkins represented Upper Howard Creek Church.

After 1832, Log Lick does not appear in North District minutes until 1844. There is no reason for this. There is no report of Log Lick elsewhere that has been discovered by this research though admittedly it has not been complete for the Elkhorn and South District for this period. They were not in Boone Creek or the Licking Associations. Later Log Lick would belong to the Red River Association which was in existence at this time, but did not leave any minutes in the Southern Baptist Seminary for the period. The messengers in 1844 were J. Curtis, William White, Thomas Raiborn and N. Hunstard. The membership was 41. There is a possibility, because of his listing in first place, that white was the minister.

There was an old Baptist minister named Thomas White that served churches in the North District Association in 1810s and 1820s. There is also a reported T. B. White who was probably minister of Upper Howard Creek after the Civil War. We may well be dealing with a family of Baptist ministers but the records are too incomplete to come to a conclusion.

Unfortunately, Log Lick was not doing well. In 1854, Log Lick reported only 20 members. James Elkins, William Elkins, William White and Charles Burgher were reported as messengers. There was a James Elkins who had during this period represented Upper Howard's Creek. We have not discovered whether this was the same man, or another James Elkins.

In 1854, the old log building was replaced by a frame house with both Baptist and Christians using the building. Unlike Mt. Carmel, it is evident from later evidence that the Christians shared in the cost of the building. Whether they bought in at a later date or shared in the building is not clear. In 1855, William Rupard was minister. In 1856, Log Lick reported William White, J. Elkin and J. Lowry with 27 members. The possibility that White is minister has improved with the placing his name first on the messenger list. If White was minister, this was his last year for William Rupard was minister at the end of that year. The 1870 North District meeting was held at Log Lick. Log Lick must have belonged to the North District. H. H. Reynolds, J. Elkins, W. White and L. Lowry were messengers.

About this time Log Lick drops out of the North District Baptist Association. It is not clear what happened to Log Lick or why. There is a news item in 1879. The Red River Baptist Association was meeting at Log Lick. The Red River Baptist Association is a gathering of "Old" Baptist churches that largely are found along the Powell, Wolfe, and Lee County lines. The Baptist Southern Seminary have only a few minutes of this association and none speak of Log Lick.

In newspaper items in the WINCHESTER DEMOCRAT, THE SUN SENTINEL and THE WINCHESTER NEWS in 1889, 1903, 1906 and 1909, a J. N. Culton is reported as minister at Log Lick. The paper does not note whether he was Baptist or Christian. The minutes of the 1900s North District Meeting report that Culton is in attendance as a messenger from the Tates Creek Predestinarian Baptist Association. Much earlier, the Licking Association of Particular Baptist reported a Tates Creek Particular Baptist Association. Unfortunatelly, the Southern Seminary does not seem to have any of their minutes and none have materialized from other sources.

Apparently Culton was welcomed at the North District and even asked to preach the introductory sermon. No information is given concerning Log Lick Church which apparently was a member of Tates Creek or at least was not a member of the North District.

When Rupard died, Culton was elected moderator of the association and, if the newspaper is right, he remained minister of Log Lick until 1909. Goshen, desperate for a minister with Rupard dead and their city brethren withdrawn, called Culton in 1905 and again in 1912 for several years.

There is another gap in the minutes of the North District through World War I. In 1924, Log Lick is listed as a member of the North District. James T. Elkin and I. F. Elkin were their messengers. C. F. Crone was listed as minister. She reported 23 members. The 1928 North District listed Log Lick but noted there was no report.

The same story of men climbing to the roof of the church and blowing a horn at the psychological movement is also told about the Log Lick Church. The story was first told by James Flannagan and often retold to contemporary audiences by Jim French. Evidently, Flannigan knew of this incident because he named Thomas F. Donaldson and M. Fritz as the culprits.

## NEW PROVIDENCE BAPTIST CHURCH
## THE KIDDVILLE EARLY BAPTIST CHURCHES

There have been three Baptist churches in the Kiddville area. The later one which was organized after the Civil War will be discussed in the third volume. The two that were in existence in the pre-Civil War days have left very little information. Their records have not been discovered in writing this book and probably have long since been destroyed. The only information we have is an occasional reference in the minutes of other churches and some passing remark elsewhere. Putting their history together is like putting together a jig saw puzzle without all the pieces.

The Indian Fields area was settled very early in the beginning of our county history. Its lands had already been surveyed and files claimed as early as 1775. Much of the land came under the control of the Goff family after 1825. Kiddville itself was late growing and did not really become a place until the 1850s.

However, the New Providence Church was organized in the Indian Field area about 1805. It is obvious from the name that the founders were aware of the Providence Baptist Church, but there is no record in the Providence minutes to show any relationship.

It was located at the mouth of Combs Creek on Lullbegrud Creek. A New Providence Church belonged to the Red River Association in 1807 with William Payne as its minister. The name of the church and the minister would indicate that it was the Indian Field Church. Payne could not have remained minister much after this date but he may have been instrumental in organizing the church.

New Providence did not seem to belong to the North District Association at this time and there are so few surviving minutes of the Red River Association that no history of it can be given. Sometime around 1822, New Providence divided and a Particular Baptist Church was organized, probably using the same building. This evidently was at the height of the Particular Baptist difficulties in Clark County. New Providence did not, however, join the Licking Association and where, if anywhere, it had its associational connections is not known. Other than there was a Particular Baptist Church, nothing more is known. Who its members were, how long it lived and when it died has never been recorded...or at least we have not been able to discover that information. It did pass away early, for by the time the Reformers were being expelled from the Baptist and were organizing their churches in Clark County, there was only one church present. There is no record of how it fared in that struggle. Bethlehem Christian Church did reach into Indian Fields and draw several of its members away, in the 1830s, however. Never being in the Boone Creek Baptist Association, Conkwright does not discuss it.

Besides the Red River minutes report, other early dates for New Providence came from vague mentions in road reports. The chances are that it died or at least discontinued activities for many years. The building may have stood, an occasional wandering minister may have held meetings in it, but the first real information on New Providence appeared in the 1822 minutes of the North District Association. There is a possibility that this group represented the non-Particular Baptist group that now sought recognition and had decided to build a church.

Deed Book 19, 1823, page 303, lists as trustees for the New Providence Church, Abraham Davenport and Vivion Daniels.

The 1832 minutes showed the church with 14 members. John B. Hayes and Vivion Daniel were messengers.

The next year the messengers were Davis Bunch and Daniel Donohoe. Its membership had grown to 19. In 1824, Vivion Daniel and Jesse Pearce were the messengers and the membership was 18. In 1827, Enoch Foxworthy was part of the delegation.

New Providence profited by the boom in religion that occurred almost everywhere during 1824 to 1830. In 1829 she reported baptizing 74 and taking 15 more by letter. Her membership was up to 108. Her messengers were James Muir, Vivion Daniels, Cuthbert Combs, and Charles Hazelrigg. Muir would move to Upper Howard Creek in the next few years. There is no record who her minister was during these years.

She did attend the rump meeting of the North District churches at Goshen in 1830. Enoch Gallop, Cuthbert Combs and Charles Hazelrigg were still her messengers. At the next meeting of the Baptist in the North District, Muir and James Fox joined the delegation. New Providence had chosen sides. She was shaken by the Reform. In 1832, she reported 77 members. Some like Daniel Donohoe, went to Bethlehem Christian Church. However, the total loss of membership between Goshen, New Providence and Lullbegrud was far greater than any gain, if any, in Bethlehem's membership. The hard fact was that literally hundreds of Baptist simply dropped out of their old churches without joining the new. Some churches, such as Providence, would win back many of these. Other would not. New Providence would be among these.

In 1834, she reported 71. She did write Goshen and request a letter for a Matilda Hanks who wished to unite with New Providence but had lost her letter from Goshen. The request was acceded to.

New Providence membership in 1836 was down to 40. Her messengers were Barnett Epperson, Sam Davenport, Thomas Allen and Robert Ware. This would indicate a shift in membership makeup. Thomas Raiburn and Ware were the messengers for 1840 and the membership remained at 40. In 1844, the membership included Zadoc Kidd, C. Daniel, Thomas Raiburn and B. Hampton. She reported 39 members. Kidd,

Robert Daniel and a Thomas Allen were messengers for 1854. The membership hung fairly steady.

During this entire period there has been no hint of who could have served New Providence as ministers. Sam Martin's article about the makeup of the county in the 1850s named a John Thompson as a Baptist minister living in Kiddville. He never served any of the Boone Creek churches or was named in the North District members so it may well be that he was minister of New Providence for at least some of this period. The Thomson family had been active members of Goshen in years preceeding these. They make a point of having no "p" in the name, but Sam Martin in his reminiscing in the paper may have put one in. It may well be that one of its members moved to Kiddville to serve New Providence.

In the old Goshen minutes there is inserted a portion of a 1870 minutes of the North District Baptist Association meeting. New Providence is not reported. There is no further mention of New Providence until the WINCHESTER DEMOCRAT reports in 1888 that R.H. Anderson had bought the deserted church, torn it down and built a house.

## EPHESUS BAPTIST CHURCH

It is quite clear that by 1840, the Boone Creek Baptist Association controlled the churches in the southern part of the county, churches that were all largely children of Providence, largely made of related families, and with close ties with one another...Providence, Mt. Olive, Boone Creek....however, the rest of the country belonged to the North District Baptist Association and took a sharply different turn theologically in the 1840s, the Boone Creek becoming missionary and the North District Primitive....New Providence, Upper Howard Creek, Goshen and the third group of Particular Baptists.. Friendship and Mt. Carmel. Not only were these churches in a different section, but they were largely made up of different families than the Boone Creek and were not nearly so inter-related. One would have to add Lullbegrud to this group just as Boone Creek has to be added to the other group.

There were signs that this arrangement was coming to pieces after 1840. The Upper Howard Creek Church divided with one faction entering into the Boone Creek. So also did Lullbegrud. The missionary factions of both churches were not strong, but they were probably as strong as the "old" faction. It is also clear that none of the "old" churches were prospering.

This restlessness among the "old" churches reached into the eastern part of the county where Goshen held firmly to its Calvinistic theology. Originally, there had been Bethlehem in that area, but Bethlehem had gone lock, stock and barrel, as the saying goes, to the Campbellites. In so doing, she had drawn the more liberal elements out of Goshen, Lullbegrud and New Providence. There were still Baptist, however, along George's Fork and Little Stoner Creeks that refused to become Campbellite and were unhappy with Goshen. Many of these people had no church affiliation. Other belonged to Upper Howard Creek and still others had their membership in the even more distant Mt. Olive. It meant an all night stay. We have noted already how Goshen made arrangements for such long distant attenders to stay in the back of the church overnight.

Out of these various groups, the first Baptist church to be established in Clark County, that was not a division of an older church, since 1810, was organized on Little Stoner Creek, and was called Ephesus.

The effort to establish Ephesus Church was lead by Edward Darnaby who had been instrumental in organizing the united Mt. Olive. In 1848, the records of Mt.Olive report that several of her members were dismissed to help organize the new church.

According to a little history based on the minutes of the Ephesus Church, written by Mrs. Harvey H. Franklin about 1938, there were 27 charter members plus seven Negro members. The minutes of Ephesus Church have been photographed by the Southern Baptist Historical Association and are also available.

In 1848, Darnaby drew together elements of these three groups and helped organize them into a church. These were Smith V. and Elizabeth Hunt Potter, Smallwood, Sarah and Thomas Action (whenever this name is used it is followed in parenthesis the name Ecton). It is presumed that the two are the same; these records are also using the name Ecton. Richard and Nancy Gordon, Thornton and Lucinda Wills, Isaiah Wills, Jonathan W. Hunt, James and Susan Acton, James and Lucinda Baker, Lewis Gordon, Horatio and Margaret Action, John E. Gordon, James and Sarah Hunt, William Baker, Lydia Ecton, John and Susan Ecton, Jesse Gordon and John D. B. Duckworth. The Negros were Linda and Sarah Ecton, Judah Gordon, Ellen Ecton, Jack and Cynthia Hunt. It is presumed that these are slaves of the families whose surnames are used. However, it is a little unusual to have surnames for slaves at this time. There is a possibility that these are free Negros. If they were slaves, as they probably were, they were certainly house servants and with close relationships with their masters. The group met in the home of Richard Gordon. The SUN SENTINEL, July 28, 1904, added more information. Ephesus began services twice a month... a luxury that only Providence could at this time afford. The second Saturday was set aside as an official business meeting day. John Hedges Goff's journal mentions Ephesus in 1852 and 1862 as a flourishing country church. From the beginning, the church appeared to be successful.

Deed Book 69, 1849, page 67, registers the transfer of property from James H. Hunt to Richard Gordon, Smallwood Acton, James E. Gordon and Jonathan Hunt, trustees of the United Baptist Church at Ephesus to build a church on Stoner Creek.

A building committee was established with James Hunt, Richard Gordon, Smallwood Acton, John R. Gordon, Jonathan Hunt, as members. John Duckworth replaced Smallwood Acton. The church was completed for $581.97.

Like the minutes of most Baptist churches, the early minutes are filled with charges of unchristian like conduct and action of the church on these charges. Rightly or wrongly, many of these charges seem to be leveled against the Negro members of the church. Not entirely however. "Immoral conduct", "drinking too much ardent spirits", etc.. were the most common charges. Discipline of the church met various reactions. In 1860 a committee was sent to call upon John W. Rupard and John D. B. Duckworth to find out why they were not attending church and asked them if they wished to continue on as members. Rupard said he did and begged forgiveness, presumedly returning to services. Duckworth said that they should erase his name from the church books.

In the back of the first volume of photographed minutes there is a list of names of members who were taken off the rolls for other than death, letter or exclusion. Mary Ballard...gone west; Agnes Redmon...joined Reformers; Cassina Taul...gone to Texas; Thomas Boone...gone to Texas; Carrie Bruce...lost sight of; Armanda Gordon...gone to Ohio. The list continued, but the restlessness of the population is easily seen. The name Thomas Boone would date this list before the Civil War. The lure of something better continually brought Kentuckians to leave their homes and head west as their fathers had done before them.

The official name of Ephesus was chosen by R. R. Gordon and adopted unanimously, the "United Baptist Church of Jesus Christ at Ephesus." So read the minutes to 1890 when the Boone Creek Association quietly dropped the use of the name United and became simply Baptist and Ephesus became the Baptist Church at Ephesus.

We note in passing that James Baker was given permission to build a house on the church property in return for care of the building. The relationship continued for in 1871, Baker broke his leg and the church promised to help.

The minutes began with a report from the church..."Fellowship was called for, all in peace."

Horatio Ecton, Richard R. Gordon and John Tipton were elected deacons for the new church. The church was admitted to the Boone Creek Association in 1848. S. V. Potts and Horatio Ecton were the messengers. The Upper Howard Creek Church sent no messengers. In 1846, this church had reported 49 members. Obviously only a small portion of these actually came to Ephesus so the establishment of Ephesus was not a net gain for the Boone Creek people. There is no indication what happened to the missing members though the Christian Church at Ruckerville began to be more active after this event.

Landrum reported T. I. Wills preaching for the Methodist April 9, 1831, and Wills' name often appeared on deeds of Methodist property. He had been baptized by immersion into the Methodist Church, but he remained on their roles as a local minister. As we will note, the Methodist organization, though depending heavily on the services of their "local" ministers, gave to them very little credit and almost no real place in the Conference. It was basically this neglect that, when Ephesus was organized close to Wills' home, he elected to turn Baptist. Ephesus, in a surprising vote, agreed to accept Wills' immersion without him have to be reimmersed. However, Wills, realizing the basic feeling of Baptist on the subject and to keep the peace...the vote was by no means unanimous, agreed to be rebaptized. From this point on, Wills became a power house amoung the Baptist ministry.

Dudley Flynn and Austin B. Wills were chosen as deacons in 1853. James Hunt was appointed to keep the Sabbath Day books. This is the first mention of Sunday School among Clark County Baptist. The Winchester Presbyterians had an operating Sunday school before the Civil War. It was operated in close relationship to the weekly school that the Presbyterian ministers directed. Sunday school was again mentioned in 1852, but evidently it was in poor health. Sunday school did not develop for in 1862, the books were sold for $9.00 with the church keeping the money.

Potts continued to serve Ephesus until 1855, but Wills remained until 1861 and then returned. He considered his home church to be Ephesus. Mrs. Franklin reported that in 1852, when John Fox was principal of the Jefferson Academy, he held graduation exercises in Ephesus. Fox is the author of such novels as "The Little Shepherd of Kingdom Come," "The Trail of the Lonesome Pine", etc.

Mt. Olive already had its famous May meeting, so Ephesus established her annual June meeting in 1852. At that time and until well after the Civil War this was a three day revival that was similar in every way to the Methodist and Cumberland Presbyterian Camp Meetings. It became one of the most important religious and social events of the year drawing literally hundreds, many of whom camp the three days.

Nathan Edmonson was ordained in 1858. James Edmonson along with Thomas Duckworth were ordained deacons. There is no reason given for the change of the Edmonson family from Goshen. James had been a minister of Goshen who followed Thomas Boone and had supported the Boone-Chenault brand of old Baptist. There is no doubt, a relationship between Goshen calling William Rupart to replace Edmonson as minister only two years earlier. We are dealing with the problem of names. This James could be a junior of the old Goshen minister. Even if this is so, the shift of the family from Goshen to Ephesus is interesting.

In 1859, Ephesus' membership stood at 57 male, 52 female and 34 Negro members for a total of 143.

Ephesus reported T. I. Wills, James Edmonson (Jr.), T. Wall, J. W. Hunt and J. F. Golden as messengers. Ephesus reported 170 members in 1862 going into the Civil War.

Ephesus tried to call George Broadus who was a Baptist minister running the Jefferson Academy at what is now Pilot View. This was one of the better private academies found scattered over the county. Broadus himself was evidently a very able and much sought after preacher, but he preferred not to tie himself down to a single church. T. I. Wills was then called and he continued to preach until 1864. Nathan Edmonson then served for a single year.

In passing, we note that William Landrum, a local Methodist minister who wrote a journal which contains information for this period, preached at Ephesus, evidently as a guest minister in August 1863, Landrum had taught school in his earlier days at Schollsville and evidently was accepted in both Baptist and Presbyterian churches as a welcome guest minister. From the beginning Ephesus had shown a willingness to cooperate with others. In 1848, a committee attended Sugar Ridge Presbyterian services.

Cyrus W. Boone organized a Sunday school at Ephesus in 1865. The Boone Creek Association was just getting interested in the Sunday school movement. In 1866, Boone reported 23 students. The Sunday school movement will be discussed in the third volume, but one must note that Cyrus Boone, L. N. Conkwright, and several others were professional school teachers who would move from community to community as their profession called. They would also immediately organize and conduct a school on Sunday at the nearest Baptist church.

Isaac Strode, a Negro, asked the church to be licensed to preach. The record reported that the church established a committee to listen to him preach and refused to grant the license...they must have done so later because Strode did begin preaching which he could not have done without the church's permission. Mrs. Franklin reports that the fourth Sunday was assigned to the Negros to hold their own services. She did not state where this was in the minutes and there is no date. Presumedly it came in 1859, but it might have been after the Civil War. This situation continued until a Negro church was built in the L. and E. Junction area.

W. D. Strode became clerk of Ephesus which he held along with the associational clerk for a quarter of a century. Ryland Dillard became minister in 1866 followed briefly in 1868 by W. B. Arvin. T. I. Wills then returned for a period that ended with his death in 1874. Belson Strode was elected deacon in 1866.

The Civil War was now over and the country had settled down to a strenuous peace time. The messengers that Ephesus sent to the association included R. R. Gordon, N. Strode and W. D. Strode and Jesse Gordon. The church reported some 136 members. The loss was substantial during the Civil War years but not disasterous. It represented the beginning of the trend in which more and more of the country leadership, landowners, young people, businessmen, etc. would abandon the country for the city.

In 1869, successful revivals brought in 23 new members by baptism. The missionary movement was now firmly established on the Boone Creek churches and this applied also to the local church. Ephesus now took the lead in establishing two new county Baptist churches. One was at Kiddville where the "Old" Baptist church was nearly dead. In dying it left behind many Baptists who still desired a church. A few of Ephesus' members lived in the Kiddville area. In one of the basic Baptist traditions to establish new churches wherever possible, Ephesus gladly sent those members to the Kiddville church. Also, in 1871, Ephesus cooperating with Mt.Olive, helped to establish the Corinth (often called Whitehall by the newspapers referring to the building the church met in). In each case successful churches appeared. However, it must be noted that when a country church gave up members for a new church, the sacrificing church often lost irreplaceable members. The fact that they would travel several miles to church showed their interest and loyalty. There were not enough people in the community to fill the gaps. However, the net gain for the Baptist movement was positive.

Thomas J. Stevenson became minister in 1874 closing the T. I. Wills era. Wills had served Ephesus off and on since its establishment. Several times he resigned when he felt that he was not getting anywhere, when it would be best for the church to have another voice. He always came back. Wills served other churches, but Ephesus was his most successful pastorate and one that owes its strength to him. He had begun his ministry as a Methodist. During his long life he was among those ministers who lived and operated out of Clark County that served the local churches faithfully. He married Joseph Emory and Anna Fisher in January of 1836. During the next half century he married 124 Clark County couples. This makes him one of the most popular ministers in the county.

George Hunt was minister briefly in 1875. Ambrose D. Rash was then minister until 1879. The messengers in 1876 to the association were Nelson Strode, Findley Wills, J. N. Conkwright, A. D. Strode, L. T. Gordon and W. D. Strode. It is not reported whether Ephesus had Sunday school during this entire period, but most of the years it did, at least in the spring, summer and fall. Most things halted during the winter when the roads became impassable. (However, J. N. Conkwright was at this time, and had been for several years, superintendent of Providence's Sunday school.) A different system appeared, in 1878 when the Sunday School superintendent was A. Fleet. Fleet was the assistant principal in the Academy in Winchester. He was also superintendent of Winchester's Sunday school. Evidently, he was interested in helping and did so in the manner that ministers did, serving several churches. It indicates how independent of the main church the Sunday school was. This development was not carried to its possible extreme. Instead the experiment seemed to end for Ephesus had no Sunday school in 1879.... or at least she did not report it to the association.

The association had established a custom of giving a brief history of one of the churches of the association, usually the host church. In 1880, the Boone Creek Association met at Ephesus and reported her history. The history noted that 270 people had been baptized in Ephesus since it was established. It now had preaching only once a month on the fourth Sunday. Seventy-four had joined by letter, 65 had been dismissed. The 1880 membership was 119. Sunday school was once again in operation with J. N. Conkwright as superintendent. In 1881, Findley Walls, W. Strode, Sam Boone, James Strode and L. N. Conkwright were messengers. She reported 125 members.

Ephesus came out strongly against dancing in 1885. This move, and similar moves in other churches at the same time, obviously instigated by the association showed an increasing interest on the part of the church in social issues. The older church minutes showed little interest in taking official positions. Sin was sin and there was no need to underline it. Curiously, Conkwright's history does not report Ephesus taking the same position against intoxicants as did Mt. Olive and Providence. This may merely have been an oversight on the part of Conkwright.

The revival season in 1887 brought 1500 people to Ephesus in a series of meetings that Simmons conducted and that was reported by the WINCHESTER DEMOCRAT. How much Sunday school was carried on during this decade is not clear. The 1883 association reported that L. N. Conkwright was superintendent of the Providence school and that Ephesus had none. Conkwright, a school teacher, changed schools and attended Providence Church. However, in 1884, W. T. Gordon was reported as superintendent. He was the first of the local people to hold the office.

Along with the social issues that now became part of the church business, the Boone Creek Association had blossomed into a modern type organization with home, foreign and local missions, education interests, and a host of other cooperative enterprises. In 1886, Ephesus gave a total of $392.00 to these cooperative causes. She also was paying her minister $240.00 a year.

J. N. Conkwright was back again in Ephesus in 1887 both as a messenger from that church, but also as moderator of the association. He was to continue as one of the most influential men in the association. Later, in the turn of the century, he was to challenge the county political machine largely on the liquor question and was badly defeated. It is a serious comment to note that influence in church affairs would not carry over to county affairs. Other messengers from Ephesus in 1887 were W. D. Strode, Findley Watts, Sam Boone, J. N. Bush, and Ecton. The power structure in a country church changes little with the years. Strode was Sunday school superintendent in 1887.

J. Pike Powers became minister in 1888, but he was a sick man and could not do the type of work he had been doing for over a decade in the county and in Montgomery County. Powers was a cashier at the Winchester Bank. He was an able minister who helped stear many country churches into a stronger position. However, he had to leave the county in 1890. Perhaps it was this that lead Ephesus to report to the association that it had no "cherry news". The Sunday school was also abandoned. The church was now meeting the second Saturday and Sunday of each month.

Into Ephesus' gloom came Richard French.

Richard French was a business man in Winchester and like all the other Frenches, very active in the Baptist church. He had been Sunday school superintendent of the Baptist Sunday school in Winchester for many years. He felt the call to preach. In 1890, at Ephesus' request, he was licensed by the Winchester Church and was ordained soon afterward. He was to serve the Ephesus Church until failing health forced him into retirement in 1913. His work with other churches was momumental. Unlike most of the ministers during this period, Richard French became virtually a full time minister, letting his business decline in his service with God. He was ordained by A. D. Rash and J. L. Southerland. T. C. Stackhouse was supposed to join in, but did not make the service. The DEMOCRAT in reporting the ordination was lavish in praise.

James French, the contemporary James French (1976), tells a story about the visit Richard French made on the aging and ill "lion of Whitehall", Cassius Clay. Clay was not the most popular man in Kentucky and was of violent disposition. French entered his house in Madison County, saw the loaded brass cannon pointed at the front door (from inside in case someone broke in), and was ushered into the living room that was stacked with guns and knives. He concluded his business with Clay and asked for permission to pray. It was granted and French got to his knees and prayed, but, as he confessed to his wife later, he kept one eye open to watch the old man. His wife remonstrated with him and asked where his faith was. French answered, "Does not the Scripture tell us to Watch and Pray"?

The messengers of Ephesus in 1891 were Richard French, W. B. Strode, W. T. Gordon and J. R. Strode. The next year the messengers were W. T. Gordon, W. D. Strode, F. Watts, Thomas Ecton and Ellis Brandenburg. The church reported 156 members. Strode was again Sunday school superintendent. Ephesus was paying to a minister $284.00 a year and raising for all causes $482.00.

Richard Gordon, one of the founding members and oldest, died in 1890. Simeon Boone and W. T. Gordon were elected deacons in 1894. Allan Rupard became a deacon in 1906. S. T. Rupard was messenger in 1891. These are new names on the list. The others reappear regularly. The DEMOCRAT reported that W. T. Gordon was Sunday school superintendent in 1895. The school met at 3 o'clock in the afternoon on Sunday and completely separate from the church worship service or business body. Like other Sunday schools at this time, it was an independent organization which was permitted by the church to use their buildings. The Baptist were beginning, even at this time however, to tie their Sunday schools into their church organization. Long been advocated by the association, they were by this time Baptist Sunday schools and seldom supported the county and state association of Sunday schools as did other denominational schools.

Gordon remained Sunday school superintendent until 1900 when there was no report of a Sunday school given to the association. Most of the next ten years, Ephesus does not report a Sunday school. The church seemed strong with good leadership. Despite the pressure by the association, a Sunday school did not seem important.

In 1901, Ephesus' messengers were W. D. Strode, Richard French, Sam M. Boone, W. T. Gordon and G. J. Hunt. She reported 133 members and paid the minister $240.00 a year. Obviously, this was $20.00 a Sunday. Her total giving was $321.00. G. J. Hunt was Sunday school superintendent in this year. However, in 1904, she once again reported no Sunday school. G. J. Hunt was again reported Sunday school superintendent in 1905, but the next year once again there was no Sunday school.

The messengers for the Ephesus Church in 1911 were Richard French, W. D. Strode, George Brandenburg, W. Gordon, John Golden and George D. Hunt. She had 114 members, paid the minister $250.00 and gave a well rounded missionary program to the association. For the first time since 1905, she reported a Sunday school with George Hunt again the superintendent. Still there were definite signs that the church was not doing well. French was not a well man. He had done magnificent work, but age and health were cutting his effectiveness. He was faced with the old problem of many a fine minister, when should he retire or change pulpits?

Ray Scot and Elis Brandenburg were elected deacons in 1913. After French retired in 1914, W. S. Taylor became minister. He was a fortunate choice for he kept Ephesus developing after the long and strong pastorate of Richard French. One of the problems that Baptist history has demonstrated over and over, is how to replace the long termed, strong minister who might have stayed a little too long for the church's well being...

For some reason Ephesus through most of this period did not report a Sunday school. In 1917, she and Corinth were the only two churches in the Boone Creek county churches that did not have a Sunday school. In the whole association less than a half dozen churches now did not have Sunday schools and those would be the weakest of the mission preaching points. Ephesus on the other hand was a strong church. Corinth more than any other of the Boone Creek churches leaned to the "Old" Baptist position. Ephesus may also have had elements of the "Old" Baptist among them. Nathan Edmonson belonged to a family that had for years been the backbone of Goshen. Brandenburg also was a Goshen family. Still, with such representatives as Strode as church clerk for so many years, it is surprising that these elements would influence the Sunday school. It is hard to believe that Ephesus had a Sunday school and did not report it.

In 1920, Ephesus conducted a very successful revival bringing more than 54 new members into the congregation. Taylor had left Ephesus in 1919 and their new minister was F. P. Peirson. He stayed until 1923 when he left to become a missionary in India.

If Ephesus had any traces of the "Old" Baptist they were contained in the newly enlarged church. In 1921 she reported a Sunday school with no one named Sunday school superintendent. However, Mrs J. T. Corey was president of the Women's Missionary Society, one of the four Boone Creek churches to have such a society...First, Central and Providence. Also in 1921, Jesse Bruen headed the Ephesus Baptist Young People's Union. Ephesus was one of the three churches in the association to have such a union...First and Central being the other two.

As Strode grew too old to carry on his functions as clerk, Jesse Bruen was elected to succeed him.

As this period closed, of all the Baptist country churches, Ephesus closed healthiest. There were some signs that she too, had weakened somewhat, but she emerged in 1920 as the strongest of the Boone Creek Baptist churches. Advocates of the congregational system of church policy, in Clark County the Baptist and the Christian churches, often criticize the Methodist churches for the moving of their ministers every few years. A study of both the Baptist and Christian churches in Clark County reveal that the median tenure of their preachers is often less than that of the Methodist. In addition, the presiding elder or district superintendent which ever his name is, exercises a continuation of program and a unity of motion that the free churches lack. The difference between Ephesus with their effective ministry, Wills, French, longer term ministers and Providence ard Mt. Olive is quite clear.

## FIRST BAPTIST CHURCH, WINCHESTER, KY

First Baptist Church in Winchester was organized in 1858. However, since this is a city church from the beginning, its history is reserved for the third volume of this history.

## MT. CARMEL BAPTIST CHURCH

The Wades Mill area of Clark County had historical ties with Bourbon County that were about as strong as she had with Clark. Just as the Van Meter Road area and the Becknerville Road area looked to Lexington, Wades Mill found North Middletown her normal shopping area. Even to the present, many of the Wades Mill people will go for medical and shopping services in North Middletown. Through much of Clark County history, North Middletown was a progressive community, perhaps not as large as Winchester, but nearly so. In the days of horse back and carriage, a mile or two was a long way and North Middletown was closer to the Wades Mill area by two or three miles. It was not until after the Civil War when the railroads missed North Middletown did North Middletown begin to decline. The very promising educational institutes in the community folded. Desperate efforts to bring a railroad failed and growth stopped and began to decline.

Even the families are different in the Wades Mill area. The Hampton-Vivion-Quisenberry-Bush-Elkin of the southern part of the county, and the Brandenburg-Hunt-Gordon-Ramsey group of the eastern part of the county were not represented.

The Mt. Carmel Baptist Church was always more a member of the Fayette-Bourbon group than Clark County. From the ealiest recorded part of her history, she belonged to the Licking Association of Particular Baptist. As such she did not go through any of the struggles that the Boone Creek and North District did. A Christian church would be established in her church which eventually would take over the area, but they were never part of the Baptist. True, the Baptist left heavy imprints on the Christian Church making it somewhat unique in the county. There was never the bitter antagonism between the two. As the Baptist weakened and the Christians strengthened, it was a merging of the children of one going over to the other.

The Christian Church more than the Baptist Church belonged to the county. In the 1890s, the local newspapers were reporting Mt. Carmel Christian Church as well as the events in the Wades Mill area when the CLARK COUNTY DEMOCRAT enlisted John Snowden as their local correspondent. He became the most vocal of all the various community correspondents.

There is no evidence how old Mt. Carmel Baptist Church was. There is a possibility that in the later 1790s there was an effort to establish a Mt. Carmel Presbyterian Church in the Wades Mill area for one petitioned the Lexington Presbytery for a minister and was assigned one on a very temporary basis with a warning that they would have to show that they were able to support a minister. The Mt. Carmel Church was never again reported. Apparently, the Presbyterians failed and soon thereafter the Mt. Carmel Baptist Church was organized for when the Licking Association minutes began, Mt. Carmel was a strong and well established church in their midst. What association she belonged to before the formation of the Licking Association has not, at this point, been discovered. There were 18 churches in the Licking in 1812. Mt. Carmel was the only Clark County church. Thomas Wright and William Cooper were messengers. She reported 25 members. There was no record of who her minister was until sometime after 1823 when Thomas Dudley would serve her for more than fifty years. Her messengers in 1817 were Wright and David Thomson. (There are two families whose names can easily be confused. Thompson and the Thomsons who bitterly protest whenever someone puts a "p" in their name.) During the next five years, these men remained her messengers and the membership shifts from 29 to 36. We should note with all these "old" Baptist churches, membership was not easily won. An experience had to accompany salvation without which one was not saved. There were always a number of very active people around each of these churches that were not members but were influential. To say a church had 29 members, does not mean that only 29 (and usually adults) would attend the services. In 1821, A. T. Darnell joined Wright as messengers. The membership was 31. Friendship joined the association in 1823, but there seemed to be little relationship between the two Clark County churches. Mt. Carmel was down to 25 members. An M. Gossett joined Wright in 1824 as messengers. Gossett would be licensed to preach by the association in 1828.

Like most churches in the middle and later 1820s, Mt. Carmel began to grow. She reported 41 members in 1927. G. Northcutt, J. M. Clarkson and J. Leach joined Wright and Gossett as messengers. In 1828, the membership had grown to 55 and in 1830 to 66. In 1831, she reported 72 and in 1833, 87. In 1837, Neal Green and D.Thomson were her messengers.

It is obvious that throughout the entire Reform struggle which so racked the other Baptist churches in Clark County, during the years of growth that was shared by most churches, Mt. Carmel did grow steadily but not spectacularly. She occupied a most desirable location in which there were no other churches but the Union Presbyterian with which to compete. The Christian church would not enter the picture until she was mortally wounded. Mt. Zion Methodist and the North Middletown churches were too far away to make serious challenges to the neighborhood. A deed was issued in 1834 by James Stewart to George Priest and Henry (illegible in records) as trustees for a Baptist church.

T. Wright, D. Thomson, T. Green, J. Stewart and R. W. Smith were messengers in 1839, she reported 98 members. A. W. Butler was among the messengers in 1841 and her membership slipped to 91.

In 1842, Alpheaus Lewis was among the membership and the membership reached an all time high of 103. In passing we note that at this time the fact that Lewis conducted one of the better known distilleries of the day, certainly of Clark County, made no difference to the religious forces of this day.

The next Licking Association minutes available were in 1845. Mt. Carmel's membership fell off to 100. These "old" Baptist churches had immensely loyal congregations. One was never an inactive member. Failure to attend church was an expelling offense. If the church was difficult to become a member of, it was also only through death that a congregation really lost members. Of course, occasionally the devil would pick one off...

In 1846, the membership began to slip more, to 98. J. Judy appeared on the messenger list. In 1849, the membership sank to 93. None of these losses are significant. It simply meant that more members were dying than joined the church. Over a decade, the difference would appear serious.

Cholera was raging throughout the country in 1849, but Wades Mill was sufficiently out of the way that the Licking Association was shifted to Mt. Carmel. T. Wright, Alpheaus Lewis, T. Green, T. Terry and E. Jones were the messengers. The membership had slipped to 91. This is normal variation for an "old" Baptist church.

The gap in the Licking Association minutes ends with 1854. Whatever it was that upset Friendship so that she left the association did not seem to effect Mt. Carmel. F. Clendennen, J. Judy, J. Terry and J. Green were the messengers. The membership fell off to 80.

In 1865, there were signs of concern in the Licking Association in that for a few years the name of the association was changed from Particular to "Old". That same concern may have been felt at Mt. Carmel in that her membership was down to 53. J. Terry, F. Clendennen, C. Posten and C. E. Stuart were messengers. The membership continues to shrink. In 1871, it had fallen to 45. Clendennen, W. Lewis, W. Scott, J. Terry and C. E. Stewart were the messengers.

The messengers remain the same combination. It is reasonable to assume that these men were also the deacons and that their families made up the Mt. Carmel Church. In 1883, Mt. Carmel was reporting 32 members. M. B. Haddon and R. Lewis were messengers.

Thomas Dudley began preaching in 1831. He was to the newspapers of Winchester a figure to be admired for old as he was in the 1870s, he was always making his appointments regardless of weather. He also provided them with some interesting history of the 1810-20 and 30 Clark County. But as it must to all things, the end of his ministry came in 1879.

As always, the question of how to replace a long time, able, and much loved minister, even if he had long overstayed his effectiveness, lay before Mt. Carmel. Unlike Goshen which immediately faced secession problems after the death of William Rupard, Mt. Carmel merely continued its slow downward trend. Goshen was in many ways at one of its strongest points when Rupart died. Mt. Carmel was already too far gone to be saved. We have the sad picture of a very large community of excellent farms and two steadily dying churches. Union Presbyterian was the second.

The CLARK COUNTY DEMOCRAT in its May 28 issues reported that H. T. Watson was preaching at Mt. Carmel. Whether this was merely for that coming Sunday or regularly was not reported.

In 1884, with a membership of 37, W. D. Thomson, R. Lewis and C. E. Stuart were messengers. The interesting fact about this delegation was R. Lewis was Negro. The great majority of pre-Civil War Clark County churches had as members Negros, mostly slave. After the Civil War many of these now free members organized their own churches. Some churches, such as Bethlehem continued with large numbers of Negros in attendance until well after World War II. There never was a Negro in any of these churches that had attained any official recognition. Other than identifying him, no comment was made in the minutes. In 1885, Mt. Carmel's membership had dropped to 32 and it sent no Lewis. There is no indication what happened to him. In passing, we should note that the largest church left in the Licking Association had only 40 members.

In 1886, the messengers were W. D. Thomson, M. B. Haddon and W. Lewis. Since the association made no comment, we assume that W. Lewis was white.

The WINCHESTER SUN, February 15, reported that William Rupard preached at the church. The paper reported that April 13, that John G. Adams was preaching at Mt. Carmel and at Upper Howard's Creek Baptist Church as well.

In 1889, A Stevenson, M. L. White and C. E. Stuart were messengers. There were 31 members.

The losses were tragic the next year, 1890. The membership was 14. Perhaps to bolster Mt. Carmel's sagging fortunes, the Licking Association met there in 1890. William Rupard was a welcomed guest and permitted to speak. The association had only ten churches with less than 300 total membership.

Sometime in 1890, the Christians in the community began to stir. Evidently they first started a Sunday school without a minister but with the weekly communion attached. John Snowden among others was a leader in this movement. They met in the Baptist church with full permission of the Baptist. Agreements were worked out between the Baptist and the Christians as to the upkeep of the church.

Evidently the Baptist willingly attended the Christian services and partook of the Christian communion. The Christians cooperated with the association when it met at Mt. Carmel helping with food, housing, etc. There was none of the hostility that erupted between Baptist and Christian in other places.

E. M. Eubank was the minister in 1894. He was from Campbellsburg, Kentucky. He and M. B. Haddon were the messengers. The church now had 18 members. There are no other reports of the Licking Association until 1909. The SUN SENTINEL did report in 1901 that a minister from Pennsylvania was holding services at Mt. Carmel. The news report did not give a name, however. In 1909, the Licking Association of Primitive Baptist met at Mt. Carmel. Eubank was moderator, but he evidently was no longer minister of Mt. Carmel. The association had only nine churches the largest of which had 27 members. The messenger from Mt. Carmel was Nettie Rogers. The church still had 9 members.

The Licking Association again met at Mt. Carmel in 1911. It had started to meet in the Old Baptist Church in Winchester but there was some differences in theological ideas so the site was shifted.

There were traces of the "old" Baptist stand in Mt. Carmel in the Christian church up to the present. The men and women have a strong tendency to sit on different sides of the church in "old" Baptist custom. Most of the Primitive churches have two doors for each of the sexes to enter. Mt. Carmel Christian Church had this until in the 1920s. There was also the custom of slipping the evangelist and sometimes the minister a donation in a handshake. As a younger generation grew more prominent, these old customs grew less discernible. The influence was still felt.

There are several Baptist churches that have appeared very briefly in Clark County history. The East Fork Baptist Church was reported by the North District Association with David Brandenburg as a messenger before 1810. The church was not reported again and much later, Brandenburg changed his membership to Goshen.

Peter Dewitt helped establish the Dewitt Creek Baptist Church. Dewitt is also spelled Jouett, and other than a brief reference in some of the family papers, there is no other information as to what happened to this church.

## THE PRESBYTERIANS

The country that gave Clark County most of its inhabitants was the mountain and sand country of Virginia and North Carolina. Then and now the country named was heavily Presbyterian. Yet, the Presbyterians did not appear in Kentucky in any where near the numbers as were Baptist. The settlers were not, as John Marshall Prewitt of Mt. Sterling in discussing the point suggested, from a class that were largely Baptist. The Boones were originally Quakers. The Bushes were Episcopalians. One does not have too look long at the Scotch and Scotch-Irish names of the settlers to see the heavy infusion of names that normally would be associated with Presbyterians. Add to these a scattering of names that were French Huegenot, one wonders what happened to the Presbyterians. It is true that for some reason the Presbyterians turned up late in Clark County.

The best source for Presbyterian history for the Clark County churches, as we have said is the newspapers. The Presbyterians have had a county history for every church except Ford which was established after the first period of this history was put out, and Mt. Tabor which is more or less out of Clark County's areas. The best historian is Robert Stuart Sanders. He has written "Gleanings from the West Lexington Presbytery, 1799 to 1935," The Ebeneazor Presbytery, 1835 to 1935, and the Lexington-Ebeneazor Presbytery, 1835 to 1950." He also has an unpublished book on the Presbyterian churches in Bourbon County in the special collection library of the University of Kentucky and other places. There are, of course, the minutes of the West Lexington Presbytery at the Louisville Presbyterian Seminary.

Our problem in dealing with Presbyterians in comparison with the Baptist associations, is their lack of Clark County history. The Baptist ministers were for the first hundred years, largely home grown boys, members of local families and ancestors of a great many local people. The Presbyterian ministers until the Civil War were largely outsiders, who lived elsewhere, and came to serve local Presbyterian churches. Even when the Presbyterians had a resident minister he seldom was a native Clark Countian, had lived in the county before serving his particular church or remained when his pastorate was over. This would be the situation of most of the county churches of all denominations after 1900. The Presbyterians showed the pattern of what would be the pattern of ministers in the future.

The Presbytery has authority of local Presbyterian churches. Usually the property of the local church was owned by the Presbytery. There were exceptions. The local Presbyterian church called its desired minister, but the Presbytery must approve the call.

The minister's family may belong to the local church, but the minister's membership was in the Presbytery. When a minister was to leave a church, this also had to have Presbytery approval. Both the call and the leaving were normally approved automatically, but it did lay in the power of the Presbytery to refuse to permit a minister from being fired by his local church. The Presbytery was the court of appeals to which factions of a local church quarrel could appeal their case. The Presbytery had the authority to enforce their decisions. They were responsible to supply a church without ministers, and, from reading of the minutes, the sending of ministers to such churches was much as the Methodist do, but the period would be monthly, with a new arrangement at the next Presbytery meeting. The difference evidently lay in the attitude. The Presbyterians in their supplying of churches were providing a stop gap arrangement rather than a permanent relationship between minister and church.

The Presbyterians always insisted on an educated minister. They flatly refused to compromise. This meant, on the frontier, a chronic shortage of ministers. Whereas the Baptist ministers were often farmers, the early Presbyterian minister inevitably organized a school. Quite often a change of ministers meant not only a new minister for the church, but a new headmaster for the school. This was particularly true of Walnut Hill in Fayette County whose relationship to Clark County resembles Lullbegrud or Boone Creek among the Baptist or Grassy Lick among the Methodist. John Lyle organized a school briefly in Winchester when he served Clark County churches. No one took over his school when he moved. Almost from the beginning of resident ministers for the Winchester Church, the Presbyterians operated a school. Sometimes this school was the Winchester Academy, other times an independent school, but there was nearly always a school.

As this period begins, there were several varieties of Presbyterians in Kentucky, but only one entered Clark County. Therefore, we do not consider the other varieties. There were also several serious divisions among the Presbyterians. In the 1820s, the only one that affected Clark County was the organization of the Cumberland Presbyterians that took place.

The first Presbyterian church in the United States according to Sanders was in 1683. The first Prebytery was assembled in Philadelphia between 1705 and 1706. The synod of Philadelphia was organized in 1716. There were other movements of the various Presbyterians being organized off and on representing the various, largely political divisions, of the Presbyterians in England and Ireland.

William Hickman, a Presbyterian, is given credit for being the first Presbyterian minister in Kentucky. There was a Morton in Harrodsburg soon after. In 1783, David Rice was in Kentucky and organized Mt. Zion and Mt. Pisgah. Walnut Hill was organized a little later, by James Crawford. The Presbytery of Transylvania was organized in 1786. Salem in Clark County was one of the 17 churches with seven ministers in the new Presbytery. A Jeremiah Frame was one of the presiding elders in this Presbytery. The Frames were to be an active family in Clark County.

Transylvania Seminary was established near Danville in 1785 and was moved to Lexington in 1788. This school began its history controlled by the Presbyterians. Henry Toulmin, Garrard's secretary of state and an admitted Universist, gained control of the college, later to be called a University in 1794, but it was back in Presbyterian hands in 1798. It was to remain there more or less for the next thirty years. No other school affected Clark County more during these years than Transylvania.

In the fall of 1786, David Rice, Adam Rankin, Andrew McClure and James Crawford met at the courthouse in Danville. Up to this time the work in Kentucky had come under the Abington Presbytery which in turn was under the Synod of New York and Philadelphia. The Synod had authorized the division of the Abington Presbytery into two organizations, the western one to be called the Transylvania Presbytery. David Rice was moderator. Ruling elders that were present, each church was represented in the Presbytery by one or more elders, were Rupert Steel, David Gray, John Bovil and Joseph Reid. James McClure was clerk. Only Crawford and McClure would play much part in Clark County history though descendents of both lived in Clark County. Jeremiah Frame, a ruling elder, but no mention of church, was seated later on. We do not know where this Frame lived, but the chances of his being related to those of Clark County and Montgomery appears good. Another minister Feral Templain joined the Presbytery.

Templain reported that he was serving churches in Jefferson and Nelson Counties (remember the size of these counties in 1786). Rice was preaching at New Providence and Whitley, McClure at Hanging Fork, Paint Lick and Irving on Stoner Creek. Crawford was also at Paint's Lick (it did not seem to be unusual for two or even three ministers to preach one month at a church), at Hingston, and the North Fork of the Elkhorn. Adam Rankin was at Glen's Creek, Licking and also at the North Fork of the Elkhorn. No locations for these churches that are recognizable today were given. However, by their names some were in Fayette County, some in Bourbon County and perhaps Hinkston was in Montgomery County.

The next Presbytery met in January 1787 at Rice's Fork on Dick's River. Ministers reported their church assignments. None seemed to have been in Clark County. Adam Rankin was preaching two Sundays at Hopewill and Templain one. Hopewell would eventually become Paris. If a minister missed a preaching assignment, he had to give reasons. Ministers evidently changed. In the October Presbytery, 1788, James McClure was preaching four Sundays at Hopewell which is interesting because he was also preaching one Sunday a month at Salem while Adam Rankin was preaching one Sunday a month. Perhaps there were more than four Sundays in a month in those days or perhaps there was an understanding that did not appear in the record.

At any rate, this is the first mention of Salem in Clark County. It was not unusual for a new church not to be reported or to be admitted to the Presbytery until well established. Salem now appears regularly in the minutes, usually being supplied ministers or asking for supplies. When a minister and a church established a relationship where he becomes that church's resident minister, this apparently is assumed and not reported in further Presbyteries until the relationship is changed.

The October 1789 meeting, Paint Lick, Silver Creek, Hopewell, Bashear, Mills Run, Walnut Hill and Ash Ridge requested that communion be held for them. At the same meeting William Scott appealed to the Presbytery from a decision of Mt. Pisgah to remove him as an elder. Apparently he was charged with inviting Baptist to attend the church frequently and even letting Methodist preach. The Presbytery supported the church.

Andrew McClure is preaching at Mt. Carmel and Salem. This is not likely the Mt. Carmel of Clark County which became Baptist. However, there is a possibility that it was. No one available among the Presbyterian sources at the Louisville Seminary seemed to know. There was Presbyterian activity in the Wades Mill area at this time. It was not unusual for several denominations to use the same building and name.

The first Presbytery in 1790 found James Crawford preaching at Salem. Andrew McClure's church requested that he be removed. Whether this included Salem is not clear since what churches McClure was serving at the time were not reported. One of the churches was Sinking Ridge and some twelve members appeared to testify in support of the ouster. None others appeared for his other churches.

The Lexington people petitioned the Presbytery for the right to build a church in Lexington. They stated it was too far for them to go to attend the established country churches. Permission was granted for the October meeting, 1790, found James Crawford serving them two Sundays a month. Whatever the outcome with McClure was not reported, but he was serving Ash Ridge for two Sundays and his standing seemed to be as good as ever. It is presumed that he had a standing appointment for the other Sundays.

The Presbytery reported that David Rice and Templain had attended the General Assembly, being gone three months and received some help from the Presbytery to do so. Meanwhile, the Synod of Virginia which was not the senior body of the Presbytery was sending out missionaries and was collecting money from the churches. For this, a list of churches appeared in the minutes. They were: Forks of Stoner, Sinking Springs, Ash Ridge, Woodford, Bethel, Lain's, Miller's Run, Mt. Pisgah, Jesamine, Walnut Hill, Salem, Silver Creek, Paint's Lick, Lincoln Courthouse, Dix River Fork, Cane Run, Danville, Chaplain's, Jackson on Harden's Creek, Poplar Neck, Penn's Run and Hopewell.

In May of 1791, Mt. Pisgah had trouble with their minister Adam Rankin. The Presbytery agreed that he should go, but suggested that Mt. Pisgah find unity. During 1791 Crawford and McClure were preaching at Salem. Cane Ridge is reported for the first time.

The February 1791, Presbytery recommended fasting as prayer as a primitive Christian effort to find the Holy Spirit. Adam Rankin was tried for what apparently was violation of Presbyterian theology. He withdrew from the Presbytery.

Two interesting things happened in April 1793. A church at Pretty Run Creek requested supplies. This apparently was in Clark County. We referred to the Mt. Carmel Church which was not reported later. This is the second stirring of the Presbyterian effort in this area. At the same time the Presbytery reported that the effort to organize new churches should not weaken the old churches. The minutes continued to say that vacant churches should give evidence when they request a minister that they are willing to support the gospel ministry. They should give the number of families involved, the general characteristics of the society, their membership, the preparation they had to support a ministry and their willingness to contribute.

This was evidently a time when Presbyterians were seeking to organize churches over the entire area. Pretty Run community must have been just one of these. An educated Presbyterian minister, with no other source of income, had to receive support. Failure to do this would mean dire trouble for the minister. Certainly this is logical and evident. On the other hand, at this time, Methodist circuit riders were meeting in cabins, in barns, bush arbors, seven days a week, wherever they could draw four or five people together. Some times they would hold services for a single family. At the same time the Baptist would gather and lacking any other minister would choose one of their own group to preach. How many fledging Baptist and Methodist churches disappeared in the struggle is impossible to say. On the other hand, a few of their impossible situations grew into strong and respectable churches. By this time in Clark County, the Baptist had at least three churches and the Methodist one with two or three preaching points. The Presbyterians now had Salem that was nearly ten years old.

This Presbytery also, for the first time, mentioned a church at Little Mountain. This community would change its name to Mt. Sterling in the next few months.

The October meeting, 1793, reports that a Joseph Howe was received as a minister member of the Presbytery. Evidently, it was Howe that had established Little Mountain. Jacob Fishback was reported minister of the Salem Presbyterian Church.

Howe does not appear again in the minutes of the Presbytery. There is no explanation for this. One wonders whether Howe might not have really belonged to another sect of the Presbyterian movement. Andrew Kinkaid is reported as minister of Little Mountain.

This theory on Howe may have some support for the October Presbytery, 1794, resolved that no church under the Presbytery's care shall make any proposals or understanding with any minister from another Presbytery or from a foreign part for the purpose to settle as their minister, or to take a subscription until authorized by this Presbytery.

We see the problems of a rapidly growing movement which now reached from churches in and around Cincinnati to what is now Louisville, to Washington and almost to the Tennessee line. Such growth meant that orthodoxy was continually being threatened. Men of uncertain ideas and theologies were posing as ministers. Other Presbyterian groups may well have been making raids on the Transylvania churches.

We had also reported in this year that Springfield, which is in the present Bath County, requested permission to build a church.

The January meeting, 1797, accepted the membership transfer of Barton Stone and John Anderson from the Orange Presbytery of North Carolina. Stone was immediately called to serve as full time minister of the Cane Ridge and Concord churches. Anderson's record is not so clearly stated, but his son was to leave the Presbyterians for the Cumberland movement and became one of the more influential and popular ministers of Clark County.

The October Presbytery, 1797, reported that Crawford was giving two Sundays to Salem and A. Howe two Sundays. It is not clear whether this is the other Howe. Initials are different, but this may have been an error. There seems to be reason to believe that they were the same man. If so, the theological differences may have been settled. Also Howe, not only working with Salem, was organizing Sugar Ridge in the western part of the county.

On the whole, these Presbytery meetings are decorously run. There is very little of the scandal that often appeared in Baptist church records, probably since the only members they had trial authority over were ministers. However, in October of 1798, one was accused of having improper relations with a Negro woman. He resigned his church and left the country. This lead to a heated discussion over slavery, which was voted to continue at a later meeting.

The March, 1799, Presbytery divided the now huge Transylvania into three. Clark County ended in West Lexington Presbytery .... West Lexington because there was already a Lexington Presbytery in Virginia. Ministers of the West Lexington Presbytery included James Crawford, Samuel Shannon, Isaac Tull, Robert Marshall, James Blythe, Joseph Howe, James West, Samuel Pennell and William Brice. The other two Presbytery were the Transylvania and the Washington Presbytery.

In 1793, the Presbyterian Church at Mt. Sterling was organized. The next year its minister, Joseph Howe, registered with the county court to marry. Despite the fact that Howe was to serve a lifetime in Mt. Sterling, four years before Montgomery County was established, and later at Sugar Ridge, no marriage ceremonies were ever filed with the county clerk. He must not have bothered to report any of his services. In 1802, the Synod of Kentucky was organized.

The first moderator of the West Lexington Presbytery was James Crawford who was then serving Walnut Hill and Salem. The revival of 1801 and following shook the Presbyterians as it did the Baptist. Being Calvinists which believed more or less in predestination, evangelism was not really satisfactory to the Presbyterian system. The extremes of emotionalism also did not fit with the educated viewpoints of the clergy. However, the pressures were too great, the Presbyterians were forced into revivalism.

This started the new light and old light dispute in the Presbyterian and Congregational Churches, but Clark County was not effected. There were other varieties of Presbyterians besides the one represented by Salem and Walnut Hill. There were Presbyterians that would not sing anything but Psalms; others that were stricter in their Calvinism. However, none of these turned up in Clark County.

Revivalism broke out again between 1825 and 1826, particularly in the form of camp meetings and in the more unemotional form of revivalism sponsored by the Reform Movement of the Campbellites. The Cumberland Presbyterians had arisen out of the earlier revival move, separating from the main body of Presbyterians over educated ministers and evangelism. Campbell called them Methodists with a Presbyterian form of church government. This was not entirely true, but it was so partially. The Cumberland Presbyterians did take one of the Presbyterian churches, Sugar Ridge and turned it into a Cumberland Church. It had been rapidly dying but now it thrived.

In 1839, the old and new school struggle broke out among the Presbyterians causing a division among the Presbytery. Once again, it did not affect any of the churches in Clark County though churches in Bourbon County divided. In 1843, the Campbell and Nathan Rice debate occurred which lasted sixteen days, was moderated by Henry Clay and exacted a great deal of excitement. Rice was an old school Presbyterian. Nothing was gained or lost by the exchange.

The Presbyterians insisted that slavery was not an issue in the old school-new school issue. It just happened that the stronger slave men were old school and the stronger new school men anti-slave.

It was not until 1866 after the Civil War when a Presbyterian minister, R. J. Breckinridge, tried to push resolutions through the Presbyterian national body that were unacceptable to most of the southern churches. Again, this did not disturb Clark County although it did split the Mt. Sterling Presbyterian Church.

Shortly after 1900, the southern Presbyterian and the Cumberland Presbyterians united to form one church. A few of the Cumberland Presbyterians refused to merge, but the majority did. The Sugar Ridge Cumberland Church that had moved to Winchester to become the Washington Avenue Cumberland Presbyterian Church was among those that merged.

Unlike the Baptist which reflected most of the struggles within the Baptist movement, the Clark County Presbyterians represented a reasonably united front against all divisions that occurred in and around her until the last few years.

## SALEM PRESBYTERIAN CHURCH

The history of Salem begins in 1786 as one of the seventeen churches that organized the Transylvania Presbytery. The history of this early period evidently has not been preserved other than references to Salem in the minutes of the Presbytery.

Jacob Fishback, for the history of Salem, is very largely the history of the Fishbacks, first appeared at one of the two preliminary meetings of the Presbyterians in 1785 as a representative, presumedly an elder, of the Fork's of Dix River Church.

He had moved to Clark County in 1787 and had become a member of the Salem Church. He was evidently immediately elevated into position as elder. In the next two centuries,Jacob, Jesse, George Taylor, William, Frederick,Hamilton Fishbacks,George Taylor, Robert Steward Taylor, Senior and Junior and Robert Stuart Taylor, III, all direct descendents of Jacob, were officers in the church.

There are no original membership lists. However, in 1811, Samuel and Susana Hayden, Richard Martin, Suzanna Robinson, Alexander Ritchie, Polly Ritchie, Mrs. Jones (no initial), Jacob and Phoebe Fishback, Andrew Wardlow, William Young, Mrs. William Young, James Young, Sr., Peggy McDonald, Mrs. Esing (no initial), Peggy Wardlow, David and Mrs. Rippy, James and Polly Vance, a total of twenty, were members of Salem. Mrs. Preston, Sally Taylor and Lucy Fishback became members in 1812. Jane Wardlow and Matilda Robertson joined in 1813. Mrs. Couchman, James Stonestreet and Mrs. McDaniel in 1812. George Taylor joined in 1816 and in 1819 Maria Dodge, William Gillespie and Louisa Price. Despite these new members, in 1819 the membership remained at 20. Death and departure took its toll.

The monthly meetings of the Presbyterian Church are called sessions. They are the same as the business meetings of a Baptist church. Salem has minutes that begin in 1819, though the records of membership go back earlier. The original minute book has been placed at the Presbyterian Historical Center at Montreat, North Carolina at the urging of Dr. Sanders. However, the contemporary clerk (1977), F. H. Fishback, has a type-written copy of those minutes. These records come down to 1845 when they stop. No one seems to know what happened to the minutes after that, or even if they were kept. Presumedly they were, but according to Mr. Fishback, there were several fires, and the Civil War, so there is no trace. They were begun again in 1892 and continue to the present.

These minutes are not as voluminous as the Goshen minutes, but they give many intimate details of the church. In 1819, Jacob Fishback represented Salem and the Transylvania Presbytery at the Kentucky

Synod. That year the church gave $7.00 to the commissioner's fund and $8.00 to missions. Apparently there was no opposition to missions as such had appeared among the Baptist and later among the Christians.

It will be necessary at this point to go back and give biographies of the earlier important ministers. None of these men, save for David Lyle, lived in Clark County. Usually they were associated with Walnut Hill.

Andrew McClure was born in Augusta, Virginia in 1755. He had been educated at Liberty Hall which would eventually become Washington and Lee. He was licensed to preach in 1783 and ordained in 1784. He visited Kentucky in 1784 but understandably returned to Virginia. He was back again in 1786 when he organized three churches, Salem, Hopewell and Sinking Springs, the last two in Bourbon County and the Hopewell church would eventually become located in Paris. McClure owned a farm in Clark County on Lower Howard Creek in what is now the edge of the Becknerville community. Despite the farm he moved to Bourbon County where he could be nearer his major churches. He continued to preach off and on at Salem which was not far from his farm in 1787 and even more rarely in 1788 and 1789. He died young, in 1793 at the age of thirty-eight. He willed his farm to his two sons, James Allen and Andrew McClure. His wife was a Rebecca Allen. He set free his slaves at the time of his death which shows the strength of the anti-slave movement at the time.

James Crawford moved into Kentucky in 1784 and organized the church at Walnut Hill in 1786. Walnut Hill was only nine miles from Salam and became sort of the senior partner in ministers for much of Salem's early history. Very early, probably by Crawford, a school was established at Walnut Hill which became one of the best in Fayette County. Sanders says that Crawford, McClure and an Adam Rankin were the ministers at Salem in 1788 and 1789. Besides Crawford and McClure, David Rice and James McConnell served. Rice probably was not much more than a visiting minister.

In 1790 Crawford was minister along with his Walnut Hill. He would be the main minister until 1798, but for several years he shared the pulpit of Salem with Robert Marshall and 1794 with Gary Allen.

Sanders' record shows only Stephen Redding as minister in 1796. However, it was Crawford, Isaac Tull and Joseph P. Howe, the Mt. Sterling minister in 1797. About this time, Howe was establishing the Sugar Ridge Prebyterian Church which may account for his occasional appearances at Salem. In 1798, Crawford was to be the minister of Salem alone. Crawford's health broke in 1798 and he was able to hold on only to Walnut Hill until he died in 1802. Some of his children became residents of Clark County.

In 1800 John Lyle became the minister of Salem and of Sugar Ridge. John Lyle was like almost everyone else in the area, a Virginian from Rockbridge County. He had been born in 1769. His education like that of McClure was at Liberty Hall. He was ordained in 1800 and Salem and Sugar Ridge were his first two churches. Lyle was to become one of the most outstanding of the Presbyterian divines. Like almost all of the Presbyterians he was also a school teacher. For Clark County, his greatest contribution in education was his educating and converting Chilton Allen. The record does not say where his school in Clark County was. The KENTUCKY GAZETTE, June 14, 1804, advertised the first boarding school for girls in Kentucky. In 1804, he wrote, "The New American and English Grammar" which was the first textbook written in Kentucky. He printed it himself being a professional printer. It was to learn printing that Chilton Allen apprenticed himself to Lyle.

During the Great Revival, 1801, revivals were held in and around Salem as well as around Owen Meeting House and Ebenezzor. Lyle's diary carried a very vivid account in which the furor of the people exalted him and their emotional excesses frightened him. However, he liked the results. Sanders says that he leaned toward the Cumberland Presbyterian position but he died in July of 1825 before he had to make any choices.

He married some forty Clark County couples, the first Presbyterian minister to register in the court book. Joseph Howe did not list his denomination. His first was September 2, 1800, Christian Best and Katy Lemon. His popularity in the county, for such a short time he was directly involved in its history, was great.

Lyle moved to Paris where he established one of the first boarding schools for girls west of the mountains. Clark County's school failed to make the records. He did not limit himself to girls, but we find him having apprenticed to him a series of boys to whom he taught printing and book bindery, both of which he did extensively during the first twenty years of the 19th century. At least two of the Kavanaugh boys and Chilton Allen learned from him.

From the WESTERN CITIZEN, April 21, 1810, we note an advertisement announcing the fact that Lyle was giving up the presidency of the Bourbon Academy and was opening another school for boys and girls. in his own home. English would cost $15.00 a year and if taught in connection with grammar, $20.00. If Latin, Greek and the Sciences were added, then the cost would be $25.00. He would be able to board a few students at 28 pounds a year. It is interesting to note the use of both American and English money...as both were still in use in 1810.

Lyle was followed at Salem by Robert Stuart. He was to serve Salem until 1825. Robert Stuart would have to be classed with Robert Elkins and James Quisenberry and perhaps one or two others as one of the most popular early ministers in Clark County. Dozens of Clark

County boys would be named Robert Stuart, or have the Stuart as a middle name in his honor. He married Benjamin Allen to Milly Allen. Despite the fact he never lived in Clark County, he still married seventeen couples. Stuart's base church was, of course, Walnut Hill where he served for forty years. Naturally, he originated in Virginia, also Rockbridge County. He was born in 1772 and was like the other Virginia born Presbyterian ministers educated at Liberty Hall. In 1798, he was teaching ancient languages at Transylvania. He married Francis Hawkins who died in childbirth in 1800. The next year he married Hannah Todd which marriage related him to one of the most powerful families in the Fayette County area.

He served Salem long and faithfully, but Winchester's Presbyterian Church was his major missionary effort. We note that his salary in 1812 was $100.00

The original church was undoubtedly a log cabin on the land belonging to Gay Prewitt. Early church people did not see any reason why they should not own the land on which their churches were placed. Cabins were cheap. Land was available. If there were any difficulties with the landowner, it was a simple manner to move the church. Logs were cheap. Labor was available. It wasn't until the church reached the point of affluence that a permanent, perhaps a brick church, was needed, that the church wanted to own its own land.

It was not until 1825 that Deed Book 20, page 539, reports that Waller and Letitia Preston deeded to George Taylor, James Stonestreet, Jesse Fishback and William Gillespie, trustees of Salem, for one shilling, an acre to be used to build a church. Along with the land went the right to use the adjoining spring. A brick church was built in 1826.

Elders in 1818 included Jacob Fishback, Samuel Hayden, Walter Preston, George Taylor and James Stonestreet. Stonestreet was also clerk of the session. This was not as important a post as the Baptist church clerk, but it was one of the responsible positions within the church. Stonestreet was still a ruling elder in 1841-42. The Synod of Kentucky, in 1821, reported Salem as having 28 members. These would be communing members, those that were eligible to take the sacraments. Walnut Hill in this year had only 37 members. The large churches in the Presbytery were Lexington first with 131 members and Frankfort with 94.

According to the minutes, Armanda Bostick transferred from the mouth of Stoner Presbyterian Church in April of 1824. In November of that year Samuel Hayden died. The area in and around Salem would be called Hayden's Corners until after 1900 when it became Beckner-ville.

Salem went without a called minister for four years after 1825. They received reasonably regular preaching but they were sent in by the Presbytery on a month by month basis and varied with those available. Had Salem been a Baptist church they would have picked one of their own young men, or perhaps a young man of a neighboring church, licensed and ordained him and continued. He may or may not have had much education. This was not the Presbyterian way. They insisted on quality. The Presbyterians felt that no minister was better if a qualified and educated minister was not available. It is this very point that caused the division with the Cumberland Presbyterians. The drain of the city church on the country was evident even at this point. Most of the original Winchester Presbyterian members had been Salem's and no doubt with such a small membership the loss of two or three families hurt. Now in 1825, Samuel D. Fishback was regretfully dismissed. He had been elected an elder in the Winchester Church.

To fill his office, Chiles Coleman was elected a ruling elder. James Stonestreet was chosen to be the elder to represent Salem at the Presbytery and Synod.

During this period, beginning about 1824 and lasting to 1830 were boom years for the Methodists and Baptists. Their churches were growing on all sides. The Sugar Ridge Cumberland Presbyterians also participated in this expansion. However, Salem, refusing to accept the revival as a method of bringing people into the church, did not show such progress. In 1826, she still reported only 28 members.

In April of 1827, the Salem Church was rocked with the charges of unchristian like conduct, drunkenness and abusive language against Walker Preston, one of the church's most important members. Unlike the Baptist, where the trials of members were conducted in the local church, the Presbyterians handled their discipline out of the Presbytery. Samuel Steel, who was then serving the Winchester Church, was appointed the moderator, and the elders of the Salem Church were to set as judge and jury. George Taylor and James Stonestreet did, but Chiles Coleman refused.

The minutes carry an elaborate transcript of the trial giving the full witness of several people. Evidently Preston had imbided too much in hard cider which was not his custom. There was disagreement on how much he had taken. His Negros, presumedly slaves, were working in the field under the supervision of Thomas Blanton. Blanton was taking it easy when Preston came and found him. An argument followed in which there was a great deal of shouting, some pushing and Preston threatened Blanton.

Preston was found guilty of unchristian like conduct, but was forgiven at his request. He continued as an elder in the church without any apparent disharmony.

July of 1827, Salem contributed $13.16 1/4 to the American Colonization Society. This was a favorite project of Henry Clay and was designed to return slaves to Africa. Liberia was started and a number of slaves were sent back to Africa where their descendents still make the backbone of the country. Salem's interest in the movement demonstrates the uneasiness of the Kentucky conscience. Salem's members were among the country's larger slaveholders. However, the anti-slavery feeling that had reached a peak in the late 1810s was beginning to die.

Eighteen twenty-seven was also a more successful, if not spectacular year for membership. In September the church received seven new members including Dorcas, a "woman of color". Dorcas was the only Negro reported member of the Salem though Negros were members of most of the Baptist and Christian churches of the time. Salem reported 31 members.

Dorcas did not remain a member long. The next year she, along with James McCall, Mary Elliott and Susan Tuttle were dismissed. The record does not give the reason but evidently they had moved. The unsettled conditions caused a constant drain of members. They caused Salem more of a problem than larger churches simply because they were so hard to replace. A few came back into the church. Betsy Fishback transferred from Boone Creek Baptist Church. This was a neighborhood Baptist church, just over the county line. Betsy had just married into the family and had gone to her husband's church. She was accepted without condition from the Boone Creek Church. Henry Venerable also joined the church, transferring from the Danville church though he moved out again within a year.

Stuart returned to Salem between 1829 to 1831. His ability immediately became apparent. Salem's membership rose to an all time high of 40 members. It must be remembered that Salem is located between Ebeneazor Methodist Church and several Baptist churches using the same building at Boone Creek. Both these churches had strong revivalistic approaches to religion. For some reason this year, Clark County including Salem were transferred to a new Presbytery, Mt. Tabor. Whether this had anything to do with Stuart again leaving Salem is not clear. Saunders lists Salem as without a minister for three years. Mt. Tabor Presbytery records show an Armond Hinkley as stated supply minister for this period. Mt. Tabor was again reunited with the West Lexington Presbytery. Between 1834 and 1835, Salem's minister was Samuel Wilson. Wilson married Albert G. Craig to Virginia Brockry in 1834. He had nine county marriages. Salem reported 38 members in 1835 and 41 in 1836.

The steady movement of membership continued. In 1832, James Preston moved to Boone County. Elder James Anderson of Winchester's church transferred to Salem and was promptly elected elder. It was obvious that Salem felt they had won a victory over their offspring in Winchester. Unfortunately, Anderson moved again, in 1834, this time to Georgetown.

Jesse Fishback and James Taylor were elected deacons in 1833.

There was another flurry of trouble in 1833 when Charles Fishback appeared before the session and confessed drunkedness and his repentence. This was in the same manner that the Baptist of the period conducted their trials of erring members. Fishback repented and was received back into the fellowship.

In September's session meeting, 1833, the church reported 46 members. Evidently Salem benefitted by the Campbellite battles. She had lost several members earlier to Mt. Zion as it declared itself to be a follower of the Reform movement. Mt. Zion was a Baptist church that had been organized in the middle '20s in the Hayden Corner community not far from Salem. It represented a more liberal element of Baptist, those who called themselves Reformers and preached a Christian union of all denominations on the basis of a simple (theirs) interpretation of the Bible. Mt. Zion, like Winchester's Friendship Baptist, went intact to the Reformer movement. There were evidently several families in Mt. Zion who preferred coming to Salem Presbyterian than going to what was left of the Boone Creek Baptist Church.

In 1833, Salem's giving consisted on $14.62 1/2 for missions, $5.00 for commissioner, $4.81 1/2 for ministerial education and $1.75 for contingency fund.

That year had the usual transfer of membership. We have reported Anderson moving to Georgetown, in June Rachel Goodwin transferred to First Presbyterian in Lexington. Walter Preston died in August. The next year Amanda Combs moved to Missouri and Chiles Coleman and family moved to Boonesboro. In 1839, J. S. Tracy moved to Missouri with his family and James Herron moved to Ohio. The once golden hope of Kentucky was not a stopping ground for those that wanted more. Jesse Fishback died this year. The minutes give us the baptisms, the deaths, the comings and the goings.

After 1836, there was a nine year period when Salem once again, according to Saunders, had no minister. In reading the reports in the Year of the Synods Salem was listed without a minister, but listed under Winchester's Presbyterian Church who had a minister at this time named Daniel Baker. Apparently Baker had some supervisory position over Salem, perhaps to help with funerals and marraiges, to occasionally help with special services and to keep some form of ministry available. The Presbytery minutes are not available for this period at the Louisville Seminary. In 1839, George McElroy became Winchester's minister and apparently continued the relationship with Salem. The same relationship existed between Sugar Ridge Presbyterian Church at Winchester. From other information, Sugar Ridge (not the Cumberland Presbyterian Church which was thriving) was not in operation despite being carried on the record books. This was a period of struggle in the Presbyterian church between the Old and New School factions. It may well have been a low period in Salem's history. The minutes report 36 members during this period.

William Y. Allen served the church between 1843 and 1844. He married Sarah Stonestreet, Jacob Fishback's granddaughter. J. J. Bullock was minister between 1848 and 1853. He was appointed

Kentucky's first superintendent of education by James Clark. W. B. Brown was minister from 1855 to 1857. J. M. Scott was minister between 1858 and 1863. We note that William Allen married Solomon Van Meter to Elizabeth Stonestreet, December 21, 1842. He had no other Clark County marriages. However, he may have been serving Salem before the date that Saunders assigns to him, perhaps as a stated supply. J. M. Scott married Richard Jefferies and Elizabeth Smith, November 27, 1856, which indicates that he was in the county before officially becoming minister for Salem. He was also minister in Winchester.

The Jefferies-Smith wedding was performed in the county clerk's office which hints at some kind of a different story. There are perhaps a dozen such marriages and usually indicates haste, problems and perhaps even a little threat of danger...and certainly of romance. He had ten other marriages during his time in Clark County.

George Fishback was elected an elder in 1841. In 1843 George Fishback became clerk. There were only 22 members. The notes reported that in this year $40.00 and a $5.00 bill on the defunct Bank of the U.S. was given for missions. In 1843, in May, Solomon Van Meter joined Salem. At this point the minutes ended until 1892.

Ezekial Foreman bought the Walnut Hill School in 1865 and was called to the church. It would be interesting to discover the exact relationship between the school and the Walnut Hill Church where a new minister would be called to one and bought the other. Did they have to go together, or could a minister take one and reject the other? Foreman also became minister of Salem.

Foreman performed a wedding ceremony for William Sensmith and Anna Fishback, June 13, 1866; this was the second church wedding performed in Clark County. This is a surprising fact. All previous marriages were done either at homes    , or clerk's office, stores, hotels, etc. The idea of marrying in a church was new. The first church wedding was October 12, 1865, when J. W. Fitch married McElroy Kohlass and Patricia Lowe Nicholas in the Winchester Methodist Church.

With the war over, Salem faced serious problems. She was now off the main road, off on a side road that led nowhere. George Fishback and Robert Stuart Taylor were the elders. Jacob Hughs, who was not a professing Christian, gave the land. In 1870, a new brick church was built and the old church passed into the hands of the Negro Baptist. Foreman left in 1872 and in 1875, was followed by the extremely interesting E. O. Guerrant. Guerrant remained minister for only a year, and served just as briefly the new Ford Presbyterian Church and the new Mt. Tabor Church before he left the county. As a minister he never again served in a Clark County church, but as a Presbyterian leader his influence was great. Later, his son was to establish a hospital in Winchester.

Guerrant was born in what became Bath County and had been educated for a doctor. However, when the Civil War came, he joined Morgan's cavalry and eventually became Morgan's adjutant. He rode the hill country on the repeated sweeps that Morgan made out of Tennessee and was deeply impressed by the needs and the poverty of the area. After the war, he went to Union Seminary in Richmond and was ordained. The Clark County churches were his first experience in the ministry. He was later to serve Mt. Sterling and help with the new Clark County churches of Ford and Mt. Tabor. Querrant went on to become minister of the First Presbyterian Church in Louisville and became the evangelist for the Presbyterian church in Kentucky. As such he established a series of medical, educational and child care centers, mostly along the railroad that ran from Winchester to Jackson and along the spurs that reached into the back country.

Meanwhile, Salem called E. E. Irwin between 1870 and 1880 for one of the sad sweet romances of Salem. He married soon after he came to Salem a beautiful girl to whom he was devoted. She died while he was at Salem and he left the church broken hearted.

Once again, Salem's ministry became erratic. The CLARK COUNTY DEMOCRAT on March 17, 1887, reported that L. R. Bridges was the minister. Services were held on the 1st and 3rd Sundays. J. P. DeVault, according to Saunders, also served in 1887. W. D. Cooper became minister in 1889 to 1891 following DeVault, both ministers tried to work out a parish by combining Mt. Tabor, Ford, the Clintonville Church and Salem.

Salem's records begin again in 1892. M. V. C. Yearman was the minister. James E. Battaile, R. Stuart Taylor and J. G. Lyle were elders. The next year the Synod's evangelist held a series of meetings (the Presbyterians preferred the words Protracted Meeting to Revival) at Salem. He was J. S. Stopper and he was most successful. Sixteen united with the church by confession and five transferred by letter. Rutherford Douglas was called for half time in 1894. He was paid $300.00 a year. J. G. Lyle was the clerk. In October of 1895, Douglas resigned to go to the Nicholasville Presbyterian Church.

The next year Salem had supplies, a William Crowe and others. In April of 1896, a W. F. Jenkins, who had just graduated from the seminary, was called with the understanding that Jenkins had applied to become a missionary in China. July of 1896, he was accepted and left the church. October of that year, W. D. Cooper was called. He was to remain until 1903 serving both Salem and Mt. Tabor.

The records show Salem paying foreign missions in 1898 $10.00, Home Missions received $3.00 and local missions received $225.00. This was about what Salem was raising for causes throughout these years. In 1900, another evangelistic service was held with five confessions and one transfer by letter. R. D. Taylor and J. G. Lyle were elected elders and D. J. Tevis and J. E. Fishback became deacons.

The West Lexington Presbytery met at Salem in 1901. This is the only record of the Presbytery meeting at Salem.

Cooper resigned in 1901. He seemed to be well liked, and there was no reason given for his resignation. He was called back to Salem in the next session and did return until 1903 when he accepted a church in Florida.

S. S. Saunders became minister from 1904 to 1905. Saunders would hold a place of influence in Salem's history until his death. W. M. Eldridge became minister in 1906 to 1908. He often supplied Salem. He was 97 years old when he preached last and was so blind that Dr. R. E. Fishback had to read the scripture.

In 1904, W. E. Fishback was elected elder. R. G. Wallis and Dr. R. E. Fishback became deasons. W. E. Fishback became clerk.

We have again the pattern of student ministers coming from seminary and leaving in a few years to larger work. The same pattern effected all the other churches with much the same results. In 1910 the Salem minister was H. H. Cassidy.

The Presbyterian movement in the county reached a low ebb in the next few years. The Ford Presbyterian Church which had begun so promisingly died with the town. Mt. Tabor grew steadily weaker and finally passed out of existence. The Clintonville Church died, the Union Presbyterian Church was staggering and Salem reached a low stage.

To save the day, William Cummings, the minister of the Presbyterian Church in Winchester, stepped into both Salem and Union. Commings had held a meeting for Salem in 1904 and had contacts with the church. He started serving Salem as minister from 1914 to 1919. Services were in the afternoon. Cummings was a very able man. To him, Salem was important and not a burden as Ebeneazor was to the Methodist city ministers. Salem responded. If she did not grow robust, at least she grew and stayed alive. In 1917 to 1921, the minister was J. S. Hagin.

Saunders also gives a list of elders and deacons but no dates. The elders were Hugh Martin, Jacob Fishback, Samuel Hayden, Walter Preston, George Taylor, James Stonestreet, Robert Stuart Taylor, Chiles Coleman, James Anderson, George Taylor Fishback, James Battaille, Joseph Glass Lyle, Robert Stuart Taylor (we presume this is a son), William Alexander Moore, Garrett Weathers, Frederick Fishback, Robert S. Taylor, J. A. Stewart. The decaons were Jesse Fishback, James F. Taylor, Robert Cunningham, Squire Turner Tevis, W. E. Fishback, Robert G. Wallis, Robert T. Fishback, Charles Marshall, Scott Wencher. Some of the elders were deacons before being elevated to the higher position.

There is not as good a reason to drop the history of Salem at 1921. With the Baptist and the Methodist, 1920 represented a valley in the life of rural churches. This was true of all denominations. The Primitive Baptist were dying all over the county or had been dead for a few years. The Missionary Baptist were just about at their weakest though it might get even a little worse in the next two decades. The Methodist rural churches were weaker in the early 1920s than any other time. A later section will show the same thing true of the Christian churches. The bad times continued for rural churches until World War II. However, with the end of the 1930s and after 1930, both the Baptist and Methodist churches show a steady increase in strength. To some degree, so will the Christian rural churches though by no means as much as the Methodist and Baptist.

However, the Presbyterians do not show the same up grade. Of the four rural churches, Salem, Mt. Tabor, Union and Ford, only Salem was to survive. There were reasons that probably could not have been avoided at Ford. Add to the fact that First Presbyterian Church in Winchester shows a stable, but relatively the same membership from 1900 to World War II and after extremely able ministers, and the slow disintegration and final merger of the Washington Street Presbyterians, questions must be raised.

It is obvious that the Becknerville area of Clark County, though a wealthy and fertile agricultural area, did not produce strong churches. Salem's neighbor, Mt. Zion Christian Church, is also a small and struggling rural church. In passing, we note that the Negro churches in the area also struggled and finally died. The neighborhood is not really strong enough to support two churches though later history will show that under certain circumstances, a very good program can be run at Salem. The problem lies in Salem's inability to reach down from the landowner groups to the tenant. It is complicated by the tendency of the landowners and the new suburban dwellers to place their membership in the town churches. Over the years the very backbone of both Salem and Mt. Zion would prefer to let the country church wither in favor of the city.

Is this bad? It certainly leaves large areas of the county where many families will not go to the city churches and have no contact with the neighborhood churches, the tenant families particularly. There is an increasing number of rural families that are not being churched by anyone. The land owning families desire a different type of church and will not give the leadership to the rural churches that is necessary for them to develop the kind of organization and program that will be effective.

There are also some problems that are particularly Presbyterian. The insistance on educated ministries makes an excellent theory, but in the case of Salem, it becomes obvious that there would be years between ministers. A church cannot thrive on such intermittant ministry. Both the Methodist and Baptist churches found answers to the problem after 1920 in different ways. The Christians were slower in finding answers.

The problem of student ministers appear at Salem as it does with the Methodist, Baptist and Christians. These young men must begin somewhere. They are in the price range of the churches they serve. Some of them are extremely good. On the whole, however, the churches do not do well under them.....or at least not as well as they did in the days where they were served by the great old country preachers. However, shifting to the other side of the argument, the days when a Stuart (Presbyterian) or a McGarvey (Christian), or French (Baptist) can stand up in a pulpit and preach and little else and can build a church are over. A church needs more than a preaching service.

There is also something in the Calvinistic approach that is difficult to present to the mass of people. It draws a certain type of intellect who appreciates its intellectual value, its dignity, its culture. It does not seem to attract the rank and file.

We will leave the history of Salem from 1920 to the present for another volume.

The history of Salem Presbyterian Church has from the very beginning been deeply involved with the Fishback family. Willis Miller Kemper's "Fishback History" gives information on several of the Fishbacks that played considerable part in the history of Clark County. They were not confined just to the Presbyterian movement. However, being close to the Fayette County lines, their ties were often closer to Lexington and Fayette County than to Winchester.

Jacob Fishback was born in Virginia in 1749. In 1771 he married a Phoebe Morgan who may have been distantly related to the Morgans of the Boone family. This again would indicate the inter-marriage of the frontier families. He first moved into east Tennessee about the same time the Bush church did, but instead of coming straight to the Clark County area he moved in 1783 to the Dix River country. Being Presbyterian, he joined David Rice's Cane Run Church that had just been organized as one of the first Presbyterian churches in Kentucky. In 1787 he moved to Clark County and settled in the area which later would be called Hayden's Corners and even later Beckner-ville. In 1806, he built a log house with black walnut and white ash. The house was expanded in 1836. He helped establish Salem and was a stern, unyielding Presbyterian elder who refused to visit even his brother-in-law on the Sabbath. He worked closely with each Presbyterian minister who served his church. He was trustee of Transylvania from 1801 to 1807. He had 11 children. Sick with rheumatic pains, he writes that he was alone having sent his family to church (February 1821) and wished that he could be there. He died in September of 1821. His wife Phoebe died in 1837 of an infected mole on her face......cancer.

Jacob had been active in farming. He supported Aaron Burr and Henry Clay both of whom visited his house... Clay often. He had been the foreman of the Federal Grand Jury that had dismissed charges against Burr in Lexington.

James Fishback was active in the establishing of the Boone Creek Association and the Kentucky Bible Society. He eventually went with the Reformers to establish the Christian Church. During the 1830s, James held a correspondance debate with Alexander Campbell in the Millinenger Harbinger.

James Fishback was a brother to Jacob. He had been born in Virginia in 1776. His brother having moved to Clark County, James joined him in 1787. In 1793-94, he attended Transylvania and the next year to the Presbyterian school at Pisgah. He began to practice medicine in Fayette County and his section of Clark County. In 1800 he returned to Virginia where he married Dorothea Christian whose mother had been a sister to Patrick Henry. He returned to Kentucky in 1801 and settled in Lexington. He taught at Transylvania in 1805 and was in the state legislature in 1808. During this period he was Presbyterian. As early as 1810, he was restless and became a Baptist joining Ambrose Dudley's Town Fork Church. He was anti-slavery and became involved in a quarrel that split that church and for a while, became a member of First Baptist. He was ordained by First Baptist as a minister. He was practicing medicine during all this period. He served the Mt. Vernon Baptist Church in Woodford County for a while. He had read Barton Stone as early as 1815 and was deeply impressed. He was even more impressed by Alexander Campbell and may have been converted to the Christian church by him. However, he remained in the Baptist church largely because of Campbell and the debate with John Walker concerning the Law and the Old Testament.

## SUGAR RIDGE PRESBYTERIAN CHURCH

The present Ecton Road roughly parallels the Mt. Sterling-Winchester Road. Between these two roads there is a very large ridge, broad on top and flanked by two broad valleys that is called Sugar Ridge. This ridge belonged to what we have called the Stoner settlement and was settled by Ramseys and others. The original road from Winchester ran down the very center of the ridge. There is still a road up there that dead ends and serves two or three families. Sometime before the Civil War, for reasons unknown it was dropped off the ridge into the valley and there the toll road was built. Even with the road on the lower levels, the ridge road continued until sometime in the 1870s when it became virtually a driveway for a few families and the church.

Sometime before 1800, perhaps even as early as 1796, Joseph Howe who had established the Presbyterian Church in Mt. Sterling in 1793 was working among the Scotch Presbyterians that inhabited the high hill. This part of Clark County had about as many ties with Mt. Sterling as with Winchester and had been desired by the early Montgomery supporters to be part of the new county.

Howe found a logical place to organize a church that would help build a powerful Presbyterian movement in the area. It was about the same time that Goshen was organizing. The Baptist had Providence, Unity and Friendship. The Methodist had the Owen Meeting House. Salem Presbyterian was ten years old. The Presbyterians were behind in the race, but not hopelessly so. It is presumed that Howe preached there until 1800. Howe was the first Presbyterian to register for the right to marry in Clark County. Saunders says that he had fifty eight marriages, but none of these were ever listed in Clark County records. They may be in Montgomery's.

In 1800 John Lyle became the minister of Sugar Ridge. In 1802, the revivalism that began at Cane Ridge spread all over the country. There were revivals both at Salem and at Sugar Ridge. Lyle's diary tells of meetings in 1801, 1802 and 1803. The 1802 meetings were in and around Sugar Ridge particularly. Lyle tells of three days of excitement. He was shocked at the disorder of the meetings, how preachers would be shouting while the congregation would be talking and laughing in private conversations...and he was appalled at the emotionalism that also appeared. He noted the disorder when boys built fires at a distance from the meeting and threw rocks at passers-by. Lyle noted that Mr. Crawford was hit. Delinquency has always been a problem. A. C. Hanks and Wright, Lyle did not know the first name, caught a couple in a barn. They thought they were man and woman in a lewd act, but they turned out to be men asleep. It is not hard to understand the Presbyterian reaction to revivalism, but at the same time, Lyle indicated he was impressed with the results.

Sugar Ridge Presbyterian Church was received into the West Lexington Presbytery in 1803. It probably had been organized for several years before this. Howe was followed by John Lyle who lived in Winchester while he served Sugar Ridge and Salem. Saunders said that Lyle founded the Bourbon Academy after leaving Winchester. Isaac Toll became minister from 1806 to 1810. Howe returned for a year and then between 1813 and 1815, William Martin. Martin became one of the most popular ministers in the county. The records show that he was fifth in the number of marriages during the first sixty to seventy years. James Quisenberry, Edward Kindred, Robert Elkins and William Morris marrying more people. His first marriage was James Gholston to Rebecca Dooley, November 14, 1814. He had one hundred and seven marriages in the county, yet very little has appeared in the records concerning him.

Deed Book 7, 1805, records that James Fowler gave to John Ramsey and John McKee for five pennies, a lot for the Presbyterian Church on Sugar Ridge. According to William Landrum some two decades later, they built a log hewn church that also doubled for a school. Sugar Ridge had one of the first continually run schools in the county. In 1817, Howe and Martin shared Sugar Ridge in a manner that was distinctly Presbyterian. As the minutes of the Presbytery reveal, the objective was to give each church at least two services a month, but it was quite common on the smaller church to divide those services between ministers. The double ministry would be a sign that the church was not doing well. Howe returned for a single ministry between 1818 and 1823. He was growing old and most of his attention was given to the Mt. Sterling Church. He had other preaching points at Springfield and in what is now Sharpsburg. His energies were running thin.

Cabel Harrison was the minister in 1824, but the church was slipping again. It was surrounded by three churches, Goshen, Lullbegrud and Bethlehem Baptist Churches that were aggressive and active. This was at a period when the Reformers were more or less accepted by the old Baptist and the division had not yet become serious. The Baptist churches were growing. The Presbyterians were simply not able to compete against that kind of pressure. The next year, Harrison, James Blythe, of the law department of Transylvania University, and Robert Shaw divided the responsibilities of Sugar Ridge. There was no minister listed for 1825. Meanwhile the Cumberland Presbyterian movement came to Clark County and found a home among Sugar Ridge's Presbyterians.

The old church continued. By this time the Winchester Presbyterian Church was growing and active. It had taken some of Sugar Ridge's membership but not many. Most of her members had originally been either Salem or unattached Presbyterians moving into the county.

The National Assembly's year book began statistics in the last years of 1820, but it is not until 1831 that Sugar Ridge is listed. In 1831, two licensees, James P. Trotter and A. W. Campbell, lived in Winchester or at least had a Winchester post office. Without naming the churches, one was reported with 70 members presumedly Winchester's Presbyterian and another 20 which would probably be Sugar Ridge. The next year, however, Trotter being listed as supply, Sugar Ridge was given 15 members.

No ministers were listed for Sugar Ridge until 1834 when William D. Young and the next year Luther H. Van Doren were listed as supply. In each case Sugar Ridge was reported with only 15 members. Alexander McKinney was listed as minister in 1837. This is the last year that Sugar Ridge appears in the statistics. The next year Union Presbyterian Church replaced it. It is reasonably certain that for all practical purposes, Sugar Ridge Presbyterian Church had been dead for ten years. There may have been an occasional meeting after that, but little effort to run a church.

William Landrum reported that the "old" Presbyterians had died out. By 1827, the Cumberland Presbyterians were in possession of the building and had a thriving and active church. There is no record of what happened. In 1826, Caleb Weedon was called by the Sugar Ridge Church as minister. Even at the time he was connected with the Cumberland Presbytery instead of the West Lexington. Already the division between the Cumberland Presbytery and West Lexington was developing.

James McCready came to Kentucky in 1896 and settled in Logan County. McCready and many other Presbyterians, as with Lyle in Clark County, were deeply impressed by the revival, by the evangelical methods used by the Methodist and Baptist, and strongly felt that the Presbyterians would have to follow suit. McCready also was ready to face up to the second problem of the Presbyterians in 1900, that was the supply of ministers.

David Rice, not a supporter of revivalism, nevertheless, saw the need for ministers and recommended taking serious young men and training them for the ministry. They would obviously not have the education desired, but they would hold the breach until the Presbyterians had developed their schools, which included Translyvania at this time, to meet the need. This was done in some of the Presbyteries. It was also criticized strongly by other Presbyteries. Some of these Presbyteries would refuse to give standing to men they felt did not meet their qualifications despite their standing in their parent prebytery.

The result was the organization in 1810 of the Cumberland Presbytery. Like many such organizations, there was no effort in the beginning to establish a new movement. However, the Cumberland Presbyterians also adopted the new revivalism, particularly the holding of camp meetings, to their use. The result was a new movement that was distinctive American. Another distinctive American, that is born on this side of the ocean, was the Disciples of Christ. Alexander Campbell described the Cumberland Presbyterians in the second volume of the Millinial Harbinger as a Methodist movement with a Presbyterian form of government.

The WINCHESTER DEMOCRAT, August 20, 1894, reporting the completion of the Washington Street Cumberland Presbyterian Church gave the history of Sugar Ridge. The Cumberland Presbyterian ministers might not have been up to the educational level of the orthodox Presbyterians, but they were still considerably higher than the educational level of the rest of the denominations. The pressure on those that fell below an acceptable level to get more education was considerable. Therefore, the Cumberland Presbyterians felt a shortage of ministers despite everything. To help correct that shortage, like the Methodist, the Cumberland Presbyterians resorted to the use of circuit riders who rode from one point to another, holding services in churches, school houses, bush arbors, homes, wherever a few people could gather together. Among these the DEMOCRAT listed were Labin Jones, Daniel Trauber, Caleb Weedon and Jesse Anderson Landrum reported he held meetings, day and night.

In 1826, it was Caleb Weedon that was called to the Sugar Ridge Church that marked the beginning of its adherence to the Cumberland Presbyterians. The call was not unanimous. A Mr. Skinner objected but evidently almost at once, the church became a center of revivalism as it well might holding the middle ground between the two strongholds of Calvinism Lullebgrud and Goshen Baptist Churches. They established an annual camp meeting that drew people, not just from the community, b t from all over Clark and Montgomery Counties and for a time revived the most famous of the Methodist camp meetings. There were extremely successful revivals in 1827 and 1840 that brought Sugar Ridge's membership close to 200 and made it the strongest Presbyterian church in the county.

Part of the success of Sugar Ridge can be assigned to its minister of long duration, Jesse Anderson, who had begun his ministry in the West Lexington Presbytery and had been won to the Cumberlands. He began riding circuit for the Cumberland Presbyterians about 1826 and included Sugar Ridge in his territory after Caleb Weedon moved elsewhere. July 6, 1837, he married J. V. Ramsey and Matilda Capp which pretty well dates his first full year at Sugar Ridge. He served the church off and on for the next thirty six years carrying him well into the post Civil War years. He was one of the most popular ministers in the county marrying more than 150 Clark County couples during his lifetime.

Sugar Ridge was one of Landrum's favorite stays. He taught school there in the late 1820s and often visited and would be invited to preach each time there was an available opening. He preached at Sugar Grove Saturday, July 1, 1831 while attending one of their camp meetings. He stayed that night with John Ramsey. In 1833, he again attended Sugar Ridge and heard ministers names Jones, Corley and Mullins. That night he stayed with Lucas Hood whose wife was a mainstay in the Grassy Lick Methodist Church. Between Weedon and Anderson was a John M. J. Cosley. In 1842, Landrum was again at Sugar Ridge to a camp meeting where men named Noel, Jones and Thompson preached. That night he stayed with Alexander Ramsey.

The library at the Presbyterian Seminary had only a few of the records of the Cumberland Presbyterians and no statistics.

The Deed Book 32, 1845, reports that John W. Redmon gave to James Ramsey, James Stevenson, Joseph Ramsey and Senaca Clark a lot on Sugar Ridge which runs through the old building and includes the cemetery. The lot will revert back to the estate if the church is disbanded. Access must be furnished it if the road for any reason is moved. A new building was erected in 1848.

One source reports John Redmon as minister in 1845. Franklin H. Ramsey and Senaca Clark were elders. Other ministers, presumedly in order were: Gregory Peck, Sterling Thomas, Ethan Hamblin, R. B. McGough, R. P. Rowe and J. H. Tanner, who served for seven years.

One problem that the Sugar Ridge people had was to find ministers who could also find other Cumberland Presbyterian churches close enough to give a reasonable parish situation. Again, it must be remembered that ministers were not expected to make parish calls, carry youth programs or have community positions such as the president of Kiwanis. Both Baptist and Christian ministers often served churches fifty miles apart. This, however, was not the usual situation. It was more common among the Christians than the Baptist among whom Mt. Olive and Providence would be served by the same minister, etc. The nearest Cumberland Presbyterian Church was in Mt. Sterling or a little beyond. It was not a strong church however, and died before Sugar Ridge. Being part of a parish that would give a Cumberland Presbyterian minister enough to survive on was always Sugar Ridge's problem after Anderson's passing. J. B. Green followed Anderson and then J. A. Ramsey and B. L. Patterson. Unfortunately, there are no dates. Landrum reported that Sugar Ridge was a strong church after the Civil War.

A Ladies Missionary Circle was operating in 1880 with Mrs. George Fry as president. At this date the only other such circle or women's group was at First Presbyterian Church in Winchester. A list of elders that had held office prior to 1894 when Sugar Ridge moved into Winchester were: Samuel Stevenson, Leonard Harmon, Joseph and Samuel Ramsey, John L. Fry, Archeleus Tanner, Franklin Watts, David Butler, Ryland D. Ramsey, James W. Turner, W. H. Ramsey, M. A. Gardner, Dr. M.S. Browne and John M. Bush. One can presume that these elders are more or less in order of their service.

The CLARK COUNTY DEMOCRAT reported B. F. Patton was minister in 1887 and that Sugar Ridge also had a Sunday school that was held before church services on the 2nd Sunday. Patton left the church in 1889.

There is no list of deacons, but the WINCHESTER SUN in 1885 reported that R. W. Tanner was a deacon in connection with another story.

The last country minister of Sugar Ridge was C. B. Clark who began his ministry in 1889. While serving the church he married Etta R. Tanner. January of 1894, he resigned in order to go to medical school.

The Sugar Ridge Presbyterians increasingly felt their isolation. The new pike had been built along the valley. The road to the church was abandoned beyond the church and the county did little or nothing to keep up the part of the road that was used. As with the other denominational rural churches, problems were increasing.

The old Baptist had already begun to feel the pinch. It was apparent with both Baptist and Christian churches. The rural climate was changing. Landowners were beginning to look toward towns for education, social contacts and religious outlets.

By 1890, more than half the membership of Sugar Ridge lived in or close to Winchester. There was no Cumberland Presbyterian church in Winchester. Winchester was booming. It was felt that if Sugar Ridge moved to Winchester it could grow into an effective church.

There followed a whirlwind of activities, mostly money raising, on the part of the Sugar Ridge people. This belongs really to the history of the Washington Avenue Church. The DEMOCRAT in April, 1899, reported the decision to move. It reported that Sugar Ridge would be sold. It was built forty years ago. The officers of the two churches were the same. There was no dissention. M. S. Browne bought the old building. The lot was sold to Preston Broughton for $325.00, J. W. Tanner bought the organ. The chandeliers, reportedly quite elaborate for a country church, pews and other furniture were bought by a committee from the Owen Chapel.

For some reason the building was resold in 1902 to J. W. R. Smith. So ended another church with a long history of service. Was the move successful? Why was it that Washington Street Presbyterian Church was able to employ a full time minister while the country church of about the same membership was not? Could Sugar Ridge have moved out on the paved road, as did Providence, Log Lick and half dozen other churches, and survived? If they had and a church had also been started in Winchester, could both of them have survived? The split in Goshen showed that it could not. However, First Baptist survived with a dozen churches in the rural areas. Ebeneazor of the Methodist lived three quarters of a century after the Winchester Methodist Church was established and died more by mishandling and perhaps even deliberate murder on the part of the Winchester Methodist, than by natural causes.

There is something sad about the reporting of finish to a church.

## FIRST PRESBYTERIAN CHURCH

Micah Taul reported that there was a Quaker Church in Winchester prior to 1810. R. J. Cotterill, in the February 16, 1915, WINCHESTER DEMOCRAT, gives a long description of the Winchester community after 1812 and casually mentions that he lost his overcoat in the Friends Meeting House. (Cotterill was not alive at the time of the newspaper article.) These two reports are the only record of a Quaker Meeting in Clark County. By 1815 it had disappeared and was largely forgotten.

Therefore, it is justified for the Presbyterians to claim that First Presbyterian Church was the first church in Winchester. It is a mistake to think of Winchester in any sense like the Winchester of the modern day. At this time Winchester had less than two hundred people of whom a third were Negro. These people came from the families of surrounding neighborhoods and on Sunday they would not hesitate to ride (carriages were still few and far between) back to their home church for a family reunion. The Methodist had two churches on either side of Winchester with the Winchester Methodist largely going to Ebeneazor. The Baptist had a church a mile or so out of town toward Strode Station, Friendship. Others would drive the longer way to Providence. Winchester was largely made up of the Bush-Quisenberry-Hampton-Haggard community. The Presbyterians had Sugar Ridge and Salem, both of these churches tended to look the other way, Sugar Ridge to Mt. Sterling and Salem to Lexington. The Presbyterians living in Winchester found it less comfortable to go to Salem than the other Winchester people to their churches.

Added to these slim facts, was the presence of an outsider and a northerner, A. Lewis, which the KENTUCKY ADVERTISER tells us was the headmaster of the Winchester Academy. Lewis was not, evidently, a Presbyterian minister like so many teachers, but he was Presbyterian. Perhaps he provided the catalyst that crystallized the Winchester Presbyterians.

At any rate, the Presbyterian Church was organized by a young Georgia minister, Robert M. Cunningham. There were eleven charter members, Mr. and Mrs. Thomas Barbee, David and Samuel Rippy, Mr. and Mrs. William Young, Suzanne D. Martin, Jane Vance, and Mr. and Mrs. James Young. None of these families are typically Providence or Methodist families unless it was Suzanne Martin. Most of them are, probably as Salem claimed, families allied with her.

This small group met at Hickman Academy. Thomas Barbee, Amziah Lewis, and Jacob Fishback were trustees. Like the Methodist trustees, they did not necessarily belong to the local church. Fishback did not but was evidently lending his prestige and influence.

In 1815, David Dodge gave the church a lot on Main Street. It was not reported when the first church was built. It was located across the street from the present Catholic Church about in the location of Ben Douglas Goff's home (1976). As late as the Civil War, the corner on which the Catholic Church is now located, was a woods called Ballard Woods. In 1812, the location was virtually in the country.

Again, the Presbyterian Church demanded that their ministers be educated.

A list of the presiding elders gives us David Rippy, the first...Thomas Barbee, Amzi Lewis, Cornelius Skinner, William Posey, Jacob Fishback, S. D. Fishback, James Anderson, Willis Collins, Dr. John Hul, William C. Simpson, James Simpson, James R. Wornall, James H. Holloway, John Taliferrie, William H. Cocke, James D. Simpson, John D. Bean, L. M. Van Meter, John M. Moore, William Logan, A. H. Hampton, Sr., Dr. I. H. McKinley, W. M. Beckner, John M. Wheeler, W. R. Philips, E. L. Uphan, C. H. Loveland, Thomas R. Talbott, George E. Motch, S. W. Willis, Charles Wilcoxen, C. M. Stagers, Joseph Richard, Eldred Bean, W. K. Sudduth, Taylor Yantis, J. B. Boxley, W. K. Elliott, J. K. Skinner, E. C. Cleland, Dr. Isaac H. Browne, E. B. Garrard, J. M. Fishback, George M. Wolfe, Lyman Ginger, William B. Spears, Lewis V. Logan, Dr. E. O. Guerrant, A. K. Landrum, Miller Ramsy, J. T. Crawford, A. R. Milby, Wallace Wood, Henry Sipe, J. Ashlan Logan, Keith Sparks, J. D. Delane, William G. Kagin, F. M. Muhlemon, W. P. Marks, R. H. Reese, Waller Bean, Russell Smith, W. P. Morgan, Jr., Francis Cricket, Wallace Rash, Walter King, Dr. R. E. Strode, Dr. S. K. McCrary (up to 1956).

Evangelism has been the major problem among the Presbyterians. Calvinistic doctrines which holds some form of predestination does not leave an aggressive role in individual salvation. The Primitive Baptist also have suffered at this point. However, the necessity of winning people to a knowledge of their salvation became quite evident.

The Presbyterians expected their men to be "divines" in the true sense. They were to be trained, specialized ministers. This accounts, in the early days, for the status of the Presbyterian ministers. In any community they were the best educated men, more so than even the lawyers and the medics. Often, where they went, they also brought education. The small frontier church was hardly strong enough financially to support a minister. He also doubled with establishing a school, as John Lyle did. There simply were not enough educated ministers to meet the demand. In the vacuum, what was called "stated supplies" were used. These were men who usually were either laymen or unordained men working for ordination. Sometimes "stated supplies" were men of other denominations. Many of these early ministers at First Presbyterian were in this category.

The CLARK COUNTY DEMOCRAT, August 27, 1879, reported that in 1816 Amziah Martin was minister of First Presbyterian. This name does not appear anywhere else. There is an Amziah Lewis and a William Martin. We suspect that the newspaper has the names confused. Martin was also minister at Sugar Ridge and as reported popular. He probably preached in Winchester also. In 1817, the church was served with a variety of ministers, James Blythe, R. W. Cunningham and Robert Stuart. The next year repeated 1817 with no one minister, but Stuart, John K. Edgar, James McCord, William Wallace and Robert Cunningham served on occasion. Samuel Crothers became minister in 1819.

Crothers was ordained in 1803 by the Associate Reform Presbyterians, a very conservative branch of the Presbyterian movement. In 1819, he converted, if that is the proper word, to the Presbyterians and took Winchester three quarter time. He was an abolitonist as were most of the ministers at this time. One of his credits was seeing Robert Fulton's first steamboat and he never tired of predicting that it would not be long before steamboats would be coming up the Kentucky.

This shifting ministry and a very small congregation is not as much of a problem in these days as it was, say when Frank Dudley in the 1890s was trying to establish the Episcopal church in Winchester. Ministers were suppose to preach. They visited the sick, buried the dead, and married the couples. They did not visit, nor did they feel obliged to be community leaders. Most of them worked elsewhere, teaching, farming and later storekeeping.

Blythe who served briefly was one of the three original professors at Transylvania. McCord later became president of Center College. Sam Steel was evidently a student minister, an immigrant from Londonberry, Ireland. He was licensed to preach in 1824 and ordained in Winchester in 1825, the first Presbyterian to be ordained in Clark County. His first marriage was Benjamin Taul to Sally Ann Capol, January 26, 1826. He married 21 couples. In 1824, the Presbyterians built their first brick church.

Like the Baptist, the period between 1800 and 1830 was a period of strife for the Presbyterians. Like the Baptist, the Presbyterians were badly divided in Europe and on the east coast. Unlike the Baptist, these divisions did not seem to migrate westward to Kentucky. They were largely jurisdictional and organizational rather than theological. Once away from their European setting, they lost their importance.

Stuart and R. H. Bishop served Winchester in 1820. Isaac Reed, Bishop and Joseph Howe divided the pulpit in 1820 and 1821. Bishop served alone in 1822. Howe, Stuart, Nathan H. Hull and John Breckinridge were ministers in 1823. Breckinridge and William Henderson served in 1824.

The first full time minister and resident minister was Samuel Steel who served between 1825 and 1828. The membership of the church was reported in 1826 as 29 members. The Presbytery records reported a J. P. Trotter, a licensee, as minister in 1828-30. He was also serving Sugar Ridge. The religious boom was on and the Winchester Presbyterian felt the effects of it. In 1830, she reported a membership of 70. Sam Steel returned to Winchester in 1832 but for some reason she was not reported in the records. Evidently Steel no longer lived in Winchester but was also the minister of Hopewell which would soon change its name to First Presbyterian in Paris. Steel resided at Hopewell. In 1833 Winchester's membership reached 124. It would be interesting to know how many refugees from the Baptist Christian struggle found peace and quiet in the Presbyterian church.

The record shows that Winchester's membership had fallen back to 50 in 1834. The minister was named Charles Stewart. There is no explanation for the drastic loss. Several theories may be offered. The Presbyterians at this stage of their evangelism, simply were not able to compete with the agressive evangelism that the Baptist, Methodist and Christians were offering. They gained for awhile because of the general atmosphere of religious excitement, but in the years following the division between the Baptist and the Christians, intense evangelistic pressure was made on all religious groups. The New Light division of the Barton Stone Churches had its effect. Basically with a Presbyterian background, the subscribers of Stone's Christian Messenger, and some other indications would show that Stone's influence in Clark County was heavy. However, unlike Bourbon and Fayette Counties, Stone's influence was largely contained in the Winchester Christian Church which has some indication of being a Stone rather than a Campbell church from the beginning. Certainly this controversy in the early 1830s before the Stone-Campbell merger was effecting the Presbyterians everywhere. At this point it is Stuart that plays the role among the Presbyterians that Thomas Rupard and James French played with the Baptist. He held the orthodox churches in the Presbyterian fold, but could not help losses.

As part of the Stone movement, though at this time independent of it, was the aggressive drive of the Christians themselves. They were not only putting pressure on the Baptist, but their vision was of a united protestantism, based on the Bible without interpretation (other than theirs). They felt it their duty to bring others into the movement. Alexander Campbell is supposed to have told Barton Stone that he made a mistake by withdrawing from the Presbyterian movement, but should have worked from within the church.

This type of pressure was also building up into a purely fraternal battle within the Presbyterians between the old school and new school forces. This would end in a sharp division of churches in the middle 1830s, but which did not divide the Presbyterians in Clark County. It may have contributed to the loss of membership however.

In passing, we note that the Sugar Ridge Cumberland Presbyterians had no problem with any of these issues and was growing and thriving during this period. In 1835, Winchester was reported vacant. In 1836, the minister was a supply by the name of Daniel

Baker. Membership was reported as 37. Once again in 1838, Winchester was vacant but Baker had stopped the loss in membership which now stood at 50. The glittering dream of the Christians had pretty largely been blocked, mostly by their own bitter intra-feuding and divisions.

The first full time resident minister of Winchester's Presbyterian Church since Steel and the first full time minister in Winchester was George W. McElroy who came to the Presbyterians in 1839. Despite his full time status, he was expected to help with Salem and the new church Union. Though he was listed as full time it is difficult to see how he could be full time with this responsibility. Evidently he did not necessarily preach at these churches, but held marriages, funerals, visited their sick when possible and supervised the supply ministers that were sent in by the Presbytery. Interestingly enough, McElroy was an old acquaintance of the county when he became its minister. He had married B. F. Couch to Elizabeth Combs, May 1, 1834, for his first county marriage. Altogether he performed nine in the county.

McElroy stayed with Winchester for four years. Henry Clay turned to McElroy to escourt 130 freed slaves back to Africa for the American Colonial Society records show that after McElroy, Winchester was supplied by Ebeneazor Bishop. Salem remained under his supervision though for the first time Union had its own minister.

W. C. Matthew served in 1842 to 1848, the membership rose to 67. Henry Grail served some in 1845. Matthew died while serving Winchester. There followed several years without a ministry. Transylvania had been lost to the Presbyterians. There apparently was no really good source of "stated supply" or ordained Presbyterian ministers. There is not any information as to the state of the church during this time. Membership had once again fallen to 44.

L. A. Lowry served in 1850 to 1855. W. S. Chaney, who had been tutor to the son of Isaac Shelby served in 1855 to 1857. He returned gain in 1862 to serve until 1870. J. M. Scott served from 1858 to 1861. During Scott's ministry, the Presbyterians built their second building and moved into it, a few blocks closer to the center of town than their first...the present (1974) Library building.

There is no record of how the division of Presbyterian Churches went over slavery other than Winchester went with the southern churches.

The outburst of evangelism in 1828 did reach First Presbyterian and some thirty new people became members. Ten years later, it was repeated, this time with some fifty people being converted, though the Presbyterian historians admitted that only sixteen of these became Presbyterians.

Though at the beginning of the Civil War, the Presbyterian Winchester Church was the smallest of the four churches, even smaller than the new Baptist church, already it had caught the idea of a city church. It had a Sunday school, a Women's Missionary Society, a full time resident minister, and through its connections with the school, a youth work. Despite its size the Winchester Presbyterian Church exercised influence in Winchester far beyond its size.

## UNION PRESBYTERIAN CHURCH

The fourth church to be organized by the Presbyterians in Clark County was Union in the Wades Mill area and it was a definite result of the taking of Sugar Ridge by the Cumberland Presbyterians. There had been a few Presbyterians in the Wades Mill area from the beginning of the county. The Transylvania Presbytery records show that there had been a request from a group on Pretty Run for a church before 1800 and that a few years later a church named Mt. Carmel was served by a supply minister for a year. In both cases, the Presbytery did not have the organization of the ministers to support such weak openings. Mt. Carmel Baptist took the name and moved into the area. There was also a Presbyterian church for a short time at North Middletown that had 64 members as early as 1832. Usually this church belonged to another Presbytery and we have made no effort to trace its history.

Still there was a large area of Clark County that was not served with any rural church other than Mt. Carmel Baptist. Stamper's Chapel had died early. An effort at a church, probably Baptist, at Thatcher's Mill also failed. Mt. Zion Methodist stood on the edge of the area and North Middletown churches on the other end. It did seem a reasonable area, however, to organize a church.

Union first appeared in the record, and Sugar Ridge disappeared, in 1838. The conquest by the Cumberland Presbyterians was now fully recognized. Union was reported with 9 members. The local Presbyterian history begins Union in 1837 with Cornelius Skinner elected elder and George Crawford as minister. The West Lexington Presbyterians do not confirm this figure. Daniel Sphar was elected in 1838 and was to remain until 1853, Skinner was to be an elder until 1848. George Anderson was elected an elder in 1838 and was to serve until 1854.

According to the West Lexington Presbytery records, Union was under the watchful eye of William Matthew of Winchester until 1842. Union Presbyterian Church got its first minister, licensee named James M. Priest. The next year the records report Alexander McKinney as minister. McKinney was another licensee.

This is not what the local Presbyterians have in their records that appear from time to time in print. They claimed that Matthews held the ministry until 1848. As senior minister he did probably have charge of these licenses that were serving Union and probably did hold the sacraments and the like.

They also report that in 1841, a Charles Philips served as minister and in 1842 Robert Davidson. Neither of these names appear in the Synodal records nor does the record show that these men were ministers. More likely they were supplies that were not recorded by the Presbytery simply because they were supplies. Occasionally, in desperation, the Presbyterians lowered their standards.

The Synodal records do not show other ministers for Union other than the supervisory presence of the Winchester ministers. However, the local Presbyterian history reports that H. V. D. Nevis served Union between 1852-1857. William Dooley was elected elder from 1846 to 1852. Isaac Skinner was elected elder in 1846 and James Allen deacon the same year.

There seems to be no information about Union during the Civil War. The newspapers did not carry Union on their mastheads. Mt. Carmel Baptist was also neglected so it may be that the Winchester papers had given the Wades Mill area to Bourbon County or at least to North Middletown. The church elected James Van Meter elder in 1876 and evidently voted to attend services in Winchester. In 1878 the church was reconstituted with J. T. Leonard as minister. William George followed between 1870 and 1874. E. O. Guerrant was the minister between 1877 and 1879. Guerrant during part of this time was also serving Salem. William Sudduth was elected elder in 1876. Phineas L. Skinner joined him in being elected elder in 1882.

One of the rare times that Union was picked up by the earliest newspapers and reported was by the CLARK COUNTY DEMOCRAT in 1878 when they reported that E. E. Erwin who was also minister of Salem served. The Presbyterian local history does not make this report.

In 1882, C. T. Thompson served as minister. He was assisted by a D. B. Ewing. Finally in 1888 Union came under the ministry of I.S. McElroy who at that time was also serving the Mt. Sterling Church.

So the same pattern for Union was to be shown for Ebeneazer of the Methodist movements. Both churches worshipped with their Winchester church, and both sought to reestablish themselves after the Civil War. The problem always remained for the Presbyterians, and that is to keep a supply of ministers that met their standards available to churches that were too small to stand by themselves.

One more effort to establish a minister at Union was made in 1889 when W. B. Cooper served. The next year Union began afternoon services using the Winchester minister James J. Chisolm. Union news now is reported regularly in the Winchester papers, particularly by the WINCHESTER DEMOCRAT. The correspondent for the DEMOCRAT was Dr. John Snowden who became one of the most active newspaper men in the county. Most correspondents would send in a little news about their community, but Snowden not only sent in considerably more news than the average correspondent but included editorial comments on Wades Mill politics, churches, social affairs and in general, presented the reader the best picture available of a rural community at the turn of the century.

Union was evidently active. In 1888, the Union Sunday school had a picnic at Holly Springs. The Sunday school was organized each spring and disbanded each fall. It was a community Sunday school merely using the Union building and meeting in the afternoons every Sunday. Charles Swift was the Sunday school superintendent in 1890. L. B. Cockrell became superintendent in 1898 and in 1900, Dr. Snowden was superintendent.

There was a genuine opportunity for a church in the Wades Mill area. Obviously the Mt. Carmel Baptist Church was failing. This left a wide rural area with little or no church life. In 1898, the church made a deliberate effort to develop in this vacuum. With help from Winchester, a minister named Gilbert Glass began a two Sunday a month program. He was replaced by a George Scott in 1900 and in 1902 Charles Martin. Evidently these men were student ministers from the Louisville Seminary. James Skinner was elected elder in 1902.

For some reason Union was not able to fill the vacuum. The Mt. Carmel Baptist Church continued to decline until it died in the 1910s, but in its place grew the Mt. Carmel Christian Church. The christians were largely members of North Middletown, or even more distant churches, and first organized a Sunday school using the Mt. Carmel Baptist building. Dr. Snowden became active in this Sunday school and eventually in the Christian church.

Here again, one can lay the failure of the Union Church on the ministerial supply. The Chrisitians did not demand an educated ministry as the Baptist did not. They were no longer bitterly aggressive as they had been. Their relationship with the surviving Mt. Carmel Baptist was excellent and many of the customs and traits of the Baptist would persist in the Mt. Carmel Church until the building of the new Mt. Carmel Christian Church building in 1972. Against these two facts, ministry and aggressive policy, the Union Presbyterians were unable to compete.

After 1902, the Presbyterians gave up. They turned to Winchester for their ministers, satisfied with an afternoon worship service. William Cunningham and S. B. Landers held services as long as they served the Winchester Church. Another Sunday school was tried in 1906 and 1907 with W. L. Eldridge and J. W. Jewell Sunday school superintendents. Both these men were from the Winchester church. By this time, however, the Christian Church had a strong and effective Sunday school. Dr. Snowden was now an elder in that church and active in the Sunday school, though he soon moved out of the area.

When Landers left the Winchester church, the Union Church gave up the struggle. The few remaining members moved to Winchester. The church building passed to Charles Berryman who bought it and turned it into a tenant house.

Once again, we find a church with a very small base and little real community support. Yet churches have grown to powerful churches with as small a base. The Wades Mill area ought to have been a good place for a church. Mt. Carmel Particular Baptist Church was a strong organization until after the death of Thomas Dudley which was in the 1870s. It was to decline steadily thereafter. Yet the Mt. Carmel Church was never a dominating church. There were no other churches in the area. For a time in the 1890s, Holly Witherspoon sponsored a chapel on Pretty Run but this church never had much strength and was always a poor man's church. Quite a few of the landlords would go to North Middletown church.

Perhaps Mt. Carmel and Union were too much alike, both conservative Calvinists. Certainly the Christian Church was able to come into the Wades Mill area at the very time Union was making its last bid for a successful church. Perhaps it was discouragement over the establishment of the Christian Church that forced Union to decide to keep a little church for their handful of people and forget about any hopes of every becoming more.

Again, there is the glaring lack of ministerial leadership, though the Calvinistic Primitive Baptist died also and did have good leadership...though not necessarily so at the end of their existence.

## THE METHODIST CHURCH

The study of Methodist churches in Clark County has turned out to be the most difficult of all the early movements in Clark County to study. The records of the Methodists are the best, and they go right back almost to the beginning of the county's history. The problem is these records are of circuits and not of churches. Only occasionally is there a hint what churches belong to the circuit. This in itself wasn't bad as long as there was but a single circuit for Clark County churches. One did not know the strength or the contribution of any particular church, but Methodism in the county is clearly reported. However, about 1840, there was a breaking up of the single circuit so that perhaps two or even three circuits would include not only Clark County churches but other county churches as well. North Middletown in Bourbon County, Grassy Lick in Montgomery County, for example, were continually linked with some Clark County churches and Buckeye and Dunaway are linked with Montgomery County churches. At this point it is impossible to separate county churches much less individual churches.

Secondly, the Methodist records and history are strongly minister centered. Such histories as Arnold's records the history of Methodist ministers. Even James Landrum's Journal which is the best record of Clark County churches before the Civil War, concerns himself largely with ministers. Yet, a glance at the marriage records show that the local preachers, usually unnamed by the early Methodist records, simply are not named, much less any description of what they do. Sometimes the obituaries will leave a little sliver of information about what churches a minister served and something on local ministers. Nothing is ever said about laymen in a single church.

Even the deeds with their list of trustees do not help much. The property of the Methodist are jointly owned and the trustess represent the circuit and not the churches. The deed does not say to what church the men belonged.

The circuit would meet quarterly in their quarterly meetings. At this time there was a report, a form to be filled out by each church and turned in at the Quarterly Conference. The minister of the circuit got one copy, presumedly for the records of the circuit. The presiding elder got a second copy for his record. Presumedly other copies went to the bishop for conference records and the like. These records must be somewhere. So far no local church has any going back more than a few decades. They generally do not have any other than membership records and these seldom are too old. None of the local sources, Asbury Library, the Mission Building in Lexington, or any of the University libraries have any. The Mission

Building did have a few years (1927-29). They were most interesting and will appear in the fourth volume and, if ever a history of Powell County is written. Presumedly the circuit record was lost when the minister moved. The presiding elder's records were probably burned on his death when his daughter-in-law cleaned up his possessions. Once the records were placed in statistics, the main office could not use the ever increasing amount of paper.

There are sources that we have not looked into....such as Vanderbilt University and the Methodist Historical Society records. If they have any such, none of those interviewed knew about them.

The best source of history was a record which painstakingly traced each church and the circuit they belonged to. The original copy is at Kentucky Wesleyan. Parts of it were in the Mission Building. There is also a history of the Montgomery County Methodist Churches that have some records of Clark County churches.

The Methodist situation in Kentucky was entirely different from those of the Methodist and Presbyterian. Both these groups had a long history that went back into Europe and into centuries. There were accepted theologies, old scisms, organizations and organizational differences that were ancient before Clark County or even Kentucky came about.

The Methodist history was contemporary with Clark County. The Wesleys were still alive. Before the American Revolution there was hardly a Methodist movement in the country. It will later be pointed out that Leroy Cole, who would be one of the more prominent Methodist in Clark County, was riding circuit at a time when there were only 36 such ministers in the entire country. Upon this young and fragile movement, came the American Revolution which cut the Methodist off entirely, first from its parent Church of England and secondly from England itself. The Wesleys were not prepared to leave the Church of England at this time, but the Americans had no choice. The Church of England was a Tory church and under a cloud of suspicion. During the war the Methodist operated with a vague sort of organization with the authority of the church largely in the presiding elders, but with very little real structure.

After the Revolution, the Wesleys, evidently reluctantly, set the American church adrift and sent them two bishops, young men and eager but without great experience, Francis Ashbury and Thomas Coke. Ashbury was to be the bishop of the southern part of the United States in which Kentucky was a part.

Methodism is arminian in theology. By this, it rejected the Calvinism that was the base of both the Baptist and the Presbyterian movement and was accepted by them as virtually indisputable. There was a small free will Baptist movement, but it never had either size or influence in the majority of the population. Methodism denied predestination but insisted on free will. It insisted on the individual part in salvation. It was therefore strongly evangelistic and heavily emotional. Shouting, moaning, jumping, tongues, etc. appalled the Calvinists but were the order of the day for the Methodist. Arnold's "History of Kentucky Methodist" tells how Presbyterian John Lyle who was then serving Salem Presbyterian Church in Clark County was appalled and astonished at the going on at the revivals that broke out all about him and included his own church.

Emotionalism was of course, the order of the day in evangelism. George Whitefield's revivals were strongly emotional and this movement was shaking the east including the congregational churches of the north. Barton Stone's movement was strongly emotional as was the later Cumberland Presbyterian revivals were also emotional, but none reached the excesses that were Methodist. This also brought about a fact that the majority of Methodist in the earlier years were converts either from the non believers or from the older churches. This did not lend for harmonious situations in communities where the Baptist and Presbyterians tended to look down on the Methodist as emotionally unstable and resented their raids on membership.

Once established, the Methodist grew rapidly. We have noted the reluctance of the Presbyterians to encourage an area that could not pretty largely support its minister. The church on Pretty Run Creek is an example. The Methodist, had it been theirs, would not have worried whether there were one or two or three families involved. It would have been included on a circuit and given some attention. Many of their preaching points fell to pieces when a key layman moved. We will call attention to several such examples in Clark County. The nature of a circuit in the early days had to be in constant flux so that even the minister could not be certain of what churches, brush arbors, barns, person's homes, log meeting houses, etc., that he would preach in on a preaching tour. The result was, howver, a very rapid growth. The Presbyterians were almost immediately passed in size. The Methodist never offered a real challenge to the Baptist or later to either the Baptist and Christian movements until well after the Civil War, at least in Kentucky. The Methodist were, however, the alternative to the Baptist movement and therefore a continual challenge.

There is another difference. The Baptist Church, as reported, thought of itself as a complete society, a miniature nation, providing for its people spiritual and material leadership. It may not have held that position consciously, but it certainly was in the Baptist mind up to and through the Civil War and into the present generation, particularly among the "old" Baptist. The Methodist were not so much concerned with the questions of material relationships, church trials, legal justice within the church, etc. There would be some of this, but essentially the Methodist were concerned with salvation or the soul which did not have to wait on God's designation, but stood ready to be had at any time. There was not a great deal of difference between the Baptist and the Presbyterians in attitude, viewpoint on religion, or the understanding of the church. There was a vast difference between these two and the Methodist.

If the Baptist and Presbyterian exerted authority over the member and his theology, the Methodist exerted authority over the minister. Asbury assumed an authority, which even the Church of England did not have or the Wesleys claim. This was the right to send a minister to whatever church the bishop, with the advice of the presiding elder or district superintendent, would deem best. This right had no appeal. A minister accepted the appointment without protest and in turn, the church accepted the minister. This would produce a great deal of unhappiness and a dozen divisions within the Methodist Church itself. It would send many an able minister, such is in Clark County, William Kavanaugh and T. I. Wills, to other movements.

It is always difficult for a member of one movement to explain the inner workers of another movement, but for one to understand Methodist history we need spend some time discussing Methodist organization.

The key factor was this appointment of ministers to their charges. No other Clark County movement does so, though there are some similarities among the early Presbyterians and some similarities among the Episcopalians. It is not to be presumed that the churches' needs or the minister's desires were not listened to. The stronger and more capable ministers certainly had a voice in where they were to go. The stronger churches also made its desires known as to when an unpopular minister should be moved or whether a popular minister should remain another year. However, this was entirely below the official organization. It would be done by delegations quietly meeting with the bishops, the presiding elder or some other important Methodist functionary to explain their problem. It had the advantage of keeping the lid on some unpleasant situations. The church knew that at conference time there would be a change and that there was no need for the angry effort to oust the unpopular minister that often occurred in other denominations.

We have made some effort to find out just how extensive this maneuvering behind the scene went. We have reached the conclusion that it is surprisingly small. The larger churches undoubtedly let their opinions be known. On the whole, both ministers and churches accepted the decisions of the organization. Certainly this is true in the early years.

The charge was not a church but a circuit. The circuit would consist of a number of churches that might range from a single strong church, a station parish, to as many as a dozen or...in one early case, 32 preaching points. A glance at the Methodist statistics, it would appear that there was a real effort to hold the circuit to about 300 to 400 members. If a circuit got larger it would be shifted and broken up into two smaller circuits. If there were too many churches or preaching points on a circuit, two or even three and once in Clark County history, four ministers would be assigned. One would be the senior minister who evidently had charge. The junior ministers were often new to the ministry. There is no indication in the minutes or the scant local records, just how these men divided the circuit. There has been some indication out of Landrum that one might preach in the morning, the other at night. Other occasions, they have appeared both at the same service. In one description, a minister was given a group of churches which he covered and presumedly the other covered the remaining churches. Obviously, there was no set pattern.

It was custom for the Methodist to move their men often. In the early days a year was the usual time. Later, the time was extended as the need fit. By 1900 a minister would stay as long as three years in a place. It might be noted that Baptist and Christian ministers averaged only about two and a half years a ministry in one place so that the difference has shrunk. Since the merger of northern and southern Methodist, the tendency was to keep a minister in a place to finish a building program, to carry on an expanded ministry or just to give a very popular minister the kind of back ground needed to use his talents to the greatest.

Beneath these men were the local ministers. These apparently were ordained men who at least had the power to marry. It is not clear in the records, or even among the ordained ministers, just what powers these local men had. Several have expressed surprise that they had the power to marry, but Clark County records show that a series of local men, who never held an offical circuit, married far more often than the regularly assigned ministers. There is no indication who these men are or what they do in the records and they are not carried as ministers on the local records.. where such local records exist. Clark County newspapers, however, show them to be men of influence and recognized reputations in the local area.

Methodist ministers do not belong to the church. They have membership in the conference in the same way that the Presbyterian ministers have their standing in the Presbytery. It is presumed that their wives and children would belong to a local church.

There are three grades of Methodist ministers, licensees or probationaries, deacons and elders. We presume that promotion from one to another came with improved education, years of experience and the approval of the conference.

Once each quarter the circuit had an official meeting of all the churches under the direction of the presiding elder. The presiding elder is in charge of a district, but in a very real way is also minister of all the churches in the district. He usually stays in office longer than the circuit ministers and provides the stability that ties the rapidly changing circuit churches together. Since he was in contact four times a year with the leadership of each circuit he was familiar with the intimate problems of each church.

At the quarterly conference, each church made its report and was given its assignments. Not only did the local church pay their share of the circuit pastor's salary but a certain amount went to the presiding elder and a smaller amount went to a bishop who was in charge of several districts. Money to support missions and other causes were also allotted to each church. It has been difficult for an outsider to discover just what happens to a Methodist church that does not come up to its assignments. Obviously many of the northern Methodist churches were delinquent on their assignments and yet little if anything was done about the problem.

From the points of view of an outsider, it is difficult to see just what function the bishop plays in the church. He ordains the elders which continues a sort of apostolic succession doctrine. He is a type of supreme court to whom appeals from ministers and churches can be carried. He presides at the conference meetings. Technically, ministerial appointments come from him. He undoubtedly has great influence and tasks in the movement as a whole, in national projects and missionary efforts. However, from the point of view of the individual layman, he is a far off beneficient power which only indirectly effects the average Methodist.

The presiding elder is the power within the system. It is his word that appointments are made. It is usually from his ranks the bishops are appointed. His recommendation can break or make a minister. An injured minister can appeal to the conference for relief but a study of the skimpy records do not show many cases where the minister won over the elder. In the early days, a minister might pass from a circuit to the eldership, come back to a circuit to be appointed elder perhaps of another district to return to the circuits. Gradually, the tendency has been to keep the presiding elders, known after the merger with the northern Methodist as district superintendents, in his office for most of the rest of his life, or move him in the same office to other perhaps more influential districts if a man of ability.

All property is owned by the conference. The conference has and does use the ability to close a church that is out of line with the conference policy. Hence, Wool's Chapel remained southern and the northern faction had to build Owen Chapel in Clark County. In 1939, when many of the Methodist churches in South Carolina refused to enter the merger, new Methodist churches were built often next door to the old building that had been locked to them. The trustees of Methodist property are responsible to the conference and represent the whole district. Clark County deeds, particularly when more than one church is on the circuit, will have trustees drawn from all the churches. The same is true of parsonages. This presents problems when churches are moved back and forth between circuits and when circuits are divided. This accounts for the sale and purchase of parsonages for various circuits in Clark County's history.

Occasionally a church retains its property. Sometimes the land is owned by individuals who will not deed it to the conference. Usually the conference will eventually relocate that church, as it did with Mt. Zion in Clark County, to land that it did own. There are occasional holdouts, however, that do not turn in their deeds. There are none such in Clark County, but Hardwick Methodist Creek Church in Powell County is one. They have argued that the deed is lost, or have just stalled over repeated efforts to bring them in line with conference policy.

The policies of the conference are binding on the local church. Actually, one can quite correctly speak of the Methodist Church in the United States for in a very real way it is an organic whole. There is no question that this power structure had caused the multitude of divisions, O'Kelley, Weslyan Methodist, the break over slavery, Protestant Methodism, Congregational Methodists, Methodist Protestant, etc., over the years. It is also certain that only through this iron control was a movement that had not reached America in 1760 able to become the second largest religious movement in the land.

Over all this structure is the Methodist Discipline. This book, revised almost yearly, lays out the rules of conduct both of the churches and ministers of the movement. It is the law book with authority. It isn't exactly a creed such as the Baptist or Presbyterians have which controls orthodoxy. It is the law book which guides and directs, limits and expands the right of a Methodist in his movement.

Finally, it is interesting to note how difficult it is for one that has been raised in Methodist discipline to understand the freedom of the congregational type churches. Likewise, it is hard for those who have been raised in congregational type churches to understand the control of the Methodist system.

The first division was lead by a Virginia presiding elder named James O'Kelly and came to a head at the famous Christmas Conference of 1786. He was perhaps the leading American Methodist, both Asbury and Coke being English importations. Frederick Abbott Norwood in "Methodist History", April 1966, described James O'Kelly:

The Methodist whom he hurt won't have him; the Disciples have forgotten him. The Christians of the old General Convention...no longer exist...an accomplished trouble maker, a thorn in Asbury's flesh, a disruptor of conventions, an inept administrator, a superficial thinker, an ambitious and proud pusher, a derisive spirit and a monumental failure...one of the key figures in the formulation of the Methodist Episcopal church...an able and devoted presiding elder...stirred the Weslyan movement in America to its depth.

He was never able to keep the extremists from tearing his movement to pieces. He was pursuaded to change the name from Republican Methodist to Christian, thus losing some who did not want to leave the name Methodist. The issue of immersion which the movement favored but did not demand tore other hunks into the body. Theological oddities haunted its edges. A sort of dualism which condensed the Trinity into two persons, had some following in South Carolina. The universalist movement found considerable support. Some of the more orthodox members went to the Presbyterian church. The sum result was an almost complete victory for Asbury. He was able to retain his control over the ministry, stopped the defection of his churches and made the rapid expansion of Methodism possible.

The O'Kelly people did establish themselves in Virginia and North Carolina and later in Georgia and Alabama. The movement was never effective in Kentucky. Nationally, it became deeply involved with the Barton Stone people, but unlike the Stone people, did not accept Campbellism. There are still churches in Kentucky that trace their history to the O'Kelly-Stone origins. They are not in Clark County.

The O'Kelly movement did effect the history of Clark County in three ways. First, it slowed the potential number of Methodist moving out of Virginia and North Carolina. These O'Kelly people were more apt to join a Baptist or Presbyterian church in their bitterness. They might also account for the early use of the "Christian" name by the larger Friendship Baptist Church division. They probably set back Methodism by a decade. The O'Kelly movement did profoundly influence Barton Stone so that his movement would eventually be called the Christian Church. Once again, we have an influence on the Winchester church. It may have been the reason why the first Methodist minister in Clark County should have played such an invisible role, despite obvious religious activity in the Methodist records.

Just another note on organization. The first Methodist churches would have what they call classes. The people who became Methodist in a circuit of any particular year would be called the Class of 17??. These classes would meet periodically in a combination of religious revival and fellowship for that group. Landrum

speaks of attending several class meetings in his early years.
The idea somewhat played out, at least in the records after the
War of 1812. Traditionally conceived, the class meeting was
designed to be the weekly exchange of religious experience with
the view of mutual education under the guidance of a leader and
is peculiar of Methodism says the April 1851 Methodist Quarterly
Review by A. J. Susnett.

W. E. Arnold's "History of Methodism in Kentucky" says:

1779: First Methodist in Kentucky was a Nicholas Reegan....
he helped build Bryan Station.

1783: First Methodist Church was established in the Danville
area.

1786: Baltimore Conference in which James O'Kelly rebelled.

## KENTUCKY CIRCUIT

1786: James How and Benjamin Ogden circuit riders...90
Methodist on circuit which includes all of Kentucky
and some of Tennessee...

1787: James Haw, Thomas Williams and Wilson Lee

A Maysville Church was organized in 1786. Circuit extended
to the Green River. There is no indication of a preaching point in
Clark County though by this time the Joshua Stampers were living in
Bryan Station. Mrs. Stamper had been converted before this move,
but her husband was converted after their move to Bryan and perhaps
after their move to Constant's Station. This would indicate that
there was some activity on Clark County about this time. It is not
illogical that in a circuit that reaches from Maysville to the
Green River, with Clark County in the middle of it, and with a
heavily settled area from Mt. Sterling to Boone Creek, that there
would be Methodist preaching points.

## LEXINGTON CIRCUIT

1788: The Kentucky Circuit is divided between the Danville
Circuit and the Lexington Circuit. Presiding
elders, Francis Poythress and James Haw.
Lexington Circuit: Peter Massie and Benjamin
Snelling.

Again, there is no indication of preaching in Clark County,
but there almost had to be. Certainly the Stampers would be a
location. There apparently was a church in the area, but presumedly it was Baptist. However, according to custom, other groups
could have used it. A single family could be a preaching point,
however, with neighbors coming and services being held in the yard,

cabin, barn - depending on the weather. 1789: Collins reports that the Methodist have 1,039 white members and 51 colored members, an increase of 227 over 1788. 1790: Bishop Asbury came to Kentucky in 1790, for the annual conference which was held in Fayette County five miles northwest of Lexington. He was guarded in his trip over the mountains by some eight ministers and eighteen frontiersmen. His trip was uneventful and he recorded finding the new graves of Indian victims. All of this Asbury recorded in his diary.

Among his preachings while in Kentucky was a time at Clarksville at the Mouth of Red River. There are two Red Rivers in Kentucky and it is not clearly stated which this Red River is. If it was Clark County there is no mention of a Clarksville in Clark County history. George Rogers Clark was of course, a hero in Kentucky. There were also Clarks in Clark County area that had come into ownership of the Red River Forge. If this is Clark County, it would indicate considerable activity of Methodism in the county.

1791: The four Owen brothers moved into Clark County out of Maryland. Lawrence Owen is described as the first Methodist minister in the county and did enter into a twenty year period of marrying Clark County couples which showed him a popular and able man. Why Owen was not a circuit rider, or why the absolute dead silence of the records concerning Owen except a mention of him in Arnold will be discussed later.

Barbabas McHenry was circuit rider for the Lexington Circuit. He is mentioned later by William Landrum and he was the circuit rider in charge of Clarksville where Asbury stopped which strengthens our argument that this was Clark County. He was at the lower end of the circuit at Bruce's Chapel at the mouth of Sulphur Fork with one or two preaching points up the form, and then over to Whipperwill Creek where there were a few societies and finally to Clarksville. A Mr. Denning always put the minister up in his home that stood some sixty yards away from the little cluster of houses called Clarksville. The night after McHenry stayed at Dennings, Indians shot through the open door and killed a Mr. Boyd who was sitting in the same chair that McHenry had sat in.

Sometime about this time, a Methodist minister named Benjamin Northcut, who was born in North Carolina about 1770, and came to Kentucky in 1786, was preaching for the Methodist in the early 1790s reported helping with a circuit that included preaching points on Indian Creek, Sugar Ridge and on Cane Ridge. Later, he was moved to Fleming County. There never was a development of these preaching points into churches, yet perhaps here is one of the answers, keeping in mind Campbell's observation that Cumberland Presbyterians were Methodist with Presbyterian government would explain why the Cumberlands were so much more successful than the ordinary Presbyterians were on Sugar Ridge...or why William Landrum seemed to be able to preach for the Cumberlands with such ease...or perhaps why it was possible for Barton Stone to lead the Cane Ridge people into Schism with the orthodox Presbyterian church.

## THE METHODIST CHURCH

## THE HINKSTON CIRCUIT

1792: The Owen's Meeting House was established. It is possible it was going even a year earlier. There do not seem to be records going back that far, only family tradition.

Clark County was also established, as this paper has noted in 1792. It reached all the way back to the Cumberland Gap. It is a sign of the importance of Montgomery County as the center of this huge mass, that the new circuit was called the Hinkston Circuit in the minds of the non politicians. There does not seem to be any record of what the various preaching points were.

1793: Francis Poynter was presiding elder and Richard Byrd was the first minister of the circuit. Limestone Circuit was the other half of the old circuit.

1793: Grassy Lick Methodist Church was established which at the time of its establishment was in Clark County but would soon become a Montgomery County church and therefore, not in this history. However, Grassy Lick Methodist Church, like Lulbegrud Baptist Church, would be closely associated at various times with Clark County.

1794: William Burke and Benjamin Larkin were appointed circuit riders. Arnold's history of the Methodist Church listed the Hindes, Martins, Kavanaughs, Scobees and Owens as leading Clark County Methodist families. One should add to that list the Stampers and Gardners.

William Burke became one of the first Methodist men who was not a resident of Clark County that need be examined more closely. He was born in Virginia in 1770 and converted to Methodism in 1791. He was the first conference secretary of the Western Conference in 1800. He was a presiding elder in 1803. Burke was assigned the task of refuting the O'Kelley dangers in Kentucky. Haw had already gone over to the O'Kelley people and Owen was in danger. There were other ministers that were disturbed. Burke's role in this dispute is the only time that Arnold's history mentions the O'Kelley division. Redmon does not even admit this much. Burke and Haw met publically in a genuine debate and Burke forced Haw to retract some of his statements concerning Bishop Asbury. Debating was at this time one of the more active spectator sports. Religious or political, they formed an important part of the era's recreation.

Burke also represented the Methodist viewpoint at the Cane Ridge Revival. The Methodist had not been included and some came to Stone's elders who were more or less responsible for the revival. They went to Barton Stone who promptly saw to it that Burke and others got a hearing.

However, Burke and his superiors got into a quarrel, the details of which are not clear. In 1813, he became a supernumerary which meant that he was no longer on circuit. He became post master in Cincinnati. He was charged with disrespect to a presiding elder and tried. The dispute raged on with several efforts at reconciliation until in 1818 he was expelled from the Methodist church. He continued to preach bold Ariminian theology until his death.

Another minister, more intimately connected with Clark County, was William Kavanaugh. He went to Lawrence Owen to be married which would indicate that Lawrence still had standing as a local minister among the Methodist. Perhaps he was again more or less accepted though he never took a circuit and the Methodist records give the local ministers little attention.

Kavanaugh was not in the best of health and he did not want to be separated from his family for weeks at a time. He asked for a location, or a station church...which was not common among the Methodist in these days. He started teaching. He helped Dr. Hinde establish Ebeneazer Church, the second of the Methodist churches in Clark County. When the Methodist failed his need to preach and did not give him an assignment, he shifted to the Episcopal movement. The Episcopal church was much smaller than the Methodist movement and largely confined to the larger communities along the Ohio River. He was given a church in Louisville and Henderson. In 1801 he registered with the Clark County Court as an Episcopalian to marry. He evidently made little, if any, effort to establish an Episcopal church in Clark County and confined his marriages largely to his own family. His first marriage in Clark County was George Moore to Polly Kavanaugh. Altogether he married nine Clark County couples, mostly relatives. He died in 1807. His children were largely small. His wife moved back to Clark County, remarried twice, but stayed Methodist. Her sons grew up Methodist ministers and her daughters married Methodist ministers. It would be interesting to wonder what would have happened had William lived to the usual age.

In 1784, a Methodist minister was paid 24 pounds a year if they needed it but no more. The money was in Pennsylvania currency which evidently was one of the more stable in the colony. In the light of the later dollar it was worth about $3.00 to an English pound. For each child under six, the circuit rider was paid 6 pounds, for each under 11, their pay was 3 pounds. In 1792, the pay of a circuit rider was $64.00 and it went up to $80.00 in 1800. For each child under seven the minister was paid %16.00 and then to 14 they were paid $24.00. It was thought that a child after fourteen ought to be able to pay his own money.

Comparatively speaking, the Baptist ministers were paid by the local churches, but since most Baptist owned a farm or a business, they were not dependent on the churches for a living. This would be true up to 1850 and would remain true among the Old Baptist. The Presbyterians were paid by the local churches but the Presbytery saw to it that the local churches would pay or else they received no ministers. The Methodist were paid by the Conference and though the money came from the churches along the circuit, in these early days the minister was not absolutely dependent on what the circuit offered. Also, there was less voluntary offering among the Methodist. The circuits were often given quotas and the churches and preaching points within the circuits were given quotas to meet. Failure to do so would effect the ministerial services they received.

Elderly or supernumeraries could be paid up to $80.00 a year. Widows also received $80.00 and $16.00 a year for ministerial orphans. In 1816, the amount rose to a $100.00 a year salary.

1798: Valentine Cook was the presiding elder. John Watson was the circuit minister. Ministers like the Presbyterian ministers who belonged to the Presbytery, belonged to the Conference. If discipline was needed, it was the conference that was the trial agent in the Methodist church. Watson was charged for improper relations with two sisters. The defense was interesting. Watson had preached in this small community and had been given shelter in a two room house for the night. The man and wife slept in one room. Watson and the two daughters went to bed in the same bed, fully clothed. The girls' brother slept before the fire on the floor. This is very close to the New England custom of bundling in which the girl and her boy would go to bed with the parents sitting before the fireplace when nights were too cold to go outside. Several safeguards were set up including a board that ran down the middle of the bed. The system seemed to work reasonably well until the French troops came to America to help in the Revolution. Evidently, the French cheated and the custom ended. At any rate, the conference must have listened to Watson's defense for he continued preaching for many years thereafter.

1799: Francis Poythress returned as presiding elder for one year. John Kobler was circuit minister.

1800: William Burke was appointed presiding elder of the Hinkston District but was replaced by William McKendree and remained presiding elder until 1804. Burke stepped down to become chief circuit minister associated with Lewis Hunt and Thomas Wilkerson. By this time, there were dozens of preaching points in the hugh Hinkston Circuit. Few could be identified by the word church or even a society. The Methodist circuit riders would hold services wherever there could be a place found to hold a hand full of people. One estimate was that these three men served some thirty-five or six preaching points. An exact number was impossible since they came and went with the Movement of the settlers. Clark County at this time had two churches, Owen Meeting House and Ebenezar Church or Meeting House as it is referred to in different records. Sometime about this period Stamper's Meeting House graduated from a preaching point into a church. In Montgomery County, Grassy Lick Methodist Church was a strong rural church. There may have been other preaching points in Clark County but they never were identified.

1801: Benjamin Larkin was the circuit minister. He converted H. H. Kavanaugh and John G. Durbin.

1802: Larkin continued as a circuit minister for the Hinkston District for a second year which was unusual for the Methodist at this time. Hezekiah Harriman was added as junior minister. Several new circuits were coming into existence at this time reducing the size of the Hinkston Circuit. Clark County was still part of this circuit though Clark and Montgomery which included Bath was about all that remained.

1803: John Granade and Harriman were the circuit ministers. William Burke became presiding elder of another district.

1804: Samuel Parker and Abdel Coleman. Arnold's history reported that Coleman became discouraged and gave up the ministry.

1805: William Burke became presiding elder of the Hinkston District which he would hold until 1807. Burke was the first Methodist circuit minister to marry in Clark County. Owen had been marrying for years. Burke's first marriage was George Taylor to Eleanor Henderson. He only married twice in the county. Kavanaugh also had several marriages in the county, but he was not a local minister. Most of his marriages were family marriages. In 1805, Richard Browning and George Atkins were the circuit ministers. Atkins was a cripple and was reported by Arnold's history as rather tactless.

1806: Joseph Williams and John Thomspon were circuit ministers.

1807: Joshua Oglesby, Henry Mallory and Elisha Bowman were circuit ministers. No reason was given for the increase in the number of ministers. There were no statistics available for these years, but presumedly the circuit was growing. Ebeneazor and Owen Meeting House were the only churches definitely organized at this time. Stamper Meeting House and Mt. Zion were probably in existence in a very primitive way.

1808: James Ward became presiding elder for these two years. Burke became senior circuit minister again. This may be the root of Burke's problems. Having served as a presiding elder for five years, he may have resented being back on the circuits and perhaps felt that the new presiding elders should not show their authority over him. Eli Truit was one of the circuit ministers. He became a missionary to the Indians in Michigan. The other circuit minister was James Blair. He had a stormy time in the Methodist movement. After he was admitted for the ministry, he was once probated, once reprimanded, once suspended and once expelled. Arnold gave no reason for such a career.

1809: John Sale became the district presiding elder. He remained so until 1813. The presiding elders stayed much longer than the ministers and provided the tie that held together the yearly ministries of the circuit riders. Richard Richards became minister. Arnold reported that he became a drunkard which wrecked his career and health but repented and reformed. Samuel Hellums was the other minister.

1810: Eli Truit was now senior minister with Henry McDonald and Henry Mallory as junior circuit ministers. Many of these ministers hardly left a mark on Clark County. Other than Owen Meeting House, Ebeneazor Meeting House and Stamper's Meeting House...perhaps Mt. Zion there were no other churches in the county. McDonald was a local convert. He had had a wild, wreckless youth of fighting, drinking, horse racing and cock fights. He became converted at Ebeneazor and went on to become a minister.

1811: Matthew Nelson and Benjamin Whoton ministers.

1812: William McMahon. There is no explanation why only one minister was assigned to the Hinkston circuit. Perhaps this represents a low point in the various churches in Clark and Montgomery Counties. Perhaps there was a shortage of ministers. The Methodist records do not say. However, the first statistics did appear, there were 1,190 white and 70 colored members officially reported. This certainly would appear to be more than one man could handle even with meetings on week days.

Usually the colored members belonged to owners who were also of that faith, but a surprising number of Negros belonged to churches when their owners did not, or even to other denominations.

1813: John Sommerville and Daniel Davison.

1814: Samuel Parker became presiding elder until 1817. William Dixon and Russel Bigelow became the circuit preachers. Usually the first name was the senior and often the older minister...or at least older in period of time as a Methodist minister. Evidently, they did not take a specific church. Often one would preach in the morning and the other in the evening. Evidently they generally went together as a team. Later, as certain churches grew strong enough to demand and get a Sunday morning service instead of whenever the minister arrived, one would take the stronger churches and the other would work the preaching points. There is unquestionably more information about these habits in letters, diaries, etc., but they have not become available.

1815: Benjamin Laker and Thomas Nelson. Membership had dropped to 908 white and 113 colored. The War of 1812 was at its height with heavy losses of young men in Clark County. There was also a general restlessness of population that sent many Kentuckians westward and northward as the war opened new areas for settlement.

1816: The ministers were Benjamin Laker and Samuel Baker. Membership in the circuit continued to drop to 831 white and 130 colored.

1817: Jonathan Stamper, Absolom Hunt and Richard Corwine were the ministers for the circuit.

Jonathan Stamper was another Clark County boy. He is important enough that there ought to be a biography about him, but none was turned up in this research. Not only were men rotated yearly or nearly so, but the Methodist seemed to move their men away from their home on the grounds that a prophet is without honor in their homes. Stamper made his first and last appearance in Clark County. He would become a prominent minister, a chaplain in the War of 1812, and represented Kentucky Methodist in conferences and assemblies nationally. He was often a presiding elder and a man of considerable influence. Arnold reported that as minister he had 32 preaching points which he covered every six weeks. There was no indication whether he did this alone, what the names of the circuits were or what the other circuit riders were doing. It is possible that these 32 preaching points were the total circuit and the three men worked them together. Mt. Zion is now definite as is Buckeye. Whether Buckeye is the same church that James Landrum reports as a child is not clear. It would be in the same area. With the exception of the Winchester churches, Clark County Methodism had reached the total number of churches it would have in the county.

The Hinkston Circuit was now abolished, or rather divided. Clark County became part of the Mt. Sterling Circuit. It may hurt Winchester's feelings, but Mt. Sterling was, at this time and would remain so until the Civil War, the larger and more important community.

The Methodist evidently would like to keep a ration of one minister for every three hundred or so members. There is no statement to this effect, but this seems to be the practice. Therefore, we can assume that after the bad days in the middle of the decade, the Methodist movement had recovered and the Hinkston Circuit had reached between 1400 and 1500 adherence and that it was divided roughly in half. It is also an indication of the importance of Mt. Sterling at this time. The name of the circuit is usually the center of operation, the stronger church grouping or the home base of the ministers.

From the basis of this history, it matters little which conference a church is in though lacking that information it makes finding statistics even harder. The Kentucky District was in existence from 1793 to 1801. Prior to that time, Kentucky was merely a circuit on an eastern district. By 1802, the movement had grown sufficiently that west of the Alleghenies was lumped into the Western Conference. Kentucky or at least Clark County's part of Kentucky became part of the Ohio Conference in 1812 and in 1821, the Kentucky Conference was organized. The Lexington district for the most part in each case, was the administrative head of the Clark County circuits.

Kathryn Owen, in speaking of her ancestors which includes Lawrence Owen, notes that they were slave holders in Maryland, but they were against slave owning when they became Methodist. Coming to Kentucky, they came as anti slave owners. This opposition to slavery continued among the Owen clan and helped make most of them supporters of the Union when the Civil War had come.

We do not take up slavery in any detail in this volume but save it for the second volume. During this period the opposition to slavery was strongly felt by many Kentuckians. Most vocal in the opposition were ministers, both Baptist and Methodist. Leroy Cole was one of the larger slave owners in Clark County in the 1810s, but he freed all his slaves before his death. His name would be closely associated with David Barrow in the anti slavery efforts of the early 19th century.

However, opposition to slavery decreases rather than increases. Much as Kentucky historians would like to overlook the fact, Kentucky became a breeding ground for slaves for the deep south once the slave trade with Africa and the West Indies was halted. "Being sold down the river" became the ultimate threat of discipline for Kentucky slaves.

There was increasing resentment of the outside abolitionists who came into Kentucky to cause trouble. Harriet Beacher Stowe wrote her absurd but impressive "Uncle Tom's Cabin" based on a Kentucky plantation. Kentucky's reaction was that of a family drawing together in face of outside criticism.

When slavery divided the Baptist, the Clark County associations and churches went along with the Southern Convention without even raising the issue. There was some anti slavery attitude among the Old Baptist that was hardly effective. When the Civil War came, the Rupards, for example, supported the northern cause.

Amont the Methodist the same movement away from slavery could be seen. Repeatedly, the Methodist Conference in Kentucky refused to condemn slavery. Pardoxically, in 1842, the Kentucky Conference firmly refused to divide as demanded by the hot heads on both sides.

The national issue came to a head with the attack on Bishop James Andrews, of Georgia, whose wife had inherited two slaves. According to the Georgia law, he did not have the legal right to free them, and the slaves themselves did not wish to be sent north. However, the problems in the issue were not considered by the radicals, and strong resolutions condemning slavery and anyone who did not take equally strong stands were passed. The division was virtually forced on Kentucky.

The General Methodist Convention met in Louisville in 1844, confirmed the division and set up the Southern Methodist church. H. H. Kavanaugh of Clark County was very active in this division.

There is nothing in the record that would show any Clark County church interested in becoming a northern or a southern Methodist church. William Landrum just doesn't mention slavery or the division of the movement. About 1850 he does note some ministers who belonged to the Southern Methodist movement as if he personally felt better with the northern movement. He doesn't say so, however. His home church, Buckeye, would eventually disappear because of the slavery issue and a northern and a southern church would replace it. Wool's Chapel, which was a development out of the Owen Meeting House, would also go through the same fate. However, in the 1840s and 50s, all of the Clark County churches appeared on the same circuits as if nothing had happened.

It is not until C. C. Thompson marries Joseph Duncan and Elizabeth Gibson, December 7, 1849, that we have a Methodist who signs the marriage book as a southern Methodist. It won't happen again until 1856 when Milton Piles marries John W. Owen to Pauline Sneed, April 10, 1856, in an obvious Wool Chapel marriage. After this, perhaps half the Methodist will state they are southern Methodist. For example, two years later when N. C. Northcutt marries Richard S. Baxter to Francis W. Owen, March 18, 1857, he claimed to be a Southern Methodist. He later joins the northern movement. Piles only married two Clark Countians, but Northcutt had seven marriages which is good for a fast moving Methodist.

In other words, the Clark County Methodist churches up to the Civil War continued in the Kentucky Conference without apparent disruption over whether a church or a minister is northern or southern. It is not entirely clear how the Kentucky Conference stood, for if men like Landrum did not record a difference, the feeling must not have been strong. Yet, the record shows that essentially Kentucky belonged to the Southern Methodist Church more out of default than intention.

However, in 1848, there were Northern Methodist agents seeking support in the south. In 1854, the Northern Methodist were organizing a Kentucky Conference. None of these really effected Clark County other than as we discuss later on. When Horatio Owen willed property to Wools Chapel, the deed was to the Southern Methodist Church.

The break between northern and southern Methodist did not really materialize until after the Civil War. Meanwhile, returning to the chronological history of the Methodist in Clark County.

William Landrum's book, "The Life and Travels of William Landrum," is the best source of information, not only of the Methodist movement in Clark County, but of much of the rest of the life in the county around 1820-1840. He was a Virginian and a second son of a Methodist family which moved to Kentucky, to Boonesboro in 1810. The next year his family moved to Upper Howard's Creek somewhere in the general vacinity of Indian Fields though he never used that name.

Very early in his life he was aware of the Hinkston Circuit. His family had a church on the land of his Uncle Thomas Landrum, a log building with a dirt floor which also doubled for a school. Unless this church is the Buckeye Methodist Church, no other mention of a Methodist church in this area has been made, nor does Landrum himself mention it again. He does mention Buckeye. Evidently his uncle sold out to go to Indiana and the church met in the home of Elijah Newham.

Landrum noted the crudity of the building...this would have to be before 1817, but noted that there were a number of churches in the circuit, Mt. Zion, King's Meeting House, Stamper's Meeting House, Ebeneazor, Owen's Meeting House, Grassy Lick, Switzer's Meeting House, Bethel, Pisgah, Mt. Gerizim (which he later identified as being in Bourbon County) and others. He noted that it was a large circuit and covered four or five counties (which would now cover most of eastern Kentucky.

Most of these churches listed are not mentioned elsewhere. They are obviously churches that one or two families sponsored... Owen, Stamper, Switzer, etc. As with the Landrum church, when the owner of the property and sponsor of the church moved off, the church often died. This would be particularly true of the Methodist being a minority in any community and looked, not exactly down upon, but more askance because of their emotionalism... not too different than the way the present "first" churches look upon the holiness and pentacostal churches in the neighborhood today.

Landrum continually reports groups meeting in homes, prayer meetings and prayer groups. Some of these were more or less permanent. A few, though only a few, would grow into Methodist societies and then into churches.

All of these were served by circuit riders. This was the same type of ministerial services that the Cumberland Presbyterians were giving their people, only on a much larger scale. Landrum was proud of the fact that even though he was on a large circuit, yet his society was served every two weeks, on a Thursday admitted, but nevertheless served. It might be noted that it was this very factor of midweek services that caused the Congregational Methodist break in the deep south in the next twenty some years. However, Landrum seemed to accept it as the best that could be done.

He names Henry McDaniel, Matthew Nelson, Benjamin Rhotum, William McMahon, James Summerville, Benjamin Lukin and others as pastors. We have a name problem here. Is Henry McDaniel the same person as Barnabus McDaniel who had served the circuit earlier. Is Benjamin Lukin the same as Benjamin Larkin or Lakin? Nelson and McMahon were circuit riders on the Hinkston...though Landrum would have to be young to remember them as circuit riders. Who was Benjamin Rhotum?

After Landrum's uncle had left the country, the worship services shifted to Elijay Newham's house. This would have to be between 1817 and 1822. He names Jonathan Stamper, Richard Corwin, Samuel Chuneworth, Joseph Marrow, Heziekial Holland, John T. Leach and Absolum Hand. These all served on the circuit. Stamper's first marriage in Clark County was Thomas Greeney and Elizabeth Dawson, January 17, 1816, Holland's first marriage was William Ellsberry to Nancy Wilkerson, March 2, 1821.

Landrum was now teaching school in the Constant Community, the general area of Strode's Station. He was still impressed by and remembered that Thursdays were the worship day for his family church.

Another feature of worship that is shared both by the Cumberland Presbyterians and the Methodist were the camp meetings. These could last weeks, as did the Cane Ridge Revival which set the pattern in the Clark County section. The participants would load their wagons down with blankets, kitchen utensils and food and camp out for the entire service. The meetings would come in the summer time after the crops had been laid by but before harvest. They were a form of recreation, a vacation away from home, that broke the monotony of hard work. Undoubtedly deeply religious, they were also strongly social. There might be a religious member or two in the family, but it also gave the young people an opportunity to meet. Strong emotions also produced strong emotions and sometimes "sin" found its way into camp. Lyle's diary reports how two Methodist circuit riders thought they had caught such sinners in a barn near a camp meeting only to find out they were men traveling together and sleeping. It gave an opportunity to listen to powerful sermons which were judged often as much on manner of delivery as on content. Many people were saved at such meetings, among these were many who did not come to the meetings with the intentions of being saved.

Arnold says the camp meetings were established as early as 1803. Around Clark County there were three centers of camp meetings that operated almost each year as well as many smaller ones on an irregular basis. These three were Owen's Meeting Ground near their Meeting House, Ebeneazor's Campgrounds in Pine Grove and one near Grassy Lick in Montgomery County.

Landrum reports going to Ebeneazor's meeting in Martin's Wood in July of 1821. He attended another earlier in the month near what is now Sharpsburg. He had been impressed by a Henry C. Bascum who looked like a lawyer orator of the time, but had the fire of a Methodist evangelist. Bascum came to Martin's Wood and repeated his performance. There were seven of these Ebeneazor camp meetings before 1830 and they moved hundreds. The Lexington Methodist movement evidently got a start out of Ebeneazor's camp meeting. Alexander Cummins was presiding elder. In 1823, Landrum reported camp meetings at Grassy Lick. He also attended camp meetings at Sugar Ridge among the Cumberland Presbyterians and reported some of their meetings were exceedingly successful. He attended a meeting at Owen's Campground in which there were 110 conversions and 6 additions to the church. It ought to be noted that the early Methodist had a difference in mind between joining the church and being converted. The former might come well before the later. Nor did it follow, as it did among the Christians, that a convert joined the church.

Between 1820 and 1830, there were at least seven camp meetings held by the Methodist and at least one by the Cumberland Presbyterians in Clark County. In 1830, August 16, there was a camp meeting at Ebeneazor. The ministers were William Holman, George W. Taylor, Richard Tydings, John Sinclair, Thomas Wallace, James Ward and a Brother Rose. August 1, there was a camp meeting at Dunaway with William Brook as the evangelist. In September there was a two day camp meeting at Mt. Zion with William Wright and William Philips preaching. Landrum reported attending others in Shelby County with Joseph Sewell presiding.

These years between 1820 and 1830, as have been reported, were boom years for nearly all religious groups. The camp meeting became very much the instrument of that religious excitement. Even the Baptist Saturday and Sunday meetings took on the flair of a camp meeting often being held in the open.

After 1830, the fire went out of the camp meeting program as it did the whole religious movement. There would be no more camp meetings at Ebeneazor. Why such a successful tool would be so abruptly abandoned is not clear. It is possible that the non religious elements including drinking and sex at the meeting had grown to such a point that the religious leaders were shocked.

The camp meetings passed from the local church almost completely in the 1830s. There would be occasional camp meetings even to the present. In 1840, there was a large camp meeting held at Oil Spring that was basically Methodist. The Cumberland Presbyterians would conduct two or three very successful camp meetings in the 1830s and 1840s. The campgrounds, semi permanent, would develop with buildings and sanitary facilities available, perhaps the most important of these, Paynter's Campground near Mt. Sterling. However, as an official arm of Methodist evangelism it ceased to be.

As indicated, it seemed customary at this time to assign an old and a young minister to each circuit. In addition, there were also the local ministers. We have already referred to Lawrence Owen. We ought also to add to this list Leroy Cole. Cole was one of the original Methodist circuit riders being converted to the ministry in 1777 when there were only 36 ministers serving some 7,000 members. At the famous Christmas Conference he was one of the 12 elders. He also had deep and disturbing contact with James O'Kelley and though there is no indication of the break, he does not seem to have the same feeling for the movement as he did. He was circuit minister for the Tar River Association in North Carolina. He married one of Dr. Hinde's daughters and moved to Clark County. At this point he settled down evidently to a local preacher status. He marries his first couple, John Rogers to December 17, 1811. He performs 44 more marriages during his life time in Clark County which places him second to Lawrence Owen in Methodist marriages performed. It may be a coincidence that he did not start marrying, despite living in Clark County for fifteen years, until after Owen had moved out of the county. In a way, Owen had married those who wanted a Methodist minister. Leroy Cole took up the obligation. Fitch whose manuscript has formed some of this information says that Cole came out of retirement for a two year tour of duty on the Mt. Sterling Circuit, but his name does not appear. Like Owen, the record largely ignores him. Like Owen, the O'Kelley influence against itineracy in the ministry or at least the forced itineracy had its effect. Cole, whose activities against slavery caused him to free his slaves, remained one of the most important figures in Clark County Methodism. Other local ministers were John Dunaway, Joseph Sewell, John Conkwright, and Martin Gillespie. There may be more since the Methodist records do not carry them, the next source is the marriage records.

METHODIST HISTORY

The new Mt. Sterling Circuit included everything from the eastern Bath County line to the Fayette boundary including all of what is now Powell County all the way into the present Breathitt. It was still a huge area, but the Red River Valley and the upper reaches of the Kentucky were still largely wilderness with sparse and isolated cabins and few settlements of any type. The circuit included Mt. Sterling, Grassy Lick, Old Fort (which was about where Camargo is today); Salem, also in southern Montgomery County; Mt. Nepo in the Kiddville area but in Montgomery County; Buckeye in the Indian Fields area closer to the Iron Works Pike which was in full operation most of these years before it became a private pike; Wren School House in the area not far from Lullbegrud in Montgomery County, Sharpsburg, Owen Meeting House, Ebeneazor, Mt. Zion, Dunaway, Stamper's Meeting House and a Proctor's Meeting House, whose location is uncertain, apparently formed the organized churches. In addition, there were three campgrounds, Ebeneazor, Owen Meeting House and Grassy Lick. There is no indication whether there were additional preaching points. None of these churches apparently were in the mountain country along the Red River and Kentucky River.

1818: Alexander Cummins became the presiding elder of the Lexington District and would hold the post until 1820. Samuel Chenowith was minister for two years. This was unusual. Joseph Morrow was the junior minister.

1819: Hesekiah Holland became the junior minister.

1820: Absolum Hunt and John R. Keatch (Leach is probably the right spelling) became Mt. Sterling Circuit ministers.

1821: Marcus Lindsay became the presiding elder until 1824. This is the longest any presiding elder of the Lexington District had held office. The practice of yearly movement of ministers was unchanged by being questioned. The Methodist movement was becoming stable. Societies had grown into churches. There were fewer preaching points that came and went with the movement of a single family. The Baptist were making steady progress and the Methodist churches were demanding more stable leadership to meet their new conditions. The frontier was gone by this time. Roads reached almost every community. Only back in the mountains that still remained nominally part of Clark County was frontier. Much of the actual leadership of the church was in the hands of the "local" minister who was unnamed in the official records. They were merely listed as numbers on the circuit.

What is more, there was need for another type of preaching than fiery evangelism. This was ideal for camp meetings, but more and more, a regular church meeting once a month, wanted more in their sermons.

1822: Josiah Whitaker and William C. Stripling became circuit ministers. William Landrum mentions that he attended a service in which Stripling spoke for five hours. Landrum evidently felt that this was sufficiently unusual to mention it in his journal, but he did not comment on it as being something radically different.

1823: John Ray was assigned to the Hinkston Circuit and Martin Flynn to the Mt. Sterling Circuit. Ray was from Clark and Montgomery Counties so they traded. This is the only incident where the wishes of the ministers apparently were permitted to effect the ministry. John Ray was one of the most popular Methodist ministers of the period. He had been a lay minister similar to Leroy Cole. His first marriage in Clark County had been Charles Gilkey to Annette McDonald. He had some six marriages over the years. He began preaching in 1801 in various circuits of the state but in 1809 he settled three miles outside of Mt. Sterling and dropped out of the itinerary. He came back in 1819 and continued until his death.

1824: William Stripling was back on the Mt. Sterling Circuit as senior minister with Fountain Pitts his junior minister. Stripling's first marriage was Wyatt Hall to Nancy Scoby (this name is spelled several different ways in the various records but presumedly is the Scobee family). He married two couples in Clark. Stripling was to become for the Campbellite Reform movement what Burke had been to the O'Kelley people. The Campbellites did not have any strong inside hold on the Methodist that they had on the Baptist. However, their message was agressively designed to bring all churches into their one fellowship and the pressure on the Methodist was to increase and reach a high point about 1835. Stripling had a series of debates with Racoon Smith in the years to follow. Fountain Pitts, according to Landrum, held a successful camp meeting at Owen Meeting House.

Landrum also reported that meetings were being held at the Academy building in Winchester. At this time Mt. Zion, Stamper's Chapel, Ebeneazor, Dunaway, Buckeye and soon Winchester formed the Methodist church in the county.

In passing we note that the Methodist approved Sunday schools in 1824. The idea, however, was not to really take ahold in Clark County until much later. Just as the Calvinists believed that those who had been saved were predestined to be saved and education would not change that one way or another, the Methodist felt that the sinner had to have an emotional experience to break the bonds of sin. Education would not materially increase the likelihood of that experience. In fact, some Methodist felt that too much education

might retard the saving process. Still, the knowledge of the
scripture never hurt anyone and both Methodist and Baptist would
take Sunday schools seriously by the Civil War.

1825: William Adams became presiding elder until 1827. Isaac
Collard and John Sinclair would be the ministers. Sinclair would
remain the next year, though still a junior. Milton Jameson would
be the senior minister in 1826 and 1827. T. N. Ralston would be
the junior minister in 1827. Collard married Joseph Fry to Prescilla Payne, June 14, 1826. He had four Clark County marriages.

Religious fervor in the county had reached its height in 1827.
Everyone but the Particular Baptist and Presbyterians were growing
by bounds and even these Calvinists showed mild improvement. The
Reforms were doubling and tripling the Baptist and organizing new
churches. The Cumberland Presbyterians were having extremely
successful revivals and took over the Sugar Ridge Church in Clark
County. The Methodist were in such a state that two more young
ministers were rushed into the circuit to handle the work, Israel
Lewis and John Y. Young. This addition took particular interest
in Methodism along the Red River. Landrum reports attending prayer
meetings of this group along with Martin Gillespie, who seemed to
be a local minister, David Smith and Elias Gardner. The Winchester
church was now established and Winchester and Mt. Sterling were
building brick buildings. Gillespie incidently married some 17
couples, his first being Harvey Gardner to Rachel Gentry, November 1, 1821. It is interesting that Gillespie becomes the marrying
Methodist minister of the county about the same time Leroy Cole
drops out of the picture. We have already noted a similar coincidence concerning Cole and Lawrence Owen. Hence, we have a chain
of Methodist, Owen, Cole and Gillespie, local ministers, but each
seemingly did the marrying of Methodist in the county. The difficulty of finding out just what the roles of these local ministers
were is still uncertain.

There is a hole in our notes concerning other laymen in these
Methodist circuits. The information lies in diaries, letters, etc.
in trunks and personal collections that so far have not been
available.

1826: Milton Jamison and John Sinclair.

1827: Milton Jamison remained for a second year and T. N.
Ralston became the junior minister.

George W. Taylor became presiding elder in 1828. The lists do
not show that Taylor was a Clark County product though both the
Taylor family and the given name George had strong roots in Clark
County. He continued as elder until 1831. The presiding elder
continued to provide the stabilizing element and maintain continuity
of effort in the picture of rapidly changing ministers serving a
dozen preaching points. With preaching once a month, a church
hardly got to know their minister. The elder at the quarterly

conference met the leadership of the church in an intimate relationship, lent to the churches ministerial services while the ministers presented an evangelistic front.

The minister of the circuit in 1828 was David D. Dyce, or (Dykes). He married Rufus Dunlop to Ann Broughton, December 11, 1828. Dyches was also a family name but there is no record whether this Dyches belonged to the same clan.

The loose leaf history of the Clark County churches which we have mentioned reports that in 1829 this circuit included Wool's Chapel, Buckeye, Snow Hill, Mt. Zion, North Middletown, Dunaway... Mrs. Matthew Dykes who gave the history of the Mt. Zion Church repeated this statement. Perhaps her source is this manuscript. However, this is the same list of churches that William Landrum reports in 1849 for the North Middletown Circuit. It would be impossible for Wool's Chapel to be in existence for Wool will not serve churches in this area until 1842. Wool's Chapel is another name for Owen Meeting House. Perhaps the manuscript writer, quoting Fitch who was writing later and knew the Owen Meeting House as Wool's Chapel, post dated the name.

Certainly at this time Owen Meeting House, Buckeye, Mt. Zion, Winchester and Ebeneazor were in existence and probably on the same circuit. Stamper's Chapel has disappeared from the list. Landrum reports attending meetings there in 1824. Joshua Stamper died in 1825 and his wife in 1826. The land that the Stampers owned was sold, and though there was a title to the church, perhaps it wasn't good enough. It would eventually be sold to Asa Bean who had already been in possession twenty years later. At any rate, Stamper's Chapel disappears from the history of Clark County churches. At a time when all other churches were booming and in an era where there were few if any other churches, it is curious why this would be so. It is an example of the unstability of the family church.

At least the Mt. Sterling Circuit had become so big that it was broken into half, the Winchester Circuit including the Clark County churches. Taylor remained its presiding elder, and John Sinclair and T. Wallace became the first minister in the new circuit. Wallace married Lesley Bostnick and Mary Ann Combs, May 18, 1831. For some reason, the Winchester Circuit had been shifted to the Rockcastle District. In 1831, John Williams was the minister and 1831 William Philips was the minister. He married John Gay and Rebecca Braton (Bratton), August 4, 1830. He married 8 couples.

In 1832, the Winchester Circuit was shifted to the Harrodsburg District and William Adams returned as presiding elder for two years. Philips remained as junior minister, but C. M. Holiday was sent as senior minister and J. Nevius as another junior minister. Holiday married William Milby and Elizabeth Dean, November 23, 1833.

He married four couples. Nevius married Thomas Morgan to Nancy Bell, September 11, 1834.

John James and Minor Cosby were the circuit ministers in 1833. James married Anderson Lowery to Catherine Niblick, October 29, 1834. James was promoted to presiding elder in 1834. He married Minor Crosley to Luise Adkins, June 25, 1834. More and more, the circuit ministers are marrying. Perhaps this is because there are more Methodist and therefore, more opportunities. Also by the 1830s, the Methodist no longer appeared to others as a wild, slightly unbalanced group of fanatics. Some of their evangelistic methods had now become standard with Baptist and Reform as well as Cumberland Presbyterians. Some of the excesses of earlier days had quietly been controlled. As the Methodist party did this, extremes would bring them up again. The Holiness movement had its roots in the 1830s. James would continue as presiding elder until 1837.

The ministers of 1824 were Henry J. Evans and S. Veach. Samuel Veach was born in 1791. He was converted in 1817; better educated than most; 1833 approved to Hinkston Circuit; in 1849 Mt. Sterling Circuit. He retired in 1831 but went to the north. The circuit reported 591 white members and 198 colored members. Methodism in the county had reached its peak. Winchester was shifted back to the Lexington District in 1835. The circuit lost membership, but this may be because of rearrangement of churches so that their figures would appear elsewhere. We note that Milton Jamison was debating John Racoon Smith and that the Reform was also pushing the Methodist. However, there was no significant loss either of ministers or members to the Christians. An occasional defection was the best the Christian church could post. No churches split or were lost.

1835: T. H. Gibbon was minister. In 1835 the Kentucky Conference voted against any stand against slavery. The issue was now becoming national and the northern Methodist were pushing heavily.

1836: Jesse Sutton was the minister.

1837: Thomas Rankin and George Merrick. Membership had slipped to 337 whites and 129 colored. There is no visible reason for this loss though there may be a reaction to the heavy religious drive of the last decade in all churches. Also, the county was losing people to the west.

1838: The district was switches back to the Lexington District. William Gunn became the presiding elder for the next three years. Elijah Madison Bosley and William McMahon were the ministers. Jesse Sutton had married a Mr. Reed to Gillis Caps, June 26, 1837, the only marriage he would perform in the county. Thomas Rankin married David Reid to Martha Woodward. Rankin married no less than nine couples during his relationship with Clark County and McMahan only the one. However, carrying the coincidence of Owen-Cole-Gillespie forward into another generation, we note that lay minister Joseph Sewell married William Hornbeck and Mary Parrish, November 9, 1833. In his ministry he would marry 18 Clark County couples. He continues the interesting fact that a lay minister seemed to carry much of the marrying in the county upon his shoulders. It is probably that the number of lay ministers are increasing with the increasing membership of the churches. Also, coming into the center of the local picture as a local preacher is John Conkwright who in October 26, 1836, married Martin Goldman to Susan Woosley and would continue to marry no less than 59 couples during his life time within Clark County.

1853: In Ralston's second year at Winchester, William C. Dandy became presiding elder for the year.

1854: John G. Bruce became presiding elder. It is important in future events to call attention to the prominent place that Bruce plays in Central Kentucky's Methodist history but also calls attention to other names such as Gunn, Harrison, Dandy and Northcutt. These men will, after the Civil War, leave the Southern Methodist Church and spearhead the Northern Methodist Movement. At this time, the Northern Methodist Movement in Kentucky is very feeble and without much hope of becoming stronger. There is little or no northern influence apparent in Clark County at this time. Bruce remained presiding elder until 1857. This is an unusually long period for a presiding elder to hold office though more and more the presiding elders were remaining in office four years. Robert Miner was the minister in 1854-55.

It was in 1854 that Ebeneazor burned and the congregation, instead of rebuilding, voted to unite with the Winchester Church. It was an unhappy marriage. Rather than make Winchester a full time church, it is now combined with Mt. Zion.

1856-57: Henry C. Northcutt becomes minister in the Winchester Station Circuit. At this point, Mt. Zion records begin with a list of ministers that have served that church. The list gives an excellent check as to what churches served with Mt. Zion.

Evidently, Mt. Zion was taken away from Winchester in 1856-57, for Mt. Zion claims Hiner served all three years whereas Finch's and the minutes show that Northcutt is at Winchester.

1858: William C. Dandy becomes presidng elder for one year. L. G. Hicks becomes minister of the Winchester-Mt. Zion Circuit or Station. Hicks would remain so until 1859. His name is reported by the Winchester Chronicle for these years. William Landrum attends Hick's final sermon.

1859: John C. Harrison becomes presiding elder until 1862.

1860: Joseph Rand served Mt. Zion and Winchester for two years.

Normally, city churches will be reported after 1860 in the third volume of this history, but unlike all the other denominational city churches, the Methodist city church and the county churches were closely tied together. The Baptist Church would not be a full time church until 1888, but it was linked with David's Fork Baptist Church which was a Fayette County church. The Presbyterian minister would at times serve country churches, but that was largely a relationship between the city minister and the country church. A Methodist circuit is a much more intimate bond than either of these cases, almost an organic union with separate preaching points.

Conkwright is also interesting in passing. Not only is he the most popular marrying person among the Methodist since Lawrence Owen, but he also was the second minister in the records to use the title Reverend. Up to this point neither the Baptist or the Christians would use the title. It was much against the Christian theology and not used by the Baptist because they preferred the title Elder. There were not enough Presbyterians in the record to set a custom. The Methodist were to become the movement that without hesitation would use the title from 1836 on...perhaps as a reflex to Baptist and Christian opposition. Conkwright also would sign himself after 1855 as Methodist Episcopal South. He was among the first to use that distinction though obviously all the Methodist at this time were in the Southern Conference.

1839: Calisle Babbitt. Babbitt married Rodney Hinde to Catherine Scholl, May 1880.

1840: Babbitt and Drummond Welbur. He married Francis T. Owen to Catherine Powers, October 21, 1841. The Kentucky Conference was held at Pynter camp group in Mt. Sterling.

1841: Benjamin Crouch became the presiding elder until 1844. Peter Taylor and John Evan (the Fitch list has Evans in parenthesis).

1842: James S. Wools and John Van Pelt. Babbitt married his first, Elam Barnard to Mary Taul in December, 1839. He would perform five marriages. John B. Ewan married Tarlton Cox to Louise Watkins May 10, 1843, for two Clark County marriages. This was well after his period in the county representing the establishments of friend- ships that would continue after the minister had left the area.

The appearance of Wool is important because of his tie with the Owen Meeting House. For some reason he makes sufficient impression on the Owen area that his name is attached to their church which be- comes Wool's Chapel for the next quarter century. This will be dis- cussed further in the Owen Chapel section. Certainly he did not appear any different than any other circuit minister and married no Clark County couples.

1843: Wools remains for the second year as the senior minister with William Kavanaugh as his junior minister. Kavanaugh was to marry William Freeman to Elizabeth Ann Huls, November 8, 1843.

1844: Josua Wilson and Evan Stevenson.

1845: Hubbard Kavanaugh comes to the Winchester Circuit to be presiding elder for two years. Joshua Wilson remains as circuit minister.

1846: John G. Bruce becomes minister. Bruce will continue the next few years to play a very important part in Clark County Methodist history. There is no record of his marrying anyone in the county despite his relationship to it. Whether this negates the theory that the number of marriages in a county is a good measure of a minister's popularity will be noted later.

Thomas Ralston, who had been circuit minister twenty years before, becomes presiding elder in 1847 with Elkaneh Johnson as minister. Only one minister is now being assigned to the circuit. Sometime during this period, certainly by 1849, the circuit is divided with Winchester and Ebeneazor in one circuit and the rest of Clark County in another. It could be that the presence of strong local preachers, that the Methodist felt that one was enough.

Nationally, a number of things were happening that deserve notice though they did not effect the Clark County Methodist movement. In 1828, the Kentucky and Tennessee Methodist were divided into different conferences. The area that directly effected the Clark County churches was growing steadily smaller. In 1830, the Methodist Protestant Church was organized. This is still part of the continuing protest that James O'Kelley began against the sending of ministers. The Methodist Protestants had presiding elders but no bishops. There were a few Methodist Protestant churches in Kentucky but on the whole, it was a northern movement and had no Clark County effects. Before the decade was out, the Congregational Methodist movement was threatening Methodism in the deep south. A rural movement, it passed largely unnoticed by Methodist historians but was influenced by the O'Kelley Republican Methodist Movement that had retained its individuality in southern Georgia and Alabama. Again, it had no real part in Clark County history.

In 1843, the Weslyan Methodist will draw from the main movement. Once again, this was largely a northern movement and closely related to the slavery question. It would not reach Clark County until after World War I.

In 1836, a church in Portland, Maine installed a pipe organ as part of its worship services. (Pianos were not yet available and harpsicords were not rugged enough for the kind of treatment church musical instruments get). The Methodist publication for Kentucky protested that "no congregation of Methodism in the Union would tolerate such an invasion of our churches." By the time organs became plentiful, it was no longer an issue in the Methodist church.

Up to this point, the Methodist Winchester Circuit contained all the churches in Clark County, Wool's Chapel(the former Owen's Meeting House), Mt. Zion, Dunaway, Buckeye and Winchester...or at least it is presumed that Buckeye was part of this circuit though the history of the Methodist in Montgomery County includes Buckeye though admitting it was in Clark County. There is a very good chance that Buckeye was affiliated with the Mt. Sterling Circuit. If this would be true, each of these churches had preaching but once a month including Winchester.

However, for the last ten years there has been a growing demand on the larger churches for a greater ministerial care. Already the Presbyterians had twice a month preaching and the Christians had full time service...the first in Winchester. They had two ministers to do it, but the establishment of the concept of full time was established.

Many of the old time circuit riders protested this change. They felt that in some way this was partiality and undue favoritism to the larger churches that could only work harm to the smaller. However, the pressure grew and as a result in 1846, Winchester became a station church. It was still not full time for with it was assigned either Ebeneazor which was usual and sometimes Mt. Zion. However, this did break up the Winchester Circuit so that it never again reformed.

There follows a period of shifting circuits and unfortunately the Methodist do not list the churches on them. Roughly, Winchester and Ebeneazor made a circuit. Mt. Zion, North Middletown, Grassy Lick, Wool's Chapel, Mt. Nepo (a Montgomery Church near Kiddville) Buckeye, Hardwick Creek, Howard's Chapel and perhaps an Estill County church. Actually for the next fifty years, until well into the 20th century, circuits are in constant flux with a variety of combinations being tried.

William Landrum in 1849 reports that this circuit includes Mt. Zion, Dunaway, North Middletown, Snow Hill, Buckeye and Wool's Chapel. There is a confusion here because Landrum himself becomes minister of the Viena Circuit in 1848 which included Buckeye. Wool's Chapel, a Kiddville Church Landrum calls Providence, but it may be the old Mt. Nepo Church and Howard's Chapel in Viena which is on the Red River in Clark County. It was at this time a promising community reaching into what is now the Log Lick area and over into Estill County.

There is a constant shifting of churches because the North Middletown Circuit was in existence in 1856, but there were no Clark County churches upon it.

The problem is which circuit should be traced out first. The best record is the circuit that served Winchester Station.

1850: William Gunn becomes presiding elder for the next three years. In 1850, Allen A. Jameson was minister of the Winchester-Ebeneazor Station.

1851: H. H. Kavanaugh who had been superintendent.

1852-53: Thomas N. Ralston who had also been a presiding elder. There is no indication of any reasons why these presiding elders should become church ministers again. It was not uncommon in the earlier days, but had become less the custom. It is possible that in those days when the Methodist movement was sinking, there was an effort to keep superior men in the churches.

1861: Joseph Rand became minister of the Winchester-Mt. Zion Circuit for two years.

1862: The record shows that T. P. C. Sheman was minister of the circuit for a year, but he does not appear on Mt. Zion's list. The possibility is that Mt. Zion was switched elsewhere for that year, but since Mt. Zion shows no name that does not belong to the circuit, it is more likely that this minister was simply omitted.

1863: John G. Bruce was again presiding elder and W. W. Chamberlain was minister for two years. In 1864, W. F. Taylor became minister during the last year of Chamberlain.

1865: Newton G. Berryman becomes presiding elder for a year and J. W. Fitch becomes minister for two years. The circuit changes now to Winchester, Mt. Zion and North Middletown. The circuit reported 135 members, but of course, it does not break it down to churches. Presumedly, Mt. Zion is the larger church, though Winchester would have to be nearly as large. A guess would be roughly a 60-50 membership with North Middletown, a very sick third member. Fitch would leave the best record of Winchester churches that is available, mostly in Kentucky Weslyan but with some pages of it in the Council of Ministries in Lexington.

Fitch was to remain the minister in 1866, but H. P. Walker began a two year presiding eldership in that year.

1867: W. T. Poynter became minister of the circuit. There is some reason to think that Grassy Lick was also on this circuit. If so, then the Winchester Circuit had degenerated from an almost full time Winchester church to a regular four church circuit. This undoubtedly was the result of the turmoil of the Civil War.

1868: G. W. Merritt became presiding elder for the next three years. There is no evidence of a northern Methodist movement in Winchester or its circuit though the Clark Memorial Methodist Church came into being during this period and belonged to the Negro district of the Northern Methodist Movement. Mt. Zion was taken off the circuit. We have no information what happened to North Middletown but it is no longer connected with Clark County churches. It passes from existence at some future date. Mt. Zion is circuited with Grassy Lick. Ebeneazor is reorganized and circuited with Winchester in 1868.

1869: F. W. Noland becomes minister of Winchester and Ebeneazor. He is minister for four years. This is the longest ministry of a Methodist minister in Clark County.

In 1871, E. P. Buckner was presiding elder and 1872, J. W. Fitch became presiding elder of the Lexington District for four years. Drummond Welburn was minister, 1973. For some reason in

1874, Mt. Zion was once again tied up with Winchester. J. R. Deering was the minister that year. Mt. Zion was switched back to Grassy Lick. Grassy Lick had spent that year in the Sharpsburg Circuit.

1875: G. W. Merrit becomes presiding elder once again and G. C. Kelley becomes the minister for another four year pastorate. T. F. Van Meter was presiding elder for one year in 1879. H. P. Walker was presiding elder in 1880 and S. S. Pentz was minister. In 1882, J. W. Mitchel was minister.

1884: J. Rand became presiding elder for four years and during the same time, J. H. Young became minister of Winchester Ebeneazor.

1888: H. P. Walker again was sent to the Lexington District as presiding elder for another four year term. He would become the presiding elder who had served longest in the Lexington District. Bruce being second with six years. For the same period J. H. Young served Winchester-Ebeneazor.

1892: J. Rand was returned to the district as presiding elder for four years to tie Walker's record. W. T. Boling became minister for two years. H. G. Henderson followed from 1894 to 1898. However, Ebeneazor died in 1896 and because this ended the country section of the Winchester Circuit, we will continue Winchester's history in the third volume of this series. The Winchester Methodist Church was the last Winchester city church to become a full time church.

## MT. ZION METHODIST CHURCH

It is possible at this point to offer what little information that is available on the Mt. Zion Methodist Church. She was probably historically the strongest of the surviving rural churches of the Methodist movement in Clark County. Being not far outside of Winchester, her affairs more than any other rural church were reported in the Winchester papers after the Civil War. The only problem is the fact that there is also a Mt. Zion Christian Church not far out of Winchester in the opposite direction. The newspapers were not always careful to distinguish which church they were reporting.

There was also a Zion Methodist Church. Mr. Stanley Clay had a poster calling for a political meeting in 1866 to meet at the Zion Methodist Church on the Mt. Sterling highway. This had to be the Mt. Zion Church and the term Zion is not used elsewhere. After the building of the new building in 1848, the church was for some ten years, referred to as the new Mt. Zion Methodist Church. Usually when a new church building was constructed, the old church in the old location would continue for a while in some function or another, as a church or as a school, hence the need for the distinction. There is no record how the old building was used.

Mt. Zion was not the first Methodist Church in the county. Owen's Meeting House, Ebeneazor, Stamper's Chapel and probably Dunaway were older than Mt. Zion. However, since she has a record of her ministers since 1856, a history of Mt. Zion helps place churches in their right circuit after this period. Also, Mt. Zion was for a while bracketed with the Winchester Church and it is, therefore, logical that we take her up at this point.

Mt. Zion Methodist Church was established sometime before 1817. There seemingly is no clear date for its establishment. In 1817, William Landrum, and he does not pinpoint the date better, one of the churches that he listed as being on the circuit of his church was Mt. Zion. The fact that it was a church would indicate that even in 1817, it was a strong church and therefore, years old at that time. It probably began as a preaching point where two or three families met to hear a Methodist preacher. It no doubt, then grew into a Methodist society still meeting in homes. When it built its first building or became a regular church is not reported in any record that has been available.

Mt. Zion was a church in the Hinkston Circuit. Therefore, all presiding elders of the Lexington District and ministers of the Hinkston Circuit served Mt. Zion. Just which ones preached regularly, if any of them, or whether they revolved taking turns, is not recorded in any of the available information.

Deed Book 16, in 1820, reports that Washington and Polly Mills deeded to John Gardner, Thomas Gardner, James Miller and William Rueben, trustees for the Methodist Episcopal Church, property on which the church was already built. As usual, these trustees represent the circuit and not the local church and it means that they were active Methodist laymen and not necessarily members of Mt. Zion. Thomas Gardner particulary appears on several other Methodist deeds. There was also a cemetary on the property which indicates the age of the church building. Landrum names the ministers serving the area to include Jonathan Stamper, Richard Corwin, Samuel Chinelworth, Joseph Farrow, Hezekial Holland, John Leach and Absolum Hand. We have already reported that the circuit which Landrum mention contained ten churches and an unknown number of preaching points. How the minister arranged the services, whether on Sunday or through the week as Landrum's home church, is not available.

In 1821, Mt. Zion became a member of the Mt. Sterling Circuit. All the ministers listed for that circuit served Mt. Zion, when and how we do not know. In 1827, a new Mt. Zion Church was built. The Fox Cousins' book reports that Flavel Vivion and Robert Bush helped build Mt. Zion's new church in that year. This does not necessarily mean that they were Methodist since most of the Vivions at this time were Upper Howard Creek Baptist. The building was finished May 8, 1927.

Landrum mentions attending "old" Mt. Zion in 1829. Was he referring to the old building? If so, what happened to the new church building? Or was he referring to the old established Mt. Zion? He called John Gardner the Apostle of Methodism in Clark County. In 1830, Landrum visited a two day meeting at Mt. Zion. A Wright (does not give the first name) and a William Philips, who would come to Mt. Zion and the Mt. Sterling Circuit in 1832 as ministers, were the speakers. There is no indication what Philips was doing at this time, whether he was a licensee getting experience or a full time minister doing evangelical work.

In 1829, Mrs. Matthew Dykes reports that the Winchester Circuit included Winchester, Dunaway, Wool's Chapel, North Middletown, Mt. Zion, Buckeye and Snow Creek. The use of Wool's Chapel instead of Owen Chapel indicates the list was a later list, but no doubt the same churches were on the circuit at this time as they were before the breakup of the Winchester Circuit which this also now created. Another problem is the circuit which included Ebeneazor was not a Clark County Circuit.

The ministers that served the Winchester Circuit until 1848 were also the ministers of Mt. Zion.

Deed Book 9, 1839, reports that Andrew Ramsey gave Thornton Wills (who later would become a Baptist minister), John W. Wills,

David Spurgeon, and George Scobee, a lot on the Little Stoner Creek to be used for a building for the Methodist church. This represents a very strong Mt. Zion trustee position rather than a circuit trusteeship. Unless it was Spurgeon, all were affiliated with Mt. Zion. This may explain why the deed lacks the usual safeguards to keep the property strictly Methodist that most of the Methodist deeds at this time and later have written in them. Instead, this deed states that all denominations when not used by Methodist could use the property. We note also a shifting of the Cumberland Sugar Ridge Ramseys towards the Methodist.

There is actually nothing in the deed book that states the property would belong to the Methodist Church at Mt. Zion. The geographical location and the names of the trustees indicate Mt. Zion.

The Legislative Manual of the House of Representatives in Kentucky reports the introduction of a bill which was routinely passed, permitting the Mt. Zion Methodist Church in Clark County to be sold in favor of the Methodist Episcopal Diocese. (We note that all church property of the Methodist is owned by the Methodist Diocese which has the last word in how it should be used.) Apparently, it took legislative permission for a church to sell its property. Presumedly this is to prevent a small group to high handedly sell church property.

As a result of this bill, Deed Book 30 shows Thorton Wills acting as trustee or commissioner in selling Lycinda Flynn the land that old Mt. Zion stood as soon as the church moves to the new location.

Landrum lists Mt. Zion, North Middletown, Mt. Zion, Buckeye, Snow Creek, Dunaway and Wool's Chapel on the North Middletown Circuit in 1847. Winchester is missing. However, in 1856, Mt. Zion is linked with Winchester in a circuit of their own. For two years, 1856 and 57, Mt. Zion was switched to another circuit, evidently with Grassy Lick. In 1858, Mt. Zion is once again linked with Winchester. In 1865, North Middletown appears linked with Winchester and Mt. Zion. There is a good possibility that Grassy Lick became part of the circuit in 1867.

The ministers of the circuit were also ministers of the Mt. Zion Church. There are no stories or reports from Mt. Zion during these years. The history of stage coaching in Kentucky mentions an accident to one of the stages near new Mt. Zion before the Civil War. In 1866 a hand bill announced a Democratic meeting at the Zion Church on the Mt. Sterling Road. There is good reason to believe that Mt. Zion was a strong church through this whole period.

In 1868, Mt. Zion is linked with Grassy Lick, a combination that would last until 1903. North Middletown apparently was the third church on this list. The presiding elders, of course, are the same as the Winchester District. The membership of the circuit in 1868 was 172. J. W. Fitch is minister for two years.

Membership of the Mt. Zion, North Middletown, Grassy Lick Circuit in 1869, J. W. Fitch's last year at Mt. Zion Circuit, was 116.

1868-69: T. G. Bosley was the minister. Membership of the three churches was 120.

1869-1870: Dr. Charles Taylor, membership was 137.

1871-1872: Dr. R. H. Reed, membership 135. Presumedly the title of doctor refers to Doctor of Divinity rather than medical doctor. It does represent in either case, a superior type of minister at this time serving country churches. This would parallel the Baptist minister such as Wills, French, Potts, etc. The country church had the best available in these days.

North Middletown is dropped from the Mt. Zion Circuit and the church is now linked with Dunaway and El Bethel. Since this information comes from the mastheads of the newspaper, the circuit could carry a fourth church. The name is the Winchester Circuit though it no longer includes Winchester's church.

1873-1874: The minister was George Smith. J. W. Fitch is presiding elder from 1873-1877.

1874-1877: John B. Deering.

1877-1878: W. W. Spates.

1878-1879: T. B. Cook. The masthead of the Winchester newspapers, whose file from this date, for either the WINCHESTER SUN or the CLARK COUNTY DEMOCRAT, is nearly complete at the University of Kentucky, reports that Mt. Zion has a Sunday school on the first and third Sundays when there is also preaching. There is no indication whether Sunday school is held on the other Sundays or how long it had been in operation. Presumedly, like most of the country Sunday schools, it is closed down in the winter and reorganized in the spring.

1878-1879: W. W. Hiner. There was another Hiner minister in the 1850s. There was never a comment on whether W. W. was Robert Hiner's son, or whether there was a relationship.

1878-1880: S. L. Robertson.

1880-1882; G. D. Turner was minister with the circuit with services on the first and third Sundays. Mt. Zion is no longer on the circuit with Dunaway and El Bethel. These are now part of the Old Fort Circuit. Mt. Zion is now linked with Grassy Lick and two times a month for each church service. The CLARK COUNTY DEMOCRAT, January 3, 1881, reported that Mt. Zion held a church supper at Vineyard, the then home of Ben Grooms. One hundred fifty people attended and $100.00 was raised. This is the first such activity reported for any church in Clark County. Considering the month, the dinner was held inside the big mansion. There is no indication whether Grooms was a Methodist or just offering his house.

The Mt. Zion Grassy Lick Circuit begins in 1882 with both churches having services twice a month.

1882-1885: B. F. Kavanaugh is the minister. This part of the Kavanaugh family which has played such an important part in Clark County and state Methodist history.

1885-1886: The minister of the circuit was T. W. Barnett. His names does not appear on Mrs. Dykes' list of Mt. Zion ministers. This was a couple of years of Clark County history where there was not a newspaper record available.

1886-1888: C. G. Nugent.

1888-1889: J. W. Fitch. This is the minister who has written the history of the Clark County churches which is found in part in the Council of Ministry and at Kentucky Weslyan. He had earlier been minister of Winchester-Ebeneazor. Evidently, he had been raised at Owen's Chapel and retired in Winchester.

1889-1894: D. B. Ware. Here again, we have an example of the trend seen in the Winchester-Ebeneazor Circuit of longer ministries. His father had been minister of the Winchester Circuit in 1854.

1894-1898: J. J. Johnson.

1898-1899: D. O. Robinson. Sunday school at 10:30, 2nd and 4th, 3 o'clock on 1st and 3rd.

1899-1903: George Froh. Evidently, Froh was a man of considerable ability. He received a good bit of attention by the newspapers during the four years he served. The fact that he served four years is a startling departure from the usual Methodist custom. However, there has been a trend to leave a man a little longer in a church than in the original days. In dealing with the Methodist itineracy, one must remember that though the circuit minister changed each year or so, the presiding elder who directed the affairs of the circuit through the quarterly meeting, stayed several years. There was also a network of local ministers whose names did not appear in the reports, yet who carried much of the load of the parish work year after year. Grassy Lick was switched to a circuit with Camargo's Old Fort Methodist Church. The name of the new circuit was Mt. Zion Circuit and included Dunaway and El Bethel. Mt. Zion had two Sundays a month.

1903-1904: J. R. Peoples. Peoples evidently was a power house of work whose activities interested the newspaper. As Froh seemingly was deeply respected, Peoples astonished. For example, March 2, 1902, he preached at Mt. Zion in the morning, at Schollsville School House at 3, and at El Bethel at 7. The SUN SENTINEL did not give his schedule for the 9th, but on the 14th he was at Wades Mill in the morning and in the afternoon (evidently using Mt. Carmel's church building still controlled by the Baptist who permitted its use to any Christian). March 3, he preached at El Bethel in the morning, Dunaway in the afternoon and Kiddville School House in the evening. The paper did not say whether this extraordinary schedule which had some features of the earlier circuit riding was a special one coming before Easter, or an effort to extend the Methodist influence. There had not been a new Methodist church in Clark County since before the Civil War except for El Bethel.

In any case, no Methodist churches appeared at any of the school houses he served.

1906-1909: W. F. Wyatt, the circuit fell back into the old pattern.

1909-1913: H. C. Wright.

1913-1917: G. W. Boswell.

1917-1918: W. W. Green.

1918-1921: W. L. Byrd.

At this point we will break the history of Mt. Zion and leave the rest for the fourth volume. Unlike the Baptist which show a definite low point in this year and steady climb in the next half century, the Methodist show less decline. There are losses that can be attributed more to the loss of all country churches due to the mobility of population.

There has not been the open divisions that have marked the Baptist either. However, unreported in the section on Methodist because they are not technically Methodist, are the appearance of the smaller and newer denominations, the various Churches of God, Nazarine, Assemblies of God, Holiness, etc. Most of that story falls into the third volume. These newer movements tend to do to the Methodist movement what the divisions did in the Baptist and Christians. There was also the undercover threat of the Holiness movement within the Methodist church itself that, though rigidly controlled among the ministers, remained like a restless stirring among the people. The fact that of all the Methodist seminaries, Asbury is the most conservative ameliorates that problem somewhat.

As this period closes, we note that now ministers are staying in their circuits three years.

## EBENEAZOR METHODIST CHURCH

With the history of the Baptist and Presbyterian denominations, we have traced the history of individual churches by the date they were established. However, since we have so much trouble coming up with Methodist church records, we have used the circuit records instead. In so doing, we have taken churches as the circuits broke off from the original county wide circuit. We will take up the two churches on the Winchester Station Circuit, the town church and Ebeneazor.

The second Methodist church to be established in Clark County was that of Ebeneazor on the Todd Road in what is now the new Pine Grove area. It was one of the truly outstanding rural churches in Kentucky's early history and certainly one of the most famous Methodist churches.

Dr. Thomas Hinde moved into Winchester about 1796 taking possession of the lands that were his reward for his services in the Revolutionary War. He moved into the neighborhood of John Martin who at this time was anything but Christian. The Salem Presbyterian Chruch was by this time an old and well established church in the general area, but its dignity and Calvinistic doctrine did not interest the good doctor. It also so happened that his daughter met at a convention a year after he arrived in Clark County, a handsome circuit rider named William Kavanaugh. The romance was fast and the marriage was performed by Lawrence Owen. Kavanaugh gave up the circuit for married life and taught school in Strode's Station. His interest in the Methodist church was as strong as that of his father-in-law. These three, with the help of the former athiest, John Martin, who had been converted by Mrs. Hinde, established Ebeneazor in 1797. The charter membership list included Dr. Hinde, Martha Hinde, William Kavanaugh, Hannah Hinde Kavanaugh, Mary Todd Hinde, John Martin, Mrs. Summers and Elizabeth Hieronymous. A church building, probably nothing but a log cabin, was erected on the property of John Martin. In 1809, the building was enlarged to hold the growing congregation. Bishop Asbury wrote that he had visited Major Martin's new chapel in Clark County.

For the next fifty years, Ebeneazor would be Clark County's strongest and largest Methodist church and one of the stronger churches in the county. During this period James Haw, Wilson Lee and Stephen Brook were the ministers. Haw was to leave the Methodist church for the O'Kelley movement.

Bishop Asbury preached in Ebeneazor on one of his several Kentucky trips, October 19, 1813. He was elaborate in his praise of the church and of Dr. Hinde.

The first recorded camp meeting in Clark County was held in Martin's Woods beside the church late in July of 1821. There would be camp meetings at Ebeneazor nearly every year for the next decade. Landrum attended services there in 1824. Besides the circuit riders, the Methodist had the services of local ministers, men who would preach, even marry and bury, but who were not assigned circuits or were on the itineracy. They ususally worked under the circuit ministers and deepened the quality of the services. Usually they were men who preached as a side line making their living either farming or with a small business. At this service a local preacher named Rucker preached a sermon on how everyone was our neighbor. He was followed by another local minister named Horace Brown whose sermon was that our neighbors are those who are in Christ. The differences between the two sermons started a hot argument between the two ministers that ended in some unneighborly fisticuffs. This type of debate was not unusual and even the concluding roughness was not always unheard of.

William Landrum reported attending camp meetings in August of 1820. Stephen Chiplie, William Holman, George W. Taylor, Richard Tydings, John Sinclair, Thomas Wallace, James Ward and a Brother Rose preached. Some of these were circuit preachers, others were local preachers from different areas. Thomas Wallace married two couples in the county, the first being May 19, 1823, and were Leslie Bostick and Mary ann Couch. John Sinclair married six couples, his first was Boswell Brion and Mary Niblic, January 7, 1830. Some of these ministers served the Mt. Sterling and Winchester Circuits. Redford's "History of Methodism in Kentucky" reports that the Lexington work was helped by these camp meetings particularly the one in 1819.

Ebeneazor grew and in 1826, a brick building replaced the old chapel. At the time it was the finest church building in the county. The church was again enlarged in 1843. John and Rachel Taylor gave the land. Samuel Morton, John Taylor, Hubbard Taylor, Calep Capps, Hubbard M. H. Taylor, Nehemiah Razzul and Henry Savry were the trustees. Once again, this was a circuit trustee board, but five were Ebeneazor members or related to Ebeneazor members. The question is which circuit? Ebeneazor apparently was often tied to a Lexington Circuit rather than Clark County. This would be in line with the influence Fayette County had in this area.

The Ebeneazor Church prospered through the religious excitement of the twenties, but lost a few members to Mt. Zion Christian when that church reconstituted itself out of the Baptist movement.

There are only so many people living in a rural area, and with three churches, Mt. Zion Christian, Salem Presbyterian, and Boone Creek Baptist in the same neighborhood, it is understandable why none of them grew much. Still, Ebeneazor was the strongest church in the Methodist movement, with the possible exception of Owen's Meeting House, during the '20s and '30s. However, by the '40s, the Winchester church had grown enough to replace it as the largest. Mt. Zion had also out distanced it in size but Owen's Meeting House, now called Wool's Chapel, had dropped to fourth place. During this period Ebeneazor belonged first to Lexington Circuit, and finally the Winchester Circuit. Some of these years Ebeneazor was circuited with Fayette County churches from what little information we have.

During this period, it is difficult to tell where Ebeneazor was circuited. In the occasional list of churches in these areas, Ebeneazor is often left off. This possibility arose late in the study of Clark County history and there has been no effort to seek whether this is true or not.

In 1848, Ebeneazor was circuited with the Winchester Methodist Church and would remain so until its death. The church burned in 1853. The county was not prospering. Population was slipping. There was a heavy exodus of people to the west. It did not seem to be a good time for building. The congregation merged with the Winchester church. The arrangement was not satisfactory. It meant a long ride to church on Sundays. It is one thing to ride out of town to visit your family and home church; it is something else again, to ride into town to church. Even when related, there is a social difference between town and country people. There are no fond memories and long unseen friends to meet on coming to town. Goshen tried to move into the city, as did the Cumberland Presbyterians; and the Union Presbyterians. It is not a matter of denomination. Only the Cumberland and Presbyterians successfully made the transition.

The merger of country churches into larger parishes is something that looks good to distant church administrators who are struggling with problems of preacher supply and mission money. It may seem to be logical to the leadership of the church. The church may even vote, as did Ebeneazor, to merge with the city church. It does not mean that it will be successfully accomplished.

Meanwhile, Landrum continued to supply personal bits of Ebeneazor's history. In 1833, he attended and preached at Ebeneazor and then stayed with Rueben Taylor. He described Taylor as one who always gave preachers a kind reception. Landrum again attended the Quarterly Conference in 1838 and reported that Thomas Rankin was the circuit minister. Rankin married nine couples in Clark County making his average one of the better ones for Methodist. His first was Davis Reid to Mary Woodward, July 5, 1838. Rankin was the Winchester Circuit's minister which would locate Ebeneazor on the Winchester Circuit at this time.

There is no information of the condition of the Winchester church in the 1850s other than that which has already been given. The merger did not create a single church parish, because we find that during this period Winchester is circuited first with Mt. Zion, then North Middletown was added to the circuit and perhaps briefly Grassy Lick.

The merger evidently did not add appreciably to Winchester's strength. If anything, Winchester was losing members from its strongest position that had been in the early 1840s.

The 1976 minister, Richard C. Brown, minister of the Cumberland Presbyterian Church in Lexington, said that a union must be a marriage in order to work. His observation is correct. If a merger merely swallows one group up so that it leaves no trace, there will be little results.

In 1868, W. T. Poynter, who was a product of the Grassy Lick Church, saw the need and tried to reconstitute Ebeneazor. The new church was built by some 20 members and two thirds of the cost was subscribed before the building was finished. In 1869, W. T. Poynter was serving both Winchester and Ebeneazor which reported a total membership of 147. The lot was obtained from James S. Lane.

However, in 1870, Ebeneazor was served by W. T. Roland who was not preaching at Winchester or any other of the Clark County churches. In 1871 Ebeneazor's minister was E. L. Southgate who also was not serving any other Clark County church.

As nearly as the skimpy records show, Ebeneazor became circuited with Wool's Chapel which was the southern Methodist split of the old Owen's Church. Since the conference owns all Methodist churches, the northern Methodist had to reconstitute and build a new church. The same situation was happening in College Hill or at this time known as Texas, in Madison County. What other church or churches were on this circuit with Ebeneazor, Wool's Chapel and College Hill? Southgate would become one of the southern Methodist better known Kentucky preachers. He was not able to save the situation. Wool's Chapel disappears and College Hill is circuited with other southern Methodist churches in Madison County. Ebeneazor is returned to a circuit with Winchester.

G. C. Kelley became Ebeneazor's minister in 1878. He was also Ebeneazor's minister holding services on the second and fourth Sunday mornings with a Sunday school. She was receiving equal time with Winchester. There is no record as to who was preaching at Ebeneazor between Southgate and Kelley. The College Hill

Circuit is reported during this period but there is no indication as to what churches were part of it. No doubt, however, Winchester suited Ebeneazor better than a circuit made up largely of Madison County churches. The distance alone made the type of organization the Methodist had difficult. There was little in common.

However, any Winchester minister in 1880 could take a long look at his parish. Winchester was on the verge of a boom with railroads and rumors of railroads being build on all sides. Both the Christian Church and the Presbyterians had full time Winchester ministers. The Baptist were still working as a part time church because of their minister. But the Baptist knew that when Stackhouse would leave them, they too would go full time. It was a courtesy to Stackhouse that for years they did not force him to decide between Winchester and David's Fork. Finally, they actually did. If the Winchester Methodist were going to meet the competition, the minister would have little time for a country appendix.

The relationship started well. A Sunday school was organized at Ebeneazor with S. S. Pents as superintendent in 1880. In 1888, T. H. Young became Sunday school superintendent.

In 1887, J. H. Young was serving the two churches, but now Ebeneazor had been cut down to one service a month. In 1890, the ministry was now to W. F. Taylor who held services at 3 in the afternoon twice a month.

The church conducted a revival in 1892, but it did not produce the expected results. The church was dead in 1896. In March of 1902, the property was sold. The church building was used as a barn and was finally torn down in 1928.

In the seventy years of its life, Ebeneazor gave thirteen ministers to the cause and one eventually became a bishop. She was directly responsible for the establishment of the Winchester church.

Why did Ebeneazor die? Next to Owen Chapel, it was the oldest. One can't say that it died because the area was poor. The Pine Grove area and that part of Fayette County close to it was and is one of the richest rural areas in Kentucky. It cannot be blamed on being in a back country, as Sugar Ridge claimed. It was on the Lexington-Winchester turnpike, a road that was macadamized before the Civil War. It is true that the Salem Presbyterian Church was barely alive during most of this period and weaker after 1900 and even more so after World War I. However, David's Fork Baptist Church was but a few miles above Ebeneazor, an old and very strong rural Baptist church. Not far away was the Macedonia Christian Church that has always been a strong capable church. The Walnut Hill Presbyterian Church was, during most of this period, a very strong organization. Mt. Zion Christian Church survived in the same area.

It seems to the observer that the same fate that destroyed Union Presbyterian Church destroyed Ebeneazor. She was not given the leadership that she needed. Originally, one might have argued that combining her with the Methodist church in Winchester was a smart idea. They formed a good size parish. However, the city church grew rapidly and was demanding. The minister lived in Winchester. It was easy for him to give a disproportionate amount of time to the city church. The opportunity was greater in the city church. It was at this point his reputation was made. Logically, if he could ride out into the country once a week, it would be just as easy for the people in the country to ride into town. No doubt he discussed this with his presiding elders and district superintendents. Even shifting to an afternoon meeting made sense. The country people always had chores to do in the mornings and evenings anyway. This made it easier to get out. Wasn't it better to come out at three and hear one of the better ministers, than come out at eleven and hear either a young man on the way up, or an old man on the way donw?

The problem that so many church planners fail to understand is that man, though a reasoning creature, is not always reasonable. Ebeneazor died when, had it been treated like the other rural churches, it might have lived.

## WINCHESTER METHODIST CHURCH

It is difficult to think of Winchester as it was in 1820. When Taul wrote his journal, he reported Winchester as having only a few hundred people that lived in a widely scattered village. Even at this, Winchester was larger than any other Kentucky community except for seven other cities, including Lexington, Louisville, etc. By 1820, there may have been a thousand people in Winchester. There were stores down Main Street and a few along Broadway. The rest of the town was built close to these commercial establishments. Hickman School was on the edge of town. There were no other real communities in Clark County. Schollsville, Kiddville, Pine Grove (perhaps the largest) or Vienna had not yet really become anything more than a country store and a smith.

Being the county seat, there was a constant migration of politicians, lawyers, and citizens with official business. It was the natural sales outlet for agricultural produce. At this time, we must confess that the taverns were more important than the churches.

The first church in Winchester had been a Quaker meeting house that was established in mystery and died unnoticed. By the time the Presbyterians sought to set up their Winchester church, the Quakers were gone. The Presbyterians had maintained a struggling little group of faithful adherents that did not really start moving until the great religous burst of the 1825s to 1830. The Presbyterians got their first resident minister about that time. There was a very strong Baptist church, Friendship, about two miles out Broadway at Strode Station. In 1820 it was preparing to tear itself in pieces over doctrine. Surrounding Winchester there was a ring of Baptist churches, Providence, Unity, Goshen being the closest. Since church was an all day affair, most people who wanted to go to church did not mind driving ten or fifteen miles to a church and back...particularly when it meant visiting with all the country cousins.

Still, there was a need for more churches in the county seat, and particularly Methodist churches. Unlike the Baptist, the Methodist churches in 1820, Ebeneazor, Owen's Chapel, probably Stamper's Chapel were not filled with inter-related families. There was not a lot of reason to go far from Winchester except to worship. Also in 1820, there were quite a few Ebeneazor families in Winchester. In those days, Ebeneazor was strong enough that, like Providence Baptist Church, it could furnish members for a city church without being hurt. Therefore, there was a religious vacuum in Winchester in 1820. Landrum reports that in 1821, the Mt. Sterling Circuit had assigned James G. Leach to spend most of his time working in Winchester and Mt. Sterling. In 1823, Landrum reported going with Newton G. Berryman to preach Saturdays and Sundays at the Academy in Winchester. He notes the lack of churches in Winchester. One can presume there were a group of Winchester residents that were interested in a Methodist church...or at least in the alternative to Calvinism that the Methodist offered.

The result of this effort was the organizing of a Methodist church in Winchester. Arnold's history says that the membership came from Ebeneazor. In 1826, the Deed Book 21, reports that Culbert and Sally Baker sold to Thomas Gardner, Caleb Capps, John Williams, George Walden and Henry Williams, acting as trustees for the circuit for a church in Winchester. The lot was on the corner of Wall Street and Fairfax. It was built of brick for Landrum noted the next year that both Winchester and Mt. Sterling had brick buildings. This building was remodeled in 1848 and rebuilt in 1876. This third building effort resulted in the embarrassing discovery that the church was sitting eight inches on the property of a neighbor named Ogden. It was reported that all was worked out satisfactorily.

It does not follow that the trustees that signed the deed for the Winchester church belonged to Winchester. They represented the circuit and their names or others like them came from the entire circuit. Their actual church membership was distributed throughout the member churches.

Landrum notes that in 1827, he was helping Brother Philips, evidently a lay minister, to hold meetings for the colored people in the basement of the Methodist church. Years later, in the 1840s, Charles Hanson reports meetings of Negros going on in the basement of the Methodist Church. This must have become a reasonably regular service and if so, it is probably the first Negro church in Clark County. Negros attended most of the other churches. There would be efforts, at least at Goshen and Ephesus by the Negros to use the church buildings for their own use.

Deed Book 30, 1840, showed that Thomas and Marie Burgess sold to John Williams, Caleb Capps and Christopher Scobee a house for a parsonage of the Winchester Circuit. The idea didn't work too well. The Winchester Circuit shifted too often. There were some ministers who had their own homes and found it easier to commute to their preaching points. By this time, the bush arbors, the two or three family gatherings in private homes, the small societies meeting in schools, had disappeared. These had grown into formal churches or had disappeared as regular preaching points. To some extent, camp meetings took their place, but in 1840, even these were running out. Religion was beginning to look more or less like present day religion.

Whatever the reason, the Methodist parsonage was sold with the blessing of the legislature, and recorded in Deed Book 38, to John Parrish for eight hundred dollars. F. B. Moss, John Williams, Samuel D. Martin and John Conkwright were the circuit trustees.

The difficulties worked out in Deed Book 38, William and Elizabeth Lewis sold to John P. Gay, John Conkwright and Jonathan Owen, trustees of the Methodist parsonage for the Winchester and North Middletown Circuits for, and at this point the deed must be avoiding the problems of the previous parsonage, use of the minister of the societies in bond, but not for the societies in themselves. The trustees obviously represented different groups. Winchester had become a station church in 1843, so the Winchester Circuit now included Winchester and a rural church or two. John Conkwright represented this church. Obviously Jonathan Owen represented Owen Chapel. John P. Gay must have represented the North Middletown Methodist Church on which we have no information.

In 1856, Ebeneazor Church is sold to Samuel Martin...nothing is said of the condition of the church after the fire. The trustees were Rueben, John and H. B. Taylors. These families now came into Winchester to church. For nearly fifteen years, Ebeneazor disappears.

Deed Book 39, reports that Mrs. Elisa C. Moss and Theodore Kohlklass, executors of the will of Frances Moss, gave to the Methodist additional property as found in the will. Jesse D. Williams, W. T. Poynter and W. M. H. Winn were the Methodist trustees.

The record shows that Winchester became a station in 1845. By this, Winchester was considered strong enough to support its own minister. However, this condition did not continue for in 1848, she was tied with Ebeneazor. Again, when Ebeneazor burned and merged with Winchester, there was another two years when she was a station church. Thereafter, she was again circuited with Mt. Zion, then with North Middletown and during the last part of the Civil War, perhaps with Grassy Lick.

With the establishment of Ebeneazor, she was once again circuited with only Ebeneazor. This brings the Winchester history up to 1860 where it will be resumed in the third volume of this work. Perhaps by that time, we will have discovered more individual church history.

Winchester's ministers are listed with the circuits names.

## DUNAWAY METHODIST CHURCH

We are now ready for the third circuit that developed in Clark County. The major representation of this circuit is the third oldest Methodist church in the county and perhaps the oldest existing Methodist church in the county, Dunaway Methodist Church. In this circuit was Buckeye which died and was replaced by El Bethel and Westbend. El Bethel was a southern Methodist church and was always circuited with Dunaway. Westbend was a northern Methodist church and is in Powell County. Therefore, we do not seek to develop Westbend history. It may or may not have been associated with the other northern Methodist churches in Clark County. There has not been any evidence yet discovered that would decide the question. We do not bring El Bethel history into play other than as she was on the circuit since she was established after 1860. Her history will appear in the third volume.

Since Dunaway is the only church on this circuit that is active today that predates the Civil War, we will combine her history with that of the circuit. Like most of the Methodist churches, Dunaway does not have a lot of written history and what she has is due almost entirely to Mrs. Dalous W. Hisle. She wrote a history as a thesis for the University of Kentucky and she has collected some of the old record and membership books.

Like Mt. Carmel Baptist Church, Dunaway sat on the edge of the county at a considerable distance from Winchester. The newspapers did not contain a great deal about its activities. On the circuit she was always over shadowed by stronger churches.

There was a pioneer settler named John Dunaway. He may have been a local preacher for the Methodist church. So far, there has been very little information concerning him. Mrs. Hisle does not mention him. She dates the founding of the church as 1815 when the Deed Book 11, 1815, recorded a deed giving one acre of property by Samuel Combs, John W. Holder and Jesse Devary to Benjamin Dunaway and John Conkwright, trustees. There was apparently a church already built on the site. Benjamin Dunaway, we believe, was a son of John Dunaway. If these assumptions are true, and they are based on the slimmest of information, then Dunaway could be much older. Landrum does not list it as a church with a recognizable name in his list of churches on the circuit in 1817. Since the deed proved that it existed at the time, and at least one of the local ministers, John Conkwright, was trustee, we know the church was either missed by Landrum or belonged to a different circuit.

Also in passing, we note that this deed was listed before the standard form of Methodist deeds appeared. There is no other deed that gives the property to the Methodist Conference. There is a possibility that the Dunaway property does not belong to the conference as most of the other property do.

It is presumed, however, that Dunaway was part of the Hinkston and Mt. Sterling Circuits. The first mention of Dunaway was by William Landrum who said that in August, 1830, he attended a camp meeting at Dunaway. The minister that held the services was William Brooks. Again, Landrum reports that in 1840, he had the funeral of Alexander Chism at Dunaway.

In 1848, the Vienna Circuit was formed. William Landrum was the circuit preacher. It is possible that Dunaway was on occasion tied in that circuit. On the whole, if there were such ties, they were temporary for Dunaway appears as part of the North Middletown Circuit until 1855.

The circuit was in existence from 1855 to 1865. The presiding elders were the same since the circuit belonged in the same district with the Winchester Circuit and the North Middletown Circuit.

The circuit was without a minister for the first two years, '55 and '56 with local ministers and John Bruce doing most of the preaching. In 1857, the circuit minister was John S. Cox. He was followed by J. L. Gragg for two years beginning in 1858.

Clark Polly was a supply minister in 1860. H. W. Abbet served in 1861. J. L. Gragg returned in 1862. No minister is reported for 1863, but Landrum was serving in 1864. The last minister of the circuit was in 1865 when James Muse served.

Fitch's history of the Clark County churches heads his list of ministers as the Vienna Circuit under Winchester. Evidently, the Winchester church, at least in the early years of the circuit, was more or less responsible. None of the ministers mentioned seemingly have had much other history in the general area. At least one, Gragg, became a northern Methodist minister.

It is at this point, Dunaway's history and the story of the northern Methodist movement merge. It is in this circuit that the most pressure is placed by the northern Methodist, and it is only in this circuit that they found any success.

It is possible that these churches, Dunaway, Buckeye, Wool's Chapel, as the Owen Church was then called, and what other churches that were associated, Providence (or Mt. Nepo in Kiddville), Howard's Chapel at Vienna, were feeling sociological differences with the richer and more influential churches that made up the rest of Clark and Montgomery Counties. At a time when the Whigs dominated the political scene, these sections that housed these churches were Democratic. When the Whigs disappeared and were replaced by the Democrats, these areas became Republican. On the whole, they were anti slave churches whose members were not among the large slave holders of one of the largest slave counties in the state. There isn't enough evidence to pursue this approach further.

Be that as it may, soon after the division in the Kentucky Methodist appeared in 1866, Roundtree Chapel was organized in the Roundtree School, a mile or so west of Dunaway Church. The information concerning the Roundtree Chapel is extremely scarce. It was serviced by M. M. Roundtree during most of its existence. Obviously, it was based on a family of Roundtrees that had sufficient influence to name the school house in the area. Mrs. Hisle says that her grandmother can remember attending Roundtree Chapel as a young girl for singing.

Roundtree Chapel appeared off and on in news items in the Winchester paper, the last being in the early 1890s when the Democrat reported a holiness revival. There was no other mention of the chapel again. Evidently it had always used the school and had no building of its own. It could not have been particularly strong. It did not seem to influence Dunaway's history much one way or another. One can presume that Dunaway as a church stood firm for the southern Methodist church, refusing to be led by old friends and ministers.

There is no record of what happened to Dunaway between 1865 and 1882. In 1866, Dunaway was served by George Gould as minister. The situation is so confused that Fitch thinks that Gould was probably with the North Middletown Circuit. He was not sure. By his own records, however, Fitch himself was serving Winchester, Mt. Zion and North Middletown. The years between this youthful assignment and the writing of his book may have dimmed his memory for the name Gould does not appear.

Ministers were going through agonies of indecision as each was called upon either to follow his state leaders into the northern Methodist church or stay with the majority in the southern church. It must have appeared at times as if whole circuits were about to change sides.

We do not know who was minister in 1871. The first indication where Dunaway is, is a remark by Fitch related to W. W. Spates in 1877. J. P. Sams was supplying Dunaway. Evidently, Sams was a local minister who was given more or less jurisdiction of Spates. No reason is given for this unusual change in the records. Therefore, it seems likely that Dunaway shared Mt. Zion's ministers back in 1872. This still leaves a two year gap between 1870 and 1872.

Dunaway was part of the Mt. Zion Circuit until 1882. Then Dunaway and El Bethel circuited with the Old Fort Chapel at Camargo in the Old Fort Circuit. In 1882, H. P. Walker was presiding elder and B. T. Kavanaugh was minister until 1814. Joseph Rand became presiding elder from 1814 to 1887.

E. P. Gifford became circuit minister in 1887 for the next two years. H. P. Walker returned to the presiding elder's position for four years in 1888. James E. Savage has written a history of Methodism in Montgomery County in which he mentions an incident concerning Dunaway. Daniel O'Rear evidently was a lay minister for he went to Dunaway Chapel on one bitter cold Sunday. He lived in what became the parsonage for the Old Fort Circuit at Camargo. He arrived at Dunaway and found no fire built. He tried to build one, but finally went to one of the nearby homes to get warm. The backs of his hands were frozen and, according to the history, he suffered for years as a result.

J. H. Williams became circuit minister for three years in 1889. Clay City was added to the circuit and a V. Daughtery was also listed as supply. He would be listed again in 1899.

1892: J. Reid became presiding elder for four years. In 1892, J. M. Wilson was minister. 1893, J. Rose, 1894, D. P. Ware returned for a year.

1895: W. W. Chamberlain held the ministry of the circuit.

1896: J. Reeves became presiding elder in 1899. B. F. Cosby became the minister in 1897 to 1899.

1899: A. Redd became the presiding elder until 1902. F. A. Savage became the circuit minister for two years. For some reason, Fitch lists Camargo, El Bethel and Dunaway as churches on the circuit.

1902: R. M. Lee was the circuit minister.

1903: The presiding elder was E. G. B. Mann and the circuit minister was again B. F. Cosby.

In 1904, Mt. Zion was returned to Dunaway and El Bethel for an all Clark County circuit and Dunaway would have the same ministers as Mt. Zion. The circuit was called the Mt. Zion Circuit.

B. F. Kavanaugh was the fourth son of William Kavanaugh. He had been converted at Ebeneazor but had moved to Texas soon thereafter. In 1882, he returned to Kentucky but despite his reputation began at the bottom of the ministerial role.

The first Dunaway Church was a log cabin that was built at a very early date. A second one was built in the 1820s that showed the Baptist influence by having two front doors, one for women and one for men. In 1896, the third building was constructed. Ben T. Wills was the chairman, J. N. Brookshire, Johnnie Tuttle, John D. Rankin, S. D. Fisher and Allen Rankin were part of the committee. Van Daugherty was also on the committee and Mrs. Hisle labels him Reverend. Wills suggested that each one of the committee put up $100.00. He figured the church would cost about $1800.00 with donated labor. Brookshire and John D. Rankin dug the foundation. Walker Brookshire, Allen and Charlie Rankin hauled the stone to the stone mason. A thunderstorm nearly broke up the corner stone ceremony. It was thought that a Newton Powell was the contractor.

The first record book showing family names of Brock, Bush, Curtin, Lawrence, Newkirk, Park and Wills families were reported in 1850 to 1860. A membership book about 1870 shows Brooks, Adams, Rankins, Brookshires, Stones, Quisenberrys, Brunners, Barrows, Osbournes, Pattersons, Curtises, Bushes, Wills, Foxes and Shimfessels members of the church. Membership in 1870 was mostly the same names that had appeared twenty years earlier showing a certain permanence of population of the area in that these would be children of the same families now reaching adulthood.

There were spells when Dunaway records picked up. In 1893, the record books show reports of quarterly meetings or even monthly meetings of the church. These are not the official quarterly meetings of the circuit. Ben T. Wills was the secretary. Wills evidently was one of the pillars of the church. Mrs. Hisle describes his piety as such that he felt that reading a newspaper was sinful, taking away of time that should be used in studying the scriptures. In that period, the church was selling to William Tuttle logs that had come off the church lot. Altogether, the church sold 7,786 feet of lumber for $19.45.

In October of 1891, the minutes report that Susie Blackwell was dropped from the membership list. The church had lost sight of her. The Sunday school was reorganized into a missionary society for the winter months. Presumedly this meant that they would meet in homes during the winter.

There are no records available until 1913 when G. W. Boswell was minister. He had visited in some of the homes and had preached at Dunaway 9 times. The next year he reported that he had travelled 532 miles, made 68 visits and had attended Quarterly Conference at El Bethel. He performed one marriage, conducted a funeral and had preached 44 times. Curiously in 1916, he reported travelling 1954 miles and had visited 144 times. He had preached 54 sermons. He had married seven couples, conducted one funeral and had assisted in two more.

There is no explanation as to why the 1916 record was so much better than 1914. However, the record gives a fairly good picture of what country ministers of any denomination in these times would do. This, of course, would not be the only religious activity of the church. The local ministers also would hold services though the record is not clear. For example, in this 1914 period, the name of Claude Shimfessel begins to appear in the record. He joined the church in 1902 and had married Evelyn Aldridge in 1907. He was licensed as a local minister in 1918. On October 1, 1973, Dunaway paid tribute to him and gave some of his record.

Claude Shimfessel in the period between 1918 and 1973 had conducted 100 revivals and had served in 100 funerals. He had travelled in the course of his ministry 35,000 miles. Most of his work was done after 1918 in the section of the county history that will be in the fourth volume. He stands for the heros of the Methodist movement, about which we have so little information. Lawrence Owen, Martin Gillespie, Leroy Cole, John Sewell, John Conkwright, V. Daughtery and others whose names we do not even have. These men must have formed a network across the county, filling in for the circuit ministers, holding revivals, performing marriages, conducting funerals, visiting the sick, raising money and a thousand other services. Almost by accident do their names appear. Much is owed to them but they get little credit.

## THE STAMPER MEETING HOUSE

Very early in his ministry in Kentucky, James Haw converted a Mrs. Jane Stamper to the Methodist church. She had been a Presbyterian and, as the Methodist historian, Redford, said in his "History of Methodism in Kentucky," was a stranger to the doctrine of the new birth. In 1791, her husband, Joshua Stamper was converted to bring together the whole family in Methodism.

The Stamper family, Joshua and Jane, according to the Deed Book 19, 1823, reported giving to the trustees, Thomas Gardner, Martin Gillespie, Elias Gardner, William Redman, Caleb Capps, Thomas Farmer, James Spillman and Stephen Scoby (this name is spelled a half dozen different ways in the record) who were trustees for the Methodist Circuit, for a church that would be and probably had been called Stamper's Meeting House. Incorporated in the deed, for the first time with Methodist deeds, was an elaborate statement that was designed to prevent anyone from stealing the Stamper Meeting House doctrinally whether or not they had the majority of the members of the Stamper Meeting House. It gave control of the property to the circuit and the Methodist church.

Stamper's Chapel was much older than 1823. William Landrum lists it as a church that was in existence in the period of his youth, perhaps 1812. Jilson says that in the KHSQ, Volume 34, that there was a Jonathan Stamper's Chapel near Major Bean as early as 1789. The 1856 Deed Book reports that Caleb Capps and John D. Gay, trustees for the Methodist Circuit, sold to Asa Bean the property of which he had been in possession for a number of years. There is no indication when it died since the Methodist records report circuits and not the churches on the circuit.

Joshua and Jane Stamper(who was a Woodrough) moved first to Boonesboro in 1779 and then on to Strode's Station. After a period they moved out of Strode's Station and then joined John Constant as one of the four families at his station. When the Indians attacked the station, Joshua had to run for his life for the stockage. Jane held open the gate.

The Stampers were deeply religious and their home from the beginning became a preaching point for the Methodist. If Jilson is right, and the Stamper's had a church in Clark County as early as 1789, they had the first Methodist church in Clark County but the record makes it the third church to be established.

Joshua died in 1827 and his wife the next year. Evidently, Stamper's Chapel died with them. There is no reason that has been discovered. It was evidently simply a family church, and when the family died, there was no one to keep it alive.

Jonathan Stamper was the son of Joshua and Jane. When he went on circuit he would return home and Redford's history describes how Jane cried and fussed over him when he returned home so tired and worn.

He became one of the more important ministers in Kentucky. He represented the district at most of the conferences for twenty years.

## BUCKEYE METHODIST CHURCH

The Landrums lived in Indian Fields. The church that William Landrum described as a youth which met in an uncle's house was probably Buckeye. We noted that when his uncle died, the church also died until it was moved to another relative's house.

The August Court, 1808, reported a road that extended from Indian Fields near the church and along a series of land owners whose names are illegible in the record until it came to the Red River Iron Works. This would probably be the Buckeye Church.

The best history and description of Buckeye is in Savage's "History of the Methodist Church in Montgomery County." As the home church of a series of Landrum ministers, he included it in his book. In 1821, Francis Landrum was one of the circuit ministers. Its ministers would, of course, be the same as those of Hinkston, Mt. Sterling, Winchester Circuits until 1848. In 1834, Rueben Landrum was admitted to the ministry. For Clark County history William Landrum is the historian.

Landrum reported helping M. M. Cosby in a two day meeting at Buckeye in 1833. He again, reported to Buckeye in 1837. He was helping Ewan Hardy in 1842.

One of the rare mention of laymen occurred in 1842 when Landrum returned to Buckeye to conduct the funeral of Mrs. William Norris. She was born in Virginia in 1771 and had come to Kentucky in 1806. She had been a strong Methodist throughout her life.

Savage describes Buckeye as a meeting house with a dirt floor and a puncheon pulpit that rested on two forked sticks. Savage says that they had service every two weeks on Thursday which was what Landrum reported. Savage obviously felt that this was the same church.

William Landrum was sent to the Louisa Circuit in 1838 according to Savage. His uncle, Rueben (not the minister), was angry and refused to go to church. When his wife asked him if he was going, he said, "Never again." And continued, "They've sent Billy to Big Sandy and he'll never get a cup of coffee to drink."

Nevertheless, his wife told him to saddle the horse. She was going. When she got there, Rueben had already arrived. He had walked across the fields while she had gone around the road. He was sitting on the men's side waiting for the first hymn.

William Landrum was a coffee drinker at a time when coffee was hard to get. He said he drank three cups for breakfast, two for lunch, two for supper and one before going to bed and slept restfully. One story is that William visited one mountain family and asked if they had any coffee. They didn't, so William gave them a few green coffee beans. After a bit, the wife came and told him it was no use. She had been boiling those beans for an hour and nothing happened.

John Goff's journal mentions Buckeye as a strong church made of Buckeye logs which gave it a name. The church was also used as a school. Later, a separate school building was built on the same lot. Goff mentioned that a Rev. Stone and William Landrum were ministers. This would then date this recollection in the 1848s and early 1850s.

In 1863, Landrum reported being with W. C. Taylor at Buckeye. Evidently, it was a strong church at that time. Soon thereafter, it disappeared from Methodist history. There is no clear reason for its death, but it is pretty obvious that it came as a result of the effort of the northern Methodist to establish a northern church in the area.

In 1876, El Bethel was established as a southern Methodist church. A few years earlier, Westbend was established as a northern Methodist church. Buckeye was somewhere between these two, though evidently closer to Westbend than El Bethel. Mrs. Ethel Wilson, treasurer of the Westbend Church in 1976, said that her grandmother had told her there were two churches at the original site of the Westbend Church. If this recollection is true, then we have again the classic example of division. The majority of Buckeye sought to unite with the northern Methodist churches but the conference controlled the church building forcing the northern Methodist to organize and build a new church. The old Buckeye struggles on for a year or so. There are no records. In the end, however, the group affiliated with the southern Methodist closed down, permitting the old building to deteriorate rapidly. Meanwhile, the southern Methodist rallied nearer to Indian Fields and organized El Bethel. How much time elapsed between the disillusion of Buckeye and the establishment of El Bethel is, at least with the present evidence, unknown.

## PROVIDENCE METHODIST CHURCH

Mrs. Nelson Gay has provided a history of El Bethel Methodist Church that was written by her father, George H. Hisle. He reports that Younger Hisle about 1850, or earlier, established a Methodist class meeting in the Indian Fields-Kiddville area. They met in the old Buckeye school. William Landrum was the minister.

It is difficult to place this story into the information from other sources. The Buckeye Church was still in operation in 1850. It did not meet in the Buckeye school, but had its own building very close to the Powell County line.

What Younger Hisle must have done was to gather together a group of Methodists, some who may have been a remnant of the old Mt. Nepo Church that once was located on Nest Egg Road just over the line in Montgomery County, and laid the foundation for a Providence Church in the new growing community of Kiddville.

William Landrum reports preaching at Providence Church in 1853. He does not label the denomination, but it would appear that had he meant Providence Baptist or Providence Christian Church, he would have made the distinction. It seems more likely he is referring to a church in Kiddville other than Buckeye. He would hardly have called Buckeye Providence without making some comment since Buckeye was his family church.

Providence evidently was part of the Vienna Circuit that was organized in 1848. After the collapse of Buckeye, Mt. Zion was circuited with Kiddville for a year or so. The Ewington Journal, October 10, 1857, reported that John Cox was preaching on the Vienna Circuit. In 1866, the conference records reported that the Vienna Circuit, which included Howard's Chapel, Vienna and Providence at Kiddville, had a total of 70 members, but no ministers. It was in 1866 that the Kentucky Methodist Church, south, met at Winchester for its yearly conference. In the next couple of years, Mt. Zion is circuited with Kiddville. Since El Bethel was not yet established this could have been the southern splinter of Buckeye or Providence.

According to Savage's "History of the Methodist in Montgomery County," there was a church called Mt. Nepo, sometimes called Lullbegrud and Nest Egg since it was located on Nest Egg Road about a mile east of Kiddville. It was built on property given Samuel and Annis Hadden and Ralph and Sally Whittsit and was located in Montgomery County. The trustees were Ebeneezer

Discon, Robert Rose, John Woodward, John Philips and Paul Talbert. The date was 1823. Presumedly the trustees represented the Mt. Sterling Circuit, but none of the names reflect the names that usually appeared on deeds in Clark County. It is possible that even before the official establishment of the Winchester Circuit, the two counties were pretty largely operated as a unit by the ministers in charge. The church building had already been built. Evidently, the church was dead and the property sold in 1849.

Savage confesses considerable ignorance on what happened next. Evidently in 1851, the church was reorganized, the property deeded back to a Montgomery County Board of Trustees. A second deed was given in 1857. Another building was built. Savage quotes a Combs as saying it was one of the largest log buildings in the area.

This could be Providence and the dates agree; this is the same church that appears on Vienna Circuit records and was called Providence. Savage talked with several Kiddville residents about the church. The Savages book was published in 1939. A grave stone of Joel Elliott who died in 1873 was uncovered in the cemetary.

There is no reason given for its death. In the 1850s, Kiddville felt itself to be a coming town. Lots were being sold. A number of businesses were established. Without doubt, the idea of resurrecting Providence from Mt. Nepo was to grow with a new and thriving community. Unfortunately for Kiddville, the railroad missed the village by three miles. Without the railroad or any other reason for its growth...it tried to become a county seat but was beaten...Kiddville fell back to a crossroad hamlet. This loss of population, plus the Civil War, plus the struggle between northern and southern Methodist, were all factors in its second death.

## HOWARD"S CHAPEL

In the Deed Book 30, 1819, Joseph and Margaret Cox gave to John Conkwright a plot of land a half mile from the Kentucky River on Upper Howard's Creek.

James Landrum mentions preaching at Howard's Chapel at the mouth of Howard's Creek in 1847. Apparently, there was a road that went directly to Mt. Sterling at that time. Such roads still exist though they would hardly be called a direct route.

In 1863, in Deed Book 40, another mention of Howard's Chapel is made when J. Patrick, Henry Schrievens and Solomon Richardson are named as trustees by the Vienna Quarterly Conference, of which J. S. Griggs was president and M. Curtin was secretary.

There is no other record of Howard's Chapel and it was never mentioned by any of the Winchester newspapers. The early names on the deeds belong to the Dunaway, Log Lick, Ruckerville area though Methodist trustees represented a circuit and not a church.

We have no record showing what happened to Howard's Creek other than one or two suggestions that Howard's Creek went with the northern Methodist. If so, it died before the Winchester newspapers became plentiful in 1870.

The unresolved question is whether Howard's Chapel is the church at Vienna that gave the circuit its name. If not, then there would have to be another church in the Vienna area. However, it is our opinion that Howard's Chapel is the Vienna Church.

## NORTHERN METHODIST

In 1844, the question of slavery came to a head in the nation and the southern delegates withdrew to form the Methodist Episcopal Church, south. Arnold's history gives an adequate enough description from a southern's point of view of the events that preceeded the division. The final break came in 1844 over Bishop J. O. Andrews of Georgia whose wife had inherited a Negro slave in a state whose laws made it impossible for him to free her. He was nevertheless, a slave holding bishop and the northern Methodist could not bear the thought. If he was permitted to remain in his chair, the northern church, which had already divided once to form the Weslyan Methodist Church, would be decimated. It was largely a question of who was to withdraw. It has not been so mentioned in any of the histories we have read but division in the north would virtually mean destruction of the Methodist movement and the creation of several Methodist movements. Division in the south would mean that the northern churches would be even more united than ever and southern Methodist would remain intact. Even then, it is pointed out, that the south merely asked for jurisdications within one church.

Arnold noted that in all this debate, the Kentucky delegation was a unit. None made speaches, but on each vote, Kentucky stood with the south. Arnold said that on return to Kentucky they found intense excitement. There was opposition to the idea of withdrawing into a southern church. In September of 1844, the Kentucky Conference met.

This conference approved the actions of the Kentucky delegation in the national meeting and endorsed all the proposals including the creation of an independent southern jurisdiction within the Methodist church. The formal report was signed by, among others, W. B. Kavanaugh and H. H. Kavanaugh both who were from Clark County, converted at Ebeneazor; H. H. Kavanaugh would serve the county churches after the war having been asked to return to the conference to help defeat the theatened northern Methodist invasion; and John Tevis who had married a Clark County girl. The organizational National Convention at Louisville was endorsed and among the delegates were men such as E. Stevenson, H. H. Kavanaugh, William Gunn, J. C. Harrison, G. W. Taylor, T. N. Ralston who either had served Clark County churches or would.

Ohio River area churches were largely opposed to the division of the Methodist church including John C. Harrison's charge as presiding elder, the Maysville District. Strong opposition also came out of Louisville and the northern Kentucky churches. There were churches and individuals all through Kentucky that opposed the division, many families leaving the Methodist church in protest.

At the Louisville Convention, T. N. Ralston who had served Clark County was elected temporary secretary. He later became assistant secretary.

In the records, the 1845 conference of the Kentucky Methodist almost unanimously aligned itself with the southern church. It was not that easy. After Louisville, Hubbard Kavanaugh rode all the way to Shelbyville with John Bruce, who had transferred from Indiana in 1841 and was already recognized as one of the ablest ministers in Kentucky, to keep him from returning to Indiana. Other ministers did leave, some without formality in their bitterness. Bitter lawsuits developed when Methodist churches in Kentucky wished to leave the Kentucky Conference for the north. They were fought and, in Kentucky courts, won mostly by the south.

Arnold makes the observation that the north was saved from the disasters which threatened it, and the south was saved from the calamities it felt would befall if they remained with the north. In a sense, both sections were satisfied.

As we reported, if there was dissatisfaction in Clark County, it did not appear in any of the records we have seen. William Landrum did not mention the division. Those churches and ministers that preferred to go to the north did so within the state affiliating with Cincinnati, Indiana and other conferences. Clark County continued as if nothing had happened until the creation of the Vienna District which looked like an effort to separate the less disturbed churches and those that might react in favor of the north. There is no report that this was the thought behind the new circuit. The churches did form a geographical and an economic unit that had more in common with each other than with, for example, Winchester or Mt. Zion. Landrum saw nothing in them other than faithful Methodist churches. I think an article in the METHODIST HISTORY, January, 1965, sums up the fact.

The article noted that at the time of the national division, only a few Kentucky ministers and churches transferred their allegiance to the northern conference. It was not that the Kentucky Methodist failed to list themselves as southern Methodist because of a desire to be northern Methodist, but because they felt that the Methodist church was the southern Methodist church, and there was no need to make further note of their allegiance.

Prior to 1866, the northern Methodist in Kentucky had only about fourteen churches with less than 3,000 members. Most of those that had felt any desire to affiliate with the northern church joined either the Indiana or Cincinnati Associations.

The Methodist Encyclopedia reports that in 1848, ministers were assigned by the northern Methodist to both Winchester and Lexington. To date, no other information is available. Who they were, or what they did is not reported. Whether they affected the shake up of the Winchester Circuit strengthening the Winchester church is not clear.

In 1853, the Kentucky Conference of the Methodist Episcopal Church was organized as the northern branch of the Methodist movement in Kentucky.

Among the districts of the new conference was one called the Maysville District. In this district there were circuits that were named Maysville, Grayson, Quincey, Ashland, Montgomery, Harrison, Augusta, Asbury, Covington and Kenton. The ministers included names such as A. H. Triplett, N. E. Taver, W. H. Black, H. M. Curry, I. F. Harmon, R. D. Larshbrock and S. F. Gaurez. Like all Methodists, their conference reports do not give a breakdown of their circuits which makes identification of local churches difficult. There is no indication of what churches were in the Montgomery Circuit which presumedly would include any Winchester members if any. It reported 200 members and two lay preachers in 1856. The next two years, it was omitted. The Montgomery Circuit that year recommended Joseph H. Bristow for licensing.

The name was changed in 1860 and the Montgomery Circuit was reported as the Stepstone Circuit of the Maysville District. This would indicate that there was at least one church in the Stepstone area which is in Montgomery County, supporting the northern movement. James Savage's "History of the Methodist in Montgomery County" reports that there was a Methodist Church at Stepstone which had been organized in 1821. Land was deeded and protected in the usual Methodist manner. A church was built. All of this, and yet, Savage reported that the church seems to have failed shortly after. It may be this shift of allegiance that caused it to fail. Savage did not mention it again or, for that matter, the division between north and south.

Besides Stepstone, there might have been other preaching points and small churches. Since it was reported infrequently, its life must have been precarious. In 1864, the circuit is again mentioned and a L. H. Pencion is assigned to it.

The situation in the state changed after the Civil War. The question of slavery had been solved by the bloody, brutal conflict. Kentuckians had been forced to choose sides. When the war was over, both sides returned. Now that the issue of the unity of the country had been settled, there were forces within the southern Methodist church that felt that the division in the Methodist movement also ought to be terminated. The Union veterans had little desire to be served by a church that was still proudly waving the Stars and Bars. It must be remembered that Clark County furnished more soldiers to the Union Army than it did to the Confederate. Roughly speaking, the Clark County Confederate came from the northern and eastern parts of the county, owned a horse and was a cavalryman...mostly with Morgan's Cavalry. The Union veteran was an infantry man or some less spectacular service than the cavalry and came from the hill country in the south and western parts of the county. As we have noted, there was also a political difference. The parts that furnished the Confederate soldiers which included Winchester were strongly and dominantly Whig. The rest of the county was Democrat. After the Civil War, the Whig section turned reluctantly, but firmly to the Democrats and the Democratic sections not so reluctantly or unanimously, but just as firmly to the Republican. This story will make up a large part of the third volume.

Also, to add to the mix, many mountaineers were already beginning to come out of the eastern mountains into the lower areas of Kentucky. Almost without exception, these would be Republican. Politics, therefore, play a very strong part of this story which, because it is covered elsewhere is neglected here. It was also a struggle between the small land owners and the large land owners.

This struggle in Clark County is uniquely Methodist. Most of the Baptist churches were located in an area where the Confederate sympathies were strongest. Baptist churches in the western and southern parts of the county were turning to the primitive form. The "old" Baptists tended to be Republican. This does not seem to be a factor in their decline. Just how much north-south politics played in this is unknown because it is invisible. William Rupart, who led these Baptists, was an ardent and a determined Republican. The Presbyterians were all in the southern areas. Sugar Ridge was the exception, but there, as it was quietly made up of more or less northern sympathizers, it voted more or less Democratic. There were sharp divisions among the Presbyterians over the same issue at the same time as the Methodist were about to fight over, but though it effected both Bourbon and Montgomery Counties, it was not felt in Clark. The Christian Church was so loosely organized that the question of slavery played no part in the county's history and the divisions that came were theological and not politically inspired.

Prior to 1866, the work of the northern branch was pretty largely limited to about ten counties. Now there was a demand that since the Civil War was over and the question of division in the nation had been decided, there was no longer justification for two Methodist movements divided on geographical lines. The result was that in 1865 in the Kentucky Conference the Methodist Episcopal Church, South, the controlling establishment, introduced a report calling for the merger of the two bodies. A minority report was offered in addition and the conference chose to support the minority report 35 to 25. Those that had supported the majority report withdrew from the southern conference. They were not hot heads or unimportant members of a movement, as so often are seceding elements.

The leader of the withdrawing group was Daniel Stevenson. He had been one of the founders of Kentucky Wesleyan College. He had been secretary to the conference. John G. Bruce was presiding elder of the Lexington District and had been for twenty years intimately associated with the central Kentucky churches. They were joined by H. C. Northcutt who had served Clark County churches and fifteen more who became known as the "Loyal Eighteen."

These united with the existing Kentucky Conference. They were appointed by the northern conference along with nine other men who joined them from out of state as if each appointment were circuits. In 1865, there were 65 appointments in the conference, 58 in '66, 75 in '67, 68 in '68. The movement claimed 10,000 members, in 1865 it had grown to 16,512. Names of out of state ministers were John D. Walsch, E. L. Shepherd, Amos Boreau, Pulaski Enright, J. J. Rainey, John Ragan, William Childer and John Godby. In addition, there were two laymen, Amos Shankle of Covington and Joshua and Fanny Speed of Louisville, who had spent and were ready to spend considerable amounts of money in the name of the new organization.

It was firmly believed with the quality of Kentucky ministers that had joined the northern conference that Methodists, Methodist churches and Methodist circuits would come over to the northern church. There was among the northern Methodist a great deal of enthusiasm and a great deal of optimistic expectations. Many ministers accepted circuits without adequate financial arrangements for their livelihood. John Bruce was one of these who settled on a small farm near Danville and worked with dedicated determination to win the churches that he had long served.

The flood of converts did not come. Here and there, churches or small groups showed interest. However, the southern Methodist moved rapidly to counter the insurrection. Strong ministers were moved into danger spots. Every resource in the Kentucky Conference of the south was bent to preserve its unity.

The northern Methodist then moved out with deliberate intentions of dividing and reorganizing circuits. The northern papers were bitter; THE METHODIST ADVOCATE, January 24, 1872, who said that the northern Methodist must look to the poor, down trodden, white people of the south under the influence of the pro-slavery, man stealing, Negro whipping, whiskey drinking, Ku Klux Klan churches to which so many belonged.

A southern writer angrily replied that religion was only a pretense to add to the political power of a sectional character, with intention to build a northern party in the south.

Actually there turned out to be very little support from the northern Methodist agencies. After the initial failure to win wide spread support, the north took only a sporadic and steadily declining interest in the south.

However, in passing, we will note that the northern Methodist Holstein Methodist Conference in eastern Tennessee and Kentucky was more successful than the Kentucky Conference. Led by David Stevenson, it brought what became Union College at Barbourville, Kentucky. This gave to the Tennessee a center for Methodist action which helped provide a continual leadership for their group.

There was only half hearted effort at starting a college. Augusta College that had a good beginning in the days before the division was allowed by both sides to die. There was no satisfactory replacement in Kentucky other than Union College which was too far away from the Blue Grass to help much.

This then, is the background for the struggle of northern Methodist sympathizers with their southern brethren. There are no details of the arguments, meetings, quarrels, bitterness that haunted Clark County churches of Buckeye, Dunaway, Wool's Chapel (Owen's Chapel) and Howard's Chapel. How much the impact was felt in Winchester and Mt. Zion is impossible to gauge. The northern Methodist did score a victory among the Negros in Winchester when the Clark Memorial Methodist Church was established after the Civil War. A second Negro Methodist was Howard's Creek Methodist Church, sometimes called Elkin. In 1881, the Negro Methodist were given their own jurisdiction in the Lexington Annual Conference of the Methodist Episcopal Church. Even here, however, the northern Methodist were not amazingly successful in that African Methodist Episcopal Church and the Colored Methodist Episcopal Church dominated the Negro Methodist field in Clark County. This history will be taken up in the third volume of this series.

The northern Methodist churches organized in Clark County the College Hill Circuit. Like their southern brethren, their conference records are carried in circuits without a breakdown as to what churches served on the circuit at any given time. Throughout most of the rest of this history, Owen's Chapel and College Hill Methodist Church are the only two churches that are absolute certainties. College Hill is in Madison County and was also the site of a school, the Texas Seminary, which was for a time, controlled by the northern Methodist church. It died. It was reorganized as a girls school with Methodist ties. This, too, dies showing the difficulties of the northern Methodist were having with their projects. Roundtree Chapel must have belonged to this circuit. For its brief life, the Corinth Methodist Church had also to be part of this circuit. Westbend is in Powell County. There may have been occasions when Westbend was in the College Hill Circuit but on the whole, it was circuited with Estill County churches.

Normally, the College Hill Circuit reported four churches, sometimes five, and one or two local ministers. One of these was Bob Eversole who also occasionally did evangelistic work with the southern Methodist, for example, at the Old Fort Chapel at Camargo. There were also two or three northern Methodist churches in the College Hill area. We have made no effort to learn anything about them other than in general they were there. Unfortunately, the College Hill Church of today has no more records than any other Methodist church, a few old membership books and that is about all.

During most of the early period, the College Hill Circuit was in the Lexington District of which John Bruce was presiding elder.

Going back in history, in 1855, the Maysville Circuit consisted of 127 white and 62 colored members. The Montgomery Circuit, 177 white and 32 Negro members with two local preachers. In 1856, the Montgomery Circuit had 200 members. There are minutes, for example, in the Council of Ministries Office of the Methodist Church in Lexington for the northern convention from 1855, but they do not give statistics or even assignments or ministerial names.

In 1867, the minister of the Montgomery Circuit was Aaron College. In 1868, the minister was N. C. Littleton. There were two churches in the circuit with 110 members and one local preacher. In 1869, B. F. Whitman was minister. The circuit voted 41 to 21 to increase the lay representation in the conference. The vote carried the conference 1659 to 1302. This would indicate that the two churches of the Montgomery Circuit had 62 members who cared enough to attend a Quarterly Meeting.

In 1869, Bruce reported to the conference that he was in contact with many churches in central Kentucky. He did not elaborate in the minutes. We will discontinue any effort to keep track of the Montgomery Circuit.

## THE TEXAS-RICHMOND CIRCUIT

The College Hill area was called Texas before it became known as the College Hill community. The circuit would take various forms. Evidently at this time, 1867, most of the churches were in the part of Madison County between Richmond and the Kentucky River. Owen's Chapel came into existence in this year. The older Wool's Chapel continued, as we have reported, tied into a southern Methodist circuit working out of College Hill as well. The minister of the Texas-Richmond Circuit in 1867 was E. M. Cole.

The circuit became the Texas-Irvin Circuit in 1868. J. G. Bruce is the presiding elder and Fred Grider is the minister. The circuit reports 228 members, two churches and two local preachers. It had 130 in three Sunday schools. College Hill and Owen's Chapel would be these two churches. We get a fairly good picture of the educational scene in 1868.

Grider's name appears in the mastheads on some of the earlier newspapers in Winchester as minister of Owen Chapel. Owen Chapel is one of the churches most commonly reported by the Winchester newspapers showing its close ties with the county and its strength as a country church.

Besides Texas Seminary which we have reported, the conference record showed other interests.

Science Hill Academy at Shelbyville is also endorsed as the best female educational institution in Kentucky for Methodists. This does not necessarily mean that Science Hill, or the Texas Seminary for that matter,were part of the northern movement. Science Hill kept good standing in both, but leaned to the southern Methodist. They would draw their next president, William Poynter, a Montgomery Methodist businessman and minister.

Sunday school work is urged and pushed. The conference claimed 111 schools at this time. Owen Chapel had one of the strongest rural Sunday schools in the county.

The conference complained of slander, misrepresentation, outrage and abuse in its effort to extend its membership, but proudly proclaimed its successes. The movement had grown from 13,997 to 17,310 in a year. Thirty churches had been added to their lists. Twenty one ministers joined the cause...the opposition as malignant and unscrupulous...in encouraging the Negro conference the minutes say "Politico-ecclesiastical spiders are trying to weave their spurious and designing nets around them..."

In all fairness, it must be admitted that the northern Methodist with their increased toleration of the Negro, were advocating unpopular causes and that they were sending ministers into areas that had no northern churches with the deliberate intention of stealing or disrupting existing churches in order to gain new churches. It is a credit to the quality of their men that they were as successful as they were and for them, unfortunately, the later leadership could not match that quality. The movement would sweep forward until about the 1880s when it would slowly be forced into a retreat that wiped out much of its earlier gains.

1869: Texas and Irving Circuit, F. Grider, 285 members, 3 churches, 64 in Sunday school, 4 schools.

1870: F. Grider, 457 members, 3 local preachers, 5 churches, 4 Sunday schools, 208 members.

1871: Frederick Grider.

1875: James Gregg.

1876: James Gregg.

1877: James Gregg.

1878: J. H. Thompson.

1879: J. H. Thompson.

1880: J. H. Thompson.

1881: J. H. Thompson.

1884: W. B. Barnett.

1885: W. B. Barnett, 432 members, 3 churches, 135 Sunday schools.

1886: J. S. Taylor, 455 members, 3 churches, 118 Sunday schools, 3 churches. The minutes show real concern over the loss of membership in the conference over the last five years of the violence that the church was meeting in the mountains, the lack of ministers...one third of the churches filled with local ministers; the isolation between churches; lack of education facilities for the ministers; poor salaries; the lack of help from the Methodist Episcopal Church as a whole, in fact, the conference felt that the northern movement had abandoned it...in short, a very depressed viewpoint on the movement that had begun so vigorously twenty years earlier.

One can see in this years report a deeper problem. The minutes confess that the southern Methodist have reasons to resent the northern Methodist that had deliberately come into their circuits and disrupted them. It was evidently also a fact that some of the northern Methodist felt the Kentucky Conference as a stumbling block between better relations between northern and southern Methodist movements.

1886: J. S. Taylor, 363 members, 4 churches, 100 Sunday schools, 4 schools. We note that seven ministers transferred out of the conference this year.

1887: G. N. Jolly is presiding elder. Frederick Grider, 354 members, 4 churches, 166 Sunday schools, 4 schools. The Owen church met on the 2nd Sunday with a weekly Sunday school. She was the only rural church with a weekly Sunday school.

1888: Frederick Grider.

1889: S. K. Ramsey, B. F. Whiteman presiding elder, no statistics.

1890: S. K. Ramsey, 556 members, 4 churches, 5 Sunday schools, 200 members.

M. M. Roundtree who was active in the area around Corinth Baptist Church...Trapp and Right Angle according to the county newspapers was reported to have a circuit in the Ashland District called Estill with a Westbend post office. The circuit reported 188 members and 5 churches. There is no indication where those churches were. Westbend, Roundtree Chapel and Corinth (Whitehall) Methodist were probably included. The other two were apt to be in Estill County.

In passing we note that the seminary at College Hill had finally expired. It had been the Ayres Academy for the last ten years, a girls school. For awhile its deed had belonged to the conference and this is a reason why it, as its predecessor, the Texas Seminary, died. The community opposition to the northern Methodist outside of their own churches was intense. Without help from non northern Methodist sources a school had little hope. Union College in Barbourville was the only institution in the northern Methodist conference that apparently managed to draw sufficient strength from Kentucky and Tennessee and from northern sources to make the grade. Again and over and over, the Kentucky Conference moans the lack of support from the northern conferences. With all the problems, the conference did note that it had grown from 4,400 members in 1865 to 30,100 in 1890. It did note that its relationship with the southern Methodist was improving.

1894: S. K. Kelly.

1895: S. W. Kelly.

1896: J. R. Howes, 513 members, 3 Sunday schools, 4 churches.

1897: J. R. Howes, 377 members.

1898: J. R. Howes, 389 members.

1900: J. R. Howes, 399 members.

1901: J. L. Sturgill.

1902: J. L. Sturgill. 394 members, 4 churches.

1904: J. E. Hopkins, 408 members, 4 churches, 3 Sunday schools.

1905: J. E. Hopkins, 290 members.

1906: J. E. Hopkins.

1907: S. M. Carrier.

1908: S. M. Carrier, 325 members, 1 local preacher.

1909: S. M. Carrier, 326 members.

1910: No minister reported, 461 members.

1911: S. F. Kelly, 375 members.

1923: The College Hill Circuit was reported to have on the circuit, College Hill, Red House and Dyersville. This means that Clark County no longer has a church among the northern Methodist. For us the chapter closes. With the kind of leadership the northern Methodist had in 1866, had their northern conferences given them the kind of backing they might well have been established. Operating almost abandoned by those northern conferences, the work was a bitter, up hill struggle against overwhelming odds. Perhaps this was best. Had there been a strong northern work in Kentucky continuing the bitterness and rivalry between the two branches, perhaps the merger between the two movements would not have occurred as it did in 1939.

Rev. L. P. Hicks died of typhoid fever while in Winchester in 1900. Judy Emily Grider died in 1900. In 1902, Frederick Grider also died. He had been a power in the Kentucky Conference and had held the College Hill Circuit throughout the years. It is obvious that the northern Methodist did not move their men as often as the southern branch. This is partly because there were not enough men to go around, and if a man was satisfied and the churches happy, they were left alone. When a young man, Grider had spent ten days on the mourner's bench seeking salvation, he was licensed to preach in 1861. He had married Judy Ann Ransdell in 1852. He had served besides his turns as minister of the College Hill Circuit as the presiding elder of the Ashland District for eight years and of the Louisville District for four years.

## OWEN"S MEETING HOUSE

The first Methodist church to be established in Clark County (unless by some chance Stamper's Meeting House was established in 1789) was Owen's Meeting House. Fortunately, the records of Owen Chapel are fairly numerous. One book had been used as a photo album. Behind the pictures were the minutes of old meetings. This is also the family church of Kathryn Owen, Clark County's best contemporary historian. She has gathered a good deal of information concerning the church.

In 1791, John, James and Lawrence Owen moved from Maryland to the Four Mile area of Clark County. Lawrence Owen had been a Methodist minister before coming to Clark County and had been intimately associated with Leroy Cole and James O'Kelley. According to the court record, Owen was licensed to marry in 1794 and during his Clark County stay, married some 78 couples. His first county marriage in 1796 was James Jackson to Polly Embre and his last was March 21, 1811, when he married David King to Harriet Watts. During this period of time, he was beaten in marriages by only Robert Elkin, James Quisenberry and William Morris. Elkin and Quisenberry's records covered nearly double the number of years in the county. In 1808, Owen lost ownership of his land and soon moved to Henry County. However, the Owen family remained the pillars of the Owen Meeting House and subsequent churches.

In 1796, Redford's history tells of a circuit rider named Thomas Scott who served a Eubank's Meeting House. This was probably the same church as Owen's Chapel, though perhaps Achilles Eubank also had a spurt of religious interest at this time.

In 1801, the Hinkston Quarterly Meeting was held at Owen's Meeting House.

Quoting Burke's Autobiography in Finley's Sketches, the historian Redford wrote: "In 1801 the quarterly meeting for Hinkston circuit was held in June at Owen's Meeting House on Four Mile Creek, commencing on Friday and breaking up on Monday morning. At this meeting was the first appearance of that astonishing revival to which we have alluded. Several professed to get religion and many more were under deep conviction for sin, and the meeting continued from Sunday morning till Monday, with but little intermission. From thence, Brother Larkin and myself proceeded in company on Monday morning to a Presbyterian sacrament at Salem Meeting House in the vicinity of Col. John Martin's...from these two meetings the heavenly flame spread in every direction.

At first appearance these meetings (i.e., camp meetings) exhibited nothing to the spectator, unacquainted with them, but a scene of confusion, such as scarce could be put into human language. They were generally opened with a sermon, at the close of which there would be a universal outcry; some bursting forth into ejaculations of prayer or thanksgiving for the truth; others breaking out in emphatical sentence or exhortation; other flying to their careless friends, with tears of compassion, beseeching them to turn to the Lord; some struck with terror and hastening through the crowd to make their escape pulling away from their relatives; other trembling, weeping, crying out for the Lord to have mercy on them; others fainting and swooning away, till every appearance of life was gone, and the extremities of the body assumed the coldness of death; others surrounding them with melodious songs or fervent prayers for their happy conversion; others collecting in circles around their variegated scene, contending with arguments of and against the work. This scene frequently continued without intermission for days and nights together...."

The bodily agitations or "exercises" attending the excitement in the beginning of this century (1800) were various, and called by various names; as "falling exercises," the "jerks," "the dancing exercise," the "laughing exercise," etc.

This revival at Owen's Meeting House was attended by David Rice and other Presbyterian ministers and Rice recorded his astonishment in his own diary. It was a preliminary to the great Cane Ridge Revival and was the characteristic example of Methodist camp meetings and revivals. The Calvinists, both Presbyterian and Baptist were shocked and confused. It isn't until the appearance of the Reform movement in Baptist under Walter Scott that the revival lost much of its exercises and was adopted by Baptists, Christians and Cumberland Presbyterians.

Besides the Owen Meeting House which was the typical log house, a camp meeting was established near the church that is generally called Owen's Camp Meeting Ground, but in at least one source, it was referred to as the Concord Meeting Ground. William Landrum attended a meeting at the campground in 1824, claiming it to be the first. The Owen Campground had permanent buildings and was better organized than either Ebeneazor's or Grassy Lick's. Landrum is again back in Owen's Meeting House in 1826 when he attended class meeting. At class meetings are those who have become Christians in a given year and form a society. They meet periodically, choose one of their own members as lay leader and conduct a combination social and revival. Landrum reports a particularly important camp meeting in 1827 with 120 converts.

Usually the camp meetings would be a large relatively cleared piece of land. There would often be some kind of crude shelter largely over the pulpit. The audience came in wagons, on horse back and by foot. The camp meeting never was really successful until wagons had become common in Kentucky. Then a farmer would load his entire family plus bedding and food and attend the meeting perhaps miles away from his home. Services were usually continuous with breaks for meals. Perhaps two or three ministers would be featured, but perhaps a dozen, lay and ordained might preach. At times two or three ministers would be speaking at different times in different places. In the beginning, there was not a lot of singing because of lack of books and song leaders. However, increasingly, ministers became skilled at singing and teaching the songs as they went. At first, the psalms were the only hymns and the Methodist quarrelled over the use of hymn books. However, by the 1820s, the singing could be heard for miles away.

About 1833, the old log church was enlarged, though there may be confusion in the record with the church and the campground. Evidently, both were used indiscriminately for church services. Church services at Owen and most Methodist churches were not like the Baptist which had a set order, and long sermons, but generally ended at a set time. Owen's services would start and perhaps continue all day, or if they broke for dinner or supper would pick up again and continue long into the night by light of flares. Sometimes services would spill over into the next day or even spontaneously into weeks. Several hundred people might attend such a service, coming from all the Methodist churches in the area. This would particularly be true in the summer and warm weather parts of the year.

Landrum reported attending Owen Meeting House in October, 1842, to a funeral of one of the Owen's. He had been a Methodist for sixty years which would make him one of the pioneers. In 1844 Landrum mentions James Wool's name.

During this period Owen Chapel belonged to the Hinkston, Mt. Sterling and Winchester Circuits and their ministers were Owen's ministers. In 1848, Wool's Chapel became part of the Vienna Circuit. She reported 60 members.

Deed Book 35, 1850 states that Horatio and Martha Owen gave to Hezekiah Owen, William K. Owen, Wilson Nicholas, D. Simpson Cast and Robert King on Four Mile, a lot on which a meeting house was erected. Evidently, the new church had already been built. The deed was carefully safe-guarded by the usual Methodist formula. The deed did say that should ever the church cease to belong to the Methodist Episcopal Church, South, the property would revert to its owner.

There is no reason why the church should be named for Wools for as far as the available records go, he was just another circuit minister.

According to Kathryn Owen, the 1851 record book reported William Gunn as presiding elder and Hezekiah and William Robey Owen as stewards. The church had 50 members. In 1851, John C. Harrison was elder and David King was stewart. In 1858, John G. Bruce was presiding elder and John W. Owen and John Cox were stewards. It is interesting to note that the circuit minister is not mentioned. The tie is really with the presiding elders.

An interesting glimpse into the activities of the old log church is found in a letter written by Allen Owen in 1924: "This is Sunday morning-Lula has gone to church, I am home by myself. As I did not sleep good last night, my thoughts went back to my childhood days.

I thought of the old log church down in the bottom on the creek. This was before you were born (letter is to his sister). The old church had wooden hinges on the door, the benches were puncheon with pegs for legs. The pulpit was fenced in so you could just see the preacher's head. There was just one song book and the preacher had that. He would line out the songs, then everybody would sing. For instance he would say:

> "A charge have I to keep, a God to glorify"
> then all would sing....
>
> "A never dying soul to save and fitted for the sky." Then all would sing, you know what I mean.

Perhaps in the mid-week Pap would say, "Jane," speaking to our Mother, Sunday is meeting day, we must go--then Mother would get ready with us children the best she could for Pap and Mother did not have much money and times were hard. This was just after the Civil War in the days of reconstruction. But poor as they were, they went to church and took Marcia and me with them.

In my imagination, I can see Mother and Aunt Marcy for she lived with us then...coming down the path through Hampton's Woods, carrying their shoes in their hands and would put them on when we got near the church. There was no pike then; I remember when the pike was made. I would black my shoes off the bottom of a pot or skillet for times were hard and we had no blacking. But I was always glad when meeting day came because Mother always had biscuits on meeting days and when the preacher came."

The old church made the news in 1879 when an item appeared in the Winchester paper: "Last Thursday night a tramp went into the old deserted church building near Pinchem in this county, to stay the night. He built himself a fire and the building caught fire and was in a fair way to be destroyed by the flames, when it was discovered by some of the citizens and extinguished."

Sometime around 1870, the chapel was abandoned and was replaced by Owen's Chapel, a frame building which stood about one-half mile west of Wool's Chapel. Probably the Owen Chapel building was built before Wool Chapel was abandoned.

In 1859 when W. Dandy was elder, J. L. Grag was the circuit minister. For some reason, Gregg was removed and a local minister named Clark Polly took over. Nancy Jane and James H. Owen were baptised under him.

There has not been any reason for the abandonment of the original Owen Meeting House and the construction of Wool's Chapel. We presume that the church had gotten in a bad state of repair and it was easier to build a new church rather than remodel the old. There never were recorded deeds for the older church building. However, what happened to Wool's Chapel is a part of the confused history of the northern Methodist movement.

For the record that Kathryn Owen reports, the presiding elders, Bruce, Gunn, Harrison were very close to the church. The Owen family had also fought in mass for the Union during the Civil War and they were the backbone of the county Republican party in the bitter political battles that followed the Civil War.

In 1864, Landrum was back on the Vienna Circuit and reports a Quarterly Conference Meeting held at Wool's Chapel. This is the last mention of the name Wool's Chapel. In 1868, Redford's history reported two Methodist churches on Muddy Creek, one northern and one southern. The southern circuit was the Madison Circuit. They were at the time evidently using the same building. However, the southern church did not survive and the southern conference closed Wool's Chapel. Kathryn Owen reports that John Wesley and Perlina Creed deeded a lot for the building of a new Methodist church. The result was Owen's Chapel, a large frame structure with four windows on each side and two front doors.

In 1880, A. Fleet organized a Sunday school at Owen's Chapel. This is interesting since A. Fleet was a Baptist and also part of the city school system. Perhaps it was in this capacity that he was called by Owen Chapel to serve. John S. Bruen was Sunday school superintendent that year.

In 1893, Owen Chapel complained that a group of young men would occasionally try to break up their services. The church complained to the Democratic sheriff and got no action. They then took steps and stopped the rowdyism. No description of these steps has been recorded. The best point is the hard fact that

Owen Chapel was not popular. One member of Antioch Christian Church but grew up at Ford, told that her father would never attend services of any kind at Owen's. Baber said that his grandfather declared that he would rather go to hell than to Owen Chapel. How widespread this feeling was, of course, cannot be said. The political climate of the times was violent.

F. L. Creed was Sunday school superintendent in 1895. The church was strong enough and active enough to buy the chandeliers and furniture of the Sugar Ridge Cumberland Presbyterian Church that had rebuilt in Winchester.

The church was active in the Sunday School Union in Clark County and hosted the county convention in 1910 and as late as 1914, her Sunday school was reported in the governmental encouraged Sunday school census.

We have not had available the records of the northern Methodist for the late teens. In 1923, the College Hill Circuit was reported to include College Hill, Red House and Dyersville. There was no Owen Chapel. The church was not officially closed, however, until 1925.

What happened to the Owen Chapel? Like the Sugar Ridge Church, it had been a strong country church, but increasingly the membership moved to Winchester. In 1901 there was a half hearted effort to organize a northern Methodist church in Winchester's northern area. However, at the same time, the Mt. Abbott Methodist Church was being organized which absorbed most of the northern Methodist in the area. There is some evidence that Mt. Abbott was not quite sure which group it would join, but the decision was for the southern church. The history of Mt. Abbott and Trinity Methodist Church is in the third volume.

James O. Grass wrote an article "Methodist Episcopal History in Kentucky," in the January issue of the Methodist Church Historical Quarterly, 1963, put his finger on the problem. In Kentucky, he stated, "The Methodist Episcopal Church often seemed sympathetic to the Republican party..." He continued to note that the end of demarcation for the northern Methodist was political. Where the Republican party was strong, the northern Methodist church was strong. During the 1890s and early 1910s, the Kentucky Republican Party nearly reached a point where it could meet the Democratic Party on equal terms. It tore itself to pieces over Theodore Roosevelt and the Bull Moose Party. It never again recovered.

Like all country churches, the Owen Chapel people were moving into town. Once in political battles in 1889, the WINCHESTER DEMOCRAT half amused and half alarmed, noted that during the year, fourteen Owen babies had been born and all were Republican. Unfortunately for the chapel, those babies grew up and moved to town. The political cloud was an added burden that the church could not overcome.

Kathryn Owen listed some ministers who presided at Owen Chapel that is not included in our record. They include T. H. Conrey, Thomas Roundtree, Rev. Nankival, Rev. Stinnett, Rev. Gardner, Charles Duncan, A. Fleet, Rev. Godby, John G. Bruce and Rev. Carmichael. Some of these were presiding elders.

Among those who served as class superintendents were: Richard Thomas Owen, John Campbell Creed, and Wallace Owen. Sunday school teachers included: Nell Owen, Wallace Owen, John C. Creed and Lucy Griggs Owen. Organists were Wallace Owen, Lucie Clifton Jones and Rebecca O. Jones.

The chapel record book gives the following class membership for the year 1875: Margaret Jane Owen, Thomas B. Owen, Mahala Creed, Emma Creed, James M. Owen, William Riley Gordon, Julia Gann Gordon, Sarah Ann Gordon, Marcia Owen, Martha E. Owen, Thomas B. Creed, Amelia Creed, William R. Owen, Rosana Owen, Maybelle Owen, Talitha Ann Jones, Laura Jane Jones, Miachel B. Owen, David Wilson Owen, Pearl M. Owen, Alice Owen, John W. Owen, II, Henry T. Owen, Elizabeth E. Irvin, Carrie B. Irvin, Fred P. Owen, Fountain Finnell, Mollie Owen, Emma L. Owen, Leona S. Owen, Mary Ellen Owen, Lou T. Owen, Fannie Owen, Myrtle Owen, Bertie Lee Owen, Alta M. Owen, Eva B. Owen, Artie Owen, Anna M. Owen, John T. Owen, Susan F. Owen, James W. Gordon, Mahala Gordon, H. S. Owen, Rebecca Owen, George W. Owen, Harriett Jane Owen, William Perry Owen, Josephine F. Owen, William O. Irvin, John W. Owen, Perlina S. Owen, Richard T. Owen, Sarah G. Owen, Wilson Owen, Mary C. Owen, John C. Creed, Julia O. Creed, Lucie Jones, John R. Jones, Mary E. Jones, William H. Jones, Permelia E. Jones, Elizabeth Owen, Sarah Owen, Mildred Owen, Francis N. Owen, William D. Owen.

The last class membership to be recorded is not dated: John C. Creed, Julia A. Creed, Lucy Owen, William P. Owen, Margaret B. Irvin, Perlina S. Owen, Richard T. Owen, Sarah G. Owen, Mary E. Owen, Mary J. Farney, Sarah J. Owen, Jennie F. Gwin, William D. Owen, Santford T. Owen, Thomas B. Creed, Emma Creed, James M. Owen, William R. Owen, Rosanna Finnell, Amelia O. Crim, Margaret L. Owen, Lizzie Owen, Maxwell G. Owen, Ruth B. Owen, Speed F. Owen, Fred W. Owen, Jesse W. Owen, Sarah M. Stafford, Will Irvin, Eliza Owen, Samuel Gwin, Alice Smith, John Smith, Henry T. Owen, Fred P. Owen, Elizageth E. Walden, Carrie B. Watts, Nellie O. Reed, Leona S. Owen, Lula O. Bush, Nancy Richardson, Myrtle O. Todd, Fannie O. Tevis, Mollis Owen, Eva B. Owen, Fountain Finnell, Thomas Irvin, Robert Richardson, Artie Owen, Mildred Owen, Hattie Owen, Mirty Farmer, Eunice Owen, McKinley Owen, Nancy Lou Owen, J. W. Smith, Lucie Jones, Hays Owen, Viola Owen, Nancy Clay Owen, Samuel Owen, Fanny Stafford, Thomas Fisher, Florence Ecton, Minnie Stafford, Algin Owen, Letha Stafford, Sherman Crim, Curtin Owen, Florence Farmer,

Maggie Farmer, Jessie Bush, Ben R. Owen, Kitty Owen, Lizzie Brown Owen, William True and Naomi Baber.

There have been references to two other Methodist churches both affiliated with the northern movement that were established since 1866. Also, the southern movement established El Bethel whose history will be considered in the third volume. Both the northern Methodist churches were short lived.

Roundtree Chapel was located in Trap. It used the Roundtree School House most of its history of which almost nothing has been discovered. The WINCHESTER DEMOCRAT did report July 13, 1894, that the church was going to dedicate its building. Other newspaper references had been given to it off and on over the last few years. Like Dunaway, it was far from Winchester and not generally reported by her newspaoer. An M. M. Roundtree, who was a northern Methodist minister, was most often affiliated with the church in these news accounts.

The other church may have actually been older. There is a possibility that the two are linked since the very few references made to it came before Roundtree Chapel was discussed by the papers. The Masons at Corinth built in the 1870s, a large frame meeting hall, the second floor of which was preserved for the fraternity and the downstairs floor for public gatherings which were largely religious. Both the Baptist and the Methodist began to use the facility and both were referred to as Whitehall Methodist or Baptist, or sometimes Corinth Methodist or Baptist. A W. H. Childer apparently was preaching there in February of 1881.

Both churches had disappeared by the turn of the century and very little information is obtainable about either one, almost none about Corinth Methodist.

## REV. LAWRENCE W. OWEN

Lawrence Owen, son of John and Elizabeth Winn Owen, was born in Maryland, February 7, 1763. He married Mary Cullom, daughter of Francis and Susannah Northcraft Cullom, circa 1781. Early United States Census records list the Culloms as residents of Frederick County, Maryland.

About the year 1788, five Owen brothers, along with the Culloms, Hukills and other families migrated from their home in Montgomery County, Maryland to Kentucky by way of the Wilderness Road. James Alfred Owen, a grandson of Lawrence, wrote in his notes of family history that the group spent the first year in Kentucky at Bullit's Lick, in what is now Bullit County, where at the time there was a rather large community engaged in making salt from a number of salt wells located there. Be that as it may, and there is no evidence to confirm or deny the story, three of the Owen brothers, Thomas, John and Lawrence finally settled on Four Mile Creek in what was then Fayette County but is now in Clark County. The first tax roll of Clark County in 1792 lists the three bothers.

Rev. Lawrence Owen purchased a part of a land grant to one John Tanner by the state of Virginia. This grant was for four hundred acres and contained a "lick and a spring," both of which were located on that part sold to Lawrence Owen. Part of the tract lay on the creek itself. This grant had been purchased through the brother of John Tanner, who claimed to have the power of attorney, by William Orear. Orear then sold it to the early settlers.

Lawrence Owen had been ordained a Methodist minister while living in Maryland and one of the first things that he did after purchasing his land in Clark County was to erect a log meeting house on a hill overlooking Four Mile Creek. Services were held regularly at Owen's campground. The community was principally Methodist, though religion played but a small part of pioneer existence at that time. From evidence gathered it would seem that Lawrence Owen and his sons started immediately to clear the land and make improvements. A church was erected on one side of the farm and deeded to the trustees along with a grove for camp-meetings. Lawrence Owen conformed to the standards of his church and opposed the practice of slavery. He took on himself and his sons the burden of clearing the virgin land and working the farm. He built a grist mill on the creek to grind the neighborhood grain and one of the huge mill stones remains embedded in the mud near the mill site and may be seen today.

In the Clark County Courthouse, Deed Book No. 1, page 116, records a bond of agreement between Lawrence Owen and Robert Clarke with Governor Isaac Shelby in the sum of 500 pounds, court money, dated November 26, 1793, and reads as follows:

Know all men by these presents that we, Lawrence Owen and Robert Clarke are held and formally bound to Isaac Shelby, Esq., Governor of Kentucky in the sum of 500 pounds court money to which payment will and truly be made to said governor. We bind ourselves, our heirs and executors, jointly and severally, firmly by these presents, sealed and dated this 26th of November, 1793, in the seond year of the Commonwealth.

The condition of the above obligation is such that whereas the above bound Lawrence Owen of the Methodist Society hath this day obtained leave of the worshipful court of Clark County to celebrate the rites of matrimony within the Commonwealth. If therefore, the said Lawrence Owen shall well and truly deem himself in the performance of the said trust, agreeable to an act of assembly regulating the solemnization of marriage, then this obligation, else to be void, shall remain in full force.

                              Signed:  Lawrence Owen
                                        Robert Clarke

This is an example of the bond that theoretically all Clark County ministers who wished to marry in Clark County were expected to execute.

A History of Henry County records: Rev. Lawrence Owen, a Methodist minister of Clark County, whose church in that county was active during the religious revival of 1801, came to Henry County and built the log Ebeneazor meeting house in 1811 on what is now the farm of Mrs. A. M. Robinson, one mile east of Smithfield. There was both a church and school at this place. Both are now defunct.

Lawrence Owen erected a grist mill on the creek and planted an orchard on his farm. Before many years a well-stocked, self-contained farm rewarded the years of hard work. Here, Lawrence lived and labored until his death on September 12, 1821. He was buried in the orchard behind his home, where he still rests. His widow continued to live at the home place until her death on June 14, 1833, when she was placed beside her husband. One of their sons, Nelson Reed, bought out the interest of the other children after the death of their father and became the owner of the Henry County farm after his mother's death. He sold it a few years later and moved to Jefferson County and the farm passed forever from Owen ownership.

After the death of Lawrence Owen, his widow and son administered the estate. They found that Lewis Schooler had never paid for the Clark County farm so they brought suit to collect the balance due. Judgment was given and the farm was put up for sale to satisfy the judgment. Nephews of Lawrence, who still resided in Clark County bought the farm and so it came back into family hands where it remained until about 1916.

Lawrence and Mary Cullom Owen were the parents of eleven children: Elizabeth, John, Anna, Ignatius, Nelson Reed, Henry B., Mary, Rebecca, Lawrence W., William McClean and Fielding Owen.

About the year 1810, Hon. Henry Clay, a promising young lawyer of Fayette County, Kentucky, received a commission from the heirs of John Tanner to sell Tanner's land grants in Kentucky on a commission basis of one third of the selling price. Clay brought suit against Lawrence Owen, claiming that the brother of John Tanner did not have legal power of attorney to sell the Four Mile Creek tract and asked for judgment against the occupants of the land for its improved value and its use for twenty years. As the two Tanners were then dead, the pioneers were unable to legally prove their title and judgment was rendered against them. Rather than lose everything, Lawrence paid for his land a second time, though it almost impoverished him.

In the year 1811, Lawrence Owen purchased from Thruston Taylor a tract in Henry County, Kentucky. Thruston Taylor, a neighbor and friend had inherited an immense tract of land there from his father. Lawrence sold his Clark County trace to Lewis Schooler and moved his family and goods to new frontiers. His married children came along and some of his neighbors also. They formed a new community at what is now Smithfield on the little Kentucky River. The Owen brothers had strong religious convictions, especially Lawrence, who devoted a great deal of his time and a considerable amount of his substance to the church. He never received any compensation as a minister, since resident ministers were not paid at this time and traveling preachers received but sixty dollars a year.

## THOMAS HINDE

Thomas Hinde was born in Oxfordshire, England, July 1737. He received the usual classical education of the new bourgeois class in England that stopped short of being aristocratic, but was probably better educated. He went to London and studied medicine under Dr. Thomas Brooke of the St. Thomas Hospital. This apparently was the finest medical education available in England in its day. In 1753, he received his surgeon's license and promptly shipped aboard His Majesty's Navy. He was rated as a surgeon and in a day when many Navy surgeons were drunkards and incompetents, his skill quickly was recognized as superior. He was quite often attached to the shops of the rating officers in a squadron.

He arrived in New York in 1757 and then served under Amhurst at Louisburg. He wintered in Halifax that winter and then was surgeon of General Wolfe's command ship in the attack on Quebec. He claimed to have been close enough to Wolfe when that general was mortally wounded to hear his last words. In Benjamin West's famous protrait of the dying Wolfe, legend has it that Hinde is the man feeling Wolfe's pulse. Lucien Beckner tried to follow up the story by writing the director of the National Galleries of Canada. The director had never heard the legend which does not mean the legend is not true. After the fall of Quebec, Hinde served at Belle's Island.

Following the end of the French and Indian Wars, Hinde took his discharge in America and found his way to Virginia where he set up practice. He was a neighbor and a friend of Patrick Henry. He also cared for the Hubbard family and married one of the daughters, Mary Hubbard.

Despite his training in the British Navy he became an ardent advocate of independence from Britain. He was a diest who saw God as the creator but as a more or less uninterested spectator in man's affairs. It was a popular view in those days of educated and intellectual minds. Technically he adhered to the Anglican Church.

He was, therefore, deeply disturbed when he discovered that his daughter had converted to Methodism which was just becoming a movement in Virginia. To stop the infection, he sent her to an aunt. The choice was bad because the aunt had also been converted to Methodism and did not stop the girl's faith.

Meanwhile, Hinde's wife converted. He thought her mentally deranged so he placed a mustard plaster upon her back to draw off the poisons. It was a painful treatment, but his wife did not reprove him but merely thanked him for an opportunity to show the depth of her faith. Hinde was deeply impressed by her attitude and did consent to attend some meetings. There he was both fascinated and rebelled by the emotional excesses he saw. He described how two young women fainted during the service and were left unattended on the floor. He left his seat and went to them, finding them more in a trance than in medical difficulty. Finally, he was reached and was converted to Methodism.

For his services during the Revolution, Patrick Henry gave him some 20,000 acres in Kentucky. He sent his young nephew, Hubbard Taylor west to survey the land, paid him in land, and began selling off much of it. Finally, he came to Kentucky himself and settled on what remained of his property which was in the Pine Grove area of Clark County.

He became a deeply religious man who built prayer shelters in various parts of his property where he could retreat for prayer. He became subject to a lot of stories. Once he was asked how salt was selling because of his interest in some salt boats on the Kentucky Rivers. He replied, "I do not know the price of salt, young man, but grace is free." Another time he went to vote. All voting in those days (until into the 1890s) was done in public. He hobbled up to the election officers and was asked who he was for. He answered in a lound voice, "Jesus Christ," every time.

It was Hinde who was given credit of converting John Martin from his athiesm and skepticism. Hinde and his family, which included William Kavanaugh, became the heart and soul of the Ebeneazor Church which in turn, became the most outstanding of the early Methodist churches in the area.

## WILLIAM KAVANAUGH

William Kavanaugh deserves more than a passing note in that he started a very remarkable Methodist family. He was one of the early pioneers in Kentucky, arriving about 1790. Like many a young man, he taught school for a living at Strode's Station. He had been a Methodist minister before coming to Kentucky having served the Franklin Circuit in Virginia. In Kentucky, he was assigned the Salt River Circuit. While attending the Kentucky Conference at Bethel in Jessamine County in 1798, he met and married Hannah Hinde whose family had just moved to Kentucky. They were married by Lawrence Owen.

Kavanaugh felt that the circuit ministry was too trying for both his health and marriage and continued as a school teacher in Clark County. Together with father-in-law's family he established Ebeneazor Methodist Church. Still feeling the call to the ministry, Kavanaugh shifted to the Episcopal Church. This movement at this time was much smaller than the Methodist movement but did not practice the circuit riding technique. They did have a number of churches in the larger towns and along the Ohio River. He also registered with the Clark County Court to have the right to marry in the county. He was the first Episcopal minister to claim that right in the county. Most of his local marriages were within the growing Kavanaugh-Hinde family. His health never good, he died in 1806 at the age of 31.

His wife returned to Winchester with her children. She had never left the Methodist church and had raised her children as Methodist. She married William Taylor in 1812 who in turn died two years later. The same year that Taylor died, she married a third time to Valentine Martin.

Mary Todd Hinde left behind nine Methodist ministers, Thomas Hinde, gransons, Leroy Kavanaugh, Hubbard Kavanaugh, who became bishop, Benjamin T. Kavanaugh, William B. Kavanaugh and Edward Southgate. Two of her daughters married Methodist ministers, one of course, was William Kavanaugh and the other was Leroy Cole.

## HUBBARD HINDE KAVANAUGH

Hubbard Hinde Kavanaugh was the third son of William Kavanaugh, and his wife, Martha Hinde. He was born June 14, 1802, after his father had become an Episcopal minister. His father died five years later. When he became an adolescent, he was apprenticed to the Presbyterian minister, John Lyle, to learn printing. In 1817, he was converted to Christ. He noted that he had an Episcopal father, a Methodist mother, was converted by a Methodist minister while traveling with a Presbyterian. He became a Methodist, however, and began in 1822 to preach the Mt. Sterling Circuit which included the Clark County churches. Later he served as pastor of Russellville, Danville, Harrodsburg, Bardstown, Springfield, Frankfort, Louisville and Maysville. Also, Covington and Winchester at one time or another.

In 1828, he married a Mrs. D. Priest Lewis. In 1837, Governor James Clark, who had known him all his life, appointed Kavanaugh the state's first superintendent of education. It became Kavanaugh's task to lay the ground work for the state's public education system. In 1851, he was elected bishop of the Methodist church. He died in 1884.

Another of William Kavanaugh's sons also became a Methodist minister. He was the fourth, Benjamin Taylor Kavanaugh. He served both Kentucky and Texas churches. In 1882, he served the Old Fort Circuit that included the Old Fort Methodist Church in Montgomery County and Mt. Zion and El Bethel in Clark County.

## CONCLUSION

The end of this volume is most arbitrary because there is so much interesting material connected with a county history that there is simply no where to end. There are continually new bits of information that come in. No doubt there remains a vast amount of material that no one knows about, letters in old trunks, diaries, books, etc. There will be a section in each volume where any new material will be recorded.

We feel that the Methodist section particularly needs additional information about local ministers, lay leaders, stewards, Sunday school superintendents, etc.

## EPILOG

The history of any county is so full and so interesting that none of it should be slighted. For this reason, we have divided this history into four volumes. The second volume will be entitled Our Good Earth, if Pearl Buck will forgive the stealing of her title. It is continuous with the end of the first volume.

We will pick up the county history and politics with 1800 using the court records, governors papers and any other source possible and bring them down to 1864 where the post Civil War politics began in earnest. We will spend a good deal of time describing the life and culture of the period between 1800 and the Civil War. Slavery will be examined in the light of history a little differently. We will examine the part that Clark Countians played in the War of 1812, in the Mexican War and in the various Indian rebellions where information is available. We will probably add the Civil War to this volume also. Actually, the war was the end of an era rather than a beginning of a new era.

In addition, we will pick up the history of the Christian Church which began in a struggle with the Baptists in the late 1820s and bring them up to date with the history of the Baptist, Presbyterians and Methodists.

We will include a number of more or less isolated incidents such as cholera and the day that the stars fell, Jackson's coming to Winchester and the life. We will spend a great deal of time discussing Clark County agriculture, particularly the shorthorn boom until it burst in 1889.

In addition, we will carry more or less complete sketches of the development of roads, taverns and hotels, the Post Office, ferries, education, Winchester, Kiddville, etc. It will be a year or so before this volume is ready. It is perhaps the hardest time to get information so any that you all can furnish will help.

## THE INDEX

An index is more than a list of names and places to find the names. It is a quick summary of the history of the county. Since county histories deal with individuals mostly, the most active individuals stand out very clearly. In the period before 1800, a number of names appear. Benjamin Allen, Junior, John Baker, Daniel and Squire Boone, David Brandenburg, Ambrose, John, Philip and William Bush, Richard Calloway, George Rogers Clark, the two Robert Clarks, Henry Clay, William Clinkenbeard, Dillard Collins, Benjamin and Cuthbert Combs, John Constant, John Donaldson, John Edwards, Robert Elkins, Achilles Eubank, John Frame, James French, Christopher and David Gist, Tom Goff, John Holder, Andrew and John Hood, William Haley, David Hampton, Josiah Hart, Richard Henderson, Richard Hickman, Robert Higgins, John Martin, James, Robert and William McMillan, Jilson Payne, James Quisenberry, Edmund Ragland, Alexander Ramsey, Joseph Scholl, Charles Scott, Thomas Scott, Isaac Shelby, Enoch Smith, John Strode, Hubbard, George, Samuel Taylor, Levi Todd, Charles Tracy, Andrew Tribble, George Washington and Original Young make up a list that appear repeatedly in the history of the county. Some of these men, the Boones, George Rogers Clark, Washington, Isaac Shelby, and Levi Todd, for example, never resided in Clark County but played an important part upon it. Enoch Smith and Jilson Payne were Montgomery County people who disappeared from Clark County history when Montgomery left. Some really represent two or three people by the same name . . . John Baker, James French, John Martin, David Hampton, etc.

What is interesting is the great number of others, who appear once or twice in some connection, or not at all, who lived, prospered and died without every doing anything that recorded their names where some historian could find them. Once in a while some list, such as a tax list, will reveal them to be prosperous men, and no doubt influential.

Also, one quickly discovers the large pioneer families, the Allens, Andersons, Bakers, Berrys, Boones, Browns, Burns, Bushes, Calloways, Clarks, Clinkenbeards, Collins, Combs, Conkwrights, Cunninghams, Daniels, Davises, Elkins, Embrys, Evans, Frenches, Gists, Goffs, Grants, Haggards, Haleys, Hamiltons, Hamptons, Harrises, Harts, Harrisons, Hickmans, Higgenses, Hieronymouses, Johnsons, Jones, Kinkaid, Landers, Lewises, Martins, McMillans, Moore, Morgan, Morton, Quisenberrys, Raglands, Ramseys, Scholls, Scotts, Smiths, Sphars, Souths, Strodes, Sudduths, Taylors, Trimbles, Vivions, Wades, Wills, and Woods. Each of these had at least five members of their family appear at least once in the records.

One can see also the dependence on Fayette County and Lexington, as, for example, compared with Bourbon County and Paris. It would be possible to add up the battles that Clark Countians fought with the British in the American Revolutionary and particularly get some impression of the effect that the Battle of Blue Licks had upon the county.

Every book of this nature should have an index. From a point of view of this Author, it has been a terrible struggle. I am not a perfectionist. I do not take well to precise and monotinous jobs. I make mistakes. Once while working with the H's, I made six mistakes in a row. I quit, but I also must have thrown away the original list of H's for when I went back to finish, I found the original list gone. I had to work back through the whole book to find the H's again. A bit later I realized that the K's were on the same original lists of the H's and I had to look back through the book for K's. If, therefore, you do not find the name you are looking for, run down the next few names and perhaps your name is just out of place.

In working on index, I am appalled at the mistakes made. In later books it has taught me to go over what I have had typed by others to see if there are mistakes. This is also one of those jobs I hate, but I am the only one that can do it. However, all the variety of spelling of a name does not necessarily lie at my door step. For example the Thomsons are very proud and insistent on the fact that there is no p in their name. Tomsons appear quite often, particularly in relation with the Old Churches. Now, should I assume that all Thompsons that appear in the records of the Old Churches are actually Thomsons? I am reasonably safe when I am dealing with a Columbus Thomson and a Columbus Thompson, but what if the name in question is C. Thompson? What is the correct spelling of a name like Hinde, or Hindes, Owen or Owens, Hoy or Hay, when the sources have both. I know what the latest spelling is, but is that what the original intent was?

This index has other problems. The author is not a geneologist. Is Robert, R. S., R. Stuart, and Stuart, the same man or four different men. For example there are at least four Eli Bruces in Clark county history. At any one time, which Eli Bruce are we dealing with? Then there is an interesting question as to whether Bruce's Chapel which was once mentioned by Landrum is related to this Bruce family.

One is impressed again with the strength of the family church. Families such as Owen, Vivion, Taylor, for example, make up the membership and strength of their respective churches. As long as a community sees its sons and daughters settling down within the midst of the community, does that church continue. On the other hand, when the children leave the community, as the Owen young people did, death rides hard upon the local church. Often, these churches have become virtually property of that family, and community rivalries and disagreements make it impossible to extend the family church beyond that small group. In any neighborhood, there are always a majority of people who do not go to church, but the sociological pressures are often such that cannot reach them. The 19th century Clake county was much more homogenious in class structure, in rural areas, than the 20th century Clark county. By this, the difference between land owners and tenants had not become so very noticable, and the large landowner had not yet deserted his community for the city. However, the divisions of politics and religious divisions, were much stronger.

We note again the relationship with other counties is different. Again, Bourbon county played almost no part in the Clark county religious history. True, there were churches in North Middletown and Clintonville both Presbyterean and Methodist and later Christian, would have a relation with Clark county churches, but these were in this case, an effort to keep alive borderline churches by affiliating them with a stronger Clark county movement. In each case the effort failed. There is little help given to a weak church by relating it to a stronger church. Again there is little influence on the part of Fayette county in the religious life of Clark, much less than political and social. True, Walnut Hill Presbyterian Church carried Salem for decades but this was the exception. Ebeneazor may have influenced Fayette county history in early Fayette county Methodist history. David Fork Baptist Church was tied with Clark county's Winchester church by ministers for quite some time, but little else. The Boone Creek Baptist Church also furnished ministerial leadership for the Boone Creek Churches, but the Boone Creek Baptist Church itself had very little influence or took very little part in Clark county affairs other than as a member of the Boone Creek Baptist Association.

On the other hand, whereas Clark county had little political or economic relations with Madison county, both the Methodist and Baptist movements in Clark and Madison county were deeply interwoven, and in the same location of Madison county. The College Hill area of Madison county, connected by a ferry to Clark county was the center of the Methodist northern movement, but Owen Chapel was always the strongest link in that circuit until near its death. The ministers lived at College Hill partly because of the College there, and the little group of northern churches in that area. The effort of the Southern Methodists to tie Ebeneazor and Wool's chapel to the College Hill work failed. Wool's chapel died, and Ebeneazor went first to Fayette circuits and finally to Winchester until it died of malnutrition. On the other hand David Chenault, whose home church was in the general area of Madison county, played an enormous part in the Baptist History of the period. Later, William Rupard was to carry that same influence back. For over a hundred years, the religious relations between Baptists in Madison and Clark county were close.

The strongest ties however, lay with Montgomery county. In the area that Montgomery county had tried to take from Clark and failed, there were always close economic, social and religious ties. Lullbegrud Baptist Church was more of a Clark county church than a Montgomery church. Her ties were with Goshen and New Providence, rather than the struggling Baptist churches that survived the Campbellite holicost of the 1830's. Grassy Lick Methodist church also was closely affiliated with Clark county, being part of a strong Mt. Zion-Grassy Lick Circuit that operated for decades as a very important unit.

By the end of the 19th century, however, these cross county lines were largely broken, and the county became a self contained religious unit as well as social and political.

We have made no effort to identify churches that are not Clark countian as to location. Where the location, at least what county, is possible without much additional study, it will be reported. Some of the nemes, Bald Eagle for example is a name of an area in present Bath county near Bethel. It is presumed that the various Bald Eagle Baptist churches were located there. No effort has been made to pin point their locations in that they have vanished decades ago.

There apparently were two Indian Creek Baptist Churches that were reported in Fayette county and Madison county Baptist associations. At first I thought it was the Clark county church being reported, but later it became obvious that it was not. I made no effort to locate it thereafter. I have made no effort to develop the Red River Baptist Association, which is not the present Red River Baptist Association, though they roughly covered the same territory. We have a pretty good history of the later Red River Association and a scattering of the Greenville Regular Baptist Association that preceded it, but we have not included it in this work. Basically it is a Powell county movement. The Old Red River Association must have died about 1920 and some of its churches belonged to the Greenville Baptist Association. The Red River, and the Tates Creek Associations did not affect Clark county history enough to be researched.

We did not mean to over emphasis the Baptist Associations over the Conferences and Presbyteries of other groups. It was just that the Baptist associations played such a large part in Clark county history where the higher eschalons of the other movements hardly affected the county as a whole. It would seem to be worthwhile to revive the North District Association, if nothing else in memory of the great men and churches that once served under her authority.

Abbett, H.W. 470
Abernaki Indians 118
Abington Presbytry 384
Abney, William 62
Action (Ecton)
   Smallwood 62, 243
Adams 473
   Benjamin 233
   John 62, 217, 359
   John G. 380
   John Quincey 222
   Nellie 300
   Simon 173, 174
       178, 241
   William 443, 444
Adkins
   James 62
   John 62
   Louise 445
   Nancy 209
   Thomas 209
African Methodist Episcopal
   Church 474
Albermarle, J.A. 219
Albermarle's Declaration
   of Independence 82
Albund, Jo Dalta 230
Aldham, Wilbur 243
Aldridge
   Evelyn 474
   William 137
Alexander
   Benjamin Sr. 62
   John 62, 93
   Rachel 288
Allansville Baptist
   Church 258, 293, 294
       299, 311, 314
       324
Allen and Selitea Act 217
Allen or Allan
   A.E. 95
   B.E. 307-310, 313
   Belle 353
   B.F. 97
   Benjamin 121, 141, 164
        223, 231, 393
   Chilton 199, 235
       238, 392
   Clifton 105
   David 121
   Elijah 137
   F.S. 296, 297, 337

Allen or Allan (continued)
   George 330
   Isaak 62
   James 137, 273, 297
       391, 416
   L. 361
   Lewis 290, 331
   Milly 393
   Rebecca 391
   Thomas 365
   T.S. 299, 300
   William 397
   William Y. 397
Allenville 125
Allenville Baptist Church
   100
Allington, Jonathan 178
Allison, John 135
Alquoinquins 12, 13, 129
Alveradado, louvada de
American Colonization Society
   394, 413
American Political Party 338
Amhurst, General 504
Ammerson, A.Y. 301
Anderson, Fort, Battle of
   138
Anderson
   Amzi 242
   Atihew 241
   George 415
   Granny 18, 20, 21
   James 62, 395, 399
   Jesse 406, 407
   J.M. 354
   John 387
   Krom 62
   Mallory 62
   Rachel 336
   R.H. 366
   Presley 58
Andrews
   James 436
   J.C. 482
Anthony
   A.H. 100
   A.M. 299
Antioch Christian Church 275
Anti-Saloon League 220
Araminism 420, 430
Ardrey, Mrs. W.P. 108
Ares, Thomas 137
Ariel Ark 37

Arnett, Theodore 200
Arnold
  Benedict 220
  John 56, 72
  W.E. 419, 421, 427-429, 422
      433, 438, 467, 482, 483
Arthur, Joseph 189
Arvan, W.B. 62, 98
Asbury, Francis 420, 422, 425
      426, 460, 461
Ashbrook, Levi 142, 335
Ashland Methodist Circuit 484
Ashland Methodist District 396
Ashley
  Josiah 335, 336
  Thomas 62
Ash Ridge Presbyterean
  Church 411
Ash Swamp 66
Assembly of God 458
Atkins, George 432
Augusta College 487
Augusta County, Va. 155
Ayers Academy 491
Babbitt, Carlisle 389
Baber
  Isham 245. 290, 331
  James 331
  Naomi 500
Bader, Jonathan 189
Badger, M. 273
Bailey
  B.B. 318
  Edmund 62
  John 89, 213, 263, 281
  Thomas 37
Baker
  A.F. 99, 100, 297, 311, 318
  Cuthbert 466
  Daniel 396, 413
  Elizabeth 84, 85
  Felix 178
  Isaac 62, 141, 205
  James 164, 368, 369
  John 7, 84, 110, 113, 152, 161
      164, 165, 166, 167, 168
      172, 173, 178, 187, 188
      189, 201, 205, 210, 215
      234, 236, 241, 339, 340
  Lucinda 368
  Mary 339
  Massa 332
  Moses 339

Baker (continued)
  Sally 466
  Samuel 434
  William
Bald Eagle Baptist Church 264
  266, 267, 284, 287
Baldwin 126
Ballard
  Bland 37
  Philip 62
Ballard's Woods 410
Ballou, T. 94
Baltimore 427
Bankertiel 233
Baptist Board of Missions
  268, 335, 357, 361
Baptist Young People's Union 376
Barbee
  Thomas 409, 410
  William 137
Barbourville 487, 491
Bardstown 507
Barker, Alconey 339
Barkham, Dennis 200
Barkley, William 62
Barnard, Elam 448
Barnes 108
  Charles 62
  Robert 62
  William 152, 167
Barnett 232
  Alexander 36
  Elijah 339
  Isaac 199
  T.W. 457
  W.B. 490
Barrow 326, 473
  Asa 114, 230, 259
  David 81, 134, 259, 263-266
      269, 274
  Hinchi Gilliam 114
  John 259, 330
  Rachel 113
Bartlett
  E.G. 279
  William 62
Barton, Josiah 52
Bascum, Henry C. 439
Basfoot Tavern 116
Bashcar Presbyterean Church 385
Bass 92
  Murry 354

Bath County 73, 80, 141, 205
        171, 262, 266, 274
        387, 398, 432, 441
Battaile, James E. 398, 399
Bauer, Maximillian 333
Baughman, John 27
Baxter
    Edmond 241, 242
    Thomas 240
Baythe, James 58, 62, 140, 141
Beachgrove Baptist Church 325
Beale, Samuel 338
Beallu
    James 192
    Leonard 17
    Zacharia 62
Bean
    Asa 444, 475
    Eldred 410
    John 62, 149, 243, 244
    John D. 410
    Major 475
    Richmond 62
Bean School 277
Bean's Creek 218
Beasley 118, 206
    62 misprint 118, 155
Beatty, James 213
Beattyville 314, 315, 326
Beaver Pond 17, 128, 156
        164, 213, 223
Beaver Pond Baptist Church
    271, 273
Beckner
    Lucien 504
    Lucius 11, 14, 15, 17, 18
        54, 56, 85, 111, 223
        231
    W.M. 54
    William 123, 225, 232, 186
        320, 410
Becknerville 123, 182, 221, 236
        377, 391, 393
Becraft, Abraham
Bedinger
    Michael 37
    Mitchell 37
Beeman, Charles 167
Begraft 142
Bell County 31
Bell
    L. 337
    Nancy 445

Belle's Island 504
Bennett
    John 68
    Joshua 78, 140
    William 58, 60
Benton, David B. 114
Berea 2
Berkley, William 62
Berry
    Benjamin 50, 52
    Elizabeth 338
    James 37, 58
    John 62, 63, 342
    Joseph 31
    Lewis 335-337
    Thomas 62, 213, 266, 335
Berryman
    Charles 418
    David 358
    Newton G. 451, 466
Best
    Christian 392
    James 62
Besuden, Beverly 222
Bethel Methodist Church 437, 506
Bethel Presbyterean Church 386
Bethlehem Baptist Church 265, 269
    274, 293, 307, 341, 243, 404
Bethlehem Christian Church
    109, 113, 116, 233, 234, 251
    258, 259, 275, 364, 365, 404
Bibb, Elisha 306, 307
Big Bone Lick 144
Bigelow, Russell 433
Biggers, William 62
Big Sandy River 478
Billings, George 25
Bird, William 52
Bishop
    Ebeneazord 413
    R.H. 411
Black, W.N. 484
Blackburn
    Samuel 24
    Joseph 241, 242
Black Fish 36
Black Hills 24
Black Hoof 17, 144
Blackgrove, Henry 263
Black Mountain Baptist Church 325
Blackwell
    Benjamin 333
    John 62

Blackwell (continued)
  Sarah 352
  Susie 465
Blair, Janice 433
Blanton, Thomas 394
Bledsoe
  Jesse 119, 201
  Joseph 328
  Lewis 357
  Moses 90, 263-266
  William 89, 328
Blue Ashe Baptist Church 264, 266
Blue Ball Precinct 111, 119
Blue Jacket 141
Blue Licks 19, 134, 236
Blue Licks, Battle of 30, 32, 48
  58, 62, 63, 65, 113, 117, 135
  143, 239, 220, 162
Blythe, James 388, 411
Bobb, James 233
Bobley, Allen 201
Bofman Ford Baptist Church
  264, 304-307
Bog's Creek Baptist Church
  281, 293
Bogg's Creek 213
Bogg's Fork Baptist Church 92
Bolger
  Edward 135
  John 135
Boling, W.T. 452
Bonapart, Napolean 151
Bomdurant, Joseph 273
Bonrey, Jack 233
Booker
  John 5, 39
  William 62
Boone 28, 37, 59, 161, 233
    329, 382, 401
  Ann 29
  Benjamin 28
  Cyrus 101, 312, 313, 371
  Daniel 18, 21, 27, 28, 29, 31
    34, 36-39, 45-48, 51
    63, 65, 71, 72, 76, 80
    81, 85, 121, 126, 143
    144, 146, 133, 135, 136
    156, 161, 114, 239, 236
    232, 230, 222, 252, 264
    485
  Edward 30, 33, 113, 205
  Elizabeth 29, 30, 32, 45
  Family 252, 264

Boone (continued)
  George 28-30, 32, 33, 195
    268, 274, 281, 304
    335
  Harriett 61
  Isaiah 33
  Isreal 34, 51, 113, 136
  James 28, 32, 34
  Jemima 32, 45
  Joseph 28, 30
  Judah 29
  Lavinia 10
  Levi 37
  Lily 205
  Martha 205
  Mary 30, 33, 28, 76, 113
  Rachel 28, 31
  Rebecca 32, 34
  Sam 28, 33, 35, 62, 85
    137, 143, 372, 373
  Samuel 281
  Sarah 31
  Squire 28, 29, 31, 33, 34, 45
    53, 85, 111, 192, 247
    281
  Thomas 33, 94, 233
Boone Creek 38, 40, 41, 184
    216, 213, 247
Boone Creek Baptist Association
  32, 51, 94, 95, 106, 83, 101
  105, 247, 262, 268-271, 280
  274-278, 286-290, 293-295,
  297, 298, 304-310, 314-318
  320, 322, 348, 351, 352, 362
  357-359, 364, 366, 367, 369
  371, 372, 375-377, 402
Boone Creek Baptist Church
  90, 92, 95, 266, 293, 300
  305, 307-309, 338, 367, 369
  383, 395, 396, 462
Boone Creek Sunday School
  Convention 313
Boonesboro or Boonesborough
  8, 9, 30, 28, 31, 36, 37
  39, 40, 42, 43, 45, 47
  49, 62, 63, 65, 70, 76
  77, 81, 85, 89, 111, 127
  131, 133, 134, 145, 155
  168, 226, 246, 239, 236
  230, 222, 217, 215, 185
  119, 329, 396, 437, 475
Boone Station 30, 58, 83, 106
    114, 143, 236, 145

Booneville 314
Booth, John 62
Bosley, T.G. 456
Boston 196
Bostick
  Amanda 393
  Leslie 461
Bostrick, Leslie 444
Boswell
  G.W. 458, 473
  John 62
  Joseph 119
  J.W. 2
  William 240
Botts, Seth 56
Bourbon Academy 392, 404
Bourbon County 1, 30, 32, 74, 77
  107, 135, 121, 132
  141, 144, 157, 175
  180, 182, 185, 239
  240, 199, 288, 304
  377, 382, 384, 388
  391, 412, 416, 419
  437, 485
Boville, John 384
Bowfield, Monnie 235
Bowman
  Abraham 137
  Elizabeth 430
  John 37, 132, 139
  Robert 137
  William 60
Bowren, Abraham 154, 159
Box, James 242
Boyd County 73, 284
Boyd, John 150
Boyle
  Mary 77
  Stephen 108, 141, 167, 207
Boyle's Station 231
Brachen Baptist Association 198
Bracken Baptist Association 265
  266, 314, 325, 340, 341
Braddock, General 16, 17, 30
  34, 144
Bradley
  Edmund 150
  John 230
Bradshaw
  John 266
  Margeret 198
Brandenburg
  Daniel 266

Brandenburg (continued)
  David 62, 198, 188, 214
    234, 349, 381
  Elis 375
  George 373
  James 62
  J.E. 301
Brandywine, Battle 60, 63, 65, 66
  67, 161, 236
Brasfield
  James 62
  Wiley 210, 215, 246
Bratton
  James 62
  Rebecca 444
Breathitt County 297, 314, 326, 44
Breckinridge
  John 152, 156, 170, 409
  R.J. 389
Brice, William 388
Bridges 201
  L.R. 398
Bright, Mary Emma 398
Brion, Boswell 461
Bristow, Joseph H. 484
Broadhus
  George 323
  W.F. 294, 307, 308
Broadhurst, W.F. 290
Broadway 7, 466
Brockery, Virginia 395
Bronaugh, A. 201, 183
Brooke, Thomas, Dr. 504
Brooking
  H.N. 336
  Robert 335
Brooks
  Abijah 165, 169, 161, 206
  Lynch 241, 242
  Stephen 336, 460
  Thomas 137
  William 439, 470
Brookshire 473
  Elias 297, 312
  J.N. 473
  Walker 473
Broughton
  Ann 444
  Preston 408
Brown (Braun)
  Ezra 62, 111
  Horace 461
  James 178, 199

Brown (Braun) (continued)
   John 150, 152, 175, 170
   John T. 254
   Oscar 24
   Richard C. 463
   Swanson 62
   W.B. 397
   William 200
Browne
   Isaac 410
   M.S. 407, 408
Browning
   James 241, 243, 245, 246
   Jonas 242
   Richard 432
Browser, William 201
Bruce
   Carrie 361
   Eli 290, 294, 295, 299
      331, 361
   John G. 447, 448, 451
      452, 470, 483
      486, 488, 489
      496, 497, 499
Bruce's Methodist Cahpel 428
Bruen
   Jesse 370
   John S. 497
Brundage
   Solomon 62
   Thomas 207
Bruner 133
   John 189, 193, 195, 205, 209
Brunswick County 259
Bruton, T. 273
Bryan
   Anderson 241
   Jonathan 211
Bryans 146
Bryan Station 74, 83, 134, 135
      136, 236, 239
      427
Bryants 233
Bryon 31, 47, 72, 151
   Morgan 53
   William 29, 31
Buchanon 62 misp.
   Fred 232
Buckeye Methodist Church
   434, 436, 437, 441, 442, 444
   419, 450, 455, 469, 470, 487
   477-479
Buckeye School 479

Buckner, E.P. 451
Bullett, Alexander 150
Bullett County 501
Bullett's Lick 501
Bullock
   Alexander 150
   Daniel 40, 62, 163, 167
   David 188, 189, 202, 205
      210, 234
   Garland 201
   J.J. 396
   Josiah 62, 159, 167, 178
   Nathaniel 242
   Patterson 199, 234
   Sustennal 205
Bunargle
   Edward 178
   John 178
Bunch, Davis 365
Bunde 233
Bunker Hill 233
Bunsford, Solomon 360
Burbridge, Luncefield 56, 62
Burgby, Nicholas 213
Burger
   Charles 273
   Nelson 266
Burgess, James 208
Burham, John 200
Burney, Tom 233
Burr, Aaron 170, 222
Burrus
   Elizabeth 85
   Frederick Tandy 81
   Jane 235
   Roger 36
   Thomas 62 misp. 9, 84, 200
   William 79
Burton, James 37
Bush 81, 134, 161, 191, 214, 225
      321, 377, 382, 409, 473
   Ambrose 81-85, 92, 93, 167,
      208, 307, 330
   C.G. 326
   Francis 62, 85
   Frank 85
   Frankie 84
   J. 97
   Jessie 500
   James 37, 62
   John 62, 84, 85, 207, 246, 407
   John V. 244
   Josiah 245

Bush (continued)
　Lucy 84
　Lula O. 499
　Nelson 185, 233, 358
　O.P. 300
　Philip 41, 62, 82, 84, 85, 88
　　　　89, 200, 207, 216, 240
　　　　241, 242-245
　R.G. 56
　Robert 62, 454
　Sarah 84, 85
　Thacker 93
　Thomas 95
　William 45, 52, 62, 72, 76, 81
　　　　82, 84, 85, 105, 109
　　　　113, 168, 172, 183, 188
　　　　207, 216, 222, 242, 243
　　　　329
　William Jr. 84, 85
Burgess
　Marie 467
　Thomas 467
Bush Creek Baptist Church 266
Bush School 230
Bush Settlement 247, 328
Bush's Landing 41, 45
Butler
　A.W. 378
　Broward 149, 159
　Edmond 62
　John 35
　Robert 200
Bybee
　Neilly
　William 233
Byrd
　Harry 31, 70, 132, 134
　Richard 429
　W.L. 458
C and O RR 6, 123
Cade, Charles 167, 168, 208
Caldwell, Williams 134, 242
Caldwell County 234, 235
Calk, William 40, 73
Calloway (Callaway) 138, 162, 185
　　　　225
　Betsy 65
　Edmond 48, 202, 246
　Elizabeth 45
　Flanders 32, 38, 46-47, 113, 327
　Francés 73
　James 47, 48, 58, 143
　John 36, 37, 46, 53

Calloway (Callaway) (continued)
　Keziah (Keziah French)
　　　　45, 55, 327
　Lydia (Mrs. Irwine) 225
　Micajah 64, 144
　Richard 32, 37, 39, 58, 63
　　　　105, 120, 134, 143
　　　　155, 207, 236
Calmes
　Marion 116
　Marquise 51, 52, 116, 118
　　　　199, 228
　William 62
Calvert, Christopher 243
Calvin, John 258, 267, 269, 308, 351
Calvinism 270-277, 285, 290-293
　　　　303-310, 334, 335, 357, 401
　　　　418-421, 441, 460, 467, 494
Camargo 155, 441, 458, 471, 472
Camden, Battle of 65-67
Camp, Robert 205
Campbell 255, 273, 286, 305, 308
　　　　352, 367, 379, 442
　Alexander 87, 92, 93, 176, 173
　　　　250, 257, 259, 267-270
　　　　284, 303, 304, 334, 335
　　　　361, 362, 396, 399, 412
　　　　426, 428
　A.W. 403
　Isaac 22
　Robert 204
　William 62, 240, 159
Campbellsburg 381
Candell, B.C. 201
Cane Creek Baptist Church 316
Cane Ridge 119
Cane Ridge Methodist Church 381
Cane Ridge Presbyterean Church
　　　　386, 401
Cane Ridge Revival 254, 255, 264
Cane Springs Baptist Church
　　(Tates Creek) 266, 277, 278
　　　　280, 272
Canewood 120
Capol, Sally Ann 411
Capp
　Caleb 461, 467, 475
　Gillis 445
　Matilda 406
Carns, Charles
Carpenter, John 62
Carr, Walter 159, 216
Carrier, S.M. 492

Carrington, Timothy 126, 284
Carroll, C.C. 323, 324
Carson
   James 290
   L.L. 399
Carter County 24, 73
Cartmill, M. 273
Caspers 233
Cassenger, Jacob 241
Cassidy
   H.H. 399
   Michael 58, 140
Cast
   A.P. 339
   D. Simpson 495
Cathacassa 17
Catherwood, John 4, 5, 9
Caveland 225
Cayuga Indians 11
Central Baptist Church 103, 311
   319, 325, 326, 375
Chadford, Cade 58, 152, 241, 339
Chadford, Glory 339
Chamberlain, W.W. 451, 472
Chaney, John 62
Chaplain's Presbyterean Church 409
Chariser, Peter 15
Charleston 196
Charm, Ebenezar 207
Cheaton
   John 208
   Micajak 180, 183, 201, 220
   Sally 208
Chenault
   David 266-275, 311, 307
   James 104
   William 62, 290
Cherokee Indians 12, 14, 16, 21
              23, 24, 32, 45
              62, 120, 129
              130, 142, 143
              155, 157, 201
              204
Chicasaw Indians 153
Childer, William 486
Chiles
   Janice Holt-nes 150
   Henry 182, 213, 215
   William 241, 243
Childs, John C. 199
Chilicothe 37, 131
Chinelworth, William 486
Chinn, Elijah 240

Chiplie, Stephen 461
Chisca 20
Chism, Elizabeth 290
Christian Church, First 249
Choctaw Indians 11, 129
Chorn, Ebenezzar 110
Christian County 234
Christian, Dorthea 402
Christian Messenger 285, 305, 411
Christmaaa Conference 425, 440
Christy
   Ambrose 41, 183, 242, 241
   J. 358
   John 241
   Joseph 243
Cinowalte, A.O. 227
Church of Christ 254
Church of England 249, 420
Churches of God 458
Cincinatti 387, 430
Cincinatti Methodist
   Conference 483
Clancy, W. 413
Clark 233, 222
   Bennett 211, 212, 240
   C.B. 408
   Charles 62
   George Rogers 13, 18, 36
                 37, 60, 70
                 138, 139, 146
                 150, 151, 220
                 219, 428
   James 1, 7, 225, 233, 245
          347, 397, 507
   Jane 259
   Jeremiah 275
   John 62
   Joseph 222, 241
   Josiah 245
   Lucile Goff 13, 14, 15, 17
              56, 63
   Mary 85
   Richard 62
   Robert Jr. 9, 40, 89, 152
               165, 168, 183
               187, 193, 196
               207, 234, 242, 243
   Robert Sr. 40, 62, 161, 168
               170, 183, 185
               197, 221, 229
   Rogers 62
   Samuel 62
   Thomas 24, 25, 180, 206

Clark (continued)
    William 224, 233
Clark County Republican Newspaper
    282
Clark House 17
Clark Memorial Methodist Church
    487
Clarksburg, W.Va.
Clarkson, J.M. 378
Clarksville 431
Clawson, Bird 234
Clay
    Cassius 227
    Green 40, 41, 185
    Henry 198, 222, 236, 244, 180
        388, 394, 402, 413, 503
Clay City 472
Clay County 73
Clear Branch Baptist Church 290
Clear Creek 24
Clear Creek Baptist Church 264
Cleland, E.C. 410
Clem
    Sally 344
    Samuel 310
Clement
    Roger 78, 134
    Sally 208
    Thomas 208
Clemmons, John 62
Clendenna, F. 379
Cleveland Landing 41
Clevenger, Stobell 227
Cliff, Glenn 153, 159, 236
Clinch River 32, 34, 59
Clinkenbeard 13, 76-78, 106
        110, 138, 145
        223
    Isaac 58
    John 58
    Joseph 62
    William 58-60, 62
        133, 134, 210
Clintonville Presbyterean Church
    398, 399
Cochran
    Emma 198
    Louis 272
Cocke, William 410
Cockrell, L.B. 417
Coke, Thomas 420, 421
Cole
    Ernest 300

Cole (continued)
    Leroy 420, 440, 442
        443, 474, 506
    Mary 85
    Robert 299, 301
Coleman
    Abdel 432
    Chiles 394, 396
    James 137
College, Aaron 488
College Hill 488, 489, 491
College Hill Methodist Church
    463, 487, 498
College Hill Methodist Circuit
    487, 488, 492
Collins
    Alexander 273, 274
    David 210
    Dillard 75, 204, 234
        242, 245
    Elijah 37, 207
    Elisha 206
    Josiah 37
    William 37
    Willis 236, 410
Colored Methodist Episcopal
    Church 487
Combs 480
    Amanda 396
    Ben 7, 12, 63, 191
    Benjamin 51, 52, 166
        167, 188
    C. 331
    Cuthbert 51, 63, 69, 118
        206, 207, 365
    Elizabeth 413
    Glenmore 3, 12
    John 245
    Joseph 63, 152, 206, 207
    Joshua 183
    Josiah 183
    Marion 117
    Mary Ann 444
    Polly 164
    Sam 118
    Samuel 11, 58, 191, 469
    William 55
Combs Creek 364
Combs Ferry 123
Comstalk 144
Conkwright (Kronhegt)
    Dolly 355
    Hercules 60, 63, 124

524

Conkwright (Kronhegt) (continued)
  John 114, 440, 446, 468
        469, 481
  John N. 93, 100, 101
          126, 198
  L.N. 313, 314, 318, 320
       325, 371, 374
  Nancy 127
  P.J. 296, 300
  Pleasant 296, 300
  S.J. 83, 84, 90, 92
       100, 116, 278, 292
       99, 295, 296, 303
       325, 326, 328, 330
       332, 336, 334, 358
  Stonewall 313
Concord Camp Ground 494
Concord Presbyterean Church 387
Congregational Methodist Church
  425, 449
Connelly (Conally)
  Arthur 212
  Thomas 19
Connor
  John 63
  Welch 63
  William 63
Conrey, T.H. 499
Constant 138, 233
  Abegail (Abegale) 207, 332
  John 37, 53, 78, 106
       133, 140, 141, 475
  Thomas 332
Constant Community
  106, 230, 232
Constant Creek 332, 334
Constant Station
Cook
  Charles 63, 65
  David
  T.B. 456
  Valentine 431
Cooley 18
Coone
  J. 273
  Nancy 336
Cooner, Jolie 204
Coons, Mrs. Wallace 277
Cooper
  Benjamin 137
  James Fenimore 46
Cooper Run Baptist Church 176

Copher
  Jesse 32, 63
  Rueben 167, 178
  William 173
Corbin
  Louis 336
  R. 41
Corinth Baptist Church 297, 311
  313, 314, 362, 371, 375, 491
  500
Corinth Methodist Church
  488, 491, 500
Corley 406
Cornelius, Isaac 336
Cornwallis, General 69
Corry, Mrs. J.I. 375
Corsica 151
Corum, John 242
Corus
  Esusa 137
  George 137
  Jacob 137
  William 137
Corwin, Richard 434
Cosley, John M. 406
Couch
  B.F. 413
  Mary Ann 461
Couchman
  Elizabeth 205
  Frederick 205
  Mrs. William 390
  William 336
Country Party 150, 170
Court Party 149, 150, 152
            160, 170, 175
Courtney, Thomas 63
Covington 507
Covington Methodist Circuit 507
Covinth Baptist Church 103
Cow Creek Baptist Church 310, 311
                              314
Cowpens, Battle of 65, 66
Cox
  Isaac 63
  John 496
  John S. 470
  Joseph 481
  Tarleton 448
  Margaret 481
Coyle, Jessie 207
Crabtree
  Isaac 241, 242

Crabtree (continued)
　John 241
Cradelbaugh, William 37
Craft, R.W. 186
Craig
　Albert 395
　Lewis 83, 84
　Robert 241
Craig Station 81, 84
Crawford
　Archibald 123, 201
　George 412
　James 152, 384-386
　　　389, 403
　John 152, 189
　J.T. 410
　William 18
Creath
　Jerry 137
　Robert 14
　Whitfield 134
Creed
　Amelia 499
　Emma 499
　F.L. 499
　John C. 499
　John Campbell 499
　Julia 499
　Mahalia 499
　N.D. 295
　Perline 499
　Thomas 499
Creek
　I.T 318
　J.I. 300
Creek Indians 129, 130, 204
Crickett, Francis 410
Crim
　Amelia 499
　Sherman 499
　Harriet 150
Crissman, Leo 281
Critchfield, Nicholas 63
Crittenden, John J. 227
Crocker
　Ann 198
　Joseph 159
Cromwell, Richard 154
Crosley (Cosley)
　B. 472
　Minor 445
　M.M. 445

Croswaithe
　Jacob 200, 213
　Philip 85
　Rueben 167
　Samuel 213
Croswaithe Station 166
Crothers, Samuel 411
Crouch
　Benjamin 448
　Mary Ann 208
　William 281
Crowe, William 398
Crump, Halley 242
Cruse, David Lee 216
Cullen (Cullom)
　Florence 125
　Francis 225, 501
　Mary 501
　Susannah Northcraft 501
Culpepper, Virginia 127
Culton, J.H. 278, 279, 354, 363
Culver, Benjamin 226
Cumberland Gap
　14, 19, 20, 48, 144
　162, 174, 201, 242, 429
Cumberland Presbyterean Church
　279, 370, 387-389, 391, 394
　404, 405, 407, 415, 421, 428
　437, 438, 443, 445, 463, 462
　494
Cumberland River 24
Cummings, William 439
Cummins, Alexander 441
　Hugh 137
　Isaac 127, 246
　John 63
　R.M. 411
　Robert 243, 399, 411
　Robert M. 409
　Waller 63, 200
　William 417
Curry, H.N. 484
Curtis 473
　J. 362
　M. 481
Custer
　Arnold 114
　William 137
Cuthbert, Ben 32
Dakota 24
Damperd, John 37
Dandy
　W. 402

Dandy (continued)
   William 447
Daniel 117, 140, 164
   Archibald 242
   A.T. 373
   Benverly 63
   James 63, 242, 245
   Jesse 63
   Peter 242
   Robert 366
   Shelby 273
   Vivian 63
   Vivon 365
Dannally, Edward 290, 294, 295
Danville 150, 152, 185, 198
       220, 384, 395, 427
       507, 486
Danville Methodist Circuit 427
Danville Presbyterean Church 386
Dark, Joseph 63
Darnell
   A.T. 373
   H. 273
Daugherty, Van 472, 473
Davenport (Davinport) 32
   Abraham 63, 365
   Sam 110, 116, 365
David Fork Baptist Church 260, 286, 447, 464
Davis 233
   B.J. 102
   James 245
   John 264
   Matthew 233
   Septimus 54, 233
   Stephen 110, 186
Davisson, John 433
Dawson
   Elizabeth 389
   Hannah 84, 85
Day
   Elizabeth
   John 63
   Sarah 30
Deal
   Eve 223
   John 242
Dean 119
   John 78
   Elizabeth 444
Deaton, Racnell 367
Deering, J.R. 452

DeLane, J.D. 410
Delhendge, Philip 204
Delonie, Pearl 214
Demeret, Martin
Democratic Party 319
Denning 428
Denton, David Barrow
de Sota 20
Detroit 51, 54, 219, 224
Detwaiet, Peter 178
DeVary, Jesse 469
Devil's Back Bone
Dewitt Baptist Church 92
Dewitt (Jouett)
   Peter, Jr. 204, 381
   Peter, Sr. 63, 204
   Robert 63
Dickenson 1, 50
   Isaac 211
Dickey
   Adam 273
   Thomas 273
Dielswack, Speller 237
Dillard 99
   Ryland 97, 371
Discon, Ebeneazer 480
Dixon, William 394
Dix River Presbyterean Church 386, 387
Dobbs, C.E. 10
Dodge, Maria 390
Donahoe 233
Donaldson (Donnelson) 63
   John 58, 63, 242, 207
       243, 244
   Patrick 33, 178, 133
   Thomas 363
Donathan, John 55
Doniphan 230
Donohue, Daniel 365
Dooley 119
   Henry 203
   Jacob 63
   John 241, 242
   Rebecca 404
   William 416
Doster, James
Dougherty, Robert 171, 174
                   178, 201
Doughlas
   Rutherford 398
   Samuel 330

Douglas
  Hugh 241
  James 49, 77
  Jane 113
  John 58, 63, 133, 137, 243
Downing
  Andrew 198
  Sam 241
  William 241
Doyle
  Dennis 294
  George 298, 56, 176
  William 288
Dozier
  Leonard 84, 85
  Rebecca 85
  Sarah 84, 85
  Suzzanah 84, 85
Drake, Benjamin 205
Dry Creek 356
Dry Creek Baptist Church
  (Ruckerville) 356
Dry Run Baptist Church 378
Duball's Centlemetic 232
Dudley
  Ambrose 87, 127, 263, 283
    284, 288, 303, 336
    339, 340, 402
  Dennis 58
  J.A. 336
  Thomas 235, 284-287, 334
    378-380, 418
  William 240, 243
Duke, T.C. 301
Dumpford 58
Dunaway
  Benjamin 418
  John 51, 125, 440, 469
    472-474
  William 198
Dunaway Station 126, 127
Duncan (Dungin)
  Charles 499
  Hannah 84, 85
  James 63, 196, 204
  John 58, 206
  Joseph 436
Dunkards 344
Dunlap
  James 241
  John 63
Dunlop, Rufus 444
Dunsmore War

Duquesne 36
Durban, John G. 432
Dyches, David D. 444
Dykes
  Cindy 103
  Clinton 103
  Jesse 127
  John 127, 203
  Mrs. Matthew 434, 454, 457
Dyersville Methodist Church
  492, 498
Eads, William 137
East Fork of Four Mile Creek
  Baptist Church 266, 267, 380
East Fork of Slate Creek Baptist
  Church 266
East Hickman Baptist Church 332
Easton
  Elissha 64
  Thomas 64, 116
Eaton, Samuel 212
Ebenezar Baptist Church 250, 399
  416
Ebeneazer Methodist Church 15, 123
Ebenezar Presbyterean Church 382
Ebenezer Cam Ground 438, 439
Ebenezer Methodist Church 395, 409
  430-433, 441-444, 447-454,
  461-465, 472, 482, 494, 505, 506
Eckert, Allan 37
Ecton (Acton)
  Allen 206
  E.A. 301
  Ellen 368
  Florence 499
  H. 359
  Horation 359, 369
  J. 359
  James 368
  John 368
  Linda 368
  Margarett 368
  Sarah 368
  Smallwood 56, 359, 368
  T.C. 101
  Thomas 368
  Woods 101
Ecton Pike 353
Edgar, John 411
Edmonson
  James 250, 258, 272, 294
    307, 310, 342
  Nathan 311, 318, 370

Edmonson (continued)
    Thomas 340, 343, 346
Edmonton, James 243
Edwards 233
    Jonathan 240
    John 141, 152, 170, 176
    William 64, 206
El Bethel Methodist Church
    456-458, 469-473, 478
    479, 500, 508
Eldridge 233
    W.E. 399
    W.L. 417
Eli (Ely), Benjamin 200
Elizabeth Baptist Church 284, 288
Elkhorn Baptist 176
Elkhorn Baptist Association
    83, 89, 92, 101, 262, 264, 274
    285, 303, 330, 333, 340, 341
Elkins
    James 266, 331, 355, 356
        358, 361
    James Jr. 361, 362
    James T. 363
    I.F. 363
    Robert 493
    Z.F. 353
Ellerzy, Peggy 113
Ellington
    Claude 142
    David 178
Elliott County 7
Elloitt
    Joel 480
    John 166, 167, 169
    Martin 204
    Mary 395
    Robert 207
    W.K. 410
Ellis
    Hezekiah 243
    Joel 208
    William 30, 200
Ellkins
    Bud 9
    E.J. 97, 99, 100
    E.G. 97
    Enoch 85, 92, 93
    Ezekial 94
    James 64, 157
    Llewellyn 95

Elkins (continued)
    Robert 40, 82, 84, 85, 88
        91, 92, 94, 101, 185
        197, 198, 234
    Ruben 246
Ellsberry, William 438
Elrod, Robert 94, 95, 307
Embree, T. 320
Embrey, John 328
Embry (Embree)
    Caleb 242
    John 64
    Joseph 82, 84, 88
    Sarah 84
    Thomas 242
Embs
    John 64
    Tarlton 358
Emory, John 328
Engle, Fred 232
Enoch Spring 212
Ephesus Baptist Church 258,
    295-299, 309-313, 315, 326
    327, 347, 358, 359, 368
    370-373, 467,
Episcopal Church 248, 382, 411
        430, 506, 507
Epperson
    Barnett 365
    Jackson 103
    John 64
    William 9
Eskippakki 13
Estes (Estre)
    Abraham 64
    Elisah 47, 64
    J. 337
    James 42
Estill County 2, 11, 32, 24, 73
        131, 133, 134, 161
        162, 176, 179, 180
        184, 246, 277, 278
        280, 291, 295, 296
        313, 314, 326, 329
        450, 488
Estill's Defeat 245
Estill, James 34, 133
Eubank
    Achilles 40-42, 50, 64, 125
        175, 183, 200, 209
        225, 242, 244, 245
    Ambrose 242, 243, 245
    E.M. 381

Eubank (continued)
   James 300
   J.G. 287
   W.T. 298
Eubank Meeting House 493
Eutaw Springs, Battle of
   57, 64, 65
Evans
   Elizabeth 257
   Henry Jr. 445
   Isaac 273
   Isaac Jr. 273
   Jabre 16
   Jacob 16
   James 64
   John 204, 448
   Mollie 257
Eversole, Bob 488
Ewan, John A. 448
Ewing, D.B. 416
Ewell, Bertram 205
Ewington Journal 289
Fains, John 202
Fairfax Church of Christ 300
Fairfax Street 246, 467
Fairlawn, Battle of 153
Fallen Timbers, Battle of
   58, 60, 140, 143, 144
Fallon, Robert 104
Farmer
   Florence 499
   John 64
   Maggie 500
   Mirty 499
   Thomas 475
   William 64
Farmer's Almanac 319
Farney
   H. 273
   Mary J. 499
Farrior, Thomas 137
Farrow, Joseph 454
Faudre, Vauchel 56, 64, 305
Faulconer, Thomas 305
Faulkner 16
Fayette County 3, 6, 9, 24
   28, 32, 73-75, 92, 97
   104, 120, 121, 138, 145
   154, 156, 157, 159, 161-
   163, 185, 199, 207, 216
   222, 225, 229, 240, 250
   259, 267, 269, 296, 288
   303, 304, 311, 383, 391

Fayette County (continued)
   393, 402, 412, 428, 447
   462, 464, 501, 503
Fear, Edmund 36, 37
Federalists 170, 174, 217
Ferguson, Charles 137
Ferral
   John 64
   Thomas 64
Field
   Barnett 207, 217
   Ezekial 137
   Thomas 13
   William 137
Fields, Zacharis 329
Fielding, Michael 237
Filson, B. 314
Fincastle County, Virginia 155
Findlay, John 1, 15, 16, 18
   21, 34, 36
Finklen, Thomas 137
Finnell
   Fountain 499
   Rosanna 499
First Baptist Church 103
First Baptist Church (Winchester
   Baptist) 258, 286, 299, 303
   325, 326, 376
First Northwestern Regular Baptist
   Association of Wisconsin 285
Fishback
   Anna 397
   Betsy 395
   Charles 396
   Frederick 390, 393, 399
   F.H. 390
   George 397
   George Hamlin 390
   George Taylor 399
   Jacob 64, 123, 175, 180, 213, 234
      304, 335, 387, 390, 393, 399
      401, 402, 409, 410
   James 268, 402, 213
   J.E. 399
   Jesse 390, 395, 399
   J.M. 410
   Samuel 394
   S.D. 473
   Robert T. 399
   R.E. 399
   William 390
Fisher
   Anna 372

Fisher
  Thomas 499
Fitch, J.W. 397, 440, 444, 451
        456, 457, 471, 472
Flaerey
  John 207
  Theresa 207
  William 207
Flannigan, James 43, 92, 121
              188, 206, 363
Flatbush, Battle of 47
Flatcreek 155, 157, 164, 178
Fleet, A. 297, 302, 372, 497, 499
Flemming County 19
Flemming,
  Brother 344
  Leroy 198
Flemmingsburg 156
Fletcher
  John 56, 64
  William 84, 85
Flint, Abram
Florence, Italy 227
Flower, William 207
Flynn
  Dudley 369
  Ezekial 115
  John 234
  Lucinda 405
  Martin 442
  Ray 101
Folley, John 137
Forbes, Hugh 164, 212, 213
Ford 6, 8, 10, 43, 127, 400
Ford, Lewis 275
Ford Presbyterean Church 397-400
Fore, Henry 336
Foreman (Forman)
  Benjamin 122
  Ezakial 397
  John 22, 122, 273
  William 64
Forks of Stoner Presbyterean
  Church 386
Forrest Grove 98, 99, 189
Fosby, William 64
Foster
  Daniel 137
  John 64
  William 56, 64, 117
Four Mile Creek 3, 5, 40, 41
            43, 52, 106
            110, 124, 213

Four Mile Creek (continued)
    216, 232, 305, 493, 495, 501
Fowler 233
  James 404
  John 64, 152, 170
Fox 127
  James 361, 371, 365
  John 370
  John Sr. 121
  John Jr. 121, 123
Foxworthy, Enoch 365
Frame
  John 167, 189, 200, 207
  William 241, 243, 245, 246
Frankfort 169, 172, 179
          184, 185, 186, 507
Frankfort Presbyterean Church 393
Franklin
  Mrs. Harvey 368, 370
  Benjamin 64
  James 243
  Rueben 56, 64, 361
  William 64
Franklin Methodist Circuit
  (Va.) 506
Franklin, State of 148
Fraser
  John 64
  Robert 152
  William 64
Frazee 189
  Drusella 332
  Moses 337, 340
Frederick, Co. Maryland 501
Frederick, Mad. 153
Freeman, William 448
French
  Charles 327
  Henry 137
  James 40, 45, 46, 64, 110
        125, 165, 173, 185, 233
        265-272, 274, 275, 307
        318, 331, 343, 346, 357
        363, 412
  Richard 199, 260, 299, 310-319
        327, 373, 376, 401, 456
  W.H. 313
Frenchburg 24
French Huegnot 382
French & Indian War 107, 504
Friendship Baptist Church
    258, 259, 266, 268, 269, 273
    274, 284, 285, 286, 305-307

531

Friendship Baptist Church (cont.)
   310, 314, 329, 335, 336, 338
   340-342, 351, 357, 360, 361
   367, 375, 403, 409, 426
Friendship Christian Church
   344, 336
Friendship Particular Baptist
   Church 335, 336
Fritz, M. 363
Froh, George 457, 458
Frost, Ebenezar 78
Fry
   John L. 407
   Joseph 443
Fues 233
Fugar, Elizabeth 333
Fulton, Robert 411
Gaitskill, Henry 121
Gallop, Enoch 365
Galloway, James 52
Gamond, James 160, 175, 176, 196
Gano, John 64, 173
Gardiner 233
Gardner 429
   Elias 443, 475
   Harvey 443
   Henry 206, 212
   John 454
   M.A. 407
   Nancy 206
   Thomas 454, 467, 475
Garrard
   E.B. 410
   James 247, 251, 257, 266, 384
Garrard County 264
Garrett School House 325
Garson, James 160, 175, 176, 196
Gatz, Benjamin 120
Gaul, John 64
Gaurez, S.F. 484
Gay 119
   James 64, 123
   John 444
   John D. 475
   John P. 468
   Nelson, Mrs. 483
General Assembly of the
   Presbyterean Church 385
General Baptist Association
   of Ky. 318
Genet, Citizen 151, 220
Geneva 351

Gentry 82
   Charles 183, 201
   Elizabeth 82
   P.T. 313
   Rachel 443
George
   Mary 90
   Nicholas 41, 58, 64, 183, 195
   William 416
George's Fork 114
George's Fork Creek 367
Georgetown 36, 395
Georgetown College 102, 318
                       322, 396
Georgetown Particular Baptist
   Church 288, 290
Germantown 62, 67, 99, 236
Gholston, James 404
Gibbon, T.H. 437
Gibbs, John 356
Gibson
   Elizabeth 436
   James 244, 246
Giddons, Isham 245
Gilkey, Charles 442
Gillespie
   Martin 440, 443, 474, 475
   William 390
Girty, Simon 70, 124, 130, 137
Gist (Guess, Gass) 180
   Christopher 14, 18, 80
                  119, 120
   David 37, 39, 64, 120
           207, 218
   George 120
   John 46
   Judith 116, 120
   Judith Belle 120
   Maria 120
   Nathanial 64, 119, 121, 207
Given, William 135
Glover, Joel 213
Godby 499
   John 486
Goe, Philip 32, 38
Goebel, William 319
Goff 54, 125, 2-4, 364
   Andrew 198
   Ben Doughlas 410
   Elisha 54, 116, 275
   John 116, 117, 118
   John Hedges 116-118, 125
                  368, 478

Goff (continued)
    Jonas 143
    Tom 54, 64, 78, 116,
        118, 126, 127, 212
Golden
    J.F. 370
    John 375
    Mary 339
Goldman, Martin 446
Goodes, William 64
Goodwin, Rachel 396
Goosey, Peter 241
Gordon 377
    Amanda 368
    James E. 274
    James W. 499
    Jesse 368
    John E. 368
    Judah 368
    Julia Gann 499
    L.T. 372
    Matilda 499
    Nancy 368
    Richard 369
    Richard E. 368, 373
    R.R. 293
    Sallie 300
    Sarah Ann 499
    W.T. 373
Goshen 343, 258, 259, 219-279
    287, 290, 294, 309, 316
    336-358, 360, 361, 365
    367, 375, 380, 462, 466
Goshen Baptist Church 90, 110,
    198
Gossett, M. 378
Gould, George 462
Gowen, James
Graham
    Edward 137
    James 137
    Little James 137
Grail, Henry 413
Granade, John 390, 404, 432
Grant
    Elizabeth 30
    John 31
    Samuel Boone 32
    Squire 31, 137
    William 3, 30
Grant Station 31
Grass, James 498

Grassy Lick 54, 75, 109, 140,
    155, 177, 178,
    211, 406, 438
Grassy Lick Baptist Church 348
Grassy Lick Methodist Church
    419, 429, 430, 437, 439,
    450-452, 455, 456, 458,
    463, 468, 494
Graves, Benjamin 243
Gravitt, James 137
Grag, J.L. 470, 490, 497
Gray, David 384, 235
Green
    Jervis 137
    Jesse 64
    Neal 378
    T. 378, 379
    Thomas 64
Greenley, Thomas 438
Greenup, Christopher 150, 171,
    338
Greenville Baptist Association
    95
Greenville Regular Baptist
    Association 289
Greenville, S.C. 318
Greenville Theological
    Institute 318
Greenway, Nathanial 64
Gregg, David 137
Grider
    Fred 489, 490, 492
    James 137
    Judy Emily 492
Griffin, Anthony 201
Griffity
    Ralph 25
    Hannah 29
    Sarah 29
Griggs
    J.R. 481
    John 64
Grigsby, Lewis 207, 241
Grimes, Robert 81
Grooms, Robert 64
Grubbs, Nancy 33
Guernsey, James 64
Guerrant, E.O. 397, 398, 410
Guildford Court House
    57, 60, 64, 65, 220
Gulliver's Travels 18, 233
Gunn, William 447, 482, 497
Gunyon, James 64

Guy 258
Hackett
  Nelson 152
  Peter 241, 242
Hadden
  Annis 479
  Samuel 479
  Nicholas 207
Haddon, M.B. 379, 381
Haggard 294, 409
  A.L. 296, 297
  Ambrose 94, 99, 100
  Bartlett 100, 292
  Bert 101
  Betsy 347
  David 294-296, 358
  D.O. 295
  Donald 290
  Elizabeth 85
  Gordon 300, 301
  James 264, 266, 292
      298, 334
  James Jr. 85, 99, 100
  James Sr. 64, 88, 99
  John 266, 293, 295
     330, 331, 64
  John Jr. 290, 292
      295, 330
  Lena 353
  Martin 82, 92, 345
     347, 349
  Mary 293
  Nathan 359
  Nathanial 82, 92, 207, 292
  Patsy 281
  Rodney 222
  T.L. 294
  William 355, 356
  Pleasant 95, 290
  Zacharia 114, 349
  Zelda 114
Haggerty, John 64
Hagin, J.S. 399
Haile, Moses 144
Hainey 119, 161
  Richard 109, 346
Hale, Moses 144
Haley (Hailey, Halley) 119, 214
  Benjamin 64
  John 40, 64
  Richard 64, 207
  William 64, 78, 108, 109
     2-3, 339

Halifax 504
Hall
  Ambrose 290
  Henry 353, 354
  John 144
  Sally 353
  Wyatt 442
Halliday, Stephen 64
Halsay, Rees 243
Hamblin, Ethan 407
Hamilton
  Edward 64
  Jones 60
  Peter 64
  William 64
Hampton 119, 125, 212
     294, 377, 409
  A.H. 295-297, 410
  A.S. 100, 101
  Audley 301
  B. 365
  David 64, 78, 110
     181, 183, 240
  D.B. 300, 301
  Henry A. 297
  James 100, 101
  Jesse 42, 294, 295, 357
  John 166, 246
  K.J. 99
  L. 295
  Philade 273
  T.W. 313
Hampton Sidney College 254
Hampton Woods 496
Hancock
  John 146
  Steven 36
  William 37
Hancock Creek 206, 212, 213
Hand, Absolom 454
Hanks
  Absolom 200
  A.C. 403
  Malinda 345, 365
Hanner, Julien 167
Hanson
  Elizabeth 203
  Garnett 205
  Charles 467
  Samuel 235
Harden County 263
Hardesty, Fannie 114

Hardon
  Enis 51
  Enos 113
Hardwick 164
  Mitchell 243
  Pleasant 167, 168
Hardwick Creek 127, 213
Hardwick Creek Methodist
  Church 425, 450
Hardwinter 5
Hardy, Ewan 477
Hargett, Peter 167
Harlan, Silas 135
Harmar 144
  John 167
  Joshua 141
Harmar, Leonard 407
Harmar's Defeat 144, 220, 239
Harmon 119
  Ephriam 115, 122
  Sampson 118
Harper
  Francis 135
  John 58
  Mathew 46
  Peter 171, 223
Harris
  Elias 51
  John 85, 204
  Joshua 64
  Mary 84, 85
  Thomas 84, 85, 202
  William 137, 168, 204, 208
Harris
  J.M. 273
  Josiah 273
Harriman, Hazekiah 432, 447
Harrison
  Alexander 213
  Caleb 404
  Daniel 163, 182, 183
  Hezekiah 200, 242
  James 64
  J.C. 482, 496, 497
  John L. 482
Harrod (Harrard)
  James 21, 26, 39, 137, 201
Harrodsburg 36, 39, 49, 77
  67, 74, 76, 132
  135, 383, 507
Harrodsburg Methodist Church
  444
Harrow, David 200

Hart
  Henry Clay 184
  Joel 227
  John 133, 137, 243
  Josiah 166, 167, 188, 189, 384
    195, 204, 217, 227
  Juddith 227
  Thomas 166
  Suzanne 153
Hart and Rochester 149, 155, 243
Hasty
  John 206
  Rebecca 206
Hathaway, David 245
Hathpenny, John 64
Hatton, Julia 245
Haw, James 460, 475, 427, 429
Hawkins
  Joe 160
  John 305
Hayden
  Ben 123
  Jeremiah 64
  William 64, 123
Haydon
  Samuel 390, 393, 399
  Suzan 390
Haydorn Corners 11, 29, 35
Haynes, Richard 343
Hays, William 32, 37, 113
Haywood, John 24
Hazelrigg,
  Charles 365
  James 198, 200
Hedges
  Jesse 36
  Joseph 64
Heidelburg Baptist Church 314
Heiett, W.P. 325
Heitt, W.P. 92, 93, 101
Heironymous
  A.S. 297
  D.G. 297
  Elizabeth 460
Hempstead
Henderson
  Eleanor 432
  H.G. 452
  Richard 26, 39, 47, 52, 219
  Sam 46
  William 64, 411
Henderson, Ky. 430
Hendrick, Pleasant 201

Henning, Judah 167, 168, 344
Henry, Patrick 123, 126, 146
    170, 219, 402
    504, 505
Henry County 493, 502
Henson, Michael Paul 22, 24
Herndon
    John 64
    William 64
Herron, James 396
Heydrick, Rachel 200
Hickle, Harry 205
Hickman
    James 11, 104, 225, 241
    Joel 64, 246
    Richard 150, 165, 167, 168
        169, 173, 174, 176
        177, 179, 183, 188
        200, 213, 217, 221
        225, 240, 241, 242
        244, 246
Hicks
    Beverly 93
    David 64
    L.P. 492
Higgins
    Joel 211
    Joseph 64
    Robert 152, 167, 189, 202
        211, 241
    Suzanna 198
    William 168, 208, 211
    Z. 351
Hill Redemption 176
Hilley, J. 352
Hinde 429
    Hannah 506
    Jane
    Martha 507
    Mary Todd 506
    Thomas 16, 123, 221
        228, 506
    Thomas, Dr. 430, 446, 506
Hiner
    Robert, 456
    W.W. 456
Hindes Creek Baptist
    Church 304, 306
Hinkston Creek 211
    nous 45
    Andrew 82
    Conrad 64, 82
    Henry 41

Hinkston Methodist Circuit
    429, 431-434, 437, 438, 442
    445, 470, 477, 495
Hinkston Presbyterean Church
    384
Hinkley, Armond 395
Hisle
    Dalous W., Mrs. 469, 471, 472
    George H. 479
    H. 301
    Minor 300
    N.G. 300
    Younger 479
Hiles 116
Hockaday
    Edmund 168, 169, 180, 207
    P.B. 199
Hogge, Robert 167, 168, 189
Hodgkins, S. 298
Holder
    John 32, 36, 37, 46, 104, 118
        161, 164, 165, 168, 169
        185, 216, 223, 226, 236
        237, 241, 242
    John W. 469
    Margaret 198
    Theodocia 105
Holder's Boat Yard 8, 11, 41, 42
    82, 145, 168
Holder's Defeat 134
Holeman
    Tandy 64, 209
    William 209
Holet, Wyatt 64
Holiday
    Francis 216
    James 64, 241
    John 64
    Stephen 64
Holiness movement 458, 459
Holland
    Jonathan 200
    Hezekiah 444, 454
Holliday, C.M.
Holloway, James H. 410
Holly Springs 417
Hollywood Springs 18
Holman, William 439, 461
Holmes, Donald 198
Holstein Methodist Conference
    354
Holstein, Michael 48
Holstein River 59

Hollmor, John 167
Hon
   Henry 354
   James 273
   Joseph 273
   William 273
Hood 138
   Andrew 106, 107, 141, 152
       165, 167, 176, 200
       234
   John 161, 167, 169
       189, 193, 202, 207
   Lucas 144, 200, 406
   Luke 109, 143
Hood Station 70, 107, 140
       150, 226, 239
Hope, George 64
Hopewell Baptist Church
   264, 267, 289
Hopewell Presbyterean Church
   384-386, 391
Hopkins 273
Horn, Jeremiah 37
Hornbeck 121, 124
   John 64
   William 446
House, Savory 446
How, Doughlas 349
Howard 228
   John 51, 58, 117
Howard Creek 51, 69, 125
Howard Methodist Church
   450, 470, 479, 481, 487
Howe 402, 404
   A. 387
   Joseph 387-392, 411
Howell Mills Baptist Church 327
Howes, J.R. 491
Hoy, Joshua 215
Hoy's Station 30, 134
Hubard 504
   Mary 504
Hubert, T.S. 300
Huddleston, John 200
Hughs
   Andrew 213
   David 167, 178, 200, 241
   Jacob 397
Hughson, Otis 300
Hukill 311
Hull, Elizabeth 300
Huls 233
   Andrew 143

Huls (continued)
   Edward 64
   Elizabeth Ann 448
   John 64
   John D. 410
   Nathan 414
   William 64
Humble
   Nellie 114
   Uriah 241
Hume, Matthew 120
Humphrey (Humphries)
   Suzzannah 84, 85
Hunt 232, 246, 379
   Absolom 434, 441
   Cynthia 368
   Elizabeth 354
   George 372, 272
   G.J. 375
   H.A. 100
   Jack 368
   James 368, 377
   Jonathan 241, 368
   R.D. 100
   Sarah 368
   Louis 431
   Nellie 296
   Robinson 246
Hunstead, N. 362
Hunter
   Jacob 137
   James 103, 207, 217
   R.D. 101
   Sarag 205
Hunton, John 310
Huron 12, 16, 129, 138
Huston, John 119
Huston Station 119
Indadus, Polly 333
Indian Creek 116, 125, 178
Indian Creek Baptist Church
   125, 267, 277, 281, 290-296
   306-308, 311, 330, 356, 361
   426
Indian Creek Methodist Church
   428
Indian Field 3, 11-16, 18, 19
       21, 22, 54, 64, 107
       116, 117, 118, 125
       144, 178, 179, 233
       268, 275, 357, 364
       437, 441, 477-479
Indian Methodist Conference 483

Ingersoll, James 339
Innes 150
Ireland
  James 22
  John 167, 168, 189
Iron Works Pike 125, 339
Iroquois 129, 130
Irvine
  Carrie 499
  Elizabeth 494
  Lydia Calloway 225
  Margaret 499
  Thomas 234, 235, 499
  Will 499
  William 499
Irving 231, 281
Irving Baptist Church 280, 314-315
Irving on Stoner Creek
  Presbyterean Church 384
Irwin, E.E. 398
Itwin
  John 246
  William 246
Jackson 305, 306
  Andrew 222, 225, 227, 288
  James 65, 241, 244, 493
  William 108
Jackson, Ky. 280
Jackson Purchass 13
Jackson's Ferry 232, 295, 305
Jackson on Harden Creek
  Presbyterean Church 386
Jacobs
  Betsy 210
  John 65
James, John 445
Jameson
  Allen A. 450
  Milton 443
Jamestown 129
January
  Ephriam 137
  James 130
Jarman
  Abner D. 94
  J. 94
  Thomas 95
Jefferies
  Richard 397
  S. 337
Jefferson Academy 371
Jefferson, Thomas 59, 71, 151
                217, 221

Jefferson County 156, 384, 502
Jeffersonville Baptist
  Church 313, 317
Jenkins, James 206
Jennings
  Isreal 65
  Williams 152
Jennings Spring 118
Jersey Campaigne 62, 67
Jessamine County 506
Jewell, Sheowen 301
Jillson
  R. 475
  Willard Rouse 11, 13, 14, 51
Johns
  Anderson
  Henry 234
John's Fork Baptist Church 264
Johnson
  Anna 84, 85
  Benjamin 84, 85
  Elkaneh 448
  Frank 84, 85
  James 273
  J.J. 457
  John 65, 85
  John M. 306, 307
  Hugh 273
  Martin 24, 56, 65, 241
  Mary 84, 85
  Nicholas 94
  Philip 65, 85
  Samuel 135
  Sarah 84, 85
  Thomas 167, 168
  William 204, 290
Johnson County 73
Jolly
  G.N. 491
  John 137
Jones
  Alexander 233
  D. 331
  E. 379
  Henry C. 280
  John 200, 201, 243
  John R. 499
  Joshua 65
  L. 273
  N. 336
  Nicholas 65
  Pamila 499
  Richard 189

Jones (continued)
  Thomas 245
  Vinah 84
  William H. 499
Jouett (Dewitt, Judy) 381
  Jack 59, 65, 222
Jouett's Creek 27
Joy Treaty 174
Judy
  David 347
  Henry 347
  J. 379
  John 133, 164, 241
Kash, William 279-281
Kaskaskia 132, 133, 219
Kavanaugh 234, 392, 429, 457
  B.F. 424, 457
  Benjamin T. 505
  Benjamin Taylor 507
  Charles 247
  H.H. 436, 457
  Hubbard 436, 448, 483
  Hubbard Hinde 507
  Leroy 506
  William 197, 234, 422
    430, 448, 460
  Mrs. William 213
Keaton, William 65
Keitley, Jacob 200
Kelly (Kelley)
  G.C. 463
  Griffin 144, 336
  James 335
  Joseph 333-335
  Stephen 200
  S.W. 491, 492
  Unknown 241
Kelso, Berryman 167
Kennedy
  John 8, 36, 52, 85
  Thomas 65, 119, 144, 240
Kenton, Simon 21, 32, 36, 82
    125, 144, 236
Kentucky Central R.R. 9
Kentucky Methodist Conference
  435, 448, 485, 487
Kerr 7
Key, Price 56, 66, 205
Kidd
  James 167
  Mrs. William 116
  Zadoc 365
Kiddville 3, 101, 116, 156

Kiddville Baptist Church
  258, 298, 311, 314
Kiddville School 458
Kiddville, Kinder 265, 312
    470, 479
  Barnabas 273
Killey, Benjamin 167
Kindred
  Edward 88, 355, 356
  Edward (Nolly) 267, 271, 293
    307, 342
  Jesse 207
King
  John 65
  William 65
King's Mountain 21, 67
Kinkaid
  Andrew 152, 242
  Arthur 169
  James 58
  Joseph 58, 65, 135, 137
  Robbin 62, 233
  Robert 65
Kirk, Julian 58, 65
Kirkham
  Robert 37
  Samuel 37
Kirkley, Berryman
Knox, Thomas 65
Kohlklass, Theodore 468
Ku Klux Klan 486
Lafayette 66
Lampton, James 352
Lamtons 167
Lander
  Charles 65
  Henry 121, 183, 201
  Jacob 65, 239
  Jonathan 65
  Matthew 204
  Tolen 189, 193, 195
Landers, S.B. 417, 418
Landrum 477
  A.D. 307
  A.K. 410
  Francis 477
  Isham 233
  Thomas 65, 437
  William 97, 106, 126, 233
    250, 293, 342, 343
    346, 352, 428, 370
    419, 426, 428, 434
    436-438, 442-444

Landrum
  William (continued)
    450, 453, 454, 461
    466, 467, 469, 470
    477, 384, 483, 494
    495, 497
Lane
  James 152, 273
  James S. 463
  Lawrence 473
  Robert 358
L. E. Railroad 314
L. and E. Junction 320
L. and N. Railroad 315
Lantor, Jonathan 178
Laramie 132
Larkin
  Benjamin 429, 432, 434, 438
  Brother 493
Larsbrook, R.D. 484
Lasseter, Dempsey 65
Lassiter, Dempsey 65
Lassity, Dan 361
Launch, Henry 65
Laurell County 73
Laurell Springs Baptist
  Church 317
Lawrence County 73
Leach
  J. 378
  John R. 441, 454
  John T. 438
  James G. 467
Leakey, Josiah 307
Lebanon 186
Ledgewood, James 65, 137
Lee
  Henry 242
  John 37
  R.M. 472
  Wilson 383, 460
Lee County 73, 201
Lemon, Katy 392
Lennox, Charles
Leonard, J.T. 416
Levee, R. 374
Lewis 119
  Alpheas 121
  Alphaeus 379
  Amaziah 235
  Amzi 409-411
  D. Priest, Mrs. 507
  Elizabeth 468

Lewis (continued)
  B.W. 379
  Isreal 443
  Nettie 198
  R. 380
  Stephen 65
  Thomas 121, 152, 154
    159, 283
  Thornton 121
  William 65, 468
Lexington 37, 74, 123, 149, 157
  161, 164, 176, 184
  185, 193, 196, 227
  304, 377, 409, 385
  451, 462, 466, 484
Lexington Annual Conference,
  Methodist Episcopal
  Church 487
Lexington, Battle of 74
Lexington and Evanston,
  L. & E. 8, 110
Lexington Methodist Church
  439, 451
Lexington Methodist District
  427, 441, 452, 453, 486, 488
Lexington Presbytery 377, 378
  385, 387, 388
Lexington Presbytery of
  Virginia 388
Lexington Reporter 5
Lexington-Winchester
  Turnpike 464
Liberty Baptist Church
  277, 278, 281, 306, 307, 353
Liberty Hall College
  228, 391-393
Licking Baptist Association
  267-270, 274, 280, 283-287
  303, 304, 309-311, 335, 338
  362, 264, 377-381
Licking Locuss Baptist
  Association 258, 259
    265, 330
Licking River 3, 135, 136
  138, 143
Limestone 36, 147, 262
Lincoln Courthouse
  Presbyterean Church 386
Lincoln
  Abraham 28, 29, 135, 159, 282
  Mordecai 29
  Nancy 29
  Sarah 29

Lincoln County 155, 156, 176, 222
Linday, Joseph 135, 137
Lindsay, Marcus 441
Linville, Nancy 30
Lipscome
  Allen 297
  Allie 299
  Nammie 299
  Nathan 268, 273
  S.A. 300
Lisle
  Henry 82
  John 90, 255
Little Rock Particular
  Baptist Church 287
Little Stone Creek 367, 455
Little, Thomas 121, 122
Little Mountain 133, 155, 164
Little Shepherd of
  Kingdon Come 121
Locus Creek Baptist Church 264
Lochland, Dorcas 93
Lockhard
  John 37
  Levi 152, 200
Log Lick 6, 126, 179, 450
Log Lick Baptist Church
  258, 259, 266, 268, 271,
  273-275, 277-282, 291
  342, 350, 360-362, 408
  481
Log Meeting House 264, 266, 281
Logan
  J. Ashley 410
  Ben 25, 26, 34, 39
    135, 136, 140, 175
  Lewis 410
  William 410
Logan County 405
Lloyd, Elizabeth 339
Logan Station 36, 49, 59, 140
London, Ky. 504
Londonderry, Ireland 339
Long Island, Battle of 63
Long Ridge Particular
  Baptist Church 284
Lone Oak School 325
Louisburg 504
Louise Methodist Church 478
Louisiana 151, 200
Louisville 75, 102, 176, 184, 185
    266, 263, 387, 398, 483
    430, 436, 466, 475

Louisville Methodist District
  492
Loveland,
  C.H. 410
  John 191
Lowe
  John 65
  William 65
Lower Bethel Baptist Church
  220, 212
Lower Howard Creek 2, 3, 41, 52
    81, 104, 181
    188
Lowes' Station 119
Lowry
  Anderson 445
  J. 362
  L. 413
  Thomas 66, 75
Lukens, Benjamin 438
Lulbegrund Baptist Church
  75, 87, 109, 116, 117
  169, 198, 233
Lullbegrud Baptist Church
  259, 264-271, 273, 276-282
  291, 311, 314, 327, 341
  343, 345, 349, 357, 361
  365, 367, 383, 404, 406
  429, 433
Lullbrgrud Methodist Church
  (Providence) 483
Lyle
  J.G. 398
  John 197, 234, 235, 383
    403, 410, 438, 563
Lulbegrun Creek 9, 17, 18, 34
    51, 206, 223
    224, 232
Macedonia Baptist Church
  87, 313, 314, 325
Macedonia Christian Church
  464
Macy, A.R. 307
Madison
  Elijah 445
  Gabriel 135
  James 185, 222
Madison County 2, 11, 30, 41, 81
    88, 89, 124, 134
    135, 156, 173, 216
    247, 262, 266, 277
    278, 304, 306, 306
    310, 311, 325, 326

Madison County (continued)
    328, 338, 347, 354, 463
    464, 487, 488, 497
Maffett, Thomas 243, 343
Magruder, Mary 75
Magruder School 235
Mahan, J.W. 370
Maigo Indians 129
Main Street 187, 246, 410
Maise, Absalom 110
Mallious, Peter 65
Mallory, Henry 432, 433
Manley
    B. 318
    Jacob 65
Mann, E.G.B. 472
Maple Street 7
Marble Creek Farm 22
Marion, James 65
Mark, Hastings 65
Marks, W.P. 410
Marrow, Joseph 438
Marsh, Jacob 339
Marshall
    Charles 399
    Gilbert 137
    Humphrey 152, 170, 174, 217
    Keith 199
    Robert 391
    Thomas 201
    Truman 183
Martin 162, 225, 429
    Amzi 235
    Charles 417
    Christopher 243
    David 200
    Elizabeth 82
    Henry 65
    Hugh 399
    J. 97
    John 37, 45, 60, 61, 65, 124
        144, 154, 159, 162, 177
        178, 180, 183, 195, 239
        241, 245, 246, 329, 460
        493
    Joseph 241
    Matthew 65
    O. 212
    Rachel 85
    Sam 366
    Samuel 161, 162, 390, 468
    Suzanne 409
    Thomas 150

Martin (continued)
    William 65, 183, 201, 404
Martin's Woods 439, 461
Mason County
Mason, fraternity 350, 500
Mason
    Henry 246
    James 268
    Pervin 333
Massie, Peter 427
Masterson, Jonathan 273
Mathis, Jimmy 77
Matthews
    W.C. 413
    William 415
Maurice, Daniel 339
Maux
    Hannah 84, 85
    Selbis 84, 85
Maxey, Asa 273
Mayslick Particular Baptist
    Church 287
Maysville 19, 36, 38
    110, 141, 156, 262
    340, 427, 501
Maysville Methodist Circuit
    484, 488
Maysville Methodist District
    482, 484
McBride 21
    Francis 137
    James 137
    William 137
McCall, James 395
McCargo, Lucy 243
McClain
    Laura 335
    Sam 335, 336
McClored 155
    John 65
McClung, Mitheny 268
McClure
    Alexander 65
    Andrew 65, 385, 384
        391, 392
    James Allen 391
McConnell
    Andrew 101
    James 391
McCord, James 411
McCormach, Wallace 101
McCourt
    Henry 209

McCourt (continued)
  John 209
McCracken, Isaac 137
McCrary, Dr. S.K. 410
McCready, James 405
McCreevey, Robert 157
McCullouch, John 65, 135
McDaniel
  Barnabas 438
  Henry 438
  John 159
  Robert 64, 207
McDonald
  Annette 442
  Bryant 124
  Francis 65
  H. 97
  Henry 433
  Rueben 274, 333
McDowell 154
  John 160
  Robert 65
McElhany, John 180
McElhassy, James 178
McEli, James 178
McElroy
  George 396, 413
  I.S. 416
McGarvey, J.D. 401
McGary
  Hugh 136
  Robert 241
McGee
  David 51, 231, 241
  William 37
McGee's Station 76, 78, 83, 104
                 105, 106, 134
                 150, 239
McGill, James 241
McGinty, Alexander 209
McGough, R.P. 407
McGuire, John 161
McHenry, Barnabas 428
McIntyre, John 58, 78, 133
McKee
  Alexander 46
  John 340, 414
  Samuel 207
McKendree, William 431
McKinley
  Alexander 311, 415
  Dr. I.H. 410

McKinney, Robert 168, 178
                   189, 208
McMahon
  James 214, 240
  Jesse 360
  Joseph 41, 244, 360
  William 240, 360, 445, 446
McMerry, Simpson 259
McMillan 43, 89, 138, 150
  Elizabeth 224
  James 14, 40, 45, 81, 89
         113, 154, 159, 161
         165, 168, 171, 175
         177, 178, 180, 206
         216, 222, 223, 224
         228, 229, 240, 241
         242
  Jonathan 58, 133, 224
  Mary 224
  Richard 40
  Robert 185, 201, 227
         240, 241
  William 45, 133, 142, 147
          152, 154, 159, 169
          179, 180, 222, 223
          225, 228, 241
McNichor, James 213
McQueen, William 65
McQuin, James 200
McWilliams 324
Meadows, Isreal 65
Means, Ky. 289
Means, William 216
Measley, Thomas 65
Mellinger Harbinger 257, 273
Menefee County 262, 289
Menninites 257
Mercer County 156
Merrick, George 445, 451
Merrill
  Andrew 65
  Nicholas 360
Merritt, G.W.
Metcalf 90
  John 65
Methodist Episcopal Church,
  South 448, 455
Methodist Protestant Church
  425, 449
Miami Indians 62, 129, 139, 141
              153, 144, 145
Milby
  A.R. 410

Milby (continued)
  William 444
Mill Creek 25
Miller
  Abraham 339, 360, 361
  Harrison 349
  Henry 137
  Humphrey 349
  John 108
  William 195, 454
Miller Run Presbyterean
  Church 386
Miller's Station 119
Millersburg 229
Millet, Jean
Mills
  Anson 334
  Polly 454
  Washington 454
Milner, Thomas 241
Milton, Jesse 241
Miner, Robert 447
Mockaby, John 178
Moffatt, William 201
Mohawk Indians 13
Monck Corners, Battle of
  67
Monmouth, Battle of 16, 64
                           65
Monroe, G.E. 337
Montgomery
  Alexander 36
  Elijah 226, 243
  James 65
Montgomery County 3, 19, 41
  58, 60, 70, 73, 74, 75, 87
  97, 101, 125, 133, 154, 157
  158, 169, 171, 177, 161, 162
  163, 179, 185, 199, 205, 206
  210, 213, 219, 240, 242, 243
  254, 259, 262-266, 274, 275
  277, 282, 289, 297, 299, 306-
  310, 314, 325, 327, 335, 348
  388, 403, 406, 419, 420, 429
  432, 433, 438, 442, 449, 450
  470, 471, 479, 480, 484, 489
  507
Montgomery County, Maryland 501
Montgomery County Methodist
  Circuit 484, 488
Montreat, N.C. 390
Moody, Patrick 65

Mooney
  James 18
  Patrick 58, 79
Moore
  George 430
  Henry 241, 243, 245
  James 241
  Jeremiah 176
  John 86, 410
  Joseph 178
  J.T. 287
  Peter 240
  Thomas 241
  Willaim 231
  William Alexander 399
Morgan
  Andrew 129
  Charles 66
  James 205
  John 66, 106, 111, 200
  John Hunt 311, 399
  Margaret 401
  Mordecai 137
  Pheobe 401
  Sarah 30
  William 30
Morgan County 241, 277
Morgan Station 60, 70, 77, 106
                     119, 132, 143
                     146, 223, 241
Mornell, Job 178
Morris
  James 66
  Robert 210
  Samuel 66
  Sarah 339
  William 329, 341, 342, 333
      356, 404, 493
Morrison
  John 74
  Thomas 66
Morrow
  Christian 246
  John 66
  Joseph 441
  Robert 209
  Thomas 66, 238
Morton 32, 270, 274, 335, 383
  John 24, 66, 246
  Jonathan 243
  Richard 32, 66, 92, 268
      304, 305
  Samuel 66, 461

Morton (continued)
  William 36, 268, 305, 306
Morton's Meeting House
  264, 266
Moseley
  Pervin 334, 335
  Thomas 267, 273
Mosley, Benjamin 66
Moss
  F.B. 468
  Frederick 216
  Mrs. Elisha C. 468
  Francis 468
Motch, George E. 410
Mound Builders 13, 129
Mountjoy, Elizabeth 176
Mounts, John 208
Mt. Abbott Methodist Church
  497
Mt. Carmel Baptist Church
  283-288, 299, 300, 303, 312
  313, 350, 359, 367, 377
  378-381, 415, 417, 418 , 469
Mt. Carmel Presbyterean Church
  377, 378
Mt. Chapel Baptist Church 345
Mt. Freedom Baptist Church 264
Mt. Gilead Baptist Church
  21, 278, 293, 303-307
Mt. Moriah Baptist Church 304
Mt. Olive Baptist Church
  259, 278, 100, 295-298, 301
  309-311, 323, 325, 361, 367
  370, 371, 375, 407
Mt. Pisgah Presbyterean Church
  383-386
Mt. Pleasant Baptist Church 264
Mt. Sterling 100, 110, 133, 142
           156, 157, 163, 165
           171, 174, 177, 179
           188, 229, 260, 386
           403, 439, 440, 448
           481
Mt. Sterling Baptist Church 101
  259, 264, 269, 271, 273, 275
  299, 314, 325, 339, 341, 357
  427
Mt. Sterling Methodist Church
  441, 467
Mt. Sterling Methodist Circuit
  434, 440-445, 449, 454,
  461, 470, 477, 480, 495

Mt. Sterling Presbyterean
  Church 388-391, 398
       404, 407
Mt. Sterling Road 213, 246
Mt. Tabor Presbtery 395
Mt. Union Baptist Church
  304, 306, 307
Mt. Vernon Baptist Church 402
Mt. Zion Baptist Church
  274, 305-307, 396
Mt. Zion Christian Church
  400, 453, 461, 462
Mt. Zion Methodist Circuit
  456, 458, 472
Mt. Zion-Grassy Lick Methodist
  Circuit 457
Mt. Zion Methodist Church
  378, 415, 425, 430-433
  439-444, 447-458, 468
Mud Lick 223
Muddy Creek 38
Muddy Creek Road 232
Muhlemon, W.P. 410
Muit (Muier)
  James 355, 356, 358, 365
  Sally 281
Munday, George 22
Munroe
  James 222
  Keith 115
Muse, James 470
Musgrove Mill, Battle 153
Myers, William 213
Mynt, Elias 121
Myor, William 66
Nade 325
Nall, E.C. 324
Natchez Trail 191
National House 17
Neeley
  Alexander 11, 18, 31
  Salley 32
Nelson
  Edward 167
  John 137
  Matthew 433, 434, 438
  William 213, 241
Nelson County 156, 263, 384
Nepo (Mt.) Methodist Church
  443, 450, 470, 480
Nest Egg Road 479
Nest Egg Methodist Church 479
Nevis, H.V.D. 416

Netherland, Benjamin 137
Nevios, William 66
Newell
   James 51
   William 51
New Freedom Baptist Church 314
New Light Controversy 314
Newman, Jonathan 24
New Orleans 42, 132, 134
        151, 288
New Pine Grove 124
New Providence Baptist Church
   265, 268, 272, 273, 276, 277
   281, 289, 309, 350, 357, 361
   365
New Providence Presbyterean Church
   384
New Salem Baptist Church 314
Newkirk 473
   Nelson 266
Newton
   George 150
   Martha 355
New York 196, 504
Nichol
   Isaac 65
   Isaiah 167, 168
   Jeremiah 167
   Joseph 61
Nicholas
   Patricia 391
   William 495
Nicholas County 22
Nicholas Presbyterean Church 398
Nicholasville Baptist Church 306
Nicholson, A.M. 301, 324
Nixon, John 137
Noble
   James 66
   Jon 66
Noe 233
   Tabitha 115
Noel, Silas
Noland
   A.C. 278
   F.W. 451
Norman, I.F. 484
Norris 66
   William 477
Northcutt
   Benjamin 428
   G.O. 378
   H.C. 436, 486

Northcutt (continued)
   Henry 447
North District Baptist Association
   65, 90, 91, 95, 213, 259
   261-269, 272-278, 281-287
   289-291, 293, 296, 303-310, 327
   328, 330-351, 354-357, 359
   360-365, 377, 381
North Fork of Red River Baptist
   Church 314
North Middletown 28, 180, 359
   415-418, 450, 455, 463
North Middletown District
   444, 450, 454, 468, 470
Northern Methodist Conference
   436, 445, 447, 451, 456, 469
   480-492, 497, 498, 500
Norton, James 137
Norwood, Frederick Abbott 425
Nowland 66
Nugent, C.G. 457
Nutt, John 137
Oakley, William 241
Oak Pond Particular Baptist
   Church 266
Oakwoods 121
O'Bryan, John 167
Ogden, Benjamin 427, 467
Oglesby, Joshua 432
O'Hara
   Daniel 66, 200
   John 66
   Patrick 66
Ohio River Methodist
   Conference 435
Ohio River Particular Baptist
   Church 266
Oil Springs 116, 120, 439
O'Kelly, James 250, 254, 425-429
               440, 442, 449
               460, 493
Oklahoma 300
Old Baptist Church 259, 287, 288
   296, 308-310, 314-316, 354
   359, 363, 370, 408, 431, 435
Oldfield, Joseph 137
Old Fort Methodist Chapel 472
Old Fort Methodist Church
   441, 458, 488, 507
Old Fort Methodist Circuit
   457, 507
Oldham
   Jesse 66

Oldham (continued)
   John 66
   Richard 66
   William 66
Old Kentucky Tele. & Tele. 10
Old-New Light Controversy 250
Oliphant, J.H. 280
Oliver
   Richard 56, 66, 124
          211, 355
   Sarah 355, 356
   William 66
Olympia Springs 64, 110, 158
          164, 223
O'Neal, John 137
Oneida Indians 13
Onondogas Indians 13
Orange County, Virginis 155, 220
Orange Presbytery of N.C. 387
O'Rear
   Daniel 65, 473
   John 66
   William 40, 501
   Wulliah 266, 273
Orsikany, Battle of 144
Osbourne 473
   George 66
Ottawa Indians 16, 17, 129
Otter Creek 72, 81
Otter Creek Baptist Church
   310, 326
Overton
   Clugh 135, 137
   Waller 214
Owen
   Alice 499
   Allen 496
   Alta 499
   Alvin 499
   Ann 501
   Anna 499
   Artie 501
   Ben R. 500
   Bertie Lee 499
   David Wilson 499
   Eliza 499
   Elizabeth 499
   Elizabeth Winn 501
   Emma L. 499
   Eunice 499
   Eva B. 499
   Fannie 499
   Fielding 503

Owen (continued)
   Francis M. 499
   Francis W. 436
   Fred P. 499
   George 499
   Harriett Jane 499
   Hayes 499
   Henry B. 503
   Henry T. 499
   Hezekiah 495, 496
   Horatio 436, 495, 125
   Ignatius 503
   James 238
   James Alfred 501
   James H. 497
   James M. 499
   Jane 496
   Jessie W. 499
   Jonathan 419, 428, 429, 432
   John 501, 503, 66, 245
   John T. 499
   John W. 436, 493, 496, 499
   John W. II 499
   Josephine 499
   Katheryn 281, 435, 493
         496, 499
   Kathryn 56, 85, 113, 116
         118, 124, 171, 191
   Lawrence 235, 355, 392, 403
         428, 429, 432, 497
         501-503
   Leona 499
   Leona S. 499
   Lizzie 499
   Lou T. 499
   McKinley 499
   Martha 495
   Martha E. 494
   Marcia 499
   Margaret J. 499
   Margaret L. 499
   Mary 503
   Mary Cullum
   Maybelle 494
   Maxwell G. 499
   Michael B. 499
   Midlred 499
   Mollie 494, 499
   Myrtle 499
   Mary E. 499
   Mary C. 499
   Nancy Clay 499
   Nancy Jane 497

Owen (continued)
  Nancy Lou 499
  Nell 499
  Nelson Reed 503
  Kitty 497
  Hattie 499
  Lucy Griggs 499
  Pearl M. 499
  Pearline 499
  Rebecca 499, 503
  Richard T. 499
  Richard Thomas 499
  Rosana 499
  Ruth B. 499
  Sam 66
  Samuel 499
  Sarah G. 499
  Sarah L. 499
  Speed 499
  Stanford 499
  Susan F. 499
  Thomas 501, 66
  Thomas B. 499
  Viola 499
  Wallace 499
  William Perry 499
  William H. 499
  William K. 499
  William R. 499
  Wilson 499
Owen Camp Ground 439
Owen Chapel 233
Owen County 284
Owen Meeting House and Chapel
  355, 392, 403, 408, 424, 429
  433-436, 442-444, 448, 449
  454, 457, 460, 462, 464, 466
  470, 487-489, 493-499
Owingsville 156, 157, 227
Owingsville Baptist Church
  259, 307, 403
Owlley
  John 66
  William
Owsley County 53, 310, 326
Pace
  Doshea 94
  John 58
  Johnny 344, 347
  W.E. 352
  Rachel 61, 167
Page
  Edward 152

Page (continued)
  John 66
  William 66
Paints Lick Presbyterean
  Church 384-386
Palmer
  James 178
  Joseph 66, 178, 198
Palt, Thomas 361
Paris 134, 288, 384, 391, 392
Parrish
  John 468
  Mary 446
  Timothy 208
  William 66
Park 473
Parker
  Alexander 240
  J. 270
  Nancy 288
  Samuel 432, 433
Particular Baptists
  257, 259, 264-270, 281, 288
  296, 303, 309, 334, 337, 338
  340, 341, 361, 367, 365, 379
Parton, W.E. 24
Parvin, Thomas 78, 106, 230, 232
Patrick 166
  J. 481
Patterson 473
  B.L. 407
  Robert 74, 135, 154
      160, 236
  T.L. 267
Patton
  B.F. 407
  George 66
  James, Mrs. 348
  Matthew 66, 125, 127
  N. 268
Payne 107
  Buckner 273
  Edward 13, 159
  James 339
  Jilson 105, 110, 161, 165
      169, 179, 180, 198
      207, 264, 266, 267
  John 273
  Priscella 443
  William 110, 178, 198, 288
      339, 340, 364
Paynter, W.T. 448
Paynter's Camp Ground 439, 448

Payton Lick 211
Peake, John 137
Pearce, Jesse 365
Peck
　Gregory 407
　James 284
Peirson, F.P. 375
Pemberton
　John 66
　Thomas 207
Pencion, L.M. 484
Pendleton 119
　Curtis 27
　D.J. 185
Penland, Mary 355
Pennell, Samuel 388
Pennington, Richard 31
Penn's Run Presbyterean
　Church 386
Pentz, S.S. 452, 464
Peoples
　John 209, 212
　J.R. 458
　Robert 115
Perkins, Alexander 137
Perry County 73
Perry
　James 37
　R.R. 303, 310
Petticorn 232
Petty
　David 109
　Francis 344, 348
　John 200
　Randall 333, 334
　Samuel 109
　Thomas 344
　William 66
Pharis Hill Christian Church 275
Philadelphia 24, 42, 205, 383
Philadelphia Confession
　256, 262, 281
Philadelphia, Synod of 383
Philips 467
　Charles 58, 415
　John 480
　Thomas 233
　William 439, 444, 454
　W.R. 410
Pickett, Thomas 235
Pigg
　Anderson 331
　Thomas 294

Pigg (continued)
　William
Pike County 73
Piles, Milton 436
Pilot Knob 1, 18, 126
Pilot View 125, 126, 370
Pinchem 8, 124, 125
Pine Grove 60, 104, 161, 222
　　　　　　460, 464, 466, 505
Pine Hill Baptist Church
　230, 288
Pine Ridge 24, 116
Pisgah College 228, 402
Pisgah Methodist Church 230, 288
Pittman, John 137
Pitts, Fountain 442
Plan of Union 289, 290, 341
Pleasant River Particular
　Baptist Church 285
Pleck, John 37
Plecker laver, John 178
Plum Creek 140
Plummer, Samuel 168, 204
　　　　　　　　208, 215
Ploague, James 169, 182, 242
Poe, E.D. 301
Point Pleasant, Battle of
　67, 68, 113, 153
Pointer, Thomas 178
Polly
　Clark 470, 497
　Drury 137
Poole (Pool)
　Anthony 193, 194, 195
　John 66
Poplar Grove Baptist Church 306
Poplar Neck Presbyterean
　Church 386
Porter
　H.G. 359
　J.J. 319
　J.W. 319
　T.J. 319
　William 243
Posey
　John 246
　William 410
Posten, C. 379
Potter
　Elizabeth Hunt 368
　Smith 368

Potts
    Smith V. 294, 295, 307-311
        325, 369, 370, 456
    S.O. 102
Poult, Michael 190
Powell
    Levin 16
    Newton 473
    Sam 213
    William 16
Powell County 1, 2, 21, 24, 25
    31, 52, 73, 96, 124, 127
    156, 162, 177, 178, 180
    213, 264, 266, 278, 288
    297, 314, 315, 325, 326
    363, 420, 425, 441, 469
    479, 488
Powell Valley Baptist Church
    280, 313, 314
Powers
    Catherine 448
    Jeremiah 167
    John 212
    J. Pike 16, 298, 299
        314, 318
Poynter (Paynter)
    W.T. 451, 419
    William 489
Poythress, Francis 427, 429
        431
Pratt, W.M. 318
Preston
    James 395
    Letitia 393
    Mrs. 390
    Robert 105
    Waller 393, 396
    Walker 396, 399
    William 49
Presbyterean Historical Center
    390
Pretty Run Creek 107, 119, 121
    126, 161, 178, 386, 415
    418, 421, 240
Prewitt (Preuit, Pruit) 137
    Gay 393
    James 189
    John Marshall 382
    Robert 66, 123, 137, 243
Priest, James M. 415
Price
    Bird 240
    Francis 200

Price (continued)
    James 263
    John 137, 240, 332
    Louise 390
Primitive Baptists 259, 288
    306, 400, 410, 418
Proctor
    Joe 133
    Nicholas 37
    Page 134
    Rueben 37
    Samuel 37
Proctor's Meeting House 441
Providence Baptist Church
    31, 83, 84, 85, 87-90, 95
    98-103, 109, 162, 232
    247, 258, 263-271,
    296-300, 303-306, 325
    328-330, 332, 336, 337
    340, 344, 348, 350, 351
    355-357, 361-364, 365
    367, 368, 376, 403, 407
    408, 409, 466
Providence Methodist Church
    450, 470, 478, 480
Providence on the Licking
    Baptist Church 273
Providence School 101
Quaker Meeting House 409, 417
Quebec 15, 143, 504
Quincy Methodist Circuit
Quisenberry 83, 294, 377, 409
        473
    A.C. 83, 85, 282, 329
    James 66, 82, 85, 94, 97
        125, 183, 197, 198
        201, 209, 264, 268-
        270, 290, 292, 293
        304, 308, 328-331
        334-338, 356, 392
        404, 493
    Joel 295
    John 205
    Lloyd 99, 100
    Milton 95
    Rachel 205
    R.B. 295
    Robert 97
    Roger 95
Rabbit Town 229
Rafferty, James 273
Ragan, John 486

Ragland
  Charles 109
  Edmund 70, 108, 109, 110
          139
  James 88
  Jane 61
  John 85
  Rhodes 212
  Thomas 362, 365
  William 109
Raiburn, Thomas 362, 265
Railsback, Daniel 244
Rainey
  Daniel 40
  J.J. 486
  John 62
  Richard 40, 146
Ralls, Harold 212
Ramey, Daniel 85, 200
Ramsey 106, 119, 377, 455
  Alexander 66, 110, 215
             234, 406
  Andrew 235, 454
  Frank 118, 407
  Franklin 407
  James 234
  John 66, 207, 234
       349, 406
  Joseph 407
  L.V. 405
  Richard 82
  S.K. 491
  William 66, 234, 349
Rand, Joseph 447, 451, 452
Randolph
  George 273
  Rueben 273
Raney, Lou 257
Rank, George 39, 40, 42
             43, 83, 84
Rankin 473
  Adam 384-386, 391
  Allen 473
  Benjamin 207
  Charlie 473
  John D. 463, 473
  Richard 207
  Thomas 445, 462
Rash
  Ambrose 372
  A.D. 285, 286, 296, 310
       311, 313, 318, 337
       338

Rash (continued)
  James 198
  Miller 353
  Tinkey 353
  W.A. 353
  Wallace 410
  William 93, 285, 286
          333-338, 354
          403
Rawlings, Pemberton 47
Ray
  D.B. 318
  John 211, 442
Rayburn, Billy 78
Raymond, George 242
Razzul, Nehemiah 461
Read, William 350
Rear (This may be the same
  as O'Rear)
  John 208
  William 208
Red House Methodist Church 498
Red Lick Baptist Church 266
Red River 9, 24, 41, 109, 142
          164, 360, 441, 443
          450
Red River Baptist Association
  278, 280, 289, 339, 354
  362-365
Red River Baptist Association
  of Tennessee 270
Red River Baptist Church
  264, 266, 329
Redd, J. 492
Redding, Stephen 391
Redman 429, 475
  George 240
  John 241
  William 66, 475
Redmond
  Agnes 360
  John W. 407
Reed 445
  Daniel 294, 295
  Isaac 411
  Nelson 502
  Nellie 499
  R.H. 456
  S.E. 353
  Thomas 294, 295
  William 273
Reegan, Nicholas 427

Reese
    Isaac 183, 201
    R.H. 410
Reeves, R.H. 472
Reform 257, 268, 270, 274-277
        282-284, 293, 304-310
        314, 327, 343-346, 349
        357, 361, 364, 365, 378
        388, 396, 402, 403, 445
Regular Baptists 176, 256-259
    262-264, 267, 268, 277, 289
    303, 321, 332, 333, 341
    343, 345
Regulators 60
Reid (Reed, Read)
    D. 293
    David 445
    Davis 462
    J. 472
    Joseph 384
    S.E. 353
    William 301, 259
Republican Methodists
    260, 426, 449
Republicans 260, 471, 485, 497
Reynolds
    Aaron 137
    George 78
    H.H. 362
    Thomas 293
Rhotum, Benjamin 438
Rice
    David 247, 383-385, 391
          399, 405, 494
    Holman 66
    Isaac 66
    John 58, 66, 230
    Nathan 388
Rice's Fork of Dix River
    Methodist Church 388
Richard, Joseph 410
Richards
    Mary 84, 85
    Robert 41, 82
    William 66
Richardson
    Isobell 288
    Lucy 339, 340
    Nancy 499
    Robert 499
    Solomon 499
Richett, Robert 335, 336
Richmond 10, 102, 280, 322, 488

Richter, George 241
Ridgeway
    Ninian 286, 343
    Zachariah 339, 357
Ries (Rees), James 213
Right Angle 491
Riley
    B.W. 304, 305
    John Adair 54
    John 66
    William 67
Ringo
    Cornelius 72, 212
    Peter 212
Robey, William 496
Ritchie
    Jane 205
    John 60, 67
    Samuel 60, 67
    Violet 205
River Raison, Battle of
    34, 226, 288, 338
Robards
    Edward 178
    George 178
Robbins, Silas 282
Roberts, John 306
Robertson
    Benjamin 67
    D.O. 457
    Matilda 390
    William 137, 231
Robinson
    George 295
    William 214
Rockbridge County 392, 393
Rockbridge Particular Baptist
    Church 285
Rock Springs Baptist
    Church 278
Rodgers, William 241
Rogers
    Barnett 135, 137
    John 440
    John C. 336, 345, 361
    Margaret 348
Roland, W.T. 463
Rollins, Pemberton 36, 37, 39
Roosevelt, Theodore 498
Rose
    Brother 439, 461
    J. 472
    James 137

Rose (continued)
  Mathias 130
  Robert 480
Roseberry, Cullum 178
Ross, Hugh 37
Roundtree
  M.M. 487, 491, 500
  Thomas 499
Roundtree Methodist Chapel
  487, 488, 491
Roundtree School 488
Routt
  David 266, 330, 331
  Don 361
  George 198
Rowe, R.P. 407
Royster, J.R. 359
Rucker 462
  J. 359
  Jacob 144
  Rueben 124
Ruckerville Baptist Church
  353, 360
Ruckerville Christian
  Church 275, 358
Ruddle, Isaac
Ruddle Station 77, 119, 132
Rule, Andrew 137
Rupard
  A.H. 265, 278
  C. 352
  Erastus 236
  John 107, 233
  John W. 368
  Joseph 233
  S. 352
  Sam 354
  Seth 352, 353
  Thomas 344, 412
  William 233, 273, 278-281
      287, 347, 350-354
      359, 362, 370, 380
      485
Russell, William 154, 160, 225
Rutledge
  James 5
  John 5, 125
  Joseph 67
Ryan
  Elisha 294
  Kate 353
  Malinda 353
  Mildred 356

Ryland
  Dillard 407
  Samule 407
  W.H. 407
Sacre, John 305
Said
  Susan 384
  William 211, 384
Sale, Job 433
Salem Baptist Church
  264, 266, 271-274
  310, 313, 317
Salem Methodist Church 441
Salem Presbyterian Church
  87, 151, 152, 234
  384-393, 396, 398-401
  403, 404, 407, 409, 416
  421, 460, 462, 493
Salem Presbytry 294, 328, 355
Salt Lick Baptist Church
  264, 271, 272
Salt River Methodist Circuit
  506
Salt River Particular Baptist
  Church 287
Salyorsville 24
Samaria Baptist Church 289
Sanders
  Nathanial 202
  Robert Stuart 382, 390-
      392, 395, 397, 398
      403, 404
  Thomas
Sandez, Elizabeth 178
Sardis Particular Baptist
  Church 287
Savage
  F.A. 472
  James E. 472, 477, 484
Savory, Henry 461
Scholl
  Francis T. 448
  Joseph 347, 349
  Lea 339
  Peter 339, 340
Scholls 28, 72, 122, 125, 233
  Abraham 58, 113, 114
  Achiles 113, 114
  Elizabeth 115
  Joseph 32, 58, 113, 114
        135, 240
  Mary 205
  Morgan 114

Scholls (continued)
   Peter 114, 136, 207
   Rachell 114
   Septimus 12, 32, 45
   William 113, 114, 233
Schollsville 21, 27, 32, 38, 71
       113-115, 125, 214
       233, 341, 458, 466
Schooler, Lewis 503
Science Hill Academy 82, 489
Scobee (Scobe) 119, 429
   Catherine 347
   Christopher 467
   George 455
   James 353
   Margaret 347
   Nancy 353, 442
   R.T. 352, 353
   Stephen 475
Scott 205
   Charles 57, 67, 116, 120, 141
       142, 201, 239, 240
   David 264
   Drury 56, 57, 67
   J.M. 413
   James 67
   John 178
   George 417
   Moses 243
   Ray 375
   Robert 137, 339
   Samuel 135, 137
   Thomas 41, 67, 157, 162, 168
       182, 183, 184, 189
       193, 195, 493
   W. 379
   Walter 267, 305, 494
   William 385
Scott County 289
Screvens, Henry 481
Scudder, R.F. 325
Searcy
   Bartlett 37, 52, 58, 137
   Howell 348
   John 137
   Rueben 37
Sebastian
   Benjamin 150
   Isaac 150
Self, John 67
Seneca Indians 7, 11-13
Senssmith, William 397

Separatist Baptist 175, 341, 351
   259, 263, 267-269, 283, 321
   332-334, 340, 357, 381, 440
   446, 474
Seqoya 120
Seveir, John 148
Seven Day Baptist 257
Sewell, John 128, 148
   Joseph 381, 440, 446, 474
   Nancy 353
Sewell Shop 128
Shackleford
   John 336
   Zacharia 85, 328
Shane 164
   John 223
Shankle, Amos 486
Shannon
   Samuel 388
   William 135
Sharp 213
   Adam 215
   George 41, 183, 213
   Litchfield 200
   Moses 266, 330
Sharpsburg 156, 157, 164, 439
Sharpsburg Baptist Church
   271, 273
Sharpsburg Methodist Church 438
Sharpsburg Methodist Circuit 452
Shawnee Indians 11, 13, 14, 18
   21, 22, 26, 45, 131, 138
   144, 223
Shay's Rebellion 148
Shearer
   W.L. 318
   W.S. 301
Shelby, Isaac 150, 151, 153, 160
   175, 178, 225, 236, 239, 240
   243, 246, 413, 502
Shelby County 287, 439
Shelbyville 229, 483, 489
Sheman, T.P.C. 450
Shepherd
   E.L. 486
   George 301
   Paul 103
   Presley 56, 67
Shimfessel 473
   Claude 474
Shinall, David 330
Shipp
   Chloe 235, 330

Shipp
  Joseph 331
Short, Moses 67
Shortridge
  Robert 114
  Samuel 133
Showduskey, Anthony 137
Shott, William 137
Shropshire, Edmond 210
Shrout, Edward 137
Shultz, J. 273
Sidebottom, John 67
Silver Creek 114
Silver Springs Presbyterean
  Church 385, 386
Simmons, J. Dallas 100, 298, 299
            311, 318
Simpson
  James D. 6, 410
  James 199
  William 410
Sinclair (St. Clair)
  Charles 84, 85
  John 439, 443, 444, 461
  Sarah 84, 85
Singleton, Edmond 137
Sipes, Henry 410
Six Principle Baptists 257
Skinner 233
  Cornelius 410, 415
  James 417
  John 183, 204, 334
  J.K. 410
  Isaac 416
  Phineus 416
  Sally 334
Slade, Ky. 289
Slade Liberty Baptist Church
  271-273
Slate Creek 140, 178, 205, 212
            223, 241, 242
Slate Union Baptist Church
  264, 266, 271, 273
Small Mountain 21
Smith
  Betsy 208
  Bill 3
  David 443
  Elizabeth 397
  Enoch 58, 157, 161, 164, 177
        178-180, 206, 226
  George 31, 137, 152, 456
  Alice 499

Smith
  Henry 208
  Jacob 14
  James 137
  J.L. 297, 298, 303-306, 327
  John 67, 129, 499
  John Racoon 87, 98, 268-274 327
                343, 357, 442, 445
  Jon 137
  Joseph 178
  J.W.R. 408
  Nancy 208
  Peggy 208
  Polly 208
  Russel 410
  R.W. 378
  Sally 208
  Sam 212
  Thomas 67, 208, 267
  William 137, 180, 189
  William Bailey 46
Smithsboro 502
Smithsfield 503
Smithson, William 347, 348
Sneed
  Charles 67
  John 67
  Pauline 436
  Snowden 67
  Thomas 67
Snow Creek Baptist Church 314
Snow Creek Methodist Church
  454, 455
Snow Hill Methodist Church
  444, 450
Snowden
  Charles 360
  David 360
  John 377, 380, 416, 417
Somerset Creek 212
Somerset Christian Church
  262, 273, 358
Sommerville, John 433
Sorrell, Christopher 20
South
  Benjamin 246
  Idom 216
  John Sr. 37
  John Jr. 37
  John the Younger 37
  Thomas 37

South District Baptist Association
    36, 85, 89, 91, 263, 264
    328, 331, 360
South Fork Red River Baptist
    Church 264-266, 271-274,
        277, 357
Southern Baptist Convention
    325, 435
Southern Methodists 436, 437, 463
    478, 480, 486-490, 497
Southern Baptist Seminary
    102, 262, 278, 283, 286, 301
    318, 362, 378
Southgate, E.L. 463, 506
Spanish Conspiracy 149, 150
Spates, W.W. 456, 471
Sparks, Kenneth 410
Spears, William B. 410
Spencer Creek Baptist Church
    264-266, 271-274, 277, 357
Spencer Creek Church of Christ
    266, 269, 273
Speed
    Joshua 486
    Fanny 486
Sphar 233
    Catherine 78
    Daniel 209, 415
    Jacob 58, 67, 78, 130
    John 167, 168
    Mathias 58, 67, 80, 140
    Rebecca 82, 140
    William 214
Spillman, James 67, 189, 193
        195, 475
Spracken, Hazel Utterby
    28, 31-33, 46
Springfield, Ky. 507
Springfield Presbyterean
    Church 404
Sprout Springs 213
Spruce Baptist Church 314
Spurgeon
    Daniel 455
    Isaac 241
    Samuel 164, 213
Stackhouse, T.C. 318
Stafford
    Fanny 499
    Letha 499
    Mimi 499
    Sarah 499
Stafford's Landing 216

Stagers, C.M. 410
Stalling, Jeremiah (Sallee) 136
Stamer, Joshua 58, 78, 121
Stamper 333, 427, 429
    Jonathan 434, 438, 454
    Joshua 427, 444, 475
    Mary 475
Stamper's Chapel 30
Stamper's Methodist Chapel
    415, 432, 433, 437, 442
    444, 453, 466, 475, 493
Stanford 39
Stanton 128, 201
Stanton, Ky. 271
Stapleton, John 36, 137
Stark
    Jeremiah 53
    Jeremina 53
Starnes
    Jacob 67
    John 67
Starns (Sterns)
    Frederick 51
    Jacob 37, 51
    Valentine 37, 51
St. Asaph 36, 59, 132, 236
St. Clair, Arthur 142, 144
        161
St. James 130
Staton Camp Baptist Church
    264, 266
Steel
    Archibald 67
    David 72
    Robert 394, 413
    Rupert 384
    Samuel 412
Steele, Andrew 137
Stephens
    J.S. 280
    James 231, 240, 243, 245
    William 133, 234
Stepstone Creek 212
Stepstone Methodist Church
    475
Stepstone Methodist Circuit
    475
Stevens, Richard 360
Stevenson
    A. 380
    E. 482
    Evan 448
    Daniel 486, 487

Stevenson (continued)
  James 413
  John 67, 137
  Samuel 407
  Thomas 318, 372
Stewart
  A. 367
  Charles 67, 183, 412
  J. 378
  J.A. 399
  James 183, 201, 214, 378
  John 31
  William 67, 137, 318
Stober, Wilson 361
Stockton, George 108
Stockton's Station 108
Stone 473, 478
  Barton 269, 304, 334, 335
        387, 402, 412, 421
        426, 428, 430
Stone Pond Baptist Church
  269
Stoner, Michael 48, 119, 144
       201
Stoner Creek 3, 11, 21, 30, 40
  52, 70, 109, 110, 114, 115
  119, 121, 136, 139, 141
  144, 155, 161, 162, 178
  201, 211-214
Stoner Creek Settlement
  125, 139
Stonestreet
  Elizabeth 397
  James 390, 393, 394
  Sarah 396
Stooper, J.S. 398
Stowe, Harriet Beecher 435
Strode
  A.D. 373
  Isaac 371
  James 143, 373
  Jeremiah 167, 241
  John 50, 52, 162, 165, 166
     188, 191, 200, 201
     204, 215, 236, 329
     332, 333
  Nelson 372
  R.E. 316
  Stephan 231
  Thomas 201
  W.D. 318, 371-373
Strode's Creek 334, 3, 50-53

Strode's Station
  58, 62, 63, 65, 117, 124
  132-136, 141-145, 162,
  164-166, 223, 225, 231
  232, 236, 239, 438, 460
  466, 475, 506
Strode Station Baptist Church
  266, 304, 332, 409
Strossberry, G.T. 99
Stucker 140
Sturgill, J.L. 491, 492
Stuart
  C.E. 379
  E 337
  Robert 392, 393, 401
       411, 412
  W.D. 354
Sudduth 168, 225
  Ezekial 141
  James 273
  Massa 107
  William 16, 30, 78, 141, 161
      164, 168, 180, 182
      183, 202, 206, 207
      208, 225, 226, 229
      230, 234, 241, 242
      244, 416
  W.D. 410
Sugar Ridge 110, 403
Sugar Ridge Methodist Church 428
Sugar Ridge Presbyterean Church
  279, 305, 353, 371, 387
  396, 404-411, 415, 439
  454, 443, 464, 485, 498
Sullivan's Island, Battle of
  63
Sulpher Fork Creek 428
Summers
  John 137
  Mrs. 460
Summerville, James 438
Susner, John 180
Susnett, A.J. 457
Sutton, Jesse 445
Swango
  Elizabeth 310, 338
  Robert 394
Swetman
  Thomas 273
  William 273
Swift
  Charles 417
  Jonathan 201

Swift Camp Baptist Church 277
Swift Silver Mine 201
Switzer's Methodist Meeting House 437
Sunday School Union 498
Sympson
  Delia 260
  James 181, 188, 195, 197, 204
Synod of Kentucky 393, 394
Synod of New York and Philadelphia 384
Synod of Virginia 385
Taes, William 198
Talbert
  Paul 480
  Thomas 410
Talbot
  Isham 67
  Paul 67
  Thomas 12, 122
Taliferrio, John 410
Tanner
  Archlus 407
  Etta 408
  John 501, 503
  J.H. 407
  J.W. 408
Tap, Hambleton 24
Tar River Methodist District 439
Tarleton 59
Tate, Charles 53
Tates Creek Baptist Association 85, 263, 264, 278, 286, 293, 303, 327, 330
Tates Creek Baptist Church 88, 262, 266, 234
Tates Creek Predestinarian Baptist Church 288, 354, 363
Taul 115
  Arthur 67
  Benjamin 183, 188, 190, 207, 210, 231, 234
  Cassina 369
  Mary 448
  Mary Jane 118
  Micah 163, 172, 183, 246, 409, 466
Tavor, N.E. 484
Taylor 214, 218, 221, 225
  Alice 222

Taylor (continued)
  Charles 456
  Dick 178
  Edward 67
  George 175, 181, 183, 195, 213, 243, 390
  George W. 439, 444, 461
  G.W. 482
  Hancock 49
  H.B. 492
  Hubbard 67, 123, 152, 155, 159, 160, 161, 165, 166-168, 174, 175, 179, 188, 202, 221, 222, 225, 228, 234, 259, 329, 461, 505
  James F. 395, 399
  John 78, 347, 461, 468
  John Pendleton 222
  Jonathan 67
  J.K. 222
  J.S. 490
  Lucy 222
  Mildred 222
  Nancy 222
  Peter 448
  Robert 78
  Robert S. 399
  Robert Stuart 390
  Robert Stuart Jr. 390
  Robert Stuart III 390
  R. Stuart 398
  Rueben 462, 468
  Stuart 397
  S.A. 102
  Sam 133
  Samuel 78, 189, 195, 235
  Thomason 222
  Thurston 235, 503
  William 506
  W.F. 450, 464
  W.S. 375
  W.C. 478
  Zacharia 227
Techumseh 36, 143
Teeter, Charles 183, 201
Templain, F. 384, 385
Templeman, Lewis 273
Tennessee 387
Terrell
  Henry 67
  Mary 198

Terry
  Enos 210
  J. 379
  T. 379
Tetter, John 241
Tevis
  Fannie O. 499
  J.D. 399
  John 482
  Julia 47, 83, 232, 399
  Peter 204
Texas, Ky. 463, 489
Texas-Irving Circuit 489, 490
Texas Richmond Methodist Circuit 489
Texas Seminary 487, 489, 491
Thames, Battle of 63
Thatcher's Mill 121
Thatcher's Mill Baptist Church 415
Thomas
  Jane
  John D. 336
  Joseph 102
  J.N. 103
  Nicholas 230
  Sterling 407
Thompson
  C.H. 324
  C.T. 416
  J.H. 490
  John 432
  C.C.
  Kessiah Hart 67
  Laurence 67
  Rodney 186
  Samuel 167
Thomson
  C. 353
  C.C. 354
  C.H. 278
  Columbus 352
  D. 378
  David 339, 341
  Elizabeth 339
  George 343, 346-348
  G.W. 341
  James 340, 341
  Lizzie 448
  Patsy 246
  W.D. 380
Thornsburg, Isaac 273
Throckmorton 235

Thurman, William 304
Thurston, Charles 39
Tinsley, William 41, 241
Tippacanoe 143
Tipton, Samuel 194
Todd
  Hannah 393
  James 155
  John 33
  Levi 135, 199, 224, 240, 241, 242
  Mary 159
  Murtle 499
  Robert 135, 154, 159, 241
  Thomas 175
Todd Road 460
Tolen, Elias 201
Toller, Peter 178
Tomlinson, Richard 137
Tory 420
Toulgier, Robert 203
Toulman, Harry 251, 257, 384
Toulmin, Harry 176
Towbridge 167
Town Fork Baptist Church 251, 257, 384
Tracy 108, 112, 161
  Asa 347, 349, 350
  B.A. 353
  Buford Allen 111
  Charles 339-342, 67, 108, 109, 146
  Erastus 108
  Joseph 343
  J.S. 396
  May 355
  Nancy 344
  Obed 348
  Roxane 354
  Sarah 339
Transylvania College 74, 153, 166, 228, 251, 384, 399, 402, 413
Transylvania Company 26, 307, 39, 71, 82, 109, 143, 158, 166, 185, 219, 223
Transylvania Presbyterey 384, 388, 390, 415
Trap 127
Trapp 491
Traube, Edward 211
Trauber, Daniel 406

Treadway 309
  John 274
Trent, William 15
Tribble
  Andrew 81, 82, 84, 85, 87, 88
       91, 262, 263, 472
       328-330
  Samuel 306
Trigg, Stephen 135, 245
Trimble
  Austin 233
  Francis 48
  Peter 33
  R. 278
  Robert 152, 199
  Sam 142
  William 12, 201
Trinity Methodist Church 498
Triplett, A.N. 484
Triplet Union Baptist Church 270
Trotter
  James 154, 159, 160
  James P. 404, 405
Truit, Eli 433
Trusdale, William 239
Tucker
  A.T. 101
  Archibald 357
  James 140
  Thomas 100
Tuggle, William 67
Tull, Isaac 388, 391
Turley
  James 213
  Leonard 273
Turner
  G.B. 457
  Smith 243
  Suzannah 85
Turpin, J.L. 324, 325
Tuscarora Indians 12, 142
Tuttle
  Johnnie 473
  Susan 395
  William 473
Tuttle's Mill 360
Twain, Mark 78
Twyman, D.R. 358
Twynian, James 137
Two Mile Creek 46, 81, 124
               205, 216, 232
Tyler, J.O. Jr. 79
Tyner 234

Tyree, William 318
Tydings, Richard 439, 461
Uncle Tom's Cabin 435
Union 435, 484, 497
Union City Baptist Church 325
Union College 487, 491
Union Presbyterean Seminary
    398-400, 413, 415-418, 462
Union Stone Branch Baptist
  Church
Unitarians 257
Unity Baptist Church
    87, 89, 125, 264-266, 268
    271, 273-277, 290-292
    294-296, 307-311, 329-332
    336, 337, 356, 357, 361
    403, 466
Universalities 176
University of Kentucky 102
Upham, E.L. 410
Upper Blue Licks 109, 134
Upper Howard's Creek
    4, 51, 87, 105, 113
    123, 125, 178, 213
Upper Howard Creek Baptist
  Church 258, 264-268, 273-277
        271, 278, 290, 293
        308, 309, 349, 350
        355-362, 365, 367
        369, 381, 454
Upper Sandusky 134
Upper Spossylvania 83
Upper White Oak Baptist
  Church 273
Vaan Landingham
  Enomi 37
  George 68
Valley Forge 57, 60, 64
Vance
  James 390
  Jane 409
  Polly 390
Vanderbuilt University 420
Van Doran, Luther A. 405
Van Meter 127
  Garrett 68
  James 416
  L.M. 410
  Solomon 397
Van Pelt, John 448
Van Sweiringer 58, 133, 178
  Thomas 78
Vardeman, Jeremiah 272, 304

Vaughn, William 334
Veach, Samuel 445
Venerable, Henry 395
Versailles 229
Vice, Nathaniel 197
Viena 9, 450, 466, 470,
    479-, 480, 483, 497
Vienna 9
Vincinnes  3, 8, 132, 139, 219
Vivon 377, 395, 119, 161, 164
  Beverly 174
  Elizabeth 290, 355
  Flavel 210, 355, 454
  Francis 81
  Harvey 355
  Henry 355
  Isaiah 355
  James 113, 124
  Jesse 113, 124, 200
  John 82, 84, 85, 210, 355
  Milton 241, 355, 357
  Nancy 355
  Thacker 355
  Thomas 92, 93, 355
  Shelby 355
  Smith 355, 356
Wade 119
  Benjamin 265
  Jacob 119
  James 241
  John 141
  Lawson 178
  Thomas 68
  Timothy 68
Wades Mill 107, 121, 126, 161
    178, 179, 235, 377
    385, 415-418, 458
Wadkins 116, 117
  William 116
Walker
  James 344, 346
  John 402
  J.D. 472
Walden
  George 467
  Elizabeth 499
Walker
  Ben 11
  James 68, 108, 189, 213
  Robert 68
  Thomas 21

Wall
  James 68
  John 68
  Ruth 84, 85
Wall, T. 370
Wallace
  Calob 150
  Robert 201
  Thomas 439, 444, 461
  William 411
Waller
  Ben 104
  John 241
  W.F. 198
Wall Street 467
Walnut Hill 229
Walnut Hill Presbyterean Church
    383-386, 397, 464
Walsch, John D. 486
Walton 300
Ward
  James 178, 183, 189
        213, 432, 461
  John 195, 235
  William 242
Warder, J.D. 318
Wardlow
  Andrew 390
  Jane 390
  Peggy 390
Ware 115
  A.B. 457
  D. 472
  John 68
  Robert 365
  Thomas 68
Warner, John 167
Warren, John 68
Warrior's Trail 12, 14-16
            19-21, 133
Washington, Fort 240
Washington, George
    17, 28, 60, 63, 66, 82
    141, 142, 143, 166, 217
Washington, Ky. 288, 340, 387
Washington and Lee 228
Washington and Lee University
    391
Washington Street 166
Washington Street Presbyterean
    Church 389, 406
Watanga River 143
Water Street 195

Watkins 344
  Louise 352
Watson 163
  John 431
Watts 117
  Barnett 260
  Carrie 499
  Fielding 234
  Franklin 407
  H.R. 352
  J.T. 358
  John T. 357
  Julius 201, 215
  W.T. 294
Wayne County 48, 246
Weathers, Garrett 399
Webb
  Austin 75, 168
  George 189, 193, 199
  John 28
  Julius 210
Weber
  John 30
  Moses 37
Webster, William 68
Weible, Daniel 210
Weldon, Abraham 333, 336
Wells
  Findlay 372
  Jacob 209
  John 208
  Mary 209
  James 355, 356
  William 338
Welburn, Drummond 448, 451
Welsch 164
  Henry 183, 201
Wencher, Scott 399
Wesley 420, 422, 426
West
  Benjamin 504
  Granny 77
  James 388
  Johnathan 288, 336
  Jerry 210
  William 68
Weslyan Methodist Conference
  429, 435
West Bend Methodist Church
  469, 478, 488, 491
West Lexington Presbytery
  393-395, 399, 405, 406
  413, 415

Wharton, Richard 213
Wheeler
  Ben 183, 204
  John M. 410
Whig Party 217
Whigs 260, 471
Whitaker, Josiah 442
Whipperwill Creek 428
White
  Catherine 260
  Elizabeth 197
  Margaret 222
  M.L. 380
  Thomas 268, 271, 273, 362
  T.B. 358
  William 362
  W.T. 358
White Ball Tavern 111
Whitefield, George 421
White Hall 491
White Oak Baptist Church
  278, 325
Whiteside
  John 213
  William 240
Whitley
  Samuel K. 360
  Mrs. Wade Hampton 210
Whitley Presbyterean Church
  342
Whitset
  Ralph 479
  Sally 479
Whitman, B.F. 488
Whoton, Benjamin 433
Wickliffe, Robert 199, 227
Wilcox 7, 29, 30
Wilcoxson
  Charles 410
  Daniel 37, 68
  Isaac 30
  Jesse 356
  Joseph 29
Wilderness Road 501
Wilderness Trail 31, 72, 81
Wilkerson
  Nancy 438
  James 149, 150, 174, 216
  Thomas 431
William and Mary College 228
Willard, William 204
Williams 108
  Aga 164

Williams (continued)
  Daniel 264
  Henry 467
  J.H. 472
  James 201, 241
  Jesse 468
  John 204, 444, 458, 468
  Joseph 432
  Lana 27
  Sister 339
  Thomas 427
William's College 127
Wills 473
  Austin 369
  Barnett 355
  Ben T. 473
  Francis 110
  Isaac 233, 234
  Isaiah 368
  John 73, 233, 243
  Maud 293
  Pricella 368
  Richard 204
  J.J. 102
  Matthew 241
  Thornton 368, 454, 455
  T.L. 295-297, 310-313, 308
    369-371, 375-393, 456
  William Jr. 68, 106
  William Sr. 68
Willson, John 137
Wilson 102, 233
  Daniel 241
  Edward 164
  Ethel 478
  Isreal 137
  J.M. 472
  J.S. 300
  Jerome 200
  John 51, 56, 68, 137
  Nathanial 241
  Ruth Wood
  S. 318
  Samuel 395
  William 200, 208, 241
Winchester
  Baseball 14
  Cemetery 79
  Rollar Mill 9
Winchester Academy
  234, 383, 409, 467

Winchester Baptist Church
  309-313, 102, 318-320
  325, 327, 338
Winchester Christian Church
  337, 464
Winchester Chronicle 447
Winchester-Ebeneazer Circuit
  450, 452, 457
Winchester Lexington Road 123
Winchester Methodist Church
  397, 408, 409, 444, 447
  449-455, 462-464, 468
  471, 483, 487
Winchester Methodist Circuit
  457, 461, 462, 470, 477
  479, 484, 495, 450, 452
  457
Winchester-Mt. Zion Methodist
  Circuit 447
Winchester Old Baptist Church
  341, 342
Winchester-Paris Road 78
Winchester Presbyterean Church
  305, 394, 396, 399, 400, 404
  405, 407-409, 412-414, 418
  464
Winchester Seminary 312
Winn
  Daniel 336
  W.M. 468
Winston 24
Wisconsin 289
Wiseman, Abner 226, 243
Witcock, John 7
Wolf County 25, 95, 123
Witherspoon, Holly 418
Wolfe County 280, 289, 297, 326
Wolfe
  George 410
  Glenn 504
Wood
  Archibald 167
  Clem 193, 194
  Daniel 68
  James 68, 298
  John 200
  Joseph 85
  Mary 463
  Micajah 52
  William 68
Woodard
  John 479
  Martha 445

Woodard (continued)
  Samuel 215
Woodford County 402
Woodford Presbyterean Church
  402
Woodford, Sally 336
Woodray, Jesse 178
Woodruff, Jesse 178
Wool, James 495
Wool's Methodist Chapel
  424, 425, 444, 448-450, 455
  470, 464, 487, 488, 496, 498
Woosley
  Susan 446
  Thomas 68
Wooten, Mrs. William R. 230
Wormell, James 410
Wray, J.L. 318
Wren Methodist Church 441
Wright, Isam 204
Wyatt, W.F. 458
Wylie, Matthew 137
Wynadot Indians 129, 133
Yadkin River 34, 47
Yale 228
Yantis, Taylor 410
Yarborough, Jon 241

Yates
  Benjamin 241
  John 200
Yearman, M.V.C. 398
Yeiser, George 99
Yokum, Jesse 137
Yorktown 57, 59, 60, 66, 67
Young
  Edwinm 273
  Frank 339
  James 268
  James, Sr. 390, 409
  James, Mrs. 409
  Jesse 207
  John 104, 169, 180, 204
  John H. 443, 452
  J.H. 464
  Original 62, 63, 65, 168
    178, 226
  Samuel 273
  T.H. 464
  William 390
  William, Mrs. 390
Zacharia 289
Zion Baptist Church 314, 317
Zion Methodist Church 453, 455

Two more comments on the index. A glance down the long list of Owen's names illustrates how strongly Republican the Owen Chappel was. Hayes, after Rutherford Hayes, McKinley after another Republican president, Speed, after the Louisville layman whose money backed the northern Methodists and kept them alive for a quarter of a century. There was no question of the loyalty of the Owen family to the Republican party during the last half of the 19th century.

Another interesting point on names is the number of people who carry ministers names. Robert Stuart was a beloved minister of Salem. His name has become a family name among the Taylors and several other area families. Ryland Dillard was also a Baptist minister who had many followers. Dillard as a given name is quite common in Clark County. There are other men whose names go back to ministers, but these are the most obvious.

www.ingramcontent.com/pod-product-compliance
Lightning Source LLC
Chambersburg PA
CBHW020631300426
44112CB00007B/83